Women, Gender, and Sexualities in Africa

Carolina Academic Press
African World Series
Toyin Falola, Series Editor

Africa, Empire and Globalization:
Essays in Honor of A. G. Hopkins
Toyin Falola, editor, and Emily Brownell, editor

African Entrepreneurship in Jos, Central Nigeria, 1902–1985
S.U. Fwatshak

An African Music and Dance Curriculum Model:
Performing Arts in Education
Modesto Amegago

Authority Stealing:
Anti-Corruption War and Democratic Politics
in Post-Military Nigeria
Wale Adebanwi

The Bukusu of Kenya:
Folktales, Culture and Social Identities
Namulundah Florence

Contemporary African Literature: New Approaches
Tanure Ojaide

Contesting Islam in Africa:
Homegrown Wahhabism and Muslim Identity in Northern Ghana, 1920–2010
Abdulai Iddrisu

Democracy in Africa:
Political Changes and Challenges
Saliba Sarsar, editor, and Julius O. Adekunle, editor

Diaspora and Imagined Nationality:
USA-Africa Dialogue and Cyberframing Nigerian Nationhood
Koleade Odutola

Food Crop Production, Hunger, and Rural Poverty in
Nigeria's Benue Area, 1920–1995
Mike Odugbo Odey

Globalization: The Politics of Global Economic Relations and International Business
N. Oluwafemi Mimiko

In Search of African Diasporas: Testimonies and Encounters
Paul Tiyambe Zeleza

Intercourse and Crosscurrents in the Atlantic World:
Calabar-British Experience, 17th–20th Centuries
David Lishilinimle Imbua

Julius Nyerere, Africa's Titan on a Global Stage:
Perspectives from Arusha to Obama
Ali A. Mazrui and Lindah L. Mhando

Local Government in South Africa Since 1994:
Leadership, Democracy, Development, and Service Delivery in a Post-Apartheid Era
Alexius Amtaika

Narrartives of Struggle:
The Philosophy and Politics of Development in Africa
John Ayotunde Isola Bewaji

Perspectives on Feminism in Africa
'Lai Olurode, editor

Pioneer, Patriot, and Nigerian Nationalist:
A Biography of the Reverend M. D. Opara, 1915–1965
Felix Ekechi

Satires of Power in Yoruba Visual Culture
Yomi Ola

The Tiv and Their Southern Neighbours, 1890–1990
Emmanuel Chiahemba Ayangaôr

The Women's War of 1929:
A History of Anti-Colonial Resistance in Eastern Nigeria
Toyin Falola and Adam Paddock

The Yoruba Frontier:
A Regional History of Community Formation,
Experience, and Changes in West Africa
Aribidesi Usman

Women, Gender, and Sexualties in Africa
Toyin Falola and Nana Akua Amponsah, editors

Women, Gender, and Sexualities in Africa

Edited by

Toyin Falola

Nana Akua Amponsah

CAROLINA ACADEMIC PRESS

Durham, North Carolina

Library of Congress Cataloging-in-Publication Data

Women, gender, and sexualities in Africa / [edited by] Toyin Falola and Nana Akua
Amponsah.
    p. cm. -- (African world series)
  Includes bibliographical references and index.
  ISBN 978-1-61163-153-1 (alk. paper)
  1. Sex role--Africa. 2. Gender expression--Africa. 3. Women--Sexual behavior--
Africa. I. Falola, Toyin. II. Amponsah, Nana Akua.

  HQ1075.5.A35W66 2012
  305.3096--dc23

2012015308

Carolina Academic Press
700 Kent Street
Durham, North Carolina 27701
Telephone (919) 489-7486
Fax (919) 493-5668
www.cap-press.com

Printed in the United States of America
2018 Printing

To Cherno And Fatou Njie,
relentless and committed supporter of the
annual conference in Austin

Contents

PART IV · WOMANHOOD, MOTHERHOOD, FEMININITY, AND HIV/AIDS

Series Editor's Preface

The *Carolina Academic Press African World Series,* inaugurated in 2010, offers significant new works in the field of African and Black World studies. The series provides scholarly and educational texts that can serve both as reference works and as readers in college classes.

Studies in the series are anchored in the existing humanistic and the social scientific traditions. Their goal, however, is the identification and elaboration of the strategic place of Africa and its Diaspora in a shifting global world. More specifically, the studies will address gaps and larger needs in the developing scholarship on Africa and the Black World.

The series intends to fill gaps in areas such as African politics, history, law, religion, culture, sociology, literature, philosophy, visual arts, art history, geography, language, health, and social welfare. Given the complex nature of Africa and its Diaspora, and the constantly shifting perspectives prompted by globalization, the series also meets a vital need for scholarship connecting knowledge with events and practices. Reflecting the fact that life in Africa continues to change, especially in the political arena, the series explores issues emanating from racial and ethnic identities, particularly those connected with the ongoing mobilization of ethnic minorities for inclusion and representation.

Toyin Falola
University of Texas at Austin

Preface and Acknowledgments

The conception of this book originated from the tenth annual conference on Africa on the subject of "Women, Gender, and Sexualities in Africa," which was held at the University of Texas at Austin in March, 2010. The main goal of the conference was to provide an avenue for scholars and professionals to dialogue issues relating to women, gender, and sexualities in Africa. The chapters in this volume not only represent a logical final step in the fulfillment of the conference's main objective, but also, it extends the dialogue to scholars in the field of women and gender studies, those interested in sexualities in Africa, and to the general reading public. In any such undertaken, many pieces would have to fall into place to make it a reality and as a result, we are indebted to numerous institutions and a number of people who supported us from the very beginning of the conference to the completion of this volume. We are grateful to all who read the manuscripts and made important suggestions as we progressed along. Our families deserve our gratitude: their patience and encouragements kept our energy and enthusiasm going in the entire process. The tremendous collaboration of all the contributors certainly made the task of finishing the volume a lot easier, and for which we cannot thank them enough.

Women, Gender, and Sexualities in Africa

Chapter 1

Introduction

Toyin Falola & Nana Akua Amponsah

This book provides a forum for scholars to engage and unravel some of the complexities and ambiguities surrounding women, gender, and sexuality, and to address the intersectionality of these issues as they relate to societal understanding of women's and men's experiences. It reflects the nuances relevant to the various dimensions of women and gender issues, and the realities and myths of African sexualities. The chapters draw on multiple disciplines to offer interdisciplinary perspectives from which to understand the diversity of women's experiences, gender issues, and sexualities as they intersect with class, race, ethnicity, and nationality. Key objectives explored include the roles that rhetorical devices of tradition and modernity play in the control of African women's bodies, and the strategies of resistance women utilize against the subjugation of their bodies and sexualities. The chapters interrogate the structures of power that exert systematic governance over a selected group of people because of their gender or sexuality and how the macro-narratives of colonialism and post-colonialism provide frameworks for understanding the micro-narratives of the empowerment and disempowerment of women. While the contributors are by no means united on the precise formulation of modes relevant in addressing problems relating to women and gender issues, they agree that ideas about women, gender, and sexuality in Africa are not "natural" categories that transcend historical forces; rather, they are shifting realities that have been impinged upon by socio-historical factors.

Conceptual and Theoretical Paradoxes

In seeking to address the socially and discursively articulated norms surrounding women, gender, and sexualities in Africa, we are immediately confronted with the conceptual problems of categorization, theorization, and terminology. The seemingly innocent category of "women," as Denise Riley puts it, "is historically and discursively constructed" and a collectivity into which female persons have been differentially positioned such that it is problematic to rely on any apparent continuity in the subject of "women" in discursive practices.[1] Perhaps, nowhere is this claim more obvious and implicated than in African social configurations where the category of "women" has various connotations and shifting representations, and thus, poses the problem of generalization if not carefully expressed. Commenting on the controversies that erupted at the 1992 "Women in Africa and the African Diaspora" conference in Nigeria, Obioma Nnaemeka suggests that the construct of "woman" may even be an empty label, which lacks any uniformed substance for the universal sisterhood of all women. According to her, attempts by some African American and British African participants to exclude the few white women who attended

---

1. Denise Riley, *"Am I That Name?" Feminism and the Category of "Women" in History* (Minneapolis: University of Minnesota Press, 1988), 1–2.

the conference based on racial and ideological differences and the objection to the presences of men at a women's conference "sketched in stark relief the complexity and heterogeneity of the category of 'woman.'"[2]

In *The Invention of Women*, Oyèrónké Oyewùmí also argues that in pre-colonial Yoruba society, for instance, "the social category 'women' — anatomically identified and assumed to be a victim and socially disadvantaged — did not exist;" rather, there were varieties of female roles. For women and men alike, seniority within the lineage was the medium of social differentiation and not a gendered division between women and men.[3] She places the imposition of "women" and "gender" categories on African societies on colonial invention; yet, as Eileen Boris points out, since Oyewùmí's postulations were based on the linguistic peculiarities of her culture, "it is difficult to derive gender ideology from grammatical neutrality."[4]

Certainly, it is not only within discursive practices that the concept, and perhaps, artificial categorization of "women" poses a challenge. Women themselves have contested the objectification of their bodies/identities and constantly have to balance simultaneously their position in societal perception and their own self-view. An excellent example is the self-reflective essay of Nwando Achebe and Bridget Teboh. As both authors contend, there are significant conceptual challenges that African women face in internalizing ones' "womanness" and "Africanness," especially in circumstances of "hybridity" — where one lives between two worlds — and instituting a sense of balance between ones' emerged identity and academic endeavors.[5] Yet, it might be feared that acknowledging such intrinsic instabilities in any blanket categorization/conceptualization of "women" equates ignoring the well-worked inclusion of women into African historiography for the indifferences of gender.

Gender, in itself, is not without conceptual difficulties. As a constituent element of social relations based on perceived sexual difference, gender is both relational and organizational. On the one hand, it "inhabits social structures, practices, and imaginations," whilst on the other, it is "an organizing principle of social structures, institutions, and practices."[6] In other words, constructs of gender provide the primary means of apportioning roles and signifying power relations; however, any change in constitution of social relations inevitably results in changes in representations of power relations.[7] Yet, the concept of gender represents much more than relational and organizational normatives. Gender resonates profoundly for discourses on women in the sense that the moment the idea of male dominance is juxtaposed with female subordination, gender surfaces as a crisis of difference and power. In the same vein, it brings out the ambivalences about the term "patriarchy," which carries powerful implications for the supposed universal "oppression" of women.

Since the 1970s, researchers interested in women and gender as well as in sexualities in Africa have found themselves, in one way or the other, confronting patriarchal notions

---

2. Obioma Nnaemeka, *Sisterhood, Feminism, and Power: From Africa to the Diaspora* (Trenton, NJ: Africa World Press, 1998), 369.

3. Oyèrónké Oyewùmí, *The Invention of Women: Making an African Sense of Western Gender Discourses* (Minneapolis: University of Minnesota Press, 1997), 79.

4. Eileen Boris, "Gender After Africa!" in Catherine M. Cole, Takyiwaa Manuh, and Stephen F. Miescher (eds.), *Africa After Gender?* (Bloomington, IN: Indiana University Press, 2007), 193.

5. Nwando Achebe and Bridget Teboh, "Dialoguing Women," in Cole, Manuh, and Miescher (eds.), *Africa After Gender?*, 63–77.

6. Michael Roper and John Tosh, *Manful Assertions: Masculinities in Britain Since 1800* (London: Routledge, 1991), 11.

7. Joan Wallach Scott, "Gender: A Useful Category of Historical Analysis," in Joan Wallach Scott, (ed.), *Gender and the Politics of History* (New York: Columbia University Press, 1988), 42.

be it African-structured or colonially-engineered. Many of the works available on patriarchy, especially those of radical feminists and Marxist feminist scholars, have focused on theorizing as well as historicizing male dominance. Often times, they have presented an indelible impression of patriarchy as resolute and fired by an indiscriminate and unswerving male devotion to controlling every aspect of life.[8] A significant polarity, however, exists among scholars as to the appropriate application and conceptualization of patriarchy to societal arrangements. Radical feminists have asserted that patriarchy involves configurations of men's misogynist control of women's sexuality and reproduction. Early Marxist feminists conceived of patriarchal domination as traversing women's reproductive exploitation and their exploitation in the capitalist market economy.

Others have countered this view by arguing that "even if control over reproduction and economic production was a necessary feature of societies, such controls need not necessarily be by men, nor need it be inimical to the interest of women."[9] Patriarchy is undoubtedly a contentious concept, and as Judith Lorber adds, "patriarchy is an overused and slippery conceptualization."[10] While the application of patriarchy holds true for women's subjugation in some cases, its understanding and implications are over simplified if it is merely dichotomized as male domination/female subordination. Oyewùmí has argued that conceiving of gender and patriarchy as the epitome of a universal female subordination is a misleading theorization because it is based on the assumption that these concepts are permeable variations in every society.[11]

Judith Bennett has also shown that a one-dimensional analysis of patriarchy shrouds the fact that the configurations of power, which uphold patriarchy, have by no means been inert. Besides being formed and reformed by different forces, women themselves have, sometimes, been the driving force behind, and have often colluded with men in patriarchal exercises, and hence, in focusing on the mechanisms of any given patriarchy, attention must be given to how those mechanisms affected different women in different ways.[12] In concurrence, Judith Butler notes:

> The very notion of patriarchy has threatened to become a universalizing concept that overrides or reduces distinct articulations of gender asymmetry in different cultural contexts. As feminism has sought to become integrally related to struggles against racialist and colonialist oppression, it has become increasingly important to resist the colonizing epistemological strategy that would subordinate different configurations of domination under the rubric of a trans-cultural notion of patriarchy.[13]

Butler's assertion captures the very essence of the conceptual struggles to understand and apply patriarchal notions in dialectical practices; in particular, when it is foregrounded as *the* source of all women's problems, and the impeding force in women's history. Admittedly, while it is almost impossible to examine the lived experiences of women without gender and patriarchal considerations, it is not sufficient to examine these con-

---

8. Kate Millet, *Sexual Politics* (Urbana: University of Illinois Press, 2000).

9. Sharon B. Stichter and Jane L. Parpart (eds.), *Patriarchy and Class: African Women in the Home and the Workforce* (Boulder, CO: Westview Press, 1988), 6. For a detailed discussion of reproduction and economic production, see Felicity Edholm, Olivia Harris, and Kate Young, "Conceptualizing Women," *Critique of Anthropology*, Vol. 3, 9, and 10, (1977): 101–30.

10. Judith Lorber, *Paradoxes of Gender* (Yale University Press, 1994), 3.

11. Oyewùmí, *The Invention of Women*, xii.

12. Judith Bennett, "Feminism and History," *Gender and History*, Vol. 1, (1989): 259–63.

13. Judith Butler, *Gender Trouble: Feminism and the Subversion of Identity* (New York: Routledge, 1990), 46.

structions as given. If anything, academic developments in this area of study have shown that no single formulation or theoretical positioning can explain the infinite complexities of social performance in the sense that constructions of gender can shift depending on class, ethnicity, and culture, among others. It can even be argued that gender is not just about the differential relations between women and men, but it is also about such things as prestige, success, status, orientation, seniority, and the interplay of these factors in Africa's social performance.

In *Africa After Gender*, Catherine M. Cole, *et al.* have equally raised important questions regarding dialoguing gender in Africa — "where did 'gender' come from, what kinds of knowledge it has and has not authorized in Africa, and how expansive or limiting the term might prove in future."[14] Granted that gender discourses have come to permeate both academic and everyday life in Africa, the term still conjures negative response as being "ill suited to local contexts and full of biased assumptions from foreign lands."[15] This is to the extent that in spite of the deluge of research works on gender in Africa, we are no closer to any consensus on its application in the African context.

Gender and patriarchy are also rooted in an understanding of the body, for gender shapes sexuality — although not in terms of sexual orientation — while patriarchy institutionalizes it. Catherine Mackinnon has argued that gender divides women and men based on the social requirement of heterosexuality and organizes social relations such that "men may dominate and women must submit."[16] This way the female body envisaged as sexually weak became connected to the gender roles ascribed to women and opened them to not only to the strength of men, but also to their protection and control. For African women, this assessment proves quite accurate in the colonial context. African women's bodies were at the center of colonial appropriation and regulation and came to represent a fraught realm of political processes, policies, laws, educational, and cultural ideologies, as well as a politicized vessel for narratives of culture, nation, tradition, modernity, authenticity, disempowerment, and empowerment in the post-colonial era.

A concise perspective on the body and sexuality, however, continues to remain problematic in the African context because of the ambivalent terminologies often used, and because of the nature of African socio-cultural outlook: discourses on sexuality, in particular, are a contentious territory. In *Unspoken Facts*, Marc Epprecht indicates that the application of such terms as homosexuality, lesbians, and gay to African sexuality have come as a "shock, embarrassment, and even to the anger of many [Africans]."[17] The uproar that met Sylvia Tamale when she openly supported the rights of homosexuals before the Ugandan Equal Opportunities Commission is a testament to this fact. Tamale describes the "ugliness, rage, revulsion, disgust, and malevolence" that the vocal homophobic public exhibited in February 2003, including calls for her "lynching" and "crucifixion."[18] From public outcries and the nationalistic hetero-normative agendas of Robert Mugabe of Zimbabwe and Sam Nujoma of Namibia, to the intellectual homophobias of Jomo Kenyatta and some of his contemporaries, we have been presented with debatable ideas on how homosexuality and "deviant" sexual behaviors are "un-Africa," "unnatural,"

---

14. Cole, Manuh, and Miescher (eds.), *Africa After Gender?*, 3–4.

15. Ibid.

16. Catherine A. Mackinnon, *Towards a Feminist Theory of the State* (Cambridge, Massachusetts: Harvard University Press, 1989).

17. Marc Epprecht, *Unspoken Facts: A History of Homosexualities in Africa* (Harare, Zimbabwe: Gays and Lesbians of Zimbabwe, 2008), 2.

18. Sylvia Tamale, "Out of the Closet: Unveiling Sexuality Discourses in Uganda," in Cole, Manuh, Miescher (eds.), *Africa After Gender,* 17–29.

and a threat to Africa's family institution. Other important personalities such as Olusegun Obasanjo of Nigeria and Jacob Zuma of South Africa have all added their voices to the "fight" against homosexuality, with many of these personalities arguing that same sex orientation was a product of the colonial modernizing enterprise.

At the same time, many have argued that it was colonialism that constructed Africa's heterosexual/hetero-normative image through ideologically motivated anthropological studies, which conjured an "idealized or exoticized natives, primitives, and other *Others*."[19] In essence, Europeans knew about same sex relationships in African societies, but engineering a "closer to nature" imagery of African sexuality devoid of the "plague" of homosexuality would justify their view of African "primitiveness" and their "civilizing" mission. Besides Epprecht, Neville Hoad, Ruth Morgan and Saskia E. Wieringa, and Stephen O. Murray and Will Roscoe, among others, have shown that Africans have historically had knowledge of, and in some societies, participate in same sex relationships although homosexuality may not necessary have been the utilized terminology.[20] The question then is why African leaders and scholars, as well as a large segment of the public, have vehemently denied and denounced same sex orientation and relationships. Epprecht intimates that the answer may have originated from the "colonial and Cold War contexts where homophobia was almost a civic duty and where Africans commonly encountered patronizing attitudes from whites, [Africans] may have feared that to produce evidence on the topic, or even to show curiosity about it, might be taken as a reproof of African dignity."[21]

Even terms like homosexual and homosexuality, which have myriad number of implicit meanings, become contentious when they are simplistically applied to all persons who do not conform to the culture of compulsory heterosexuality, eventually feeding into stereotyping and sexual discrimination. With African women, the colonial obsession with racial differences and patriarchal didactics resulted in the labeling of their bodies as the exoticized "other" and hyper-sexualized with such categorizations scripting female sexuality as negative and locating it as extreme and profuse beyond that perceived as normal, moral, and socially acceptable. The above suggests that the application or imposition of theories, terminologies, and categories on complex social relations need careful consideration, and as Epprecht suggests, there is no "direct and predictable relationship between the physical body (sex), social behavior (gender) and sexual feeling (sexuality)" because relations between these sets are constantly negotiated.[22]

Clearly, ideas about women, gender, and sexualities involve much more than the designation or naming that society assigns to it.[23] They entail forceful instabilities and implications in their meanings and are widely ramified concepts, which can be used in either a general or more specific sense. None is fixed in an unproblematic, easily discernable way to allow uncomplicated identification and discourse. There is, thus, a need for a constant dialogue that redefines women's experiences and moves the discourses on gender

---

19. Epprecht, *Heterosexual Africa? The History of an Idea from the Age of Exploration to the Age of AIDS* (Athens, Ohio: Ohio University Press, 2008), 34.

20. See Neville W. Hoad, *African Intimacies: Race, Homosexuality, and Globalization* (Minneapolis, MN: University of Minnesota Press, 2007); Ruth Morgan and Saskia E. Wieringa (eds.), *Tommy Boys, Lesbian Men, and Ancestral Wives: Female Same-Sex Practices in Africa* (South Africa: Jacana Media Ltd, 2005); and Stephen O. Murray and Will Roscoe (eds.), *Boy-Wives and Female Husbands: Studies in African Homosexualities* (New York: Palgrave, 1998).

21. Epprecht, *Heterosexual Africa?*, 131.

22. Epprecht, *Unspoken Facts*, 11.

23. Jeffery Weeks, *Sexuality and its Discontents* (London, 1985), 122.

and sexuality beyond their static and ambiguous representations. The need is even more imperative in these times of identity formations, femininity and masculinity contestations, and sexual liberation and openness. It requires the adoption of a new approach that focuses on the nuances and complexities of these issues and prevents discourses on women, gender, and sexualities from becoming objects of analysis onto themselves, but a means of reflecting on individual and collective identities and differences as well as an avenue for negotiating discursive practices and social strategies.

Historiographical Perspectives

In the last few decades since the project of writing of African women back into history began, researchers have constructed and reconstructed the experiences of women in concrete African social structures. New ways of thinking and envisioning women, gender, and sexuality issues in Africa picked up momentum directly or indirectly to the binary politics of private/public, women/men, tradition/modernity, production/reproduction, formal/informal, and heterosexual/homosexual. A significant number of scholarships have emerged, many of which have explored the conceptions and contestations surrounding gendered normative practices, African sexual notions, and women statuses in both the public and private spheres. In the 1970s and 1980s, writers such as Ester Boserup, Edna G. Bay, and Margaret Jean Hay and Sharon Stichter sought to understand African women's subordination by focusing on the dichotomy of the sexes, conceived in terms of control over economic production.

These scholars have suggested that although a gendered division of labor was a feature of African social arrangements, it allowed the crossing of boundaries and reversal of roles, which was systematically derailed by the introduction of colonial market economy. Colonialism effectively eroded whatever socio-economic autonomy African women's exercised through such things as cash cropping, facilitation of male migration to urban and mining centers, denying women's access to agricultural technology, financial resources, and global markets, and relegating women to reproductive labor. This has especially been expressed in Marxist feminism where women's subordination and exploitation is articulated as having emanated from the concept of nature/nurture dichotomy, which linked women with reproductive roles and men with the control of economic production. This understanding purports that even though women are the means of reproduction, patriarchal structures grant the "rights to the progeny to the husband's community." This exploitation of women's reproductive labor provides the platform for women's subordination to men established through women's "inability to acquire a status based on rights in the means of production."[24]

Nonetheless, some scholars have contested the conceptualization of women's lower status through the lens of their reproductive roles. In her *Sisters and Wives*, Karen Sacks argues that the economic transformation African societies experienced was the result of their historical encounter with European rule, which changed both the basic mode of production and women's relations to the resources of production.[25] In effect, the economic

---

24. Stichter and Parpart, *Patriarchy and Class,* 5.
25. Karen Sacks, *Sisters and Wives: The Past and Future of Sexual Equality* (Urbana, IL: University of Illinois Press, 1979).

changes had a greater impact on women's social, economic, and political statuses more so than their ability to bear children. Margaret M. Lock and Patricia Alice Kaufert have also cautioned against the intransigent stereotyping of women's lives as equivalent to reproduction; instead to focus on bringing out the different dimensions of women's experiences.[26] Other researchers have established that the control of women's sexuality and fertility has direct links with patriarchal tendencies that either existed in African societies or were introduced by the European colonizing mission. Lynn M. Thomas, for example, has located the cementation of colonial political control in the restructuring and regulation of Kenyan women's sexuality and reproduction. As with their other colonies, the British colonial authority readily transferred their patriarchic orientation into Kenya by interfering in women's reproduction as a way of not just subjugating women, but also, reinforcing their paternity over the entire population.[27]

In a more recent publication, Adeline Masquelier in *Women and Islamic Revival in a West African Town* has documented how Muslim practices in Dogondoutchi, Niger literally and symbolically fashioned socio-political, religious, and economic spaces around women, their bodies, and their sexualities. She notes that Islamic revivals that emerged in Dogondoutchi in the aftermath of the French invasion, both empowered and disempowered women as they sought ways to define authentic Islamic practices. On the one hand, regulating women's visibility and autonomy became vital parts of the moralizing discourses as most of the revivalist movements viewed the spread of immorality as directly related to the failure of society to control women's sexuality. On the other hand, women actively participated in the movements by reconstructing and redefining Muslim traditions and religious identities through such mediums as defying marriage reforms and husbands' authority, ignoring restrictions and directives from religious leaders, or dressing and behaving in public in certain ways.[28]

The above discourses, directly or indirectly, have all been situated in a historical trend that embodies colonial and African ideas of patriarchy and women's subsumed statuses. Although not so stated, the theoretical application of patriarchy — control of men over women — juxtaposed with colonialism overshadows the conscious choices of women as well as women's collaborative relationship with men. African women's history and issues revolving around gender and sexuality are not only that of subjugation, or even that of women's empowerment, as some have argued; rather it is the totality of experiences including the mundane. It is about women's everyday needs and aspirations, their successes and failures, their compassions and transgressions, and about their glee and grief. As Signe Arnfred in *Rethinking Sexualities in Africa* has suggested, the conceptualization of gender and sexuality discourses must move beyond that structured by the colonial pejorative imagery of women and men and their sexualities.[29] Indeed, not only is it vital for an academic re-imagination of the dialectic conceptions surrounding women, but we are presented with a unique opportunity to provide essential socio-cultural and historical perspectives needed to appreciate the changing dynamics of women, gender, and sexuality issues in contemporary Africa.

26. Margaret M. Lock and Patricia Alice Kaufert (eds.), *Pragmatic Women and Body Politics* (Cambridge: Cambridge University Press, 1998).

27. Lynn M. Thomas, *Politics of the Womb: Women, Reproduction, and the State in Kenya* (Berkeley and Los Angeles, CA: University of California Press, 2003).

28. Adeline Masquelier, *Women and Islamic Revival in a West African Town* (Bloomington, IN: Indiana University Press, 2009).

29. Signe Arnfred, *Re-thinking Sexualities in Africa* (Uppsala, Sweden: Almqvist &Wiksell Tryckeri AB, 2005).

Imaging New Paradigms

We began this introduction by focusing on the ambiguities, complexities, and contestations that have come to be associated with dialoguing women, gender, and sexualities in Africa. Although it may seem peculiar to have spent so much time discussing the problematics of these issues, yet, it is precisely by virtue of the conceptual and theoretical uncertainties and assumptions that is allowing us move beyond the subjugated/victimhood paradigms that have tended to frame discourses on women, gender, and sexuality in Africa into engaging critical re-imagination and questioning. As a conceptual exercise, let us for a moment assume that African women have been "rescued" from their historical obscurity and "restored" to their rightful place in history: their oppression and struggles brought to the forefront; their power and agency explored; their indispensable roles in society explored; and gender and sexuality issues deftly examined from both within and outside the continent.

The fundamental question that then confronts us is not whether the time has come to shelf these issues. Rather, it is whether the paradigmatic frameworks used to examine them have promoted new dimensions to the discourse and whether the visibility has engendered sensitivity to the realities, commonalities, and divergences of women's experiences and not just academic perforce mediated by impractical visions and ideological divide. As Kolawole argues,

> grass-root women are not concerned about conceptualization, which is considered as an academic preoccupation, but in belief and in practice; many prefer a position that enhances women's conditions and opportunities for participation in development that does not alienate men, that does not jeopardize the esteemed family system, and that celebrates motherhood. This provides a meeting point between grass-root women and scholars, between working class and middle-class women, between theory and practice, and between concept and activism.[30]

Indeed, many researchers recognize the need to re-conceptualize women and gender discourses in Africa and to engender new paradigms that unpack the baggage of western feminist theorization to the African experience. Changes in how we engage these issues began in the 1980s, intensified in the 1990s, and are almost at a tipping point in recent years. Some researchers have envisioned women's struggles as microcosmic of the broader struggles Africans face and adjust to, and the fight for women's rights as a fight for human rights. Others have visualized women and gender issues through the principles of "self-reclamation" and "self-naming," based in part on African philosophical thought on naming and identity, and on the notion that an outsider can hardly understand the experiences and struggles of another, and hence, provide the appropriate naming/solutions for such experiences and struggles.[31]

African women writers, in particular, vigorously began to present their stories as they saw and experienced them. Their voices and perspectives became grounded in the paradigmatic trend of "self-naming" couched on the concept of "womanism" as espoused by Alice Walker, Chikwenye Okonjo Ogunyemi, and Clenora Hudson-Weems as an alternative to the concept of gender. While each of these authors developed their idea of womanism as an independent and distinct conceptualization, together, they formed the "basis for an interpolated field of theory and praxis," which Layli Phillips argues, has been utilized

---

30. Mary Kolawole, "Re-Conceptualizing African Gender Theory: Feminism, Womanism and the *Arere* Metsphor," in Arnfred, *Re-thinking Sexualities in Africa*, 253.
31. Ibid.

by "a host of people to follow."[32] Filtering out the minute differences between the three conceptions, womanism represented:

> the idea of a social change rooted in Black women's and other women of color's everyday experiences and everyday methods of problem solving in everyday spaces, extended to the problem of ending all forms of oppression for all people, restoring the balance between people and the environment/nature, and reconciling human life with spiritual dimension.[33]

Because womanism coheres around ideas of motherhood, spirituality, community, hospitality, healing, mutual aid, and self-help, it becomes particularly congruent to the realities of African women's expectations and experiences, and hence, more appealing to both African scholars and grass-root activism. In the more than three decades since womanism was first championed, it has generated heated debates and avid associations, but as we go forward, the challenge is not just the recognition of the multiple implications of class, ethnicity, culture, environment, and politics in dialoguing women's issues, but the shortfalls of these emphases and concepts as well. Such an approach is vital for charting new pathways. For instance, while womanism provided, for many, a more acceptable mode for analyzing and understanding women and gender issues in Africa than feminism, and its stance on sexuality remains non-specific.

As Phillips points out, "womanist perspectives on sexuality are as diverse as sexuality itself, [with Hudson-Weems rejecting homosexuality outright] yet, womanism still opposes oppression based on sexuality."[34] Phillips, herself, argues otherwise, but the undeniable fact is, discourses on African sexualities do not fill the confines of contemporary conceptualizations, be it womanism, feminism, and other (isms). There is the need for the re-imagination of new paradigms and analytical frameworks that, for example, 'remembers' homosexual Africa to heterosexual Africa, debunks notions of sexual non-conformity as destabilizing to African social structures, and defuses the idea that African women are sitting targets of African patriarchal and gender restrictions needing to be saved and protected. Victim-narrative model, extensively used in sexuality and health dialogues, shrouds core structural problems in African countries that in the end disenfranchise both women and men.

For example, the general assumption that women, much more than men, want to prevent HIV/AIDS, but cannot, and that there is a one-way traffic—men to women—in the spread of the disease, disengages important social, economic, and political under-pinnings of the HIV/AIDS problem, as well as women's own agency in their daily choices. Although it is essential for the retention of our prior knowledge about women and gender dialectical practices, we need replacement paradigms that speak to how social structures create gendered normative performance for both women and men. Such paradigms would topple the idea of men's monolithic dominance and women's universal subordination.

Overview of Chapters

The contributors to this volume have engaged many of the issues we have discussed above in the four thematic parts of this book. Consisting of five chapters, Part One, "Contesting Sexualities and the African Woman's Body," engages the appropriation of the

---

32. Layli Phillips (ed.), *The Womanist Reader* (New York: Routledge, 2006), xx.
33. Ibid.
34. Ibid., xxxvii.

African female body as a site for narratives of culture and nation, of authenticity, and of empowerment and disempowerment. It analyzes the flexibility and fluidity of sex roles and how women, in particular, create spaces of resistance and agency for themselves and their communities.

As Naminata Diabate demonstrates in the opening chapter, ambivalences about African women's sexuality and bodies abound more often in discursive practices than the reality on the ground demonstrates. More importantly, she points out that portrayals have been framed in terms of disempowerment and pathologically such that discourses of HIV/AIDS, rape, prostitution, and clitorecdomy and studies on African women (West African) and tradition, have been "polarized between the construction of tradition as oppressive and its recuperation by reactionary scholarship as authentically West African." Using Jean Pierre Bekolo's 2005 film, *Les Saignantes* (The Bloodletters), which is about the empowering nature of Beti women's sexuality through the *Mevoungou*, a traditional Beti female secret society, Diabate examines the ways in which the director structured the film to resemble a *Mevoungou* ritual. According to Diabate, Bekolo's aim was to use the film both as a medium of "purification" against the corruption of the postcolonial state and to portray how women utilize the power of their sexuality to not only shape and protect their communities, but also to guard against patriarchal tendencies.

Diabate argues that in "the postcolonial context where traditional and cultural practices and beliefs are under siege, Bekolo's invocation, transposition, and adaptation of the Mevoungou ritual works as a reminder to contemporary continental and diasporic young African women of the power women draw from their sexual bodies." Indeed, Bekolo's application of the "tradition" as a facilitator of women's sexual empowerment and Diabate's dialectical analysis both challenge "western feminists' view of 'tradition' as the locus of women's subordination and 'modernity' as the path to women's liberation." The application of western values and understandings reaffirms discourses that "others" the African woman's body and sexuality and ignores endogamous factors necessary for unambiguous interpretation of African sexuality.

Like Diabate, Z'étoile Imma and Jacqueline-Bethel Mougoué, in chapters three and four deftly adopt important literary works on the African body and sexuality to elucidate how African writers responded to the colonial imagery of the African body and how they have mapped their own interpretations of African sexualities in the post-colonial context. Adopting the poetry of Dambudzo Marechera, Imma describes how the author's work conveys "multiple ruptures central to a dynamic post/neo-colonial identity" and situates the African body as "the ultimate site of cross cultural anxiety and possibility." Imam examines Marechera's utilization of sexual violence to describe the intimate anguish of cross-cultural and postcolonial contacts, and how within the same context, he complicates his literary interpretation of the sexual violence. The ambiguities and the squalor the colonial contact and constructions engendered in Marechera's poems take on a more gendered and contemporary angle in Jacqueline-Bethel Mougoué discussion of British women travelers' narratives about African women. Analyzing five of such travel narratives, Mougoué's argues, "Like their Victorian counterparts, modern British female travelers expressed ideologies of Western cultural superiority and assumptions about 'normative' gender roles within zones of contact with African women."

According to Mougoué, the pejorative sexual notions laden in these narratives were anchored on the presumed assumptions about African women's physiology and over-heightened sexuality. Mougoué's approach opens an innovative angle for dialoguing African women's sexuality and gender issues by moving away from male representations to female representations. The key here is the recognition of the intersection of sexuality, race, class, and gender and the opportunity to envisage these intersections from a feminine angle. Aderonke Adesola Adesanya in chapter five extends the dialogue on gender and sexuality using Yoruba artistic representations. According to Adesanya, Yoruba art offers an endless avenue to engage the social realities of Yoruba culture and it is here that he identifies ambivalence in gender representations and the appropriation of feminine sexuality for the collective interest of the society. The paradigmatic frameworks of victimhood and empowerment are posited to be indexes in Yoruba verbal and visual arts and as Adesanya sees it, it is only when we unite the above paradigms that we will appreciate and understand the position and status of women in Yoruba culture.

Following a similar line of thought as Diabate, Imma, Mougoué, and Adesanya although not from a literary or artistic point of view, Mary A. Nyangweso Wangila explores in chapter six the "multiple layers of sexual controls" African woman's sexuality is normally subjected to and the reasons behind the sexual control in the religions of Judaism, Christianity, and Islam. Nyangweso argues that, very often, patriarchal structures have been used as the index for analyzing female sexuality; yet, the matrix surrounding the different layers of patriarchal structures expressed through various cultural norms and religion have not received the needed attention. There is, thus, the need to deconstruct and disentangle not just the ambiguities about women's sexuality, but to isolate the multiple factors that inform the norms of sexual control and account for the statuses of African women's sexuality. In chapter seven, Felix Kiruthu, Martha Musalia, and Mildred Ndeda offer a counter argument to the general view that African women lacked any power in regards to their sexuality in both pre-colonial and colonial Africa. While not refuting the influence of African-based social constraints and colonial systematic gender restructuring, they give more credence to women's ability to engender spaces of influence for themselves, arguing that although the degree of control varied from one society to the other, African women had some level of control over their sexuality during these periods.

African women challenged both colonial authorities and African patriarchal notions in order to maintain control over their sexual rights. The authors demonstrate that in central Kenya, Kikuyu women showed hardiness and resilience in their resistance struggles against the authorities during the female circumcision controversy in the 1920s and 1930s, just so their sexuality would not be re-ordered. The women adopted a variety of resistance mechanisms, including migrating to "urban centers in spite of a spirited effort by Kikuyu patriarchs and colonial government to contain them in the reserves," and marrying men from other communities against the protests of the families. The sexual politics that played out among the Kikuyu was not exclusive to the region. Indeed, the clash between women, who fought to preserve their sexuality and control of their bodies, and colonial and African patriarchal authorities, who aimed to control female sexuality, have been demonstrated in many societies and presented to us through various mediums.

The three chapters under Part Two, "Homosexuality and Identity Politics," continue the discourse on African sexuality, but this time, tackling the not-so-openly-talked about, and often avoided, subject of homosexuality, particularly from the African point of view. The three chapters examine notions of homosexuality from the African perspective and the contestations over western ideological influences on African sexuality and identity formation. Collectively, these various discourses are unified under the theoretical concern of examining the avenues by which women and men have historically dealt with gender and sexuality, and how they continue to deal with the gendered outcomes of contemporary changes to co-construct future sexual identities and configurations on the African continent. In chapter eight, Caroline Tushabe draws on Marlon Ross' "Beyond the Closet Paradigm as Raceless" to analyze the politics of sexual freedom, colonial political legacies, and constitutional protections in Uganda.

As Tushabe describes it, the Ugandan legislative body since the colonial period, has one way or the other, enacted laws intended to punish persons perceived as sexual "nonconformists" and to protect traditional family values from "deviate" sexual behaviors. Tushabe argues that while the Uganda's legislative machinery may believe it is defining itself and constructing "a progressive 'civilized' system of sexuality," the opposite is true since such a stand, for example, supports the colonial construction of "primitive" African sexuality. Instead, she calls for a decolonized "thinking that re-members the knowledge, languages, communities, and practices" of the Ugandan people and rejects every aspect of the colonial project meant to restructure African sexuality. The chapter openly forces the confrontation of one of the fundamental questions on sexuality in Africa. That is whether homosexuality has always existed in "traditional" African social arrangements or whether outside contact constructed it into the African consciousness. Ebunoluwa Olufemi Oduwole discusses this question using the Yoruba as a case study in chapter nine. She suggests that the linguistic and conceptual formulations of Yoruba society indicate the presence of homosexual thought and practices, although activities connected with homosexuality were covertly undertaken until the influence of Western cultures took it "out of the closet," to use Marlon Ross' "Beyond the Closet Paradigm." She argues that while modernity may have promoted spaces of identity and belonging for homosexuals, those who are openly embracing their sexual orientation and identity face strong religious and cultural condemnation and their sexual freedom in the future remains uncertain.

As chapter nine shows, social unacceptability and stigmatization of same sex individuals is not unique to any one African society. Kathleen O'Mara in chapter ten looks at the social networks and micro communities that same sex individuals have had to create for themselves in the concealed spaces of Accra, Ghana. There, their activities are "concealed" from public scrutiny because Ghana's "sodomy laws, police entrapment and extortion, condemnatory charismatic and Pentecostal Christian public discourse, and general public antipathy to non-normative sexual expressions," have prevented an open embrace of sexual difference. Nevertheless, lgbtiq (lesbian, gay, bi-sexual, transgender, intersex, and queer) individuals have come together to establish a vibrant community that ensures the material and emotional wellbeing and spaces of social agency for its members. Extending the geography further, Janeske Botes analyzes, in the chapter eleven, the representation of gay men in South African gay print media advertisements. Her chapter is based on the premise that media shapes our perception of both individual and collective identity and operates as a site of narratives of social formulations and reformulations. She posits that a deliberate perversion exists in gay media advertisements that favor heterosexual imagery of masculinity. She also points out that misrepresentations of the masculinity of gay men intersect with race, age, and the physical traits of the men who appear in gay advertisements.

The four chapters under Part Three, "Gendered Nationalism, Gendered Resistance," focus on dress culture and the application of patriarchal control beyond the realm of domesticity; the complementary, yet antagonistic relationship between modernity and tradition; ideas of nationalism as structured in gender differences; and gender-based resistance strategies. In chapter twelve, Danielle Porter's examination of Mobutu's Authenticity campaign in the late 1960s and early 1970s, sets the stage in reviewing how ideas of cultural nationalism could, indeed, be crouched on patriarchal tendencies and in gendered notions. She describes how Mobutu forced men to re-adopt the wearing of traditional Congolese (Democratic Republic of Congo/Zaire) clothing as a sign of national pride and a defiance of colonial legacies—the slogan adopted was "down with the suit."

Surprisingly, African women, whom we have been told over and over again that they are almost always at the worse end of male domination and social restriction, somewhat escaped this dictatorial initiative.

Porter writes, "Women were an afterthought in the Authenticity campaign; [they] were simply told to wear traditional clothing and hairstyles, which was relatively vague compared to [dressing directives giving to] their male counterparts." Was the lack of focus on women a gendered perception that saw women as only good for reproductive roles and domestic responsibilities, and hence, not suited for an exercise of nationalism? Was it to the benefit of women that Mobutu focused on Congolese men, or was Mobutu's focus on men as result of his own gender partiality? To answer these questions and many more, Porter discusses the Authenticity program, the SAPE (Société Ambianceurs et Persons Élégants) movement, and the later Sapeur movement which emerged in the 1970s and 1980s; all geared toward dress culture and all almost nearly excluding women's active participation. She argues that not only were these events important features in Congolese history, but also, during these periods, women were actively participating in "political discourses, the workforce, and their communities," and therefore warrant an analytical insight that contextualizes the politics of women's absence in the broader history of the Democratic Republic of Congo (Zaire) in the 1970s and 1980s.

Like Porter, Jonathan Shaw (chapter thirteen) offers insights into Mobutu's Authenticity project, with a greater emphasis on exploring some of the theoretical questions we have raised around notions of patriarchy and gender. Shaw takes a comparative approach by drawing parallels between Mobutu's Congo/Zaire and Nyerere's Tanzania from the period each man instituted his version of "'traditionalist' national re-imagination projects" to the mid-1990s when they both lost their hold on political power. In the case of "Mobutism," Shaw shows that during the period of "Authenticite," Congolese/Zairians not only had to accept the idea of a nation with an "ultimate 'father' (Baba Mobutu) and 'mother' (Mama Mobutu)," but they also had to emulate the models these concepts presented.

Here, he questions the impact the spiritualization and politicization of fatherhood posed to the familial understandings and representations of gender identity in Congolese society as well as the possible connections between Congolese constructions of male and female identity and the contemporary sexual violence the conflict areas of eastern Congo is experiencing. On the Tanzanian front, the *Ujamaa* project, which at its core emphasized the principles of freedom, equality, unity, and traditional African family-hood, formed the basis of Nyerere's social and economic development strategy. Among the many changes the *Ujamaa* project initiated, it constructed/reconstructed gender roles in the country. Shaw argues that Mobutu's Authenticite was modeled after Nyerere's *Ujamaa* and both programs leave us to confront the gender re-conceptualizations that occurred.

In chapter fourteen, Alicia Decker also looks at the political dimensions of gender construction and reconstruction. We learn from her analyses that like many post-colonial African leaders, the political underpinnings of gender was not lost on Idi Amin, however, he was perhaps, one of the few who manipulated the social implications of gender to enhanced his political dominance. Decker confronts the question of whether Amin was a feminist or a foe by elevating women to high political positions at certain points in his administration and demoting them when their presence did not suit his political ambitions. Amin's actions, while Decker admits, positioned him in a light where he might be considered a supporter of women's rights, he was certainly not for a "genuine empowerment of women as he strategically manipulated the social ideologies femininity and masculinity to consolidate and maintain his tenuous grasp on power." By her arguments, it becomes clear that women's participation in Amin's government, while it symbolized important victories for women's empowerment and equal rights, they were merely symbolic than literal, as they did not significantly alter the structure of masculinity in post-colonial Ugandan politics.

In chapter fifteen, Marie Grace Brown takes us back to the colonial period by revisiting the issue of nationalism and dress culture from the perspective of women's power and resistance against the colonial imposition. As Brown outlines it, the first women's political party in the Sudan, the Sudanese Women's Union, proclaimed in 1952 that the adoption of the *tobe* (bolt of cloth) "as the national costume was an integral part of women's progress and their access to increased economic and social rights." Initially, only married women in Northern Sudan wore the *tobe*, but this changed in the mid-twentieth century when it became the preferred national uniform of midwives, nurses, and students. According to Brown, the wearing of *tobe* was an appropriate symbol of resistance to colonial rule and a nationalist pride for the members of the Sudanese Women's Union at a period when Sudan was gearing up toward its bid for political independence from British colonial rule.

Nevertheless, she points out that scholarship that only positions nationalism and dress culture into severe poles of opposition against westernization and imperialism fails to explain the nuances of the symbolism of clothing. Brown, therefore, argues that the "*tobe*, though a 'traditional garment,' acquired a new meaning as a symbol of discipline and power under colonial rule." In this sense, the *tobe* represented not only nationalist desires, but also, it allowed women who did not want to challenge local, Islamic, or colonial standards of modesty to appear in public areas without apprehension. Furthermore, it enabled women in public service who adopted it as their official uniform to create a visible Sudanese presence in the colonial administration. The constellation of symbolic messages encoded in the *tobe* allowed women of the Sudanese Women's Union who wore it to bear, simultaneously, Sudanese cultural traditions and to have a powerful non-confrontational medium of engaging colonial rule.

In the chapters of Porter, Shaw, Decker, and Brown, modernity and tradition take on the antagonistic relationship seen in the employment of traditional values and cultures to counter colonialism and its resultant modern values in the post-colonial period. Modernity and tradition play out in chapter sixteen by Sati U. Fwatshak, but his point of entry speaks to how historical, social, and economic transformations challenged and restructured the traditional division of labor and reversed sex roles in a gender ordered society. He describes how some Nigerian men have managed to break the gender barrier through their appropriation of a previously feminine sphere of control—the braiding industry. Fwatshak raises important questions about the "sexualization" of occupations and the complications such constructions could mean for the relationship between women and men. Fwatshak's line of analysis suggests that modern trends, at certain points in time, produced "places" of agency not just for African women, but also for African men seeking to break from stringent traditional social arrangements and to function in a new world order, although, at other times, modernity was a strong medium for obliterating traditional values. Furthermore, it shows that men, and not always women, can equally be subjected to the restrictions of social configurations and that the idea of male dominance/female submission is one-dimensional.

While maintaining the general theoretical and discursive trends of controlled sexuality/empowered sexuality, colonial construction/post-colonial reconstruction, male-domination/female subordination, and modernity/tradition raised in the preceding chapters, the five chapters under Part Four, "Womanhood, Motherhood, Femininity and HIV/AIDS," change directions slightly. The chapters under this section examine the themes of health and reproduction as tools for negotiating social relations and for strengthening kinship ties; womanhood and motherhood as constructed in the African understanding; the gendered nature of HIV/AIDS in Africa and the "weaponization" of HIV/AIDS in conflict times; and the femininity of the practice of medicine. Chapter seventeen by Bridget Teboh approaches the issue of women's essence as grounded in their reproductive roles through the examination of pregnancy as a powerful stage in a Cameroonian woman's lifecycle. In the reproductive life cycle she describes, womanhood in the Moghamo belief system is socially geared toward achieving motherhood, and this phenomenon has been heightened since the beginning of the twentieth century. The causative factors for this social emphasis emanated from political and economic changes and its impact on women's lives, and women's fears of social ostracization due to infertility. Within Teboh's application of reproduction as a social mode of defining women's lives, pregnancy becomes a "metaphor of life," and fertility/infertility a tool for revealing the dynamics of gender inequity between women and men. The chapter revisits the idea of "women equal reproduction" by analyzing not just the social imposition on women's reproductive role, but also women's own choices and complacency in achieving motherhood.

Chapter eighteen by Andréa Souza Lobo extends the dialogue on women and their reproductive roles from the context of the social construction of motherhood. In her empirical research in the Cape Verde, she focuses on the relationships women build among themselves in the upbringing of children, particularly the often-overlooked roles of grandmothers in these relationships. Souza Lobo shows that the concept of motherhood in Cape Verde is achieved in stages, beginning with birthing mothers and ending with grandmothers. In other words, motherhood is not fully achieved until a woman becomes a grandmother, and it generally takes the coordinated efforts of two generations of women to achieve the full realization of maternity. This system ensures that women, within a family structure, maintain connections in order to continue the shared responsibilities of mothering.

Chapter nineteen by Gretchen du Plessis and Heidi Celliers considers the conceptual changes that occur in African motherhood when it has been impinged upon by uncontrollable factors. In other words, the chapter provides insight into some of the experiences of South African women living with an HIV-positive diagnosis and the changes in perception that occur in a woman's motherhood status following such a diagnosis. They argue that there is "the need for a conceptual shift in the notion of empowerment in order to understand the constrained decisions" women living with HIV make on a daily basis. While accepting the fact that women are in the majority of people affected or infected with HIV/AIDS in Africa, they reject the gendering of the disease as a feminine quandary and the "vulnerability paradigm" that has been used to analyze the disease for such a categorization overshadows and stifles wider engagement of the HIV/AIDS pandemic on the continent. What du Plessis and Celliers stress is retelling the stories of these women as that of a "celebration of the beauty and strength" of women who, on a daily basis, contend with the inflictions of the disease on their physical bodies and the disruptions in their personal lives as well as deal with the responsibility of caring for others.

Aginam Obijiofor presents the next case study on HIV/AIDS and the "weaponization" of the disease during wars and conflicts. Chapter twenty "traces the missing links between HIV/AIDS, wars/conflicts, and victims of rape in reconstructing post-war societies through the process of Disarmament, Demobilization, and Re-integration." Obijiofor explains that besides the many hardships the AIDS pandemic has visited on Africans, the factors of war have unleashed a complex and, perhaps, a frightening dimension with the blanket sexual assaults and rape that combatants perpetuate against women. Focusing on selected post-conflict states including Rwanda, Democratic Republic of the Congo, Sierra Leone, and Liberia, Obijiofor argues that not only was the raping of women deployed as a systematic tool of warfare in the conflicts in these countries, but also, there was a "willful" transmission of HIV to the rape victims. Undoubtedly, HIV/AIDS has visited a greater burden on African women than on African men, and as du Plessis and Celliers indicate the gendering of HIV/AIDS positions women at the worse end and leaves them there, while at the same time, obscuring the wider problems of social degradation, political ineptness, and healthcare inadequacies.

There are, however, certain instances, as Yaw Sarkodie Agyeman shows in the last chapter, when gendering plays to the status enhancement of women. Examining the social construct of femininity in the practice of medicine among the Asante of Ghana, Agyeman indicates that the materiality of aduro (medicine) is gendered in such ways that both animate and inanimate objects are regarded either as feminine or as masculine, but it is the feminine aspect that takes precedence. He argues that the distinct contradictions and the ambiguities that abound in the application of femaleness in the practice of medicine are purposefully constructed to enable practitioners to tap women's spiritual qualities. This bestows on the female figure some level of reverence in a practice that men generally dominate.

As several of the chapters in this volume recognize, African women, in their collective history, have long experienced adversities from both colonial and African patriarchal structures that sought to reorder their sexuality and construct appropriate gender roles for them. Contemporary changes have not necessarily made women's lives any easier; however, as it has equally been shown, African women's experiences have not always been that of victimization and struggle against diseases, gender normative practices, and patriarchies. Women have historically exercised influence and power in their various communities, and where they had no influence, they have created spaces of autonomy for themselves. More importantly, African women have utilized a myriad of avenues to resist the appropriation and control of their bodies and sexuality initiated as part of colonial imperialist agenda or in the name of nationalism. Given the current debates on African sexualities and the struggles both women and men face about their sexualities on the continent, we hope that the chapters here have engendered a shift that embraces broader perspectives on women, gender, and sexualities in Africa.

Part I

Contesting Sexualities and the African Woman's Body

Ambivalence towards the African Woman's Body: Jean Pierre Bekolo's *Les Saignantes* (The Bloodletters) and the Mevoungou

Naminata Diabate

Questions related to West African women's sexuality have been predominantly framed in disempowering and pathological terms. HIV/AIDS, rape as weapon of war, marital rape, "corrective rape," prostitution, and female circumcision constitute well-known subjects in the field. Similarly, most critical works on African women and "traditions" have been polarized between the construction of "tradition" as oppressive and its uncritical recuperation as positive. The nexus of what I call the pervasive picture of negative sexualities and tradition would, it seems, portray an utterly depressing image of female bodies.

However, using Jean Pierre Bekolo's 2005 postmodern film *Les Saignantes*, I argue that there is more to African women's bodies than pathology and stigma. To do so, I explore how *Les Saignantes* shows a rather empowering nature of female bodies through its adaptation of the Mevoungou, the ritual of the powerful female secret society of the Beti of Cameroon. A conventionally women-centered ritual, the power of the Mevoungou is predicated upon the clitoris; and it is performed to restore prosperity to the entire community as well as to empower its members against patriarchal practices.[1] Bekolo structures the film like a Mevoungou ritual to purify allegorically the corrupt postcolonial state, to move it from failed decolonization and nominal independence to real independence while suggesting the power of women's bodies in shaping communities.

Of *Les Saignantes*

With the English title *The Bloodettes, Les Saignantes* was produced in 2005 and previewed during the 2005 Toronto International Film Festival (TIFF) and the 2007 Cannes Film Festival. Several scholars and film critics including Kenneth Harrow, Olivier Barlet, and Olivier Tchouaffe have compellingly analyzed the film as a political critique of the postcolonial state as well as its subversion of genre and gender dynamic. But, what

---

1. Philippe Laburthe-Tolra, *Les seigneurs de la forêt* (Paris: Publications de la Sorbonne, 1981); Jean Pierre Ombolo, *Sexe et Société en Afrique Noire: l'Anthropologie Sexuelle Beti: essai analytique, critique, et comparatif* (Paris: L'Harmattan, 1990); Jeanne-Françoise Vincent, *Femmes beti entre deux mondes: entretiens dans la foret du Cameroun* (Paris: Karthala, 2001).

has not been noted is how at times, the film resists negative stereotypes of West African women's bodies.

Set circa 2025 in a postcolonial West African state, the mystical and ritual-laden film features two young sexy women who operate in official spaces, engaging in transactional sex for business contracts.[2] However, the decadent and corrupted state of the country forces the intervention of the Mevoungou to take possession of their bodies and direct them from their individual concerns towards a community-oriented mission. As they execute their mission of purifying the diseased postcolonial state, the protagonists also undergo their own purification.

The film opens with a sexual encounter between Majolie (Adele Ado) and a high ranking state official and ends with his death. Panicked and frustrated over the loss of her sexual investment, Majolie calls her best friend Chouchou (Dorelia Calmel) to help her dispose of the lifeless body. The disposal of the body leads them to explore the various socio-economic strata where corruption, decadence, and death lurk. Following their mistreatment of the corpse, "les Saignantes," the titular characters, take it to the butcher shop and have an animalized butcher decapitate it while passing it for a "load of fresh meat, prime beef." However, the butcher miraculously recognizes the body of the *Secrétaire General du Cabinet Civil* (SGCC) by tasting it; but, he proceeds to separate the head and the testicles from the body. Later, with the realization that they will possibly land other business deals during the SGCC's funeral, Majolie and Chouchou, already in possession of the head, work to reconstitute the body by visiting a mortuary where an alcoholic middle-aged mortician, who upon receiving a bribe, provides them with a body that matches the head. The re-constitution of the SGCC's body with a random and unnamed body, found at the mortuary, suggests the interchangeability of all bodies in the postcolonial state; in this way the film begins to destabilize the exceptionality of the ruling body.

In order to strike the business deal at the funeral, Majolie and Chouchou attempt to seduce the State Minister (Emile Abossolo Mbo). But, an intelligent man, a sex maniac, and a voodoo adept, the Minister proves to be more insightful and challenges the protagonists. At the end of the film, strengthened and purified, they use their supernatural powers in a type of martial arts dance scene to defeat the State Minister. Through the invisible force, acquired during their purification process and that flows through their bodies, Majolie and Chouchou throw waves of energy at the minister weakening him and, by extension, the corrupt elite. Additionally, they succeed in wresting away from him and his corrupt entourage a van load of cash, yet roam the streets of poor neighborhoods in order to escape state-sponsored forces. Even though the film does not feature the victory over the corrupt ruling class, it suggests empowering female characters and the positive powers of their bodies.

Now an established filmmaker on the West African cinema scene, Bekolo achieves continental and international recognition in 1992 at the age of 26 thanks to his debut film, *Quartier Mozart*. To overcome the challenges of distributing his film in Duala, Cameroun, a city with two main commercial theatres, Bekolo screened it in the city Town Hall for weeks and advertised it on cabs. The making and distribution of *Quartier Mozart* demonstrate Bekolo's innovative and maverick spirit, which *les Saignantes* reinforces with

---

2. Most published scholarly works on Les Saignantes have described Majolie and Chouchou as prostitutes. I argue against that label because sex trade is not their exclusive source of income. In fact, they use sexual favors to obtain business deals and to gain leverage in Cameroonian high social and political ranks. Transactional sex rather than prostitution best describes their activities.

the metaphorical and literal emasculation of the male ruling class. In fact, the film seeks to shake up the status quo because it was inspired by a real life experience.

In an interview in 2005, Bekolo explained how he discovered the corruption in the postcolonial state and the influence that the 'misused' female sexuality-reduced here to transactional sex—has on the ruling body: "During a stay in Cameroon, I wanted to meet a Minister but I didn't succeed. A young woman told me she could sort it out for me. I quickly understood it was a network and I could have met the whole government that way! These young women control the workings of the system and they have a certain power" (Interview Barlet and Bekolo 2005, my translation). As a filmmaker, Bekolo therefore used cinema to explore, in unsettling ways, the degeneration in the postcolonial state as well as the crippling influence of women's bodies on the body politic.

Female Body and the Diseased Postcolonial State

By featuring female protagonists who appropriate spaces traditionally defined as male, wield the phallic symbol—the guns in the 'shooting position'—and stand up like men rather than squat down to urinate, the director seeks to reclaim a feminine modality of power in a space where women's bodies are considered to be instrumental in the corruption of the state and where masculine symbols have failed. In several interviews, Bekolo explains his choice of female protagonists and highlights the thread between female bodies, moral contamination, and the ills of the postcolonial state. To Akin Adesokan, he says:

> I had the idea that if I focused on women, I would really touch on very sensitive issues in society. I was trying to make a film about Cameroon, and so it was important to bring up the issue of women's relationship with men in power. That is a sensitive issue, and it would seem more interesting than if the central characters were to be boys. Also, *there is a connection between the idea of human corruption and girls.*[3] (my emphasis)

Then, with Claire Schaffner, Bekolo frames women as instruments to draw attention to questions that would otherwise remain without interest, adding: "Concerning the girls, they become interesting when they adopt an ambivalent behavior because everyone gets involved: traditions, the police.... *It will be less radical if the characters were male. The girls allow me to politicize my views of society*" (my emphasis and translation).[4] From these answers, it appears that women occupy a crucial position in the postcolonial state; but, unfortunately, they seem to contribute to its decadence. Their actions justify the centuries-old patriarchal beliefs that stigmatize women's bodies as source of moral contamination.

By juxtaposing his interviews with the film, it appears that Bekolo's reading of women's bodies is a web of contradictions. On one hand, he acknowledges their importance in the advancement of the postcolonial state and seems to argue that long term solutions to its ills will be unsustainable without addressing questions related to women's status and

---

3. Akin Adesokan, "The Challenges of Aesthetic Populism: An Interview with Jean-Pierre Bekolo," *Postcolonial Text* Vol. 4.1. (2008). http://postcolonial.org/index.php/pct/article/view/771/538 (accessed August 20, 2009).

4. "Quant aux filles, elles sont un sujet intéressant car lorsqu'elles ont un comportement ambivalent, tout le monde s'en mêle: les traditions, la police ... C'est moins radical lorsqu'il s'agit de garçons. Elles me permettent de politiser mon regard sur la société," interview with Schaffner.fa 02 RTF.rtf.

conditions. On the other, he makes a questionable and exploitative move with the statement: "it would seem more interesting than if the central characters were to be boys," which turns women into metaphors in his political critique of the postcolonial state as well as marketing instruments. Bekolo's instrumentalization of women somewhat resonates with that of nationalist movements and their uses of women's images as sites of cultural interiority to advance their decolonizing agenda, without any regards to women's conditions.[5]

Perhaps the pervasive belief in the dangerous powers of female bodies has led the director to consider them as the antidote to the ills of the postcolonial state; in other words to set up the poison as the cure. Although problematic, the director's answers are refreshing because they move beyond reified categories. Any rigid distinction between power and powerlessness, the body as a site of subjugation or resistance is unproductive at best and dangerous at worst. To use the poison as the cure, he draws from the past, from women-centered and community-oriented rituals. In the precolonial Beti society, female bodies were marshaled for the communal good, which can be considered a complex practice because it turned women's bodies into objects in the service of the collective. But, contrary to the precolonial Beti society, Bekolo's imaginary postcolonial state sees them as exclusively destructive. And it is this unitary thinking that *Les Saignantes* seeks to undermine. In the same vein, the director is not interested in upholding the values of a specific gender of sex, he moves away from rigid categories, adapting the women-centered ritual to the point of degendering and defeminizing it. This film is a 'photoshopped' version of the grim reality that he experienced and the software serving to 'beautify' or heal the image is the Mevoungou ritual. The dialogue between anthropological texts on the Mevoungou and Bekolo's film adaptation demonstrates the director's artistic intervention in recuperating the precolonial cultural practice. In the postcolonial context where traditional beliefs are under siege, Bekolo's invocation of the Mevoungou ritual works as a reminder to contemporary continental and diasporic young African women of women's bodily powers.

As one of the most revered female secret societies of the Beti and due to its cultural significance in studies of power configurations, the Mevoungou has received considerable anthropological attention.[6] Yet, its secret nature challenges any exhaustive account of it. The use of anthropological texts to contextualize the film is fraught with tension because they cannot be taken at face value. Indeed, they should be understood in the larger and contentious conversation around cultural anthropology and its subjects. In his seminal *The Invention of Africa* (1988), V. Y. Mudimbé argues anthropology's role in reifying Africans and their cultures as abnormally different. According to him, the thought-objects of anthropology were partially constructed outside of their "original" context and incorporated in an ideological matrix of power/knowledge: "The anthropologist did not seem to respect the immanence of human experience and went on to organize, at scientific expense, methods and ways of ideological reduction: concrete social experiences

---

5. Elleke Boehmer, "Transfiguring the Colonial Body into Narrative," *Novel*, Vol. 3 (1991): 268–77.

6. Laburthe-Tolra, "Le Mevoungou et les rituels féminins a Minlaaba," (1985); "Initiations et sociétés secrètes au Cameroun: Essai sur la religion beti" (1981); Marie-Paule Bochet de Thé "Rites et associations traditionnelles chez les femmes beti du sud du Cameroun" (1985), Vincent, "Femmes beti entre deux mondes: Entretiens dans la foret du Cameroun" (2001); Charles Gueboguo, "Manifestations et facteurs explicatifs de l'homosexualité a Yaoundé et Douala." http://semgai.free.fr/doc_et_pdf/Gueboguo_memoire_maitrise.pdf (2002) (accessed August 5, 2009).

were looked at and interpreted from the normativity of a political discourse and its initiatives" (89). Mudimbé's argument serves as a cautionary measure against investing the value of science in the descriptions of the Mevoungou as well as rejecting anthropological texts, which remain one of the limited options of making contact with the ritual.

The Mevoungou and/in Anthropological Texts

The recovery and the larger dissemination of an extinct female ritual speak to the social and political intervention of the film. The task is made even more compelling because in the early decades of missionization, German missionaries abolished many Beti indigenous rituals including the Mevoungou (Mviena 1970, Vincent 2001). Bekolo, himself a Beti, never experienced the ritual or heard about it until he read *Le tombeau du soleil: a novel* by French anthropologist Philippe Laburthe-Tolra (2005).[7] Although the novel form may have 'popularized' the ritual, French and Cameroonian anthropologists including Jean-Pierre Ombolo, Charles Gueboguo, Jeanne-Françoise Vincent, Philippe Laburthe-Tolra, and Marie-Paule Bochet de Thé have published on the Mevoungou since the 1950s.

Anthropologists report that the Mevoungou ritual was typically performed during periods of hardship, draught, unsatisfactory hunting sessions, and in cases of thievery or witchcraft. Under those challenging circumstances, men would request that women perform the ritual, more specifically that they summoned female mystical powers, believed to stem from their connectedness to the earth. In *Traditions et Transition: entretiens avec des femmes beti du Cameroun* (1976), Vincent provides an overview of the ritual based on seventeen interviews she conducted with Beti women in 1967 and 1971. Most of the accounts are based on reports and hearsay as only three of the sixteen interviewees most in their sixties actually participated in it. Not surprisingly, the interviewees differ on the significance of the ritual to the point of contradicting one another. For example, Cressence thinks the ritual and its festivities are a way for women to eat elaborate meals, since men daily enjoy those meals at the expense of women and children. Others define it as a ritual of purification, initiation, protection against evil eyes, celebration of femininity, and resistance against male domination.

According to Vincent's interviews, in the Beti cosmogony, the Mevoungou is a secret society built around the cult of the "*evu.*" Located in women's bellies, precisely in their clitorises, the *evu* is a magical gland that embodies both good and evil and when activated, is capable of giving life and taking it. The location of the gland explains why the power of the Mevoungou is predicated upon the clitoris, which is seen as the exterior physical site of this powerful gland. The leader of the society, called the mother of Mevoungou, *Mevoungou Mba* in Beti, is chosen based on the large size of her clitoris, which is believed to represent her power and fecundity. She is a woman past menopause and no longer engages in heterosexual intercourse.

---

7. Ironically, Bekolo's contact with the ritual became possible via a French anthropologist and Laburthe-Tolra as the link shows the possible non-linearity in the perpetuation and transmission of cultures.

Although the society's membership is exclusively female, the entire community of men and women reap the benefits of its activities. The interview subjects of Vincent's monograph describe the Mevoungou purification ritual as a two-part ceremony (public and private). The public ceremony reunites the entire village while the private/secret one is exclusively attended by the initiated and the candidates for the secret society. The secret ceremony starts with the mother of Mevoungou undressing and inviting the participants to undress before she swears them to secrecy. Then, they invoke a ceremonial package composed of various roots, ashes, medicinal leaves, and centipedes among others. The composition of the package reinforces the belief in women's connectedness to nature. Later, women dance around and jump over the fire while invoking the Mevoungou "symbolized as the package" to take their lives should they be guilty of a wrongdoing or to retaliate against those who offend them. The rest of the ceremony consists in transmitting the power of the package to the clitoris of the mother of Mevoungou and to those of the other women. If the ritual is performed to unmask wrongdoers, the village expects them to confess or an outbreak of diseases ranging from swelling to various skin conditions will unmask them.

In 1985, Laburthe-Tolra published *Initiations et sociétés sécrètes*. This study draws heavily from several sources: Vincent's interviews, Bochet de Thé's dissertation (1970), and German anthropologist Gunther Tessmann's 1913 reports. Laburthe-Tolra defines the ritual "as a means of protection and a way of eliminating evil forces for both men and women," confirming its importance as well as the occasions of its performance.[8] However, he silences much of the 'messiness' of Vincent's interview subjects reducing their complex and indeterminable descriptions to the rite of passage for young girls and the night-long ritual of purification and sanitation performed by married women. Importantly, however, he confirms Vincent's report that the mother of Mevoungou is chosen based on the large size of her *evu* (her clitoris), which is believed to symbolize the extent of her power and fertility.[9] The criteria for choosing the mother of Mevoungou lead Laburthe-Tolra to observe that the Mevoungou is a "celebration of the clitoris and of feminine power."[10] Adoration of the clitoris explains why, in Beti culture, its excision is the ultimate punishment for adulterous women. Expanding Vincent's descriptions, the anthropologist describes that after the transmission of the power of the clitoris to the package, women rub, massage, admire, tickle, and stretch out the clitoris to give it the allure of a virile organ. Participants then mimic intercourse with older women in the conventional masculine role and the younger ones in the feminine. Throughout the ritual, women make fun of men's genitals, degrading them while celebrating women's. In the middle of the night, the package is burnt and its ash is divided into three portions. The first portion is buried with a centipede in front of the hut of the organizer, the second is made into a package to represent the Mevoungou, and the third is sprinkled on rooftops and around the village. According to Laburthe-Tolra's account, women spend the rest of the night dancing, singing, eating, conjuring, examining, and praising members with prominent clitorises. Most anthropological reports show consistencies in the importance of women's bodies in

---

8. Laburthe-Tolra, *Le tombeau du soleil: Chronique des Bendzo* (Paris: Jacob, 1986); "Le Mevungu apparaissait comme un moyen de protection et d'élimination des maléfices au yeux de tous, femmes et hommes," "Le mevungu et les rituels féminins à Minlaaba" (1985), 235.

9. Vincent, *Traditions et transitions, entretiens avec des femmes beti du Sud Cameroun* (ORSTOM: Berger Levrault, 1976); *Femmes beti entre deux mondes: entretiens dans la foret du Cameroun* (Paris: Karthala, 2001).

10. "Le Mevungu en revanche, se présente clairement, du moins pour ses adeptes, comme une célébration du clitoris et de la puissance féminine," Ibid, 234.

restoring social balance and prosperity to the community, but they differ on other uses that may appear subversive to patriarchal values.

Desexualizing the Historical Ritual

Two French feminist anthropologists, Bochet de Thé and Vincent, argue that the Mevoungou was also a means of women's resistance against male domination. Vincent believes that the rituals function, among other uses, as "retaliatory actions deliberately taken by women against men" and Bochet de Thé adds that it is a means for women to "affirm their personality, reinforce their productivity and to engage in a double sexuality" that is sanctioned lesbianism.[11] However, most male anthropologists and intellectuals, whether French or Cameroonian, dismiss these subversive aspects. For instance, Charles Gueboguo claims that the descriptions of the ritual suggest that it is a celebration of women's sexual organs and power and admits that it does contain homosexual gestures. However, he opposes its eroticization, arguing that its most important use was for procreation. For Laburthe-Tolra, the ritual was not a means of resistance but, a celebration of women's sexual organs. He suggests that it resembles a desperate plan to summon the powers of nature to heal the community rather than the constitution of a female world of pleasures.

Cameroonian intellectuals, including Catholic priests Paul Mviena and Isadore Tabi, as well as Bekolo himself, echo Laburthe-Tolra and Gueboguo in critiquing the sexualized interpretations they think French feminist anthropologists bring to bear on the ritual. Mviena argues that the ignorance of its real significance and the misinterpretations by colonialists justified its abolition. The Catholic priest pleads that the Mevoungou be not regarded as "un Sabbath des lesbiennes" (a Sabbath of lesbians) because it was exclusively performed for procreation and social purposes. In 2005, almost 30 years after Mviena, Bekolo desexualizes the ritual claiming that it focuses on a force of nature, women's sexual organs, to heal the community and did not implicate sexual relations: "In Beti, the same root [Mevoungou] refers to cohabitation, offspring, progenitor … — at least around fifteen words with no relation to the sexual" (My translation).[12] Despite the director's words, *Les Saignantes* still shows women engaging in joyful sexual intimacy with one another for purposes of their own pleasure and self-discovery.

It is intriguing that those who desexualize the ritual are men even though the ritual is forbidden to them. I would argue that the desexualization goes beyond the cultural battle between French anthropologists and Cameroonian intellectuals to enter a gendered landscape. Although the research necessary to argue that rubbing clitorises provoke pleasures lies beyond the scope of this chapter, I would argue that by desexualizing the ritual, male observers deny women who performed the Mevoungou the possibility of experiencing sexual and erotic pleasures. Women's enjoyment of sexual pleasures during the ritual should not be contradictory to or annihilate its 'spiritual' and patriarchal aspects. To completely evacuate possible pleasures associated with the ritual is to 'hijack' Beti women's bodies. And as a postcolonial African feminist critic, I seek here to reclaim the power of the body without its stigma. Whether the ritual is oriented toward purification

---

11. "Pour elles, c'était le moyen d'affirmer leur personnalité, de renforcer leur fécondité et de réaliser une double sexualité" 248.

12. "Being African and modern at the same time," "En beti, la même racine désigne le concubinage, la descendance, le procréateur etc. au moins une dizaine de termes sans rapport avec l'acte sexuel."

or for women's self-empowerment and resistance against men's tyrannical practices, *Les Saignantes* shows the positive aspects of female bodies.

Les Saignantes as an Adaptation of the Mevoungou Ritual

"Mevoungou was the foundation on which the society of tomorrow was being built…. It's really a Mevoungou we all needed in this country." Postscript, *Les Saignantes*

The filmic adaptation of the Mevoungou is, at times, very consistent with anthropological descriptions of the ritual; but at other times, it transforms, degenders, and even suggests fear and ambivalence toward it. To re-create the atmosphere and the participants, various parts of the film are tailored to mimic the 'original' ritual. The necessity of the ritual is unequivocal as the off-screen voice gravely declares after the shocking scene of sex, horror, and death: "Mevoungou has fallen on us like a bad dream. Now this country has a chance to escape from the darkness." And later: "Mevoungou was inviting us to join the dance." The ambivalence about the ritual is reflected in these descriptions as "fallen on us like a bad dream" and "inviting us to join the dance." This juxtaposition of coercion and invitation, of a frightening event and a joyous celebration, is unmistakable. The use of the communal plural third person is an invitation to the viewer to join the community of men and women that need purification through women's creative and healing powers, even if at times, the film downplays the importance of female powers by degendering the Mevoungou.

The centrality of the ritual is established through the timing of its definition, after a blackout, a moment of heightened confusion. With the intense curiosity, the viewer becomes more receptive to the off-screen voice and her definition:

Mevoungou is neither a living being nor a thing. Mevoungou is not a place much less a moment. Mevoungou is neither a desire nor a state of mind. Because Mevoungou is something we see, we live and experience but cannot quite define. We don't decide to see Mevoungou. Mevoungou appears to you. Mevoungou invites itself.

Like a dormant entity ready to manifest itself in unforeseen and challenging circumstances, the Mevoungou escapes the control of *les saignantes* and takes possession of their beings. Here, it is adapted to the demands of a more globalized world because unlike the tangible ceremonial package in the ritual, it is framed in intangible terms. From its original setting, the village, the ritual is relocated in the postcolonial city where corruption reeks. The Mevoungou is no longer time and place-specific and exclusive to Beti women much less the prerogative of a specific gender. In the film, it is cast as gender neutral with the use of the singular third personal "it."

While, the nighttime setting of the film corresponds to the conventional time of the Mevoungou ritual, the low-key lighting of the opening scene and the diffuse shadows and pools of light set the tone and create a thriller atmosphere. In addition to the low-key lighting, the use of red, orange, green, and blue as dominant colors reflects the realm of the paranormal, dazzling and unsettling the viewer. The off-screen voice, that of a mature woman, is a compelling device that forces the viewer to pay closer attention to the content and also to behoove her to consider the larger implications of the issues tackled in the film. In an additive logic, the role of the off-screen voice seems to straddle polar opposites. Like in the conventional film noir, it gives *Les Saignantes* a haunting note while serving as a soothing and reassuring voice that reinforces the maternal and nurturing associations with women. As an omniscient narrator and a guide, the voice informs the viewer of the development of the plot and provides information that would otherwise be unknown to her.

To re-create the passivity of men and the activity of women, several scenes of the movie show men sitting in *maquis* drinking or lying down like the SGCC while Majolie and Chouchou and the five elderly women are active.[13] Not only the long shots of the men in *maquis* drown their voices suggesting the fruitless nature of their conversations, but they also create indistinct and impersonal figures, incapable of curing the rampant corruption. Through the device, most men in the film and, by implication, in the postcolonial state, are cast as shadowy figures. In contrast to the passive roles in which most men are confined at the beginning of the film, close-up shots of the protagonists and the initiated reflect their importance to the upcoming ritual. And the viewer clearly identifies them and hears their voices and conversations.

The opening scene with Majolie and the SGCC reflects the differences between men and women. In the sexual encounter, Majolie is literally and metaphorically in the elevated position and the SGCC is in the lower position. Wearing only a bra with her pubic hair exposed, she gyrates over the old man and executes the 'shooting position' while suspended in a harness.[14] The scene proves provocative and titillating in its withholding of details since the absence of dialogue preceding and during contributes to the suspense level and raises the viewer's feeling of unease. After a moment, Majolie springs on and jumps away from the man. Using the prerogatives of the empowered position, she finally chooses the moment of contact between the bodies, which turns out to be unusual.

Speaking of unusual occurrences, the scene also reverses the normalized hierarchies of gender and seniority with two unexpected juxtapositions.

The first unusual juxtaposition, a metaphor of the inequitable power dynamic, is contrary to the prescribed social norms because the West African imaginary considers the woman and a young one, for that matter, as the one who should be actively penetrated and dominated, placed physically underneath her social superior. The reversal of the conventional gender dynamic with the male in the bottom position, with arms extended like an infant waiting for a savior-like, maternal figure and the young woman, who like a savior figure, an angel comes to rescue a man in distress is potentially offensive to the collective imagination.

The second unexpected juxtaposition is the death or rather the sacrifice of the SGCC for a more prosperous State. Majolie's 'shooting position' and the gyrating and engulfing movements of her hips take the welcoming and obedient male body from the terrain of the superficially pleasurable into that of submission, war, and death. The new terrain represents what Georges Bataille names the erotic, where death is a constant presence.[15] The death of

---

13. The maquis in Francophone West Africa refers to a bar, usually frequented by men.

14. "The shooting position" or "La position du tir" is a dance move created by young artists to imitate the shooting positions of soldiers and rebels. The dance originated from Cote d'Ivoire in the year 2002 following the armed rebellion. The integration of celebration and death, two seemingly contradictory phenomena, reflects the creativity in the postcolony and the ability to turn traumatic events into regenerating ones. Also, with the inclusion of an Ivorian dance in a Cameroonian-directed film, Bekolo demonstrates his ability to produce a cinema that transcends national boundaries.

15. Georges Bataille, *Death and Sensuality: a Study of Eroticism and the Taboo* (New York: Walker, 1962).

the SGCC subverts the image of the beautiful and sexy young African woman as a source of pleasure for the enjoyment of the affluent. Unlike the conventional reading of a female body as annihilating, the film shows it as purifying, for Majolie, now the embodiment of the Mevoungou, purifies the community by extracting a member of the corrupt ruling regime. The scene, which pushes the erotic boundaries in West African cinema, represents the female body and its sexuality as powerful and positive, a bold departure from pathologizing images.

No ritual is complete without the assistance of the initiated, represented here by five elderly women in red and blue headscarves with serious and authoritative demeanors — one of these women is Chouchou's mother. In the film, under their guidance, the younger women dominate spaces traditionally considered male. Through visual effects, the viewer witnesses the ways in which the initiated protect Majolie and Chouchou. For example, in the middle of the film, when the police suspect the protagonists' subversive activities, Inspector Rokko goes to Chouchou's mother's house to arrest them. In his search, he is caressed by four women who are invisible to him; they lift his gun and move him in an instant from the house to a hospital.

Figure 1. The initiated. Courtesy of Quartier Mozart Films.

In order to perform the purification ritual of the diseased state, the protagonists need to undergo their own initiation, which they complete not through a clitoris-centric session but, through a dance session. In fact, consistent with anthropological descriptions of the ritual, dance moves and ritualistic movements permeate the film. While Majolie and Chouchou may appear terrifying and zombie-like, they are actually conforming to the demands of the ritual. For example, during the fight with the State Minister, they perform dance-like movements to emit waves of energy that neutralize the enemy; however, the last blow to him was possible after they tapped into their genital powers by going through orgasmic spasms.

The most elaborate dance occurs in the middle of the film, and from it Majolie and Chouchou come out as re-created. After they reject the clitoral session, a point I shall analyze later, and enter Chouchou's bedroom, the powerful voice of the iconic Brenda Fassie singing "Vuli Ndlela" throws them in a dancing frenzy during which they change several outfits and embody several women. *Vulindlela*, a Zulu word for "to open the way," seems the most suitable incantation for a transformational session.[16] At a dizzying pace, created by the doubling and tripling of the shots, Majolie and Chouchou metamorphose from sexy to modest, from young to old, and from trashy to respectable. In fact, their movements take them into the spiritual realm where they embody several beings and live several lives, continuously creating and evacuating identities. The doubling and tripling shots condense time and space and reject the comfortable position of sameness and immobility by creating an uncanny sense of estrangement and familiarity. Reflecting on the role of dance in ritual performances, John Conteh Morgan writes that the movements are "not used in the representational mode, that is, to signify but instead to create psychological states... [they] are the inevitable elixir, as it were, for the performers' transition into liminal states of trance and religious performance."[17]

The power invested in songs and dances becomes obvious when the off-screen voice triumphantly announces: "Our Mevoungou had rediscovered its integrity. It could no longer accept the slightest insult. We were ready for the final phase." Through the dancing frenzy, the protagonists recover their integrity, come out as new born women, and ready to deliver the last blow to the enemy. Following their purification, they attend the SGCC's funeral and subsequently disarm the Minister.

The scene of metamorphoses is made even more compelling with Bekolo's use of the mirror. While dancing, Majolie and Chouchou gaze into a mirror and watch their appearances change. That experience displaces the reliance on other entities and propels self-reliance; as a result, they are purified and cease being instruments of the system. The specular image is reminiscent of the Lacanian mirror stage and provides the protagonists a triumphant turning point in their identity formation.[18] They have reached their completeness and integrity, unlike in the previous stage characterized by 'unco-ordination' and fragmentation.[19] To create the new Majolie and Chouchou, Bekolo creatively combines the occult powers of the Beti cosmogony and the Lacanian theory of the mirror stage.

Radical Departure from the Clitoris-Centric Ritual

While dance movements permeate the film, the appreciation of the clitoris, a crucial aspect of original ritual, disappears from the filmic adaptation. When protecting the young women from corrupt leaders and state forces, the initiated attempt to perform Chouchou's initiation and purification. Similar to the 'original' ritual, they need to appreciate Chouchou's clitoris in order to consolidate the success of the ritual. After re-

---

16. For a translation of the term "vulindlela" see fa 02 RTF.rtfhttp://www.gov.bw/cgi-bin/news.cgi?d=20010827.

17. John Conteh Morgan, *Theatre and Drama in Francophone Africa: A Critical Introduction* (Cambridge: Cambridge University Press, 1994), 31.

18. Jacques Lacan, *Écrits* (Paris: Éditions du Seuil, 1966). In *Écrits*, Lacan defines the mirror stage as the period between the ages of six to eighteen months in which the child recognizes his reflection in the mirror. The experience is accompanied by an affairement jubilatoire and a connaissance paranoiaque, a celebratory and affirmative self-recognition and the realization of the child's separateness and disunity from the mother and the world (19).

19. Fragmentation is a pervasive theme in the movie: the fragmentation of the SGCC's body, of the state, and of les saignantes.

constituting the SGCC's body, the protagonists go to Chouchou's house where the initiated are waiting for them to examine Chouchou's clitoris. The examination and the rubbing, feeding, and stretching of the clitoris will empower Chouchou since the size of her *evu*, clitoris, would correspond to the level of her mystical powers. However, Majolie mocks the practice and teases her friend: "They want to see your clitoris" to which Chouchou answers in a song: "They can't see my clitoris." On this aspect of the ritual, Chouchou and the initiated seem positioned on different ideological platforms, precolonial and postcolonial. While the initiated stay up all night expecting to consolidate the purification, Chouchou mocks their attempt through a song. Her refusal to comply with all the rules of the ritual is symptomatic of contemporary continental West African young women's rejection of most cultural and traditional rituals and practices. And postcolonial African states, in their majority, condone such rejection as Cyprien Fisiy argues: "Postcolonial authorities see the belief in witchcraft and other occult forces as creating a basic impediment to development initiatives in Africa." Aspiring to 'modern' forms of being, the ruling classes' position in comfortable oppositions modernity to rituals which they construct as markers of primitive societies.[20] Ironically though, while they publicly disavow occultist practices, they resort to them for their personal gains just like the State Minister in the film. It is therefore subversive in the eyes of the ruling classes that *Les Saignantes* advocates an intelligent use of occult forces such as the Mevoungou as an antidote to the failures of the postcolonial state.

The disappearance of the clitoris from the purification ritual, as a result of the protagonists' choice to undergo their own initiation under the guidance of the late South African singer Brenda Fassie constitutes a double-edged undertaking. And several reasons, often contradictory, may explain the director's choice. Rather than praising the clitoris, the director makes the choice of a performative cliché of female sexuality, trying on clothes, thereby degendering and defeminizing what had been at least physically an exclusively female genital ritual. As shown earlier, the film is not devoid of sex, it just seems to avoid an extensive female same-sex erotic practices as prescribed in the ritual to reclaim a more acceptable and palatable heterosexuality, even if gendered roles are reversed in the opening scene. Although *Les Saignantes* suggests female sexual empowerment, it does not go as far as to endorse a full blown erotic autonomy, which in its view might have contributed to practices such as transactional sex. In other words, female sexuality should be consigned within certain parameters.

But rather than consider the disappearance of the clitoris as a patriarchal practice, one can also see it as the director's need to get around the challenges of representing the clitoris to a mass audience. Perhaps, out of respect, he refrains from showing the clitoris, which would amount to divulgating the secrecy around the ritual and or violating women's bodies. The director's choice seems to echo Anne-Laure Folly's claim that "Any action of unveiling [sex] amounts to violating it."[21] Unlike anthropological texts and their extensive descriptions of the ritual, Bekolo's medium, a visual performance is more limiting. Also, perhaps Chouchou's rejection of the clitoral session may suggest the filmmaker's rejection of a singular and nativist view of precolonial rituals and practices. So, against die-hard 'traditionalists' with their *a la lettre* prescriptions and proscriptions regarding anything ritual, Bekolo decides to break loose from age-long constraints. He does delocalize and transform the ritual, adapting it to a more global audience and to

20. For more on the opposition of ritual to modernity, see the introduction to Jean and John Comaroff's anthology *Modernity and its Malcontents: Ritual and Power in Postcolonial Africa* (Chicago: Chicago University Press, 1993).

21. Alexis Tcheuyap, "Hors cadre: Le sexe dans le cinéma africain," *CinémAction*, Vol. 106 (2003): 37–40.

the demands of the screen. Instead of confining the ritual to some nativist framework, his adaptation becomes a more relevant approach and considers the larger context. In sum, whether the ritual is clitoris-centric or not, there is still something retained about female genital power by undergoing purification at the hands of powerful older women, seen as artists and healers.

Emasculation, Dismemberment, Theophagy: Purifying the Postcolonial State

In their journey to purify the state, female protagonists and the Mevoungou deploy an array of modes of purification, including sacrifice, decapitation, emasculation, and theophagy. According to Vincent's descriptions, oftentimes the ritual includes the sacrifice of a chicken or goat whose blood is used for purification. Similar to but unlike the historical ritual, in the film, a sacrifice is the *sine qua non* condition for a more prosperous State. But, instead of a goat or chicken, we have the SGCC, more specifically an elite body. After undergoing their own purification, the young women are now ready to purify the community by sacrificing a member of the corrupt ruling regime so the community can enter, albeit momentarily, a period of prosperity. In that vein, the title of the film, *Les Saignantes*, which means cruel women or those predisposed to inflict pain in French, resonates with the mission that Majolie and Chouchou have to execute: purify the diseased state. They administer the cure through bloodletting, upon which I think the title ought to be translated as "The Bloodletters" rather than "The Bleeders" or "The Bloodettes."[22]

Most often, the film portrays the protagonists with vampire-like qualities, operating at nights and with prominent lips, glistening and bloodshot eyes—created by color contact lenses. Unlike the conventional readings of vampires as destructive, here in the film they represent positive entities on the mission to save the postcolonial state. The 2009 revealing poster of the film emphasize their bloodsucking qualities. They show the young women as the devourers of the corrupt ruling elite and engaged in an economy of emasculation, eating, and *devoration*.

As part of the purification and a moment of women's empowerment, Chouchou and Majolie's degradation of the SGCC's testicles is a section of the film that literalizes anthropological descriptions of the Mevoungou ritual. After the protagonists have the butcher decapitate the body and take a break from their macabre experiences, they use the package representing the SGCC's testicles as their toy and Majolie rhetorically asks: "The Secretary General of the Civil Cabinet's balls?" Her question is more for the viewer than her friend. With it, the director seeks to avoid any ambiguity as to what the protagonists are about to do. Toying with the SGCC's testicles shows how young women dare disrespect corrupt old men, supposed pillars of patriarchy and holders of social and political powers. Insulting and degrading men's genitals are key aspects of the night-long Mevoungou ritual. With regards to that aspect, Laburthe-Tolra reports that German anthropologist Gunther Tessmann found the Mevoungou songs so outrageous and de-

---

22. In their 2007 essay on *Les Saignantes*, Celine Dewaele and Olivier Barlet translated the title as "The Bloodletters," which I think accurately reflects the spirit of the film.

Figure 2. Poster of Film 2009. Courtesy of Quartier Mozart Films.

grading that he could not report them.[23] Bekolo's adaptation of the abuse of men's genitals is interesting because it goes beyond the insult to have Majolie and Chouchou literally toy with and kick a small package shaped like male testicles. Kicking the SGCC's balls, insulting his manhood, constitutes his ultimate defeat as a man, especially in a culture where male genitals are invested with the power of a weapon. According to

---

23. Laburthe-Tolra (1985), 238.

Mbembé, the penis is an instrument of production of docile bodies in the postcolony because "[T]he violence of the penis that 'makes' a hole in a woman is undistinguishable from that of the gun that dangles and awaits its prey." Not only genitals are crucial in reproductive functions, they also serve as contractual power regulating relationships between men and women. In an additive logic, their disappearance, a recurrent allegory in West African films, is synonymous with the collapse of the postcolonial state.[24] Consequently, *Les Saignantes'* symbolic and literal emasculation of the ruling class is in itself a painful and humiliating blow to the imaginary patriarchy and dictatorship, and the use of young women as the agents of emasculation constitutes the humiliation of the highest order.

While degrading the SGCC's testicles draws from the described ritual, the scene of the sacrifice does not. Instead of a secret and an all female scene of sacrifice, the director creates a public and a mix-gendered performance. The public decapitation of the SGCC's body is an example of the excessive visual display of power, characteristic of ancient European regimes.[25] It also sets him up as an example and leaves the State, literally and figuratively, without its head and testicles, in a disarticulated and infertile state. This gory and uncomfortable act of violence is not pointless for it helps rid the State of a corrupt and cancerous body. The SGCC's body, metaphorical and literal, is the abject that ought to be cut from the social skin in need of purification.

Although the decapitation and the emasculation scenes create a malaise and unsettle the viewer, they also empower her by reversing the social hierarchy, potentially turning the SGCC's body into meat for the people's consumption. This consumption suggests the possibility of sacrificing and consuming the entire decayed system. The potential ingestion of the SGCC's body becomes a practice of cannibalism. In the film, we see a shift in the structure of perception of cannibalism, from its reading in colonialist writings as a sign of "absolute difference" between the natives and the colonialists to a form of domination in the postcolony.[26] Indeed in the discursive economy of colonialism, cannibalism, real or imaginary, was constructed as a sign of the natives' backwardness and heathenish nature and consequently used to justify the colonizing mission. The film's reversal of the trope of cannibalism contributes to its overall message of doing away with reified practices.

The film becomes more compelling as we move from cannibalism to theophagy, a higher level of subversion. Just like in Mbembe's postcolony, here the 'worshippers' devour the 'gods.' Their act is subversive if we consider how the corrupt postcolonial elite metaphorically and literally feed on the resources of the State and its people. I think that the film suggests a symbolic theophagy as a means of turning the postcolonial state into a self-sufficient and an organic State capable of flourishing without the handouts of the international financial institutions. The power that Majolie, Chouchou, and the Mevoungou have harnessed to purify the State threatens the authorities so much so that the police officer informs the Minister of Homeland Security and, by extension, the President, of the imminent threat that women are plotting against their rule. The supposed or real

---

24. See Sembene Ousmane's *Xala* (1975), Souleymane Cisse's *Yeleen* (1987), and Benoit Lamy and Ngangura Mweze's *La Vie Est Belle* (Life is Rosy) (1987), and Bekolo's *Quartier Mozart* (1992).

25. Michel Foucault, *Discipline and Punish: the Birth of the Prison* (New York: Vintage, 1979).

26. Stephen Greenblatt, *Marvelous Possessions: The Wonder of the New World* (Oxford: Oxford University Press, 1991); In *From Communication to Cannibalism*, Maggie Kilgour identifies in the act of eating a negotiation of a power dynamic in which the eater is the consumed. See Kilgour, *From Communication to Cannibalism: An Anatomy of Metaphors of Incorporation* (Princeton: Princeton University Press, 1990).

threat to the State speaks to women's contribution to the reconfiguration of the new post-colonial state. By choosing female characters as active agents in the new formulation, the film empowers them and reclaims their sexual bodies without the stigma of pathology or degeneracy.

Conclusion

In this essay, I argue that there is more to African women's sexuality than HIV/AIDS, rape as weapon of war, and female circumcision. Through a postcolonial feminist reading of Bekolo's political critique, I explore how the film retrieves an important precolonial ritual of the powerful female secret society of the Beti of Cameroon, giving women's rites the power to heal the postcolonial state. Despite the fear of the Mevoungou and, by implication, of women's bodies, which the off-screen voice conveys as: "Mevoungou is a serious thing that would either destroy us and or the country. We would have to use Mevoungou and get rid of it quickly if we want to survive,"[27] the film still features the image of positive female sexuality.

Our reading of the film and its representation of the women-centered ritual displaces the conventional reading of African women's sexual bodies as sites of oppression and pathologization. In the postcolonial context where traditional and cultural practices and beliefs are under siege, the film, as a performance of the Mevoungou ritual, works as a reminder that women's bodies can be positive forces. It also contradicts Western feminists' view of tradition as the locus of women's subordination and modernity as the path to their liberation, a view Signe Arnfred explains: "The general idea is that women's subordination belongs to tradition and to the past, whereas women's emancipation—or gender equality, as the current terminology has it—belongs to modernity and to the future."[28] This bifurcation has never served African women nor African feminist theory well.

References

Adesokan, Akin. "The Challenges of Aesthetic Populism: An Interview with Jean-Pierre Bekolo." *Postcolonial Text* Vol. 4.1. (2008). http://postcolonial.org/index.php/pct/article/view/771/538. (Accessed August 20, 2009).

Arnfred, Signe. "Simone De Beauvoir In Africa: 'Woman = The Second Sex?' Issues of African Feminist Thought." *Jenda: A Journal of Culture and African Women Studies* Vol. 2.1 (2002).

Barlet, Olivier. "Etre à la fois africain et contemporain: entretien avec Jean-Pierre Bekolo." *Africultures.* (July 2005).

_____. "*Les Saignantes*, The Bloodletters by Jean Pierre Bekolo." *Africultures.* (June 2007).

Bataille, Georges. *Death and Sensuality: a Study of Eroticism and the Taboo.* New York: Walker, 1962.

Boehmer, Elleke. "Transfiguring the Colonial Body into Narrative." *Novel* Vol. 3 (1991): 268–77.

---

27. Laburthe-Tolra.
28. Signe Arnfred, "Simone De Beauvoir In Africa: 'Woman = The Second Sex?' Issues of African Feminist Thought," *Jenda: A Journal of Culture and African Women Studies,* Vol. 2.1 (2002).

Bochet de Thé, Marie-Paule. *La femme dans la dynamique de la société béti 1887–1966.* Doctoral Dissertation, Université de la Sorbonne, Paris V, 1970.

_____. "Rites et associations traditionnelles chez les femmes béti du sud du Cameroun." *Femmes du Cameroun: mères pacifiques, femmes rebelles.* ean Claude Barbier, (ed.). 245–83. Paris: Karthala, 1985.

Comaroff, Jean and John. "Introduction" in *Modernity and its Malcontents: Ritual and Power in Postcolonial Africa.* Jean and John Comaroff (eds.). Chicago: Chicago University Press, 1993.

Foucault, Michel. *Discipline and Punish: the Birth of the Prison.* New York: Vintage, 1979.

Gueboguo, Charles. "Manifestations et facteurs explicatifs de l'homosexualité a Yaoundé et Douala." (2002). http://semgai.free.fr/doc_et_pdf/Gueboguo_memoire_maitrise.pdf.(Accessed August 5, 2009).

Greenblatt, Stephen. *Marvelous Possessions: The Wonder of the New World.* Oxford: Oxford University Press, 1991.

Harrow, Kenneth. "Let Me Tell You about Bekolo's Latest Film, *Les Saignantes,* but First …" 2006 ALA conference paper. http://www.msu.edu/~harrow/recent/LesSaignantesALApaper.htm. (Accessed July 23, 2008).

_____. "What's an Old Man Like You Doing with a Saignante Like Me?" In *Facts, Fiction, and African Creative Imaginations,* Toyin Falola and Fallou Ngom, (eds.). New York: Routledge, 2009. 190–206.

Kilgour, Maggie. *From Communication to Cannibalism: An Anatomy of Metaphors of Incorporation.* Princeton: Princeton University Press, 1990.

Laburthe-Tolra, Philippe. *Le tombeau du soleil: Chronique des Bendzo.* Paris: Jacob, 1986.

_____. *Initiations et sociétés secrètes au Cameroun: Essai sur la religion beti.* Paris: Karthala, 1985.

_____. *Les seigneurs de la forêt.* Paris: Publications de la Sorbonne, 1981.

Lacan, Jacques. *Écrits.* Paris: Éditions du Seuil, 1966.

Les Saignantes. DVD. Directed by Jean-Pierre Bekolo, 2005. France, Cameroon: Quartier Mozart Films, 2009.

Mbembe, Achille. *On the postcolony: Studies on the History of Society and Culture.* Berkeley: University of California Press, 2001.

Morgan, John Conteh. *Theatre and Drama in Francophone Africa: A Critical Introduction.* Cambridge: Cambridge University Press, 1994.

Mviena, Paul. *Univers culturel et religieux du peuple beti.* Douala: St. Paul, 1970.

Mudimbé, V.Y. *The Invention of Africa: Gnosis, Philosophy, and the Order of Knowledge.* Bloomington: Indiana University Press, 1988.

Ombolo, Jean Pierre. *Sexe et Société en Afrique Noire: l'Anthropologie Sexuelle Beti: essai analytique, critique, et comparatif.* Paris: L'Harmattan, 1990.

Osinubi, Taiwo A. "Cognition's Warp: African Films on Near-Future Risk." *African Identities* Vol. 7:2 (2009): 255–74.

Quartier Mozart. VHS. Directed by Jean-Pierre Bekolo. France, Cameroon: Une production Kola Case. 1992.

Schaffner, Claire. "Interview with Jean Pierre Bekolo: *Les Saignantes,* film Africain d'anticipation." *Afrik.com* (May 2009).

Stam, Robert. *Subversive Pleasures: Bakhtin, Cultural Criticism, and Film.* Baltimore: John Hopkins University Press, 1989.

Tabi, Isadore. *La théologie des rites Beti: essai d'explication religieuse des rites Beti et ses implications socio-culturelles.* Yaounde: AMAC-CEN, n.d.

Tcheuyap, Alexie. "Hors cadre: Le sexe dans le cinéma africain." *CinémAction.* Vol. 106 (2003): 37–40.

Tchouaffe, Olivier. "Homosexuality and the Politics of Sex, Respectability and Power in Postcolonial Cameroon." *Postamble.* Vol. 2. 2 (2006): 4–15.

Tsala, Abbé. T. "Mœurs et coutumes des Ewôndô." *Etudes camerounaises.* Vol. 56 (1958): 8–112.

Vincent, Jeanne-Françoise. *Traditions et transitions, entretiens avec des femmes beti du Sud Cameroun.* ORSTOM: Berger Levrault, 1976.

_____. *Femmes beti entre deux mondes: entretiens dans la foret du Cameroun.* Paris: Karthala, 2001.

Chapter 3

"I am the Rape": Exile, Sexual Violence, and the Body in the Poems of Dambudzo Marechera

Z'étoile Imma

A product of colonized Rhodesia, imperial England, and liberated Zimbabwe, the poetry of Dambudzo Marechera, embodies a crisis of double consciousness[1] that is often ubiquitous within postcolonial imaginaries. Submerged in the rituals of rebellion, Marechera's poetics narrate the violence of domination, sexual transgression, exile, and return, with a language of obscenity, rage, irony, humor, and despair. Manipulating a discourse of erotic violence, Marechera's poems express the multiple ruptures central to a dynamic post/neo-colonial identity and reveal a compulsive focus on the body as the ultimate site of cross cultural anxiety and possibility. Often heralded as a post-Black, proto-anti-nationalist writer, Marechera's work is often read as working to "erase national, sexual and generic boundaries."[2] And yet by situating the sexualized visceral as the particular location on which colonization and decolonization is both violently inscribed and disavowed, Marechera's poems enact a shifting gender politic that contain a perilous mapping of racialized bodies in struggle. Thus, in this essay, I seek to explore the ways in which Marechera employs sexual violence to describe the intimate anguish of cross-cultural, postcolonial contact. Moreover, I intend to show how Marechera's use of sexual violence as a metaphor that seeks to articulate a liberatory language is complicated as it ultimately reinforces a discourse of oppressive and destructive regimes.

A difficult and challenging presence in the rubric of African literature, Marechera's poetic work has often been displaced to the margins of the writer's oeuvre. Perhaps due to the fact the most of his poems were consistently deemed unsuitable for publication by English and Zimbabwean publishers and were actively censored by the Zimbabwe Censorship Board. Thus, the only collection of his poetic works, *Cemetery of Mind,* was published posthumously. Nevertheless, Marechera wrote poetry consistently throughout his short troubled life and, as his biographer Flora Veit-Wild asserts, his poems "bear witness to his emotional conflicts as well as the social changes around him."[3] While the reasons for the overwhelming critical neglect of Marechera's poetry may be multifarious, the prevalence of brutal and obscene images that mark his literary landscape make Marechera's writing a thorny confrontation with the grotesque and violent that cannot be easily digested.

---

1. See W. E. B. DuBois, *The Souls of Black Folk* (New York: Penguin Books, 1989), 5.
2. Jane Bryce, "Inside/Out: Body and Sexuality in Dambudzo Marechera's Fiction," in Flora Veit-Wild and Anthony Chennells (eds.), *Emerging Perspectives on Dambudzo Marechera* (Trenton, NJ: Africa World Press, 1999), 223.
3. Flora Veit-Wild, *Dambudzo Marechera: A Source Book on His Life and Work* (London: Hans Zell Publishers, 1992), 348.

His poems written during his London years,[4] years that were marked by the war in Rhodesia, his expulsion from Oxford University, imprisonment, a lifestyle charted by homelessness, poverty, squatting, and excesses of alcoholism, show a preoccupation with sexual violence as a repetitive trope. Poems such as "I am the Rape," "Emptied Hearts," "Smash, Grab, Run," and "I Ain't Got My Balls (On the Chip On My Shoulder)," written in London from 1979 to 1980, point, through the titles alone, to Marechera's fascination with the body and violence. Exile was a bewildering and enraging, yet artistically fecund experience for Marechera given his prolific achievements that propelled the acclaimed novel *House of Hunger* set in the ghettos of Zimbabwe. However, as his poems reveal London as discursively imagined and experiential felt by Marechera that was in itself also a battle ground. Indeed, as critic Annie Gagiano has noted, Marechera discussed "the terrible anxieties of exile"[5] in several interviews and explained this more fully in 1986 after he returned to Zimbabwe by saying:

> My experience of Oxford University was loneliness and a certain questioning of why I found myself in a strange environment ... Some of my friends had gone off to join the freedom fighters, some like myself, found ourselves in countries where all we wanted to do was ... survive mentally ... hospitalize ourselves ... our generation had more or less been raped and like any other rape case we could never really recover from the psychological consequences.[6]

"Down and out in the streets of London,"[7] Marechera was keenly attentive to the Empire's use of violence through the mechanisms of war, racism, enforced poverty, and language and surveillance. Rape became an all encompassing metaphor to explore the corrosive effects of colonization and exile as an African experience. Hence, he attempted to construct his own language of sexual violence to articulate a resistance to domination as well as to subvert his own alienation and isolation. Displaced, dislocated, and excruciatingly aware of the body, the poetic persona of Marechera's London poems speaks violence on the body as means of illuminating the brutality of the colonial contact.

Sexual Violence as (Post) Colonial Response

In poem "I am the Rape," Marechera endeavors to wrench violence beyond the binaries of the Manichean world, a world that marks the Black body as the silent-objectified Other. With the title of the poem, which is repeated as the first line, Marechera subverts grammatical conventions to conflate victim and agent in the poem. Thus the rape, an event, a happening, a crime, becomes an identity, a definition of a self, one that merges the subject and object, rapist and raped, inside a dangerous matrix of complicity. "I am the rape." With this unsettling assertion, the voice of this London poem demands that this is a sexual violence that must be shared by the exploited and the exploiters. This blurring of agent and victim continues in the body of the poem:

---

4. Zimbabwean Dambudzo Marechera lived in Britain from 1974 to 1982. A large portion of his most acclaimed work, including *House of Hunger*, which won the Guardian Prize for Fiction in 1979, was written while he was in exile.

5. Annie Gagiano, *Achebe, Head, Marechera: On Power and Change in Africa* (London: Lynne Reiner Publishers, 2000).

6. Ibid.

7. David Pattison, *No Room for Cowardice: A View of the Life and Times of Dambudzo Marechera* (Trenton, NJ: Africa World Press, 2001).

I am the rape
Marked on the map
The unpredictable savage
Set down on the page
The obsequious laborer
Who will never be emperor[8]

The "I" of the poem names his objectification and yet in doing so subverts it. The power of "I" as subject cannot be entirely diminished though there is an overt acceptance of disempowerment—the laborer, the savage, the one who will never be emperor—these are familiar brandings of one without full agency. Yet with a voice bold and assertive, the poem maintains a representation of a body that is in sharp contrast to the narrative voice. Again, it is with irony, that the one who is marked as object bluntly commands his subjectivity. Marechera's poem continues with

My lips have rhythm
My lips an anthem
My arms a reckoning
My feet a flight
My eyes black sunlight
My hair dreadlocks[9]

With tone rocking with drum rhythm, a meter of militancy with its repetitive staccato, the personae describes himself in fragments, in body parts that point to a sum of physical attributes, not a cohesive whole, it is a body deconstructed. This deconstructive element could describe Marechera's recognition of the instability of the body, and by extension the instability of its identity. However, this stanza also performs a mapping of the Black body, a coded inventory that suggests an inherent strength "my lips an anthem," a concord resistance, "my arms a reckoning" an imminent integrity, "my eyes black sunlight," all this a royalty, a beauty unquestionably tied to Blackness.

This Black subject has identified himself first in the language of the hegemony (in the first stanza), then secondly in his own reclaiming idiom (second stanza). And it is the force of this reclamation that offers him the potency to speak directly to the colonizer with a mocking, sing song expression. The once objectified Black body, though fragmented, is firm enough to demand, "Sit on the truth out at sea/Shit the shit when you go out to tea."[10] The flippant usage of the body's banality, sipping tea and shitting shit "bears witness to Marechera's conscious transgression of the boundaries of social acceptability."[11] Additionally, it recalls that Marechera is invested in exposing the violence of everyday life, colonialism's aggressive reach from the public spheres into most mundane and intimate space of the private. Given the discrepancy between how the Black body is constructed by the colonizer and how the colonized then constructs himself, from the discourse that the poem encodes, the reader knows, that a very similar and intimate violence that must inevitably come as a boomerang back onto the bodies of the Empire.

Thus, not to disappoint, the persona continues, "Don't want to hear what ears hear/Don't want to see what eyes see/Your white body writhing underneath/All the centuries of my

---

8. "Marechera, Dambudzo," in Flora Veit-Wild (ed.) *Cemetery of Mind: Collected Poems of Dambudzo Marechera* (Harare: Baobab Books, 1992), 30.
9. Ibid.
10. Ibid.
11. Bryce, "Inside/Out," 227.

wayward fear."[12] Now the white body is marked—a stubborn deafness, blindness, vulnerability—this is now the victimized body. Interestingly, the wholeness of the white body does not extend the same agency or beauty the narrator dispelled on the Black body. This wholeness is shaped by disability, inability, and refusal to function in accordance with the normative, "don't want to see what eyes see." Are the eyes that see those of the oppressed, exploited, the colonized? The poem performs a subtle reversal in casting the white body as mismanaged and polluted, while the colonized Black subject whose eyes see and ears hear—presumably the truth.

It is not until the final couplet of the third stanza, that Marechera's "I am the Rape" discloses the violence the title harkens. The white body writhing underneath is the injured party and the victim of sexual violence performed by the Black body. For Marechera's poetics of violence is not sufficient for these two bodies to exist in close proximity caught in a rhetorical struggle in the small space of the poem, it is not enough for the colonized Body to reclaim his dignity in language. No this poet is obliged to propel their contact to most intimate act of violation. In Marechera's poem sexual violence is described as analogous to postcolonial contact. These repeating tropes of rape and violent sex are central to the poet's lexicon because as critic Jane Bryce asserts, "images of torture, rape, horrific violence, filth and disease proliferate precisely because of the physicality to which they point. The body is the concrete expression of all the abstractions by which the powerful, those in command of discourse, the controllers of language and lives, oppress the powerless, the voiceless."[13] Implicitly, penetration becomes a route through which power and powerless are made visible. In discussing his novel *Black Sunlight*, Marechera declared, "penetration becomes an entrance into that other world from which one can view all the atrocities."[14] And I assert that penetration functions similarly in his poems. So that the body with its multiple orifices becomes the site where bodies cross racial and national boundaries and enter and see the atrocity—the violence of their association. This entering, this intercourse, is certainly not an easy serene exploration of unity or difference; rather it is a paradoxical mantling and dismantling of power and powerlessness through erotic pain and bitter pleasure.

Nevertheless, rape as a metaphor, while a powerful linguistic means to usurp the colonizer's overwhelming extent of power over the colonized in the colonial and postcolonial reality, is not without its discursive, material, and cultural baggage. The Black body that from before this juncture in the poem appears implicitly genderless is now constructed as masculine as the personae is made "rapist" in matters of semiotic seconds, and by extension the white writing body is immediately feminized. Helliwell has explained, "In the eyes of rapists that act of rape marks them 'as real men' and marks their victims as not men, that is, feminine." In this iconography the masculine body (along with the 'masculine' psyche) is viewed as hard, penetrative, and aggressive, in contrast to the soft, vulnerable and violable "feminine sexuality and psyche. Rape both reproduces and marks pronounced sexual polarity."[15] Although Marechera attempts to utilize the violent trope of rape to signify corporeal transformations that might lead to dissolution of boundaries and/or a reversal of power dynamics, rape as a metaphor ultimately fixes the agent/victim binary in gendered terms.

---

12. Marechera, *Cemetery of Mind*, 30.
13. Bryce, "Inside/Out," 225.
14. Veit-Wild, *Dambudzo Marechera*, 219.
15. Christine Helliwell, " 'Its Only a Penis': Rape, Feminism and Difference," *Signs*. 25.3 (Spring 2000): 789–816, 797.

It is important also to note, that while the "I" and "you" of the poem are not gendered, the act of rape reifies gender difference. As Rus Erwin Funk discusses in his analysis of male-to-male rape, "... if there is any doubt, that rape is a gendered crime, that doubt gets erased when examining the verbal abuse used during the commission of a rape. Men who are raped are often called 'bitches,' 'sluts,' 'whores,' 'women,' 'girls' and other gendered terms."[16] Thus the use of feminization (or emasculation) as a postcolonial resistance strategy signifies not a breakdown in hegemonic social order but a power struggle for the maintenance of a certain kind of social order, and as feminist theorist Henrietta Moore has argued, violence in itself is most often already gendered and sexualized in its nature.[17] This claim may not stretch universally to explain all types of violence, nor should it assume to do so; however, within the Western regimes of colonial violence on the Black body, feminization of that body is a central fixture in the procedures of white supremacist patriarchal domination.

That Marechera described his own experience of colonization and exile as having been raped illustrates his awareness of the colonial mechanisms that sought to feminize the African body, to construct it as vulnerable, soft, weak, and enterable. Nonetheless, the recasting of this feminization on a white body does not discharge his poetics from the limiting confines of sexist discourse. In the words of poet Audre Lorde, can the tools of the master dismantle the master's house?[18] Furthermore, these tools of the master, this gendering matrix, reinforces the invisibility of the Black female body as this repeating myth of the Black male rapist continues to disappear Black female agency and victimization. The colonial conflict is cast once again as a triangular struggle—white male, Black male, and white female—as main actors in a sexual clash over bodies, freedoms, and rights. While this myth had and continues to have cultural capital in the West, as historian Pamela Scully has noted, a focus on this triangle had led to relatively few detailed studies on the realities and discourses that have lead to Black women's sexual subjection as the myth of the "Black male rapist" has proved a more fascinating topic in its discursive form.

Even so, from the slave plantations in Jamaica to the Senegalese infantries stationed in France, the myth of the "Black male rapist" has been a powerful means to dehumanize and subjugate Black peoples. Furthermore, this discourse of Black male's inherent sexual insatiability and proclivity for violence performed very particular tasks in the white settler colonies. Discussing rape in Southern African colonies Scully writes, "rape became a powerful means of discussing anti-colonial revolts ... the myth of the Black male rapist who through overexposure to civilization came to desire white women also embodied a more generalized anxiety and ambivalence about the appropriate limits of the civilizing mission."[19] And as Scully goes on to discuss, this myth was often rendered to refine constructions of whiteness and stabilize the boundaries between colonized and colonizer as well to police transgressive sexual behaviors.[20]

---

16. Rus Ervin Funk, "Queer Men and Sexual Assault: What Being Raped Says About Being a Man," in Christopher N. Kendall and Wayne Martino (eds.) *Gendered Outcasts and Sexual Outlaws: Sexual Oppression and Gender Hierarchies in Queer Men's Lives* (Binghamton: The Haworth Press, 2006).

17. Henrietta Moore, "The Problem of Explaining Violence in the Social Sciences," in Penelope Harvey and Peter Gow (eds.) *Sex and Violence: Issues in Representation and Experience* (New York: Routledge, 1994), 154.

18. Audre Lorde, *Sister Outsider* (Berkeley: The Crossing Press, 1984), 110.

19. Pamela Scully, "Rape, Race and Colonial Culture: The Sexual Politics of Identity in Ninetieth Century Cape Colony, South Africa," *The American Historical Review*, 100.2 (April 1995): 335–59, 338.

20. Ibid., 339–41.

Given that Marechera "articulated his view of sexuality as intrinsically political"[21] declaring that "almost everything one does reeks actually of sex,"[22] his use of rape as metaphor and his pointed use of the "Black male rapist" myth should be not considered an unconscious slippage into fantasy. Instead, Marechera is interested in making what is deemed transgression and what been hidden known. Thus Gagiano's reading that the poem "'I am the Rape' imagines cross racial sex as a form of international vengeance"[23] can raise important questions regarding the construction of Black masculinity on the text of the sexually violated white female body. Rape as Black male vengeance as a means to validate Black masculinity gained an astonishing popular currency in what has come to define Black Power rhetorics on race and gender. I am thinking in particularly of Eldridge Cleaver who wrote in 1968s *Soul on Ice*:

> I became a rapist ... Rape was an insurrectionary act. It delighted me that I was defying and trampling upon the white man's law, upon his system of values, that I was defiling his women ... I felt I was getting revenge ... I wanted to send waves of consternation throughout the white race.[24]

Significantly, Cleaver's revenge strategy locates the white female body as the site of violation. By dominating her body, he can then attack the entire white race. The object of rage is the female body and yet her flesh is only a medium through which his language of wrath can be expressed; the female body becomes the text that the Black male finally empowered can write. And as Robert Reid Pharr portends, "again women act only as conduits by which social relations, relations that take place exclusively between men, are represented. Cleaver may indeed be raping Black and white women, but it is white men whom he intends to hurt."[25]

While Cleaver's gender problematics send a terrifying message, his use of violence as a language points to the symbolic power of the visceral. Cleaver, later after his incarceration, discusses how writing saved his life and made him human. And yet his writing on the flesh of the white woman body is clearly constructed as a rite of passage, a practice school of writing of a different sort. While most apparently disturbing, like Marechera's metaphoric rape, these Black male personas use violence as a "grotesque cultural logic." This writing is not madness, unrestrained, chaotic, or feral; instead it is a careful semiotics that overrules violence as excessive passion and replaces this representation with a diabolical ordering of bodies and body parts in pain, which become "macabre forms of cultural design and violent predictability."[26] As with Cleaver, in Marechera's revenge-fantasy poem, if read as such, the white body—feminized—becomes the synecdoche on which centuries of Black anguish can be written.

Yet unlike Cleaver's use sexual violence, Marechera poetic narrator is caught in the destructive and generative possibilities of violence on the body as a continuous movement outside of a progress narrative of redemption. Just as one Black body can harbor centuries of wayward fear beyond temporal boundaries, his final stanza describes, "the electric shocks that seized my testicles/which you now eat with the lips of a sunrise," violence is a repetitive cycle of trauma in which "perpetrator and victim are constantly exchanging position."[27] And yet, Marechera's poetic language reveals an ironic erotic play that conflates

21. Bryce, "Inside/Out," 231.
22. Ibid.
23. Gagiano, *Achebe, Head, Marechera*, 221.
24. Eldridge Cleaver, *Soul on Ice* (New York City: Laurel Books, 1968), 14.
25. Robert F. Reid-Pharr, "Tearing the Goats Flesh: Homosexuality, Abjection and the Production of a Late Twentieth-Century Black Masculinity," *Studies in the Novel*, 28.3 (Fall 1996): 372–95, 379.
26. Vigdis Broch-Due (ed.), *Violence and Belonging: the Quest for Identity in Post-colonial Africa* (London: Routledge, 2005), 24.
27. Ibid., 25.

pleasure and pain, and significantly disturbs a strict binary construction of sensation. Though the lips of a sunrise may herald brighter days of freedom beyond violence, the poem's last couplet re-enacts the sexual violence of rape once again. Thus, "I am the Rape" performs a liberatory violence that is nevertheless entrapped in the rituals of domination it has assisted to create.

The (Post) Colonial/ Cross Cultural as the Vulgar Body

In his much-acclaimed polemic, *On the Postcolony*, Achille Mbembe writes against the Bakhtinian notion of the grotesque and the obscene to show how the postcolonial African state often organizes an aesthetic of vulgarity to "dramatize its own magnificence" and "confirm state legitimacy" and control the body of the subject.[28] While Mikhail Bakhtin's work illustrates how the grotesque and obscene are manipulated by the folk (ordinary people) as means of resistance to dominant "officialdom,"[29] Mbembe asserts that within the sphere of the *postcolony*, the state also, and more forcefully, directs a theatrics of excess and vulgarity as a vehicle to produce maximum repression and control of the masses.[30] Similar to the folk culture that Bakhtin describes, in this state performance of the obscene "the body [becomes] the principle locale of the idioms and fantasies used in depicting power."[31] Since the body is the central site for mechanisms of domination — with the gluttonous often huge phallic body of "officialdom" and the subjugated, starved, feminized, mutilated, or murdered body of the dominated — responses to state power often reflect this violence through linguistic debauchery. Thus from both directions, within the multi-tiered discourse of the public sphere, there is an "obsession with orifices, odors and genital organs" used to both critique and reinforce power and violence, so that postcolonial jokes, slogans, reportage, and creative work are often marked by language of lecherous excess.[32]

It is this double usage of the obscene that Marechera's poetics explore. In 1980, as Zimbabwe claimed national independence, Marechera, exiled in London, wrote the chore-opoem "Portrait of a Black Artist in London." While offering a titular nod to James Joyce, selections entitled "I Aint Got My Balls (On the Chip On My Shoulder)" configure, like "I Am the Rape," sexual violence and the erotic of violence as recurring tropes in the poetic lexicon in this much longer text. And as the title denotes, subtlety is not the mechanism operating here. The language is coarse, raunchy, and profane with lines like "Wipe your arse you're in Buckingham palace,"[33] and, "In a pub in Great Russell Hall/Strapped in sheets of beer/Truly fucked down to my Jungian balls."[34] Although Marechera submitted several versions to his British editors, it is not entirely surprising that the choreopoem was found unsuitable for publication by Heinemann editors and was never published. Notwithstanding, Marechera performed the piece at a reading of

---

28. Achille Mbembe, *On the Postcolony* (Berkeley: University of California Press, 2001), 103–105.
29. Mikhail Bahktin, *Rabelais and his World*, trans. Helene Isowolsky (Bloomington: Indiana University Press, 1984).
30. Mbembe, *On the Postcolony*, 107.
31. Ibid.
32. Ibid.
33. Veit-Wild, *Dambudzo Marechera*, 266.
34. Ibid., 260.

Zimbabwe poems and prose, held at the Africa Centre in 1980.[35] Having been published posthumously by Flora Veit-Weid in abridged form, the work defies boundaries of genre as it contains lyrical, narrative, and dramatic stylistic elements. Nonetheless, Marechera's sardonic spillage in this particular poetic work exemplifies Mbembe's conceptualization of the postcolonial aesthetic of vulgarity. It is an illuminating addition to Marechera's canon as it illustrates his preoccupation with sexual violence as a fecund trope for imagining the trauma of post-coloniality.

Yet in "I Aint Got My Balls (On the Chip On My Shoulder)" Marechera employs the metaphor of sexual violence to disclose the brutal experience of the colonialism on a Black body in exile, traversing beyond Mbembe's framework of the post-independence African nation as the post-colony. In "I Aint Got My Balls (On the Chip On My Shoulder)" the banal violations that mark the post-colony are relocated, or more aptly, are found in the proceeding site, the locus of Western hegemony, the heart-sphere of Empire: Britain. According to Marechera's poetics, the perversions of power are demonstrated with full potency on the Black body in exile in England, so that the "London" of his poems is the central landscape where postcolonial violence is practiced and defined as metaphoric rape and sexual violence. Marechera writes:

What's your Big
Daddy like?
A knife twisted in my voice!
Underline it quietly   White and Big
                                                       And blue

With a shining helmet
It shines brighter than burning rain

                                                       Is his name White
                                                       And Law
Rammed it down my throat up my arse it slammed my eardrums
                                                       Did you hear his voice
                                                       Give you genteel choice
A liquorice stick the magistrates licked
His balls jammed against my lips I couldn't breathe and gagged
All right, all right let's go on to the next thing.
                                                       Whitelaw![36]

Indeed what Audre Lorde described as the "right to dominance"[37] is made visceral through act of sexual violence in Marechera's poem. Yet as the state is personified as the rapist father figure, a perverse intimacy is revealed as the colonial figure is made not only patriarch but "Daddy." Marechera with typical acidic wit conflates colonizer/state with a term that echoes Judeo-Christian creator, priest, slave master, and progenitor. While much could be said about this metaphor from psychoanalytic and/or queer perspectives, reading these figures as historical tropes of imperial domination offers insight into the complex registers of Western patriarchal control. As "Daddy," the great phallus of Empire is perversely familiar and made known through of his recurring acts of abuse. "Daddy" as the state, "the magistrate," carefully produces an excessively masculine ritual of rape upon the body

---

35. Both Veit-Wild and Patterson discuss this controversial reading in which Marechera ignored his 20 minute allocation and defiantly read the entire 60 page manuscript of "Portrait of a Black Artist in London." Dramatic episodes such as this firmly established Marechera as the *enfant terrible* of African literature.

36. Veit-Wild, *Dambudzo Marechera*, 260–61.

37. Lorde, *Sister Outsider*, 45.

of the child/Other. That the state is singularized as an enormous phallus, "White and Big and Blue," serves as a totem for the colonizing regime's recurring attempts to dominate the colonized through state systems designed to inscribe the naturalness of white paternal superiority. Furthermore, as Houston Baker asserts, "the PHALLUS is not a material object but a signifier of the Father, or better, the Father's LAW."[38]

Hence, this familiar violation seeks not only physical entry into, but legislative dominion over, the Black body. "Whitelaw" as a name for the father figure/state exposes the deep-seated ties between patriarchy, violence, white supremacy, and state power. For the personae of the poem, this naming serves as recognition of what the Black subject as a colonized-immigrant in London is frightfully aware of: government jurisdiction can at times be a most dangerous adversary for the Black body in exile. In his everyday life, Marechera was often confronted state surveillance and control. After being expelled from Oxford University, he struggled to survive as a Black writer in London with no fixed income and no consistent housing. And though Marechera seemed to revel in his writer-tramp lifestyle, according to the London district police he was classified as a vagrant and especially as the "sus-laws" were in full effect during his exile years, he often was imprisoned for days, weeks, or months at a time. The sus-laws were the informal name for a stop and search law that permitted a police officer to act on suspicion, or 'sus,' alone. The law was widely believed to have been abused by the Metropolitan Police in order to harass young black men.[39]

It is clear from the riots that exploded in reaction to these laws in London, Brixton, and other urban working class districts, that those most affected by this legislation did not view police presence in their neighborhoods and imprisonment of so called truants as reformative. The rage and fear of being harassed and incarcerated is a repetitive articulation in the selections from Marechera's "Portrait of a Black Artist in London." While the themes of police brutality are most certainly not unique to Marechera, it is his employment of obscene and brash images and metaphors that propel the reader to view the different mechanisms of white supremacist state control as invasive and traumatic as perpetual rape. It is the state and its law that are "rammed [it] down my throat up my arse it slammed by eardrums"[40] and thus the Black body is dehumanized and made orifice by the brutal intrusion of the State's phallocentric exercise of control. And as Mbembe asserts, "to exercise authority is, above all, to tire out the bodies of those under it, to disempower them not so much to increase their productivity as to ensure the maximum docility."[41] Forced into compliance, the speaker of the poem "c[an't] breathe"[42] beyond his violation.

Yet unlike the lyrical voice that inhabits "I am the Rape," "I Aint Got My Balls (On The Chip On My Shoulder)" is performative, disjointed, and multi-voiced, none of the voices are detached from the experience of domination. While the form suggests disparate positionalities and differing subjectivities, sexual violence executed by "Daddy" binds the voices as an ensemble of victims. The multiplicities, however, may signify the single, though representative, exiled subject, the hybrid scum "who in the white world ... encounters difficulties in the development of his bodily schema."[43] The voices of the poem

38. Houston Baker, *Workings of Spirit: The Poetics of Afro-American Writing* (Chicago: University of Chicago Press, 1991), 145.

39. Cindi John, "The Legacy of the Brixton Riots," *BBC News*, April 5, 2006, Accessed February 21, 2007. http://news.bbc.co.uk/2/hi/uk_news/4854556.stm.

40. Veit-Wild, *Dambudzo Marechera*, 263.

41. Mbembe, *On the Postcolony*, 110.

42. Veit-Wild, *Dambudzo Marechera*, 264.

43. Frantz Fanon, *White Skins, Black Masks* (New York: Grove Press, 1967), 110.

express that for the Other to be exiled "on an island that contained millions of whites,"[44] is to be made hyper-corporeal. The Black body or bodies are referred to as "we niggers ... we [who] got through somehow in spite of Whitelaw/In spite of Webster/In spite of Maggie."[45] Earlier in the poem, the Black body is caught in a hostile hybrid condition, where there is an attempt to claim power in this reverse colonization; yet, in the hegemonic space of white supremacist Britain, the Black body is defiled and degraded. Thus, for the once colonized now immigrant African in London as Gagiano declares, "naturalization is seemingly unachievable."[46] Consequently, the speakers of the poem alternatively express the anguish, discomfort, disbelief, self-censoring, and rage that is an articulation the "tearing cloth of exile."[47]

Alongside these dynamics of victimization, however, there is voice of aggressive resistance in this work as well. Most overtly the poem itself stands as response to the dehumanizing processes of the (post)colonial experience. With its vulgar language and experiential form, "I Aint Got My Balls (On the Chip On My Shoulder)" embodies a raw, reckless and violent urgency that attacks and strips bare the pervasive discourses of Eurocentric modernity and reveals "progress" as an ideology that validates racial hierarchies and acts of State violence. Usurping the signatures of state violence and inverting these acts into metaphor, Marechera uses linguistic sexual violence to "enact the subject into being."[48] Beginning with the title, which serves as a chorus throughout the poem, "I Aint Got My Balls (On the Chip On My Shoulder)" most obstinately laments the speaker's castration. His "balls" are a present absence as throughout the piece the speaker(s) scream, "I TOLD YOU I AINT GOT MY BALLS."[49] Interestingly with his use of "aint" Marechera adopts a term from African American vernacular to express the negation of his masculinity.

Thus, the poet invokes a historical thread that links the emasculation and torture of the Black male body from the enslavement epoch to the centuries of colonialism in Southern Africa. The habitually silenced narrative of lynching, castration, and mutilation of the Black male body is foregrounded in this repeating line through the poem with a thoroughly macabre affect. That this disquieting image is pronounced almost flippantly does not abjure its significance. While the castration of the speaker may be read as symbolic, as to portray the cultural maiming indicative of colonialism, this image triggers the very real castrations on the Black body that were practiced by state licensed mobs in the Jim Crow South as well as at hands of colonial soldiers in prison camps during anti-colonial military resistance movements in Africa.[50] With this candid reference to castration alongside images of rape, Marechera pushes to the surface the sexualized underpinnings of these particular acts of violence. Rape and castration are co-configured not as paralleled acts binary bound by gender difference, but instead as twin sets of violence enacted on the Black body, now unequivocally racialized through this humiliation. Ironically, however, it is the same violence that impels this voice to speak despite the "knife twisted in [his/her] voice."[51]

---

44. Dambudzo Marechera, *Black Sunlight* (London: Heinemann Press, 1980), 78.
45. Veit-Wild, *Dambudzo Marechera*, 250.
46. Gagiano, *Achebe, Head, Marechera*, 220.
47. Marechera, *Black Sunlight*, 61.
48. Broch-Due, *Violence*, 19.
49. Veit-Wild, *Dambudzo Marechera*, 261.
50. A most horrific example is discussed in Josiah Mwangi Kariuki's memoir, *Mau Mau Detainee*. The war veteran describes how a number of prisoners were castrated at Nyangwethu Camp by colonial guards as means to force confessions.
51. Veit-Wild, *Dambudzo Marechera*, 259.

Through the voicing of sexual violence, Marechera's poem embodies a raw, and at times reckless, will to power that spits a passionate barrage against injustice. Though victimized, the speaker who declares "I aint got my balls" demands that brutality and vulgarity of Empire be exposed. It is the voice that commands every heavy stone of imperialistic power be overturned.[52] Accordingly, Marechera tackles the myth of the Black male rapist again this piece. The persona declares:

> All those Miss Piggies they always say
> > I wouldn't let a nigger so much as come
> Come within a mile of my cunt
> They always say
> > I wouldn't let a nigger so much as think
> Of loving my daughter
> They always did say
> > Niggers talk about equal rights but the actual freedom they want is
> To rape Miss Piggy ...
> All those Miss Piggies they always declare
> > Invited him to tea next thing he leaped onto my ham
> Accepted to dance with him next thing he tried to screw me into the floor
> > SCREW ME OFF THE FLOOR
> > HA HA HA HA HA.[53]

Marechera's determination to offend reaches its excessive pinnacle in the "Miss Piggy" passages. The poetic cocktail of profanity, conversational speech, and ribald absurdity is meant to oust the all hypocritical proprieties and the pretensions of power. There is no innocence to protect for the colonized-immigrant, so with no mercy this voice transforms even the puppet celebrity[54] into a twisted metaphor to signify the complex matrix of racism, desire, violence, and anxiety that permeate the hegemonic Western discourse regarding interracial sex. The poet uses "they always say" with a subversive authority as the narrator speaks the discourse of white supremacy, enacting a disturbing ventriloquism. The once silenced Other now speaks the vernacular of whiteness in a ironic reversal through which the obsessive imagining of the Black male body as over-sexualized rapist-savage is revealed as a most necessary construction within the repertoire of white supremacy.

"Miss Piggy" as a stand-in for the white woman is odious at best. Yet, similar to "I Am The Rape" Marechera remains centered on this duo—mirroring the historical (anti-) coupling of this pair in the popular imagination of the West. The white woman figure emerges consistently throughout "I Aint Got My Balls (On the Chip On My Shoulder)" as the a kind of foil for Black male persona.[55] In un-naming her "Miss Piggy," however, Marechera works to dehumanize the white female body through a reversal. Here Marechera recasts representations of the Black body as bestial and savage and applies this damning

---

52. Gagiano, *Achebe, Head, Marechera*, 204.

53. Veit-Wild, *Dambudzo Marechera*, 255.

54. The Miss Piggy puppet, 'superstar' of the Muppets television series, continues to be a iconic figure. Hyper-feminine, Miss Piggy's determination to secure her romantic status with her beau Kermit the Frog reveals her aggressive need to be coupled. Ironically, Miss Piggy first appeared in second pilot show for the series, entitled the "The Muppets: The End of Sex and Violence" in 1975. At its beginning, the show was geared entirely at an adult audience and fostered a dark and absurdist humor. It is possible, though unlikely, that Marechera had viewed this episode and is using this figure of "Miss Piggy" with a deeper metaphoric texture than I imagine here.

55. Black women as victims of sexual violence are seemingly disappeared or at least submerged within the Black male narrative inside this text.

caricature onto the body that most often signifies vulnerability and sentimentality. To "Miss Piggy-ify" the white female body is an act linguistic trickery that holds challenging implications. Interestingly, although Jane Bryce has argued that Marechera fascination with the abject body in his fictional works succeeds in erasing racial and gender boundaries,[56] these poems propose a re-centering on the body and fixed racial identities as a means of recognizing them as "instruments of power and control."[57]

Marechera does not erase racial categories; instead he moves them, plays with them, exaggerates them, reassigns them across the binary, so that the arbitrariness and social weight of racial and sexual constructions are disrupted, illuminated, and inveigled. Racial and gender boundaries and voices may be blurred, but they are not expunged, and this in work of Marechera is frighteningly compelling. Therefore, the exuberant laughter at the end of "I Aint Got My Balls (On the Chip on My Shoulder)" may signal the Miss Piggy's sexual pleasure, her satisfaction in inspiring the Black male's uncontrollable desire or the speaker's sardonic recognition of the banal reproduction of Black male sexualized criminality. Caught in the dangerous terrain of interracial sex and sexual violence the polyvocal "HA HA HA HA HA" is haunting, bitter, and provocative.

In some sense Dambudzo Marechera in life and in work was caught in the contradictions of revenge and violence as performed on the body. Speaking of a struggles to free himself from the discourse of interracial sex as revenge he confessed to Flora Veit-Wild in an a interview done in 1987, "even when I am making love to her I find that I am actually with my whole self trying to fool myself that I am revenging myself against the whole white race. Afterwards of course, one realizes that it was simply an illusion that one can revenge oneself on history."[58] Yet, in exile in 1980, when he described himself as "one of England's walking wounded,"[59] the illusion of sexual violence as a liberatory directive against colonialism's damning history was the urgent impulse that propelled one of African literature's most strident voices to create.

References

Baker, Houston. *Workings of Spirit: The Poetics of Afro-American Writing.* Chicago: University of Chicago Press, 1991.

Bakhtin, Mikhail. *Rabelais and His World.* Trans, Helene Isowolsky. Bloomingdale: Indiana University Press, 1984.

Bhahba, Homi. *The Location of Culture.* London: Routledge, 1994.

Broch-Due, Vigdis. "Violence and Belonging: Analytical Reflections." In Vigdis Broch-Due (ed.), *Violence and Belonging: the Quest for Identity in Post-colonial Africa.* London: Routledge, 2005. 1–36.

Bryce, Jane. "Inside/Out: Body and Sexuality in Dambudzo Marechera's Fiction." In Flora Veit-Wild and Anthony Chennells (eds.), *Emerging Perspectives on Dambudzo Marechera*, Trenton, NJ: Africa World Press, 1999. 221–232.

Buuck, David. "African Doppenlganger: Hybridity and Identity in the Work of Dambudzo Marechera." *Research in African Literatures*: 28.2 (1997): 118–31.

---

56. Bryce, "Inside/Out," 223.
57. Gagiano, *Achebe, Head, Marechera*, 218.
58. Veit-Wild, *Dambudzo Marechera*, 260.
59. Gagiano, *Achebe, Head, Marechera*, 214.

Cleaver, Eldridge. *Soul on Ice*. New York City: Laurel Books, 1968.

DuBois, W.E.B. *The Souls of Black Folk*. New York: Penguin Books, 1989.

Fanon, Frantz. *Black Skin White Masks*. New York City: Grove Press, 1967.

———. *The Wretched of the Earth*. New York City: Grove Press, 1963.

Funk, Rus Ervin. "Queer Men and Sexual Assault: What Being Raped Says About Being a Man." In Christopher N. Kendall and Wayne Martino (eds.) *Gendered Outcasts and Sexual Outlaws: Sexual Oppression and Gender Hierarchies in Queer Men's Lives*. Binghamton: The Haworth Press, 2006, 131–46.

Gagiano, Annie. *Achebe, Head, Marechera: On Power and Change in Africa*. London: Lynne Reiner Publishers, 2000.

Helliwell, Christine. "'Its Only a Penis': Rape, Feminism and Difference." *Signs*. 25.3 (Spring 2000): 789–816.

Hesford, Wendy. "Reading Rape Stories: Material Rhetoric and the Trauma of Representation." *College English*. 62.2 (Nov 1999): 192–221.

John, Cindi. "The Legacy of the Brixton Riots" *BBC News*, April 5, 2006. Accessed February 21, 2007. http://news.bbc.co.uk/2/hi/uk_news/4854556.stm.

Kariuki, Josiah Mwangi. *Mau Mau Detainee: Account by a Kenya African on His Experience in Detention Camps 1953–1960*. Oxford: Oxford University Press, 1975.

Kristeva, Julia. *Powers of Horror: An Essay on Abjection*. New York City: Columbia University Press, 1982.

Lorde, Audre. *Sister Outsider*. Berkeley: The Crossing Press, 1984.

Marechera, Dambudzo. *Cemetery of Mind: Collected Poems of Dambudzo Marechera*. Flora Veit-Wild (ed.). Harare: Baobab Books, 1992.

Marechera, Dambudzo. *The House of Hunger*. London: Heineman Books, 1978.

Mbembe, Achille. *On the Postcolony*. Berkeley: University of California Press, 2001.

Moore, Henrietta. "The Problem of Explaining Violence in the Social Sciences." In Penelope Harvey and Peter Gow (eds.), *Sex and Violence: Issues in Representation and Experience*. New York: Routledge, 1994. 138–55.

Pattison, David. *No Room for Cowardice: A View of the Life and Times of Dambudzo Marechera*. Trenton, NJ: Africa World Press. 2001.

Peterson, Kirsten Holst. *An Articulate Anger: Dambudzo Marechera: 1952–87*. Sydney: Dangaroo Press, 1988.

Reid-Pharr, Robert F. "Tearing the Goats Flesh: Homosexuality, Abjection and the Production of a Late Twentieth-Century Black Masculinity." *Studies in the Novel*, 28.3 (Fall 1996): 372–95.

Scully, Pamela. "Rape, Race and Colonial Culture: The Sexual Politics of Identity in Ninetieth Century Cape Colony, South Africa." *The American Historical Review*, 100.2 (April 1995): 335–59.

Veit-Wild, Flora. *Dambudzo Marechera: A Source Book on His Life and Work*. London: Hans Zell Publishers. 1992.

Vincent, Kerry. "Liminal Positions: Dambudzo Marechera's The House of Hunger and Black Sunlight." *English Studies*: 42.2 (1999): 49–65.

Chapter 4

Big Buttocks and Sultry Behavior: Perceptions of Post-Colonial African Women in British Women's Travel Narratives

Jacqueline-Bethel Mougoué

Upon entering Gabon for the first time, British traveler Christina Dodwell, who was appalled, reported this about the African country:

> Gabon was by far the most primitive country I visited ... The eating of human flesh was often a privilege reserved for men only; the women had an equally primitive habit and it was one in which they excelled. Female natures were not gentle and soft; they didn't lead a gentle, soft life. Their ways were hard and cruel, they were often vicious and spiteful to each other, and their revenge was through poisons. Some of the types of poisons were cunning and fairly harmless, like the ones to which they apparently addicted their unsuspecting husbands, administering a dose each day in his food. It guaranteed that the husband would never leave them, and if he did then within three or four days he would come back with a craving for home cooking. Woe betide the person who aroused a woman's wrath. One of their favorite poisons was made from the finely chopped whiskers of wildcats, and when the person ate or drank these hairs they would catch in their stomach lining causing ulcers and a great deal of pain.[1]

The above observations were published in Dodwell's travel account, *Travels with Fortune: An African Adventure.* In this excerpt, the author has meticulously detailed her views of the level of civilization in Gabon. She has additionally made gendered assumptions about the people, such as how Gabonese women supposedly kept their marriages intact with the use of poisons. Furthermore, Dodwel has concluded that Africans refused to change and would rather stay in their "primitive" state. What is remarkable about the traveler's beliefs about Gabonese culture and life is that it seems as if it were ripped out of the travel narratives of Victorian women—stories about Africa that were peppered with Western superiority and disregard for African societies and cultures. However, Dodwell's travel narrative about Africa was published in 1979, after the independence of most African countries, and during the period in which there was increased academic awareness and a re-examining of African cultures through historical and culturally sensitive lenses.

Modern British women, like Dodwell, who traveled abroad in the post-colonial period, were not a new phenomenon. During the nineteenth century, Victorian women journeyed

---

1. Christina Dodwell, *Travels with Fortune: An African Adventure* (London: W.H. Allen, 1979), 158–59.

53

to various continents like Africa and South America to explore worlds beyond the domains of their households.[2] Most British women, regardless of their period, who traveled to Africa encountered African women in contact zones—spaces in which people usually geographically and historically separated encountered one another and established relationships.[3] British women often recorded their experiences in diaries and journals, and frequently published them in forms of memoirs and adventure books. The travel accounts are significant in that they illuminate the historical narratives of both British and African women. However, we must be careful not to take British women's convictions about post-colonial African women at face value or for absolute truth. There is no denying that there is a great deal to learn about post-colonial African women from the travel accounts of British women. Nevertheless, I argue that like their Victorian counterparts, late twentieth-century British female travelers expressed ideologies of western cultural superiority and assumptions about "normative" western gender roles within zones of contact with post-colonial African women. I will highlight three significant themes of westernized cultural and gendered social assumptions modern British women expressed about African women. These themes are anchored in perceptions about African women's physical traits, gender roles and duties, and their perceived patterns of sexuality.

The travel narratives of five modern British women travelers will be discussed in this chapter. The travelers are Eva Davison, Christina Dodwell, Mary Anne Fitzgerald, Hazel Jackson, and Robin Page. All of the women visited Africa in the post-colonial period and traveled throughout the entire African continent, with the exception of Davison who stayed mostly in West Africa.[4] The women's reasons for traveling throughout Africa varied. Davison went to West Africa for humanitarian and religious purposes; she went to be a nurse in Christian missionary clinics. She recorded her experiences in *They Two Went On* (1979). Page first went to Africa in 1974 to visit her sister who worked at a Christian mission hospital in Zaire.[5] From there she proceeded to travel to East and Southern Africa. She published her accounts as *Dust in a Dark Continent* (1989). Fitzgerald was a journalist who lived in Kenya for twenty-two years. She was jailed after publishing articles that President Daniel Moi's government deemed politically threatening. Fitzgerald was finally deported out of Kenya, thereby giving her the opportunity to travel throughout the continent, with the resulting publication: *Nomad: Journeys from Samburu* (1992). Jackson was born in colonial Nigeria, though she did not grow up in the country. Her interest in the continent began when her parents took her to Kenya in 1983 for her eighteenth birthday. Her account, *Into Africa* (1997), chronicles her return to the continent in 1994. Like Jackson, Dodwell was also born in colonial Nigeria. She lived there until she was six, after which she and her family returned to Britain. A worldwide traveler, Dodwell, became a fervent explorer of Africa starting in 1975. She recounted her travels of Africa in two books, *Travels with Fortune: an African Adventure* (1979) and *Travels with Pegasus: a Microlight Journey across West Africa* (1990).

---

2. Rebecca Stefoff, *Women of the World: Women Travelers and Explorers* (New York: Oxford University Press, 1992), 8, 10. The most prominent women explorers of the Victorian period were Gertrude Bell, Isabella Bird, Mary Henrietta Kingsley, and Harriet Martineu.

3. Mary Pratt, *Imperial Eyes: Travel Writing and Transculturation* (London: New York: Routledge, 1992), 6.

4. "Post-colonial" refers to the period after 1960 in which most African countries gained independence from their European colonizers.

5. Zaire was the name of present day Democratic Republic of the Congo between October 27, 1971 and May 17, 1997.

Travel Differences and Similarities between Victorian Women and Modern British Women

My work diverges from the traditional scholarship about the travel narratives of British women in that I am specifically interested in focusing on modern British women in the middle to late twentieth-century who explored post-colonial Africa (1960–1997). Recent academic works have failed to analyze the travel writings of modern British women. Instead, current discourse of the field is embedded in the travel accounts of Victorian women in the colonial period.

There are significant factors that differentiate modern British female travelers from their Victorian counterparts. The historical contexts in which both groups of women voyaged to Africa differed. Victorian women who journeyed to colonial Africa were symbolic representatives of the British Empire. On the other hand, modern women were traveling to politically independent African countries. Another compelling difference between the two groups of women was the access they had to opportunities of travel. Katherine Frank identified four types of Victorian women who traveled to Africa in the nineteenth century: government wives or daughters, women explorers-travelers, ethnographers, and anthropologists.[6] A fifth type of woman who traveled to Africa, either alone or with female companionship, went to the continent with loose goals of "learning."[7] However, modern British women who traveled to post-colonial Africa cannot be boxed into such neat categories as their Victorian predecessors. They went to the continent for various purposes: as missionaries, with family members for vacation and leisure, as volunteers for international organizations, for educational goals, or for business networking. The main point is that modern British females who traveled to Africa went there for a broad range of reasons — reasons that were endless and not limited to a specific scope.

An additional distinction between Victorian and modern women was the different gender notions and expectations of their times. Patricia Romero writes that Victorian women's "opportunities to study were limited; the household was their domain, not the larger world of ideas and events. Women were expected to be good wives and mothers. If they did not marry, they were expected to keep house for their male relatives or quietly earn a living in a genteel way, perhaps by giving drawing lessons or doing embroidery."[8] Due to such pervasive ideologies of gender roles, Victorian women felt pressured not to explore Africa unlike their male counterparts. Seen as a dark and terrifying place only for males, women were perceived as being too feminine and weak to voyage to the continent, especially if it was alone.[9] Consequently, women who felt the urge to wander into the "dark" continent felt that they had to justify their travel. Katherine Frank concludes that women travelers "felt that they had no business going there unless they could perform some sort of public service by studying, observing, nurturing, healing, [or] even saving."[10]

---

6. Katherine Frank, "Voyages Out: Nineteenth-Century Women Travelers in Africa," in Janet Sharistanian (ed.) *Gender, Ideology, and Action: Historical Perspectives on Women's Public Lives* (Westport, Connecticut: Greenwood Press, 1986), 73–74.

7. Maria H. Frawley, *A Wider Range: Travel Writing by Women in Victorian England* (Rutherford, N.J.: Fairleigh Dickinson University Press, 1994), 22–23.

8. Patricia W. Romero, *Women's Voices on Africa: A Century of Travel Writings* (New York: M. Wiener Publishers, 1992), 4.

9. Ibid.

10. Frank, "Voyages Out," 70.

Modern British women faced little of the same obstacles that their predecessors dealt with; British gender notions and expectations differed greatly in Britain from the 1960s to the present. Though many scholars question if women's positions in British society have continuous strands from the Victorian era, it is evident that modern women have more opportunities in being able to travel to Africa.[11] For example, women often have their own source of income and do not fully rely on their husband's or family's income.[12] This makes it easier therefore for women to travel overseas and fully fund themselves. Additionally, though Africa may still be perceived as a dangerous place by the British, a woman who travels to the continent is not perceived as stepping out of her expected gender roles and duties.

Despite vast differences, there are similar characteristics that link Victorian and modern British women travelers. Both groups of women often recorded their experiences in diaries and journals and published them. The women also exhibited similar cultural and racial supremacy while in Africa, though the levels and forms of these ethnocentrisms may have differed. It can also be argued that both groups of women represented imperialism and colonialism. Frank writes that when Victorian women traveled to Africa, their identity derived from their white skins rather than for their gender.[13] In Africa, Victorian women were representatives of the British Empire and symbolized prestige and power that were linked to their skin color. Though the British, or the French, no longer colonized any of the African countries modern women visited, they still represented neo-colonialism. Wunyabari Maloba argues that globalization is a new form of imperialism and colonialism.[14] He stresses that post-colonial African countries still face western exploitation: "The old networks of Western exploitation and domination of the third world still remain intact … What is clearly evident is that current globalization affirms the structure and operation of imperialism … Theoretically, and especially operationally, globalization has to be seen as being essentially imperialism."[15] Globalization has helped to cement neo-colonialism and allow former western colonial powers to maintain control of former colonies through political and economic avenues. Therefore, modern female travelers in post-colonial Africa did not only represent themselves individually; these women epitomized western imperialism and neo-colonialism.

Zones of Contact: The African Woman Participant

In this chapter, I give historical agency to African women by weaving in their historical accounts.[16] Only the lives of Western and Central African women are emphasized in the chapter. Unfortunately, it is difficult to briefly summarize an overarching historical background of post-colonial Western and Central African women. Catherine Coquery-Vidrovitch points out that "Africa is too large and its types of social organization too

---

11. Jane Lewis, *Women in Britain Since 1945: Women, Family, Work, and the State in the Post-War Years* (Oxford, UK: Blackwell, 1992), 1–10.

12. Ibid., 2–3.

13. Frank, "Voyages Out," 72.

14. Wunyabari Maloba, *African Women in Revolution* (Trenton, New Jersey: Africa World Press, Inc., 2007), 181–82.

15. Ibid., 182.

16. The Western and Central African countries that are highlighted in this paper are Cameroon, the Central African Republic, the Democratic Republic of Congo (also referred to as Zaire in this paper), Gambia, Ghana, Mali, Mauritania, Morocco, Niger, Nigeria, and Senegal.

varied to allow a detailed description of [the] African woman's tasks."[17] She further elucidates that it "is perhaps even less possible today than before to speak of [the] African woman."[18] Western and Central Africa women vary from women in the urban centers to those in the countryside, from highly educated women to those who do not have any western education.[19] Consequently, it is difficult to make one single general explanation about the lives of African women.

'Dark' Days in Primitive Africa

We must start at the beginning to understand the ways in which British women discerned and interacted with Western and Central African women. The title of the published diaries and journals alone represent the myriad notions of Africa the women held. For example, Robin Page's book title, *Dust in a Dark Continent*, encompasses the long held popular British view of Africa as a "dark continent."[20] Maria Frawley articulates that for Victorian women, "[t]ravel to Africa was taken as a 'step in the darkest dark' where 'no Englishwomen yet had gone' "[21] Frank asserts that for many nineteenth century explorers, Africa was more than a geographical place; it was the land of fabulous bears, gold, and diamonds, and was the Dark Continent.[22] She further elaborates that the " 'darkness' or 'blankness' that the great African explorers of the nineteenth century hoped to illuminate or fill in was the source of Africa's enormous appeal."[23] This analysis of nineteenth century explorers of Africa can be applied to modern British female explores like Page. The very title of Page's book hints at her risky adventures in the 'dark' continent.

Under the umbrella perspective of Africa as a 'dark' place are the presumptions that the continent is diseased and full of primitive, savage, violent, and heathen people. African feminist and scholar Oyèrónké Oyewùmí writes that in today's period, perceptions of Africa as a violent and evil place has been integral in depicting the region as the "dark continent" and its women as the "heart of darkness."[24] Such viewpoints are evident in the travel narrative of Eva Davison.

For example, after arriving in Ghana, Davison fearfully records the 'savage' behavior of the Konkomba people in a town named Yendi: "The Konkomba people were easily provoked and often a fight would break out over yams, women, or just a drunken brawl. Deaths were not infrequent at this time and some terrible wounds were inflicted. You can imagine how they liked a fight when the Government sent sixteen policemen to reside in the village."[25] Later, after witnessing a funeral in the town, Davison refers to it as a "pagan

---

17. Catherine Coquery-Vidrovitch, *African Women: A Modern History* (Boulder: Westview Press, 1997), 11.

18. Ibid., 200.

19. Ibid., 11.

20. Cheryl McEwan, *Gender, Geography, and Empire: Victorian Women Travellers in West Africa* (Aldershot, Hampshire, England: Ashgate, 2000), 150.

21. Frawley, *A Wider Range*, 13.

22. Frank, "Voyages Out," 67.

23. Ibid., 68.

24. Oyèrónké Oyewùmí, "The White Woman's Burden: African Women in Western Feminist Discourse," in Oyèrónké Oyewùmí (ed.) *African Women and Feminism: Reflecting on the Politics of Sisterhood*, (Trenton, NJ: Africa World Press, 2003), 32.

25. Ibid., 90.

funeral site."[26] Finally, while still in northern Ghana, Davison remarked about the inhabitants of Nakpanduri: "The Bimobas were primitive folk."[27]

The British women also expressed feelings of cultural superiority in their travel accounts. For example, the women believed British culture to be the zenith of civilization. Throughout their voyages, the women desperately looked for manifestations of 'civilization.' For instance, Hazel Jackson repeatedly equated civilization with the presence of western goods. While camping out in Morocco with her travel companions, she stated about their meal: "We ate very well; it didn't feel like we were in Morocco at all, as I had a good old fisherman's pie."[28] While traveling through Mauritania, Jackson wrote after a night's sleep in a tent, "We had a much civilized breakfast at the table and set off to do business at 9 a.m."[29] After staying in a hotel in Senegal, Jackson exclaimed, "All decided to have breakfast in the hotel on the veranda by the pool. Très civilisé [very civilized]!"[30] Finally, in Mali, Jackson gives a Liberian man looking for a job a Western shirt "so that he could look smart enough to get a job."[31]

The presence of western cultural habits and the appearance of white Westerners were perceived as evidence of civilization and modernity. Jackson was appalled at the supposed lack of modern traits in Mauritanians after being invited for tea at a woman's home. She remarked, "It [the tea] was mighty strong and very, very sweet. No wonder they all had rotten teeth. They clean it with a twig thing that they chew at the end and rub it against their teeth, and then they just sit there with it in their mouth."[32] After arriving in Bamenda Cameroon, Dodwell observed about the city: "Bamenda was more civilized than we had imagined, with electricity and many white faces."[33] Jackson's observations are similar to those of Victorian women who believed that Africans could only "advance" through westernization.[34] According to Jackson, Africa is only westernized when there are visible traces of western cultural habits and traits.

Another significant view that the women held about Africa was that it was unchanging. For example, Page commented about Zaire:

> Zaire, it seemed to me, was the typical face of the new Black-Africa—proud, independent, chaotic, stretching out to reach for the material possessions of the first World, but with feet firmly planted in the Third ... Away from the seat of government old Africa remained virtually unchanged as it had for hundreds of years: T-shirts, tin-cans, new brief-cases and the occasional lorry or Japanese pick-up truck being the main reminders that the world outside had changed and was still changing. If aid was suddenly cut off and those who administered it went home, then the jungle would again assert its authority, with the foliage closing in high above, shutting out the shafts of new light.[35]

Though Page recognizes the political independence of Zaire and the country's attempts to obtain materials from the 'First World,' she still hints that most of the country, and Africa overall, are unchanged. Dodwell also believes that Africa is unchanging when she is in Kukawa, a town in the Northeastern Nigerian state of Borno. After explaining about the

---

26. Ibid., 91.
27. Ibid., 97.
28. Jackson, *Into Africa* (London: Minerva Press, 1997), 18.
29. Ibid., 19.
30. Ibid., 45.
31. Ibid., 60.
32. Ibid., 39.
33. Dodwell, 57.
34. McEwan, *Gender, Geography, and Empire*, 149.
35. Robin Page, *Dust in a Dark Continent* (London: Claridge Press, 1989), 45.

people and culture of the Bornu Empire from hundreds of years ago, Dodwell concludes as she observes the present-day villagers: "I doubted the scene was much changed."[36] Oyewùmí argues that the belief that Africa is static and unchanging is ahistorical.[37] Oyewùmí further stresses that within anthropology, there are major critiques against the "tendency to treat the present circumstances of the so called traditional cultures as if they were identical to past circumstances."[38] The same critiques can be applied to the modern British women's travel accounts. Except for the random western goods, Africa, according to the women, will always be the same. It is this view of Africa, among others, that influenced the female travelers' perceptions, encounters, and experiences with African women.

Plaited Hair and Body Markings: African Women's Physical Traits

Physical traits and forms of bodily adornment have often been areas of fascination in cross-cultural encounters and understandings of gender.[39] Tony Ballantyne and Antoinette Burton emphasize that the body has arguably been crucial to the experiences of these contacts.[40] Cheryl McEwan writes that Victorian women who traveled to Africa noted physical descriptions of indigenous African women, frequently describing their patterns of dress and commenting on the physical attractiveness of the women.[41] This was no exception for modern British women who voyaged to post-colonial Western and Central Africa. For example, Dodwell was captivated with Cameroonian women's outwardly appearances and recorded:

> Some of the women looked entirely different to those we had seen before; they were tall, slim-hipped, fine-boned and very graceful. Though their skin was equally black, their faces were delicate with Hamitic features, and they had tribal markings like stars and arrows. Nose rings were worn by most of them, loops of cowerie shells were threaded up and down the rims of their ears, and their black hair was woolly but very long, often reaching to their shoulders in twenty or thirty tight tassels. They wore ragged leather loin clothes and went bare chested like most of the other women in the bush—it was only around the towns that women were obliged, or preferred, to cover their breasts.[42]

Jackson also noticed the physical attributes of African women when she traveled through the Central African Republic (CAR): "The women in CAR were quite unusual looking with sharp features; some were quite beautiful. They were from Chad apparently—the men were really black. There was actually quite a racial mixture here, with an Arabic influence, and it was very Muslim."[43] Though the women made numerous notes on the

---

36. Dodwell, *Travels with Pegasus: A Microlight Journey Across West Africa* (New York: Walker, 1990), 58.
37. Oyewùmí, "The White Woman's Burden," 30.
38. Ibid.
39. Heidi Gengenbach, "Tattooed Secrets: Women's History in Magude District, Southern Mozambique," in Tony Ballantyne and Antoinette Burton (eds.) *Bodies in Contact: Rethinking Colonial Encounters in World History*, (Durham, N.C.: Duke University Press, 2005), 253.
40. Tony Ballantyne and Antoinette Burton, "Postscript: Bodies, Genders, Empires: Reimagining World Histories," *Bodies in Contact*, 406.
41. McEwan, *Gender, Geography, and Empire*, 157.
42. Dodwell, *Travels with Fortune*, 47–48.
43. Jackson, *Into Africa*, 143.

overall physical appearances of African women, they often focused on specific features, such as hair and body markings.

The British women frequently imposed their cultural notions of physical beauty when observing the physical traits of Western and Central African women. These viewpoints were often tied to the women's skin tones. For example, both Jackson and Page identified "beautiful" African women as those that were fair-skinned and had European features. While spending time playing with Mauritanian children, Jackson remarked, "I passed the time with kids. One little girl was especially pretty and we had a dance. She was slightly fairer-skinned than the others and had beautiful hair."[44] In the Democratic Republic of Congo, Page spent time with Africans in the town of Mbandaka. While resting with the women of the town on a Sunday afternoon, she observed young girls and women braiding each other's hair:

> The young girls would spend hours braiding their hair in complicated patterns; the most beautiful girl was a 'mulatto'—where Portuguese and African blood had mixed to create a most attractive girl with a pale skin, sparkling eyes and a ready smile. Her hair was tied in long spikes and her light colour was said to be of great appeal to the men and youths of the village.[45]

Though the women described the physical attributes of African women in great detail, many times just expressing plain curiosity, it is evident that they viewed these physical traits from the podiums of western cultural superiority.

"Beasts of Burden:" African Women's Gender Roles and Duties

The travel narratives of modern British women list the assorted gender roles and duties of Western and Central African women. It must be emphasized that many of these observations were made of rural Western and Central African women. Though the British women did encounter African women in urban settings, they frequently only noticed them when they were prostitutes. The women were especially interested in African women's household duties and chores, African gender relations, and overwhelmingly, polygamy.

The first conclusion that many of the British women made about African women was that they worked harder than African men. When in Zaire, Page wrote that "nearly all the men classified themselves as hunters or fisherman ... But for many of the men life was easy, as most followed the manly pursuits of fishing, hunting, and sitting under trees."[46] She then continues by describing the long tedious daily tasks of Zairian women:

> For the women life was different, leaving the village at dawn with empty baskets on their backs; the trails of bare footprints along the numerous sandy tracks ... Often they would walk miles each day to work in the gardens on which each family depended for most of its food ... From mid-morning to mid-day the homeward trek began, with the women, Equatorial Africa's only beasts of burden, loaded up with firewood and food. The young girls in their early teens thrived on the physical work, being upright and attractive with straight necks, board

---

44. Ibid., 39.
45. Page, *Dust in a Dark Continent*, 32.
46. Ibid., 29–30.

shoulders, rounded well-developed biceps and generous firm breasts ... Deportment was not attained by balancing books on their heads at finishing schools, but by carrying baskets loaded with wood strapped to their foreheads, and buckets of water carried on their heads. Sadly, the physical work inevitably took its [toll], and after a lifetime of toil and bearing a succession of children, the old women were left bowed, wizened and shuffling, but still working without complaint. Once home, the work of cooking and preparing manioc would begin.... the women of the village worked their gardens and kwanga pools six days a week ... The only time the men condescend to visit the kwanga pools was when they went to collect yard-long worms to use as fish bait ... Sunday was the only say when most of the women could rest.[47]

Page's report clearly indicates her belief that African women are hard workers while their male counterparts are lazy and fish all day. Page's viewpoint is similar to those of Victorian women who evoked stereotypes of downtrodden African women whom they believed to be oppressed and unhappy with their plight.[48]

Page failed to recognize the differing yet complementary contributions West and Central African women and men make in sustaining a household's subsistence. Niara Sudarkasa has stressed the complementary division of labor among African women and men:

In most African societies, as elsewhere, the division of labor among sexual lines promoted reciprocity of effort. If men were farmers, women were food processors and traders. Where women and men were engaged in the same productive activity ... they produced different items. Among the Ibo [of Nigeria], females and males grew different crops; among the Yoruba [of Nigeria], female and male weavers produced different types of cloth on different types of looms ... In the management and disposal of their incomes, the activities of African women and men also were separate but coordinated ... women and men had different responsibilities ... a husband might be primarily responsible for the construction and upkeep of the home and the provision of staple foods, while the wife (or more probably the wives) assumed responsibilities for non-staple foods and the daily needs of her children.[49]

Furthermore, Page's conclusion in believing that African men's fishing and hunting activities are signs of laziness is an error. She does not take into account that both activities greatly contribute to a household's subsistence. Page has clearly imposed western ideas about proper gender roles by believing that fishing and hunting are leisure sports for African men as they are for British men. Page's outlook brings to mind the perceptions early Europeans had of Native American men. Like Page, many European men were confused as to why Native American women toiled the fields while men sat by in supposed idleness. Kathleen Brown writes that "English commentators reacted with disapproval to seeing women perform work relegated to laboring men in England while Indian men pursued activities associated with English aristocracy."[50] These activities then, and today,

---

47. Ibid., 30–32.
48. McEwan, *Gender, Geography, and Empire*, 157.
49. Niara Sudarkasa, "The 'Status of Women' in Indigenous African Societies," in Rosalyn Terborg-Penn and Andrea Benton Rushing (eds.) *Women in Africa and the African Diaspora: A Reader* (Washington, DC: Howard University Press, 1996), 82.
50. See Katherine Brown, "The Anglo-Algonquian Gender Frontier," in Nancy Shoemaker (ed.) *Negotiators of Change: Historical Perspectives of Native American Women* (New York: Routledge, 1995), 33. Also see David Smits, "The 'Squaw Drudge': A Prime Index of Savagism," in Rebecca Kugel and Lucy Eldersveld Murphy (eds.) *Native Women's History in Eastern North America before 1900* (Lincoln: University of Nebraska Press, 2007), 33.

were perceived as not being true works of labor, but leisure activities.[51] This misunderstanding of the gender division of labor in Africa creates faulty understandings and distorted conclusions.

The travel accounts also highlighted African women's household duties and outdoor chores. Coquery-Vidrovitch writes that unlike women in the west, African women's household duties are not limited to the house and that many women contribute to the whole household's subsistence by managing their own fields and sometimes their own herd of cattle.[52] Sudarkasa reveals that "African women were farmers, traders, and crafts producers in different parts of the continent. It is equally well documented that their economic roles were at once public and private. Women worked outside the home in order to meet the responsibilities placed upon them in their roles as mothers, wives, sisters, daughters, members of guilds, chiefs, or citizens."[53]

Davison and Dodwell noticed the varied household duties of African women. In Nakpanduri, Ghana, Davison commented about the Bimobas women: "Most of the women folk spent their days going into the bush to chop wood for their fires, going to the well or a river for water twice a day, pounding out grain, cooking outside in the yard and caring for their children."[54] In a Nigerian town, Dodwell described the organized gender duties of the people:

> [The] Village was surprisingly strictly organized and each person had their role to fulfill. It was the work of men to build the huts and keep them repaired, to erect and renew the pens for the animals, to clear the bush and undergrowth from places that the women had decided to cultivate, to make tools and weapons, to go fishing, hunting, or gathering, or to be craftsmen. The women's duties were to fetch water, to till the land, and to provide food for the families.[55]

Dodwell also underlined African women's roles in the preparation of food. While looking for water in Nigeria, Dodwell arrived in a village and observed women gathered in the center shelling and pounding guinea corn.[56] Dodwell also stumbled upon Pygmy women in Niger cooking, "Later we saw a spiral of smoke coming from a pygmies' hunting camp ... Outside it sat three children and a woman busy breaking open the boiled shell of a water tortoise. She would then add its meat to the pot of soup simmering on the fire."[57] Later, still in Niger, Dodwell stopped at a fishing camp and reported, "The fishing camp was deserted except for one woman, skinning manioc, a root that needs to soak for four days in water ... She would use the offcuts for baiting her prawn traps. The smoke rack above her fire held an assortment of small scaleless catfish."[58] Though I have argued that the British women's travel narratives were riddled with western superiority and pervasive western cultural ideologies, I do not dismiss the fact that many times their accounts are full of useful knowledge. Such is the circumstance of the observations the women made about African women's household tasks for it provides much historical insight.

---

51. Ibid.
52. Coquery-Vidrovitch, *African Women*, 11.
53. Sudarkasa, "The 'Status of Women,'" 81–82.
54. Davison, *They Two Went On*, 97.
55. Dodwell, *Travel with Fortune*, 26.
56. Ibid., 35.
57. Dodwell, *Travels with Pegasus*, 20.
58. Ibid., 21.

British women also took note of proper gender relations between African women and men. When in Niger, Dodwell engaged in a conversation about Tuareg gender relations with a man named Sulieman. She learned:

> He said that if men were in the company of unknown women they usually kept their face covered, not even opening their veil to drink tea, which could be sipped from below its folds. I think this was connected to the belief that the soul could escape through a man's mouth. For him as an enlightened town Tuareg, the most shocking thing about foreign women tourists was their skimpy clothing, and he wished they could know how offensive their mini shorts were to local people.[59]

Unfortunately, Dodwell does not provide reactionary comments to Sulieman wish that western women stopped wearing mini shorts in Niger. Perhaps it is because she herself wore them while in the country! Later, while in Tabalak, Niger, Dodwell learns about gender relations and expected marriage roles in an African marriage from a conversation with a local Tuareg man. She narrates that the man "had taken a second wife because his first one was no good. She kept running off home and made his life miserable. He had divorced her some time ago but she then insisted on coming back, only to give him a hard time. 'She was never like that when we were courting, but when we married, she changed.' He hoped that by marrying another, the first wife would come to her senses, though for the moment she was insanely jealous."[60] It is tempting to conclude from Dodwell's observation that the man's wife was not a good wife because she kept running away and not fulfilling her expected gender tasks, such as cooking. However, Dodwell fails to acknowledge that perhaps the wife was unhappy in the marriage. Rebecca Popenoe writes that among the Tuaregs and Azawagh Arabs of Niger, women who were unhappy in their marriages often "escaped" from their husbands to a neighboring house or to their parents' home,[61] Popenoe further adds that many women did this for various reasons, such as their husbands mistreating them.[62]

Later while in Mali, Dodwell also notates the gender relations of Tuareg women in the country while speaking to a Tuareg chief. She remembers:

> What struck me really absurd was when he said that a woman may never speak to more than five categories of men during her whole life — her father, her brothers, her husband, her sons, and her husband's sons. If any other man speaks to her she is forbidden to reply. I couldn't resist showing him a postcard of Queen Elizabeth, pointing out that Britain's greatest chief is a women, while our country is governed by the second most important woman, Margaret Thatcher. The chief's expression was aghast and he sent some words of sympathy to David. Unfortunately David was feeling too tired to take part in the conversation and was lying down with his eyes shut. Without understanding French, it must have been boring to him, and a blow for the chief, since for a Tuareg [man] it's an insult to have to speak to a woman. But I couldn't help that.[63]

---

59. Ibid., 78–80.
60. Ibid., 106.
61. Rebecca Popenoe, *Feeding Desire: Fatness, Beauty, and Sexuality among a Saharan People* (London: Routledge, 2004), 101
62. Ibid.
63. Ibid., 145.

When Dodwell is in Mauritania she writes, "Strictly an Islamic country, I was aware of the complete difference between Mali and Mauritania. Various men shook hands with David but not with me, instead they put their hand to their chest and salute, unable to touch a strange woman."[64] It is evident that Dodwell is keenly aware of African gender relations and even notices when the relations change from country to country. However, as exemplified in her conversation with the Tuareg chief, she does not seem to accept the validity of the relations. Instead, she imposes her western concepts of gender relations by telling the chief that in Britain things are different—women hold political power as queens and prime ministers. Dodwell's actions seem to shout falsely that African societies are male-dominated and are anti-women because they seem to deny female power and agency.

Finally, the practice of polygamy in Africa was widely acknowledged in the travel narratives. The women were quite occupied with this form of marriage and consistently noticed how many wives African men had. While among the Fulani of Cameroon, Dodwell reported, "The chief had over fifty wives, most of whom were inherited from the previous chief who died aged 100."[65] In Nigeria, Dodwell stated, "We ended up at a mountain-top village whose chief had forty-four wives."[66] In the Central African Republic, Fitzgerald recounts that the country's former president "had several official wives and at least fifty-four children."[67] She adds, "There had been scores of mistresses and girlfriends ... Each wife was kept secluded in a separate villa. His number one wife was Catherine ... his second wife was La Roumaine ..."[68] In many of these observations, there is little regard for the African woman and her lifestyle. Instead, she is thought of a numeric agent who is bought or inherited. There is minimal thought to how polygamy may benefit women, such as having an economic role in guaranteeing women the autonomy and human dignity they need.[69] Though African wives in polygamous marriages are acknowledged in the travel narratives, their experiences are silenced and thus not validated.[70]

The women's perceptions of polygamy stem from two different historical contexts. First, the modern British women outlooks were a clear a continuum from their Victorian counterparts. McEwan has written that in nineteenth-century Britain, "polygamy was perceived as immoral means of maintaining the subservience of African women. According to the prevailing view, African women in polygamous marriages were treated as chattels." [71] Therefore, Victorian women who traveled to Africa viewed polygamy as uncivilized and gave little thought to how it was a fundamental aspect of the structure of many African societies.[72] Victorian female travelers disdained polygamy because of their own cultural backgrounds. Modern British women travelers also had similar feelings towards polygamy. Back home in Britain, the home and family were believed to be havens of peace and security.[73] Furthermore, the bedrock of these beliefs was on the emphasis on monogamous couples. It is no wonder then that modern women emphasized their preoccupation with polygamy in their travel accounts.

---

64. Ibid., 190.
65. Dodwell, *Travels with Fortune*, 66.
66. Dodwell, *Travels with Pegasus*, 47.
67. Fitzgerald, *Nomad*, 150.
68. Ibid.
69. Molara Ogundipe-Leslie, *Recreating Ourselves: African Women and Critical Transformation* (Trenton, NJ: Africa World Press, 1994), 228.
70. Oyewùmí, "The White Woman's Burden," 34.
71. McEwan, *Gender, Geography, and Empire*, 159.
72. Ibid., 160.
73. Lewis, *Women in Britain since 1945*, 12.

British feminist movements in the 1970s–1980s may have also influenced the female travelers' views of African polygamous marriages. For example, the Women's Liberation Movement argued in the 1970s that "the family was as much a source of women's subordination in society as discrimination in the public sphere."[74] Such movements were often regarded as "anti-family" because they dismissed assumptions that the traditional family structure should be desirable.[75] For example, during the 1980s, many British feminists stressed that women should not be dependent on men, and they argued for the need to disaggregate the family and to treat its adult members as individuals.[76] The female travelers may have carried these changing attitudes towards men and family in Britain overseas. Perceiving marriage as a way to subordinate women, the women many have been shocked to see *multiple* African women married to one man. This may explain why the women were obsessed with counting how many wives African men had. This counting may have been translated to how many women were being subordinated and oppressed by the hardships of marriage. The factors that may have influenced British women's views of polygamous marriages are indeed contradictory. On one hand, the women valued 'traditional' marriages while in Africa, and on the other hand, they viewed marriage, particularly polygamy, as being oppressive.

The Hypnotic Sexuality of African Women

The sexuality of African women has long dominated Africanist scholarship. The preoccupation with African women's sexuality has been extended to the travel narratives of modern British women. For instance, Fitzgerald states "Africans regard sex without inhibition. For them it is a rite of passage to be celebrated as well as the biological means to propagating the tribe. This is why Africa exudes a libidinous sensuality."[77] Fitzgerald has generalized African sexuality without regards to the diverse attitudes Africans have towards it. In fact, while in Bangui, Central African Republic, Fitzgerald is disappointed that African women in the city were not representing her notion of African hypersexuality. She disappointedly reports, "Here ... people were so perfunctory about sex it had as much poetry as ladling food into your mouth. That was the key to Bangui. All the subtlety and allure had been ironed out of it."[78] To Fitzgerald, there is only one concept of African sexuality that should be embraced—that all Africans are hypersexual and frivolous about sexual acts. This ideology is not valid for all African countries as confirmed by Rebecca Popenoe on her gendered anthropological study of the Azawagh Arabs in Niger. The Azawagh Arabs perceive sex as a paramount ordering principle of life.[79] Therefore, one's sexuality and sexual acts are carefully organized and guarded. For example, Popenoe writes that the Azawagh Arabs believe that to "eat with too apparent pleasure and eagerness ... readily raises the specter of rapacious sexual lusts."[80] Consequently, women and girls must evince distaste of food to avoid sexualizing their bodies and enticing interest in sex.[81]

---

74. Ibid., 35.
75. Ibid.
76. Ibid., 36.
77. Fitzgerald, *Nomad*, 143.
78. Ibid.
79. Popenoe, 191.
80. Ibid., 192–93.
81. Ibid.

The physical features of African women are also intertwined with perspectives of African women's sexuality. For example, Fitzgerald and Jackson took detailed notes about the buttocks of African women and how it exuded sexuality. Fitzgerald reported:

> You stare at women whose bounteous backsides, encased in brightly patterned cloth, gyrate beneath the plates of mangos or cassava they are carrying on their heads. That hypnotic shifting of weight from left buttock to right buttock to left to right is such a triumph of female sexuality that you couldn't help grinning. At first you are so delirious you don't even mind the equivalent public display of masculinity.[82]

Fitzgerald clearly indicated that the buttocks of African women exude so much sexuality that one can almost become delirious from the mere sight of them! Jackson too is fascinated with the buttocks of African women, specifically those of Senegalese prostitutes, "There were loads of hookers around too, who were quite amusing to watch. They were some outrageous clothes and their bottoms stuck out so much you could stand your beer bottle on them!"[83]

Prostitution is another preoccupation with African women's sexuality. This attention to African prostitution is not limited to travel narratives but to writings about African women overall. African scholar, Oyèrónké Oyewùmí, points out that "one of the recurrent images of African womanhood in feminist writings is that of prostitution."[84] The scholar argues that in "the literature, the impression created is that African women, apart from being peasants, traders, wives, clerks, child-care workers or, whatever, are also prostitutes. This image of the prostitute cannot be separated from the association of Africans with strong sexual desire."[85] Jackson reported her sight of prostitutes in a Nigerian bar: "There were a lot of ladies of the night—if you know what I mean—looking very sultry. They would just sit at a table on their own, checking out other girls. Neil and I just sat and watched ... Then two black girls came and sat with us, who were really amusing. One was from Somalia and was drunk, but we had a good chat. All the hookers come up and greet you like you are old friends; they're really friendly and nice."[86]

Conclusion

An increasing number of British women are traveling to the African continent, leaving their footprints behind, and altering the landscapes via their travel accounts. Despite the many faulty and problematic perceptions of post-colonial African women, we cannot dismiss the valuable information British women's travel narratives provide. The accounts provide fresh insights into how citizens of former colonial empires are viewing post-colonial Africa. However, we must read the information about African women through lenses that take into account, and contextualize, the historical background of the writers and the women they highlight. Admittedly, there has been a shifting paradigm that has started to include more information on the people that British women travelers interacted with, such as Cheryl McEwan's *Gender, Geography and Empire*. However, more analysis of the women the travelers interacted with, colonial and post-colonial, will aid in redressing

---

82. Fitzgerald, *Nomad*, 142–43.
83. Jackson, *Into Africa*, 47.
84. Oyewùmí, 36.
85. Ibid.
86. Jackson, *Into Africa*, 77–78.

the imbalance in the discourse. After all, there is more than one participant within zones of contact.

References

Primary Sources

Davison, Eva. *They Two Went On.* London: Evangel Press, 1979.

_____. *Travels with Fortune: An African Adventure.* London: W.H. Allen, 1979.

_____. *Travels with Pegasus: A Microlight Journey across West Africa.* New York: Walker, 1990.

Fitzgerald, Mary Anne. *Nomad: Journeys from Samburu.* New York: Viking Press, 1993.

Jackson, Hazel. *Into Africa.* London: Minerva Press, 1997.

Page, Robin. *Dust in a Dark Continent.* London: Claridge Press, 1989.

Secondary Sources

Ballantyne, Tony and Antoinette M. Burton. "Postscript: Bodies, Genders, Empires: Reimagining World Histories." In *Bodies in Contact: Rethinking Colonial Encounters in World History*, Tony Ballantyne and Antoinette Burton (eds.) Durham, N.C.: Duke University Press, 2005, 405–23.

Brown, Katherine. "The Anglo-Algonquian Gender Frontier." In *Negotiators of Change: Historical Perspectives of Native American Women.* Nancy Shoemaker (ed.) New York: Routledge, 1995, 26–48.

Buettner, Elizabeth. *Empire Families: Britons and Late Imperial India.* Oxford: Oxford University Press, 2004.

Bush, Barbara. "Gender and Empire: The Twentieth Century." In *Gender and Empire.* Philippa Levine (ed.) New York: Oxford University Press, 2004. 77–111.

Coquery-Vidrovitch, Catherine. *African Women: A Modern History.* Boulder: Westview Press, 1997.

Frank, Katherine. "Voyages Out: Nineteenth-Century Women Travelers in Africa." In *Gender, Ideology, and Action: Historical Perspectives on Women's Public Lives*, Janet Sharistanian (ed.) Westport, Connecticut: Greenwood Press, 1986, 67–94.

Frawley, Maria H. *A Wider Range: Travel Writing by Women in Victorian England.* Rutherford, N.J.: Fairleigh Dickinson University Press, 1994.

Gengenbach, Heidi. "Tattooed Secrets: Women's History in Magude District, Southern Mozambique." In *Bodies in Contact: Rethinking Colonial Encounters in World History*, Tony Ballantyne and Antoinette Burton (eds.) Durham, N.C.: Duke University Press, 2005. 253–73.

Harper, Lila. *Solitary Travelers: Nineteenth-Century Women's Travel Narratives and the Scientific Vocation.* Cranbury, NJ: Associated University Press, 2001.

Lawrence, Karen. *Penelope Voyages: Women and Travel in the British Literary Tradition.* Ithaca: Cornell University Press, 1994.

Lewis, Jane. *Women in Britain Since 1945: Women, Family, Work, and the State in the Post-War Years.* Oxford, UK: Blackwell, 1992.

Maloba, Wunyabari. *African Women in Revolution*. Trenton, New Jersey: Africa World Press, Inc., 2007.

McEwan, Cheryl. *Gender, Geography, and Empire: Victorian Women Travellers in West Africa*. Aldershot, Hampshire, England: Ashgate, 2000.

Ogundipe-Leslie, Molara. *Recreating Ourselves: African Women and Critical Transformation*. Trenton, NJ: Africa World Press, 1994.

Oyewùmí, Oyèrónké. "The White Woman's Burden: African Women in Western Feminist Discourse." In *African Women and Feminism: Reflecting on the Politics of Sisterhood*. Oyèrónké Oyewùmí (ed.) Trenton, NJ: Africa World Press, 2003, 25–43.

Popenoe, Rebecca. *Feeding Desire: Fatness, Beauty, and Sexuality among a Saharan People*. London: Routledge, 2004.

Pratt, Mary Louise. *Imperial Eyes: Travel Writing and Transculturation*. London: Routledge, 1992.

Romero, *Patricia W. Women's Voices on Africa: A Century of Travel Writings*. New York: M. Wiener Publishers, 1992.

Smits, David. "The 'Squaw Drudge': A Prime Index of Savagism." In *Native Women's History in Eastern North America before 1900* Rebecca Kugel and Lucy Eldersveld Murphy (eds.) Lincoln: University of Nebraska Press, 2007, 27–49.

Stefoff, Rebecca. *Women of the World: Women Travelers and Explorers*. New York: Oxford University Press, 1992.

Sudarkasa, Niara. "The 'Status of Women' in Indigenous African Societies." In *Women in Africa and the African Diaspora: A Reader*, Rosalyn Terborg-Penn and Andrea Benton Rushing (eds.) Washington, DC: Howard University Press, 1996, 73–87.

Chapter 5

Of Silences, Bended Knees and Sexuality: Insights on the Gendered (Re)Presentations in Yorùbá Art

Adérónké Adésolá Adésànyà

The Yorùbá of southwestern Nigeria are creators of rich lore, vintage and vibrant verbal and visual expressions that continue to fascinate scholars and present ideas for contemplation. These art genres offer a rich reservoir of data relevant to understanding the Yorùbá worldview and explicating the peculiarities of their lore. At each flip of the coin, one gets interesting and dynamic insights into the cultural vista of the people, an understanding of the notion of double sense and an unending search for the Yorùbá. Diplomacy is a craft perfected in Yorùbá culture as exemplified in the expression 'sòtún sòsì má ba ibì kan jé.'[1] In fact, one cannot truly comprehend the Yorùbá, in a given sense of the word and in view of the dynamic and vibrant expressions that the culture presents to the investigator, without examining the verbal and the visual arts of the people. It is from them that one gets a foregrounding of how they conceive hierarchy, power, gender relations, and sexuality, fecundity and sundry issues peculiar to them. Yorùbá arts are essentially eloquent: They are in a given sense cultural windows of endless lore; trajectories and repositories of indigenous tradition that present the social realities of the Yorùbá, and provide memory, which reinforce the consciousness of the past in the present.

In the eloquence of Yorùbá arts, however, I identify some ambivalence in gender representations, the problem with historical accounts, the muting of the female gender, the appropriation of her sexuality for the collective interest of the society, and consider what the works of male and female artists indicate about their notion of gender. I also note that sex and power are underlying premises for artistic representations. Two contrasting views about women in the Yorùbá society and their representation in Yorùbá art are worth considering in this chapter. One is the argument that women are subjugated in the Yorùbá society and that the indexes of this domination are noticeable in their verbal and visual arts. The other is that Yorùbá women occupied privileged positions in the past and over time lost their foothold as a result of the institutionalization of patriarchy. Both views are right and I will attempt to unite them shortly. In the meantime, I will make some theoretical consideration.

I consider the perspectives of Elaine Showalter (1979)[2] and Lisa Tuttle (1986) on feminist literary criticism and the body of works they have examined relevant to my discussion.

---

1. This simply refers to the capacity of the Yorùbá as master of intrigues and diplomacy.

2. Although the thrust of Elaine Showalter's studies concern mental health and female representation, she uses her studies as platforms for reviewing subjectivity and advocated a rethinking of women issues using gendered lens. See "Feminist Criticism in the Wilderness," *Critical Inquiry*, Vol. 8, 2 (1981): 179–205; *The Female Malady: Women, Madness, and English Culture, 1830–1980* (New York, Penguin Books, 1987); *Hystories: Hysterical Epidemics and Modern Culture* (New York: Columbia

Why use feminist literary criticism? It becomes necessary based on the premise that a writer does with her pen what an artist does with her media. Feminist literary criticism focuses on representations of women in literature and the rationale for such representations. The theory is applicable to the visual arts in the way it is applied to literature. However, the shortcomings of feminist literary criticism includes the fact that (i) it is essentially about politics and polemics; and (ii) it has strong theoretical affiliations with Marxist sociology. These somehow underscore the relevance of feminist literary criticism to this study. Although feminist literary criticism provides insight into men's worldview on women, exposes what men have thought women to be and should be, this approach has a tendency to take women's subjugation for granted and presents it as inevitable—a seemingly patriarchal position within a feminist mould. Thus, instead of relying on the larger feminist literary criticism, I focus on its subsets, mainly on two aspects, namely, 'feminist critique' and 'gynocritique.'[3]

Tuttle has defined feminist theory and by extension feminist critique as asking new questions of old texts. She cites the goals of feminist criticism as: (1) To develop and uncover a female tradition of writing, (2) to interpret symbolism of women's writing so that it will not be lost or ignored by the male point of view, (3) to rediscover old texts, (4) to analyze women writers and their writings from a female perspective, (5) to resist sexism in literature, and (6) to increase awareness of the sexual politics of language and style.[4] Feminist critique awakens a sexual code in a text, focuses on the image of women and their stereotypes in art. It highlights their exploitation and manipulation and analyzes them as signs in semiotic systems. In line with the ideology propounded by exponents of feminist critique, I attempt to raise new questions about old texts in Yorùbá culture. Gynocritique departs from looking at women through male gazes to developing a framework for the analysis of women's art. It argues for new models that are based on their experience and useful for studying their works. The theory highlights women as writers and readers, provides a platform for women to interpret male art (including writings) and to re-present themselves and the "other." While I find this quite useful in my discussion, for the most part, my discussion of Yorùbá arts and my interrogation of the representation of women in them derive essentially from the feminist critique ideology.

In order to seek new questions from old texts, I will now return to the subject of subjugation and the much debated privileged position of women in the Yorùbá society. Let me restate that the issues of gender inequality, gender bias, and/or discrimination in the Yorùbá society have been subjects of controversy in existing literature. While some scholars insist that gender inequality exists, and in the process of researching broader subjects have sought to re-write and revisit representations of women[5] scholars including Bolanle Awe, J. Atanda, S. O. Babayemi and Oyeronke Oyewumi have posited differently by advancing the view that Yorùbá women were indeed prominent in Yorùbá history and

---

University Press, 1997); *Inventing Herself: Claiming a Feminist Intellectual Heritage* (New York: Scribner, 2000).

3. The body of works developed by Showalter on this subject is particularly instructive. See "Towards a Feminist Poetics," in M. Jacobus (ed.), Women Writing about Women (London, UK: Croom Helm, 1979), 25–33, 34–6.

4. Lisa Tuttle, *Encyclopedia of Feminism* (Santa Barbara, CA: Greenwood Press, 1986), 184.

5. Ade Adeeghe, "The Other Half of the Story: Nigerian Women Telling Tales," in Stewart Brown (ed.), *The Pressures of the Text: Orality, Texts and Telling of Tales* (Great Briton: University of Birmingham/African Studies Series, 1995); Aderonke Adesanya, "Women in Contemporary Nigerian Art," *Isese: Journal of Folklore*, Vol. 2, I & 2 (2000): 25–36.

have highlighted areas of their prominence.[6] Toyin Falola offers a critique of the latter group and describes them as engaging in a scholarship of "archaeology of queens" whereby they go into archives and single out a few women who attained prominence in the annals of Yorùbá history, and take these examples to be basis for gender equality within the Yorùbá matrix.[7] Using the example of *Iya Lekuleja*, he discusses this in his memoir *A Mouth Sweeter Than Salt*, but admits that there are indeed powerful women in the Yorùbá society.

One wonders however, how the power and influence of such women have not engendered the collective visibility and emancipation for women. Why have they not been able to influence, challenge, or transform the dominant patriarchal structure, which Oyewunmi locates its origin as beginning from the colonial period? What holds true to date in spite of the few successful and prominent women in Yorùbá history, is that their successes, even in their respective endeavors including their roles in traditional religions and agrarian economy, have been largely by what that patriarchal culture permitted.[8] Their successes were even short-lived in the sense that when their wealth and influence threatened the universe of men in their society such women suffered sudden eclipse. Indeed, what the literature has established about patriarchy is that male dominance must be maintained at all cost and at all levels because, as Eva Figes notes "the person who dominates cannot conceive of any alternative but to be dominated in turn."[9]

The need to query the status quo, and as Tuttle advanced, 'to question the texts,'[10] is brought to the fore now and then without any significant change. Indeed, Carolyn Heilbrun's submission about women writers is apposite.[11] She argues in 'Women Writers and Female Characters: The Failure of Imagination' that women fail to see themselves beyond the spaces defined for them by men, that women novelists fail to imagine female characters as strong as themselves, and notes how women along with men write women as backdrops in literature:

> Women's most persistent problem has been to discover for herself an identity not limited by custom or defined by attachment to some man. Remarkably, her search for identity has been even less successful within the world of fiction than outside it, leaving us until very recently with a situation largely unchanged for more than two millennia: men as writers have created women characters with autonomy, with a self that is not ancillary, not described by a relationship — wife, mother, daughter, mistress, chief assistant. Women writers, however, when they wished to create an individual filling more than a symbiotic role, projected

6. Bolanle Awe, "The Iyalode in the Traditional Political System," in A. Schlegel (ed.), *Sexual Stratification: A Cross-Cultural View* (New York: Columbia University Press, 1977), 144–60; S. O. Babayemi, "The Fall and Rise of Old Oyo c. 1760–1905: A Study in the Traditional Culture of an African Polity," (Ph.D. Dissertation, Centre for West African Studies, University of Birmingham, England, 1979); Oyeronke Oyewunmi, *The Invention of Women: Making an African Sense of Western Gender Discourses* (Minnesota: University of Minnesota Press, 1997).

7. Toyin Falola, "Gender, Business, and Space Control: Yoruba Market Women and Power," in Bessie House-Midamba and Felix K. Ekechi (eds.), *African Market and Economic Power: The Role of Women in African Economic Development (Westport, Connecticut: Greenwood Press, 1995), 33.*

8. See Ojo Olatunji's work on Yorùbá women farmers in "More than Farmers' Wives: Yoruba Women and Cash Crop Production, c. 1920–1957," in Adebayo Oyebade (ed.), *The Transformation of Nigeria* (Trenton, New Jersey: Africa World Press, 2002), 383–404.

9. Eva Figes, *Patriarchal Attitudes* (London: MacMillan Education Ltd., 1986), 45.

10. Tuttle, *Encyclopedia of Feminism* 184.

11. Carolyn Heilbrun, *Reinvention of Womanhood* (New York: W.W Norton and Company, 1979), 71–92.

their ideal of autonomy onto a male character, leaving the heroines to find their role in subservience, or change of name, or both.[12]

Whether performing culturally assigned symbiotic roles or individual role, a similar ideology informs the (increasing) acceptance of the stereotypical way women are depicted in Yorùbá art and indeed African art as the norm. Some scholars even consider such representations as indexes of valorization rather than denigration. For instance, Barbara Thompson argues that "Western sexualization and pathologizing of the African female body sharply contrasts with traditional African ideologies of womanhood, in which women were honored and depicted in the visual and performing arts as givers of life, as guardians of moral integrity, and as cornerstones of family continuity and communal unity."[13] One of the major submissions of Babatunde Lawal's study on Gèlèdé is that the representation of the sexes in symbiotic cultural ascribed roles as exemplified in Gèlèdé spectacle promotes social harmony.[14] This idea, that is, the recognition of the complementarity of the sexes in promoting social cohesion, is underscored in the study of Anita Glaze on the Senufo. She drew attention to how among these people the female arena of power and arts produced by women complements those of men. She submits that men's and women's arts "combine in a vital process whereby conflicts and tensions, in both a real and an ideological sense, are harmonized and resolved."[15] The Drewals highlight the import of feminine power, and its strong connection with masquerade tradition and influence on the wellbeing of the Yorùbá society.[16]

Altogether, the scholars' interesting perspectives and their ideas converge in a pattern that seems to endorse the popular cultural representations in Yorùbá art, and in the equally very interesting pattern, they also adopt the characteristic diplomacy of the Yorùbá 'sòtún sòsì má ba ibì kan jé.' Though the arguments of the scholars are based on well researched data, still, there is a need to ask new questions from the old visual texts which they have examined and re-examine the oral data which informed their submissions. Given the fact that African societies are largely patriarchal would the conclusion of the scholars have been different if matriarchy was the predominant structure in African societies? Are women in the Yorùbá society indeed a powerful or exploited group, or both? At any rate, I will summarily use the visual and verbal data that I present in this study to answer these questions and examine the notion of equality in the Yorùbá society, revise the assumptions in literature and some misleading concepts about gender representations in Yorùbá art, offer new insights into, and add new dimensions to the subject.

From the feminist critique perspective, what the verbal and visual expressions of the Yorùbá articulate about the sexes are not difficult to interpret. First, there is clearly gender differentiation in the iconographic representation of male and female: the male occupies a position of influence and domination, and expresses overt power while the female occupies position of submission, supplication and communicates covert power. Though power rests with the two genders, taken together, there is great distinction. As Oyeronke

---

12. Ibid., 73.

13. Barbara Thompson, "The African Female Body in the Cultural Imagination," in *Black Womanhood: Images, Icons and Ideologies of the Human Body* (Hanover, New Hampshire: Hood Museum of Art, 2008), 29.

14. Babatunde Lawal, *The Gelede Spectacle: Art, Gender and Social Harmony in an African Culture* (Seattle: University of Washington Press, 1996), 71–97.

15. Anita Glaze, *Art and Death in a Senufo Village* (Bloomington: Indiana University Press, 1981), xii.

16. Henry John Drewal and Margaret Thompson Drewal, *Gelede, Art and Female Power Among the Yoruba* (Bloomington, Indiana: Indiana University Press, 1983).

Oyewunmi aptly puts it, "the male is the norm, the female is the exception, it is a pattern in which power is believed to inhere in maleness in and of itself."[17] The male is the privileged "other" in any African society and "given the fact that African figurative sculpture is primarily made and used by and for men, this paradigm has left little room for locating women's arts within the broader traditional cultural milieu, much less for discussion of how ideologies of African womanhood have been constructed and visually expressed by and for women."[18]

Secondly, the representations of the sexes derive their currency and orientation from a threefold patriarchy: patriarchy of colonialism, patriarchy of religion, and patriarchy of culture. In terms of the patriarchy of religion, if one factors the notion that men make gods in Africa into the discourse it is easy to understand what shapes ideas of religion and spaces of power in traditional religious institutions in Africa and how women more often than not assume subsidiary position in such spaces. In uniting patriarchy of religion with culture, men manipulate cultural spaces to entrench male hegemony to the detriment of women. Colonialism simply reinforced existing patriarchal structure. Patriarchy of colonialism or state patriarchy was European in content and intent, meant to entrenched British hegemony while granting little space at the lowest echelon to the native Africans (men) and totally excluding women who were categorized as the "Other." Thus, whether at the level of religion, culture or colonial imagination or realities women lost a foothold while men gained ascendancy.

The threefold patriarchy also influenced significantly on existing pre-colonial structures. To start with, chroniclers began distorting historical data while documenting Yorùbá history. There were set agenda to preserve emerging hegemonic structures to promote male supremacy and jettison the egalitarian Yorùbá culture that provided equal political space for both male and female. If the natives/colonized experienced grave dislocation and lost their history as a result of European incursion and invasion of their cultural space, for "African women the tragedy deepened in that colonial experience threw them to the very bottom of a history that was not theirs."[19] Women lost foothold to patriarchy by installments. In the tradition of origin of the Yorùbá, reference to the deities who descended from the sky to establish Yorubaland has always identified men and not women as founders even though a woman was among them. According to Ifá, there were sixteen gods, all male, and a seventeenth a woman who was initially despised by the male gods.

Òsun of the cooling waters fame and an entity fondly called "arí pepe kó ide sí" (she who has a shelf to store brass) because of her abundant brass wealth was initially ignored by the sixteen male gods before calamitous circumstances forced them to seek her assistance. Adepegba, citing Odù Òsé Tura, an Ifá verse, provides insight into this primeval event:

> She was the seventeenth of the primordial orisa and was at first not involved in the management of the world because she alone was a woman. But the earlier sixteen deities were having problems until they went to God for direction and were told to invite Òsun to all that they wanted to do, for normalcy to be restored ... she should be involved because she was as powerful as men.[20]

---

17. Oyewunmi, *The Invention of Women*, 30.
18. Thompson, "The African Female Body in Cultural Imagination," 30.
19. Oyewunmi, *The Invention of Women*, 153.
20. Cornelius O. Adepegba, "Òsun and Brass: An Insight into Yoruba Symbology," in Joseph M. Murphy and Mei-Mei Sanford (eds.), *Òsun Across the Waters: A Yoruba Goddess in Africa and the Americas* (Bloomington: Indiana University Press, 2001), 106–7.

This account indicates that the Yorùbá tradition recognizes the fact that women are indispensable to men. However, in admitting their importance women acquire a cultural label, which Rowland Abiodun alludes to in his summary of the encounter between Òsun and the sixteen male òrìsà: "Disguised here, however, is the ambivalent attitude of men towards women." This can be attributed to the belief that, like Òsun, women of any age are potential aje who possess "eye," the "bird power."[21] Any reference to powerful or "exceptional" women in the context of Yorùbá tradition of origin has always been derogatory or satirically salutatory.[22] In most cases, they are vilified and labeled as witches that ought to be placated to avoid their wrath, dangerous caprices and by implication, destruction of the society.

Women, whether young or old but predominantly older women, can be characterized as witches if they manifest extraordinary power. In fact, the Yorùbá consider old women who have passed the age of menopause as potentially dangerous irrespective of any good that they have to offer. An example of this phenomenon is found in the Ketu migration story documented by E. D. Babatunde, which refers one of the women who helped the migrants to establish at Ketu as a sorcerer.[23] Falola also contributes to the debate in his discussion of Ìyá Lékuléja, a powerful diminutive woman in Ibadan society of the 1950s who on the one hand, many ran to for help whenever they experienced normal to threatening health issues.[24] They desperately sought her herbal and sundry ingredients for all diseases, but on the other hand, avoided her like a plague for fear of her capricious tendency. Because she knew too much, could heal all manners of diseases, largely distanced herself from worldly concerns and refrained from fraternizing with people, many weaved mysterious stories around her to the degree that only those who really could not avoid going to her for their medicinal cures hurried to her stall where she sold various charms and herbs to make purchases. The irony in the denigrating cultural labeling of powerful women such as Ìyá Lékuléja and other old women is that, if men exhibited similar powers, they are simply wizards. A wizard, a male equivalent of a witch has a positive connotation in contrast to the universal perception of a witch as an entity capable of dangerous manifestations.

It is also necessary to do a feminist critique of Yorùbá history in view of the fact that undermining the position of women in Yorùbá society is as old as the foundations of the society itself where men and their gods have manipulated the structure of the society and knowledge production to advance patriarchal ideology. For instance, Yorùbá lore hardly recognized women as founders of Yorùbá chiefdoms and settlements except in mythology. Even the reference to Odùdùwa, progenitor of the Yorùbá, as possibly female has remained a subject of debate.[25] In historical reality, or put differently, in written history authored by men, female rulers do not exist; their universe is permitted in mythology. Thus, the universe and memory of Oba Jomijomi Jepojepo Òtòmpòrò níyùn of Òyó, Oba Púpúpú of Òndó, Èyékùnrin àfin of Ìjerò Èkìtì, and Oba of Ife, and a few of female rulers 'graciously' recalled in human memory exists in Yorùbá mythology.

21. Rowland Abiodun, "Hidden Power: Osun, the Sixteenth Odu," in Joseph M. Murphy and Mei-Mei Sanford (eds.), *Osun Across the Waters: Yoruba Goddess in Africa and the Americas*, 7.

22. Even the term undermines the capabilities of women. When they demonstrate abilities contrary to the expectation of the society, they are regarded as exceptional and acquire cultural labels.

23. E. D. Babatunde, "Ketu Myths and the Status of Women: A Structural Interpretation of Some Yoruba Myths," *African Notes*, Vol. XII, 1 & 2 (1988): 131–143.

24. Falola, *A Mouth Sweeter Than Salt* (Ann Arbor, MI: The University of Michigan Press, 2004), 170–176.

25. See A. K. Ajisafe, *The Law and Customs of the Yoruba People* (Lagos, Nigeria: CMS Bookshop, 1924); Geoffery Parrinder, *African Mythology* (London: Hamlyn, 1967); Bolaji Idowu, *Olodumare: God in Yoruba Beliefs* (London: Longman, 1962), 24–27.

Indeed, Samuel Johnson, the chronicler of Òyó history actually brought the knowledge of some of them to light. Oyewunmi rightly raised fundamental questions about the 'suspect' history which effaced women rulers from the king list of Òyó in her book *The Invention of Women*, and took a number of historians to task on how their scholarship is implicated in the distortion of Yorùbá history and misrepresentation of cultural ethos. The paradigms presented in Yorùbá myths, which portray the few female rulers as tyrannical and evil, can be interpreted as a patriarchal attempt to explain away the displacement of female rulers. Patriarchal, too, is the reversal of gender roles in Yorùbá kingdoms where women once ruled.[26] At Ilésá, female rulership was obliterated because a particular female king called Adérèmí could not manage and defend Ilésá against external aggression, hence, her people resolved to subsequently elect male warrior rulers.[27] Also among the Òndó where it is recalled that a woman called Púpúpú, was the first ruler, male ascendancy is now the norm and the Olóbùn title, a ceremonial position has been created as a commemorative title and token for women. The Olóbùn, who is otherwise known as ba Obìnrin (female ruler) but not a king in the real sense of the word, and her chiefs are influential in the installation rites and ceremonies of the Òsemàwé, the monarch of Òndó. These examples are some part of the premise on which those who advance the argument that women occupy powerful positions in Yorùbá society hinge their debate.

Although mythology and court tradition of some Yorùbá kingdoms posit that women once ruled such kingdoms, Yorùbá art, like Yorùbá chronicle, is silent on them. In the ancient art traditions of Ifè, Òwò and Èsìé royal women appear or scholars interpret, in consonance with the manipulated Yorùbá history, their images as queens and not kings. If Yorùbá art including woodcarvings are indeed tangible historical data then one begins to question these ancient texts for the missing gender. Without any form of ambiguity, Yorùbá sculptures of the royalty present the gender of the rulers as predominantly male. Although the images are not actual representations of specific monarchs, the visual references to only men as kings indicate some lopsidedness and perhaps highlight a patriarchal agenda on the part of the artists, custodians of culture, historians to mute the female gender.

Socially learned norms govern artistic productions in the Yorùbá society to the degree that certain icons remain sacrosanct, men as kings, priests, riders, and hunters, women as queens, mothers, maidens, and genuflecting worshippers. In view of their socialization training and the media, men produce much of these art forms used in sacred and secular contexts; thus, they have the choice of subject matter and the advantage to control the form. The edge that men have over the women allows them to create forms that articulate and entrench patriarchy. Indeed, one could safely argue that Yorùbá male artists use the repertoire to extend hegemonic structures. Traditional Yorùbá art mirrors the people's religious practices. Highly gendered are the art forms produced for the gods or consecrated for his/her worship. Integral to Yorùbá rituals are the issues of sex and gender. Gender in Yorùbá art is subject to socio-cultural influences; they are idioms of relations between different power structures and political figures.

Gender is also historical and political and is subject to transformation by prevalent political and financial interests. Men and women play specific roles that are expedient to worship and ritual. In some rituals and related or other spectacles, men dominate. In others, powerful women, especially those who have reached menopause, take charge of the rituals. Men play key roles in Yorùbá masquerade traditions and male-centered cults'

---

26. Lawal, *The Gelede Spectacle: Art, Gender, and Social Harmony in an African Culture*, 267.
27. Harold Courlander, *Tales of Yoruba Gods and Heroes* (Greenwich, Connecticut: Fawcett, 1973), 114–16.

initiation ceremonies. Women, too, have their spectacles but such do not exclude men though the number of men who are attracted to female performance is quite negligible. Henry Drewal notes that in male-directed and male-centered masquerade performances women are more restricted.[28] The Yorùbá concept of power finds expression in the construction of gender and in its manifestations in social and religious contexts.

Another area where royal women suffered neglect in the memory of the Yorùbá and an index that seem to strengthen the idea that female rulers only exist in Yorùbá mythology and not in their chronicles, is in the content and performance of oríkì. The quintessential characterization panegyric poetry of the Yorùbá that celebrates the intrinsic and extrinsic qualities, and addresses the good and bad attributes of the object of praise.[29] Women build the repertoire and perform most oríkì, whether the oríkì orílè or personal oríkì of rulers of specific Yorùbá kingdoms. Majority of Yorùbá oríkì orílè and other traditions of origin indicate men as founders, reinforcing the idea of patriarchy. Concerning personal oríkì of Yorùbá monarchs, the praise poems of Aláàfin Abíódún, Aólè, and Babáyemí Ìtíolú alias Sàngó of Old Òyó kingdom, are popular and well documented in existing literature.[30] They are also celebrated in *Yùngbà-kíkùn*, a female-authored rárà restricted to and distinctive of the Òyó noble household.[31] Memorized in oríkì too are the attributes, achievements and pageantry of male kings of other Yorùbá kingdoms.

The Yorùbá Cosmos, Oriki and Aesthetic Topicalities

The Yorùbá society, like most African cultures, is essentially patriarchal. No matter how the notion is stiffly opposed by contemporary feminists in the Yorùbá society, women depended, and largely still depend on men for status and respectability. That patriarchy is a widespread phenomenon, well grounded but masked all over the world, and that the culture of male dominance is not an African 'disease' is well established in literature.[32] Women derive definition by their relationship with men and there is largely no room for the expression of female power without the endorsement of male hegemonic structure. Traditional expectations in the Yorùbá society and the same can be said of African societies, are such that women are supposed to achieve lasting contentment only when they marry. Their needs and aspirations are inextricably linked if not subsumed to those of their husbands. Omoniwa informs that,

---

28. Henry Drewal, "Flaming Crowns Cooling Waters: Masquerades of the Ijebu-Yoruba," *African Arts*, Vol. 20, 1 (1986): 32–41, 99–100.

29. Ogundeji classifies oríkì as a speech, recitative and even chant mode of Yorùbá oral poetry and describes it as basic to all other poetic forms. He posits that it constitutes one of the critical standards for assessing excellence in poetic performance. See P. Adedotun Ogundeji "Ritual as Theatre, Theatre as Ritual: The Nigerian Example," *Isese Monograph Series*, Vol. 2, 1 (2000): 1–40: 26.

30. For a rich panegyric on Sango refer to John Pemberton III, "The Oyo Empire," in Henry Drewal, John Pemberton, Allen Wardwell, and Rowland Abiodun, *Yoruba: Nine Centuries of African Art and Thought* (New York: The Center for African Art in Association with Harry N. Abrams, 1989), 159–162.

31. A. Olateju "Yungba Royal Chant: A Specialised Yoruba Oral Poetry Type," *Oye: Ogun Journal of Arts*, Vol. IV (1988): 54–68; O.B. Jegede "Court Poetry Tradition and Performance in Nigeria," (PhD Dissertation, Department of English, University of Ibadan, Ibadan, 2002).

32. Mojubaoluwa Okome, "What Women, Whose Development? A Critical Analysis of Reformist Evangelism on African Women," in Oyeronke Oyewumi (ed.), *African Women and Feminism* (Trenton, NJ: Africa World Press, 2003), 84, 87.

Through the performance modes and feature types of his art, the Yorùbá oral poet is able to perform a variety of functions, which project him as critic, historian, moralist, religious commentator or reformer. These functions make him a unique artist; that is, one who is deeply committed to the propagation of the shared values and experiences of his people in their day-to-day strive for stability, order and progress. From traditional through modern times, Yorùbá oral poetry has functioned as an invaluable transmitter of the customs, beliefs and practices of society. Taboos, mores and all other communal lore inevitably find expression in the peoples' poetry. In this way, the oral poet is able to convey values, which invest the community with a sense of identity, and reinforce its commitment to common goals and social ideals.[33]

Yorùbá *oríkì* performance, a rich repertoire, includes oríkì àbíjo/ìnagije/bòròkìnί (personal praise poem), oríkì orίle (lineage panegyric poetry), oríkì ìlú (panegyric of towns), among others. Though both male and female perform some genres, the corpus is largely a woman's art. Some oríkì are developed for the individual to foreground his/her origin and celebrate his/her achievements. Others celebrate the origin and achievements of towns. The performances take place in an informal or semi-formal setting and most of these performances remain the exclusive preserve of women. However, it is an art largely created and celebrated for men in the sense that they have a greater percentage of the various forms of *oríkì* in the Yorùbá society. As Karin Barber rightly observes, "The more outstanding the person, the greater the number of *oríkì* that will be added. For this reason, men acquire more than women, and important men acquire more than ordinary men."[34] Barber's observation bears testimony to the fact that men have more visibility that is social and political, and a higher ranking than women do in the traditional Yorùbá society. Ironically, women through their customary performance of various *oríkì* (personal, lineage, town, etc) serve as currency and channels for such male visibility to happen. They use their artistry as *oríkì* chanters to negotiate and expand cultural and political space for men. Mojubaoluwa Okome presents an interesting account of Yorùbá *oríkì* that questions the position of Barber.

Based on her understanding of the Yorùbá culture, Okome argues that both men and women performed the *oríkì*, and that all members of her family irrespective of gender and age share the same *oríkì orίlè* and that each family has its own distinctive *oríkì* contrary to what Barber holds on the gender of chanters and the performance of *oríkì*. Her submissions, factual as they appear, also contradict contemporary practices. At family gatherings, ceremonies and communal events will confirm that *oríkì* genre is essentially a female art. The practice is even more pronounced in contemporary period. The few exceptions to the norm are royal court bards who praise the universe, achievements and ancestors of a king. Increasingly in contemporary period, street miscreants and urchins found in cities who have now developed new genre of 'oríkì'—a type of free style eulogy that has no historical precedents—to praise personages they encounter at public events in order to get some money from them.[35] I have chosen to refer to this free form/*oríkì* as 'pedestrian panegyric' more essentially because it is developed from and for, performed and dispensed with on the street.

---

33. Olanrewaju Omoniwa, "The Yorùbá Oral Poet as a Religious and Heroic Archetype," *Nigerian Heritage: Journal of the National Museum and Monuments*, Vol. 2 (1993): 109.

34. Karin Barber, *I Could Speak Until Tomorrow: Oríkì. Women, and the Past in a Yoruba Town* (Edinburgh: Edinburgh University Press, 1991), 69.

35. These are popularly known as 'alright sa' a cognomen derived from their customary salutation of their object of praise usually wealthy men and women.

Yorùbá *oríkì* is political in content and form in the sense that the chanter recognizes and celebrates the political space of the person for whom the *oríkì* is performed. Pemberton III notes that "Oriki celebrate in rhythm, rhyme, and word play the iwa (status, essential character, fundamental nature) of the person or god whose praise is heralded. As in every performance, the singer of an oriki not only acknowledges the presence and power of the subject of praise, but through verbal imagery evokes the reality that she or he praises."[36] For instance, *Yùngbà-kíkùn*, a type of *rárà* in which the wives of the Aláàfin (monarch) of Òyó engage in occasional *oríkì* performances with accompaniments of stick-drumming on the back of upturned gourds in (mortar) basins filled with water (igbá-títí), is a celebration of the political space, clout and pageantry of the Aláàfin. His wives chant with vigor and relish the great achievements of their monarch-husband.

In fact, it is expedient for the wives to master the *oríkì* in order to be part of the performance. Older wives train the younger wives who have just joined the royal household in the artistry of praising the monarch. In doing this, both trainer and trainee recognize the importance of the *oríkì* to the universe of the Oba whose prominence derives from this and several other celebrations and is most fully established and most securely located in his glory, when he is enhanced by the royal oríkì. In effect, by mastering the *yùngbà-kíkùn*, the wives of the Aláàfin not only eulogize and celebrate their royal husband they also metaphorically reinforce his ancestry. The audience of *yùngbà* chant comprises the monarch, his chiefs and few select guests.[37] As they listen to the Aláàfin's praise singing by his wives, who are in a sense his profilers and political campaigners, the political space of the Oba becomes more defined, more elevated, more established and more exclusive. As oríkì chanted by women celebrates and empowers important personages such as kings and chiefs, so it does to the gods:

> Orisa and other spiritual beings are treated in the same way: oríkì uttered to them both empower them, and localize them in the human community whether through possession or more simply by securing their presence at a shrine. Every fourth day, an orisa's devotees perform an early morning ceremony at its household shrine. Food or just kola is offered; the orisa's acceptance is solicited; prayers and incantations are uttered; and one of the women chants the oríkì of the orisa. Without the oríkì, the presence of the orisa could not be secured.[38]

Women chant most *oríkì* whether for men or the gods is in recognition of, on the one hand, the vocative and evocative effect of the genre and its import for empowerment, and on the other hand, the political space that men occupy.[39] Women even go beyond the palaces and sacred arenas to warfronts singing praises of and empowering warlords, in most cases, to victory. Barber observes that *oríkì* formed one of the significant elements of motivation for Yorùbá warriors in the nineteenth century when they go to battle. To psyche warriors to victory and achieve their purpose *oríkì* performers would scream, in an urgent and feverish manner, and thus, with such intensity advance the process of empowerment. When warriors return victorious, they move up the political ladder in the society and women add more praise songs highlighting their conquest to their *oríkì*

---

36. Pemberton III, "The Oyo Empire," 159.

37. Olateju, "Yungba Royal Chant," 54–68; Ademola Dasylva, "Identity and Memory in Omoboyode Arowa's Oríkì performance in (Yorùbá) Èkìtì Dialect," *African and Asian Studies*, Vol. 6, 1 & 2 (2007): 173–200.

38. Barber, *I Could Speak Until Tomorrow*, 76–77.

39. That women more often than men perform oriki is well established in literature. Sango pipe is performed by women. Wives of Olowe also performed praise songs in honor of their husband. See Pemberton III, "The Oyo Empire" 1989: 159–161.

Figure 1. In praise of Sango, god of thunder. Oya is seen here performing Sango pipe at the opening of Centre for Black Culture and International Understanding in Osogbo, January 8, 2009. Photo: Aderonke Adesanya.

Figure 2. Front view of Oya while performing Sango pipe. Photo: Aderonke Adesanya

repertoire.[40] Thus, *oríkì* is not only a medium of empowerment, it also a currency that women consciously and unconsciously use to acknowledge and concede a superior political space to men.

However, as society changes new roles and new attitudes are assigned to artists and to art. Artists also become more sensitive to their roles depending on the nature of society in which they operate, and by so doing they begin to redefine the artistic idioms. Omóbóyòdé Àrowá, a traditional poet, defies the norm by developing a unique and radical genre. Dasylva examined Àrowá's gender specific poetry in which the poet negotiates a highly nuanced cultural (and political?) space as a woman chanter and succeeds in inscribing and re-inscribing self in her oríkì corpus.[41] She also confronts male hegemony in her texts. These approaches make her oríkì text performance one of the most developed oríkì poetic performances in indigenous Yorùbá oral poetry, and demonstrate her ethnographic and psychosocial knowledge of her environment and how it in turn, engenders her inscription of self in her *oríkì* corpus. Aspects of her poetry are examined in the later part of this essay.

Hegemony, Gender and Headship: Male Kings and Warriors in Yorùbá Art

In the context of Yorùbá art forms that are gendered one has to bear in mind that hegemony does not rest with the audience rather it rests solely with those who construct, maintain, and sustain the instruments of hegemony. We have argued that Yorùbá culture is patriarchal and the hegemony of the male in that society is palpably entrenched to the degree that the very notion of subjugation of a particular sex is lost on the "privilege other" (the male) and the "unprivileged other" (the female) remains politically unconscious or oblivious of her subjugation. Although Margaret Drewal cautions on the use of an asymmetrical model to analyze the relationship between male and female in the Yorùbá society and argues that power does not always resides in the male side of the equation,[42] one is encouraged to think otherwise given the realities that the data on traditional Yorùbá verbal and visual arts present.

Scholars have long been concerned about the relationship between art and the social order, and whether art reflects societal values or correspond to the same structural principle as the social organization.[43] In the absence of literacy, art was indeed a means of documentation for the preliterate society of the Yorùbá. It is through their verbal performances (including songs, poetry, proverbs, folktales, mythical traditions, etc.) and visual representations that mores and lore of the society were transmitted. It is also through these forms that one gets an understanding of the notion of power, gender, and sexuality, among other issues in this milieu. Although in some Yorùbá art one gets a hint of equality of the sexes as exemplified by the paired brass objects of the Osugbo in other genres inequality of the sexes clearly manifest. In verandah posts iconography, door panels registers or in freestanding figures, men appear as riders, warriors, kings, and priests. Representations of women as riders are absent in Yorùbá art in spite of the

40. Barber, *I Could Speak Until Tomorrow*, 76–77.
41. Dasylva, "Identity and Memory in Omoboyode Arowa's Oríkì Performance in (Yorùbá) Ekiti Dialect," 173–200.
42. Margaret Drewal, *Yoruba Ritual: Performers, Play and Agency* (Bloomington, IN: Indiana University Press, 1992).
43. Oyewunmi, *The Invention of Women*, 112.

fact that in Yorùbá traditional and contemporary histories note that affluent Yorùbá women owned several horses and even rode them. The practice has even not stopped as one observes in contemporary Ijebuland, female chiefs own and ride horses during Id-El Kabir and Ojúde-Oba festivals. Equestrians are symbols of sacred and political power. In the nineteenth century, equestrians were a common feature on Yorùbá landscape. However, because they were mostly used for war campaigns and in view of the fact that popular historical account identify men as having fought in such wars, artists depict men as riders, and historians alike discuss what the artists and oral tradition have passed to them in literature.

Gender, Memory and the Masking Tradition of the Yorùbá

One must remark that the art forms used in the masking tradition of the Yorùbá provide us with copious examples of gender agenda that is pursued in such cultural cult icons, paraphernalia and associated performances. For over two decades, scholars have observed and critiqued the cross-dressing phenomenon in Yorùbá religions whereby male possession priests wear female clothing and adorn their head with female coiffures.[44] There are four Yorùbá deities, or òrìsà, which require masks, staffs, bowls, and carved figures: Ifá (divination), Èsù/Elegba (trickster), Ògún (iron and war) and Sàngó (lightning and thunder). Of the four, Sàngó appears to have the most elaborate repertoire of arts. The profusion of sculptures produced for Sàngó worship includes altar bowls (apere), carved mortars (odó Sàngó), dancewands (osé Sàngó), altar pedestals, figured posts, figured pots, carved stools and sculpted axes, to mention a few. A greater percentage of these paraphernalia have feminine images adorning them. One may wonder why the use of feminine images and not masculine ones? The answer lies in the fact that feminine images are propitiatory.

Yorùbá masks and masked figures recreate and preserve the people's pre-colonial, colonial, and postcolonial experience. Masks are not mere artistic creation, but communicative objects. They embody a variety of meanings that, if properly studied, can help illuminate rich history of the Yorùbá. Besides their use for ancestor veneration and commemoration of historical events, Yorùbá masks and masques serve political ends. They are used as instruments of community power and serve both coercive and hegemonic purposes. In Yorùbá masking tradition, we find a lot of trading places between the sexes. It is common to find the swapping of sex roles in Yorùbá egungun performance. Although men play prominent roles as maskers, women are nonetheless significant. Women create the costume, chant, and sing songs that add luster to the spectacle.

Mothering and Modernity

In Yorùbá art, the depiction of women as reproductive objects and as nurturers and caregivers is common. Tunji Azeez notes that in Yorùbá belief, any object with reproductive

---

44. The list include Parrinder, *Religion in an African City* (Westport, Connecticut: Negro Universities Press, 1972); Babayemi, "The Fall and Rise of the Oyo Empire 1860–1905"; Margaret Drewal, "Art and Trance Among Yoruba Sango Devotees," *African Arts*, Vol. 20, 1 (1986): 60–67, 98–99.

tendencies is automatically termed as "female."[45] The application of such terms as "motherness," or femaleness, is not limited to human beings rather it is also applied to vegetal things such as trees and inanimate objects such as a piece of stone; hence, a pawpaw tree which does not produce fruits is seen as male, while that which produces fruits is seen as female. The Yorùbá call an infertile woman a curse and an "ak ìb p" (male pawpaw) to her nuptial family, meaning something which is not productive. Fecundity is a necessity and infertility is abhorred in African societies. It explains the high premium societies in Africa place on the child as the pride of motherhood. Many folktales and myths abound which explain the position of indigenous African societies on fertility and infertility in the woman. It is no surprise therefore that the Yorùbá artist mirrors societal expectation in the way he portrays a woman in sculpture as mother, an evidence of fruitfulness.

Such fruitfulness contributes not only to the individual's enhanced image but generates inalienable wealth for the society. Even this significant contribution to humanity is not lost on people from other cultures living in African societies as Helen Callaway says concerning European women in colonial Nigeria that giving birth is recognized as the most essential female function of all.[46] The Yorùbá worldview about women, their reproductive power, and their expected contribution to the society has not changed even with the advent of modernity. Women who fail to conceive within the first few years into their marriage are usually traumatized and strive through various means including using modern and traditional medicine to overcome their childlessness.

Patriarchy and diplomacy, two strong ideological structures within the Yorùbá world, are united at different levels. At one level, men recognize and deploy diplomacy to acknowledge the abstract (covert) power of women as mothers, wives, priestesses, and or goddesses. For instance, in masquerade performance such as the Gèlèdé, it is the recognition of feminine power that makes men to acquiesce to and cautiously mediate and negotiate the universe of women in other not to incur their wrath. Gèlèdé is about appeasing àjé or 'the mothers' who control fertility, life, and the death of children through dance, mask, costume, and poetry. At another level, the recognition of feminine power and its implication on the society (understood as a threat to male hegemony) if not controlled encourages them to use patriarchy to curtail such female powers. The curtailment is done in different ways; by sanction, banishment, or death. In the past, the mother of an Oba elect was not allowed to live, but was asked "to go to sleep."[47] That is, to commit suicide, in order to prevent her from exercising and exerting her extreme influence on her son, who is the king and by implication the father of the community, highly reverenced and to whom all his subjects defer.

However, we see another manifestation of the ambivalence of male attitude towards female power in the way women as wives or metaphorical mothers of the society are depicted on an imposing scale behind Yorùbá kings. They are in such instances representing support and communicating allegiance to the king and his domain. Olówè of Ìsè made some excellent examples of such carvings where he deliberately emphasized the scale of the woman in order to communicate visually her abstract (covert) power.[48] A woman

---

45. Tunji Azeez, "Of Feminism and Yoruba Gender Relations: A Study of Wole Soyinka," in Toyin Falola and Ann Genova (eds.), *Yoruba Creativity: Fiction, language, Life and Songs* (Trenton, NJ: Africa World Press, 2005), 38–39.

46. Helen Callaway, *Gender, Culture, Empire: European Women in Colonial Nigeria* (Oxford: MacMillan Press/St. Anthony's College, 1987).

47. Samuel Johnson, *The History of the Yorubas* (Lagos: CSS Bookshops, 1921), 63.

48. Roselyn Walker, *Anonymous Has a Name: Olowe of Ise: A Yoruba Sculptor to Kings*, (Washington, D C: National Museum of African Art, 1998).

behind the throne is a common concept in Yorùbá word and world and in every kingdom there are women who provide immeasurable support to ensure its stability.[49] One pillar, also by Olówè, formerly at the courtyard of the Ògògà of Ìkéré relates a traditional custom, which allows the Olorì of the Ògògà to place the beaded crown on his head. He must never peer into this crown, which in a way represents the hidden and enormous power of "*awon aje*," that is witches, those entities who are tagged "powerful, awesome mothers of the society" and who support the king's enthronement. In fact, no Yorùbá king must glimpse the inner core of his crown. The visual metaphor and the indigenous code is clear. Peering into the recess of the crown is tantamount to a child looking into the vagina of his mother.

Women are the *òpómúléró* that is, the pillars behind a throne, the support on which the fate of the community rests. As *òpómúléró*, the image of the Olorì of the Ògògà, standing behind the king "visually expresses the importance of her support for the king's ability to effectively rule his people. The queen's role as support is further emphasized by her caryatid function in physically balancing the verandah roof on her head."[50] In that sculptural idiom the idea that the woman as mother, nurturer, and caregiver shoulders the burdens of the society is conveyed. Without the support of powerful women, the Ògògà cannot effectively rule. In the same vein, the people of Òsogbo in a song acknowledge the supportive role of Òsun to the throne thus: "Who does not know that it is Òsun who enables the Oba to rule?"[51] I have cited the example of the prominent role the Olóbùn plays in the installation of the Òsemàwé of Òndó. Every Yorùbá monarch knows the importance of women to the success of his reign and as such avoids doing things that may incur their wrath.

Oba Williams Ayeni, the late Òràngún of Ìlá-Òràngún, attested to the universality of feminine power in the Yorùbá world and its tangential importance to the successes and failures of kingdoms in a declarative voice: "Without 'the mothers' I could not rule."[52] Women who support the throne are depicted as birds on Yorùbá crowns. The confluence of bird motif on the crown indicates that the swift powerful mothers oversee the secular and sacred engagements and endeavors of the Oba and ensure that he does not misstep. As sacred birds on royal crowns, they are known as sacred mothers "àwon ayé" or "àjé" who act as mothers to the entire community and are more often than not appeased, and entreated to ensure the growth and well-being of the society. In fact, the Yorùbá are especially enamored with the concept of growth, increase and multiplication, to the degree that they amplify the concept "in their mother and child configurations"[53] and offer sacrifice to the sacred mothers so that the society may be regenerated through copulation between and procreation of both male and female.

To underscore the role of women as mothers, nurturers and caregivers, essentially as society conceives of them and constructs their worldview, they are usually depicted either breast-feeding or carrying a child on their back and are sometimes surrounded by children. Carrying the baby on the back communicates nurturing, mothering and bonding, and

---

49. There are several ideas in Yoruba verbal expressions conveying the support that women provide to individuals and the community.

50. Judith Perani and Fred T. Smith, *Visual Arts of Africa: Gender, Power, and Life Cycle Rituals* (Upper Saddle River, NJ: Prentice Hall, 1998), 140.

51. Murphy and Sanford (eds.), "Introduction," *Osun Across the Waters: A Yoruba Goddess in Africa and the Americas*, 6.

52. Pemberton III, The Carvers of North East," Henry Drewal, Pemberton, et al., *Yoruba: Nine Centuries of African Art and Thought*, 210.

53. Dele Jegede, "Anatomy of a Housepost," *Ife Studies in Literature and the Arts*, (1985): 68.

is typical of African women. It contrasts sharply with the way babies are carried in pouches or pushchairs as it is common in other cultures of the world. This image, from the African point of view, is nurturing, mediatory and communicates bonding between mother and child. The African baby-on-the-back model creates the context of security for the baby, a maternal security that even adult males crave. When men are distressed, irrespective of their age, young or old, they crave for maternal succor. Obododinma's takes an example from the Igbo culture to illustrate this point:

> When a man is being persecuted by his kinsmen, or has to seek refuge from for some other reasons, the most likely place he runs to is the village or town from which his father married his mother, in short, to his maternal home. This maternal home stands in symbolic relation to the mother's body, the site of his security as a baby.[54]

The above was what the epic hero Okonkwo in Chinua Achebe's *Things Fall Apart* did when calamity befell him. He sought refuge with his mother's kinsmen. Even when powerful men including kings and warriors come to a crossroad, they seek help from powerful 'mothers' believing that 'yèyé omo níí gba omo' meaning a mother never fails to heed the cry of her child. The African believes that there is an eternal bond between mother and child (established during pregnancy and through the nursing period) which does not exist at the same degree between father and child. Whether as a woman offering her breast to nurture another or as a genuflecting bowl-carrying gift, the female figure communicates maternal attributes of sacrifice (giving of her body) and selflessness. Women have always served as mediatory channels, hence, the use of genuflecting female images in ritual ambience.

As Henry Drewal notes: "images of women in ritual contexts and mother and child figures represent much more than symbols of fertility, they communicate sexual abstinence, inner cleanliness, ritual purity, female force, and spirituality."[55] Mother and child "compositions seen in Ifá tapper ... and the figurated bowl ... denote a state of ritual purity; for during the long nursing period (2–3 years among Yorùbá) when the child is carried on the back, a woman's menstruation is suppressed and she practices sexual abstinence."[56] The centrality of women as mediums to gods such as Sàngó and Sòpònná has also been underscored in the literature. The *arugbá Sàngó*, the large female figure with outstretched arms balancing her headload, which contains the *edun àrá*, thundercelts of Sàngó, is the principal sculpture found on Sàngó shrines in Ìgbómìnà and Èkìtì towns. The female figure surmounting or surmounted by thundercelts is also found in shrine sculptures and dancewands of the thunder god.[57] Babatunde Lawal states that the female body is the ideal choice for this scared service essentially because of the resilience that allows it to bear children without serious injury.[58] Thus, it is customary to find even male

54. Oha Obododinma, "Embodying Women's Stories: The Dialogue with Femininity in the artworks of Peju Layiwola and Elizabeth Olowu," *Of Bronzes and Prints: A Mother/Daughter Perspective*. An Exhibition Catalogue Goethe Institut, Lagos 14th–25th June, 2003: 12.

55. Henry Drewal, "Art and the Perception of Women in Yoruba Culture," *Cahiers d'Etudes Africaines*, Vol. 17, 4 (1977): 5.

56. Ibid.

57. Pemberton III, "The Oyo Empire," 159, 161–169.

58. Lawal, "Orilonise: The Hermeneutics of the Head and Hairstyles among the Yoruba," in Roy Sieber and Frank Herreman (eds.), *Hair in African Art* (New York: The Museum of African Art, 2000), 92–109.

devotees of Yorùbá gods assuming feminine profile in order to present themselves as women/wives objects of submission to their patron deities.

Just as the female body is considered expedient to sacrifice, appeasement and submission to the gods and goddesses her sexuality is also greatly compromised. Of the two sexes, the power and the sexuality of the female appear to be more visually expressed in Yorùbá art and is the most appropriated in ritual contexts. Women have three powers: (i) the power of their nakedness and by inference, sexuality; (ii) the power of persuasion and potent spirituality on which the society from ordinary folks to priests and kings depend to connect the sacred spaces and spiritual entities; and (iii) the power of submission. All three are harnessed visually and figuratively as seen in the representation of the female on bended knees in cult icons of Ifá and Sàngó, and literally as in the example of the sacred possession of body, private and public life of the *arugbá Òsun* Òsogbo. It is in view of the examples above that I consider the female, in this study, as the 'property' of the community.

Nude Female, Male Eyes: The Nexus between Nudity of Women and Sacred Power

Since male carvers produce most of traditional Yorùbá woodcarvings, we can argue that in depicting women, the female body comes under intense male scrutiny in the creative enterprise. The artist serves as the eye of the society, a proxy for the desire of gods and the collective interest of men. Even the language of discussing depictions of women is sex specific: it is explorative of the various parts of the body of the female form. The anatomically detail and adornment come under the full glare of the creator, the critic, and the observer. The gaze is a practiced one, trained in the western notion of looking and seeing the sexes. Critiques of this notion including feminists have concluded that the gaze is always male and the analyses highly nuanced. To wit: Nude females like most figures in Yorùbá art are depicted in the prime of life as exemplified by the firmness fleshiness and erectness of their breasts. Even the female in mother and child icon has firm erect breasts in spite of the fact that the breasts of mothers who have nursed a number of children do not remain as firm as they were during the prenatal state. It is interesting to note that in traditional Yorùbá society the female subject under masculine gaze is seen in similar light. A palace attendant I met at Ìsè-Èkìtì during my fieldwork in 1996 told me that firm breasts of the female figure in Yorùbá art announce youthfulness not only of the image and also the aesthetic ideals of the community or personality that commissioned the form. In essence, a youthful nude female mirrors many abstract ideas including vitality, ever-greenness, purity, and stateliness of the community.

Where the focus is on other social values such as ìwàpèlé (cool headedness) the sexuality of the female is still highlighted as in the highly nuanced visual articulation of her genitalia and in the accentuation of her protruding breasts. The nudity of female figure, whether as sacred or secular objects, is a constant aesthetic index and derives from cultural and ritual requirements. There is an unwritten code that is worked into the aesthetic program that a female figure must be youthful and sensual, appealing and pleasing. Ordinarily the Yorùbá consider a person who goes naked partially or totally in public to be insane, and repugnant to the eye. However, it is interesting to note that the people's idea of beauty, purity, and even power stem from human, especially female, nakedness. The privatization or seclusion and covering of the body lead to the idea that its exposure is offensive to

Figure 3. Left and right: Mother and child and bowl presenter.

public morality; it essentially typifies a violation of public privacy and may convey a release of power. The naked body may be understood as private or public. The private body is exposed in the confines of a person's room or secluded space while the public body is usually expressed in sculptures. The Yorùbá public is not averse to the expression of nudity in traditional arts as many traditional figural sculptures, especially female ones, appear in the nude. Yorùbá artists depict women in the nude, except when carrying a baby on their back, and by so doing reflect shared beliefs and expectations. One shared concept among the Yorùbá is that women's nudity and sexuality encapsulate their covert power, which they believe could threaten social harmony. Hence, the pubic is hardly made public except at the instance of extreme provocation. Only a sane person would provoke a woman to strip herself naked. At that instance she transform into a vital force that can be destructive.

Concealment of male power is also a necessity in worship, appeasement, and ritual. While a genuflecting woman on a cult object remains the epitome of humility necessary for the propitiation of the gods conveys the traditional symbol of Yorùbá life that signifies submission to authority and salutation to an elder and or the gods in social and religious contexts, the cultural codes about the male figure contrast these values. The political space which men occupy in the society, their engagement in warfare in the past, their propensity to dominate their space and assert authority situate them as contending forces with the deities. Using a female and not a male to express submission is the Yorùbá's sheer recognition of the need to conceal male power in the face of the gods. Concealment of male power is necessary for other reasons: protection from powerful women. Since men occupy considerable visible political and religious spaces of the Yoruba world, they require support and protection from the invisible spheres, which women dominate. While men display overt authority, women covertly control it. We get a sense of this power play and symbolism in typical Yoruba Oba's crown crowned at the apex with bird imagery, symbol of covert female power. The power dynamics is also visually coded in bird imagery (female power) on Osanyin's staff and herbalist's staff, both symbols of male religious authority. The overt roles of men in public space increase their vulnerability and expose them to entities (ajogun, ayé and àjé, especially women) that are not physical but extremely powerful, formidable enough to shape or destroy their destinies.

Male power, like his genitalia, is overt, provocative and may be offensive and or challenging to the universe of the gods while female power, like her genitalia too, is covert and hidden, non-confrontational and persuasive, qualities which endear them to the gods.[59] The avoidance of confrontation with the universe of the gods is thus necessary and negotiated through the female who possesses covert power and is more submissive in ritual ambience. This quality is also the basis why men in a bid to appear submissive in the face of the gods cross-dress by wearing female ensemble and hairdos. This is the case with Sàngó priests, who deliberately wear large skirts and adorn their heads with different styles of female coiffures,[60] to demonstrate their allegiance and total submission to god-king Sàngó.[61] During the Igogo festival at Òwò, the Olówò and his chiefs assume feminine appearance wearing blouses and big skirts to disguise their masculinity. In a sense, this gender positioning in the face of the gods simply emphasize the dichotomy between the sexes in sacred and secular ambience. The power of women is recognized in the former while it is consciously and unconsciously subjugated to those of men in the latter.

---

59. The hidden power of the female genitalia is comparable to what Abiodun describes as eégún, the concealed power of ancestors. Interestingly eegun also alludes to female genitalia because they are hidden. The clitoris in particular is traditionally regarded as possessing concealed power, which women can use to achieve whatever they desire. See Abiodun, "Hidden Power: Òsun, the Sixteenth Odu", Murphy and Sanford (eds.) *Òsun Across the Waters: A Yoruba Goddess in Africa and the Americas*, 24.

60. Lawal avers that the practice of men wearing female hairstyle in Sango cult does not transform the male priest into a 'wife' at least not in the literal sense but it does present the priest as feminized entity prepared to please the thunder god. See Lawal, "*Orilonise*," 164.

61. This presentation has been given other interpretation such as the idea of homosexuality in Yoruba Sango cult.

Still some further comments on ìwàpèlé and representation of women in Yorùbá art. A genuflecting woman in Yorùbá woodcarving is a symbol of prayer and is the height of submission in the Yorùbá society and is an expression of iwàpèlé.[62] Ìwàpèlé is inextricably linked to prayer. We note that iwàpèlé and other virtues such as patience and humility are expected of, and conceded to, women in the Yorùbá culture, the same may be true of most African societies. The Yorùbá believe that patience is a necessary virtue for every woman, the absence of which may spell doom for or encourage people to cast aspersions on the individual female or the homestead or society, which she represents. To avoid sanction, shame, and the possibility of doom, the Yorùbá do not ignore but rather resort to prayer as a lifeline from time to time. To make supplication to the deities effective the Yorùbá believe the image of female is most suitable to be used as mediatory and or placatory channel. Whether in the worship of Ifá, Sàngó, Èsù and Òsun, among other Yorùbá gods, the image of a genuflecting woman is indispensable. I have had cause to disagree on this notion.

The question I have asked some Yorùbá artists, priests and a number of elders is, what makes the female figure more suitable than the male figure in a sculptural idiom suggesting supplication? I got responses such as: (i) culture shaped the idea; (ii) women traditionally kneel to greet their elders, and even the Yorùbá concept of ìkúnlè abiyamo stems from the recognition that women submit by kneeling in order to surmount obstacles; and (iii) Yorùbá artists normally carve figures from a single block of wood and it is impossible to situate a prostrating male within such a format. While the latter is a straightforward explanation, the first two are not, for a number of reasons. First, who determines what culture stipulates? Second, if the purpose of the genuflecting figure is to express piety and submission in traditional worship, I therefore ask, do men not kneel to pray in other faiths? Whatever informed the widespread depiction of female genuflecting figure in Yorùbá art has to do more to do with male hegemony than anything else. In Ifá it is found on and even referred to as agèrè ifá or ìb rí ifá, and among Òsun and Sàngó devotees it is called arugbá, meaning "the one who carries the calabash holding the sacred items" for the òrìsà.[63] In a sense, the agèrè and arugbá are proxies for devotees. Women, when carrying receptacles as in the case of the real arugbá Òsun of Òsogbo and the sculpted versions for Sàngó and Òsun cults, automatically become receptacles — conveyors of sacrifices and victuals of the gods and bearers of burdens of the community. Margaret Drewal describes them as ritual containers "a primary symbol of female power."[64]

Even priests and priestesses of different Yorùbá gods and goddesses recognize how powerful the image of the woman, as mediatory object, is to worship.[65] Herbert Cole, cited in Drewal and Drewal, alludes to this fact in his book, Icons:

> Yoruba diviners, when ordering their cups for palmnuts from sculptors, favor those depicting a woman with one child or more. One such diviner, also a sage analyst of his own art and culture, identifies the woman holding these cups as containers themselves.[66]

---

62. Iwàpèlé means good character and comeliness.

63. Abiodun, "Hidden Power," 27.

64. Margaret Drewal, "Performers Play, Agency, Empire: Yoruba Ritual Process," (PhD Dissertation, New York University, 1989), 320.

65. Òsun priestess Doyin Olosun who I interviewed at Osogbo in November 2009 notes that women are expedient to success in sacrifice to deities. According to her, they are 'owó èrò' the calming cooling potent mediums, and represent the height of appeasement.

66. Henry Drewal and Margaret Drewal, Gelede: Art and Feminine Power, 67.

Divination reflects the universe of the deities and the ideal world human beings. With each receptacle created for the cult, the artist conveyed visual ideas about the Yorùbá society and culture. The object is thus an art of the people, a collective possession. In receptacles that have caryatids, the female genuflecting figure is the dominant subject and the preference for such an icon is already established. Divination tappers too always have a genuflecting female figure but we find an exception to this typical representation in The Trout Gallery exhibition catalogue.[67] Here we see a genuflecting nude male on the divination tapper. Like the genuflecting female, he also signifies submission to authority: the authority of the deities. The icon illustrates man's willingness to accept his destiny as dictated by the gods. The nudity of the form also refers to the solemnity of divination. However, when a nude pregnant woman is depicted on any cult icon, the sculptural message is both literal and spiritual. The icon also connotes a different power, a trajectory of life, a channel of wisdom, a passageway into life for man and a channel of rebirth for the gods. Truly, the womb embodies the ontological nexus, which indicates humanity's cornucopia of possibilities and experiences.[68] As the owners of the womb, women incubate the essence, spirituality, wisdom, and ideas of men and gods. Pemberton describes her power as that on which ultimately, the society depends and she "conceals in her womb the future promise of the community."[69]

A female figure with headload depicted in Yorùbá art presents a different idea and consciousness. Yorùbá women, like their African counterparts in other parts of the continent, characteristically carry on their head sundry loads, which may be calabashes and or baskets or other receptacles used for carrying food, cloth and other assortments of goods ranging from food, cloth and other items. Their ability to cope with headloads is elevated to the level of sacred duty as female genuflecting figures, which carry headloads such as thundercelts of Sàngó, the ritual *igbá* (calabash or carved wooden containers of cult paraphernalia) of Òrúnmìlà, Èsù, Òsun and other gods.[70] However, beyond this, we see a multiplicity of ideas experienced and expressed by the Yorùbá artist. With each kneeling female figure, the Yorùbá artist communicates abstract ideas of sexuality, servitude, and submission. I had a deeper understanding of the degree of submission of the female devotees of Òsun to the deity and to the community when I encountered the current *arugbá of Òsun* at Òsogbo in late 2009. The young woman once chosen as arugbá summarily loses her independence, has no life of her own independent of what the community demands of her until she is relieved of her duties when she decides to get married. According to Doyin Olosun, the sexuality of arugbá is also controlled as she must essentially maintain her chastity throughout the period of her service to the goddess and community in order to remain pure to perform her ritual roles. She is thus confined within the ancient town of Òsogbo where she is properly groomed and chaperoned. She cannot even venture to go to school outside the community.[71]

Although a young maiden is not chosen to serve the Sàngó cult as seen in the case of Òsun, a sculpted image of a female acts as surrogate. Where a kneeling female figure

67. The Trout Gallary, "African objects of Prestige and Personal Adornment from the Permanent Collection," Art Exhibit (February 4 to March 5, 1994).

68. Driedre L. Badejo, "Authority and Discourse in Orin Odún Òsun," in Murphy and Sanford (eds.), *Òsun Across the Waters*, 139.

69. Pemberton III, "The Oyo Empire," 197.

70. A secular task typically performed by women as men rarely carried headloads; the exception being human porterage during the pre-colonial era documented by Ogunremi and contemporary practices where male meat sellers in cities such as Ibadan and Lagos and vendors of other articles now place their articles of trade on their heads in markets and on the streets.

71. Oral communication with Doyin Olosun and the current arugba of Osun, Osogbo town, November 2009.

Figure 4. Doyin Olosun. Photo credit: Aderonke Adesanya, Osogbo town November 2009.

bearing the *edun àrá* (thunder celts) on her head appear in a sculptural idiom of Sàngó cult it basically indicates the figurative mounting characteristic of the god of thunder. Sàngó typically mounts his devotees, meaning that the òrìsà is figuratively "enthroned" on a devotee's head. Margaret Drewal elaborates on the idea of the mounted female:

> On one level, head-loading pose reflects actual behaviour ... On another, it alludes to the female as receptacle, and to her head as container for the power of the deity. Both these ideas are conveyed in western Yorubaland during festivals when large sculptures are placed in basins containing the vital force of particular

deities that are then placed on the heads of priestesses before they proceed to a nearby stream to gather water and herbs. As the basins are mounted on their heads the priestesses go instantly into possession trance.[72]

The image of the woman in cult icon of the Sàngó connotes covert power, and a genuflecting nude female codifies this hidden power and the representation is deliberate. When male devotees of the god cross-dress, that is, when they wear female-like garments (long skirt called bànté, tòbí or wàbì) and spot sùkú hairdos, they do so for a number of reasons. First, they are reflecting their submission to the god-king Sàngó. Second, they need to hide male power, which in a given sense could be taken as a challenge to the universe of the god, and third, to emphasize priest/wife metaphor, project femininity and present their bodies for the customary mounting of the thunder god.

Gender in the Eyes of Yorùbá Male Artists

How does the Yorùbá male artist perceive the feminine gender and how does this perception shape his creative expressions? To answer these questions, I have selected the works of a number of Yorùbá woodcarvers, dead and alive, old and new such as Àreògún (c. 1880–1954) of Osí-Ìlorin, Olówè of Ìsè (d. 1938) Ìsè-Èkìtì, Èkìtì region, Làmídì Fákéye (c. 1925–2010) and Bísí Fákéye (b. 1945) of Ìlá-Òràngún to see the extent to which culture shapes their creativity and particularly their representation of women.

Three different lenses will be applied in my analyses of the works of the artists, namely, a cultural lens, a patriarchal lens, and a feminist type. A cultural lens seeks in the artistic representations conformity to tradition; a patriarchal one regulates, authorizes, and scrutinizes the form to ensure that it does not negate the existing male hegemony while a feminist lens demands change and transformation. A feminist lens reveals how the artists through their works endorse patriarchal imagery, speak to the nuances of the Yorùbá culture and invariably promote its continuity.

Seen from a cultural lens, a common strand runs through the works of Àreògún, Olówè and Làmídì Fákéye in terms of the topicalities of their oeuvres. Apart from adhering to an established canon style, Yorùbá artists follow similar thematic traditions with distinctions occurring in their works in terms of regional and individual styles. While ensuring the iconographic appropriateness of the forms they create, they also demonstrate extraordinary artistic imagination in their rendition of common themes such as horserider, arugbá, ìbejì, mother and child figures, among others. They also visually articulate or interpret proverbs, wise sayings, myths, stories and events gleaned from their individual experiences, acquired through cultural training and as they are passed to them by their patrons. The artists conform to time honored sculptural idiom which present the sexes in culture-specific roles.

Throughout his creative career Àreògún followed cultural registers in rendering his form. In an arugbá piece carved by him and documented by Pemberton, he condenses his conception of the Yorùbá cosmos, the Yorùbá's notion of power, gender, and identity into visual metaphors transforming the superlative arugbá piece into a cultural icon. Àreògún's arugbá illustrate multiple layers of ideas including the connection between feminine power and the sacred universe of the thunder god. As Pemberton explains:

---

72. Margaret Drewal, "Art and Trance among Yoruba Shango Devotees," *African Arts* Vol. 20, 1 (1986): 61.

Areogun's arugba Sango represents the burden and power of the devotee of Sango. It tells the celebrant about herself. The great central figure and those surrounding her are figures of composure and graceful power, even when kneeling as supplicants. She carries on her head the burden and power of Sango. It is not her physical ability to carry weights, but her ase that is the very life and defines the iwa of the Sango worshipper. The bowl is a metaphor of the devotee's womb. It contains the evidence of Sango's power, a power, which strikes unexpectedly, transforming and sometimes destroying, but also giving life.[73]

Here, I see the male gaze manifesting again in Àreògún's malecentric creation and Pemberton's reading of the visual text. What is however not lost to the feminist eye is Àreògún copious and uncritical representation of the feminine gender. Uniting the two texts, I note that the female figure is presented as a beast of burden, a sacrificial lamb and scapegoat that must bear the wrath of Sango when he loses his habitual temper. Opposites coalesce in the sculptural idiom; bravery contrasts vulnerability, strength contrasts fragility.

Let us turn to another Yorùbá artist, Olówè of Ìsè, an extraordinary and distinguished artist of the twentieth century who played many parts in his society during his lifetime. He was a woodcarver to a number of Yorùbá kings in the Èkìtì region. He lived in the palace of the Àrìnjalè and made several woodcarvings for his royal domain. He was also a native fully integrated into the traditional religion and the mores of his people. The artist produced both sacred and secular objects, and many of his works reflect life within the palace walls and associated spectacle of the royalty. He also documented other events such as war and violence as he possibly witnessed some of them. Copious reference the artists made to Yorùbá cultural idioms as seen in his repertoire and in his depiction of women are also quite illuminating. As a culture enthusiast, Olówè's carvings, especially the door panels that he produced in the pre-colonial era, comment on cultural themes and motifs such as role positioning, role sharing, dress forms, hairstyles, war, slavery, rituals and human developmental and transitional phases including birth, adulthood and death.

Pemberton describes Olówè as a master carver who understood the symbols of power in Yorùbá society. In the sculpture of the king and queen, hierarchic sculptural form accords with the relationship of male and female powers. Male power is visible (in the authority of the king), female power is concealed (in the metaphor of the woman standing behind the throne and king as well as the iconic bird on the crown of the king). In conveying in lucid form the typical role positioning of the sexes and their active participation in the Yorùbá society, Olówè depicts men as drummers, warriors on horseback, priests and kings while women appear as mothers and maidens, nurturers and caregivers. Men as riders in veranda posts and door panels epitomize forceful domineering male power over domains and territories and recall their role in the Yorùbá wars of the nineteenth century.

It is interesting to note how Olówè, Àreògún and other Yorùbá artists before and after them render horse riders and kings as essentially male and not male and female. Was warfare predominantly a male affair throughout Yorùbá history such that in the art forms that recalls the events of war men became the topicality? Oyewunmi avers, "Warfare, which in many cultures is constructed as a masculine enterprise, was not projected as such in Yorubaland. Because effectiveness in war involved control of mystical and supernatural forces, much of which was controlled by iyá mì i òsòròngà (metaphysical

---

73. Pemberton III, "The Oyo Empire," 163.

mothers—sometimes inappropriately called witches), it was not possible to reduce par-ticipation in war to gender questions."[74] Similarly, the stereotypic depiction of men as warriors on horseback is called to question given the fact that, as Oyewunmi notes, women in Yorùbá history engaged in combat and emerged as war heroines. She cites the example of Aláàfin Òròmpòtò who led Oyo to war against the Borgu in the battle of Ilayi.[75]

One gets a glimpse of how violence played out in Olówè's society from one of his many large carvings. Rituals involving human sacrifice were a common feature in the pre-colonial times. The practice was outlawed after the establishment of British rule in the late nineteenth century. Olówè provided visual records of such gory events as in the example on doors the artist made for the Ògògà of Ìkéré (c. 1910–14) and the Àrìnjalè of Ìsè-Èkìtì. On the Àrìnjalè's door, he depicted a woman, possibly a victim of human sacrifice, in spread-eagle position with birds pecking at her eyes. In the past both male and female were used for human sacrifice depending on who was caught or the gender recommended for such a ritual. It therefore implies that the artists could have depicted a male or female figure. However, Olówè chose to represent a female as the victim. In ancient Ife human sacrifices featured and visual reminders such as a terracotta piece showing a decapitated male body, lying naked on a potsherd, gagged heads in bronze, and terracotta appear in Frank Willett's book, Ife in the History of West African Sculpture.[76] The realism of the figures suggests that they may have been sculpted from life models.

I have noted in this essay that figures in Yorùbá art are typically depicted in the nude. Occasionally brief clothing such as a skirt, knickers (bànté), sòkòtò and even beads are indicated to provide covering for the pubic region of both male and female. More often than not, the female figures are depicted nude. While nude figures of children (including ibeji figures) or men may not necessarily convey strong aesthetic codes, the nude female is a site for many cultural ideas. Generally, the nude forms in the early works of Olówè (especially those produced pre-1910) highlight cultural ideas such as the notion of beauty, purity, innocence, tenderness (in the case of nude maidens and mothers) reverence, dep-rivation, captivity (in the case of nude male) in traditional Yorubaland during the colonial period.[77] Nude women holding their breasts in their hands with tiers of beads dangling around their waists are characteristic of Olówè's works of the pre-colonial period. Perhaps the artists recorded particular spectacular events where maidens danced to entertain visitors to the palace. Olówè was also fond of creating very elaborate coiffure on the heads of the female figures in his works. This characteristic is a reflection of the milieu in which the artist developed his forms.

Women in the Èkìtì region are particularly noted for elaborate hairstyles. Wives of the Oba, chiefs and even princesses have variety of styles, which they wear. The hairstyles evident on the female figures are documentary evidence of hairstyles typical of the period and visual reminders of the artist's closeness to royal domains. He was a palace artist privileged to observe at close range the various intricate hairstyles including sùkú, agogo (cockscomb) and their variants that Obas' wives (oloris) and brides in Èkìtì-Yorùbá country

---

74. Oyewunmi, Invention of Women, 65.

75. Ibid., 65–66.

76. Frank Willett, Ife in the History of West African Sculpture (London: Thames and Hudson, 1967), 64.

77. In the past, it was easy to identify these virtues in a woman and easier to distinguish a virgin (who normally has firm pointed breast and other tell tale signs obvious because of her nudity) from other women in a crowd.

wore as occasion demanded. In the past, it was easy to distinguish a married woman from an unmarried woman by their hairstyles. As Lawal notes, "Spinsters wore simpler forms of the ojompeti, ipako elede, or koroba styles. Brides and housewives ... sported some intricate versions of the agogo and panumo styles. Wives of kings (olori) frequently distinguished themselves in public with elaborate versions of the sùkú style with long knot in the middle of the head."[78] From the various visual commentaries found in the work of Olówè, to a large extent one could conclude that the artist, much like Àreògún the master artist from Osi-Ilorin who provided visually eloquent narratives of his society in his carvings, Olówè too represented the Yorùbá world the way he experienced it and in the manner the society deemed appropriate.

Làmídì Fákéye and Bisi Fákéye, his cousin along with other Fákéye siblings inherited the tradition bequeathed to them by their forebears and artistry learnt from their Osi-Opin masters. Given this background, it presupposes the fact that they also created forms in conformity with tradition. However, in view of other influences, which influenced the career of the two artists, there emerged some distinctions between their work and those of Àreògún and Olówè. With the Roman Catholic serving as a catalyst, Làmídì took his woodcarving style beyond the characteristic tradition passed on to him by his Osi Opin masters. For his new patrons that required Yorùbá forms created for Christian purposes, he developed images based on the scriptures occasionally interfacing these with traditional iconography. What did Làmídì do differently with images carved for Christian patrons? He created figures that were draped, male and female wear apparels. And as the new subject matter dictated new forms, the female figures were no longer depicted on bended knees. However, this does not mean that he totally abandoned the traditional themes and formats; rather he continued to produce the time-honored images for local and foreign collectors. As for Bisi whose relocation to cosmopolitan vista of Lagos has encouraged exploration of new ideas while he gradually modifies old ones, the idea of female supplicant is given new meaning.[79] He called one of such carvings *Humble Giver*. The sculptor, in addressing the representation of women in Yorùbá, much like his forerunners, simply pours old wine into new wineskin. He also unites cultural and historical memory of Yorùbá men and women, the nuances of the society and her politics in contemporary expressions.

Gender in the Eyes of Female Artists: Contemporary Transformations

Just as female writers have started writing alternate stories in order to properly locate, (or to follow Oyewunmi's argument) to reinvent their gender in history and to redress whatever misrepresentation of women that exist within their milieu, female artists are also increasingly seeking and creating new identities for themselves. While resisting gender categorization, the 'patriarchalization' of creative locations and cultural spaces some Yorùbá women have sought redefinitions. These radicalization and transformations are noticeable in the oeuvres of some contemporary Yorùbá women artists such as Omoboyode Àrowà, a revolutionary Èkìtì-Yorùbá female poet, Abatan, the female potter and Adefowora Onabanjo, a Yorùbá female woodcarver whose works I have examined here, they present

---

78. Lawal, "Orilonise," 98.
79. Adesanya, "Old Wine, New Wineskin: The Woodcarvings of the Fakeye Family," in *Modern History of Visual Art in Southern Nigeria* (Ibadan, Nigeria: IFRA, 2003), 1–23.

Figure 5. Sola Fakeye, son of Bisi Fakeye poses with *Pregnant Mother*, one of his father's contemporary representations of Yoruba women. On the right is a carving entitled *The Supplicant*. Photo credit: Aderonke Adesanya, January 2007.

new vistas for looking at the art of Yorùbá women. In the verbal arts, Omoboyode Àrowà verbal artistry illustrates how Yorùbá women have virtually begun the crusade to construct for themselves new social realities while not totally abandoning the culture-rich Yorùbá verbal art traditions.

In constructing new genres, they redefine and re-inscribe themselves, challenge the status quo and the universe of men. Omobóyòdé Àrowà's oríkì which Dasylva describes as "having a consciousness that aims at deconstructing, re-locating, re-situating, re-defining and re-inscribing self in a manner that subverts existing cultural boundaries and syntax of 'fabricated' role of the woman in a patriarchal society"[80] is revolutionary in content and form. The chanter's crusade to re-present the self (as a woman) and to deride patriarchy is exemplified in the way she lampoons her father, a king and his domain, a greedy chieftain, and almost everything that a male represents in her worldview. Àrowà's representation of her father as crooked and lacking in physiognomic attraction is in a way a subtle deconstruction of the male gender, drawing attention to his lacking in physical and moral *finesse* to warrant that usual man/woman lustful relationship, the biological link or paternal bond notwithstanding. The gender twist and derision of masculinity in her chant is very apparent in the way she describes her father as ugly in contrast to her praise of the physical beauty and comeliness of Ajogun, her intimate female friend. In taking to task another male, she selects a king whose domain (Ijero-Èkìtì) is considered popular in the Èkìtì region of Yorubaland and in crafty but terse verses, she summarily dismisses such idea of popularity of the Ijero royalty and his kingdom.

An excerpt from Dasylva's summary of the poet's assessment of the town:

---

80. Dasylva, "Identity and Memory in Omoboyode Arowa's Oríkì performance in (Yorùbá) Èkìtì Dialect," 173–200.

In Ijero town, sun-baked dung litters the streets. The drinking ponds are covered with fresh faeces, while dried faeces that are large enough to cover drinking pots constitute a peculiar mess. Ijero, by the chanter's assessment, and regardless of the fact that the town has a king (Oba), again a male, is the dirtiest town in the whole of Ekiti, and it is her reason for celebrating it. According to the chanter, Ijero claims her greatness (popularity) only in filth, an indictment on the patriarchy.[81]

In contrast to women writers, women in the visual arts have been less radical in their approach to aesthetic topicalities and have generally focused on crossing artistic boundaries. I have noted how in the past Yorùbá women were restricted to practice feminine crafts such as pottery, embroidery, basketry, dye cloth, and sometimes calabash carvings. Some of them engaged in shrine wall paintings, beadwork, body decoration, leatherwork, and cloth weaving.

Women and men's art were clearly defined and often constitute very separate spheres of activity. While women did and still do all the aforementioned genres of art, and men carved wood and stone and also forge metals as well as work in other media that are within the exclusive domain of men, there has been a shift in artistic production. Women have since entered into spheres traditionally dominated by men. For example, the Hausa aluminum spoon industry, once rooted in the traditional male art of silver-smithing, now includes women as well as men. The practice of such artistry in Yorubaland has thus included women. Similarly, more women are increasingly participating in metalsmithing (gold and silver), a task once reserved for men. Iron blacksmithing, a profession traditionally restricted to men now involve women who assist in the process and even smelt the iron itself as found among the Oyo Yorùbá, where the blacksmith's wives and daughters will pound the ore, wash it in the river, burn it in the furnace.[82] Another exception to the norm, and by no means the only example is Adefowora Onabanjo, a female woodcarver that Margaret Drewal saw in the Ijebu town of Imodi-Imosan. She is the granddaughter of a carver who learnt woodcarving and specialized in carving twin figures. In Drewal's view, she is only one among many who nevertheless contravened the normal practice and had the power to "act otherwise."[83] Acting otherwise however is demonstrated only in the artist's successful crossing artistic barrier and entering the male-centered woodcarving profession. It does not translate to the reinvention of women and their representation in Yorùbá woodcarving.

Conclusion

Artistic presentations and representations, whether verbal or visual, of the Yorùbá articulate the social realities and the universe of the people. Gender representation in Yorùbá art is generally informed by patriarchal ideologies, which simultaneously undermine and celebrate women. Women are valorized in creative expressions as essential supports to the family, lineage, and the community. They are also depicted in highly nuanced sexual context. However, the icons, which project them as valorized subjects also indicate their vulnerability and hint at the exploitation of female sexuality for common good of the society. From the old to new creative expressions of the Yorùbá, the vulnerability of women is reinforced in spite of the over celebrated notion

81. Ibid.
82. Lisa Aronson, "Women in the Arts" in Margaret Jean Hay and Sharon Stichter (eds.) *African Women South of the Sahara* (London, New York: Longman, 1984), 122–143.
83. Margaret Drewal, *Yoruba Ritual: Performers, Play and Agency*.

of their enormous power in traditional society. The representations, which reinforce patriarchy, fulfill the collective interest of the society, and meet the desires of both deities. The male artist who carves culturally approved images does so to fulfill societal expectations. He is not persuaded to do otherwise. Yet the representations have sociological implications for the women are perceived and how women see themselves. They also have implication for reinventing the past and the shaping of contemporary history. Yet it has been rightly argued that, "Women's voices must be heard in concert with as well as apart from men's voices if the passageway between birth and ancestry is to remain eternally well-traveled."[84]

The representations in Yorùbá art also explicate the concept of power among the Yorùbá. For the male, power means authority while for the female, power means influence and support. However, are these mutually reinforcing? The continuous striving to balance the power of the sexes in Yorùbá society is the height of diplomacy. Diplomacy however does not enable equality; it rather creates platforms for compromise heavily discounted by women. On the idea of whether there could be a change, radical transformations in the way women are represented in Yorùbá art, two options are apparent: First, that women engender such radicalization themselves by writing and creating alternate histories and images. The second option follows the arguments of Fatton, Figes and others who hold similar ideological position that women can only achieve power, visibility, and autonomy only if men/patriarchy/culture will allow it, that women remain on the periphery for the elusive change to come from men.

References

Abiodun, Rowland. "Woman in Yoruba Religious Images." *African Languages and Cultures.* Vol. 2, 1 (1989): 1–18.

_____. "Hidden Power: Òsun, the Sixteenth Odu." In Joseph M. Murphy and Mei-Mei Sanford eds. *Òsun Across the Waters: A Yoruba Goddess in Africa and the Americas.* Bloomington: Indiana University Press, 2001.

Adeghe, Ade. "The Other Half of the Story: Nigerian Women Telling Tales." In Stewart Brown. Ed. *The Pressures of the Text: Orality, Texts and Telling of Tales.* Birmingham, IN: University of Birmingham African Studies Series, 1995.

Adepegba, Cornelius. "Òsun and Brass: An Insight into Yoruba Symbology." In Joseph M. Murphy and Mei-Mei Sanford. Eds. *Òsun Across the Waters: A Yoruba Goddess in Africa and the Americas.* Bloomington: Indiana University Press, 2001.

Adesanya, Aderonke. "Women in Contemporary Nigerian Art." *Isese: Journal of Folklore.* Vol. 2. I & 2 (2000): 25–36.

_____. "Old Wine, New Wineskin: The Woodcarvings of the Fakeye Family." In Laurent Fouchard. *Modern History of Visual Art in Southern Nigeria.* Ibadan, Nigeria: IFRA 2003.

Ajisafe, A. K. *The Law and Customs of the Yoruba People.* Lagos, Nigeria: CMS Bookshop, 1924.

Aronson, Lisa. "Women in the Arts." In Margaret Jean Hay and Sharon Stichter. Eds. *African Women South of the Sahara.* London, New York: Longman, 1984.

---

84. Badejo, "Authority and Discourse in Orin Odún Òsun," 128–139.

Awe, Bolanle. "The Iyalode in the Traditional Political System." In A. Schlegel. Ed. *Sexual Stratification: A Cross-Cultural View*. New York: Columbia University Press, 1977.

_____. "The Yoruba Woman in Traditional Society." *Gangan: A Magazine of Oyo State of Nigeria*. Ibadan: Sketch Publishing Company, 1979.

Azeez, Tunji. "Of Feminism and Yoruba Gender Relations: A Study of Wole Soyinka." In Toyin Falola and Ann Genova. Eds. *Yoruba Creativity: Fiction, language, Life and Songs*. Trenton, NJ: Africa World Press, 2005.

Babatunde E. D. "Ketu Myths and the Status of Women: A Structural Interpretation of Some Yoruba Myths." *African Notes*. Vol. XII. 1 & 2 (1988): 131–143.

Babayemi, S. O. "The Fall and Rise of Old Oyo c. 1760–1905: A Study in the Traditional Culture of an African Polity." Ph.D. Dissertation, Centre for West African Studies, University of Birmingham, England, 1979.

Badejo, Driedre. L. "Authority and Discourse in Orin Odún Òsun." In Joseph M. Murphy and Mei-Mei Sanford, Eds. *Òsun Across the Waters: A Yoruba Goddess in Africa and the Americas*. Bloomington: Indiana University Press, 2001.

Barber, Karin. *I Could Speak Until Tomorrow: Oríkì. Women, and the Past in a Yoruba Town*. Edinburgh: Edinburgh University Press, 1991.

Brown, Stewart. *The Pressures of the Text: Orality, Texts and Telling of Tale*. Birmingham: University of Birmingham African Studies Series, 1995.

Courlander, Harold. *Tales of Yoruba Gods and Heroes*. Greenwich, Connecticut: Fawcett, 1973.

Dasylva, Ademola. O. "Identity and Memory in Omoboyode Arowa's Oríkì performance in (Yorùbá) Ekiti Dialect." *African and Asian Studies*. Vol. 6.1&2 (2007): 173–200.

Drewal, Henry J. "Hidden Presence and Visual Command." *Traditional Art of the Nigerian Peoples: The Ratner Collection*. Washington. D. C: Museum of African Art, 1977.

Drewal, Margaret. "Art and Trance among Yoruba Shango Devotees." *African Arts*. Vol. 20. 1 (1986): 60–67, 98–99.

_____. *Yoruba Ritual: Performers, Play and Agency*. Bloomington and Indianapolis: Indiana University Press, 1992.

Falola, Toyin. "Gender, Business, and Space Control: Yoruba Market Women and Power." In Bessie House-Midamba and Felix K. Ekechi. Eds. *African Market and Economic Power: The Role of Women in African Economic Development*. Westport, Connecticut: Greenwood Press, 1995.

_____. *A Mouth Sweeter than Salt: An African Memoir*. Ann Arbor, Michigan: The University of Michigan Press, 2004.

_____ and Ann Genova. Eds. *Orisa: Yoruba Gods and Spiritual Identity in Africa and the Diaspora*. Trenton, NJ: Africa World Press, 2005.

Figes, Eva. *Patriarchal Attitudes*. London: Macmillan Education Ltd, 1986.

Glaze, Anita. *Art and Death in a Senufo Village*. Bloomington: Indiana University Press, 1981.

Heilburn, Carolyn. *Reinvention of Womanhood*. New York: W.W Norton and Company, 1979.

Idowu, Bolaji. *Olodumare: God in Yoruba Beliefs*. London: Longman, 1962.

Jegede, Dele. "Anatomy of a Housepost." *Ife Studies in Literature and the Arts*. 1985.

Jegede, O. B. "Court Poetry Tradition and Performance in Nigeria." PhD Dissertation, Department of English, University of Ibadan, Ibadan, 2002.

Johnson, Samuel. *The History of the Yorubas.* Lagos: CSS Bookshops, 1921.

Lawal, Babatunde. *The Gelede Spectacle, Art, Gender and Social Harmony among the Yoruba.* Seattle: University of Washington Press, 1996.

_____. "Orilonise: The Hermeneutics of the Head and Hairstyles among the Yoruba." In Roy Sieber and Frank Herreman. Eds. *Hair in African Art.* New York: The Museum of African Art, 2000.

Mojubaoluwa Okome. "What Women, Whose Development? A Critical Analysis of Reformist Evangelism on African Women." In Oyeronke Oyewumi. Ed. *African Women and Feminism* Trenton, NJ: Africa World Press, 2003.

Murphy, Joseph M. and Mei-Mei Sanford. Eds. *Òsun Across the Waters: A Yoruba Goddess in Africa and the Americas.* Bloomington: Indiana University Press, 2001.

Ogundeji, P. Adedotun. "Ritual as Theatre, Theatre as Ritual: The Nigerian Example." *Isese Monograph Series.* Vol. 2. 1 (2000): 1–40.

Ojo, Olatunji. "More than Farmers' Wives: Yoruba Women and Cash Crop Production, c. 1920–1957." In Adebayo Oyebade. Ed. *The Transformation of Nigeria.* Trenton, NJ: Africa World Press.

Olateju, A. "Yungba Royal Chant: A Specialised Yoruba Oral Poetry Type." *Oye: Ogun Journal of Arts.* Vol. 4 (1988): 54–68.

Omoniwa, Olarewaju. "The Yorùbá Oral Poet as a Religious and Heroic Archetype." *Nigerian Heritage: Journal of the National Museum and Monuments.* Vol. 2. (1993): 109–119.

Oyewunmi, Oyeronke. *The Invention of Women: Making African Sense Western Gender Discourses.* Minnesota: University of Minnesota Press, 1997.

Parrinder, Geoffery. *African Mythology.* London: Hamlyn, 1967.

_____. *Religion in an African City.* Westport, Connecticut: Negro Universities Press, 1972.

Pemberton III, John. "The Oyo Empire." In Henry John Drewal, John Pemberton, Rowland Abiodun, and Allen Wardwell. *Yoruba: Nine Centuries of African Art and Thought.* New York: The Center for African Art in Association with Harry N. Abrams, 1989.

_____. "The Carvers of North East." In Henry John Drewal, John Pemberton, Rowland Abiodun, and Allen Wardwell, *Yoruba: Nine Centuries of African Art and Thought,* New York: The Center for African Art in association with Harry N. Abrams, 1989.

Perani, Judith and Fred T. Smith. *Visual Arts of Africa: Gender, Power, and Life Cycle Rituals.* Upper Saddle River, NJ: Prentice Hall, 1998.

Showalter, Elaine. "Towards a Feminist Poetics." In M. Jacobus. Ed. Women Writing about Women London, UK: Croom Helm, (1979), pp. 25–33; 34–6.

_____. "Feminist Criticism in the Wilderness." *Critical Inquiry.* Vol. 8. 2 (1981): 179–205.

_____. *The Female Malady: Women, Madness, and English Culture, 1830–1980.* New York, Penguin Books, 1987.

_____. *Hystories: Hysterical Epidemics and Modern* Culture. New York: Columbia University Press, 1997.

_____. *Inventing Herself: Claiming a Feminist Intellectual Heritage.* New York: Scribner, 2000.

Thompson, Barbara. "The African Female Body in the Cultural Imagination." In Barbara Thompson. Ed. *Black Womanhood: Images, Icons and Ideologies of the Human Body.* Hanover, New Hampshire: Hood Museum of Art/Dartmouth College, 2008.

Tuttle, Lisa. *Encyclopedia of Feminism.* Harlow: Longman, 1986.

Walker, Roselyn. *Anonymous Has a Name: Olowe of Ise: A Yoruba Sculptor to Kings.* Washington, D.C: National Museum of African Art, 1998).

Willett, Frank. *Ife in the History of West African Sculpture.* London: Thames and Hudson, 1967.

Chapter 6

Western Religions and Female Sexuality: Engaging Dualistic Thinking in Attitudes to African Women's Sexuality

Mary Nyangweso Wangila

An attempt to understand any aspect of women's experience must seek to examine the social cultural patterns that inform such experience. Therefore, it is appropriate that an analysis of women's experience should explore gender relations in the communities they are situated. Just like any social concept draws from cultural influence over a period, conceptions of sexuality in Africa draws from a complex history of African heritage. The role of religion in this concept is significant as it draws its authority from sacred ideological sources that help to sanction social practices. It is difficult to discuss sexuality without discussing gender not because the two are social constructs, but because they are intricately interconnected. Simply defined, sexuality is a human experience and expression of oneself as a sexual being. Gender on the other hand is the social condition of being female or male. As social constructs, both sexuality and gender define the experience of being male or female in a particular culture.[1]

Control of sexuality is a significant factor in social organization. Sexuality is often controlled because it is frequently viewed by most societies as a potential disruptive force of social order. Every society has its own definition of what constitutes normal or moral behavior. Attitudes and behavior toward sex, sexual orientation, and members of the opposite sex are categorized into moral, normal, and natural, or unnatural, abnormal, and immoral. Most often the trend to police sexuality is common in societies where family name and reputation are key to power and status, including the protection of property inheritance.[2] In such societies, the behavior of one member of the family reflects badly on all. Under such conditions total respectability and confidence of paternity is considered essential. With such regulation, limited knowledge about sexuality is ensured by the perpetuation of various myths about the negative consequences of disapproved sex acts. Most often, sex is tied to family reproduction of children and the inheritance of possession. Pleasure is discounted totally especially for women.

---

1. Elaine Graham, "Gender," in Paul B. Clarke and Andrew Linzey (eds.), *Dictionary of Ethics, Theology and Society*, (New York: Routledge, 1969), 396.
2. Rutter Swartz, Pepper Schwartz, and Virginia Rutter, *The Gender of Sexuality* (London: Pine Forge Press, 1998), 74.

Why Control Female Sexuality?

Female sexuality has been the target of control in most societies because as Sherry Ortner and Rosemary Radford Ruether argue, it is viewed as threatening and polluting to higher male (culture).[3] According to Ortner, the universal devaluation of women is based on the cultural assumption of the hierarchy of culture over nature. Culture, which is viewed as the sphere of human control, is equated to the male sphere, while nature viewed as dependant is equated to the women's sphere. Women are equated to nature because, as Ruether observes, their physiological processes are not only viewed as "dangerous and polluting to higher (male) culture, but also because her social roles are regarded as inferior to those of males, falling lower on the nature-culture hierarchy."[4] But this cultural symbol of woman is inconsistent. Whereas femaleness is perceived as representative of devalued parts of the self and the roles that service them, woman as mother, as original source of life, primary mediator of nature and culture is also seen as possessing powers of life and all that supports and inspires the human (male). By equating a woman to nature, her despised sexuality is also portrayed as powerful, and as a symbol of the divine therefore dangerous. It is a force that can "tempt and distract men from their duties."[5] In some communities, women's sexual desires are considered insatiable and a woman's presence is considered too seductive for even the most disciplined of men to resist.

Some have argued that women's ability to reproduce life and to produce blood that is not related to a wound is threatening to men's power. Because women are said to possess power to create next generations, a power that men do not have, men resorted to controlling their sexuality in order to control this power. Ruether explains:

> The first subjugation of woman is the subjugation of her womb, the subjugation of access to her body, so that she should not choose her own beloved or explore the pleasures of her own body but that her body and its fruits should belong first to her father, who would sell or trade her to her husband. She must be delivered as undamaged goods, duly inspected, any signs of previous use punished by death. Only the male to whom she has been legally handed over may put his seed in her body, so that he can be sure that the children that emerge from her body belong to him, pass on his name, inherit his property.[6]

Because of this attitude, women in most societies are not allowed to explore and express their sexuality freely and openly without fear of reprimand. This is because they are often associated with the flesh, and prohibited against performing certain duties such as the priestly office duties or to achieve ultimate state of salvation because of the allegedly impurity of their bodies. Restrictions or some form of physical or psychological control is ensured in order to conform to these prohibitions. Both unmarried and married women are controlled in different ways.[7]

---

3. Sherry B. Ortner, "Is Female to male as Nature Is to Culture?" in M. Z. Rosaldo and L. Lamphere (eds.), *Woman, Culture and Society* (Stanford: Stanford University Press, 1974), 67–87. See also Judith Shapiro, "Cross-Cultural Perspectives on Sexual Differentiation," in Herant A. Katchadourian (ed.), *Human Sexuality: A Comparative and Developmental Perspective* (London: University of California Press, 1979), 269, 308; and Rosemary Radford Ruether, *Sexism and God-Talk: Toward a Feminist Theology* (Boston: Beacon Press 1993), 72.

4. Ruether, *Sexism and God Talk*, 72.

5. Ibid., 75. See also Amy Levine, "Sexuality," in Serenity Young (ed.), *Encyclopedia of Women and World Religion* Vol. 2 (New York: Macmillan Reference USA. 1999), 889.

6. Ruether, *Sexism and God-Talk*, 260.

7. Judith Shapiro, "Cross-Cultural Perspectives on Sexual Differentiation," in Herant A. Katchadourian (ed.), *Human Sexuality: A Comparative and Developmental Perspective* (London:

Sexuality is a vital topic for feminist social theorists because women's oppression is so often expressed through it. Feminists have often located sexuality within the theory of gender inequality; a critical term for the social hierarchy of men over women. Such a theory treats sexuality as a construct of male power. According to a feminist, Catharine Mackinnon, sexuality is a dimension through which gender pervasively occurs. It is "where dominance eroticized defines the imperatives of masculinity, submission eroticized defines femininity."[8] This means that sexuality is an area where distinctive features of women's status as second class are mostly seen, where dynamics of inequality of sexes are clearly manifested.

The control of women's sexuality is a reflection of higher forms of power control; the power that they draw from patriarchal notions of male dominance and female submission, male power and female powerlessness.[9] As such, sexual pleasure — the cycle of arousal, desire, and orgasm — is often seen as a basic, 'natural' and pre-social need that should not be denied to anybody, while social injustices such as rape, sexual harassment, abuse of girls, prostitution, and pornography are viewed as acts of dominance expressed through sexuality.[10] It is on this basis that the repression of female sexuality is considered a violation of women's basic rights.

Religion and African Women's Sexuality

Sexuality occupies the attention of many religions because many of human attitudes toward sexuality are embedded in value systems of any society. Control of sexuality is a powerful way of promoting morality in the society. All religions have teachings about sexual behavior that reflect a larger understanding of the sexual nature of humans and procreation. Most religions tie sexuality to the production of children. Deviant sexual practices are often condemned by religions because they are considered disorderly, a threat to social order, religious institutions, or to the society as a whole. In most African communities, women's sexuality and fertility are at the core of religion. Whereas indigenous religions have influenced attitudes towards female sexuality, the influence of Christianity and Islam in Africa is significant as well. An overview of each religion's influence suffices to illustrate the argument.

a) Indigenous View

Quite often, when we speak of African women's sexuality, we quickly think of indigenous practices such as polygamy, female circumcision otherwise known as female genital cutting, widow inheritance, etc. These indigenous values often described as primitive, barbaric, superstitious, and uncivilized are not necessarily so, as they borrow a lot from western

---

University of California Press, 1979), 291.

8. Catharine A. Mackinnon, "A Feminist/Political Approach: Pleasure under Patriarchy" in James H. Geer and William T. O'Donohue (eds.), *Theories of Human Sexuality* (New York: Plenum Press, 1987), 69.

9. Catharine A. Mackinnon, "'Sexuality' From Toward a Feminist Theory of State," in Wendy K. Kolmar and Frances Bartkowski (eds.), *Feminist Theory A Reader* (Toronto: Mayfield Publishing Company, 2000), 438.

10. Celia Kitzinger, "Problematizing Pleasure: Radical Feminist Deconstructions of Sexuality and Power," in H. Lorraine Radtke and Hendrikusj Stam (eds.), *Power/Gender Social Relations in Theory and Practice* (London: Sage Publications, 1994), 194.

dualist thinking, a fact that will be illustrated in the coming pages. Since Africans embrace a holistic approach to life in which every cultural behavior is perceived in relation to corporate relations in the community, it is important that female sexuality must be seen in the broader sense of female control. It is important that the socialization process is appreciated in order to fully interrogate female sexual control in particular.

Most African norms and modes of ethical conduct are based on an 'African' worldview that perceives the individual in holistic, communal terms and the decisive role of the community in the individual's life. According to holism, all life entities, including human experience, are not only interconnected, they are also supplementary and complementary to each other. In other words, every social phenomenon is dependent and therefore defined by other social phenomenon. Without one entity, the other is not only devalued, it loses its validity and meaning. The concept of holism was propounded first by Jan Smut (1920). The holistic notion that "the whole is greater than the sum of the parts" is fundamental to understanding African corporate worldviews and especially how social behavior and roles are interrelated with other aspects of experience and role of the community as a whole. By implication, therefore, sexuality as a social phenomenon must be understood as part of the whole, often in relation to social needs of a community. In the African indigenous systems, sexuality cannot and should not be seen as an entity in itself. It is always conceived as serving the needs of the entire community. Consequently, an African women's sexuality is valued, respected, and acknowledged in relation to the expectations of a woman's role in society.

Consequently, the African concept of sexuality is not an entity in itself. It is part of the whole. Sexuality is not only understood in relation to an individual's marital relations but in relation to the role of marriage, social status, spiritual matters, and social ideologies in the maintenance of a given community. Attitudes towards women's sexuality are based not on the individual level, but on the community's attitude towards femaleness and maleness, puberty and fertility rites, marriage, and widowhood, as well as how these relate to the community's welfare. Referring to this experience, Elizabeth Amoah, an African feminist, explains appropriately how an African woman's identity is more than the biological, physical, and socio-economic dimensions. It is also about the religious and spiritual dimensions.[11] Western views of sexuality have moved beyond this basic sociological understanding to focus on the individual alone, a concept that is often perceived as alien to the African concept of the human. In this paper, I argue that western dualist notions that inform individualism are gaining ground in contemporary Africa to be ignored.

In most African communities, what is considered the norm in sexuality is often confined within marriage. This is because sexuality is perceived as a means of reproduction intended to ensure that children born are cared for properly. Therefore, a heterosexual union is considered as the norm; any deviant behavior is stigmatized and severely punished. That is why in most African societies homosexual and bisexual behavior is considered inappropriate. Often, femininity is often associated with reproduction, care taking, generosity, modesty, and the dignity of perseverance, obedience, submissiveness, conformity, and dependence. Masculinity, on the other hand, is associated with virility, strength, authority, power, leadership, and the ability to bear physical pain, to offer protection, and provide economic sustenance as breadwinners. The values that are generally inculcated in the individual from early childhood are expected of boys when they are told that "men don't cry," and likewise

---

11. Elizabeth Amoah, "Violence and Women's Bodies in African Perspective," in Mary J. Mananzan, Mercy A. Oduyoye, Elsa Tamez, J. Shannon Clarkson, Mary C. Grey, and Letty Russell (eds.), *Women Resisting Violence: Spirituality for Life* (Maryknoll NY: Orbis Books, 1996), 84.

girls are told not to insult boys or show aggression often associated with males. Attitude toward men's strength and women's weaknesses is usually translated in marriage so that even in sexual relations, the woman's sexual role is expected to be more or less marginal or passive. She is not expected to take initiative in sexual activities such as courtship, show desire to have sexual intercourse, or even give an indication that she is enjoying sex, otherwise she takes the risk of being branded a prostitute.

Gender roles are instilled in children as early as when they are born. Among the Kikuyu for instance, when a girl is born, Mbiti explains, a mother screams four times and the father cuts four sugar canes and places the waste craps on the left side of the house. If it is a boy the mother screams five times and the father cuts five sugar canes as a symbol of his higher role in society. A child who, from then is a public property, belongs to the entire community and is no longer the property of one person. Sugar cane symbolizes the fact that these children should be treated as expected of their gender. From birth onwards the parents and the community at large instill into children gender expectations. In most cases, girls are brought up to embrace household duties such as house care, fetching water and firewood, and treating boys and men as superior entities. Boys on the other hand are taught to embrace masculine duties such as hunting, sitting with elderly men to learn leadership wisdom, and to protect their families.[12]

At puberty, an individual is considered ready for adulthood and consequent responsibilities. At this time, a sharp distinction between maleness and femaleness is made. While men enter into the world of power, girls are instructed in matters of womanhood such as sexual games, menstruation taboos, and the 'secret' of childbirth. For instance, a girl is taught moral values about the sanctity and purity of her body and how to remain clean and undefiled sexually until marriage. Emphasis on maintaining one's virginity is a common method used by most communities to maintain purity among women. Although it is important to note that some communities such as the Kikuyu and the Akamba allow premarital sexual activities, penetration is not allowed because virginity has to be maintained. Sexual activities allowed before marriage include only the fondling of each other's genitals as a means of instilling self-control in the youth. Among the Kikuyu this practice is known as *ngwiko*.[13] As Davidson observes, "newly initiated youth of both sexes were allowed to sleep together and engage in sexual play and experimentation without intercourse under a strict code of behavior in a communally controlled environment designed to prohibit premarital pregnancy."[14] During the circumcision ritual, one of the excisor ensures that initiates are virgin. Those who are not virgins during this time are considered a disgrace to their families and can face embarrassment by being exempted from attending important initiation rituals.

It is important to point out, however, that, whereas virginity is stressed in most communities, some communities do not worry about premarital sex since it is viewed as preparation for adult life. During puberty also, women are advised on how to be good wives. A good wife is one who cooks good and fast meals for her husband and the whole household, is obedient to her husband in all matters, follows his dictates, and respects

---

12. John S. Mbiti, *African Religions and Philosophy* (London: Heinemann Educational Books, 1989).

13. Jean Davidson, *Voices from Mutira: Change in the Lives of Rural Gikuyu Women, 1910–1995*, (London: Lynne Rienner Publishers, 1996), 11. See also Jomo Kenyatta, *Facing Mount Kenya: The Tribal Life of the Gikuyu* (New York: Vintage Books, 1962 (1938)), 152–156; and Joshua W. Sepembwa, *African Traditional Norms and their Implications for Christianity* (St Augustine: Steyler Verlag, 1983), 90.

14. Davidson, *Voices from Mutira,* 11.

and obeys her in-laws. The initiate girl is slowly introduced to matters of sexuality. Apart from reference to sex organs and sexual activities, which is usually made through the admonitions and ridicule of initiates and in songs sang during puberty rituals, the initiate is introduced to themes revolving around subordination, power, authority, and challenge. After marriage, chastity is expected from married women with infidelity receiving severe punishment, including divorce. Most women fear to be divorced not only because it is a stigma, but also because a divorced woman and her parents are often required to go through the painful ordeal of returning dowry, which most often is already shared and utilized by family members and extended relations

Control of sexuality is clearly manifest in the idea of purity, which becomes an aspect of focus at the onset of menstruation and infertility. This is another subject of importance during puberty time. Menstruation is considered unclean and dangerous. In most communities, a menstruating woman is taught to avoid certain people or places in case she contaminates them. Menstruation blood is considered dangerous such that any contact with certain people is believed to render all their powers impotent and inactive, a sign of how powerful the ability to bleed is perceived. For instance, a woman in this state is not allowed to fetch water in certain rivers, greet or talk to the chief, address her husband directly, or visit shrines. In some communities a girl who has not had her first menstruation is forbidden to have intercourse because such an act is believed to bring misfortune to the whole community.[15] In case a menstruating woman happens to have intercourse, a purification rite must be performed because misfortunes may occur that may cause infertility.[16] Infertility is dreaded in most African communities because childlessness could lead to dissolution of marriages.[17] Among most communities, begetting children is a way of attaining personal and communal immortality since the longer an individual is remembered in his or her community the more immortal he/she is believed to be.[18] As the giver of life, a woman is considered the intermediary between existence and non-existence.[19]

In marriage, sexual control is exercised through an emphasis on procreation and the role of women in matters related to sex. Marriage is given a central place in most African communities because it controls procreation. Marriage strengthens and reestablishes the community. It brings together not only the two individuals getting married but also the extensive kinship groups to which the individuals belong. In other words, marriage is a community contract. It does not only signify solidarity with ancestors, but also implies fertility and a transmission of life that not only concern the survival of the individual, but also of the community. Marriage establishes a fellowship with the living, the dead, and the unborn. As Bujo rightly argues, marriage is the "narration of one's ancestors, one's biography, and the writing of one's autobiography."[20] In other words, it is a way of conquering death on the individual and community level. For this reason, procreation is the transmission of life, a fundamental responsibility of all. Since most communities circumcise girls at an early age, early marriages are encouraged in order for girls to maintain

---

15. It is a tragedy that with the coming of HIV/AIDS in Africa, men are defiling children under the misconceived belief that an HIV positive man who sleeps with a virgin will be cured.

16. Amoah, "Violence and Women's Bodies in African Perspective," 140.

17. Musimbi K. Kanyoro, *Introducing Feminist Cultural Hermeneutics: An African Perspective* (Cleveland: The Pilgrim Press. 2002), 15–16.

18. Benezet Bujo, *Foundations of an African Ethic: Beyond the Universal Claims of Western Morality* (New York: The Crossroad Publishing Company, 2000), 36. See also Mbiti, *African Religions and Philosophy*, 25–27.

19. Joshua W. Sepembwa, *African Traditional Norms and their Implications for Christianity*. St Augustine: Steyler Verlag, 1983), 90.

20. Bujo, *Foundations of an African Ethic*, 36.

virginity until their wedding night. In case a girl becomes pregnant before marriage, the man responsible is obliged to marry her.[21] Among the Maasai for instance, marriages are arranged for daughters as young as twelve years.

In marriage, a man is given exclusive rights over his wife's body and sexuality. Some men take advantage of this privilege to commit all forms of abuse on women. For instance, wife battering and other violent acts are justified in terms of such rights. In most communities, it is the responsibility and the privilege for man to 'discipline' his wife or wives in order to subdue them and keep them to their proper position. Among the Kikuyu as previously mentioned, men are encouraged to beat their wives at least once otherwise the curse of their ancestors would catch up with them.[22] This kind of discipline is found in other communities such as the Luyia, the Luo, and the Kisii, among others. In addition, in most communities, rape in marriage is unheard of simply because sex is believed to be a husband's right at all times. Men expect sex on demand and enforce this privilege through a variety of means. In some communities denying your husband sex is a good reason for wife beating.

In most communities, sex is only allowed within the institution of marriage. Uncontrolled sex outside of marriage is seen as contamination of one's lineage, clan, and the community at large with 'bad' blood. It is believed that sexual intercourse contributes to a happy and successful marriage. Because of this, young brides are usually advised not to deny their husbands sex under any circumstances. Although adultery is prohibited, married men are allowed to seduce unmarried women with an intention of marrying them since polygamy is allowed. Women may be allowed to have sex outside marriage only with their husbands consent. This culturally acceptable practice is usually very secretive and rare. Such a union is considered a sign of hospitality as among the Maasai or intended to provide children for an impotent man. The children born out of such a relationship are her husband's. Mbiti explains:

> There are areas where sex is used as an expression of hospitality. This means that when a man visits another, the custom is for the host to give his wife (or daughter or sister) to the guest so that the two can sleep together ... among the Maasai, members of one group who were initiated in the same batch, are entitled to have sexual relations with the wives of fellow members.[23]

As indicated earlier 'widow inheritance' is another method used to control women's sexuality. In most communities, a widow is not allowed to have sexual intercourse for a prescribed period. This period can be as long as a year, depending on community, after which she can remarry (be 'inherited'). A widow who violates this rule is believed to bring misfortune to herself and to the community at large. Although widow inheritance ensures that a woman's sexual needs are taken care of, this practice controls the sexual freedom of a widow. Her remarriage to the brother of her deceased husband is meant to control the possibility of contamination of the family, or clan, with 'outside blood' and to ensure inheritance stays in the family, also indicating that she is property. Children born in such remarriages are believed to belong to the diseased husband.

Although initiation rituals may grant women an opportunity to express their displeasure with the social system including how their sexuality is perceived, as Henrietta Moore

---

21. Amour, "Violence and Women's Bodies in African Perspective," 91.

22. Wanjiku Mukabi Kabira, "Images of Women in African Oral Literature: An Overview of Images of Women in Gikuyu Oral Narratives," in A. Bukenya, M.K. Wanjiku, and O. Okombo (eds.), *Understanding Oral Literature* (Nairobi: Nairobi University Press, 1994), 81.

23. Mbiti, *African Religions and Philosophy*, 143.

validly observes, instances of resistance are very rare and thus ineffective to change things. Moore explains how women from the Marakwet community who participate in initiation rituals take this opportunity to ridicule men's selfish sexual desires and consequent dependence on women. Sometimes they criticize men's inability to satisfy women's sexual needs.[24] She explains:

> If a man treats his wife badly, she may call together other women to abuse the man as a warning. Women tie the hands and legs of the man and beat him. Then the man cries out, 'Leave me alone, I'll give you a goat, — I'll give you two goats,' until women agree. Then the man goes and gives the women one or two he-goats — whatever the man agreed. Then the women slaughter the goats and divide between them (sic).[25]

The control of female sexuality in indigenous religions is often transmitted through religious stories. Myths, folktales, and songs tell of the consequences of disobedience, especially where sexuality is concerned. Often, tales of misfortunes such as infertility, barrenness, and the death of siblings, husbands, oneself, or close relatives are prevalent. Stereotypes about women's need to be pure, virgin, and passive during intercourse and courageous during female circumcision are reinforced through stories to promote compliance. Discipline through wife battering is religiously sanctioned to reinforce female subordination in all matters including passivity during sexual intercourse.

Among the Kikuyu, for instance, there is a myth about the need for a woman to be protected from herself because she is capable of involving herself in self-destructive activities and therefore she needs to be protected for her own good. Kabira narrates:

> 'Wandang'otho'... gets married and he is very good to his wife. He decides to go on a journey. He spends eight days building a fence around his home to protect his wife and then tells his wife not to answer if anybody calls. The woman is therefore left safely protected. When the man goes, an ogre comes and calls:
> Wandang'otho
> Wandang'otho is not in, says the woman.
> Where is he?
> He has gone to make spears.
> To do what with the spears?
> To kill the ogres.
> The ogre in the meantime removes one of the branches of the fence. He comes everyday and repeats the same thing. Eventually the hole is big enough and the ogre enters and eats the woman.[26]

Another story, called Wagaciairi, tells of how wives run away from their husbands and get married to men who turn out to be ogres. Their 'dedicated' husbands realize the sufferings they go through so they save them and take them home where under their 'protection' the women live 'happily' ever after.[27] These stories communicate the message that a woman needs to be protected from herself because of her irresponsible, stupid, and senseless nature. She is capable of engaging in self-destructive activities. Unless controlled, women are incapable of running their families because they are disloyal and easily cheated. They need to be disciplined too as a reminder that they need to stay in their place.

---

24. Henriettah Moore, *Space, Text and Gender: An Anthropological Study of the Marakwet of Kenya* (London: Cambridge University Press, Moore, 1986), 175.

25. Ibid., 177.

26. Kabira, "Images of Women in African Oral Literature" 80.

27. Ibid., 81

Another justification for female sexual control emanates from stereotypical assumption that her sexuality is defiling. Among the Kalenjin, religious stories convey women's sexuality as defiling. Women are considered unclean and unfit to come into close proximity with the gods. Ironically, virgins were used as sacrifice because the best gift a community can offer to a god or a monster is the body of a virgin woman.[28] This contradiction can be explained in two ways. First, the sacrifice of virgins is drawn from the common attitude of women as sex objects. The best gift a community can offer a god or a monster is the body of a woman with whom no man has slept; hence the insistence on virginity in most communities. Second, only those who are powerless in society would participate without resistance in a ritual that ultimately involves their death. The narrative of virgin girls being sacrificed for rain is quite prevalent in most Kenyan communities.

Passivity in marriage is particularly effective where sexual control is concerned. If a woman cannot negotiate her sexuality such as initiating sexual union, she is unable to negotiate on other matters relating to her sexuality such as family planning, condom use when in suspicion of sexually transmitted diseases such as HIV/AIDs, rape, and other forms of sexual abuse. Ultimately such a woman is vulnerable to abuse, diseases, and even death. In most marriages, women are expected to be passive partners otherwise they face discipline from their husbands. The Kalenjin and the Maasai share a story about how a wife who refused to be subordinate must face discipline. Chesaina explains:

> Two friends were coming from a beer party. Rero told his friend "These days, these women of ours are behaving differently from long ago. They are becoming too inquisitive. Every time we go anywhere they must ask where we have been. I think it is high time we disciplined them." On hearing this, Arap Suge was angry because he knew his wife was a friend of Rero's wife and he knew that whatever Rero was experiencing from his wife had been discussed by the two women. Above all, Arap Suge believed strongly that a woman had no right to question her husband. He therefore supported Rero that they discipline their wives that night by beating them severely. They agreed to lock the doors before starting on the beating so that the wives would not … run away.… Arap Suge beat his wife almost to death.[29]

It is apparent from the foregoing that the African concept of sexuality conforms to the holistic, corporate, and functional roles of the society. While a holistic approach is and should be admired for its emphasis on the importance of functionalism, interrelatedness, and most importantly complementarity, when unchecked, holism may subsume and infringe upon the rights of some individuals in any society. This aspect finds elaboration in the later pages. Important to remember is the fact that sexuality is important for human welfare just as it is important for social organization. As a basic human right sexuality is an expression of humans of their essence as sexual beings. All humans should be able to claim, explore, and enjoy their own sexual rights. It is on this basis that female circumcision, widow inheritance, and polygamy find critique in feminist and human rights discourse. The control of female sexuality in these culturally legitimate African practices defies notions of human rights. African women's sexuality must be acknowledged as important, necessary, and a right if social justice is to be extended to the women folk on the continent of Africa.

---

28. Ciarunji Chesaina, "Images of Women in African Oral Literature: A Case Study of the Kalenjin and the Maasai Oral Narrative," in A. Bukenya, M.K. Wanjiku, and O. Okombo (eds.), *Understanding Oral Literature*, 88.

29. Ibid., 89.

b) A Christian View

Christian teachings about female sexuality must also be seen in the broader context of sexual and female control. This is because they draw from Judeo Christian assumptions that God's primary creation is man, not woman. Since woman is believed to have been created from a man's crooked rib, she is secondary and inferior to man. It is also based on the assumption that man was not the primary agent of man's 'fall' or man's expulsion from the Garden of Eden, hence all 'daughters of Eve' are to be regarded with hatred, suspicion, and contempt. Finally, a woman was created not only from man, but also for man, which makes her existence merely instrumental and not of fundamental importance.[30]

Christian control of sexuality is exemplified in teachings about male dominance, female subordination, monogamy, celibacy, sex for procreation only, and abstinence until marriage. Christian attitudes toward sexuality are often legitimized through Christian stories such as the myth about the original sin in which Eve is blamed for causing the fall of Adam. According to this myth, recorded in Genesis 2–3, the serpent tempts Adam and Eve. Because Eve was tempted to eat from the tree of knowledge by a serpent telling her that it will make her more like God and it will not lead to death. She was blamed for succumbing to the temptation and for giving the fruit to Adam, who eats of it as well. When God asks them about what they have done, Adam blamed Eve and Eve blamed the serpent. God curses the snake, "Upon thy belly shalt thou go, and dust shalt thou eat all the days of thy life."[31] God then curses Adam and Eve with hard labor and with pain in childbirth, and banishes them from his garden, setting a cherub at the gate to bar their way to "the tree of life lest he put out his hand ... and eat, and live forever."[32] This narrative is often used to justify male dominance and female submission.

The teachings of prominent Christian teachers such as St. Paul and St. Augustine also serve as points of reference for the Christian attitude toward sexuality. For instance, Paul's teaching about women's submission to their husbands is interpreted to include sexual submission. In Ephesians 5:22–26, Paul writes, "Wives, submit to your husbands as to the Lord. For the husband is the head of the wife as Christ is the head of the church, his body, of which he is the savior. Now as the church submits to Christ, so also wives should submit to their husbands in everything."[33] Furthermore, he writes in Colossians 3:18, "Wives, submit to your husbands, as is fitting in the Lord."[34] Finally, in I Corinthian 3:16–17, Paul reminds Christian converts about the need to remain holy. The verse reads, "Do you not know that you are God's temple and that God's spirit dwells in you? If anyone destroys God's temple, God will destroy that person. For God's temple is holy, and you are that temple,"[35] referring to sexual defilement.

Church fathers' teachings on sexuality have particularly influenced a Christian attitude towards female sexuality. St. Augustine of Hippo for instance taught that any sexual activity that did not lead to procreation was sinful. Like Paul, he advocated celibacy as the most desirable lifestyle for a Christian. For both Paul and St. Augustine, marriage was permitted only for the purpose of procreation. To St. Augustine, any kind of non-

---

30. Riffat, Hassan, "An Islamic Perspective," in Jeanne Betcher (ed.), *Women, Religion and Sexuality: Studies on the Impact of Religious Teachings on Women* (Philadelphia: Trinity Press International. Hassan, 1991), 100.
31. The Holy Bible, "Genesis 2–3."
32. Ibid.
33. Ibid., "Ephesians 5:22–26."
34. Ibid., "Colossians 3:18."
35. Ibid., "I Corinthian 3:16–17."

procreative sex—from masturbation to homosexuality to the use of contraceptives—was sinful. He used the sin of Onan broadly to justify the need to control sexuality. According to this narrative recorded in Genesis 38:4–8, Onan, the son of Judah and Shuah, was instructed by Judah to marry his brother's wife Tamar, "and raise up seed to thy brother."[36] The Lord had killed Er, Onan's brother, for wickedness. However, Onan did not want to have children by his brother's wife. The narrative continues: "And Onan knew that the seed should not be his; and it came to pass, when he went in unto his brother's wife, that he spilled it on the ground, lest that he should give seed to his brother."[37] This misdeed displeased the Lord "wherefore he slew him also."[38] To St. Augustine, Onan was punished for engaging in sex that was not meant for procreation.

In Christianity, therefore, sexuality has been portrayed as evil and should be avoided at all costs as illustrated in teachings about abstinence, celibacy, and sex for procreation. What is implied in this attitude is the fact that Christians should not only denounce their sexual bodies by remaining virgin, but also shun and despise any activity that leads to sex that is not intended for procreation. Women's sexuality is especially targeted in sexual control because a violation of sexual norms is likely to be detected through the loss of hymen and the possibility of becoming pregnant. In addition, their sexuality is often defined by the needs of men. The general assumption is that if women are controlled, controlling men will be easier.

Christian teachings are powerful sources for attitudes about sexuality in Kenya since the majority of Kenyans are Christians. Catholics and some women in Kenya believe the Catholic Church and some African Independent Churches' (AIC) teachings about procreation, abortion, and contraceptives strongly. Most Kenyan Catholic women embrace the matriological tradition of the 'Virgin Mary' as a model of the feminine. Mary's virginity and obedience is embraced as a model for women to emulate. Matters pertaining to sex education, family planning, condom use to protect against sexually transmitted infections (STIs), HIV/AIDS, and abortion have been highly controversial in Kenya, largely due to the teachings of the Catholic Church. The Protestant church is also influential in teachings on abstinence and contraception.

The role of the African Initiated Churches, also known as African Independent Churches, continues to define Kenya women's sexuality. These churches are particularly important to examine because they incorporate both indigenous and Christian teachings into their worship. Some AIC usually teach about the need to uphold virginity until marriage and fidelity within marriage, as well as discourage the use of contraceptives and abortion by calling them sinful. The Bible is often quoted to justify the subordination of women. It is believed by some evangelical Christians that "if women keep to their traditions of subjugation, they will have a lot of blessings."[39]

It is important to note that Christian teachings about sexuality did not only introduce new ideas of sexuality among Kenyans, they also reinforced existing ones. These Christian teachings reinforce indigenous beliefs that sex is a man's right and should be given on demands. In these patriarchal communities, the domination of men and the subjugation of women were reinforced by Christian ideologies about women. The control of women's sexuality was reinforced by Christian ideas of virginity, fidelity, monogamy, and the view of sex as a tool for procreation. The practice of female circumcision finds justification in

---

36. Ibid., "Genesis 38:4–8."
37. Ibid.
38. Ibid.
39. Kabira, "Images of Women in African Oral Literature" 78.

religious ideas such as women's submissiveness, the control of sexuality, and the need for purity and fidelity among Christian women. Although some indigenous practices such as polygamy, female circumcision, and widow 'inheritance' are despised by mainline churches, AIC's that embrace indigenous attitudes to women's sexuality reinforced attitudes to these practices by incorporating practices such as female circumcision and polygamy in their teachings. For instance, the African Independent Pentecostal church and Akorino churches promote sexual control of women by allowing members to practice polygamy and female circumcision.[40] Currently, a new sect in Kenya known as the Thaai Fraternity Kenya, also known as *Mungiki*, claims to promote African values such as female circumcision and polygamy.[41]

c) Islamic View

Islamic attitudes towards sexuality are not vastly different from that of Christianity as they draw from same Judeo-Christian values. Important to remember, however, is the fact that some claims about female sexuality are not necessarily in the Qur'an. Although Islamic moral teachings are drawn from the Qur'an, Hadith, and the Shariah, there are inconsistencies in these sources regarding female sexuality, and some of these inconsistencies are attributed to cultural notions that existed in pre-Islamic Arabia. Like Christians, Muslims generally believe that women are not equal to men. Men are perceived to be 'above women' or to have 'a degree of advantage' over them. This belief draws from general Judeo-Christian assumptions discussed above. In Islam, Riffat Hassan argues for the pre-Islamic culture of Arabs, especially the notion of *ird*-honor of the Bedouin Arabs, is instrumental to the way women are viewed in Muslim communities.

Christians and Muslims both believe that Adam was God's primary creation and that Eve was made from Adam's rib, a myth rooted in the Yahwist account of creation in Genesis 2:18–24. Although this myth of Eve as having been created from Adam's ribs has no basis in the Qur'anic account of human creation, it is believed to have entered the Islamic tradition directly through the Hadith. Muslims also belief that since a woman caused the fall of man, an allegation that the Qur'an does not even mention, a woman is a tempter, deceiver, and seducer of man. The association of the fall with sexuality and the perpetuation of the myth of the feminine as evil is a Christian influence. Women are seen as agents of sexuality, which is regarded as the Shaitan's (devil's) chief instrument for defeating God's plan. The belief that woman was created for man is not only found in the Hadith, some Qur'anic passages also support this claim. Sura 4:34 and Sura 2:288 are generally cited in support of the contention that men have a degree of 'advantage' over women. Sura 4:34 reads:

> Men are the managers of the affairs of women because Allah has made the one superior to the other and because men spend all of their wealth on women. Virtuous women are, therefore, obedient; they guard their rights carefully in their absence under the care and watch of Allah. As for those women whose defiance you have cause to fear, admonish them and keep them apart from your bed and beat them. Then, if they submit to you, do not look for excuses to punish them: note it well that there is Allah above you, who is Supreme and Great.[42]

---

40. John Murray, "Varieties of Kikuyu Independent Churches," in David Barrett, George K. Mambo, Janice McLaughlin, and Malcolm J. McVeigh (eds.), *Kenya Churches Handbook: The Development of Kenyan Christianity 1498–1973* (Kisumu: Evangel Publishing House, 1973), 129.

41. Kim Longinotto, *The Day I Will Never Forget*, (Film) (London: Women Make Movies, 2002).

42. Hassan, "An Islamic Perspective," 110.

Hadith describes a virtuous woman as one who pleases and obeys her husband at all times. According to Hassan, Hadith's teachings about female sexuality are heavily influenced by the Bedouin notion of *ird*. Bedouin Arabs notion of *ird*—honor and "shame"—was linked with the ideas of women's chastity and sexual behavior. This idea dominated past Mediterranean societies; *ird* was considered sacred. Bedouin Arabs were so fearful of having their *ird* compromised by their daughters' loss of chastity that they were willing to kill those who violated this ideal. The practice of infanticide, common in pre-Islamic Arabia, was informed by this notion of honor. This practice was seen as a way to strictly control women's sexuality. Although the term *ird* does not appear in the Qur'an, most Muslim men's concept of honor is shaped by this idea. Women's sexuality is seen as men's possession. A woman is perceived to be 'oversexed' and therefore incapable of controlling her sexual desires, in contrast to men who possess greater reason and rationality (*aqel*).[43] As oversexed, women must be protected from themselves and men should be protected from women.

Because of this Bedouin notion of honor, Muslim women's bodies are subjected to external social controls. Women are believed to differ from men in the amount of *nafs*— an animal life force that includes lusts, emotions, and desires—and *aqel*—or reason and rationality, which includes the ability to control one's emotions and to behave in socially appropriate ways. Whereas men are thought to develop considerable *aqel* as they mature, the amount that women are able to develop is les.[44] Therefore, women are said to be governed by their carnal natures and to be less intelligent than men. Consequently, they are unable to exercise conscious restraint.

The nature, purpose, and boundaries of female sexuality in Islam is further defined by circumscribing sexuality through dress or other restrictive measures such as virginity until marriage, female circumcision, denial of birth control, and the institution of *purdah* (segregation and veiling of women). These are perceived as symbols intended to promote honor.[45] Virginity symbolizes chastity; it is a social contract into which a girl must be initiated by other women. Girls' are encouraged to remain virgin until marriage. This is ascertained the night of her wedding by a red spot of blood on white sheets.[46] Birth control is discouraged not only because it interferes with God's procreation purposes, but also because it promotes promiscuity and unchaste behavior that would go contrary to notions of Islam. Fertility is valued because birth control and abortion are morally wrong.[47]

The institution of *purdah* protects women from their supposed wild sexual emotions. *Purdah* is a policy, which is part of the notion of *qawama*, an Arabic word meaning guardianship and authority. This notion originates from verse 4:34 of the Qur'an. According to this verse, "men have *qawama* over women because of the advantage they [men] have over them [women] and because they [men] spend their property in supporting them [women]."[48] The Sharia interprets this verse to mean that men as a group are the guardians

---

43. Esther K. Hicks, *Infibulation: Female Mutilation in Islamic Northeastern Africa* (London: Transactions Publishers, 1996), 74.

44. Janice Boddy, *Wombs and Alien Spirits: Women, Men and the Zar Cult in Northern Sudan* (Madison: The University of Wisconsin Press, 1989), 53. The idea discussed here is comparable to the Greek and Christian notion of dualism where femininity is considered inferior.

45. Hassan, "An Islamic Perspective," 116–18.

46. Sami Awad Aldeeb Abu-Sahlieh, *Male and Female Circumcision: Among Jews, Christians and Muslims: Religious, Medical, Social and Legal Debate* (Warren Center, PA: Shangri-La Publications, 2001), 220.

47. Hassan, "An Islamic Perspective," 119.

48. An-Na'im Abdullah Ahmed, "Human Rights in the Muslim World," in Henry J. Steiner and Philip Alston (eds.), *International Human Rights in Context: Law, Politics, Morals* (Oxford: Clarendon Press. 1996), 214.

of and superior to women, as a group, and the men of a particular family are the guardians of and superior to the women of that family. *Purdah* ensures that women (married and unmarried) are kept in isolation from men and strangers. *Purdah* translates into elaborate rules restricting the free expression of emotion, physical touching, laughter, and the insistence on or male relative chaperone for all women. In some communities, wooden bars are installed on windows to ensure that the person inside is able to see out while the one outside cannot see inside.[49] This is because of the belief that women are too tempting to be exposed or empowered.

Related to the institution of *purdah* is the institution of *al-hijab*, the veil. The veil originates from Sure 24:31, 33:33, 33:53, and 33:59. The veil means more than requiring women to cover their bodies and faces in public. According to Sharia's interpretation of these Qura'nic verses, women are supposed to stay at home and not leave except when required to by urgent necessity. When they are permitted to go outside the home, they must do so with their bodies and faces covered. According to An Na'im, "al hijab tends to reinforce women's inability to hold public office and restricts access to public life. This is because women are not supposed to participate in public life, because they must not mix with men even in public places."[50] Veiling is seen to protect men from the lustful temptation that women allegedly embody and from potentially abusive, invasive attention from men.[51] Veils cover from their heads to toes to prevent others from seeing even their eyes. Most Muslim communities believe that the Qur'an gives Muslim women the right to work, earn money, and go about her daily business without fear of sexual harassment. To ensure this they should be veiled (Sura 4: An Nisa 37).

Contesting Dualist Thinking

To understand attitudes towards sexuality in Africa, it is important to go beyond indigenous values. As indicated above, teachings about African female sexuality draw from multiple value systems, including indigenous, Christian, and Islamic teachings. What is common to all these sources is the fact that they all sanction male dominance, female subordination, and, consequently, control of female sexuality. They all base their justification of female control on dualist assumptions. The fundamental question in this essay regards the origin of this mindset. The essay explores how dualist thinking continues to influence attitudes towards female sexuality and how a deconstruction of this mindset is necessary to transform attitudes and general behavior toward the African woman.

Dualism is the doctrinal assumption that reality consists of two basic opposing elements, typically the mind and matter (or mind and body), or good and evil. One of the elements in each pair is often deemed superior to the other. In religion, for example, a 'dualist' is someone who believes that good and evil—or God and the Devil—are independent and more or less equal forces always at conflict in the world. They believe that, ultimately, God will triumph. Dualist thinking is rooted in Greek thoughts of renowned philosophers such as Plato and Aristotle.

---

49. *The Gender of Sexuality*, 73.
50. An Na'im, "Human Rights in the Muslim World," 215.
51. Shapiro, Judith. "Cross-Cultural Perspectives on Sexual Differentiation," in *Human Sexuality: A Comparative and Developmental Perspective* ed. Herant A. Katchadourian, 269–308, London: University of California Press.1979, 22. It is important to note that today veiling is seen as an "emblem of political, economic and cultural emancipation and as a means of asserting their multifaceted identities." See Nawal Saadawi, *The Nawaal El Saadawi Reader* (London: Zed Book, 1997), 95.

Gnostics and Manicheans popularly embraced dualist philosophy, which was prevalent during the Hellenistic period. Gnostics, who believed that divine knowledge (mystical knowledge) rather than faith was the key to salvation, drew on Greek dualist thinking. Manichianism, a religion founded by a Persian prophet Mani in the latter half of the third century, taught Zoroastrian brand of dualism. Western dualism is often contested because it is intertwined with power relations, often relations that draw legitimization from social evolutionism, eurocentricism, and imperialism, all of which influence attitudes toward African women's sexuality.

In religion, dualism categorizes the world into superior and inferior entities. This Greek notion of the world, composed of the spirit and the material body with the former being viewed as good and the later as evil, became popular in explaining God as spirit and the body as material. The soul (spirit) is said to represent the good, while the body is seen as representing evil. According to dualist mindset, life was perceived as a conflict between good and evil, between the desires of the soul and the pleasures of the body. Sex is equated with the desires of the body, which make it evil. Sex is perceived as evil not only because it is pleasurable but because it also leads to procreation and the imprisonment of good souls.[52] Unfortunately, dualist ideology has been expanded to justify social structures, including patriarchal hierarchies, to the point of identifying masculinity with transcendence, rationality, logos, and femininity with immanence, emotionality, and Eros.[53] It is the general assumption that the higher reality, often identified with the male, must dominate and control the lower reality—the female. It is believed that the female threatens the male domain.

Within Christianity, for instance, dualistic notions are apparent in the thoughts of renowned Christian apostles such as St. Paul, Church fathers like St. Augustine of Hippo, Tertullian, and early Christian theologians such as Thomas Aquinas. This is because dualism influenced Christianity through the incorporation of the thought of early Christian church fathers, many of whom had been raised in dualistic scholarly traditions. Both Manichaeism and Gnosticism were two major rivals of Christianity, and thus significant in transmitting dualistic ideas into Judaism, Christianity, and Islam as we know them today. St. Paul and St. John's teachings have been interpreted to reflect Gnostic and Manichean influence. The dualistic thinking of important churchmen in like St. Augustine of Hippo and Thomas Aquinas exerted great influence upon Medieval Christianity and scholasticism and are still very influential in Christian theology today.[54]

Among church fathers, the sexual ideas of St. Augustine have mostly profoundly influenced the Christian view of sexuality. Although born to a Catholic mother and a pagan father, Augustine was later influenced by the Manichean dualist doctrine, which he believed offered deeper insights into the nature of good and evil than those he found in his mothers simple Catholicism. St Augustine practiced Manicheanism for nine years before he converted to Christianity.[55] Manichean dualist teachings explained his sexual struggles, which he regarded as evil sexual desires. Manicheanism offered him an outlet

52. Vern L.Bullough, "A Historical Perspective," in James H. Geer and William T. O'Donohue (eds.), *Theories of Human Sexuality* (New York: Plenum Press, 1987), 50; Ruether, *Sexism and God-Talk*, 78–79.

53. Penelope Washbourn, "Process Thought and a Theology of Sexuality," in James H. Grace (ed.), *God, Sex and the Social Project* (New York: The Edwin Mellen Press 1978).

54. Cf. Liu Xiaofeng (ed.), *Collection of Western Religious Philosophy in 20'11 Century*, Vol. I (Shanghai: Press, 1991), 174.

55. Manicheanism and Gnosticism, two major rivals of Christianity, were important in transmitting dualistic ideas.

for his sexual expression since it allowed birth control, which his mother's religion did not. Although his mother, who detested Manicheanism, pressured him to give up Manicheanim and recommit to Catholicism, Augustine's transformative vision in which a voice told him to read Roman 13:14 led him to shun women and sex as evil desires that must be avoided and controlled. Roman 13:14 reads, "Arm yourself with the Lord Jesus Christ and spent no more thought on nature or nature's appetites."[56] From then onwards, he shunned women as sexual temptations, as any relation with them would always involve sexual attraction.

His teachings about procreation as the only purpose of sexual union are reflective of Manichean dualist thinking. He believed that the body is the work of the devil, and the propagation of the body is evil as well. Marriage is the institutional means of procreation and is therefore also evil. Sexual activity is of little importance as long as conception is avoided. This is because it affects the body alone and not the spirit. As Bulluogh observes, Augustine's "ideas about the evilness of sex led him to conclude that any sexual activity that did not lead to procreation, not performed in the proper position (i.e. male on top) and not using the appropriate part of the anatomy (i.e. penis and vagina) was sinful."[57] Although celibacy was for him the most desirable state, like Paul he permitted marriage only for the purpose of procreation. He interpreted the sin of Onan broadly to imply that any kind of non-procreative sex from masturbation to homosexuality to the use of contraceptives was sinful. Even procreative sex in an improper position was sinful. These teachings about the sinful nature of sexuality have heavily influenced Christian attitudes.

Because of his dualist mindset, the Christian Church father Tertullian described women as representatives of evil and a sexual fleshy body that needs redemption. A woman is depicted as temptress: the wily wanton and seductress who destroy a man's innocence. The scapegoating of Eve in the fall of Adam makes all women guilty for sexual temptation. For instance, in a letter to his wife, the Latin Church Father Tertullian wrote:

> And do you not know that you are Eve? God's sentence hangs still over all your sex and his punishment weighs down upon you. You are the devils gateway. You are the unsealer of that forbidden tree. You are the first deserter of the divine law. You are she who persuaded him whom the devil was not valiant enough to attack. You destroyed so easily God's image man. On account of your desert, that is death, even the Son of God had to die.[58]

Augustine reiterates this view about women when he describes women as incomplete beings whose purpose was only to serve as vehicles of procreation.[59]

Dualist teachings of church fathers such as Augustine found legitimacy in scriptural teachings, especially the Genesis creation and temptation story, as well as Paul's teachings discussed earlier. The condemnation of certain sexual activities, such as adultery and homosexuality, are considered reflective of the dualist thinking prevalent at the time. A number of stories have been analyzed to illustrate this point. For instance, the story of Adam and Eve is often used to sanction dualistic assumptions about sexuality and especially how ideal godly human behavior can be derailed by sexual instincts. This story becomes the first religious incident in Christianity where a woman is perceived as oversexed and hence she needs to be dominated and controlled. The story of Onan in Genesis 38:7–10

---

56. The Holy Bible, "Roman 13:14."
57. Vern L. Bullough, "A Historical Perspective," in *Theories of Human Sexuality*, 49–62.
58. Tertullian De Cultu, *Feminarum*, 1.1; Ruether, *Sexism and God-Talk* 167.
59. Augustine, Saint. 1950. *The City of God*. New York: The Modern Library, Translated by Marcus Dods D.D. XIV 464–471.

has been interpreted as promoting similar assumptions about female sexuality. According to this story, God only permits sex for procreation and as only a necessary evil. The depiction of the Virgin Mary, the mother of Jesus, as having conceived immaculately and therefore not engaging in any sex at all is illustrative of attitudes towards sex.[60] The world that looked down upon sex in preference of celibacy could not imagine the son of God having been brought into the world through the most defiling of acts—sex. It was therefore important that Jesus be conceived through the Holy Spirit. Those who are familiar with the development of the Christian doctrine may recall the bloodshed that characterized the controversy that surrounded the nature of Jesus. Was he fully human or fully God? Central to this controversy was how to reconcile dualist assumptions prevalent at the time that a good God (the Holy Spirit) could take on a human 'defiled body.'

The portrayal of Jesus as an asexual person is another example of dualist influence. As the son of God, Jesus could not involve himself in defiling behavior that has to do with sex. Most importantly, Jesus could not be involved with a woman because a woman was in essence defiling. The denial of the sexual needs of Jesus as God conforms to dualist assumptions that Jesus could have been married, and that a woman, a temptress could possess that power that Mary Magdalene possessed. It is no surprise that the only way to control her power was to control her sexuality—turn her into a prostitute. That was enough to destroy the legacy she built in the development of the church of Christ. And for poor Jesus, if he indeed had a daughter, dualism took it all away. The contemporary debate about the Da Vinci code revolves around this dualism, sexuality, and the status of women in Christianity.

Islamic teachings on female sexuality are also influenced by dualist mindset. According to Riffat Hassan, inconsistencies in Islamic sources draw from pre-Islamic cultural norms, some of which draw from dualist influence in the Hellenism world that Judeo-Christian values existed alongside Islam. Without belaboring the point, it is important to note that Judaism, Islam, and Christianity have been influenced by the same values and ideologies; specifically, that one significant point of contact is the influence of dualism. Although the Qur'an has tried to circumvent negative attributes associated with sexuality by affirming it as integral part of God's plan for humankind, Hassan is right in observing that most Muslims hold dualistic notions that sexuality is opposed to spirituality. This is clearly illustrated in the Islamic view discussed above. The influence of dualist ideology on African through Christianity and Islam is apparent in attitudes expressed toward female sexuality in most African communities. While indigenous practices draw from a patriarchal system that display some kind of dualist mentality, a reinforcement of this mentality by western religions—Christianity and Islam—contribute significantly toward challenges to transform attitudes towards women's experience.

Toward the Deconstruction of a Dualist Mindset

In contesting dualist thinking, feminists have tended to promote a holistic thinking, an approach that is indigenous and complementary in its approach. This approach promotes a mindset that acknowledges the significance of every aspect of nature, including different human experiences. Thus female sexuality is given its due as a significant human

---

60. Bullough, "A Historical Perspective," 52.

experience, one that no one should be denied. This implies the need for a deconstruction of dualist mindset that is prevalent in religions practiced in Africa. Such as deconstruction must involve re-interpretation of religious values, indigenous, foreign, or western, in order to highlight the basic human rights of African women.

Christian feminists Rosemary Radford Ruether (1993) and Sherry Ortner (1974) have observed that Augustine's views reinforce the dualistic dichotomization of feminine from masculine and the assumptions that masculinity is superior to femininity. This attitude is responsible for the control of female sexuality. Like Christian feminists, Muslim feminists like Hassan, El Saadawi, Amina Wadud, and Asma Barlas have argued that Islam is essentially egalitarian. Dualist ideals within the religion are as a result of influence of Graeco-Roman philosophy and Manicheanism that was prevalent at the time of Prophet Muhammad. These dualist ideals have not only corrupted Allah's message of love, equality, and justice for all, it has corrupted his message by sanctioning female dominance and the control of female sexuality.

In the Qur'an, for instance, heterosexual marriage is affirmed as the human need for sexual satisfaction and intimacy, which is natural. It protects human beings, especially men, from immorality by providing them with a religious framework in which their sexual and other energies can be channeled constructively. According to the Qur'an, God did not prescribe monasticism, which the followers of Jesus imposed upon themselves. Renunciation of the world and celibacy are not required of those who wish to dedicate their lives to the service of God or to spiritual pursuit.[61] Unfortunately, Hassan argues, this Qur'anic attitude towards sexuality is not reflected in Muslim attitudes towards women's sexuality. While Muslims are to draw their teachings of sexuality from the Qur'an and Hadith, the cumulative (Jewish, Christian, Hellenistic, Bedouin, and other) biases against women, which existed in the Arab-Islamic culture of the early centuries of Islam, have infiltrated the Islamic tradition, undermining the Qur'an's egalitarian message.[62]

Muslim feminists have rejected Islamic practices such as *purdah* and *al-hijab* because they do not reflect the egalitarianism that Allah intended for all Muslims. According to Hassan, the notion of *purdah* is not in the Qur'an. In Sura 4:15, confinement to the home is prescribed as a punishment for unchaste women. The Qur'anic law of modesty addressed to men and women tells women not to dress or act as sex objects.[63] A Muslim feminist scholar from Egypt, El Saadawi, sees *purdah* as a patriarchal pervasion of the Qur'an. According to her, the authentic identity of a Muslim woman is not to be veiled and that the veil is not even authentically part of Islamic dress. It is a practice reverted to by fundamentalist movements in order to return to the culture where women are dominated by men.[64] Commenting on this role of religion in sanctioning sexist attitudes, El Saadawi observes that all religions of the world, both eastern and western, have patriarchal principles as far as the submission of women to men is concerned.[65]

Feminists condemn practices such as female circumcision because it existed in pre-Islamic Arabia as a form of sexual control, long before Islam was instituted as a religion. This practice conformed not only to the Bedouin concept of *ird*—honor that discriminated against the girl on the assumption that the feminine and sexuality are evil, corruptible, and dishonorable. The practice that existed before Islam most likely found legitimacy in

---

61. Hassan, "An Islamic Perspective," 98–99.
62. Ibid., 116.
63. Ibid., 119.
64. Nawal Saadawi. *The Nawal El Saadawi Reader* (London: Zed Books, 1997), 95.
65. Ibid., 73.

helenist the Judeo-Christian mindset that was prevalent in Arabia at the time. The need to control sexual desire and the activities of women was deeply rooted in the need to ensure women's purity, particularly to ensure that these woman's children truly belonged to their husbands.[66] Virginity was a fundamental way of ensuring that women did not bring irreparable shame to their family though misbehavior.[67] Although the need to distinguish Arabic and African cultural practices from religious practices is fundamental in empowering women, it is mostly important to deconstruct dualist mindset that informs patriarchy and sexism in order to transform attitudes about female sexuality in Africa.

The introduction of Islam to Africa reinforced traditional notions of honor and women's sexuality, also found in some indigenous African communities. Ideas of virginity, circumcision, widow remarriage, and polygamy were renewed as legitimate. In Africa, a woman's sexuality is perceived as a men's possession. Most African Muslim communities practice *purdah* as a way of protecting women from sexual pervasion.[68] African Muslims who circumcise their daughter regard the practice as a cardinal religious duty in Islam necessary to curb and socialize sexual desires. As I found out in my 2007 study, some informants described female circumcision, as "an injunction of Islam required of every Muslim."[69]

While in this paper I advocate a holistic approach, it is important to acknowledge the fact that this approach can sometimes leans toward social functionalism. Unchecked social functionalism can easily subsume and infringe upon the rights of the individuals, especially in corporate societies. As a basic human right, sexuality is an expression of human essence as sexual beings. All humans should claim, explore, and enjoy their own sexual rights without inhibition. It is on this basis that female circumcision, widow inheritance, and polygamy find critique in feminist and human rights discourse. While the control of female sexuality is culturally legitimate, it is time that Africans changed practice that defy notions of human rights. African woman's sexuality must be acknowledged as important, necessary, and a right if social justice is to be extended to the women folk on the continent of Africa.

Conclusion

In this paper, I highlighted how complex factors affect the sexuality of the Africa woman. Efforts to transform her situation must acknowledge this, especially how interconnected these factors are. In particular, I discussed how western dualist thinking has influenced attitudes towards women and their sexuality. I argued that to understand an African woman's experience one must appreciate her holistic worldview and appreciate her complementary roles in society. A holistic approach that I advocate is one way of acknowledging how social experience is interconnected and complementary. I note that while it is true that modern notions of human rights are essential in the valuation and validation of the human worth of the woman, and consequently her sexuality, this valuation

---

66. Fran Hosken, *The Hosken Report, Genital and Sexual Mutilation of Females* (Lexington, MA: Women's International Network News, 1993), 118.

67. Janice Boddy, *Wombs and Alien Spirits: Women, Men and the Zar Cult in Northern Sudan* (Madison: The University of Wisconsin Press, 1989), 53.

68. It is important to note that in Kenya veiling is also seen as a sign of respect among some Muslim women.

69. Mary Nyangweso Wangila, *Female Circumcision: The Interplay between Religion, Gender and Culture* (New York: Maryknoll, Orbis books, 2007).

should be viewed in a holistic, complementary worldview in which women and their sexuality is respected and acknowledged as valuable as much as any other experience.

Moreover, I discussed the significance of religion in defining women's sexuality and how this role in intertwined in patriarchal and dualist structures of the society that have demonized her sexuality as non-essential, defiling, and evil. I have explained how religion operates within 'ruling relations' and how it conforms to structural and cultural attitudes about women.[70] By sanctioning cultural stereotypes emanating from Arab, western, and indigenous cultures; religion acts as a powerful instrument of social legitimization. Stereotypes sanctioned by religion are often internalized as the norm by members of communities within which specific religions operate.

I conclude the paper by recommending the need for deconstruction of the dualist mindset that informs patriarchal and sexist attitudes. I indicate that, as the most powerful institutions for legitimizing patriarchy, sexism, and the control of female sexuality, religion possesses the ability to serve as an agent for the deconstruction of a dualist mindset that promotes sexism. Religion has social capital potential for addressing issues that women in Africa continue to face in the light of human rights. In order to change the religious justification of unjust and outdated social practices, religion must draw upon the authority it possesses to deconstruct dualist thinking that undermines the human rights of women. The same persuasive authority of religion that is embedded in human rights values can dismantle the persuasive authority of religion that helped instill dualist thoughts in these religions. This is the task of sensitized religious leaders. Religious leaders that must be willing to decode oppressive dualist assumptions about women in order to promote the human worth and human rights of the African woman. These rights include the right to sexuality, a freedom of choice in matters pertaining to sexuality, such as the right to divorce a man who has been infected by HIV/AIDs, or to refuse marriage to a polygamous man. African religious leaders must embrace this task in order empower African women to emancipate themselves from sexist practices that are sanctioned by religions.

References

Abu-Sahlieh, Sami Awad Aldeeb. *Male and Female Circumcision: Among Jews, Christians and Muslims: Religious, Medical, Social and Legal Debate.* Warren Center, PA: Shangri-La Publications, 2001.

Amoah, Elizabeth. "Violence and Women's Bodies in African Perspective." In Mary J. Mananzan, Mercy A. Oduyoye, Elsa Tamez, J. Shannon Clarkson, Mary C. Grey, and Letty Russell (eds.) *Women Resisting Violence: Spirituality for Life.* Maryknoll, NY: Orbis Books, 1996.

_____. "Femaleness: Akan Concepts and Practices." In Jeanne Beecher (ed.), *Women Religion and Sexuality: Studies on the Impact of Religious Teachings on Women.* Philadelphia: Trinity Press International, 1991.

An-Na'im, Abdullah Ahmed. "Human Rights in the Muslim World." In Henry J. Steiner and Philip Alston (eds.) *International Human Rights in Context: Law, Politics, Morals.* Oxford: Clarendon Press, 1996.

_____. "Islam, Sharia and Human Rights." In Henry J. Steiner and Philip Alston (eds.) *International Human Rights in Context: Law, Politics, Morals.* Oxford: Clarendon Press, 1996.

70. Dorothy Smith, *Writing the Social Critique: Theory and Investigations* (London: University of Toronto Press, 1997).

Augustine, Saint. *The City of God*. Translated by Marcus Dods. New York: The Modern Library, D.D. XIV, 1950.

Brown, Karen McCarthy. "Fundamentalism and the Control of Women." In John S. Hawley (ed.) *Fundamentalism and Gender*. New York: Oxford University Press, 1994.

Berger, Peter. *The Sacred Canopy*. New York: Anchor Books, 1969.

Boddy, Janice. *Wombs and Alien Spirits: Women, Men and the Zar Cult in Northern Sudan*. Madison: The University of Wisconsin Press, 1989.

Bujo, Benezet. *Foundations of an African Ethic: Beyond the Universal Claims of Western Morality*. New York: The Crossroad Publishing Company, 2000.

Bullough, Vern L. "A Historical Perspective." In James H. Geer and William T. O'Donohue (eds.) *Theories of Human Sexuality*. New York: Plenum Press, 1978.

Chesaina, Ciarunji. "Images of Women in African Oral Literature: A Case Study of the Kalenjin and the Maasai Oral Narative." In A. Bukenya, M.K. Wanjiku, and O. Okombo (eds.) *Understanding Oral Literature* Nairobi: Nairobi University Press, 1994.

Davidson, Jean. *Voices from Mutira: Change in the Lives of Rural Gikuyu Women, 1910–1995*, 2nd ed. London: Lynne Rienner Publishers, 1996.

DeLamater, John. "A Sociological Approach." In James H. Geer and William T. O'Donohue (eds.) *Theories of Human Sexuality*. New York: Plenum Press, 1978.

El Saadawi, Nawal. *The Nawal El Saadawi Reader*. London: Zed Books, 1997.

_____. *The Hidden Faces of Eve: Women in the Arab World*. Boston: Beacon Press, 1980.

Gagnon, John H. "The Interaction of Gender Roles and Sexual Conduct," In Herant A. Katchadourian (ed.)*Human Sexuality: A Comparative and Developmental Perspective*. London: University of California Press, 1979.

Graham, Elaine. "Gender." In Paul B. Clarke and Andrew Linzey (eds.) *Dictionary of Ethics, Theology and Society*. New York: Routledge, 1995.

Hassan, Riffat. "An Islamic Perspective." In Jeanne Betcher (ed.) *Women, Religion and Sexuality: Studies on the Impact of Religious Teachings on Women*. Philadelphia: Trinity Press International, 1991.

Hicks, Esther K. *Infibulation: Female Mutilation in Islamic Northeastern Africa*. London: Transactions Publishers, 1996.

Hosken, Fran P. *The Hosken Report, Genital and Sexual Mutilation of Females*, 4th Edition, Lexington, MA: Women's International Network News, 1993.

Kabira, Wanjiku Mukabi. "Images of Women in African Oral Literature: An Overview of Images of Women in Gikuyu Oral Narratives." In A. Bukenya, M.K. Wanjiku, and O. Okombo (eds.) *Understanding Oral Literature*. Nairobi: Nairobi University Press, 1994.

Kanyoro, Musimbi K. *Introducing Feminist Cultural Hermeneutics: An African Perspective*. Cleveland: The Pilgrim Press, 2002.

Kenyatta, Jomo. Facing Mount Kenya: The Tribal Life of the Gikuyu. New York: Vintage Books, 1962 (1938).

Kitzinger, Celia. "Problematizing Pleasure: Radical Feminist Deconstructions of Sexuality and Power." In H. Lorraine Radtke and Hendrikusj Stam (eds.) *Power/Gender* Social Relations in Theory and Practice. London: Sage Publications, 1994.

Levine, Amy. "Sexuality." In Serenity Young, (ed.) *Encyclopedia of Women and World Religion* Vol. 2. New York: Macmillan Reference USA, 1999.

Levinson, Pnina Nave. "Women and Sexuality: Traditions and Progress." In Jeanne Beecher (ed.) *Women, Religion and Sexuality: Studies on the Impact of Religious Teachings on Women.* Philadelphia: Trinity Press International, 1991.

Mackinnon, Catharine A. " 'Sexuality' From Toward a Feminist Theory of State." In Wendy K. Kolmar and Frances Bartkowski. *Feminist Theory A Reader.* Toronto: Mayfield Publishing Company, 2000.

_____. "A Feminist/Political Approach: Pleasure Under Patriarchy." In James H. Geer and William T. O'Donohue (eds.) *Theories of Human Sexuality.* New York: Plenum Press, 1987.

Mbiti, John S. *African Religions and Philosophy.* London: Heinemann Educational Books, 1989.

_____. *Concepts of God in Africa.* London: S.P.C.K., 1970.

Moore, Henriettah. *Space, Text and Gender: An Anthropological Study of the Marakwet of Kenya.* London: Cambridge University Press, 1986.

Murray, John. "Varieties of Kikuyu Independent Churches" In David Barrett, George K. Mambo, Janice McLaughlin, Malcolm J. McVeigh (eds.) *Kenya Churches Handbook: The Development of Kenyan Christianity 1498–1973,* Kisumu: Evangel Publishing House, 1973.

Nelson, Harold D. *Kenya: A Country Study.* Washington D.C.: The American University, 1984.

Ortner, Sherry B. "Introduction: Accounting for Sexual Meanings." In S. Ortner and H. Whitehead (eds.) *Sexual Meanings: The Cultural Construction of Gender and Sexuality.* Cambridge: Cambridge University Press, 1981.

_____. "Is Female to Male as Nature is to Culture?" In M.Z. Rosaldo and L. Lamphere (eds.) *Woman, Culture and Society.* Stanford: Stanford University Press, 1974.

Ruether, Rosemary Radford. *Sexism and God-Talk: Toward a Feminist Theology.* Boston: Beacon Press, 1993.

Shapiro, Judith. "Cross-Cultural Perspectives on Sexual Differentiation." In Herant A. Katchadourian (ed.) *Human Sexuality: A Comparative and Developmental Perspective.* California: University of California Press, 1979.

Smith, Dorothy. *Writing the Social Critique: Theory and Investigations.* London: University of Toronto Press, 1999.

Smuts J. C. *Holism and Evolution.* Cape Town: N & S Press, 1987 (1926).

Sepembwa, Joshua W. *African Traditional Norms and their Implications for Christianity.* St. Augustine: Steyler Verlag, 1983.

Swartz, Rutter, Pepper Schwartz, and Virginia Rutter. *The Gender of Sexuality.* London: Pine Forge Press, 1998.

Tertullian, De Cultu Feminarum, cited in Radford Ruether. *Sexism and God-Talk: toward a Feminist Theology.* Boston: Beacon Press, 1993.

Wangila, Mary Nyangweso. *Female Circumcision: The Interplay between Religion, Gender and Culture.* Maryknoll NY: Orbis books, 2007.

Washbourn, Penelope. "Process Thought and a Theology of Sexuality." In James H. Grace (ed.) *God, Sex and the Social Project.* New York: The Edwin Mellen Press, 1978.

Chapter 7

The Struggle for Sexual Rights among the Kikuyu Women of Central Kenya, 1918–2002

Felix Kiruthu, Martha Wangari Musalia &
Mildred Jalang'o-Ndeda

Following independence in 1963, the Kenyan government embarked on a program of national development with the aim of eradicating poverty, disease, and ignorance. Today, four decades after British colonialism, women in particular are challenging the fulfillment of these aspirations, the majority of whom are still battling poverty. Ironically, although they comprise over half of the population (52 per cent), and therefore play an important part in the development of the country, women are still marginalized.[1] During colonialism, women suffered from a lack of economic resources, which were mainly under the control of the men. They also suffered from the political oppression of the harsh colonial administration. Many scholars have correctly observed that African women have suffered double jeopardy since colonialism. In the post independence era, women are expected to excel in their domestic duties of managing their homes while at the same time they are expected to excel in the work place.

One area that is yet to receive due attention in regards to the status of women in Africa, particularly in Kenya, is the extent to which women have been able to control or modify their sexual relations with men. This is mainly because women's sexuality is controlled by legal, cultural, and social constraints. The prevailing dearth of information on this subject has further compounded the HIV/AIDS calamity in Africa. Traditionally, the discourse addressing women in Africa perceive them as a group without agency. They are depicted as victims of local, national, and global processes that have affected their reproductive and productive roles.[2] Although the power of African women to change their status quo has greatly

been underestimated, they have nonetheless been engaged in a never-ending daily struggle to improve their condition; a struggle that includes agitation for their sexual rights, in spite of many obstacles. Sexual rights include the right to choose a partner; the right to decide freely on matters related to one's sexuality without fear of violence; the right of access to confidential health services; and the right of all persons to express their sexual orientation.

African women have struggled for their sexual rights in various ways since the pre-colonial era. They struggled not only in the face of colonial restrictions on the mobility

---

1. FIDA, "A Shadow Report to the 5th, and 6th Combined Report of the Government of Kenya," The 39th Session of the UN Committee in New York, July 3 to August 10, 2007.

2. Mary Kinyanjui, *Kamweretho: Urban Women Speaking Out: Social Economy, Rights and Politics of Motherhood* (Institute for Development Studies, University of Nairobi, 2009).

of women, but also in the face of exploitation by their male counterparts. In Kenya, for instance, this struggle is demonstrated through the resilience of Kikuyu women during the female circumcision controversy in the 1920s and 1930s, and by many other women who moved into urban centers despite efforts by male patriarchs and the colonial government to contain them in the reserves. In addition, some African women married men from other communities in spite of spirited protests from their kith and kin. With the expansion of educational opportunities in the post-independence era, many African women were able to substantially improve their socio-economic status. Buoyed by the international media and women activists who embarked on a crusade to liberate women, their sexual rights have been further enhanced. Nevertheless, since pre-colonial times, the struggle for sexual freedom is intertwined with the struggle for economic and political power. Given that women are yet to achieve all these rights, it follows that their struggles continue.

The Pre-Colonial Era

The Kikuyu are the largest ethnic community in Kenya, occupying the hilly and fertile region of central Kenya. At independence, they occupied five districts: Kiambu, Murang'a, Nyeri, Kirinyaga, and Nyandarua. The claim that Kikuyu women had scant freedom before the advent of colonialism in Africa is perhaps grossly exaggerated. Women had freedom not only to carry out long distance trade, but also in sexual relations. Jomo Kenyatta states that, among the Kikuyu, both boys and girls were taught rules and regulations governing sex during the circumcision right of passage.[3] Indeed, such initiates were also allowed to practice some kind of limited intercourse called *nguiko*, which involved fondling. Moreover, boys and girls were free to dance together during social ceremonies after this stage of their life.

Sarah Boulanger observes that when the Christian missionaries arrived in Kenya during colonialism, they begun to oppose *irua* (circumcision) as they did not see it as a positive rite of passage, but rather as a heathen act.[4] However, some new African Christian converts still sought and procured circumcision (sometimes against the wishes of their parents) as they were aware of the great significance of circumcision in the community. Kenyatta goes on to state that girls were not coerced to marry someone they did not like. They could choose to reject an unsuitable suitor. This does not mean, however, that some practices did not seek to control women's sexuality. For instance, girls had to undergo clitoridectomy, ostensibly in a bid to suppress their sexual urge, among other reasons. This practice ensured that sexual intercourse mainly served the interests of the society in terms of procreation and the production of food to sustain the community.

It is not surprising therefore that, among the Kikuyu, polygamy was viewed as both economically and socially advantageous. The practice was favored by both men and women for a variety reasons. The first of which, as Ester Boserup observes, was because it ensured that men did not take part in farm activity and could in turn devote more time to governance and other affairs for the welfare of the community.[5] Children from polygamous marriages provided the required farm labor, and polygamous unions fostered

---

3. Jomo Kenyatta, *Facing Mount Kenya: The Tribal Life of the Gikuyu* (New York: Vintage, 1965).
4. Sarah Boulanger, "Women's Activism for Gender Equality in Africa," *Wagadu*, Vol. 6 (2008).
5. Ester Boserup, *The Conditions of Agriculture Growth: The Economics of Agrarian Change Under Population Pressure* (Chicago: Aldine, 1965).

the linkage of clans since a man was only allowed to marry from other clans. Furthermore, a man with a large homestead was highly respected as this symbolized wealth and prestige. This notion was further strengthened by the fact that a man with many daughters was likely to acquire enormous wealth in the form of livestock, once he married off his daughters. Polygamy also solved the problem of sexual access by men during the long post partum period prescribed by the society.

Polygamy has been viewed by many as tantamount to depriving women their full sexual rights; however, the situation was much more complex. The fact that polygamy was widely practiced does not mean that women in such unions did not enjoy sexual rights in Kikuyu society. Seniority in terms of age among women came with some benefits. Indeed, it is the first wife, in most cases, who suggested that the husband acquire another wife. In some instances, they even helped to choose a good co-wife in order to ensure a harmonious relationship in the family. Oruboloye observes that among the Yoruba women of West Africa, having a co-wife was celebrated since it allowed the woman to observe the full post-partum period of sexual abstinence without any sexual advances from her husband, and to withdraw from sexual obligations without his protest when she reached an advanced age.[6] Similarly, polygamy was accepted as a healthy practice for the community as it solved a variety of problems, including bareness. Thus, if a man's wife were unable to bear children, he would acquire a second wife with the blessings of his first wife. Among other things, this avoided divorce and marital tension between the man and his first wife. The Kikuyu community also allowed a woman whose husband died without siring children to marry a wife.[7] However, in such a situation, the 'wife' would get a piece of land and access other property of her 'husband' in return for companionship and children.

The Impact of Colonial Conquest and State Formation on Kikuyu Women

Pre-colonial societies within what is now Kenya were drawn slowly into an expanding world economy through conquest, the imposition of taxes, and the development of a cash economy. With the advent of colonial invasion in the second half of the 19th century, the socio-economic, not to mention political, situation in most African societies was disrupted. The colonial state was dominated by men, and therefore the policies it developed were not focused on gender parity. It was no wonder then that women felt less empowered during colonialism, much more than during the pre-colonial times when some safeguards were instituted by custom for their benefit. It is argued here that many of the forces that continue to oppress women in Africa today arise from the distortion of gender relations during colonialism.[8]

The policy of encouraging white settlers to occupy and acquire large tracts of land for farming in Kenya was propounded by Charles Eliot, the first British Commissioner to British East Africa Protectorate.[9] Eliot was concerned that the British government had

---

6. Israel Orubuloye, John Caldwell, et al., *Sexual Networking and Aids in Sub-Saharan Africa* (Canberra: The Australian National University, 1994).

7. Kenyatta, *Facing Mount Kenya.*

8. Shadrack Nasong'o and Theodore Ayot, "Women in Kenya's Politics of Transition and Democratization," in Murunga Godwin and Shadrack Nasong'o (eds.), *Kenya: The Struggle for Democracy* (Dakar: CODESRIA, 2007).

9. William Robert Ochieng, *A History of Kenya* (Nairobi: MacMillan, 1985).

spent a considerable amount of British taxpayers' money on the construction of the railway and in the administration costs in the colony, and wanted the colony to pay for these expenses. In Kenya, the European settlers and the Christian missionaries acquired property in some of the best arable lands, especially near Nairobi, the headquarters of the colonial government. As Lord Delamare observed, land without labor was of no use. Consequently, a number of colonial ordinances were enacted to facilitate the acquisition of African land by the Europeans in Kenya. These included the Crown lands Ordinance of 1901 and 1902. However, the most notorious was the Crown lands Ordinance of 1915, which stated that Africans were tenants at the will of the British Crown. This implied that communities could be moved from their ancestral land if the colonial officers deemed it necessary. Since much of this land was from the Kikuyu, the lives of many members of the community were disrupted, both men and women. The productive male population was pushed out of agriculture and forced into wage labor, mainly as migrant laborers either on plantations or in urban centers; while the women were left in the impoverished rural areas.[10]

It has been observed that the designated African Reserves were deliberately overcrowded as the white settlers did not want Africans to be self-sufficient. Lord Delamare, the leader of the White settlers in Kenya, emphasized in his 1912 appeal to the Labor Commission that the African Reserves should be small enough to discourage a self-supporting level of production among Africans. This strategy profoundly affected the social fabric of Kenya, especially the roles of men and women. The colonial administration was manned by men, who were by products of the Victorian era. Subsequently, they introduced the Victorian biases of male superiority in colonial Africa.[11] Men were supposed to be the breadwinners, while women were to be confined to homes. Wage labor targeted men through taxation.[12] Women were not encouraged to engage in wage labor and remained behind in the traditional subsistence sectors. Ironically, African men were paid low wages, not only in the White settler plantations but also in urban centers, so that the burden of raising and sustaining the family fell on women in the rural areas.[13] The colonial logic was that since the African male left his wife or wives in the Reserves, they should cater for their livelihood as they could live on the food they produced. Moreover, due to prevailing sexist attitudes, the colonial administration sought the support of chiefs and male elders to promote social control of women. However, the colonial government was not consistent in its policies — for there were times when it suited its interests to have women conduct activities such as trading in urban centers.

The Female Circumcision Controversy

One of the African cultural practices that clashed with the Euro-Christian values in colonial Kenya was female circumcision. By 1906, Christian missionaries in Central Kenya were out to fight clitoridectomy, or female circumcision, which was an old customary tradition not only among the Kikuyu, but also among several other Kenyan communities. At the forefront of this crusade against female circumcision rite was the Church of Scotland

---

10. Jalang'o-Ndeda, "The Impact of Male Labor Migration on Rural Women: A Case Study of Siaya District, 1894–1963" (Ph.D. Thesis, Kenyatta University, 1991).

11. Boulanger, "Women's Activism for Gender Equality in Africa."

12. Anar Visram, "Gender Politics and the State: A Study of Kenya and Zimbabwe" (Master's Thesis, Department of Political Science, Simon Fraser University, 1994).

13. Claire Robertson, *Trouble Showed the Way: Women, Men, and Trade in the Nairobi Area, 1890–1990* (Bloomington: Indiana University Press, 1997).

Mission from its bases in Tumu Tumu (Nyeri) and Thogoto, in Kikuyu (now Kabete). Upon becoming the head of the Kikuyu hospital in 1906, Dr. John W. Arthur embarked on a serious struggle against the practice of female circumcision. The missionaries argued that female circumcision was a barbaric and cruel act that caused intense pain to the women. They also argued that it made the women vulnerable during childbirth as the scar left after the healing would make the body stiff when giving birth. These arguments seemed to work in some instances, as, by 1915, some Kikuyu girls who converted to Christianity had rejected circumcision altogether. At the same time, many girls who had been forcibly baptized sought to be circumcised at whatever cost. Dr. Arthur's criticism of female circumcision was mainly based on the argument that uncircumcised girls were successfully bearing children.[14] Unfortunately, the missionaries lost sight of the social implications that would accompany the eradication of the practice among women. They erroneously believed that circumcision had no value and only caused pain and physical trauma.

As already noted, by 1915 the number of Kikuyu converts had greatly increased, and a number of girls in mission schools were beginning to reject the practice due to the influence of the Christian missionaries who convinced them that it was a satanic practice that should be ignored at all costs. Some Christian converts even escaped from home so as to avoid circumcision and the accompanying rituals altogether. It should be noted that this was a big struggle among the Kikuyu girls. In 1915, the Church of Scotland Mission Tumu Tumu allowed the procedure to be carried out but on the condition that the operation was to be performed in the absence of the accompanying ceremonies. A traditional circumciser (muruithia) was asked to operate on the girls, while Dr. H.R.A. Philip, a medical missionary, observed. It is reported that the experience shocked and irked the missionary so much that he called for the abandonment of the practice by all the protestant missions in the country. These included the Church Missionary Society, Gospel Missionary Society, African Inland Mission, and Church of Scotland Mission. A medical statement to justify this condemnation of female circumcision cited the inability to have intercourse and possible death during childbirth, as well as the infection of the bladder during childbirth.[15] Coincidentally, while the missionaries viewed the pain endured during circumcision as torturing the girls, the Kikuyu women viewed this as a necessary rite of passage.

The circumcision controversy became a major cause of division and acrimony in Kikuyu society during the 1920s. The Kikuyu Central Association, which was formed at Fort Hall in 1925, was at the forefront of defending the practice. In 1928, for instance, a baraza was convened by the colonial government in Nyeri town to discuss the issue of female circumcision, among other issues. The meeting was attended by Paramount Kinyanjui and Jomo Kenyatta, in his capacity as the General Secretary of the KCA. In the meeting, the KCA declared that it would contest for the forthcoming Local Native Council elections on a platform of preserving the community's customs, especially circumcision of girls. This public declaration brought the KCA into open conflict with the Church of Scotland Mission throughout Central Kenya.[16] The church responded by waging an all-out campaign against female circumcision. It is alleged that the CSM sponsored the formation of a political association, the Kikuyu Progressive Party, which comprised staunch CSM educated followers to contest Local Native Council elections against the KCA.

---

14. Boulanger, "Women's Activism for Gender Equality in Africa."
15. Tabitha Kanogo, *African Womanhood in Colonial Kenya* (Oxford: James Currey, 2005).
16. John Nottingham, and Carl G. Rosberg, *The Myth of Mau Mau: Nationalism in Kenya* (Nairobi: East African Publishing House 1966).

The female circumcision controversy had serious consequences for Kikuyu society, and more so on the Kikuyu women themselves whose bodies became a major site for contestation between different groups. Some of the propaganda being spread by the KCA and its supporters was that the Europeans opposed female circumcision so that they could marry the uncircumcised girls. Besides being viewed as immature and worthless, such girls were viewed as a great security risk to the community, ostensibly because they could easily sell off or give away the communal land to foreigners since they could not be entrusted with the secrets of the community. The hostility between those who supported the KCA over the issue of circumcision of women and the Christian converts created a major cleavage in the society, whose undercurrents are still being experienced to date. This hostility was accentuated in 1929, when the Protestant missionaries declared that female circumcision was evil. Consequently, all the parents who supported female circumcision were expelled from the mission churches and their children were barred from attending mission schools. The Christian converts were also called upon to thumbprint (kirore) their signature to signify their unequivocal support for the repudiation of the cultural practice.[17] As a result, two opposing groups emerged: on the one hand the diehard Kikuyu supporters of cultural traditions (Karing'a group), and, on the other, the loyalists who supported the Christian missionaries (the *Kirore group*). The term *kirore* was applied to those who appended their thumbprint in support of the missionaries over the controversy. This group was subjected to humiliation by the rest of the Kikuyu society, which saw them as sell-outs. *Muthirigu*, a Kikuyu adaptation of a coastal song with a rousing chorus and unlimited number of improvised verses, was sang as a way of abusing the missionaries, Christian converts, and the African chiefs and headmen, all over Kikuyu land.[18]

The woman's body continued to be used as a battleground for the contestation of power between the missionaries, the KCA, and the colonial government. Jomo Kenyatta, the KCA secretary general and editor of the KCA journal, *muiguithania* (conciliator), vigorously defended the practice of female circumcision as a beautiful and an important cultural practice for the community. Following the fallout between the supporters of the practice and the Christian converts, Kikuyu independent schools were started by members of the community in order to accommodate the children who were expelled from mission schools and to impart a spirit of nationalism among the children in the community. The difficulties encountered by these girls during this controversy should be appreciated, as all the different groups, which apparently were all male-dominated, made what they considered to be the right decision over the fate of the helpless girls, many of whom were circumcised against their will.

Consequently, the colonial government entered into the female circumcision controversy more openly in 1930, when it passed a new ordinance equating circumcision without consent to a felony. Subsequently, a number of people were arrested and punished for defying this ordinance. Kanogo highlights one case where a man and a traditional circumciser were fined by the colonial government for forcing his daughter to go through the rite.[19] Unfortunately, whereas such an action possibly discouraged many people from forcing the girls to undergo the rite, it also left such girls in a lot of trouble as they would

---

17. Felix Kiruthu, "A History of the Colonial Laborers of Nyeri Township, 1902 to 1945" (Master's Thesis, Nairobi: Kenyatta University, 1997); see also Boulanger, "Women's Activism for Gender Equality in Africa."

18. Kanogo, *Squatters: The Roots of Mau Mau* (Nairobi: James Currey, 1987).

19. Ngugi wa Thiong'o, *Dreams in a Time of War: A Childhood Memoire* (New York, Pantheon Books, 2010); Boulanger, "Women's Activism for Gender Equality in Africa"; Kanogo, *African Womanhood in Colonial Kenya*.

now face not only ridicule and humiliation from fellow age mates, but also rejection by their families. For the Kikuyu, an uncircumcised person is a child and can never be respected as an adult. While a big uncircumcised boy (*kihii*) was regarded as lacking decorum and could easily be excused whenever he misbehaved, uncircumcised girls (*irigu*) were viewed as ritually unclean (dirty) and encountered a harsher rebuke than their male counterparts.

Equally depressing was the situation of the girls from Christian families who defied parental authority in order to undergo circumcision. The dilemma experienced by such girls is illustrated by Ngugi Wa Thiong'o in his book, *The River Between*, where one of the main characters, Muthoni, is forced to run away from home in order to be circumcised. The difficulties encountered by the Kikuyu girls also arose from the fact that the rite conferred some level of authority on women.[20] As Boulanger and Robertson have observed, female circumcision signified the passage from childhood to adulthood, and therefore conferred upon initiates' authority over junior women. It also gave women power within their own age-set, separating them from the men. Age-sets and age-grades were highly respected by both women and men. Kikuyu age-grades performed a variety of functions in the society that were anchored on the rite of circumcision, which acted as a license for one to gain membership to these important associations in society. Such age sets performed a wide variety of functions, including judgment, mutual aid, initiation into womanhood, and discipline enforcement among women. In addition, an age-grade system allowed for control of younger lineage females as well as dependent males by women. Such power among the women helped to moderate male power in the society. As Nasong'o and Ayot observe, although male domination existed in the ideological structure of the pre-colonial African communities, this was mitigated by sexual dualism, to the extent that women had areas of social life in which they predominated. They enjoyed a certain amount of social control in their capacity as co-wives, mothers, daughters, and aunts, as well as elder women. By fighting female circumcision, missionaries eroded the gains made by women in terms of status, power, and solidarity in the community.[21] It is therefore not surprising that older women were at the forefront of defending the rite of female circumcision.

Social Control on Women's Mobility to Urban Centers

Colonialism in Africa interfered with communities' way of life, and Kikuyu elders were overly concerned about the influence of the urban life on their women and girls from the very outset. In particular, elders were worried that women's procreative powers would be greatly undermined by their mobility to urban centers. Of particular concern was the access by women to the larger urban centers, especially Nairobi. Elder received reports that, at the advent of colonialism, even young girls from rural areas were getting corrupted by the new capitalist economy. Some girls were reported to have used the excuse of trading in order to engage in prostitution. Men became afraid that if the community's women travelled to Nairobi, they were likely to become prostitutes. Apparently, such women were

---

20. Ngugi wa Thiong'o, *The River Between*, (Nairobi: Heinneman, 1965).

21. See Robertson, *Trouble Showed the Way*; Visram, "Gender Politics and the State"; Nasong'o and Ayot, "Women in Kenya's Politics of Transition and Democratization" in Murunga, G., and Nasong'o, S. (eds.): *Kenya: The Struggle for Democracy,* (Dakar: CODESRIA, 2007); Boulanger, "Women's Activism for Gender Equality in Africa."

feared because of the danger they were likely to pose to the society. They were believed to have rejected the authority of their fathers and their husbands, and were now exploiting both men's bodies and possessions.

Women's mobility, especially with a view to trading, became a serious issue during the First World War when large battalions of male soldiers were garrisoned in Nairobi and other parts of central Kenya. Some of these soldiers were Africans from other parts of the British Empire, such as Nigeria, Uganda, and Ghana. Kariokor Depot (Carrier corps) in Nairobi was one of the areas housing such soldiers.[22] These developments further attracted many women traders to Nairobi. It should be noted that women traders who controlled their own incomes not only threatened individual men's control, but the survival of the entire clan. Obviously, this situation bothered male elders, who responded by trying to stop women from accessing Nairobi for trading purposes, and they were supported by the upcoming Kikuyu politicians. However, not all the Kikuyu men were against women accessing Nairobi.

Indeed, the women who succeeded in prostitution and other trades were able to gain a foothold due to the support they got from some of the men. In particular, young unmarried men were great beneficiaries of this system. This indicates that even among the males, there were differences in the way women in the urban centers were viewed. Harry Thuku, the leader of the East African Association, had the solid backing of such Kikuyu women residing in Nairobi. On the other hand, male elders, led by Chief Kinyanjui, led the crusade of preventing women from accessing the town. It should be noted that, in his area, men were more opposed to the movement of women into urban centers; in particular because males from Kiambu area usually sought wage labor while at the same time continued farming on their small farms, aided by their wives who provided labor. Chief Kinyanjui even set up patrols to prohibit women from going to trade in Nairobi in spite of the government's warning through the District Commissioner in the late 1920s. In allowing the women to trade in Nairobi, the DC was not motivated by the need to promote the activities of women as a group. Rather, he wanted to facilitate this trade, as it was proving difficult for the urban population to access some of the services and produce provided by the women for the predominantly male population.

Efforts to control the trading activity of women by the Kikuyu elders continued during the 1930s and the 1940s. In Nyeri Township in Central Kenya, some elders were given express authority by the Local Native Council to stop young women from boarding public buses to Nairobi unless they were to be accommodated by male relatives. The Nairobi Municipal Native Affairs Officer, Eric Davies, was not willing to back such controls. In his view, prostitution, which involved domestic services in addition to sex, was a necessary part of African urban life and saved the cost of housing African laborers, a great problem given the small wage paid to the African urban labor force in Nairobi. He reported that the 8:1 male to female sex ratio in Nairobi in the late 1930s created a huge demand for prostitutes and encouraged young women to leave home. Nevertheless, many colonial servants joined the male elders, missionaries, and the Kikuyu politicians in trying to control the mobility of women. This was particularly done through legislation and social control. The fact that missionaries supported such measures highlights the complex situation of Kenyan women during colonialism.

It should be noted that a myriad of factors contributed to the movement of women to urban centers such as Nairobi in colonial Kenya. Many women were obviously searching

---

22. Felix Kiruthu, "The History of the informal Enterprises in Kenya: A Case Study of the Artisan Sub-Sector of Nairobi, 1899–1998" (Ph.D. Dissertation, Nairobi. Kenyatta University, 2007).

for a means of livelihood to fend for themselves and their families. In addition, a number of rural obligations further compounded the colonial environment given that most of the men had already left the Reserves in search of wage labor. In the late 1940s, it was the women of Murang'a who initiated a boycott against forced labor; such as the one against the requirement to dig terraces to prevent soil erosion. In some cases, women were escaping from oppressive unions, especially abusive husbands. The new arrangements provided a way of escaping such authority without punishment from the family. Attempts to control women's movement and status in Kikuyuland highlight the difficulty of drawing a line between women's bodies, sexuality, and labor.

As the colonial government and the Kikuyu elders contested the control of women's labor, women and girls negotiated their economic and social sexual mobility through their own individual concepts of personhood. It was apparent that even the men were not united in the social control of women. The male elders who could easily have access to women wanted to exert social control. Moreover, many of the male elders were unhappy about the possibility of losing a potential bride price in the event that their daughters went to stay in the urban centers. On the other hand, younger males in the urban centers had no problem with this arrangement. This social cleavage between the men was a blessing in disguise for the women who wanted more freedom.[23]

As the introduction of the capitalist mode of production continued to weaken the kinship structures of the community, it became very difficult for elders and headmen to control the movement of junior men and women. This is because colonialism heralded new opportunities, especially in the sphere of bride wealth system. For instance, wage earning young men were able to secure a wife without the assistance of elders. Given that bride wealth could be transacted using cash, junior men were able to have some more freedom. However, it was more difficult for women as they found it difficult to join wage labor, while young men could join the patriarchal class using money earned, and subsequently gained female labor power. The Mau Mau War that erupted in Kenya against the British from 1947 presented a serious challenge to the Kikuyu women in their struggle for sexual rights.

With the British declaration of the Jock Scott operation in 1954, Kikuyu, Embu, and Meru men in Nairobi were either arrested or detained, while their women and children were put into trucks and sent to the rural areas. Moreover, in Central Kenya, the government introduced the villagization programme with a view to cutting off the Mau Mau guerillas in the Aberdare and Mount Kenya forests from food, weapons, medicines, and other essential needs.[24] It would take years before some of the families would see their loved ones again. Given that many African men died either in the forests, in detention centers, or in prisons during the Mau Mau War, many women never got to see their children and husbands alive. Moreover, many others lived in great agony, not knowing whether their loved ones were dead or alive. In the face of this great challenge, some of the home guards, including the colonial police, chiefs, and headmen, are believed to have taken advantage of such miserable women for selfish sexual fulfillment. In his book, *A Grain of Wheat*, Ngugi wa Thiong'o narrates how some women were forced to have sex in return for disclosure on the whereabouts of their children and spouses or on when their husbands would be freed from detention or prison.[25] When eventually such men came back home,

---

23. Caroline Elkins, *Britain's Gulag: The Brutal End of the Empire in Kenya* (London: Jonathan Cape Ltd., 2005).

24. Robertson, *Trouble Showed the Way*, 99; Kiruthu, "A History of the Colonial Laborers"; Kanogo, *Squatters*.

25. Ngugi wa Thiong'o, *A Grain of Wheat* (London, Heinemann 1988).

they would find that their wives had given birth to children they had not sired, a factor that drove many men and women either to commit suicide or to break up their families. The horrors encountered particularly by the women during this period require more analysis. Some brave women had to endure loss of life, multiple rapes, and untold humiliation in a bid to protect the hideouts of relatives, including their husbands, children, and siblings, and consequently shield them from being arrested by the colonial forces.

Another impact of colonial capitalism on Kikuyu women was the eventual denial of land ownership. During the Mau Mau War, in 1954, a land reform program known as the Swynnerton Plan was introduced. Its aim was to convert the traditional land tenure system to private land ownership, with a view to consolidating the scattered land parcels, registration, and adjudication.[26] Unfortunately, the targeted beneficiaries of the program were the progressive male farmers. These were mainly the loyalists who supported the colonial government during the Mau Mau War. Many families did not benefit from this program, especially if the head of the family supported the Mau Mau movement. Consequently, cash crop agriculture expanded tremendously among the small-scale Kikuyu farmers, as the country moved towards political independence. The unfortunate impact of this expansion, however, was that women's labor was now shifted from food production to cash production. At the same time, more labor obligations were added to women. In the final analysis, land reform excluded women from formal land ownership, but at the same time denied them rights to land, which they had hitherto enjoyed under the traditional land tenure system.

Traditionally, women controlled and distributed what they produced. Thus, they wielded power and had considerable control over their own lives.[27] After the Swynnerton Plan, which privatized land ownership, men had an edge over the women with regard to the access of financial services and other economic resources. They could now obtain loans from financial institutions using land as collateral. Moreover, although cash crops like coffee, tea, and pyrethrum were mainly produced using the women's labor, they were generally regarded as belonging to the males. With time, men were able to easily dispose of the land without the consent of their wives, something that could not have happened during the pre-colonial times. This disparity in terms of economic resources negatively impacted the sexual rights of women.

Political Independence and the Struggle for Sexual Rights

Kenya attained political independence in 1963, with Jomo Kenyatta as the first Prime Minister, who later became the first President of the Republic of Kenya. In spite of the fact that women participated in the nationalist movement alongside the men, after independence women did not reap as much in terms of accessing political power and economic resources. Nevertheless, the independence constitution contained a bill of rights and promised equal rights in the society for both men and women. Thus, in theory, women had as much space as men in politics, social situation, and the economy, as well as access

---

26. Winfred Kamau, Esther Wangari, and Anne Kinyua, "Globalization and Its Impact on Women in the Third World," *Gender Discrimination: A Global Perspective Forum on Public Policy 290*, Vol. 1. 3 (2005).

27. Nasong'o and Ayot, "Women in Kenya's Politics of Transition and Democratization."

to other opportunities. However, there were many areas where women were still disadvantaged as compared to their male counterparts. This was the case among most communities, including the Kikuyu, in spite of boasting a large population of western educated women. For instance, women could not inherit ancestral land, as this was not enshrined in the constitution.[28]

Although a number of women's organizations such as the National Council of Women of Kenya (NCWK) and the Maendeleo ya Wanawake Organization fought for more rights for Kenyan women after independence, the focus was in areas such as the provision of more educational opportunities for women and girls, better maternal and child facilities, etc. Cases of sexual violence such as rape and battering were treated rather casually for many years. It was common for women who reported cases of rape or battering to be put under such harrowing experiences in court that many of them abandoned further attempts at getting the culprits punished. Moreover, given that most women had no access to land and other resources, they for a long time avoided taking their husbands to court due to fear of being kicked out of their matrimonial homes and possibly lose their children. In most cases, girls who had children out of wedlock have had to bring up such children single-handedly as the law has not been strict on the issue of paternal responsibility. Similarly, many women lost the right to bury their husbands, especially because the right to bury one's husband almost automatically guaranteed property rights to the woman. The late husband's relatives usually capitalized on this and used all means at their disposal to disinherit the widow.

Inequalities in marriage continued to grow, especially after political independence opened up more opportunities for economic accumulation through acquisition of title deeds for land, as it was the men who became the chief custodians of the land titles. According to Wangari and others, land remains one of the most crucial resources for women's basic livelihoods, especially in rural areas. Food for subsistence is acquired from such land, in addition to firewood and family shelter. Secondly, it is difficult for one to access loans from financial institutions without collateral (such as land) in Kenya. However, kinship and marriage ties closely define access to land, and this is largely determined by a person's marital status. Most Kenyan women have been excluded not only from the control of land, but also from control of other key economic resources, simply by lack of access to land. Apart from land ownership, married women in the public service were for a long time denied a house allowance. This disadvantage meant that their economic options were limited in comparison to their male counterparts Maathai.[29] Moreover, in the face of serious financial difficulties, most families withdrew girls from school in order to support the boys in the family mainly due to gender bias regarding the perceived higher value of boys' education over that of girls.

Many of the young women who left home upon dropping out of school found that opportunities for employment were extremely few. Many such girls were desperate, having been locked out of education either due to lack of school fees or due to pregnancy. While a boy would get away with a fine for impregnating a fellow schoolmate, the punishment for girls was harsh. It was only after the 1990s that such girls were allowed to go back to a different school to complete their education. The only opportunities available for girls who dropped out were the least desirable, such as those involving domestic work and working as attendants in pubs. Those engaged in such capacity have suffered from untold

---

28. Kanogo, *Squatters*; Visram, "Gender Politics and the State."
29. Kamau, Wangari, and Kinyua, "Globalization and Its Impact on Women in the Third World"; Maathai Wangari, *Unbowed: A Memoire* (New York: Anchor Books, 2007).

humiliation and exploitation from working women and from men. It is not surprising, therefore, that many young girls ended up as commercial sex workers. Due to a lack of adequate economic and social support for young girls, many have been enticed to join 'sex tourism' as victims by greedy entrepreneurs. Such women end up as sex slaves in the western world, while others end up as illegal immigrants working in deplorable conditions. The Kenyan media has from time to time highlighted cases of women who have ended up in different parts of the world as a result of being enticed into sex tourism, many of them ending up in near slave situations in Europe, Saudi Arabia, and the USA.[30] The trafficking of women and prostitution are a violation of women's sexual rights, since this undermines the right to freedom and safety of the person, as well as lowering one's bodily integrity.

In addition to the girls who are enticed into sex tourism outside the country, there are many others who are lured into the main urban centers, especially Nairobi, and the coastal towns such as Mombasa and Malindi. Wangari and others have observed that many girls end up in military bases. Thus, the existence of foreign military bases has given rise to a different kind of commerce involving women, with the full blessings of governments.[31] By so doing, women's bodies have been exploited to establish global political alliances. Since the 1990s, Samburu, Kikuyu, and Masaai women have been accusing the British soldiers in Kenya of having raped them in the Dol Dol area, north of Nanyuki town. Their accusations have been corroborated by Amnesty International, which has documented serious allegations against the British soldiers training in Kenya since 1965.[32] There is no doubt that some of the so-called rape victims were enticed with money by the British soldiers.

Ironically, although the Kenyan government acknowledges that the main reason women turn to prostitution is poverty, it is largely women who are singled out for punishment for engaging in prostitution, while the men involved usually go scot-free. In Kenya, there is an entrenched culture characterized by the Nairobi City Council askaris and police staging raids on the notorious red light streets, such as Koinange Street in Nairobi, with the aim of arresting prostitutes. Many women are usually caught and ferried to court in a most inhuman manner. Sometimes they are transported in open trucks and taken to court where they are either fined or sent to serve a term in prison. It is argued that women's poverty in particular stems from the entrenched discrimination against women in education, employment, and property ownership. Given this economic disempowerment, they have few options but to turn to commercial sex or other abusive relationships where they are exposed to exploitation; they therefore need to be protected rather than punished.[33]

In 1987, the struggle for women's rights increased by Mrs. Wambui Otieno over the right to bury her late husband, S. M. Otieno, a famous criminal lawyer who died of natural causes in 1986. Early in 1987, Mrs Otieno was taken to court by her late husband's clan, Umira Kager, who wanted to bury their clansman in the rural home in Siaya. Wambui, on the other hand, preferred that the body be buried in Upper Matasia Ngong, near Nairobi. Stamp observes that the S. M. Otieno burial saga illustrates the relations between women and the state in most countries. Moreover, it also points out the subtle

30. Rose Omondi, "Gender and the Economy of Sex Tourism in Kenya's Coastal Resorts," A paper presented at the International Symposium on "Global Economic and Political Systems and Women's struggle for Global Justice," Norway, September, 2003; Antony Kitimo, "Kenyan Family Wants Mysterious Death of Kin in Lebanon Probed," *Saturday Nation*, September 25, 2010.

31. Kamau, Wangari, and Kinyua, "Globalization and Its Impact on Women in the Third World."

32. Amnesty International, "British Soldiers Training in Kenya," www.amnestyusa.org/2009 (Accessed on March 15 2009).

33. FIDA, "A Shadow Report."

ways in which gender relations are implicated in political processes of the society. Wambui's struggle in court to bury her late husband has a symbolic victory in terms of the quest for justice not only for Kikuyu women, but also for all the women in Kenya. Today, her burial contest with the husband's is still quoted by both men and women in Kenya to symbolize the character of a tough woman. Wambui was a pioneer in the struggle for women's sexual rights in several ways. First, she played an important role in terms of overcoming ethnic barriers to marry members of other ethnic communities. Having been introduced to Otieno, who was a Luo, in the 1950s by her own father, she went ahead and married him in 1963, defying both her Kikuyu customs and all expectations of a Kikuyu woman by both family and peers. It should be noted that even during her prolonged court tussle with the husband's clan, she did not get a lot of political support from the Kikuyu men. Patricia Stamp attributes this lukewarm support to the way she challenged patriarchal values and practices.[34] Wambui argued her case as a wife, mother, Christian, and as a Kenyan citizen, rather than as a feminist. Later in life, she defied tradition in her old age to marry a man young enough to be her grandson, again defying custom.

Although Wambui did not win the burial case against her husband's clan, her struggle has inspired many women in Kenya to fight for the welfare of women. For example, the NCWK mounted a campaign to correct flaws in Kenya's statutes pertaining to women's rights. The Organization observed that while widows acquired property rights upon their husbands' death, it was silent on the question of burial. For example, the Law of Marriage and Divorce Bill that sought to grant women equal status and the Succession Act that sought to allow widows to administer their husbands' property were referred to customary law, which is either unclear or discriminatory against the women. According to Njoki Wamai, the statute law in Kenya potentially gives property rights to married women. The principles imply that even in customary marriages, women have equal rights in matrimonial property. However, problems arise in dividing matrimonial property on divorce or separation, especially where the property is registered solely in the husband's name.[35] The situation becomes more complex in cases where the relatives of the deceased husband contest for property, as well as other competing women and children from another marriage. Moreover, the law of succession has discriminatory provisions such as when the woman is supposed to forfeit her interest in her husband's estate in case she remarries. It should be noted that the same condition is not imposed on a widower who wants to remarry. Thus, the ability of a woman to claim property rights under either the married Women's Property Act or Succession Law depends on her ability to establish her marital status.

In addition, evidence shows that, in most instances, the male-dominated Kenyan parliament does not give gender issues the attention they deserve. Whenever bills pertaining to women's concerns are introduced before parliament, they are either taken casually or defeated. In 1990, for instance, there were only two women out of 177 members of parliament in Kenya. It was only after the 1992 multi-party elections that the number of women parliamentarians increased to six. Out of the 222 MPs in the 2002 general elections, only 18 were women, eight of whom were nominated to parliament. Due to this disproportionate voice of men in parliament, women MPs are unable to push successfully for policies that would give more benefit to women.[36] Another case in point was the Sexual

---

34. Patricia Stamp, "Burying Otieno: The Politics of Gender and Ethnicity in Kenya," *The Journal of Women, Culture, and Society*, Vol. 16. 4 (1991).

35. Njoki Wamai, *Women and Poverty (Land Rights Ownership)*, A policy brief on the Kenyan Situation prepared for the African Women Rights Observatory, 2008.

36. Visram, "Gender Politics and the State;" and FIDA, "A Shadow Report."

Offences Bill that was introduced by a nominated Member of Parliament, Njoki Ndung'u, in 2006, with a view to curbing rape and other sexual offences, especially against women, which was greatly opposed by male politicians. Issues such as the right of women to procure an abortion have also not been given the attention they deserve. The problem originates at the level of political parties. Very few of the political parties grant women senior party positions, especially the powerful political parties in the country.[37] Moreover, in spite of the guarantees in the constitution that both males and females are eligible to contest for civic and parliamentary seats in Kenya, actualization of this goal was defeated by the requirements of large sums of money and a lack of political will to support the enhancement of women's participation in political and public life at the national level.

Even the mainstream women organizations in Kenya, such as the Maendeleo ya Wanawake Organization, have not succeeded in fighting for enhanced rights for women. This could be explained by the fact that these organizations are often afraid of provoking the wrath of their male patrons. For instance, women politicians did not want to support openly Wambui Otieno in the burial saga due to the fear of a backlash from their male patrons and constituencies, although they were privately extremely sympathetic to Wambui's cause. This could be explained by the fact that most of the elite women who have accessed positions of power in Kenya have in most cases succeeded only due to the support of male politicians. It is therefore not surprising that class interests supersede the issues of women. Such elite women therefore defend class interests to the detriment of poorer women. Since the male-dominated state in Africa virtually blocks the majority of women from joining the ruling class, some women have aligned themselves with powerful men, a phenomena referred to as femocracy by Amina Mama.[38]

Maendeleo ya Wanawake, the largest women's organization in Kenya, has a long history of control by the government since its formation in 1952. The colonial government then wanted to divert the attention of western educated women from nationalist politics during the Mau Mau, and instead have them channel their energy to activities such as homecare. Good hygiene, cookery, and home craft skills such as tailoring were emphasized. The idea was for the Organization to mould women to be good homemakers. This was quite consistent with the objectives of colonial education for the girl-child in Kenya. Under colonial rule, academic education for girls was not given emphasis. Rather, western education mainly targeted men who supplied the labor needs of the capitalist society. Consequently, education for girls consisted of the "three Bs," namely baby, bath, and broom. It was only in the 1950s that the colonial authorities saw the need to produce a class of educated women who would be suitable partners to the emerging African elite. The MYWO fell into this scheme. After independence, the new male politicians sought to use the organization as an avenue for reaching out to women for the purpose of political mobilization. In 1987, the Organization declared that it was affiliated to the ruling party KANU. This was at a time when President Moi's government was facing tough opposition from pro-democracy crusaders. The strategy of affiliating the Maendeleo ya Wanawake Organization to KANU was therefore undertaken in order to forestall any attempt by the opposition to access the support of Kenyan women.[39]

As already observed, the participation of women in Kenya's political arena and decision-making processes goes back to the pre-colonial period. Their systematic political

---

37. Njoki Wane, "Sexual Violence and HIV aids Risks in Kenyan and Ugandan schools: Implications for Educational Policy Development," *Journal of Contemporary Issues in Education*, Vol. 4. 1 (2009): 71–91.

38. Nasong'o and Ayot, "Women in Kenya's Politics of Transition and Democratization."

39. Kamau, Wangari, and Kinyua, "Globalization and Its Impact on Women in the Third World," 299.

marginalization, however, has roots in the colonial legacy that continues to be actively perpetuated by the political elite. The prevailing socio-cultural factors have been used by the political class to keep them out of power, in addition to laws and policies enacted by the post independence government. As a response to this lethargic attitude towards the elimination of discrimination against women, a number of women civil society groups began to address women's issues from the 1980s. In 1991, a number of Kenyan women decided that enough was enough: they were tired of the style of politics under President Daniel Moi's reign in Kenya, who had introduced an atmosphere of fear and insecurity in politics. This fear was further entrenched as people who spoke out against the government would be thrown into prison or detention. However, a group of women defied this culture of fear after watching helplessly as their sons and husbands were incarcerated in prison on flimsy grounds. Mothers, sisters, wives, and daughters of political detainees were stripped naked at Uhuru Park in a symbolic act meant to curse Moi's government for refusing to release their kin.[40] In particular, the Government was being cursed for unleashing an armed police to beat up and tear gas the unarmed women, whose only crime was to congregate in solidarity with their children. The women were fighting for their rights as mothers, wives, sisters, and daughters.

When Wangari Maathai successfully campaigned against the allocation of Uhuru Park to the KANU-owned Kenya Times Media Trust for commercial development in 1989, her personhood and humanity came under a scathing attack not only from President Moi, but also from his sycophants in Parliament. They capitalized on her marital status as a divorcee, which they not only questioned but also ridiculed. As in many other countries, the status of women is further complicated by the dichotomization of the social space into private and public in Kenya. As Amutabi observes, the dressing down of Professor Maathai as a divorcee was based on the perception that as a woman she ought to have been happily married and preoccupied with family duties, including taking care of her husband and children, rather than campaigning against environmental destruction. The fact that the women's struggle has borne some positive changes is perhaps best illustrated by Wangari Maathai's story. By the 1990s, many male skeptics in Kenya had begun to see her point in condemning environmental destruction and other undemocratic practices by the male politicians in Kenya. Her crusade against attempts by a group aligned to former President Moi to grab Karura Forest near Nairobi won her great backing from the entire Kenyan public.[41] Nevertheless, it must be noted that even after winning the Tetu constituency parliamentary seat and being awarded the 2004 Nobel Peace Prize, she did not rise beyond the portfolio of an assistant minister, although she was arguably one of the most knowledgeable professors on environmental issues globally.

Wangari Maathai and other strong Kenyan women helped to inspire many women in the region to struggle harder for their rights. Organizations such as the Federation of Kenyan Women Lawyers (FIDA) and the Coalition of Women Against Violence (COWA) took up the mantle in fighting violations against women such as the trafficking of women and children, wife battering, and other types of violence against women. Section 82 of Kenya's first post-independence constitution was identified by these organizations as negatively affecting women, while at the same time giving undue advantage to men. It

---

40. AWC Features, *A Journey of Courage: Kenyan Women's Experiences of the 2002 General Elections* (Nairobi. AWC Features, 2004).

41. Maurice Amutabi, "Intellectuals and the Democratization Process in Kenya," in Shadrack Nasong'o and Godwin Murunga (eds.), *Kenya: The Struggle for Democracy* (Dakar: CODESRIA, 2007), 183; Wangari, *Unbowed*.

provides that no law shall make a provision that is discriminatory.[42] By doing so, and by omitting 'sex' as a basis for discrimination, it restricts women's fundamental human rights. Between 2000 and 2002, women civil society organizations went a step further and began to agitate for new laws to protect the women of Kenya. Some of the groups even went to the extent of drafting gender-friendly laws such as the Equality Bill, Affirmative Action Bill, and the Family Protection Bill. It has been realized that concerning citizenship in Kenya, for instance, Kenyan women were disadvantaged by the first post-independence constitution, which provided that determination rested with the male. This implied that a father's nationality determined not only the nationality of the children, but also that of the spouse. This situation made it difficult for Kenyan women to legalize the citizenship of their spouses and children and therefore placed tension on the family. Although this unfair situation has been corrected by the new constitution, which was promulgated by President Mwai Kibaki on August 27, 2010, it was previously supported by men, who argued that granting citizenship to a non-citizen male who marries a Kenyan woman would expose Kenyan women to exploitation from male aliens seeking a short cut to Kenyan citizenship.

Wangari Kamau and Kinyua observe that one of the unfortunate effects of the human rights regime that accompanied globalization is that it provides room for hiding the underlying economic and social inequalities in societies, especially in regard to women. Fortunately, unlike the men in Kenya, women have developed new survival strategies in the face of the harsh realities of globalization. Munguti and others argue that Kenyan women have developed new survival strategies, which she calls "invisible adjustment."[43] She adds that women are capable of making adjustment policies socially possible by increasing their own economic activities by working harder. They have also developed an elastic concept of time, whereby they not only work for long hours but also engage in multi-tasking. Similarly, Mary Kinyanjui observes that, even within the context of urban centers, Kenyan women have used their strong social and religious networks to overcome socio-economic hardships.[44] Such networks range from prayer groups, merry go-rounds, and business support groups, among many others. *Kamweretho*, a new aspect of social organization among Kikuyu women helps to cement not only their social relations, but also relations between women and their parents, especially in Central Kenya, Nakuru District, and other areas around Nairobi. According to Kinyanjui, its main purpose is the expression of gratitude to parents, more so to one's mother, while at the same time seeking her blessings. The ceremony can be traced from the 'women merry go-rounds,' and other women organizations, some of which can be traced to the traditional '*ngwatio*' organization among the Kikuyu.[45] Such support networks facilitate women's participation in socio-economic and political spheres. It is curious to note that men have not made similar efforts, especially in the rural areas of Central Kenya, and the few groups that were established have been short-lived. This could partly explain the magnitude of hopelessness as the men struggle to make ends meet in the absence of a good social support network like that of their women counterparts. *Kamweretho* is described as follows:

---

42. FIDA, "A Shadow Report"; Nasong'o and Ayot, "Women in Kenya's Politics of Transition and Democratization."

43. FIDA, "A Shadow Report"; Kamau, Wangari, and Kinyua, "Globalization and Its Impact on Women in the Third World."

44. K. Munguti, E. Kabul, M. Isoilo, and E. Kamaara, "The Implications of Economic Reforms on Gender Relations: The Case of Poor Households in Kisumu Slums," in Tamboura Diawara (ed.), *Gender, Economic Integration, Governance and Methods of Contraceptives* (Dakar: AAWORD, 2002); Mary Kinyanjui, "Informal Enterprise is a Path to Women to Urban Dynamism in Nairobi," A Working Paper presented to the International Development Center, Open University, United Kingdom, 2008.

45. Kinyanjui, *Kamweretho*; Stamp, "Burying Otieno."

The ceremony begins with women dancing to songs announcing their arrival in the host's home. These categories of songs not only announce arrival but also state the purpose of the visit. They also convey a message geared towards situating the girl child in the home. One chorus in the entrance songs "*mucii wi Karaitu ndwagagwo gucerwo,*" meaning that a home with a girl child will always have visitors, tells of the advantages of having a girl child in the home. This chorus contrasts with the traditional Kikuyu saying which praises the boy child by stating that *Mucii wina kahii ndukaga kurigwo mutwe* meaning that a home with a boy child will one day slaughter a goat. The saying implies that a boy child will bring festivities and celebration even in the poorest of the homes. The women gathered to receive the visitors at the host's home reciprocate with song and dance and welcome the visitors.[46]

According to Kinyanjui, in *Kamweretho*, women are speaking out the politics of motherhood and constructing a discourse, which is likely to shape the future of motherhood among the Kikuyu. Motherhood is presented in an institutional context with clearly defined tasks, rules, and regulations. The women seek to elevate motherhood status in society and underscore the important role of a woman not only as a mother, but also as a daughter and sister in the community. It should be noted that as early as 2002, some Kikuyu women were reported as having started paying dowry to their parents. These developments could be explained in terms of the erosion of the male economic power that accompanied globalization in Africa. Although *Kamweretho* dances have become very popular in Central Kenya, they have also aroused some criticism from the clergy, especially within the Anglican Church in Central Kenya. In addition, some men also see the *Kamweretho* organization as a strategy to undermine the husband as the head of the family in a home.

A number of factors could explain this new social development in the Kikuyu society. First, many Kikuyu women feel insecure in their marriages if the dowry is not paid, especially because they stand the risk of being disinherited in the event that their spouse dies since the husband's relatives could argue that the marriage was not sealed through payment of dowry. Secondly, women also express the fear of missing parental blessings in the event of nonpayment of dowry. Indeed, misfortunes in the family are usually attributed to denial of such blessings. Thus, gifts given during *kamweretho*, which include money, clothes, and utensils, are meant to appease the parents. Finally, Kikuyu traditional customs demand that a mother cannot receive a dowry for her daughter unless her own dowry has been paid. Kikuyu women are overcoming this hurdle by paying their own dowry so that they can be able to receive dowry for their children. By so doing, their singlehood status is recognized, qualifying them to inherit property from their parents.[47]

These new dynamics have important implications on gender relations in the Kikuyu society and require a thorough analysis. First, contrary to the Kikuyu traditions that expect men to pay dowry, women can now pay dowry as long as they feel economically stable. By implication, this means that masculinity should not be understood only in terms of biological attributes. Secondly, and even more importantly, Kikuyu women have given men a strong signal that contrary to societal expectations, marriage is just one option for women, as they can as well remain unmarried. It is noteworthy that even the

---

46. Ibid.

47. Ibid.; Amuyunzu-Nyamongo and Francis Pual, "Collapsing Livelihoods and the Crisis of Masculinities in Rural Kenya," in Bannon, Ian, and Maria Correia (eds.), *The Other Half of Gender: Men's Issues in Development* (Washington, DC: The World Bank, 2006).

elderly have also felt the impact of the rapid changes in gender relations in society. The Presbyterian Church of East Africa, for instance, raised the alarm in the 1980s on the awkward situation of a number of male elders whose spouses traveled out of the country and failed to return. Some of the women initially visited their children in the Diaspora, but remained, as they were escaping from the social and economic frustrations in the country during the globalization era.

Alternatively, many of the Kikuyu younger males responded to the new challenges that accompanied globalization by increasingly turning to the consumption of illegal cheap brews. Nyamongo and Francis observe that younger men are consuming alcohol more than the consumption level of the elderly. Given their idleness in the rural areas due to unemployment, young men increasingly spend a lot of precious time, consuming alcohol. This in turn has led to terrible consequences for families. Since the men are perpetually drunk, it is impossible for them to contribute towards family welfare such as in the area of food production. This hopelessness among men has not only frustrated, but also annoyed many women all over Central Kenya, and in urban centers such as Nairobi where consumption of alcohol is notorious. Several demonstrations have been organized by the women to protest against the brews, including a protest by a group of Kikuyu women who blocked the busy Nakuru-Nairobi highway for an hour to demand tougher laws against the businesspeople behind these brews, which have wrought untold misery to the members of the community. Many men are reported to have not only become economically unproductive, but have also been unable to fulfill their conjugal obligations to their spouses as the consumption of the illegal liquors has made them sexually inept. The *World Health Organization Global Report on Alcohol* (2004) reported several incidents of alcoholic related deaths in the slums of Nairobi by the year 2000. On November 22, 1998, six people were charged in court for brewing and distributing an illegal alcoholic brew and thereby causing the deaths of 140 people in Nairobi and the neighboring Kiambu district. During the same month, another 20 people became irreversibly blind as a result of consuming the lethal liquor, while 400 people were admitted to hospital suffering from alcohol poisoning.[48]

Another issue facing Kenyan women are militias. In Central Kenya, Nairobi, and some parts of the Rift Valley, an organization comprising mainly Kikuyu youths, the *mungiki*, has caused havoc since the 1980s. Despite having started out as a cultural organization, the *mungiki* militia has in the course of time metamorphosed into a ruthless gang, extorting money from business people with impunity, and on a number of occasions, forcefully circumcising women.[49] A number of analysts have concluded that this organization is symptomatic of a masculinity crisis in the society. With the government crackdown on such illegal militias, women have borne the pain of seeing their children and spouses lose their lives. Sadly, since 1991, many families have been displaced during every general election in Kenya, and women have consistently been the main victims of political violence as they are unable to flee and leave their children behind.

Following the disputed 2007 presidential elections in Kenya, the country experienced a bloody post-election violence, which claimed more than 1200 lives and displaced an estimated 350,000 people, mainly women and children.[50] Some of the internally displaced

48. World Health Organization, "Global Status Report on Alcohol," (Geneva: Switzerland, 2004).

49. Margaret Gecaga, "Religious Movements and Democratization in Kenya: Between the Sacred and the Profane," in Shadrack Nasong'o and Godwin Murunga (eds.), *Kenya: The Struggle for Democracy* (Dakar: CODESRIA, 2007).

50. J. Biegon, "Electoral violence and Fragility in Africa: Drawing Lessons from Kenya's Experience in the 2007/2008 Post Election Violence," A Paper presented at a Conference on Financial Markets, Adverse Shocks and Coping Strategies in Fragile Countries in Accra, Ghana, May 21 to 23, 2009.

persons are still living in intolerable conditions in Internally Displaced Persons (IDPs) camps. Many of them have suffered from various infections due to lack of proper food, shelter, and medicine. Moreover, men have often taken advantage of such conditions to coerce girls to have sex in return for food or other favors. It is important to note that at the height of the post-election crisis, a good number of Kikuyu women who had married spouses from ethnic communities that were supporting the Orange Democratic Party were either abandoned or kicked out of their homes by their in-laws.

On a brighter side, women have made many gains. In the area of land ownership, most families in Central Kenya have seen the necessity of allocating land to unmarried or divorced sisters. In addition, more girls than boys are now completing primary and secondary education in Central Kenya, and with better results. The cumulative advantage of these changes will translate into more rights for women. As women become more economically empowered through acquisition of western education and through sheer discipline and hard work, men will have no choice but to recognize that things have changed.

Conclusion

It is clear that the issue of sexual rights for women is intertwined with the socio-economic and political situation in a country. Therefore, the struggles of the Agikuyu women reflect the experiences of most women in Kenya. It is apparent that the pre-colonial societal structures among the Kenyan communities had clear safeguards against the mistreatment of women. Even polygamy was structured with a view to maintaining marital harmony, and all children were catered for economically and socially. Unfortunately, the forces of globalization began to interfere with the safeguards in society. The Christian missionaries and the colonial officials initially pioneered these changes as they sought to entrench capitalist values in Kenya. The destabilization that took place due to the alienation of land, the introduction of taxes, and the subsequent migration of males in search of wage labor contributed to the disruption of the community and undermined the sexual rights of women.

Even after political independence, women did not attain equal rights with their male counterparts. Land, the most important economic resource, especially the ancestral land, remained in the hands of men, as brothers, fathers, or spouses. Thus, whereas men could acquire financial services based on land titles, women were largely left out. In the absence of sufficient economic resources, women were edged out of the political arena by the men as illustrated by the dismal performance of women politicians in subsequent elections, in spite of the fact that many male politicians have sailed through parliamentary or civic elections due to groundwork and campaign strategies of their spouses or other women relations. Given that sexual rights intersect with other rights, including human development issues, efforts must be made to ensure decent wages and conditions for all workers.

The weakening and the economic dependence of women compromise their negotiating power to discuss the terms of their sexual relations. Ultimately, this makes them vulnerable to sexually transmitted diseases, which include HIV/AIDS. However, the new constitution promulgated by the government of Kenya on August 27, 2010 has addressed most of the constitutional shortcomings that prevented women from enjoying equal sexual rights with their male counterparts in the country. Most importantly, a number of gains have been achieved by women due to persistent advocacy and their social genius in negotiating for opportunities not only with their male counterparts, but also among themselves. Women like Wambui Otieno and Wangari Maathai have led the way by demonstrating that there cannot be true democracy unless the government recognizes the rights of women.

References

Amnesty International. "British Soldiers Training in Kenya," www.amnestyusa.org/2009. Accessed on March 15, 2009.

Amuyunzu-Nyamongo, Mary and Francis Paul. "Collapsing Livelihoods and the Crisis of Masculinities in Rural Kenya." In Bannon, Ian and Maria Correia (eds.) *The Other Half of Gender: Men's Issues in Development.* Washington, DC: The World Bank, 2006.

AWC Features. *A Journey of Courage: Kenyan Women's Experiences of the 2002 General Elections.* Nairobi. AWC Features, 2004.

Amutabi, Maurice."Intellectuals and the Democratization Process in Kenya." In Shadrack Nasong'o and Godwin Murunga (eds.) *Kenya: The Struggle for Democracy.* Dakar: CODESRIA, 2007.

Biegon, J. "Electoral violence and Fragility in Africa: Drawing Lessons from Kenya's Experience in the 2007/2008 Post Election Violence." A Paper presented to the Conference on Financial Markets, Adverse Shocks, and Coping Strategies in Fragile Countries, Accra, Ghana. May 21 to 23, 2009.

Boserup, Ester. *The Conditions of Agriculture Growth: The Economics of Agrarian Change Under Population Pressure.* Chicago: Aldine, 1965.

Boulanger, Sarah. "Women's Activism for Gender Equality in Africa." *Wagadu*, Vol.6 (2008). Elkins, Caroline. *Britain's Gulag: The Brutal End of the Empire in Kenya.* London: Jonathan Cape Ltd., 2005.

FIDA. "A Shadow Report to the 5th and 6th Combined Report of the Government of Kenya." The 39th Session of the UN Committee in New York. July 23 to August 10, 2007.

Gecaga, Margaret. "Religious Movements and Democratization in Kenya: Between the Sacred and the Profane." In Shadrack Nasong'o and Godwin Murunga (eds.) *Kenya: The Struggle for Democracy.* Dakar: CODESRIA, 2007.

Jalang'o-Ndeda. "The Impact of Male Labor Migration on Rural Women: A Case Study of Siaya District, 1894–1963." Ph.D. Thesis, Kenyatta University, year 1991.

Kagwanja, Peter. "Facing Mount Kenya or Facing Mecca: The Mungiki Ethnic Violence and Politics of the Moi Succession in Kenya, 1997 to 2002." *African Affairs: The Journal of the Royal African Society*, Vol. 102 (2003).

Kanogo, Tabitha. *Squatters: The Roots of Mau Mau.* Nairobi: James Currey, 1987.

_____. *African Womanhood in Colonial Kenya.* Oxford: James Currey, 2005.

Kenyatta Jomo. *Facing Mount Kenya: The Tribal Life of the Gikuyu.* New York: Vintage, 1965.

Kinyanjui, Mary. "Informal Enterprise is a Path to Women to Urban Dynamism in Nairobi." A Working Paper presented to the International Development Center. Open University, United Kingdom, 2008.

_____. *Kamweretho: Urban Women Speaking Out: Social Economy, Rights and Politics of Motherhood.* Institute for Development Studies, University of Nairobi, 2009.

Kiruthu, Felix. "A History of the Colonial Laborers of Nyeri Township, 1902 to 1945." Master's Thesis. Nairobi: Kenyatta University, 1997.

_____. "The History of the informal Enterprises in Kenya: A Case Study of the Artisan Sub-Sector of Nairobi, 1899–1998." Ph.D. Dissertation. Nairobi. Kenyatta University, 2007.

Kitimo, Antony. "Kenyan Family Wants Mysterious Death of Kin in Lebanon Probed." *Saturday Nation*, September 25, 2010.

Maathai, Wangari. *Unbowed: A Memoire*. New York: Anchor Books, 2007.

Mueller, Susanne. "The Political Economy of Kenya's Crisis." *Journal of East African Studies*. Vol. 2. 2 (2008): 185–210.

Munguti, K., Kabul E., Isoilo, M. and Kamaara E. "The Implications of Economic Reforms on Gender Relations: The Case of Poor Households in Kisumu Slums." In Tamboura Diawara (ed.) *Gender, Economic Integration, Governance and Methods of Contraceptives*. Dakar: AAWORD, 2002.

Nasong'o, Shadrack and Ayot Theodore. "Women in Kenya's Politics of Transition and Democratization." In Murunga Godwin and Shadrack Nasong'o (eds.) *Kenya: The Struggle for Democracy*. Dakar: CODESRIA, 2007.

Ngugi wa Thiong'o. *The River Between*. London: Heinemann, 1965.

_____. *A Grain of Wheat*. London: Heinemann, 1988.

_____. *Dreams in a Time of War: A Childhood Memoire*. New York: Pantheon Books, 2010.

Nottingham, John and Carl G. Rosberg. *The Myth of Mau Mau: Nationalism in Kenya*. Nairobi: East African Publishing House, 1966.

Robertson, Claire. *Trouble Showed the Way: Women, Men, and Trade in the Nairobi Area, 1890–1990*. Bloomington: Indiana University Press, 1997.

Ochieng, William Robert. *A History of Kenya*. Nairobi: MacMillan, 1985.

Omondi, Rose. "Gender and the Economy of Sex Tourism in Kenya's Coastal Resorts." A paper presented at the International Symposium on "Global Economic and Political Systems and Women's struggle for Global Justice." Tromso, Norway. September 24–26, 2003.

Orubuloye, Israel O., John Caldwel, Pat Caldwel, and Gigi Santow. *Sexual Networking and Aids in Sub-Saharan Africa*. Canberra: The Australian National University, 1994.

Stamp, Patricia. "Burying Otieno: The Politics of Gender and Ethnicity in Kenya." *The Journal of Women, Culture, and Society*. Vol. 16. 4 (1991).

Visram, Anar. "Gender Politics and the State: A Study of Kenya and Zimbabwe." Master's Thesis. Department of Political Science, Simon Fraser University, 1988.

Wamai, Njoki. "Women and Poverty (Land Rights Ownership)." A policy brief on the Kenyan Situation prepared for the African Women Rights Observatory, 2008.

Wane, Njoki. "Sexual Violence and HIV aids Risks in Kenyan and Ugandan schools: Implications for Educational Policy Development." *Journal of Contemporary Issues in Education*. Vol. 4. 1 (2009): 71–91.

Wangari, E. W. Kamau, and A.M. Kinyua. "Globalization and Its Impact on Women in the Third World." *Gender Discrimination: A Global Perspective Forum on Public Policy 290*. Vol. 1. 3 (2005).

World Health Organization. "Global Status Report on Alcohol." Geneva: Switzerland, 2004.

Part II

Homosexuality and Identity Politics

Chapter 8

Decolonizing Homosexuality in Uganda as a Human Rights Process

Caroline Tushabe

In the last few decades in the U.S. and Western Europe, the closet paradigm has influenced and oriented much of queer theory and lesbian, gay, bisexual, transgender, intersex, and queer (lgbtiq) studies. Eve K. Sedgwick's work on epistemology of the closet has influenced how we think about the social hierarchical system of the oppressive heterosexual majority system and the subordinate homosexual minority. Sedgwick exposes the complexities of self-knowledge and experiences of the homosexual minority marked by the closet in the sexual hierarchy, at least in the U.S. and Western Europe.[1] The hierarchy is maintained through oppressive practices that gain legitimacy through state policies that enforce silence or the closet. Meanwhile, the closet framework has proliferated beyond both geographical and intellectual Euro-American boundaries, intensifying theoretical and activist work in mapping homosexuality across cultures.

The closet paradigm has fostered the notion that all non-sex-crossing (non heterosexual) sexual experience that does not have Constitutional visibility or whose reading does not spell public visibility is marked by the closet. The closet, theorized as an act of power-knowledge relations, investigates the public privileges enjoyed by heterosexualities and the confining nature inherent in the invisible space relegated to non sex-crossing sexualities. According to Steven Seidman, the condition of the closet and the culture of "kicking its door open," are trapped within the colonial heteronormative culture. Seidman defines this culture as one that thrives on "repression and pollution" because it fosters "the idea that heterosexual and homosexual are antithetical" and indigenous non-sex-crossing desires are antithetical to homosexuality.[2] Given this sense, the fight for sexual freedom for indigenous/colonized people, particularly in Uganda, and Africa as a whole, necessitates that we rethink the closet paradigm and homosexual identity and that we engage practices of decolonization.

Homosexuality in Western hegemonic discourses represents a progressive system of sexuality, one that is impossible in colonized communities since their European colonizers understood them as only capable of unthinking beast-like sexual behavior. According to Murray and Roscoe, homosexuality as a marker of civilized cultures became a model for unsophisticated systems of sexuality in colonized cultures marked primitive by colonial ideology.[3] In the politics of sexual freedom, the closet paradigm follows the logic of

---

1. Sedgwick asserts that the closet is symptomatic of ways in which a society organizes identities and lives, and this organization is ahistorical and incomplete.
2. Steven Seidman, "From Identity to Queer Politics: Shifts in Normative Heterosexuality and the Meaning of Citizenship," *Citizenship Studies* 5 (2001): 321.
3. In their preface, "All Very Confusing" to their edited volume, *Boy Wives and Female Husbands: Studies in African Homosexualities,* xi, Stephen O. Murray and Will Roscoe elaborate the colonial construction of homosexuality in Africa, whereby European colonialists undertook the categorization of differences between them and those that they invaded and colonized. Africans were categorized as

progressive sexuality that was initially introduced through colonial control and erasures of those cultures marked as primitive. The logic of progressive sexuality distinguishes primitive from progressive, simple from sophisticated, and pre-modern from modern sexualities. This categorization divides bodies into identities and spaces as though space is always purified and homogenized. Indeed, according to Murray and Roscoe, African indigenous non sex-crossing sexualities were not to mix and contaminate modern homosexuality, a progressive and sophisticated order whose consciousness is made legitimate by the closet.

In his article, "Beyond the Closet as Raceless," Marlon Ross notes that the closet paradigm in the U.S. functions as an essential vehicle for narrating homosexuality as a necessary progress from dark secrecy to open consciousness.[4] Ross complicates homosexual identities arguing that the closet paradigm is inherently flawed when it emphasizes the difference between "dark secrecy" and "open consciousness" by disregarding bodies that are marked by race and always closeted. Drawing from scholars in Great Britain, Ross notes that Weeks takes the closet as "an essential step in the evolution of modern homosexual consciousness" because it not only challenged the binary between heterosexual and homosexual, but it also proved itself to be as modern as hetero sexuality in the Euro-American system of sexuality.[5] The practice of coming out of the closet is therefore central to sexual politics of homosexual lifestyle and homosexual identities of gay and lesbian. In other words, the closet is a definitive articulation of modern and progressive homosexuality.

A short yet complicated question from Ross's argument asks, how do black bodies appeal to the closet? Those of us who embody "unsophisticated" pre-modern indigenous non sex-crossing sexualities are, according to the hegemonic discourse of progressive homosexuality, an unknown entity to politics of sexual freedom. In the proliferation of the closet paradigm beyond geographical and epistemological boundaries of Western Europe and the U.S., we are weighed down by the dilemma of how the colonial ideology functions in our appeal to the closet. For us, 'coming out as lesbian or gay' requires collaboration with colonial ideologies by viewing our cultures, bodies, sexualities, and spaces as primitive and without political agency. We are impelled to adapt to modern sexual identities and the politics of the closet that "purify" our cultures, bodies, sexualities, and spaces of their primitiveness. This shift adorns modern sexual identities as the only ones that provide legitimate self-knowledge and enables legitimate exposure of sexual oppression. Although modern sexual identities establish themselves as the basis for political power, they fail to challenge colonial sexual oppression against colonized people by building on the colonial hierarchies of sexualities. The colonial hierarchical categorization of unsophisticated and sophisticated systems of sexuality necessitates collective identities that are easily confinable for a people to access or be denied legal protection and state recognition.

'primitive' and 'savages' who could not have afforded a hierarchical system of sexuality that divides heterosexuality from homosexuality. In the colonizers' sense the African savages had to be closer to nature and therefore heterosexual, and their "sexual energies and outlets devoted exclusively to their natural purpose: biological reproduction" (xi). The absence of normalized and purified demarcations between hetero and homo sexualities, the ambiguous notion of whether sexuality is an identity, and the absence of codes marking homosexuality as an aberrant disqualified African systems of sexuality from progressive sexuality.

4. Marlon Ross, "Beyond the Closet as Raceless Paradigm," in E. Patrick Johnson and Mae G. Henderson, (eds.) *Black Queer Studies: A Critical Anthology* (Durham, NC: Duke University Press, 2005), 162.

5. 5 Ibid., 164.

Narratives of the closet in the U.S. and Western Europe helped construct a public identity that exposes the location, the closed-up-ness and alienation of homosexual bodies and their experiences from public space by the oppressive heterosexual identity and system. This, in many ways, compelled language that affords some space to homosexuals in public streets. However, as identity categories tend to homogenize collective activity, sexual identity politics proved to undermine the complexities of race and failed to engage race theory.[6] Similarly, the politics of sexual freedom in Africa generally follow identity-based politics and theorize the closet as an avenue for political force. While sexual freedom is what all peoples of the world who live under repressive regimes desire, the closet paradigm does not provide the strategies that different contexts require. In Uganda, for example, the closet paradigm fails to engage critically the logics of colonialism and to explore alternative possibilities for agency amongst indigenous non-sex-crossing experiences. I do not argue, however, that the cultural production of sexual identities and cultural representation in Uganda are reducible to or subsumed under lgbtiq identity politics in the U.S. or Western Europe. Rather, I am interested more broadly in how the decolonization of the closet produces subjects that challenge colonial and imperial globalization in both the practicability of politics of sexual freedom and Constitutional protections. Spurlin observes that when we privilege collective identities in theorizing and movement activity across borders, we have to acknowledge that we are vulnerable to reinventing colonial and imperialist practices in favor of political utility while failing to decolonize cultural and epistemological oppressions.

The rush to theorize dissident sexualities in transnational terms and to account for the emergence of new social formations of same-sex desires, though important, may potentially risk obscuring or overriding the histories and cultural specifications of lived experience and material existence in local contexts and how these might impinge on Western understandings of sexual difference.[7] Centering local knowledge without dislodging the transnational is crucial because borders are not simply geographic but rather are epistemic, such that articulations of sexual freedom in the local where epistemology of the closet emerges may be damaging to the epistemic articulations in the local where it is reinvented.

Contextualizing the Local

Not all scholars who have mapped homosexuality, particularly in Uganda and Africa in general, use the term "closet." Nonetheless, the closet is assumed in lgbtiq theoretical framework and political activism. For instance, Tamale has deployed the concept of the closet, while Wairinga and Saskia, among others, have used notions of coming out and silence. What is agreeable to all of these scholars regarding homosexuality in Africa is that Africans deny homosexuality and are silent about it. Accordingly, the closet in Uganda is not marked so much by the sense of hiding one's homosexuality, but rather of denying that homosexuality exists both by those marked primitive (Africans) and homosexuals (non-sex-crossing postcolonial beings who are more advanced than pre-modern beings, but are not as modern as those in Western Europe and the U.S.). In some African states, including South Africa, where the transition from apartheid to democracy has fostered

---

6. 6 For extended discussion see also Audre Laurde (1984); Roderick A. Ferguson (2004); and Marlon Ross (2005).

7. 7 William J. Spurlin, *Imperialism Within the Margins: Queer Representation and the Politics of Culture in South Africa* (New York: Palgrave Macmillan, 2006), 18.

Constitutional inclusion of sexual orientation, Uganda, Zimbabwe, Kenya, and Nigeria, state figures have strongly claimed that homosexuality is un-African and an import of the West. While this sense of 'denial' is based on the desire for Africans to dissociate themselves from colonial identifications of primitivism, I argue that the denial becomes a textual production because local knowledge and indigenous non sex-crossing desires have been denied agency since colonization.

A typical example of such textual production of denial appears in Bleys' reference to the kings of Buganda (Uganda) and Dahomey (southern Benin) during early stages of colonialism. Bleys' intention is to expose the denial and silencing of homosexuality, yet the implicit information is more telling of different possibilities than of denial and silence:

> Alarmed by the well known images [of homosexuality] of the Dahomey of West-Africa, British missionaries thus felt compelled to sanction Mwanga, the leader of the Baganda (Uganda), from 1884 till 1897. He maintained a 'herem' full of pageboys and resisted Christianization as it became clear that anal intercourse had to be renounced. As gradually more and more boys, who had converted to either Protestantism or Catholicism, refused sexual services to Mwanga and his entourage, a conflict arose. When his favorite pageboy Mwafu resisted as well, Mwanga went into paroxysm of rage and several boys were killed. It is said that about one hundred boys, later turned into the Martyrs of Uganda.[8]

Mwanga the epitome of colonial homosexuality is not the Mwanga that desired other men who work in his court. Rather, it is the Christian-resistant Mwanga, on whom, by law, a new identity (from a Euro-cultural understanding of non sex-crossing desire) is imposed. By resisting Christianity, Mwanga simultaneously resisted the identity homosexual and the link between homosexuality and aberration. Mwanga's gesture here is significant, not because he resisted Christianity but because he refused to deny knowing the person he already knows—the Mwanga who desires and shares erotic energy with other men. Mwanga bears the impetus of colonial misidentification as a homosexual due to his rebellious act against Christianity that could only be further constrained by the inherited colonial penal code that prohibits homosexuality in the Constitution of postcolonial Uganda. The Mwanga narrative reiterates the construction of Uganda as a colonially nationalist identity that is forced to privilege masculinist heterosexuality and represses non sex-crossing desires.

In scholarly analyses, Mwanga's desire as a site of resistance against colonialism is barely explored but used to mark and map homosexuality and homosexual identity in Uganda. As such, Mwanga's narrative has always been analyzed in relation to political power and nationalism, masking the colonial repressive and oppressive apparatus at work, and confusing both as liberation and progressive undertakings, while totally ignoring the cultural imperialism within which homosexuality was constructed and forced onto Africans. While non sex-crossing or same-sex desire may be universal across cultures, the ways in which this desire is known, expressed, identified, and experienced, as well as its meaning, are all cultural specific. The debate does damage and erases non-sex-crossing sexualities in Uganda and Africa as a whole when it follows the logic of abrasive colonial cultural control and Christian morality to conflate sexual actions with sexual identity as self-identity. This self does not only become morally deficient but also insignificant and disposable.

For that matter, Mwanga's narrative loses its significance in adequately locating the political and historical agency of decolonization that non-sex-crossing intimacies in

---

8. 8 Rudi C. Bleys, *The Geography of Perversion: Male to Male Sexual Behavior Outside the West and the Ethnographic Imagination, 1750–1918* (New York: New York University Press, 1995), 172.

Uganda can envisage because homosexuality is always presented as identity and privileged in legal rights and Constitutional provisions. Privileging homosexual identity overshadows the meaning and the significance of non-sex-crossing desires in Uganda that have no knowledge of homosexual identity and may not be dependent on gender relations. Here, I am thinking of such understanding as stipulated in the nineteenth century constructions of gender and sexuality in Europe and in Africa under direct colonial rule. There has never been, in the same accounts of Mwanga's sexuality, any acknowledgement of the difference between Baganda's and British Empires' attitude toward non-sex-crossing sexualities. The privileged narratives of Mwanga rely solely on his political disempowerment by Christianity and colonialism, portraying Mwanga as a power hungry ruler who used sex as a weapon of control of the young men.[9] Textual analyses and political rhetoric do not acknowledge that sexual intimacy between people of same sex was not culturally criminalized prior to European control and that Mwanga was not closeted.

Meanwhile the British introduction of homosexuality as a sexual identity criminalized non sex-crossing sexual intimacies, declaring them aberrant. It is through this act of criminalization that the closet is imagined. As Ross elaborates,

> the coming out of closet paradigm has been such a compelling way of fixing homosexual identification exactly because it enables this powerful narrative of progress, not only in terms of the psychosexual development of an individual and the sociopolitical birth and growth of a legitimate sexual minority group, but also more fundamentally is a doorway marking the threshold between up-to-date fashions of sexuality and all the outmoded, anachronistic others.[10]

The colonial penal code that criminalizes Mwanga and others in Uganda dismembers one's being, outmodes non-sex-crossing desires in colonized cultures, and renders such desires out of existence and with *no legitimate language*. The stipulation that the nineteenth-century discursive invention of sexual identities by the sciences of sexology, psychoanalysis, and criminology is representative of all non hetero sexual beings and desires founds the denial of indigenous languages a chance at decolonization and articulation of their non sex-crossing knowledges, legally and socially. Their knowledge and histories continue to be lodged within the language and meanings of the closet paradigm and the notions of silence and denial.

Although the closet is a metaphor for a space in which something is hidden and in which structures of colonial power and domination oppress others, the closet does not necessarily open avenues to ask questions that address non-sex-crossing desires cross-culturally, especially those that challenge Euro-American empires and the dichotomous knowledges of homosexuality and heterosexuality. Sustaining the dichotomy as Ross explains privileges the closet as the "principle for sexual experience, knowledge, and politics [which] effectively diminishes and disables the full engagement with potential insights from race theory" and other cultures.[11] The closet paradigm, thus, erases other possibilities of being where gender exists as a colonial imposition in which homo/hetero, unsophisticated/sophisticated, and pre-modern/modern dichotomy is intelligible. Confronting this dichotomy is the work and practice of decolonization, which seeks to redress colonial and global erasures of indigenous knowledge of multiple possibilities. For colonized peoples who center decolonization, the closet paradigm does little to dismantle the colonial structure of homosexuality but seeks to save the person who

---

9. 9 For a detailed discussion, see Hoad (2007).
10. 10 Ross, 162.
11. 11 Ibid., 163

embodies the colonial structure of homosexuality. The closet paradoxically re-identifies both the pre-modern and postcolonial persons out of existence because they only exist either outside the closet or by acknowledging what one becomes as a result of the closet experience. Those who exist outside the closet are not politically visible; they lose their voice and their lives because the closet forecloses all possibilities for them unlike the post-colonial homosexual who exists by proxy to modern homosexuality as might be claimed in the Mwanga phenomenon.

Available analyses of Mwanga's phenomenon seek to create a sort of evolutionary logic that is particular to colonial construction of who is human and who is not: civilized and uncivilized, primitive and progressive, simple and sophisticated. Although the closet paradigm falls short of engaging possibilities viable for those marked outside modern sexuality, adopting the closet paradigm in Uganda makes the homosexual body epitomized by Mwanga phenomenon an archival embodiment of success of colonial project and imperialist notions of liberation. While erased by the logic of modern sexuality articulated in the penal code prohibiting homosexuality, the postcolonial Ugandan homosexual is made visible through colonial constructions of homosexuality and global sexual identities of lgbiq by proxy to modern homosexuality.

Making Claim and Making Relation to Global Sexual Identities

I would like to proceed here with a myth of *ebihindi* that my grandmother told me when I was growing up as a way to explore the sense of making claim and making relation to global sexual identities. *Ebihindi* are people who transition from one form of being to another. In the village I was raised there was a tree called *omusisa* by the *akayanja* or swamp. The myth explains that at night *ebihindi* would gather under the *omusisa* and make fire, dance, and change from female to male, to half female and half male, and to one whole of four parts consisting of one fourth of each. At dawn, *ebihindi* reverse their being and reintegrate themselves into community. The ethic of the myth is that there exist different possibilities of being and that we ought to respect the existence of this difference. There is also a notion that people *know* and this *knowing* requires no finger pointing or public discussion.

The myth does not closet *ebihindi* nor does it seek visibility in the contemporary politics of sexuality that appeals to the closet. The myth affords existence and respect for difference, community integration, and positions within community knowledge of and space for *ebihindi*. Upon hearing this myth, I found 'solid' home within community. The myth afforded me a place of belonging, a space for self-knowledge and meaning of my existence in community because my desires and differences were articulated in my culture's cosmology. Similarly, it makes sense when lesbians in Europe and the U.S. trace their sense of self as lesbians back to Sappho of the Island of Lesbos. However, when they claim that history, what becomes of mine within the politics of global sexual identities? In what ways can politics of sexual freedom *de-colonize* the colonial constructions of homosexuality and erasures of indigenous non-sex-crossing experience so that I can reclaim a transformative and new sense of self?

Because of our colonial positioning as indigenous non-sex-crossing colonized people of Uganda, we are casualties of time, entangled within the difference between making claim and making relation to global sexual identities of lgbtiq. Making claim that we *are* homosexuals, lesbians, gays, or queers by association via such colonial constructions of sexuality and gender, and making relation to identities that are genealogically intelligible within specific histories and cultures, renders us *only* a people of colonial imagination. Our claim does not make those histories our histories nor does it offer the same avenues, as in those histories and cultures, to achieve sexual freedom. As it turns out in both cases of making claim and making relation to global sexual identities, colonized peoples of Uganda whose sexual desires do not cross sex actually do not become the subject of the politics of sexual freedom, Constitutionally and theoretically. The language that addresses the oppression of non-heterosexual beings focuses only on the product of colonial constructed homosexual. This person must deny self in order to be addressed by the colonial language and meanings of homosexuality.

Moreover, those whose genealogy of homosexuality is intelligible within their histories and cultures can make claim to the human rights provisions without troubling the framework. That being the case, making claim and making relation to global sexual identities without troubling the human rights framework further alienates non sex-crossing bodies from claims of human rights. Otherwise, Ugandans would have to do two things: 1) to affix ourselves to this genealogy of global sexual identities and continue in the practices of self-erasure; and 2) continue to be obedient to the colonial creation of who is human through the dismemberment of self by sexual identities that sustain the systemic oppressive apparatus that pervades communities with histories of colonialism.

Repositioning Human Rights Framework

Though it has evolved and progressed over the years to include the once excluded issues of colonized peoples, women, and sexual minorities, the human rights discourse is still trapped in practices of formalization that do not go far enough to exploit the power and knowledge of local and indigenous subjects. These local and indigenous subjects are the victims of human rights abuses born of capitalism, colonial legacies, and imperial globalization.[12] Human rights protections are still monitored within the existing categories that are fundamental to the logics of hierarchies of civilized and uncivilized, sophisticated and unsophisticated, and progressive and primitive systems of race, sexual, and gender oppression.

Universal discourses of freedom and principles of human rights must be contextualized within local knowledge in respect to the relationship indigenous people have not only to land, but also to language. As Walter Mignolo explains, "languages are not something human beings *have* but they are part of what human beings *are*. Languages are embedded in the body and memories (geo-historically located) of each person" (emphasis original).[13] The origins of identities like 'lesbian' and 'gay' or even 'queer' cannot possibly articulate the sexual subjectivities and erotic play enacted in indigenous languages such as Rukiga speaking community that integrates *ebihindi* in cosmologies of a people without self erasure. Our histories of colonialism cannot be denied. As such, I advocate processes of decolonization with a locally contextualized approach to human rights by integrating local and global knowledge that affirm the dignity and liberation of colonized peoples.

---

12. 12 Sonia Corrêa, Rosalind P. Petchesky, and Richard Parker, *Sexuality, Health and Human Rights* (New York: Routledge, 2008), 162.

13. 13 Walter D. Mignolo and Madina V. Tlostanova, "Theorizing from the Borders: Shifting to Goe- and Body-Politics of Knowledge." *European Journal of Social Theory* 9 (2006): 207.

Because of our particular contexts there is need for a different kind openness — a decolonial strategy — to our particular subjectivities that is fundamental to unravel the challenging and epistemic questions that emerge from particular peoples, places, and time. That way, for example, we arrive at different epistemic shifts when we seek to know how Mwanga was told not to love the men he found himself loving; why he was told not to love the people he was supposed to love. It is not only that Mwanga enjoyed sexual intimacy with other men, but rather other things happened: the police and criminalization, punishment and the prison system, stigma and condemnation, aberration and sin, and the divide between human and non-human (in the colonial sense of white and black people categorization), moral and immoral, all in relation to the state and sexuality.

Human rights are necessary but inadequate without confronting beliefs and practices of racialism, and political investment in de-centering both the heterosexual as *the only human* and progressive sexuality in the case of homo and hetero hierarchies. This de-centering is important in dislodging the Euro-American empires as they rely on racial and gender processes of dehumanization. In this racialized and gendered framework, the construction of homosexual and heterosexual identity for colonized people remains tied to the subjection of self. The self-identity that colonial constructions of homosexuality imposed on us, supposedly, as a means to our self-knowledge, impedes our self-knowledge as it forecloses processes and avenues for a politic of decolonization. Only a human rights discourse that is invested in de-colonial practices could help change the way we think and see others.

References

Bleys, Rudi C. *The Geography of Perversion: Male to Male Sexual Behavior Outside the West and the Ethnographic Imagination, 1750–1918.* New York: New York University Press, 1995.

Corrêa, Sonia, Rosalind P. and Richard Parker. *Sexuality, Health and Human Rights.* New York: Routledge, 2008.

Hoad, Neville. *African Intimacies: Race, Homosexuality, and Globalization.* Minneapolis: University of Minnesota, 1997.

Murray, Stephen O. and Will Roscoe, (eds.) *Boy-Wives and Female Husbands: Studies of African Homosexualities.* New York: Palgrave, 1998.

Ross, Marlon. "Beyond the Closet as Raceless Paradigm." In E. Patrick Johnson and Mae G. Henderson, (eds.) *Black Queer Studies: A Critical Anthology.* Durham: Duke University Press, 2005, 161–89.

Sedgwick, Eve K. *Epistemology of the Closet.* Berkeley: University of California Press, 1990.

Seidman, Steven. "From Identity to Queer Politics: Shifts in Normative Heterosexuality and the Meaning of Citizenship." *Citizenship Studies* 5 (2001): 321–28.

Spurlin, William J. *Imperialism Within the Margins: Queer Representation and the Politics of Culture in Southern Africa.* New York: Palgrave Macmillan, 2006.

Mignolo, Walter D. and Tlostanova V. Madina. "Theorizing from the Borders: Shifting to Geo- and Body-Politics of Knowledge." *European Journal of Social Theory* 9 (2006): 205–221.

Chapter 9

The Reality of Homosexuality in Africa: The Yoruba Example

Ebunoluwa O. Oduwole

Homosexuality has been a source of moral concern to philosophers, feminists, the church, and the family. In many societies, people condemn homosexual acts as immoral, and, hence, subject those deemed homosexual to social discrimination, verbal abuse, harassment, and assault in society. Some countries even have laws prohibiting homosexuality. This chapter focuses on homosexuality in Africa using the Yoruba as a case study. The Yoruba are a group of people from the southwestern part of Nigeria in West Africa. Besides being found in Nigeria, the Yoruba can also be found in diasporic places such as Cuba, Brazil, Haiti, and in the Republic of Benin. They are a people that are bound together with a strong sense of culture. They have a unique language and set of religious and philosophical beliefs. The Yoruba culture is rich in ideas, beliefs, and thoughts and they express their worldview in proverbs, folktales, aphorisms, folklores, idioms, and practical beliefs. We shall be making some claims on the Yoruba view on to the issue of homosexuality from an x-ray of the African culture through proverbs, folkloric sayings, day-to-day sayings, and the Ifa literary corpus.

The Ifa literary corpus, upon which this chapter shall draw its arguments on homosexuality, is one of the richest sources of Yoruba beliefs, ideas, and thought. The Ifa corpus pre-dates Western civilization. According to Abimbola, Ifa as a body of knowledge and academic discipline has been preserved and disseminated with such care as to ensure that the essential ingredients of the system are transmitted without much corruption.[1] Ifa is not only a repository of knowledge but also an academic discipline. Through Ifa, we can establish many ideas about the belief system of the Yoruba, and thus, we will draw some philosophical arguments about the view of the Yoruba from it. Our position in this chapter is that although homosexuality is neither unheard of nor inconceivable in traditional Yoruba culture, it is a taboo because it runs contrary to the cultural notions, ideas, beliefs, and worldview. Homosexuality is discouraged because it is contrary to the Yoruba family concept, and from that perspective, it is generally frowned upon. It is also seen as morally unjustifiable, for which we will examine the grounds for this position.

Homosexuality in Africa

This chapter considers two major issues on the question of homosexuality; first, is its existence and second, its morality. We need to prove its existence in Africa, particularly

---

1. Wande Abimbola, "Ifa as a Body of Knowledge and as an Academic Discipline," *Journal of Cultures and Ideas*, Vol. 1. 1 (1983), 1.

among the Yoruba, before we discuss whether it is morally justifiable or not. There are two opposing views on the existence of homosexuality in African culture. One view argues that homosexuality did not exist in African societies, and indeed, was unheard of in many African cultures prior to Africa's contact with European colonial rulers. A May 2007 Immigration and Refugee Board of Canada information response stated that homosexuality is considered "taboo" in Nigeria; very few people are openly gay. Homosexuals are generally treated as outcasts by society and are often disowned by their own families. It further states that homosexuality is unacceptable both in the Christian-dominated south and the Muslim-dominated north.[2] The most recent United Kingdom Home Office Operational Guidance Note for assessing asylum claims from Nigeria states that the country's sodomy laws "also contribute to the climate of intolerance towards gay men and young men who discover that they are gay tend to hide the fact as they fear being ostracized or thrown out of the family home if their homosexuality became known."[3]

The opposing views are ready to deny the above claims that homosexuality is alien to African traditional culture and that it is the result of the corrupt influence from Western colonization. Leo Igwe, a humanist, shares this opposing view. In his discussion of homosexuality, he claims that homosexuals have always existed in Africa.[4] In his opinion, gay sex is as old as Africans in Africa are, and predates the contact with Arab and Western cultures. However, as in other cultures, gays in Africa have until recently been in the "closet," expressing their sexual emotions and orientation in private. Heterosexuality is the norm. Due to high infant mortality rates, many African societies place great emphasis on procreation, childbearing, and reproductive sex, but have been accommodative of people with other sexual preferences and proclivities. Homosexuals in Africa may also practice heterosexual relationships to bear children and to live "normal lives." That is why some say there are no gays in Africa.

Igwe further claims that the Igbo in Nigeria recognize and practice same-sex marriages among women for procreative purposes. He agrees that traditionally a homosexual relationship does not enjoy equal status and recognition as a heterosexual relationship, which is considered to have procreative (and reproductive) value. However, he argues that what is actually un-African is not homosexuality or same-sex marriages, but homophobia—the fear, hatred, persecution, and liquidation of gays and lesbians. What is actually imported to Africa from other cultures is the idea that gay persons should be hunted down, incarcerated, or killed.

Rather than colonization influencing the African reaction to homosexuality, Igwe is of the view that colonialism has caused the intolerance to homosexuality in Africa. To him, the persecution of homosexuals in contemporary Africa has some roots in the continent's colonial experience. In his defence, he states that for centuries Arab and Western imperialists scrambled, partitioned, and colonized most parts of Africa. Western imperialists forced on these colonies their social, cultural, and political ideologies. Unfortunately, at independence most African countries blindly adopted the laws and constitutions of their erstwhile colonizers. The law prohibiting homosexuality is one of such laws. For instance, the former British colonies—Nigeria, Kenya, Uganda, and Ghana—adopted the British common law, which until the 1960s prohibited homosexuality;

---

2. A May 2007 Immigration and Refugee Board of Canada (IRB) Information Response," *www.mrtrrt.gov.au/articledocument* (Accessed February 4, 2008).

3. UK Home Office, Operational Guidance Note: Nigeria, November 26, 2007, Section 3.13.5-Attachment.

4. 1 L. Igwe, "Humanism and Homosexuality," http://www.iheu.org (Accessed on February 4, 2008).

while the Islamic majority states adopted the shari'a law—introduced to Africa by Islamic missonaries—which sanctions death for gay sex. Therefore, homosexuality is a crime in most African countries due to colonial legislation that African governments have refused to review.[5]

Christian and Islamic Homophobia

What prevailed in Africa was not necessarily religion-based homophobia because, before the advent of Christianity and Islam, Africans had practiced traditional religion, which was in agreement with their tolerant and secretive attitude to sex. What we have today in Africa is a Christian and Islamic-based homophobia fuelled and fostered by the primitive and anachronistic teachings in the Bible and the Koran. For centuries, foreign missionaries invaded Africa and forced the people to abandon their religion, culture, and tradition, and embrace the outdated doctrines and dogmas of these homophobic faiths that now dominate the continent. Thus, today, Africa is a homophobic society thanks mainly to Christianity and Islam. In Nigeria, Uganda, Egypt, and Algeria, Christian and Islamic groups oppose attempts to decriminalize homosexuality and legalize gay marriage, citing the provisions in the Bible and the Koran.[6]

Igwe's point of view is, with all intent and purpose, carefully stated. However, his claim cannot be a priori asserted. He did not justify his claims and assertions. A careful look at oral traditions would have given an insight into the views of the Igbo, which is his reference point. Mezu, in his reaction to Igwe's claim, argues that there is nothing like same gender marriage in Igboland.16 He considers Igwe's assertions as a figment of his imagination not based on history, anthropology, sociology, or even mythology. The next section hopes to meet with Igwe's inadequacies; thus, providing enough grounds for making philosophical assumptions.

Homosexuality and Yoruba Culture

Otura Goriirete is an Odu Ifa excerpt that gives a vivid account of homosexuality. The Odu says:

Okunrin meji sun botonrigin botonrigin

Okunrin meji sun botonrigin botonrigin

Obinrin meji sun botonrigin botonrigin

Ka lo mu okunrin kan

Ka lo mu obinrin kan

O di libilibi

A dia fun Erifobogbile

Babalawo ori difa fun ori

Ori n lo mule ibudo

---

5. Ibid.
6. Ibid.

Won ni ki ori rubo

Ma sowo ma jere

Ori je n bi egbewa lomo

Ma sowo ma jere

Two men are copulating

Two men are copulating

Two women are copulating

Two women are mating

Why don't we take a man?

And then take a woman

Therein lies enjoyment and fulfillment

Divination was made for Erifobogbile

The (Primordial) Head's diviner divined for it too

When head was to site a domicile

Head was told to offer a sacrifice

May I trade and make profits

My (Primordial) head, may I have two thousand children

May I trade and make profits.[7]

Erifobogbile literally means, "River uses her vagina to acquire land." This Odu (Ifa verse) means that a spiritual quest was made for Erifobogbile when she wanted to site a dwelling place. She was told that for her troubles to be profitable, she needed to mate with a male (rather than a female like herself). This is to enable her to have offspring to fill the land she wanted to acquire for domiciliary. Let us also consider these folkloric sayings:

Oju re pon kankan bi oju adofuro

His eyes are red like the eyes of one who has sex through the anus.

And this proverb:

A ri kan se kan lo mu obinrin gbe omu egbe re jo

It is idleness that causes a woman to fondle her mate's breast.[8]

Some Philosophical Implications and Arguments for Procreation

From the above Ifa verse, folk saying, and proverb we can deduce some points and arguments on homosexuality. It is clear that the concept is not inconceivable; however, not

---

7. S. Mezu, "There is No Tradition of Same Gender Marriage in Igboland," www.scribd.com (Accessed on February 4, 2008).

8. This Odu Ifa verse was given in the course of research by a renowned Ifa priest: Chief Ayo Agbato in Ogere Remo, Ogun State of Nigeria.

all inconceivable thoughts are beneficial. The first argument that comes out of these is what can be labeled as the argument from procreation. That is, sexual organs are for procreation; anything short of this is not appreciated nor is it a useful exercise, but rather an exercise in futility. This amounts to an unnatural misuse. If our sexual organs have the function of procreation, then the only natural use is for procreation. The pleasure of heterosexuality is even better appreciated if it leads to procreation. Following this view, the argument that comes out is that it will be both unnatural and immoral to use an organ for what it is not meant for or for what is not its primary function.

The second argument that may be deduced is that homosexuality threatens the family. The Yoruba hold the family in high esteem. Family values are not only preserved but also guarded jealously because it is where the society is preserved and life made bearable for all. The family unit is made up of a father, mother, and children who do not necessarily need to be biological children. The communal life of the Yoruba supports this very strongly. Against this background, there is no way a family can be formed without two sexes coming together. The coming together of two sexes from two different backgrounds not only forms the basis of marriage but also procreation.

For Yoruba peoples, marriage is the focus of existence, the point where all the members of a given community meet: those who are living, their ancestors, and generations yet born. History is often repeated, reviewed, and revitalized during marriage. It is a performance in which two families, villages, or towns come together in a union. Everyone becomes an actor or actress and not just a spectator.[9] Marriage is thus considered a duty, a requirement from the corporate society, and a rhythm of life in which everyone must participate. Failure to get married means one is sub-human, or has rejected society, and society rejects him in return. If one does not marry, he is seen as a rebel, an irresponsible person, a lawbreaker, abnormal and, perhaps, not even a human being. It may also be assumed that such a person is an impotent.

Therefore, marriage and procreation are intricately intertwined in many African societies. The two form a unity that cannot be separated. Without children, a marriage is not complete. To choose to marry and not give birth to children is almost alien to Yoruba thought. Procreation serves the purpose of first reproducing the husband and wife biologically. Secondly, within the idea of reincarnation, the spiritual reproduction of grandparents and great grandparents is also established. Thirdly, it is seen as a means of perpetuating the chain of the family, clan, or society at large: just as person who has no descendants quenches the fire of reincarnation in terms of physical and spiritual personalities, so does the community, family, or clan lose its descendants when marriages do not produce children. This points to lack of fruitfulness and posterity.

The Yoruba also consider that marriage without procreation means the cutting of contact with the living-dead or ancestors. This is because there will be no one to either remember or pour libation on such ancestors. There will be no one to carry on the values of the family. By implication, it is possible to say that the name of such family or families will go into extinction. These are the reasons why in Yoruba society everyone strives to get married and bear children. To then think of getting married to the same sex, a union that cannot produce children, means not only running the family into extinction, but it is also an aberration, a misnomer, and an exercise contrary to Yoruba cultural norms. It is considered a sub-human act and an action that is shameful, can be cursed, and is not to be tolerated. It is no wonder the Yoruba consider it a taboo.

---

9. John Mbiti, *African Religions and Philosophy* (London: Heinemann, 1982), 133.

It is possible to argue that culture is dynamic; it is subject to change. For example, homosexual couples could adopt children if the essence of their marriage is for procreation and to maintain a family. For the Yoruba, this argument is irrelevant because child adoption is equally a cultural aberration. The institution of a family that includes extended family makes adoption unnecessary. The nuclear family is made up of the father, mother, and biological children, whereas the Yoruba setup of the family is much wider. It includes the father, mother, biological children, grandparents, uncles, aunts, and their children, brothers and sisters who have their own children, and other immediate relatives.

These large family units are so close to each other that a barren couple need not adopt children formally from outside the home. The children of aunties and uncles, brothers and sisters are enough to fulfill the idea of motherhood or fatherhood that a woman or man may be facing or expected to face. It is even common practice for children to be sent to live with relatives and such children are counted as members of such families where they happen to live. However, the foundation of a respected family is the father and mother. Even where the father or mother is dead or unreliable there will always be a reliable father figure or mother figure. That is why the Yoruba says:

Baba ku baba ku

The biological father has died but there is still a father.

Immanuel Kant's deontologism comes in handy here. It lends credence to the Yoruba view and supports the immorality of homosexuality from the Yoruba point of view. Homosexuality as a maxim cannot be universalized. Kant says that there is therefore but one categorical imperative, namely, "Act only on that maxim whereby thou canst at the same time will that it should become a universal law."[10] Apart from the universality principle, such an act must not be self-contradictory or inconsistent with itself. Suicide, for example, is not consistent with man's nature of life and survival.

Applying the above principle to homosexuality, one will realize that it cannot be universal. Following the line of Immanuel Kant, we can ask what if everyone becomes homosexual and engages in homosexual marriage? If enough human beings become homosexual and engage exclusively in the act, fewer and fewer children will be conceived and the human race will go into extinction. Homosexuality is inconsistent with human nature of procreation as a continuation of the human race. Although it is possible to argue that the human race is already overpopulated and homosexuality and homosexual marriage is by choice.

The argument that homosexuality is by choice will not be tenable since in Kant's theory we are to consider ourselves as members of the legislative body. There is no exception to the rule. Based on cultural values, the Yoruba generally reject, condemn, and do not tolerate homosexuality. It is possible for a critic to argue that culture is dynamic and is about the experience of man. Since the experience of man in life changes, it is expected that culture will change. It is when culture is dynamic that we can have human development. There is no dispute that culture is dynamic, but this argument is not substantive because culture has to be productive in all of its ramifications. To some Yoruba, there is no productivity in homosexual marriages as it does not lead to the bearing of ones children. Where is the human development when man, who is supposed to be the developed and agent of development, runs into extinction? Who then will do the development?

---

10. Immanuel Kant, "Fundamental Principles of the Metaphysic of Morals," in William Frankena and John Granrose (eds.), *Introductory Readings in Ethics* (New Jersey: Prentice, 1974), 117.

Besides, some argue that for the Yoruba, any marriage contract outside that prescribed by culture does not give personal growth and fulfillment that it does not contribute to their sense of worth and adjusted personality but a maladjusted life. Coming from this cultural background, coupled with the Christian religion, it is not surprising that most African Bishops and Archbishops find homosexuality and homosexual marriage difficult to accept or even tolerate. For instance, Archbishop Akinola of the Anglican Church opposes same-sex blessings, the ordination of non-celibate homosexuals, or, indeed, any homosexual or same-sex union practice. He argues that God instituted marriage between man and woman, among other reasons, for procreation.[11] To Akinola, to set aside this divine arrangement in preference to self-centred perversion is an assault on the sovereignty of God. He sees homosexuality as an abuse of a man's body just as much as lesbianism is. He reiterates that God created two persons—male and female. In Akinola's argument, the world of homosexuals has created a third, a homosexual, neither male nor female, or both male and female—a strange two-in-one human. Akinola further argues that the practice of homosexuality, in his understanding of the scripture, is the enthronement of self-will and human weakness, and a rejection of God's order and will. Using strong words, Akinola believes that homosexuality does violence to nature; a rebellion against God.[12]

Before I conclude the chapter, let me imagine some arguments that may come up as reactions to the position advanced by Akinola. It may be argued that sex is a private matter; it is a business between two consenting adults. Therefore, whether it is homosexual or heterosexual does not matter. However, where communal sense is very strong, they may refuse to accept that sex is a private matter. An individual does not live for himself alone but for the community, whatever the repercussions of his acts he does not bear them alone. That is why the Yoruba say:

Ti ara ile eni ba nje kokoro ti ko da

kurukere re ko ni je ka sun loru.

If a neighbor is eating poison and we keep quiet

When he starts to react to it in the night we will not be able to sleep.

In other words, the discomfort of one, if not discouraged, could lead to the discomfort of others. To think in the Yoruba manner, who will take care of homosexuals when they grow old—there will be no children to do this. This can only be achieved in a family setup. The family is the basic unit through which society thrives in terms of peace, unity, and cultural values; values that prolong the existence of man, that bring prosperity and joy.

It has been argued that castigating homosexuals is against human freedom and rights. Many scholars have criticized this communal nature of African societies, arguing that the communal emphasis of African cultures stifles individuality and does not allow for human rights and freedom. When we talk about freedom, we need to note that there is no absolute freedom. The whole essence of morality is to curb the excesses of freedom. Freedom exercised without consideration for the existence of others is not freedom but selfishness. The Yoruba are strongly averse to selfishness and self-centeredness.[13]

---

11. Peter Akinola, "Why I Object to Homosexuality and Same-Sex Unions," www.anglican-nig.org (Accessed on February 4, 2008).

12. Ibid.

13. Bolaji Idowu, *Olodumare: God in Yoruba Belief* (London: Longman, 1962), 157.

Conclusion

Following from the exposition of Ifa literary corpus and Yoruba worldview, it can be established that the idea of homosexual acts and relationships is not inconceivable to the Yoruba. A further analysis shows that the Yoruba consider it inhuman, unproductive, and futile. Even the gods do not see it as fitting unto man. Besides, the cultural values, which the Yoruba hold in high esteem, run contrary to the practice of homosexual acts, marriages, and relationships. The influence of Western culture no doubt aggravated the practice of homosexuality in Yoruba society. Recent reactions from various quarters go further to confirm the intolerance and unacceptability of homosexual acts in Yoruba society. As such, it cannot be seen as an issue that needs repackaging and redelivery.

References

Abimbola, Wande. "Ifa as a Body of Knowledge an as an Academic Discipline." *Journal of Cultures and Ideas.* Vol. 1. 1 (1983): 1-11.

Akinola, Peter. "Why I Object to Homosexuality and Same-Sex Unions," www.anglican-nig.org/Pri_obj_Homo.html.

Augustine. *Confessions.* trans. by E.B. Pussy. London: Dent, 1909. III, VII: 15.

Bentham, Jeremy. "Homosexuality: An Essay on 'Pederasty.'" In Baker Robert and Elliston Fredrick (eds.). *Philosophy and Sex.* Buffalo: Prometheus, 1984.

_____. "Offences Against One's Self: Pederasty." *Journal of Homosexuality.* Vol. 4 (1978): 390.

Holy Bible, King James Version.

Idowu, Bolaji. *Olodumare: God in Yoruba Belief.* London: Longman, 1962.

Igwe, Leo. "Humanism and Homosexuality in Africa." http://www.iheu.org. Accessed on February 4, 2008.

Kant, Immanuel. *Lectures on Ethics.* trans. by Louis Infield. New York: Harper and Row, 1963.

_____. "Fundamental Principles of the Metaphysics of Morals." In William Frankena and John Granrose (eds.). *Introductory Readings in Ethics.* New Jersey: Prentice, 1974.

Mbiti, John. African Religions and Philosophy. London: Heinemann.1982.

Ruse, M. "The Morality of Homosexuality." In Robert and Fredrick, *Philosophy and Sex.* New York: Prometheus Books, 1984.

UK Home Office. "Operational Guidance Note: Nigeria." November 26, 2007. Section 3.13.5-Attachment.

Chapter 10

Kodjo Besia, Supi, Yags and Eagles: Being Tacit Subjects and Non-Normative Citizens in Contemporary Ghana

Kathleen O'Mara

Intragender loving social networks of men and women have formed in urban Ghana since the mid 1990s, forming the base of micro-communities in metropolitan Accra. These networks have multiplied by example and building group inter-connections without openly acknowledging their existence, much like local social networks elsewhere in the global south where anti-homosexual sentiment and public discourse make presenting a "public face" deeply threatening.[1] In fact, in September 2006, Ghana reached the web and blogosphere with a moral panic about gays and lesbians incited by a radio announcement of a rumored "forthcoming gay conference."[2] Although no conference was actually organized, the suggestion produced weeks of condemnation in pulpits, newspapers, and blogs, as well as radio and television. Homosexuality was uniformly described as an "unnatural, bestial, satanic, deviant, and un-Ghanaian by Christian, Muslim, and elected government leaders."[3]

That statement left little doubt about the risks of intragender love, and demonstrated the churches' and the media's work in reproducing the colonial category of the African sexual deviant as a renewed target for abuse. Ruth, for example, a twenty-two year old self identified lesbian, recounted her experience in 2008: "my neighbor set me up, sent her little sister to my place to watch a video, later she knocked on my door … the girl ran out saying I tried to have sex with her. I didn't! The older sister called police." As a result, Ruth had to give the older girl her cell phone and "eighty (Ghana) cedis to the police." Extortion and verbal abuse are common, and to some individuals, it seems to be increasing alongside anti-gay radio commentaries and newspaper reports.

In 2009, the legal situation and safety of lgbt Africans gained intensified international attention as individuals in several countries resisted the laws and cultural constraints on their freedom to live as they wished. The proposed *Anti-Homosexuality Bill, No. 18*, in Uganda's parliament in October 2009, broadened the criminalization of homosexuality,

---

1. Kathleen O'Mara, "Homophobia and Building Queer Community in Urban Ghana," *Phoebe: Journal of Gender and Cultural Critiques* 19, 1 (2007): 35–46.

2. BBC News, "Ghanaian gay conference banned," http://news.bbc.co.uk/2/hi/africa/5305658.stm. 1 September 2006, accessed March 6, 2007.

3. D. Ireland, "Ghana: Media Leads Anti-Gay Witch-Hunt," http://www.zmag.org/content/showarticle.cfm?ItemID=1106, September 21, 2006, accessed January 9, 2007.

even setting out the death penalty for some offenses. Condemnations from the global north came swiftly, especially from the U.S. Congress and the European Union, eventually leading to the bill's nullification. At approximately the same time, two men in Malawi were arrested for holding a symbolic traditional wedding ceremony. Two Kenyan men "married" in the UK in 2009 gave rise to great public condemnation in their homeland, and the suspension from competition of Caster Semenya, the eighteen-year old South African record breaker of the women's 800 meter run at the Berlin *World Championships* on suspicion of not being a "real woman" added to global scrutiny of African sexualities.[4] International gay rights and human rights groups' protests highlighted the hegemony of Western portrayals of African lives. Shining the public spotlight on African countries exposes the problem of understanding how various Africans express same sex intimacy, live and think about their sexuality and social lives, and even how the history of African sexualities may be written, precisely because the subject is complicated by Western narratives, concepts, and agendas. As in Western discussions, there is a strong focus on male sexual intimacies, which further diminishes public acknowledgement of women's non-normative sexualities.

Foundational concepts of sexuality studies such as gender and race, as Oyéronké Oyewùmí and Maria Lugones argue, are colonial constructs and part of the Euro-centered capitalist axis of modernity, not indigenous West African notions.[5] Local, indigenous modes of thinking, naming, and integrating difference are stifled by the force of Western hegemonic discourse about social identities and individual rights. In this conflict, the Western concept of the closet intersects with human rights as the "right to come out" into the open and drives the macro-level discussion as one of individual rights and preferences, though the characterization may not make sense in many African communities. Whether arguments focus on individual rights denied, sinfulness, or homosexuality as a foreign import, they reflect colonial constructions of an "underdeveloped" African sexuality versus a "developed" Western one, which contemporary critics such as Marlon Ross have urged researchers to reject and replace with a reconsideration of theories of sexual identity of racialized and colonized minorities everywhere.[6]

In Ghana, homosexuality is predominantly perceived as a sign of Westernization, which in a proper African nationalist reading is inappropriate for a decolonized subject position. Indeed, the Western category of homosexual, as queer theorists such as Michel Foucault and Jonathan Ned Katz have detailed, arose in the mid-late nineteenth century as an aspect of social discipline and the modern power-knowledge regime, a time, which equally coincided with European expansion into Africa.[7] Rather than a useful universal concept, the Western closet does not reflect the variety and complexity of African same sex intimacies, present or past, especially women's. Therefore, as Henriette Gunkel argues for South African women's same sex relationships and Thomas Walle for diasporic Arabs, it is more illuminating to regard same sex physical intimacy and sexual relations as positions on a continuum, not a split between friendships and homosexual relations, especially since

---

4. C. Clary, "Gender Test after a Gold Medal Finish." http://www.nytimes.com/2009/08/20/sports/20runner.html?_r=1, accessed September 15, 2010.

5. Maria Lugones, "The Coloniality of Gender," *World and Knowledges Otherwise* (Spring 2008) 1–9; Oyeronke Oyewumi, *The Invention of Women: Making Sense of Western Gender Discourses* (Minn: U MN Press, 1997), 32–33.

6. Marlon B. Ross, "Beyond the Closet as Raceless Paradigm," in E. P. Johnson and M.G. Henderson, (eds.) *Black Queer Studies* (Durham: Duke U.P., 2005), 181.

7. Michel Foucault, *The History of Sexuality, An Introduction,* (NY: Random House, 1978) 18–36; Jonathan Ned Katz, "The Invention of Heterosexuality," *Socialist Review* 20 (1990): 7–14.

the positions individuals occupy on the continuum at a given moment are flexible.[8] Opposing this malleability, the Western closet serves to fix the non-normative African subject in a Western model that is ill fitting.

This chapter is drawn from research for a larger study of new urban communities in contemporary Ghana.[9] It is inspired by Marlon Ross's analysis and concern with racist characterizations of black sexualities and that of Carlos Decena whose work on immigrant Dominican gay men argued that by adopting a tacit sexual subjecthood, the men disrupted the idea of the Western closet. That is, they could be both "in and out" of the "closet" as tacit subjects since their sexual and romantic practices were understood, knowable to those who were assumed to have the necessary skills to "read" their behavior, i.e., relatives, friends, and other lgbt individuals.[10] This chapter supports this reading as key to comprehending and building a history of African sexualities and focuses on women's intragender sexual lives as well as men's lives.

Discursive Practices

Silence in Ghanaian languages is a discursively contextual and variable tactic. Although some read silence on homosexuality as a strategy of suppression of non-normative sexuality, as it has functioned in the West, silence reflects indigenous preferences for discretion and indirect speech about sexual matters and can be called normative.[11] Silence equally serves to protect against social hostility and arrest. Rather than inevitably repressive, an act of concealment of sexual practice upholds social protocol about what it means to be visible or invisible within ordinary sites like the family, the church, or in the community. Such discretion equally maintains social space for ambiguous expressions of homosociality and building community, whereas the opposite invites familial rejection, violence, and is perceived as culturally inappropriate. Similar to communities of color in the United States, such as African Americans, Latinos, and Asian Americans, whose members often refuse visibility and labeling, Ghanaian intragender loving networks employ similar strategies and resist or find irrelevant the dominant Western model of 'coming out.' Rather than building community through the individual shared experience of coming out and realizing an 'authentic' core person, they construct intragender affiliated networks through local community building and claiming expressions of Ghanaian-ness and citizenship. This

---

8. Henriette Gunkel, " 'What's Identity Got To Do With It?' Rethinking Intimacy and Homosociality in Contemporary South Africa," *NORA-Nordic Journal of Feminist and Gender Research*, 17, 3 (2009): 208; Thomas Michael Walle, "Making places of intimacy—Ethnicity, friendship and masculinities in Oslo," *NORA-Nordic Journal of Feminist and Gender Studies*, 15, 2–3 (2007): 149; see also, Eve Kosofsky Sedgwick, *The Epistemology of the Closet* (Berkeley: University of California Press, 1990), 83–90 on the homosocial-homosexual continuum.

9. LGBT is used therein as an umbrella term for same sex intimate persons who by and large see this aspect of themselves as ongoing and social. It is not employed to include all MSM or WSW. Not capitalizing the letters is to counter the assumed importance of the acronym; The data for this chapter draws from two dozen life story interviews, as described by Paul Thompson, *The Voice of the Past: Oral History*, 3rd Edition (Oxford: OUP 2000). They were conducted between 2005 and 2010 and transcribed by this writer though Teye Moncar and Nii Richard Cudjoe translated from Ga and Twi and co-interviewed *won hegbemei*. The author's position as *obruni* (white/foreign), outsider and as insider, lesbian, should be noted as a factor affecting the interviews.

10. Carlos Ulises Decena, "Tacit Subjects," *GLQ: A Journal of Lesbian and Gay Studies* 14, 2–3 (2008): 340–41.

11. Serena O. Dankwa, "It's a Silent Trade': Female Same-Sex Intimacies in Post Colonial Ghana," *Nordic Journal of Feminist and Gender Research* 17, 3 (2009): 194.

opens the possibility, as Arnfred suggests, of re-conceptualizing "silence" not as oppressive but as comprising "different types of silence," understanding that linguistic practices of discretion and indirection only "prevent discursive, not sexual acts."[12] The following discussion incorporates a consideration of social and discursive practices among men and women in Accra who express same sex intimacy through processes which combine indigenous expressions of homosociality, friendship, community building, and recently by selectively appropriating organizational practices of global NGOs.

The centrality of discretion among Africans has been examined in recent studies of same sex intimacy by Epprecht, Pierce, Hoad, Gaudio, and Dankwa.[13] In Ghana as in northern Nigeria and southern Africa, the subjects for this project indicated that discretion was unquestioned, and prohibits public displays of affection or discussion of sexual lives, especially activities outside of marriage. Norms of homosociality, however, carve space for ambiguity. Cynthia, for example, stressed the acceptance of her relationship with her primary girlfriend by her mother and grandmother, "She has a key to my room and stays when I am not there. My Mum calls her daughter." Kin terms are ambiguous and key signifiers, with different meanings to those in the know. She noted that her girlfriend's family, "love me so much … her fiancé has called me … to talk with me about her!" When an acquaintance of his suggested the two were doing *supi* (i.e., lesbian relationship), he asked, and Cynthia said, "I told him, absolutely no."

The term *supi* is less ambiguous than it once was, having evolved to mean lesbian or gay from its original reference to intense emotional ties between adolescent girls commonly made at boarding schools or other homosocial spaces, and involving an exchange of gifts and love letters and that could involve erotic intimacies. The senior *supi* protected and supported the younger girl who in turn ran errands for her senior. While *supi* is still understood as a non-sexual close friendship by many in Ghana, Dankwa has detailed the dual impact of Pentecostal-Charismatic churches and the media in demonizing "supi-supi lesbianism" since the mid-1990s.[14] Among the women subjects discussed here, none self identified as being or doing "*supi*," and preferred lesbian as a term or *igbyomo* (husband) to describe the particular relationship.

Intergenerational discussions of sexual matters are shameful, although most subjects believed their parents and siblings "knew" about their partners and friends. As Alex said, "My mum would never ask, nor my brothers. My cousin gave me such trouble, after this man who was living with me created a scene; she told my other cousins … and now I cannot see many of them." These norms, rooted in Ghana's dominant ethno-linguistic group, the Akan, extend to other ethnicities, including the Ga of Accra. While not everyone may be able to read the signs, there are those who apprehend who is *saso*, *kodjo besia*, or gay or an eagle, a lesbian or in *supi-supi* relationships.[15] Rather than a using a category

---

12. Signe Arnefred, "African Sexuality/Sexuality in Africa: Tales and Silences," in Arnefred (ed.), *Re-thinking Sexualities in Africa* (Uppsala: Nordic Afrika Institute, 2004), 73.

13. Dankwa, "It's a Silent Trade," 194; M. Epprecht, *Hungochani: The History of a Dissident Sexuality in Southern Africa* (Montreal: McGill-Queen's University Press, 2004); R. Gaudio, *Allah Made Us: Sexual Outlaws in an Islamic African City* (Chicester: Wiley-Blackwell, 2009); Stephen. Pierce, "Identity, Performance and Secrecy: Gendered life and the 'modern' in northern Nigeria," *Feminist Studies* 33, 3 (2007): 539–45.

14. Dankwa, "It's a Silent Trade," 193–96.

15. Dankwa,"It's a Silent Trade," 193–96; Decena, "Tacit Subjects," 340–42. Charles Guebogo, "Penser les 'droits' des homosexual/les en Afrique: du sens et de la puissance de l'action associative militante au Cameroun," *Canadian Journal of African Studies* 43, 1 (2009): 130–32.

rooted in a Western white experience, it is useful to conceptualize such individuals as tacit subjects, which enables us to see the complexities of their practices and the complicities that frame their social relations, their erotic attachments, and social practices generally.

The rise of urban social networks and communities appears similar whether in the mid-twentieth century U.S. or contemporary Accra, sharing certain features of urban subcultures. The trajectory of community growth is similar, e.g., building a minority 'geography' of social sites, and networks of information sharing and group recreation. The economics of sub-cultural group growth results in public spaces as male spaces, whereas women's socializing is private, more hidden unless a social event is jointly attended by both men and women, identified as a yag-eagle affair. Homophobic public discourse in Ghana, and Africa generally, tends to be read by outsiders as the unfolding of a gay historical meta-narrative like that of the U.S., UK, or Netherlands, only decades later. However, that view both reflects the racism and sexism of the colonial project, the global north as 'developed pacesetter' and validates the local fear of a foreign-imported narrative unfolding. Instead, struggles for indigenous expressions of same sex intimacy should be identified as part of the process of new sexual identity communities coming into being in an environment where same sex intimacies are changing, labeled homosexual, and condemned as not authentically Ghanaian. They straddle the divide between accepting and rejecting the Western sexuality identity regime and the homosocial continuum of African societies.[16]

Contemporary Ghanaian networks demonstrate alternative approaches to living as sexual citizens, i.e., they quietly build community and do not directly demand human rights. This community building is tactically a practice of indirection and domestication, a locally centered, at times even a neighborhood process. Visible to those in the know, it includes Ghanaianizing the discourse and creating fictive kin, e.g., gay daughters, lesbian sons, eagle senior brothers, and for men it involves constructing a small subcultural lexicon, and increasingly utilizing the knowledge and practices of NGOs to create formal organizations to address group needs. In this way, the communities offer an alternate paradigm of subjecthood, different from the Enlightenment model of progress: gay subjectivity as stage one of social transformation.

Same Sex Intimate Practices

The historical record on sexual difference in Ghana is scant, largely confined to colonial police and public health records concerned with prostitution and sexually transmitted diseases, but records in Ghana demonstrate British colonial efforts to regulate male and female sexual behaviors.[17] In mining Ghanaian culture for historical examples, *won hegbemei* emerge as a category of people known in the present and past as non-normative because they are possessed by spirits enabling them to justifiably have same sex partners. To acknowledge indigenous antecedents is only one way to situate sexual difference and to counter the Western paradigm in which the closet and coming out serve as the basic

---

16. Gunkel, "What's Identity got to Do With It?" 210.
17. NAG/National Archives of Ghana, ADM 11/1/922, Extracts from Criminal Codes; ADM, 11/1/922, Houses of ill fame, *The Gold Coast Independent*, September 19, 1925; ADM, 11/1/922, False Celebacy, Gold Coast Times, August 29, 1925; NAG, RG 3/1/304, T.E. Kyei, Some notes on marriage and divorce among the Ashantis.

tenet of non-normative sexual experience and politics,[18] particularly since such religious antecedents are found in a number of African cultures.[19] These professionals include: *wontsemei*, or spirit mediums, which include many women, *wulomei*, priests who tend shrines, and *tsofatsomei*, herbalists. A popular nickname for *wontsemei* is *kodjo besia* (male), which describes MSM, *Men who have sex with men*; some women are said to be doing *supi*.

In this discussion, certain assumptions about sexual difference are employed, i.e., that identities are fluid and permeable and that 'community' as constructed in discourse is also a social construction which exists largely in the minds of its members. As Bucholtz and Hall argue, "gender does not have the same meanings across space and time, but is instead a local production."[20] The development of lgbt Accra communities reflects this "communities of practice" perspective, which views social identities as multiple and fluid and arising through social and discursive practice. In contemporary Accra, intragender networks are articulated within a local community, marked in part by a shared geography. Although sexual identity is unspoken or expressed in indigenous language, and formed in the face of stigma, a sense of community develops around shared knowledge, experiences, and social location. As Bucholtz emphasizes, individuals "engage in multiple identity practices simultaneously," moving from one identity to another ... meaning, that it is the result of a local production, realized differently by different members of a community.[21] Thus, friendship networks and the role they play in bringing together potential partners and friends often begin on football pitches, schools, hair salons, public baths, or cafés, and then grow into larger social groups based on same sex intimate relationships. Over time, restaurants, bars, and local nightclubs become part of the geography of difference. For the subjects interviewed, the spots are far ranging but not numerous, a bar in Bukom, a restaurant in Osu, a nightclub in Kokomemle, a café in Nungua.

To comprehend non-normative subjectivities, it is useful to consider the approach of Liz Morrish, who applies Charles Clark's idea of concealment to explicate discursive practices of lgbt communities in the global north. That is, she points out that one can conceal from part of an audience and reveal to another in using a code that depends on mutual knowledge, e.g., some Ghanaian men use a specialist lexicon.[22] Another practice is disguisement to deceive a listener, a practice that some men also use, especially when speaking in risky spaces. Women, on the other hand, use kin terms, allusion, and gestures to express desire, which formally is concealment. Women are particularly cautious about dressing or appearing non-normative. A person's social location is also relevant as elite men, for example, might have more status to risk but more power to resist a social penalty. Kwesi, age forty-one, a shop owner successfully fought a blackmailer, taking him to court "with help from a clever lawyer!"

---

18. See Stephen O.Murray and Will Roscoe (eds.), *Boy Wives and Female Husbands* (NY: St. Martin's, 1998), intro; Saskia Wieringa, "Women Marriages and other same sex practices: Historical reflections on African women's same-sex relations," in Ruth Morgan and Saskia Wieringa (eds.), *Tommy Boys, Lesbian Men and Ancestral Wives* (Johannesburg: Jacana Media, 2005).

19. See *Tommy Boys, Lesbian Men, Ancestral Wives*, chapter 7.

20. Mary Bucholtz and Kira Hall, "Theorizing Identity in Language and Sexuality Research," *Language in Society* 33 (2004): 503–506.

21. Ibid., 504.

22. Liz Morrish and Helen Sauntson, *New Perspectives on Language and Sexualities* (Houndsmills: Palgrave, 2007), 99–101.

Communities of sexual difference in Africa remain under-examined beyond southern Africa where a number of studies have explored lgbt cultures, histories, memoirs, etc.[23] In Ghana as elsewhere in Africa, heterosexual marriage and procreation are social expectations,[24] which do not require the "suppression of same sex desires and behaviors" as much as not allow such "preferences to supplant procreation."[25] Scholars have identified a range of historical evidence of same sex intimacy across sub-Saharan Africa, including woman-woman marriage as an option, especially to produce offspring for a male relative, enhance the status of a female husband, or as the right of a spirit possessed sangoma-healer.[26] Though a binary gender concept came to dominate as the major idiom of sexuality in colonial and post-colonial eras, there is no reason to assume, as Oyewùmí has argued for the Yoruba, that a concept of gender predates European entry with the slave trade and colonialism.[27]

The relatively new urban networks of intragender identified individuals in Accra share particular characteristics with communities elsewhere in Africa, especially South Africa, e.g., the presence of tommy boys or HIV prevention health counselors and activists, which influence other Africans through human rights and health NGOs.[28] Ghanaians over thirty also describe *supi* relationships at boarding school that resonate with "mummy-baby" ones in southern Africa.[29] The majority of the Accra subjects comprised individuals between twenty-two and forty, underemployed urban working poor: most attended junior secondary school and a few completed senior secondary school; few have been heterosexually married or had children; almost all lived alone, with a partner, or a parent; and most under age thirty-five self identified as gay or lesbian, using English, more than Ga and Asante-Twi words. No one was wealthy or in an elite profession. Indeed, most subjects were self-employed vendors, cooks, artists, and tailors, though some worked in hotels or as community health advocates. Ga, comprised the majority interviewed, though a number

---

23. See William Leap, "Does the Past Matter: Exploring Cape Town Area Black Gay Men's Recollections of Spatial Transgression during Late Apartheid," unpub. paper presented at *13th Annual Lavender Languages and Linguistics Conference*, American University, February 10–12, 2006; S. Wieringa and R. Morgan (eds.), *Tommy Boys, Lesbian Men and Ancestral Wives*; Cameron and M. Gevisser, *Defiant Desire* (London: Routledge, 1995).

24. Stephen O. Murray and Will Roscoe's anthology *Boy Wives and Female Husbands* typifies foundational research on African sexualities. The essays demonstrate that African same sex patterns of behavior are diverse, and as Gaudio and Amory show in that volume, may employ distinct language to describe non-normative masculine and feminine behaviors. Wieringa and Blackwood's *Female Desire* included discussions of women's same sex relationships in southern and eastern Africa. Arnefred's anthology *Rethinking Sexualities in Africa* is a groundbreaking decolonial feminist anthology. Many earlier researchers on African homo/sexualities emphasized alternative genders or "third sex" categories, e.g., ghanith. Murray and Roscoe claim that what is missing in the African inventory of same sex patterns is an identity and "lifestyle" in which homosexual relationships are primary. S. Murray and W. Roscoe (eds.), *Boy Wives and Female Husbands: Studies of African Homosexualities* (NY: St. Martins, 1998); Saskia Wieringa and Evelyn Blackwood, *Female Desires* (NY: Columbia University press, 1999); S. Arnefred (ed.), *Re-thinking Sexualities in Africa*.

25. Nii Ajen, "West African Homoeroticisms: West African Men Who Have Sex with Men," in Murray, and Roscoe (eds.), *Boy Wives and Female Husbands*, 133.

26. N. Nkabinde with R. Morgan, "This has happened since ancient times … it's something you are born with: ancestral wives among same-sex sangomas in South Africa," *Tommy Boys, Lesbian men and Ancestral Wives*, 234–41.

27. Oyewumi, *The Invention of Women*, 30–35.

28. Wieringa and Morgan, *Tommy Boys*, 99–101, 112–18.

29. Gunkel, "What's Identity Got To Do With It?" 207–10.

were Asante, Fante, and Ewe. The *wontsemei* interviewed largely met gender expectations, married (and divorced) and had children.

Ghana's Social and Legal Context

Ghana, a post colonial developing country economically experienced its nadir in the 1980s, which was a period marked by the onset of Christian revivalism, a process contributing in Charismatic and Pentecostal forms to a deeply heteronormative culture.[30] Moreover, British colonial era anti-sodomy laws remain in force, (as in other Anglophone states, e.g., Nigeria, Uganda) notably Article 104 of the Ghana criminal code states that,

> whoever is guilty of unnatural carnal knowledge (a) of any person sixteen years or over without his consent shall be guilty of first degree felony, and liable on conviction to imprisonment for a term of not less than five years and not more than twenty-five years; or (b) of any person with his consent or of any animal, is guilty of a misdemeanor. (12 Jan 1961)[31]

The sodomy law, which lumps together rape, homosexuality, and bestiality, sustains a matrix of colonial era power relations and discursively frames public attitudes. Both men and women have been prosecuted and imprisoned in the past decade: four gay men in August 2003 who were tried for "unlawful carnal knowledge" and "indecent exposure" were sentenced to two years imprisonment for exchanging photos with a Norwegian man for money and gifts. In August 2005, a lesbian was charged with practicing unnatural sex, for "luring an 18 year old girl into lesbianism."[32]

International human rights organizations have reported police entrapment of gay men in Ghana, which many men such as Alex, Kofi, Michael, Isaac, Jacob, and Prince affirmed. Violence against those perceived to be lgbt is intertwined with Ghana's economy, one of high unemployment, underemployment, and where lgbt individuals are known as legally unprotected. Extortion and violence have framed identity and community for men and women. Chris noted, "I used to go to clubs ... now I just stay at home." Gay bashing is reported in the press, as in BBC's 2007 report on Joseph Afful and his four friends attacked in Accra.[33] Michael, a video actor claimed assault was a major problem, "People who are not gay find the spot where we hang out ... hide and attack gays." Verbal abuse of those perceived or known to be lgbt is endemic; resisting verbal abuse can be equally dangerous. Mercy, a self-employed artist age thirty, was returning from the market to her home and woman partner when an "older man cursed me, calling me lesbian, evil." When he would not stop, she swung a newly purchased broom at his face, causing a bloody nose. He called the police who arrested her and kept her in jail over

---

30. Paul Gifford, *Ghana's New Christianity: Pentecostalism in a Globalising African Economy* (London: Hurst, 2004), 89–128.

31. UNHCR, "Ghana treatment of homosexuals by society and authorities and availability of state protection; names and activities of groups or associations promoting homosexual rights," http://www.unhcr.org/refworld/type,queryresponse,GHA,45fl1473820,0.html; Zachary, http://www.sodomylaws.org, accessed February 16, 2010.

32. J.Jacques, and F. Gbolu, "Social Justice-Same Sex, Different Rights," Ghanaian Chronicle, June 22, 2005, *Behind the Mask*, http://www.mask.org.za/article.php?cat=ghana&id=255; Hanson, "No room for gays and Lesbians," *Public Agenda*, May 21, 2007, http://allafrica.com/, accessed February 18, 2010.

33. O. Ryan, "Ghana's Secret Gay Community," BBC News, March 14, 2007, http://news.bbc.co.uk/2/hi/africa/6445337.stm 14 March 2007, accessed October 12, 2007.

two weeks until her "step-father secured several hundred cedi so the police would let" her go. Blackmail, entrapment, and bribery all comprise elements of the surveillance regime, which shapes lgbt subjecthood.

Extortion of intragender loving women occurs where they live. Cynthia's narrative, repeated by a number of women in their twenties, was typical:

> This girl ... I go to church with her ... She wanted to watch a movie with me ... She was sitting on my bed. She wants me to hold her, so it came to a point where we were making out ... later she called me and said she need(s) money ... so I told her I'd give her some money. Later her boyfriend ... said he'd tell people I'm lesbian ... He wanted about 150 Ghana cedi. I was afraid ... I went ... sold my t.v. ... got 130 cedi ($90). I gave it to him.

This threat of exposure leaves young women hyper-vigilant; some like Cindy, a young athlete, try to live in compounds where other "lesbians" (the word she uses) live with partners. Even there they are taunted by neighbors who call them "*supi*," though she stressed they deny it and explain, "We are sports girls. This is how we dress ... We love football!" For some women the threat of arrest creates a tragic drama where the partners are forever separated. Caroline described having to move from her grandmother's house and only occasionally contact her girlfriend, a frustrating situation of three years duration.

The problem began with the girlfriend's "senior brother" asking to date Caroline, and when she turned him down, he became suspicious. Sometime later, he saw the two together and asked rather aggressively, "What are you doing with my sister?" They ignored him but the next day, "We were in my room when my grandmother called me on the cell phone and said, 'Hide! He's here with the police.' We did not come out till after eight that night. We climbed the wall to her neighbor's, then her house." Fearful of the authorities, Caroline hid for several weeks, but enroute to football training one day, the brother "stopped me with the C.I.D. (police) ... and they arrested me." She had to borrow one hundred twenty Ghana cedi to give the police and "give her brother my laptop." Fearful of returning home although her "grandmother needs" her, she took a new primary partner and lives with her, but remains attached and involved with her former girlfriend

Surveillance is a key aspect of socially (re)producing the non-normative subject. As a strategy of control it is accomplished by penetrating the individual's consciousness and encouraging self-restraint, thereby nudging the person to be obedient to cultural norms. This panopticon is another Western construct and maintains continuity with the colonial regime as the previous fundamental structure of social inequality and state regulation. Western homophobia has migrated; indeed, it is fostered by Christian Westerners such as the anti-gay interventions of 2008–2009 in Uganda by American evangelicals claiming there is an international gay agenda.[34] Cyber-technologies of hate have intensified this regime and created new opportunities for exploitation. Alex claimed he knew "two dozen men ... blackmailed," and others "beat and robbed by email planned dates." Nii who ran "blackmail trainings" reported, "Men who have gone into hiding ... pay and pay and fear for their life." Jacob, age twenty-four, who moves back and forth between Accra and Cape Coast, stressed that "blackmail is worse in Cape Coast" and that victims are never "left alone ... they must pay, pay." He knew several men who ran away and never returned and one who he assumed to have been killed. Two strategies have developed to combat this problem although very few people actively address it: Western NGO data collection

---

34. Barry Bearak, "Same-Sex Couple Stir Fears of 'Gay Agenda,'" http://www.nytimes.com/2010/02/14/world/africa/14malawi.html, October 12, 2007.

and periodic trainings on avoiding blackmail; and local lgbt networks meeting at information exchange sites, e.g., house parties, sporting events.

Making Non-Normative Subjects

Ghanaians who attend secondary school often reside there, producing "first experience" narratives that invoke British stereotypes of boys' public school "deviance." They are similar to 'mummy-baby' school girl relationships detailed by Gunkel,[35] and like "coming out" on campus stories of American college students in that the narratives are nearly identical,[36] and contribute to a discursive regime or dominant narrative as Foucault detailed, a group of statements formulated elsewhere and repeated, acknowledged to be truthful and involving exact description, and defined conditions of existence.[37] The West's discursive regime of coming out of the closet privileges the act of self-naming, accepting one's same sex emotions and disclosing them to others, whereas the Ghanaians' narratives tell about a partner, an experience, not the recognition of an authentic self.

The Ghanaian discourse is outside/alongside the closet and not part of an identity continuum that privileges leaving the closet as evolved and modern. Women in their thirties in particular related these narratives. Gina, age twenty-eight when first interviewed, described a first encounter with her prefect, a senior girl, at boarding school who when she was "asleep would come to me ... like a man and woman" and with whom she remained in a relationship for twelve years, stressing that a woman partner "has rights over you, like a husband's." She acknowledged, as did Evelyn, a hair stylist in her thirties, that not all girls doing *supi* moved from intense friends to a "man and woman" relationship, indicating that several homosocial spaces and cultural practices allow women's intimacy.[38]

A generational and class difference appears in women's narratives. Women age thirty years or older spoke about initial same sex relationships in secondary school and family pressure to marry. Gina, for example, when first interviewed was ending her long-term relationship and within two years married a Nigerian man and had a child; however, she remained on the periphery of a women's network and dated within it. Women in their early twenties now have multiple partners, socialize inter-network, and dress in football clothing as well as in conventional women's dresses. As with other subcultures, there are efforts made to mark membership with clothing and accessories unknown to outsiders. To some degree, the political economy of the surveillance regime encourages individuals to enlarge the number of their partners to avoid a solitary existence. It is women over thirty who tend to self-present as mature and heteronormative, largely to avoid suspicion according to Gina and Amelemegbe, although Esi was an exception. In her late thirties, she always wears football and men's clothing. It is the threat of exposure not family pressures that structures homosocial networks. Emphasizing the tacit understanding of sexual difference, Amelemegbe noted, "My mother knows, my brother knows. We do not talk about it."

---

35. H. Gunkel, "What's Identity Got To Do With It?" 212–16.

36. Kathleen O'Mara, "Historicising Outsiders on Campus: the re/production of Lesbian and Gay Insiders," *Journal of Gender Studies* 6, 1(1997): 28; K. O'Mara. "Queers Performing on Campus," *Phoebe* 11, 2 (1999): 48–49.

37. M. Foucault, "Politics and the Study of Discourse," *Ideology and Consciousness* 3 (1978): 7–26.

38. Dankwah. "It's a Silent Trade," 199–200.

Indigenizing Discourse

MSW:	WSW:
saso (buddy), *yag* (backslang)	eagle (macho), *supi* (girl love)
kodjo besiya (Twi), nunjo (Ga)	yaa'mah (Twi), zimah (Ga)
—acts/looks like a woman	—acts/looks like a man
Yaa Asantewa—queen	Prempeh II—king

Gender binaries and local cultural references mark the rather small lexicon, which belongs largely to men who also employ Ghanaian history to signify same sex affiliations, invoking the Asante state, the most powerful pre-colonial entity, which for decades militarily resisted (1807–96) the British. The last campaign, in 1900–1901, was an uprising led by Yaa Asantewa, the Queen Mother of Ejisu, whose name men invoke in naming a leader. In this way, they can claim patriotism, citizenship, and armed motherhood. Akan societies, Stephan Miescher argues, possess a "long history of contested masculinity and femininity," with rival notions of masculinity, the ɔpanyin (an elderly mediator with good advice) and ɔbirɛmpɔn (wealthy and generous).[39] This lexicon reveals two strategies of an evolving community: a domestication and incorporation of non-normative sexuality to local culture through inventing playful new expressions of it,[40] and employing a rhetoric of ambiguity rooted in Akan discursive practices of discretion that uphold tacit understandings.

Viola, age thirty-three, is one example of a male tacit subject. He lives in a building on his mother's property where she welcomes his fictive kin and community: "My friends helped me give my Mum a good drink up for her birthday." His father, a businessman, who died in late 2009, never commented about his boyfriends nor raised marital expectations. At his father's funeral reception, his three dozen close friends sat adjacent to his family who knew how the deceased had welcomed his closest friends. Viola is proud "my little nephews call me Auntie!" In this way he and his extended family and friends are complicit in nurturing a non-normative community for which he is a leader: "I bring people together to talk over our problems, to arrange social affairs ... birthday parties, weddings, funerals, all yag or eagle affairs."

Esi, age thirty-nine, also known as Paa Joe, is Viola's female equivalent. Although her father and twenty-one year old daughter tacitly accept her partner as kin, the subject is never discussed and she accommodates them by toning down her dress and self expression in their presence, i.e., she wears loose shirts and "speaks like a woman ... in higher voice." Short and stocky with nearly shaved hair, on the street Esi 'passes' as a man, which makes everyday life both easier and more complicated: few male challengers and a few more questions about her work as a football coach for teenagers and a 'farm team' for future professional footballers. Her partner Sadie's family, who live in Bukom, "accept" her as a "son-in-law" and have urged her to marry Sadie, a position of acceptance that Paa Joe/Esi claims "only the Ga of Bukom" would take, in contrast to her own natal community of La/Labadi-Accra.

Both Viola and Paa Joe reveal how a "community of practice" is thus constituted through combining a tacit understanding of sexual practices; men's use of a small lexicon; men and women claiming particular public spaces such as bars and eateries, football fields, and community centers; and constructing self-help networks and bestowing recognition

---

39. Stephan Miescher, *Making Men in Ghana* (Bloomington: Indiana University Press, 2005), 8, 12.

40. Kwesi Yankah, "Power and the circuit of formal talk," *Journal of Folklore Research* 28, 1 (1991): 18.

on network leaders. Until recently, these efforts have been invisible and distinct from the developed world's model of lgbt 'freedom' with NGOs, i.e., wage a legal campaign for gay rights, a strategy associated with the West as opposed to grassroots community service and domestication of difference. Thus, it is relevant to examine any intersections with indigenous non-normatives, *won hegbemei*.

Intersections of Sexual Difference

One man, Nathaniel, and two women, Ansa and Pattey, were forthcoming in explaining themselves. Nathaniel lives in his small family house located in Bukom, old Accra, near the beach and Korle Bu Lagoon. His personal narrative and Ansa's are typical of *won hegbemei*. He was raised Anglican and she was raised Methodist. His family had *wontsemei* in the family line, though he did not plan on becoming one until his late teens when he started having dreams, and one day was mounted by an unidentified spirit, went blind, and lost his memory for hours afterwards. Taken by his family to several different *wontsemei*, *tsofatsemei*, and *wulomei*, he was diagnosed as having a powerful spirit with twin personalities to have filled him: the female goddess called Mami Wata, a well known West African deity associated with commodities and destructive forces, and a male god, Bentum, who lives under the sea. Ansa, a cloth vendor, about forty years old, also described a spiritual assault that began in Nsawam one day and ended in Bukom the next. It was later determined that she had been chosen as a vehicle for expressing the will of the family fishing god called Ansa.

Both Nathaniel and Ansa provide spiritual guidance and medicine to same sex intimate clients. Nathaniel who claims he is able to cure most diseases, e.g., heart trouble, high blood pressure, diabetes, and depression, as well as treating the loss of a partner or wish to acquire one, claims that medicine he fabricated from wood, charcoal, hair from the ex-lovers' comb, etc., brought one man back to his client, keeping the pair together for one year more. Nathaniel said he is *kodjo besia* and has two men with whom he is close. Ansa, who dresses "like a *wulo*" by "choice" discussed courting her partner: "First, I take her as a friend, then we dated, then we came to a love relationship." Fearful of losing the woman, she explained, "I am jealous … if I see her with someone else. I'm like a viper and I'll bite." She asserted that "her neighbors know" of her relationship with her partner, but "they do not bother" her.

Pattey, a priest from Tema from a family of *wulomei*, was the most resistant to Ga expectations for women. She interacts with 'lay' networks of eagles in a way the other two do not. She had never been heterosexually married, had children, or raised a partner's child and lived openly. "Everyone knows … that I am eagle. I was born with (an) interest in women." She says that her god is Dantu and that she was "born into being a priest." Pattey proudly reported, "Neighbors have come to me and said 'if you are an eagle, then I want to be one,' though they use the word *supi*. I am so strong they want that strength." Lonely and searching for a partner, someone to "help with (working funerals) … and to support one another," Pattey's self-presentation contrasts with Ansa's and Nathaniel's for whom the unspoken forecloses social or community acknowledgement. They are tacit subjects and respected for their spiritual powers. Pattey, however, said she disapproved of "publishing your business" on radio or TV, which was a reference to the 2006 moral panic begun on Joy F.M. radio. All three religious practitioners manifest indigenous intragender affiliation and the use of indigenous professionals as community support.

Among community leaders, Lartey was the individual called "Yaa Asantewa," the queen mother, an honor he acknowledged by asserting that his being gay is "a gift from God ... God created me to become somebody." His statements demonstrate the way individuals speak and are spoken about in locally meaningful terms and their strategy for domestication of non-normative social practices and identities. In this process, they indigenize new forms of sexual difference and 'yag' the culture. Lartey models himself after a much-admired man, King Bennett, who died in 2005, and who a number of men identified as an exemplary leader because he acted on behalf of a local community neighborhood, sponsoring a youth football team, and making "loans to fishermen," and simultaneously was a leader of a non-normative community. Lartey and Spiffy were King Bennett's gay daughters. They spoke of his home as their ancestral village though it was not. Until 2005, Lartey owned a drinking spot in Tema and he stressed the importance of building and keeping spaces for social life. "We (would) meet friends there, drink there ... have meetings ... I tell how it is to be gay, even to the chief and the head of police ... God gave it to us, we have to give it back." Lartey positioned himself as a new Ɔpanyin, a man of reputation, good at mediating and offering advice.

Both Lartey and Viola perform at times as ókyeame, the indigenous "linguist," the intermediary between the king and the people,[41] though now the role is an orator in a triad between government offices, social institutions, and community. The dominant position of men in Ghanaian society creates opportunities for Lartey or Viola not as easily duplicated by women. Men recount contacts that are more extensive with different "gay" professionals. Viola reported, "I arranged for some friends to get married ... I know a gay pastor, two lawyers, doctors." Women are more reluctant to assume leadership beyond a small circle though pairs of women in different neighborhoods, including Esi/Paa Joe and her co-coach, have reached beyond their neighborhood network, to make common cause with other eagles and lesbians around community service and employment. Reflecting their deep community consciousness, Viola and Lartey have mentored several groups of neighborhood-based women, which resulted in 2009 in their forming a new human rights organization, Sister to Sister for Social Justice and Empowerment (SSSJE). It is a volunteer organization, which merges neighborhood networks into one group and demonstrates women's efforts to be community leaders, gain respect for community service, and for some to claim non-normative sexual citizenship.

The stated mission of SSSJE is to work towards the education and economic betterment of all women regardless of age, religion, ethnicity, sexual identity, or occupation through outreach on health, athletics, and sex education. The leadership group shares scarce economic resources and social knowledge, provides emotional and kin work, and is building a larger sense of unity for a half dozen neighborhood networks in Accra. The young women, most who identify as lesbian, have thus initiated, as in other African nations, a human rights and women's organization because a lgbt organization would be perceived as too militant.[42] Regardless, as social contract theory claims, the women's actions and obligations to 'community' reveal their engagement in active citizenship. Viola specifically expresses an awareness of that when he says, "I love Ghana so much! I love our men! They know I am a diva!"

---

41. Kwesi Yankah, *Speaking for the Chief: Okyeame and the Politics of Akan Royal Oratory* (Bloomington: Indiana University Press, 1995), 24–31.

42. Charles Guebogo, "Penser les 'droits' des homosexual/les en Afrique: du sens et de la puissance de l'action associative militante au Cameroun," *Canadian Journal of African Studies* 43, 1 (2009): 131–132.

Conclusions

What the personal testimony of being gay, or eagle, support is Judith Butler's assertion that the "foundationist reasoning of identity politics" is off the mark; that is, "that an identity must be in place for ... political action to take place." Rather, the "doer," the non-normative self, one's subjectivity is "constructed in and through the deed."[43] For these Ghanaians, this is a process of repetition in serving the community. Linking networks of lgbt community members, introducing friends to one another for potential partnering, gathering for birthday parties and video viewings, attending funerals, loaning funds to those in need, linking football teams for games and sponsors, advocating for those in legal trouble or in need of health care, and in general providing support to their community. They are, tacitly, challenging heteronormativity, claiming community and citizenship, and quietly enacting what Butler calls identity politics, another imported concept, which fails to illuminate their complicated social relations and connections to community.

In multiple ways, Viola, Lartey, Esi and SSSJE leaders claim non-normative citizenship by reframing indigenous roles, institutions, and discourses. This strategy disrupts the colonial, Christian argument that same sex intimate relationships are a white, Western import and disrupts the Western metanarrative of "coming out" with its emphasis on the individual, instead placing the speaking non-normative subject in a relationship to indigenous culture that asserts cultural "authentification and authority."[44] In the totality of their social and discursive practices, these emergent non-normative Ghanaian communities reject the Enlightenment project of progress and development, especially as applied to sexual practices and identities and social discourse. Implicitly, they recommend abandoning Western hegemonic paradigms of human sexuality.

Interviews

Alex Y., February 4, 2010

Amelemegbe N., January 18, 2007

Caroline A., February 4, 2010

Chris I., February 25, 2005

Cynthia T., February 3, 2010

Evelyn M., November 2, 2007

Esi C., May 12, 2010

Gina A., January 13, 2006

Kofi D., January 22, 2007

Kwesi L, April 27, 2010

Lartey O., January 13, 2006, November 29, 2007

Mercy M., May 2, 2010

---

43. Judith Butler, *Gender Trouble: Feminism and the Subversion of Identity* (NY: Routledge, 1990), 142.
44. Mary Bucholtz and Kira Hall, "Theorizing Identity," 506–509.

Nathaniel B., October 30, 2007, January 11, 2009

Nicolina A., October 29, 2007

Nii, F., January 22, 2007, January 13, 2009

Pattey l., November 20, 2007, January 13, 2009

Prince M., January 17, 2006, October 25, 2007

Ruth N., February 5, 2010

Spiffy M., February 25, 2005

Viola M., January 12, 2006, November 16, 2007

References

Ajen, Nii. "West African Homoeroticisms: West African Men Who have Sex with Men." In Murray, Stephen and Roscoe, Will. (eds.) *Boy Wives and Female Husbands: Studies of African Homosexualities.* NY: St. Martins, 1998.

Arnefred, Signe. (ed.) *Re-thinking Sexualities in Africa.* Uppsala: Nordic Afrika Institute, 2004.

BBC News, "Ghanaian gay conference banned." http://news.bbc.co.uk/2/hi/africa/5305658.stm. Accessed September 1, 2006.

Bearak, Barry. "Same-Sex Couple Stir Fears of a 'Gay Agenda.'" http://www.nytimes.com/2010/02/14/world/africa/14malawi.html? Accessed April 27, 2010.

Broni, Y. "Joy FM had a homosexual on a program and my oh my." *Accra Mail.*http://alafrica.com/stories/200608291000.html. Accessed August 29, 2006.

Bucholtz, Mary and Kira Hall. "Theorizing Identity in Language and Sexuality Research." *Language in Society* 33 (2004): 469–515.

Butler, Judith. *Gender Trouble: Feminism and the Subversion of Identity.* New York: Routledge, 1990.

Clary, Christopher."Gender Test after a Gold Medal Finish." http://www.nytimes.com/2009/08/20/sports/20runner.html?_r=1. Accessed September 15, 2010.

Dankwa, Serena Owusu. "'It's a Silent Trade': Female Same-Sex Intimacies in Post-Colonial Ghana," *NORA-Nordic Journal of Feminist and Gender Research* 17, 3 (2009): 192–205.

Decena, Carlos Ulises. "*Tacit* Subjects," *GLQ: A Journal of Lesbian and Gay Studies* 14, 2–3 (2008): 339–59.

Epprecht, Marc. *Hungochani: The History of a Dissident Sexuality in Southern Africa.* Montreal: McGill-Queen's University Press, 2004.

Foucault, Michel. *The History of Sexuality, An Introduction.* NY: Random House, 1978.

_____. "Politics and the Study of Discourse." *Ideology and Consciousness.* 3 (1978): 7–26.

Gaudio, Rudolf. *Allah Made Us: Sexual Outlaws in an Islamic African City.* Chicester: Wiley-Blackwell, 2009.

Gevisser, Mark and Edwin Cameron (eds.) *Defiant Desire.* New York: Routledge, 1995.

Gifford, Paul. *Ghana's New Christianity: Pentecostalism in a Globalising African Economy.* London: Hurst, 2004.

Gueboguo, Charles. "Penser les 'droits' des homosexual/les en Afrique: du sens et de la puissance de l'action associative militante au Cameroun." *Canadian Journal of African Studies* 43, 1 (2009): 129–50.

Gunkel, Henriette. " 'What's Identity Got To Do With It?' Rethinking Intimacy and Homosociality in Contemporary South Africa." *NORA-Nordic journal of Feminist and Gender Research* 17, 3 (2009): 206–21.

Hanson, J. "No room for gays and Lesbians." *Public Agenda*, May 21, 2007. http://allafrica.com/. Accessed February 18, 2010.

Human rights Watch. "Uganda's Anti-Homosexuality Bill." http://www.hrw.org/en/news/2009/10/15/uganda-ant-homosexuality-bill-threatens-liberties-and-human-rights-defenders. Accessed January 20, 2009.

Ireland, D. "Ghana: Media Leads Anti-Gay Witch-Hunt." http://www.zmag.org/content/showarticle.cfm?ItemID=1106. Accessed September 21, 2006.

Jacques, J. and F. Gbolu. "Social Justice-Same Sex, Different Rights." *Ghanaian Chronicle*, June 22, 2005, *Behind the Mask*, http://www.mask.org.za/article.php?cat=ghana&id=255. Accessed April 4, 2007.

Katz, Jonathan Ned. "The Invention of Heterosexuality." *Socialist Review* 20 (1990): 7–34.

Lugones, Maria. "The Coloniality of Gender." *World and Knowledge Otherwise* 2, dossier 2 (Spring 2008): 1–17.

Miescher, Stephen. *Making Men in Ghana.* Bloomington: Indiana University Press, 2005.

Morgan, Ruth and Saskia Weiringa (eds.) *Tommy Boys, Lesbian Men and Ancestral Wives: female same-sex practices in Africa.* Johannesburg: Jacana Media Ltd., 2005.

Morrish, Liz and Helen Sauntson. *New Perspectives on Language and Sexual Identity* Houndsmills, UK: Palgrave Macmillan, 2007.

Murray, Stephen and Roscoe, Will (eds.) *Boy Wives and Female Husbands: Studies of African Homosexualities.* New York: St. Martins, 1998.

Nkabinde, Nkunzi with Morgan, Ruth. "This has happened since ancient times … it's something you are born with: ancestral wives amongst same-sex sangomas in South Africa." In R. Morgan and S. Weiringa. Johannesburg: Jacarana Media, 2005. 261–78.

O'Mara, Kathleen, (eds.) *Tommy Boys, Lesbian Men, Ancestral Wives.* "Historicising Outsiders on Campus: the re/production of Lesbian and Gay Insiders." *Journal of Gender Studies* 6, 1 (1997): 17–31.

_____. "Queers Performing on Campus: Concealment and Revelation by Students of Color in the 1990s." *Phoebe: Journal of Gender and Cultural Critiques* 11, 2 (1999): 43–50.

_____. "Homophobia and Building Queer Community in Urban Ghana." *Phoebe: Journal of Gender and Cultural Critiques* 19, 1 (2007): 35–46.

Oyěwùmí, Oyéronke. *The Invention of Women: Making Sense of Western Gender Discourses.* Minneapolis: University of Minnesota Press, 1997.

Pierce, Steven. "Identity, Performance and Secrecy: Gendered life and the 'modern' in northern Nigeria." *Feminist Studies* 33, 3 (2007): 539–65.

Ryan, O. "Ghana's secret gay community." http://news.bbc.co.uk/2/hi/africa/6445337.stm. March 14, 2007.

Ross, Marlon B. "Beyond the Closet as Raceless Paradigm." In E. Patrick Johnson and Mae G. Henderson. *Black Queer Studies*. Durham: Duke University Press, 2005. 161–89.

Rubin. http://www.huffingtonpost.com/ariel-rubin/ugandas-anti-homosexuality_397090.html. Accessed February 17, 2010.

Sedgwick, Eve Kosofsky. *The Epistemology of the Closet*. Berkeley: University of California Press, 1990.

Walle, Thomas M. "Making places of intimacy-Ethnicity, friendship and masculinities in Oslo." *NORA-Nordic Journal of Feminist and Gender Research* 15, 2–3 (2007): 144–57.

Wieringa, Saskia and Morgan, Ruth. *Tommy Boys, Lesbian Men and Ancestral Wives*. Johannesburg: Jacana Media, 2005.

Yankah, Kwesi. "Power and the circuit of formal talk." *Journal of Folklore Research* 28, 1 (1991): 1–22.

Yankah, Kwesi. *Speaking for the Chief: Okyeame and the Politics of Akan Royal Oratory*. Bloomington: Indiana University Press, 1995.

Chapter 11

Advertising as Reality? Defining Gay in South African Gay Print Media

Janeske Botes

This chapter is the product of research conducted in late 2007. While researching representations of homosexuality in the media, I noticed that, especially in an African context, homosexuality and its television manifestations received extensive research focus, while other mediums were sidelined. A few years later, I still notice this gap in gender representation research, and so, this chapter aims to start filling that gap. South Africa, one of the few countries worldwide where civil unions between gay men are legal, has an established gay press in the form of three prominent gay magazines: *Gay Pages*, *Wrapped*, and *EXIT*. *Gay Pages* has been in circulation for fourteen years, and *Wrapped* was launched in 2006. *EXIT* is South Africa's only lesbian and gay publication. Established in 1985, it is the longest circulating homosexual publication in the country.

All three magazines cater for the same target market, allowing for an analysis of some of the representations found within these publications. In doing so, conclusions can be drawn around the presumed gay identity in South Africa and questions can be asked about from where these representations stem. It is first necessary to present the definition of "gay" that will be used for this chapter. While homosexuality includes both gay men and lesbian women,[1] I am choosing to use the term "gay," which refers to male persons "desiring sexual contact exclusively with members of their own sex."[2] Hence, for the purposes of this research, the term "gay" will be used predominantly, with the terms "homosexual" or 'homosexuality' referring to broader realms of "gayness."

Kaczorowski situates homosexuality within gay and lesbian studies, which consider how ideas of homosexuality and its opposite, heterosexuality, have been defined both socially and historically.[3] This is an especially important field of research, as noted by Ellis fifty-four years ago, in his work on the impact of heterosexual culture on homosexuals.[4] More recently, Dennis Altman has linked this field of research to globalization. Altman demonstrates in his book, *Global Sex*, that there is a relationship between globalization and sexual identities.[5] Just as people and information are now able to transcend borders,

1. Richard Dyer, "Believing in Fairies: The Author and the Homosexual," in Diana Fuss (ed.) *Inside/Out: Lesbian Theories, Gay Theories* (New York: Routledge, 1991), 186.
2. Matthew D. Johnson, "Homosexuality," http://www.glbtq.com/social-sciences/homosexuality.html, accessed August 25, 2007.
3. Craig Kaczorowski, "Gay, Lesbian, and Queer Studies," http://www.glbtq.com/social-sciences/gay_lesbian_queer_studies,2.html, accessed August 25, 2007.
4. Albert Ellis, "The Influence of Heterosexual Culture," in Donald Webster Cory (ed.) *Homosexuality: A Cross Cultural Approach* (New York: The Julian Press, Inc., 1956), 415–19.
5. Dennis Altman, *Global Sex* (Chicago: The University of Chicago Press, 2001), 86.

so too can ideas around identity, and therefore sexual identity: "The question is not whether homosexuality exists ... but how people incorporate homosexual behavior into their sense of self." Anthony Giddens confirms this connection, explaining that the global outlook created by globalization has led to people looking to sources outside their immediate domestic environment to assist in creating their sense of identity.[6] A potential problem with this phenomenon is the possible eradication of cultural differences between people and societies, which, in this research, manifests itself in the observation that more Western ideas of homosexuality are found in South African gay print media.

James Weinrich and Walter Williams support this observation in stating that Western homosexualities, which include gay identities, strongly resemble the identities seen worldwide today.[7] In locating this comment within the print medium realm, Gillian Dyer connects this resemblance to advertising, as it provokes the manipulation of social attitudes.[8] This manipulation is carried out through the persuasion advertising employs in order to convince consumers to purchase the specific product.[9] The various ideas and representations inherent in *Gay Pages*, *Wrapped*, and *EXIT* will now be presented. Due to the physical placement of specific products in these publications, the broad categories of analysis will firstly consider car advertisements, followed by other product and service advertisements. Advertisements for venues, meetings (phone sex, dating portals), and the classifieds have not formed part of this analysis. Various areas of discussion, including language, race, product, physical appearance, and age will be focused upon in order to further consider representations within all the advertisements.

Advertisements: Cars

Jean Kilbourne postulates that advertisements, along with selling products, also aim to "sell values, images, and concepts of success and worth, love and sexuality, popularity and normalcy."[10] A total of eleven car advertisements were found in *Gay Pages* and *Wrapped* in 2007. Twelve car advertisements were found in the same magazines in 2009. *EXIT* featured none, in both time periods. Of the eleven advertisements featured in 2007, four include people: three feature men and one features a woman. The 2009 car advertisements include three men, but they are all placed as secondary to the car being advertised. The roles they fulfill are that of drivers of the vehicles, whereas most of the 2007 advertisements place people as central aspects of the advertisement. Brands include Jaguar, Smart, Diahatsu, Cadillac, Audi, Jeep, Alfa Romeo, Nissan, Suzuki, Honda, and BMW, with Mercedes-Benz, Fiat, Lexus, and Porsche advertisements featured multiple times in both magazines.

Many of these advertisements are replicated for the homosexual market targeted by these publications, implying that these car advertisements appeal to both gay and

---

6. Anthony Giddens, *Sociology* (Cambridge: Polity Press, 2001), 56.

7. James D.Weinrich, and Walter L. Williams, "Strange Customs, Familiar Lives: Homosexualities in Other Cultures," in John C. Gonsiorek and James D. Weinrich (eds.) *Homosexuality: Research Implications for Public Policy* (California: Sage Publications, Ltd., 1991), 59.

8. Gillian Dyer, *Advertising as Communication* (London: Routledge, 1982), 2.

9. Ingrid Porter, ""Reading" Advertisements," http://www.newsweekeducation.com/extras/ad.php, accessed August 28, 2007.

10. Jean Kilbourne, "Beauty and the beast of advertising," in Gail Dines and Jean M. Humes (eds.) *Gender, Race and Class in Media* (California: Sage Publications, Inc., 1989), 121.

heterosexual men.[11] Despite this, Paul Messaris notes that persuasion through images must often be supported by words. However, in the instance of luxury products, such as many of the car brands mentioned earlier, explicit notions of status through language are unusual.[12] Many of the car advertisements contradict this point—the text is often a focal point of the advertisement. A Daihatsu advertisement (see Figure 1 below) in the 2007 *Gay Pages* features a young, smiling black man alongside the text: "Have a fling!"

Another Daihatsu model is also advertised on this page, which is interesting in that it juxtaposes the two dominant ideas of gay identities—"Have a fling!" aligns with Jamie Gough's ideas of an effeminate gay male, which typically involves the exhibition of the limp wrist whilst screaming and lisping in conversation, often seen as a sure sign of a gay man.[13] Christo Cilliersalso highlights the use of the color pink in visually labeling a gay man as effeminate.[14] Vito Russo in his landmark study on homosexuality in movies, *The Celluloid Closet*, notes that "sissies," or more effeminate men, are "yardsticks for measuring the virility of the men around them," indicating that gay men are either effeminate or not.[15] The second idea of gay identity seen below—"Tough never looked this good"—incorporates the more masculine, more heterosexual gay male16 through the ideas associated with the word "tough."

A Dodge Caliber advertisement in *Wrapped* shows the vehicle being tattooed in a tattoo parlor, with text commenting that "It's anything but cute." The stance against effeminate gay men is repeated, supporting Tim Bergling's comment that assumptions of sexuality are based on years of cultural programming.[16] Hence, the idea of a tattoo parlor as a "masculine," and therefore, heterosexual, establishment, and of tattoos as a "masculine" trait, is circulated. This is also encapsulated in the tattoo artist, who has tattoos across both arms.

Heterosexual identities are clearly the focus in a Cadillac advertisement in *Gay Pages*. It depicts a woman, which is quite interesting, as the advertisement is placed in a gay magazine. Anne Cronin explains that this advertisement presents the woman as a "conventional 'status symbol' tied to notions of tradition, exclusivity, craftsmanship and prestige," hence aligning with a very traditionally masculine viewpoint.[17] Yet, the text reads, "The new measure of success," implying the relatively recent introduction of gay men as prominent consumers in society.[18]

This advertisement is an example of "gay window advertising." Advertisers were initially hesitant to advertise both for and within the gay market, as their product would be labeled

11. Rebecca Phillips, "Advertisers' Strategies to Target Gay Audiences in Attitude and Gay Times," http://www.aber.ac.uk/media/Students/rrp9601.html, accessed August 28, 2007.

12. Paul Messaris, *Visual Persuasion: The Role of Images in Advertising* (California: Sage Publications, Inc., 1997), 219, 226.

13. Jamie Gough, "Theories of sexual identity and the masculinization of the gay man," in Simon Shepherd and Mick Wallis (eds.) *Coming on Strong: Gay Politics and Culture* (London: Unwin Hyman Ltd., 1989), 119.

14. Christo Cilliers, "Media and Sexual Orientation: The Portrayal of Gays and Lesbians," in Pieter J. Fourie (ed.) *Media Studies Volume 2: Policy, Management and Media Representation* (Cape Town: Juta & Co., 2008), 332.

15. Vito Russo, *The Celluloid Closet: Homosexuality in the Movies* (New York: Harper & Row, Publishers, 1987), 16.

16. Tim Bergling, *Sissyphobia: Gay Men and Effeminate Behavior* (New York: Harrington Park Press, 2001), 27.

17. Anne M. Cronin, *Advertising and Consumer Citizenship: Gender, Images and Rights* (London: Routledge, 2000), 62.

18. Fred Fejes, "Advertising and the Political Economy of Lesbian/Gay Identity," in G. Dines and J.M. Humes (eds.) *Gender, Race and Class in Media* (California: Sage Publications, Inc., 2003), 213, 314.

Figure 1. Daihatsu advertisement from *Gay Pages* © 2007 Gay Pages.

as "gay." Rand explains that the "gay window advertising" technique was then utilized, where advertisements in mainstream publications were constructed to appeal to gay and lesbian consumers, whilst simultaneously remaining appropriate for heterosexual consumers. Many more examples of this are seen in the magazines, as discussed below. Despite this advertising technique and its prevalence within South African gay print media, the use of a woman as a reminder of cultural notions of triumph and accomplishment indicates that this heterosexual interpretation of her image is forcing heterosexual masculinities to remain in the gay realm.

Many of the other car advertisements specifically utilize language to send a message to the homosexual market. A Jeep advertisement in *Gay Pages* reads, "Wrangler and Wrangler Unlimited," "A New Species from Jeep." These "new species" can be interpreted as applying to the gay consumer—a new market for Jeep to cater for, aside from the traditional heterosexual market. Some of this market will be effeminate, but they are a 'new species' to target, regardless. Furthermore, the photographs of the cars are taped to a wall, for display and admiration—this can be related to the gay market within which they are advertising. They are a new market to adapt to, so they will be researched and analyzed to ensure the success of the advertising campaign. This observation aligns with Robert Goldman's assertion that advertisements contain deep social assumptions of which consumers are often unaware.[19]

A Jaguar advertisement (Figure 4) in *Gay Pages* shows a man on the left, looking over his shoulder at the reader, while the Jaguar is on the right, positioned so as to indicate that it

---

19. Robert Goldman, *Reading Ads Socially* (London: Routledge, 1992), 1.

Figure 2. Dodge advertisement from *Wrapped* © 2007 Wrapped.

can drive off the page. The text is placed above the man: "Gorgeous demands your immediate attention," with "gorgeous" referring to both man and car. As the man is walking away and the car is positioned to drive away, the reader must focus immediately and decide which of the two is the "gorgeous" requiring attention. This observation contradicts Messaris's earlier observation on the subtlety of status in car advertisements, via the language used. This advertisement is also an example of gay window advertising—the "gorgeous" can be assumed to be the car for heterosexual men, while the man will be a consideration for gay men.

Other examples of language that can possibly appeal more to a gay market abound. A Porsche advertisement in *Gay Pages* asks: "What's wrong with dressing up for a workout?" The words "dressing up" include effeminate gay men as a target market for this car. Less effeminate gay men will presumably not be concerned with dressing up and appearance, as it is not a very traditional masculine activity. The words "want" and "need" are used in two advertisements in 2009. The first is for Mercedes-Benz and reads: "Some cars you want. Some cars you need. Some cars you want to need." The second is for Nissan, and states, quite similarly to the former, "Want? Need? Same difference." These two words have rather explicit connotations for the gay market as a common stereotype is that gay men are very promiscuous.

The ideas of 'want' and 'need' are merged in these advertisements, indicating that gay men can, and will, blur the line between these two feelings. This will be highlighted again in other product advertisements. The races observed in the advertisements featuring people highlight a major issue in gay advertising today. Donald Donham notes that,

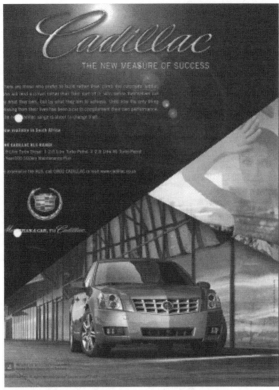

Figure 3.   Cadillac advertisement from *Gay Pages* © 2007 Gay Pages.

Figure 4.   Jaguar advertisement from *Gay Pages* © 2007 Gay Pages.

especially in South Africa, the notion of a black gay man is still a much stigmatized one.[20] Therefore, it can be noted that, in 2007, one of the four car advertisements with people feature a black man. The other three depict white men and a white woman. In 2009, none of the three car advertisements featuring people included black men.

Advertisements: Other Products and Services

Advertisements that fall into this category include products such as computers, laptops, broadband Internet, gay lifestyle websites, dog food, cologne, razors, clothing, skin products, nutrition products, adult shops, pornography websites, lubricant, jewelry, furniture, home wares, and alcohol. Services advertised include graphic and web designers, body treatments, personal trainers, dentists, medical aids, hospital plans, airlines, travel agencies, cruises, and counseling. This broad range of products and services, in addition to the cars discussed previously, highlight the common view of gay men as upscale and wealthy. In South Africa, this manifests itself into the idea of the "Pink Rand," referring to the buying power of gay men.[21] This notion has greatly assisted in attracting advertisers to gay media, as they believe gay men display the following traits: "Above average income, highly educated, travels a lot, and buys all the new electronic toys and gadgets."[22]

In total, there are four Mecer advertisements (two from 2007 and two from 2009) and one advertisement for broadband Internet, from 2007. These advertisements are indicative of the technological lifestyles gay men often have, which John Campbell aligns specifically with Internet usage.[23] Furthermore, *Wrapped* presents two advertisements for a new gay lifestyle website in 2007, mamba, which is also advertised in *EXIT* during both 2007 and 2009 (displaying both a white and black plastic doll). A graphic and web design company advertises in *Wrapped*, and a gay pornography website advertises in *EXIT*. A common theme throughout these advertisements is the use of physical appearance, as well as the specific physical appearance of the men presented in order to sell the products. Gough explains that the dominant image of gay men has gradually become more masculine (rather than effeminate), with much focus placed on the male body. Richard Kaye supports this in writing that images of the male body have permeated culture, especially gay culture.[24] Here, one sees men at work, plastic dolls, and an attractive face to sell products associated with technology and the Internet. All of these, as will be observed below, firmly position their ideas of gay men within a more masculine sphere, avoiding the depiction of effeminate men. Furthermore, the four Mecer advertisements are all possible examples of "gay window advertising." Heterosexuals would, perhaps, interpret the groups of people and the single men at work as examples of people at work, whereas a gay man may pick up on the isolation of the man in Figure 5, the focus on the single man in Figure 6 and 8, and the group of (possibly, gay) men at work in Figure 7, and so, view and read these images through a different framework.

---

20. Donald L. Donham, "Freeing South Africa: The 'Modernization' of Male-Male Sexuality in Soweto," in Jennifer Robertson (ed.) *Same-Sex Cultures and Sexualities: An Anthropological Reader* (UK: Blackwell Publishing, Ltd., 2005), 264.

21. Marketingweb, "The Power of Pink," http://www.marketingweb.co.za/marketingweb/view/marketingweb, accessed August 28, 2007.

22. Jay Rosen, "Out Magazine's National Reach," *The New York Times*, March 7, 1994.

23. John Edward Campbell, *Getting It Online: Cyberspace, Gay Male Sexuality, and Embodied Identity* (New York: Harrington Park Press, 2004), 9.

24. Richard Kaye, *The Male Mystique* (USA: Hunter College, 2000).

Figure 5. Mecer advertisement from *Gay Pages* © 2007 Gay Pages.

Figure 6. Mecer advertisement from *Gay Pages* © 2007 Gay Pages.

Figure 7. Mecer advertisement from *Gay Pages* © 2009 Gay Pages.

Figure 8. Mecer advertisement from *Gay Pages* © 2009 Gay Pages.

Figure 9. K-9 Holistic Dog Food advertisement from *Gay Pages* © 2007 Gay Pages.

Figure 10. Philips advertisement from *Gay Pages* © 2007 Gay Pages.

Another interesting use of the male body is the advertisement for K-9 dog food. The advertisement portrays a muscular, tanned, topless gay man holding his dog. The gay male here contradicts some conventions identified by Philip Locke as representing attractive gay males — the dark hair on his arms and chest, as well as his facial hair, is rare amongst gay males portrayed in the media.[25] Physically, he looks very masculine, but his gaze towards his dog, as well as the use of pink in the advertisement, indicates that he is more of an effeminate gay male. This physical contradiction is also seen in a cologne and adult shop advertisement, where hairy men are used to sell very intimate and sexual products.

This is interesting, as gay males are predominantly viewed as hair-less, a view upheld by the Philips razor advertisement in *Gay Pages*. Two kiwifruits are shown — one has been shaved, the other remains untouched. The text states: "Simplicity is shaving yourself wherever you want," and later explains that "It's the safe and easy way to shave and trim everything from the neck down: chest, back, legs, armpits, buttocks … exotic fruit?" This aligns with Dyer's observation that male sexuality is represented through symbolism, a characteristic often seen in gay media.[26]

This is generally seen across the board in advertising in both heterosexual and gay media — the body and the notion of sex are used to sell a product. Locke further notes

---

25. Philip Locke, "Male images in the gay mass media and bear-oriented magazines: Analysis and contrast," in Les Wright (ed.) *The bear book: Readings in the history and evolution of a gay male subculture* (New York: Harrington Park Press, 1997), 103–40.

26. Dyer, "Male Sexuality in the Media," in Andy Metcalf and Martin Humphries (eds.) *The Sexuality of Men* (London: Pluto Press, 1985), 29.

Figure 11. Cetaphil advertisement from *Gay Pages* © 2007 Gay Pages.

Figure 12. Cape Medical Plan advertisement from *Gay Pages* © 2009 Gay Pages.

that the bodies are almost always slim, toned, and muscular, which further links to the advertisements focused on body and skin treatments, products, medical aid, and cologne. The focus on sex and the body also incorporates the adult shop and pornography website advertisements in *EXIT*. The Cetaphil advertisement (see Figure 11, below) in *Gay Pages* features a large, dominant image of a topless man in tight underwear, busy shaving. In this instance, Dyer's explanation that the focus of male sexuality is "overwhelmingly centered on the genitals, especially the penis," is clearly seen. When the penis is not shown, the idea of arousal and sex is clearly portrayed. 29 This is noted in advertisements for FMO (the models are wearing tight underwear, with exposed chests); Cape Medical Plan (a naked man is viewed from the side, and the text "We care for our members" is positioned next to where his penis would be); Laser Hair Removal (a man is busy undressing and his chest is exposed); and a Personal Trainer (a tattooed man, presumably the trainer, is topless, kneeling, with his face turned towards the camera) advertisements. An interesting contradiction is noted in the Angel for Men advertisement, which presents an attractive, topless, well-built, hair-less gay man advertising a product called "Angel." The sexuality of the advertisement is communicated to the reader through this contradiction between language and visuals. This again highlights Messaris's argument that persuasion through images must often be supported by words.

The Brett Goldman advertisement in *Gay Pages* and the Energie advertisement in *Wrapped* are the two clothing brands advertised in 2007 that depict fully clothed men. The males in Brett Goldman's advertisement are wearing formal suits and are posing for the camera on a set. The one dressed in black is holding a flower down to the one in gold. Furthermore, as he is standing, while the other is sitting, so that dominant heterosexual roles are reinforced. The standing man is the "man" in this image, while the other is the "woman"—this is a common belief around gay relationships, which many gay men seek

Figure 13. Brett Goldman advertisement from *Gay Pages* © 2007 Gay Pages.

Figure 14. Tiger of Sweden advertisement from *Wrapped* © 2009 Wrapped.

to dispel.[27] The Energie advertisement depicts five men leaning against a wall, with one looking away from the rest, as if to rest his head on his neighbor's shoulder. Despite the models being fully clothed, this position hints quite strongly at the presumed homosexual relations in the image.

A Tiger of Sweden advertisement, in *Wrapped* in 2009, features a man and a woman. The man is the dominant character, while the woman has a more secondary position—she is reflected in a mirror, and is standing deep in shadow. While this can be interpreted as "gay window advertising," another interpretation can view the inclusion of the woman as a reminder of heterosexual sexual identity. The inclusion of women in gay print media advertisements during both time periods considered here points to the idea that gay men still need heterosexual reminders of identity, perhaps in case they realize they may be wrong in their pursuit of homosexuality.

Two jewelry advertisements, both appearing in 2007, represent the union of a gay couple, which is legal in South Africa.[28] The union of a couple reinforces the previous belief of there being a 'male' and 'female' figure in a gay relationship. These figures are strongly disputed, as each gay relationship is unique. The advertisements for furniture and home ware can both be seen to contribute to the issues of roles in a gay unity, as they imply settling down and unity. This, however, is one reading another focuses on gay men being able to afford expensive goods for their homes, which again links to the "Pink Rand" concept.

---

27. Donald Webster Cory, *The Homosexual in America: A Subjective Approach* (New York: Greenberg: Publisher, 1951), 149.

28. Behind the Mask, "South Africa," http://www.mask.org.za/index.php?page=southafrica, accessed August 25, 2007.

Figure 15. Club Travel advertisement from *Gay Pages* © 2009 Gay Pages.

A new observation is the appearance of two holiday advertisements — they appear in *Gay Pages* and *EXIT*, both in 2009. The former advertises Club Travel, a travel agency, and the latter a cruise line.

This advertisement is clearly targeted for the gay market; men are the only sex that features, and there is extensive focus on the male body. However, there are no black men represented. Overall, the representation of black men is limited, with the black plastic dolls found in the mamba website advertisement and the inclusion of a black torso in a Body Renewal advertisement are the only black male representations present in the 2007 and 2009 *Gay Pages*, *Wrapped*, and *EXIT* editions.

This is a major inconsistency in representations of South African gay men. The majority of the population is black, so it can be assumed that a fair number of black men are gay. However, if one considers the lack of racial diversity in the advertisements in these three publications, it is obvious that this element of the gay population is being sidelined by advertisers. This raises questions about the class that the advertisers expect the magazines to be targeting. In a country where race relations form an integral part of history, the shortage of black representation in the gay press 16 years after South Africa's transition to a democracy is troubling.

Further stereotypes that are perpetuated, and that serves to 'other' homosexuals even more in the print media realm, include the abundance of young, or youthful looking men. Figure 6 (the second Mecer advertisement) is an exception, as he is older. However, he is clean-shaven and busy with technology, so, through utilizing the 'gay window advertising' technique, one can assume he is gay. Phillips writes that the dominance of young men

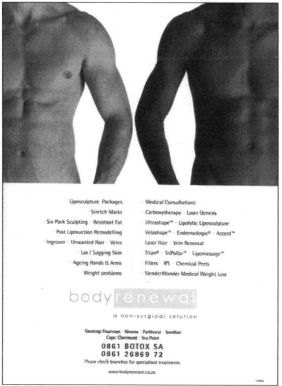

Figure 16. Body Renewal advertisement from *Gay Pages* © 2009 Gay Pages.

"reinforces the homosexual stereotype of gay men as predators as voiced by many homophobic heterosexuals." It also offers an inaccurate portrayal of gay men in South Africa.

The examples presented in this paper show that the representations of gay men in South African gay magazines are often skewed in favor of more traditional, heterosexual representations of masculinity. These representations often have Western roots, thereby indicating that Western cultural ideas and representations of homosexuality frequently form the basis of domestic representations. Hence, misrepresentations regarding race, physical appearances, and age have been shown to exist. These include the lack of representation of black gay men, a very specific and highly sexualized physical appearance (which quite clearly does not focus on effeminate gay men), and a vast majority of representations of young gay men. Within car advertisements, it was found that "gay window advertising" is common, along with the more blatant use of heterosexual masculinities. The use of language within gay advertisements also plays a relevant role in the interpretation and analysis of a product. The specific focus upon advertisements selling products and services was necessary in order to show that the idea of the "Pink Rand" also plays an inherent role in the advertising process for this specific market. Therefore, it can be concluded that there are skewed and often unreal, and unrepresentative representations of race, physical appearance, and age within advertisements in the South African gay print media realm.

References

Altman, Dennis. *Global Sex.* Chicago: The University of Chicago Press, 2001.

Behind the Mask. "South Africa." http://www.mask.org.za/index.php?page=southafrica Accessed August 25, 2007.

Bergling, Tim. *Sissyphobia: Gay Men and Effeminate Behavior.* New York: Harrington Park Press, 2001.

Blasius, Mark. "Ethos of Lesbian and Gay Existence." *Political Theory.* Vol. 20 (1992): 642–71.

Campbell, J.E. *Getting It Online: Cyberspace, Gay Male Sexuality, and Embodied Identity.* New York: Harrington Park Press, 2004.

Cilliers, Christo. "Media and Sexual Orientation: The Portrayal of Gays and Lesbians." In Pieter J. Fourie (ed.) *Media Studies Volume 2: Policy, Management and Media Representation.* 2nd ed. Cape Town: Juta & Co., 2008, 331–58.

Cory, Donald Webster. *The Homosexual in America: A Subjective Approach.* New York: Greenberg: Publisher, 1951.

Cronin, Anne M. *Advertising and Consumer Citizenship: Gender, Images and Rights.* London: Routledge, 2000.

Donham, Donald L. "Freeing South Africa: The 'Modernization' of Male-Male Sexuality in Soweto." In Jennifer Robertson (ed.) *Same-Sex Cultures and Sexualities: An Anthropological Reader.* UK: Blackwell Publishing, Ltd., 2005, 261–78.

Dyer, Gillian. *Advertising as Communication.* London: Routledge, 1982.

Dyer, Richard. "Male Sexuality in the Media." In A. Metcalf and M. Humphries (eds.) *The Sexuality of Men.* London: Pluto Press, 1985, 28–43.

Dyer, Richard. "Believing in Fairies: The Author and the Homosexual." In Diana Fuss (ed.) *Inside/Out: Lesbian Theories, Gay Theories.* New York: Routledge, 1991, 185–201.

Ellis, Albert. "The Influence of Heterosexual Culture." In Donald W. Cory (ed.) *Homosexuality: A Cross Cultural Approach.* New York: The Julian Press, Inc., 1956, 415–19.

Fejes, Fred. "Advertising and the Political Economy of Lesbian/Gay Identity." In Gail Dines and Jean M. Humes (eds.) *Gender, Race and Class in Media.* California: Sage Publications, Inc., 2003, 212–22.

Giddens, Anthony. *Sociology.* 4th ed. Cambridge: Polity Press, 2001.

Goldman, Robert. *Reading Ads Socially.* London: Routledge, 1992.

Gough, Jamie. "Theories of sexual identity and the masculinization of the gay man." In Simon Shepherd and Mick Wallis (eds.) *Coming on Strong: Gay Politics and Culture.* London: Unwin Hyman Ltd., 1989, 119–36.

Johnson, Matthew D. "Homosexuality." http://www.glbtq.com/social-sciences/homosexuality.html. Accessed August 25, 2007.

Kaczorowski, Craig. "Gay, Lesbian, and Queer Studies." http://www.glbtq.com/social-sciences/gay_lesbian_queer_studies,2.html. Accessed August 25, 2007.

Kaye, Richard. *The Male Mystique.* USA: Hunter College, 2000.

Kilbourne, Jean. "Beauty and the beast of advertising." In Gail Dines and Jean M. Humes (eds.) *Gender, Race and Class in Media.* California: Sage Publications, Inc., 1989, 121–25.

Locke, Philip. "Male images in the gay mass media and bear-oriented magazines: Analysis and contrast." In Les Wright (ed.) *The bear book: Readings in the history and evolution of a gay male subculture*. New York: Harrington Park Press, 1997, 103–40.

Marketingweb. "The Power of Pink." http://www.marketingweb.co.za/marketingweb/view/marketingweb. Accessed August 28, 2007.

McIntosh, Mary. "The Homosexual Role." In E. Stein (ed.) *Forms of Desire: Sexual Orientation and the Social Constructionist Controversy*. London: Routledge, 1992. 25–42.

Messaris, Paul. *Visual Persuasion: The Role of Images in Advertising*. California: Sage Publications, Inc., 1997.

Norton, Rictor. "Homosexual Identities." http://www.infopt.demon.co.uk/social08.htm. Accessed August 25, 2007.

Phillips, Rebecca. "Advertisers' Strategies to Target Gay Audiences in Attitude and Gay Times." http://www.aber.ac.uk/media/Students/rrp9601.html. Accessed August 28, 2007.

Pillard, Richard C. "Masculinity and Femininity in Homosexuality: 'Inversion' Revisited." In John C. Gonsiorek and James D. Weinrich (eds.) *Homosexuality: Research Implications for Public Polic*. California: Sage Publications, Ltd., 1991, 32–43.

Porter, Ingrid. "Reading" Advertisements." http://www.newsweekeducation.com/extras/ad.php. Accessed August 28, 2007.

Rand, Erica. "Advertising and Consumerism." http://www.glbtq.com/arts/ad_consume.html. Accessed August 28, 2007.

Rosen, Jay. "Out Magazine's National Reach." *The New York Times*, March 7, 1994.

Russo, Vito. *The Celluloid Closet: Homosexuality in the Movies*. New York: Harper & Row, Publishers, 1987.

Shugart, Helene A. "Reinventing Privilege: The New (Gay) Man in Contemporary Popular Media." *Critical Studies in Media Communication* 20 (2003): 67–91.

Weinrich, James D. and Williams, Walter L. "Strange Customs, Familiar Lives: Homosexualities in Other Cultures." In John C. Gonsiorek and James D. Weinrich (eds.) *Homosexuality: Research Implications for Public Policy*. California: Sage Publications, Ltd., 1991, 44–59.

Part III

Gendered Nationalism, Gendered Resistance

Chapter 12

Dressing the Part: Dress Culture, Gender, Compliance, and Resistance in Mobutu's Zaire

Danielle Porter Sanchez

The movement known as the SAPE (*la Société Ambianceurs et Persons Élégants*) emerged in Congo-Brazzaville following colonialism and spread to Congo-Zaire during the latter half of the twentieth century. The *sapeur* movement was characterized by men wearing expensive European clothing and listening to Rumba in the bars of Kinshasa and Brazzaville. The word *sapeur* comes from the French slang word *sape*, which means, "to dress with class." While the movement served as a means to empower those that dressed elegantly, its followers were predominately male. This is intriguing because it hints at important questions relating to dress, political expression, identity, and gender in the post-colony.

During Mobutu's Authenticity campaign, the state dictated that citizens had to wear traditional Zairian clothing. The Authenticity movement primarily centered upon men, especially in the realm of dress culture. For Congolese men, Authenticity was synonymous with the *abacost*, which was derived from the French phrase, *a bas le costume*, or "Down with the suit!" Mobutu decreed that Zairian men had to wear the *abacost*. At the same time, it seems that women were an afterthought in the Authenticity campaign; women were simply told to wear traditional clothing and hairstyles, which was relatively vague compared to their male counterparts.

Authenticity and the *sapeur* movement are significant because they emerged at approximately the same period in Congolese history, but more importantly, they represent an ongoing discussion of politics and the nation in Mobutu's Zaire through the medium of dress culture. Furthermore, the relative exclusion of women in both of these contexts relating to politics and dress culture is important to understand because it is representative of a larger discussion of gendered domains and political activism against the colonial and postcolonial state in Central Africa. These two examples thoroughly underscore the question of whose voices (or patterns of dress) matter in the political discourses of a given society, and whose voices are considered less important.

Through the work of Hildi Hendrickson and others regarding dress culture, it is clear that the act of wearing clothing is more than just assembling random colors and pieces of cloth. In *Clothing and Difference: Embodied Identities in Colonial and Post-Colonial Africa*, Hendrickson argues, "clothing and other treatments of the body are primary symbols in the performances through which modernity—and therefore history—have been conceived, constructed, and challenged in Africa."[1] Thus, the act of wearing clothing

---

1. Hildi Hendrickson, *Clothing and Difference: Embodied Identities in Colonial and Post-Colonial Africa* (Durham: Duke University Press, 1996), 13.

is much more than putting a piece of cloth on one's body; instead, it is representative of the negotiation of one's values and understanding of society and one's place within it.

This chapter will demonstrate that women were excluded or marginalized in these two unique movements as a result of gender discrimination in the colonial state, and Mobutu's emphasis on creating a nation among men in order to secure his place as the head of state. Women were actively involved in political discourses, the workforce, and their communities; therefore, by overlooking their presence in the realms of politics and dress culture, one is missing a major part of Zairian life in the 1970s and 1980s.

Discrimination and the Construction of the *Sapeur* Movement

The man in Figure 1 lives the life of the *sapeur*.[2] The *sapeur* dresses himself well. One may ask why he is characterized as a male; the reason for this is because of the influence of traditional culture, colonialism, and modern politics within Congo-Brazzaville and the Democratic Republic of the Congo. While few have thoroughly addressed the issue of the *sapeur* in modern historical discourses, the *sapeur* is incredibly important to the history of the Congo due to the politicization of the movement that arose out of a long history of brutality and abuses. Furthermore, few scholars and journalists have given attention to the relative lack of women in the movement.[3] The lack of information regarding women in the *sapeur* movement can be contributed to the historiography on the subject matter that initially focuses on the involvement of working-class males in Brazzaville and then transitions to the shift of the movement to socioeconomically disadvantaged males in Leopoldville/Kinshasa. Much of the work on the *sapeur* to date has looked at the movements within Brazzaville and Kinshasa independently of each other.[4] The fact that the *sapeur* movement transferred from Brazzaville to Leopoldville/Kinshasa was not a coincidence. The *sapeur* movement could have potentially moved anywhere in Francophone Africa, but it moved to Kinshasa for a reason. Their similar colonial pasts, histories of violence, and cultural background facilitated the spread of the movement to Kinshasa where it thrived in the period following independence.

Despite the arbitrary borders drawn during the Berlin Conference, there was a sense of fluidity in between Kinshasa and Brazzaville that colonialism could not necessarily erase with ease. By neglecting these crucial linkages and looking at the *sapeur* movement as solely a Zairian phenomenon during the 1970s and 1980s, one is not able to comprehend the longer history of gender imbalance that shaped the movement in Brazzaville that

---

2. I took this photograph while conducting research in Brazzaville during the summer of 2011. I stumbled into a *sapeur* shop on the outskirts of the administrative center of Brazzaville and was greeted by the owner, a self-proclaimed *sapeur* (although his attire was scaled down for work). Nevertheless, once he found out that I was researching the politics and culture of *sapeurs,* he threw on a tie, hat, and jacket that was a few sizes too small and insisted upon being photographed. He continued posing until he was happy with the photographic results. In the series of photographs, he posed and offered various shots of each article of clothing (including his intricately tied cravat and fancy socks). To these gentlemen, elegance is necessary, even when their outfits are scaled down during the week. Additionally, the photograph also displays the vast variety of colorful suits that the *sapeurs* of Brazzaville gravitate towards during their weekly exhibitions each and every Sunday in Bacongo.

3. Including Justin-Daniel Gandoulou's groundbreaking works, *Entre Paris à Bacongo* and *Dandies à Bacongo*.

4. Ibid.

Figure 1. Man dressed in the elegant manner of a *sapeur*; Brazzaville.

eventually spread into Kinshasa. Scholars and journalists, including the celebrated work of Justin-Daniel Gandoulou, have incorrectly labeled the beginning of the *sapeur* movement as colonialism or World War II. By beginning the story of the *sapeur* with one of these two instances, one completely removes all history and agency from the Congolese *sapeurs*. One conveniently forgets the longer history of politics, culture, and society that began before the relatively brief period of colonial rule and places all of the power of the *sapeur* movement in the hands of the colonizer. Instead, one should recognize the longer history of the *sapeur* movement and the fact that Africans were not blank canvases or hangers that Europeans could decorate to fit their needs.

While the origins of the *sapeur* movement did not emerge until colonialism, it is still important to contextualize this with the cultural background that was central to the identity of the Bakongo in Brazzaville and Kinshasa. Central Africans had a history and culture that predated colonialism and informed their decisions regarding clothing in the twentieth century.[5] Dress was an important method of expressing social status in the

5. Georges Balandier's *Daily Life in the Kingdom of the Kongo from the Sixteenth to the Eighteenth Century* provides an excellent discussion of cultural, social, and political history in the Kongo before colonialism. Similarly, Joel Tishken provides a brief background of the cultural history of the Bakongo in "Central Africa: Peoples and States" in *Africa, volume 1: African History Before 1885*, 215–217. In

Bakongo kingdom in the pre-colonial period. According to Martin, elaborate clothing was a symbol of status and prestige in the Bakongo kingdom of Loango.[6] She states, "In seventeenth-century Loango, foreign visitors marveled at the prestige raphia cloth worn by powerful individuals, likening it to velvet, taffeta, satin, and damask. Specialized royal weavers produced cloths which might be worn only with the ruler's permission, while lesser-quality cloths were worn by ordinary people."[7] The symbolic nature of clothing as a marker of status continued to inform ideas of dress among the Bakongo in the colonial and post-colonial period, as we will see in the pages that follow.

The origins of the *sapeur* movement began to emerge in colonial Brazzaville during the 1920s, when houseboys began wearing the castoffs of their European masters. At this point, the movement was not overtly political or unique, in fact, according to Ch. Didier Gondola in his article, "Dream and Drama: The Search for Elegance Among Congolese Youth," it was still greatly fueled by European concepts of prosperity rather than the mere desire of Africans to follow the trends of the French colonizer:

> Social prestige in the colonial city did not consist so much in having several houseboys — something that was within reach of even the *Petits-blancs* — but in having several "civilized" or "enlightened" servants. Some masters did not hesitate to give their used clothing to their houseboys, who showed off their clothes as much to enhance their master's reputation as to increase their own social status in the eyes of other African city dwellers.[8]

This sort of behavior is significant because it illustrates the close linkages the movement had to European overconsumption during this period. Furthermore, it exemplifies the notion that the French perceived their houseboys as mere hangers and status symbols with no sort of history or culture that could define their being as otherwise.

Despite their available options, many Congolese men during this period consciously chose to wear the cast-offs of their masters.[9] This decision was informed by the key linkages between the cultural background of clothing, status, and advancement within the colonial society. While Congolese men that were working as houseboys for Europeans certainly did not have a glamorous job, access to European goods (not limited to dress) at this time meant something quite significant in Congolese society. As Martin states, "Most Africans observed whites from a distance, but servants who looked after their employers' clothes were conduits of information … confirming the association of power, clothing, and display."[10] Martin's assertion is interesting because it emphasizes this longer history of clothing and understandings of status that houseboys brought with them into their jobs on a daily basis.

The understanding of why these men accepted the cast-offs and chose to live and work in such a Eurocentric context cannot solely be related to status symbols because doing so would negate the history of colonial violence in Congo-Brazzaville. Segregation and oppression were prevalent in colonial Brazzaville and had a profound impact on daily life

---

Africa Adorned, Angela Fisher discusses representation and traditional dress among many African societies, including the Bakongo in Central Africa.

6. Phyllis Martin, "Contesting Clothes in Colonial Brazzaville," *The Journal of African History*, 35 (1994): 402.

7. Ibid., 403.

8. Ch. Didier Gondola, "Dream and Drama: The Search for Elegance among Congolese Youth," *African Studies Review*, 42 (1999): 26.

9. Ibid.

10. Martin, *Leisure and Society in Colonial Brazzaville*, 159.

in the colony. That being said, how could one overcome these violent memories and realities of daily life to essentially mimic the colonizer? While there is no easy answer to this question, the reality of the situation is the fact that compliance and access to European goods often meant advancement within society and much needed perks from one's previous master.

Food and job shortages were often present in colonial Brazzaville, especially following World War I.[11] Thus, choosing to adopt the clothing of the colonizer was never a black and white decision because many significant factors, including survival, had to be considered. The growing number of African houseboys wearing European clothing was not representative of the mere export of European high fashion to Africa. Rather, it represented the social, cultural, and political contexts in which people lived in colonial Brazzaville. Furthermore, Martin argues that before colonialism, royal families controlled valuable cloth; colonialism gave access to cloth and clothing to anyone with cash, which symbolized a renegotiation of status and social differentiation.[12] Thus, gaining access to European clothing in the colony allowed these men to renegotiate their statuses within society in a manner that represented a longer cultural history.

With time, the *sapeur* movement began to shift away from modes of access that centered upon the passing down of used clothes from masters to houseboys.[13] The 1930s represented a sort of independence from French monopolies on access to high fashion. In Gabrielle Vassal's *Français, Belges et Portugais en Afrique*, a clear divergence from the original patterns of consumption of European dress among the Congolese becomes quite evident. She argues that it was quite common for houseboys to sacrifice great lengths, including giving up food, to acquire European goods.[14] The beginning of this divergence also coincides with the spread of this new sense of consumerism from the houseboys of Brazzaville society to others within the colony.[15] The spread of this new phenomenon is not to be confused with the *coastmen* of the 1930s. The *coastmen* were men from other parts of Africa that were sent to Brazzaville to serve in Brazzaville's early labor force. They eventually accumulated enough cash to dress like their European counterparts. The *coastmen* attempted to live the European lifestyle as much as possible, and Africans in Brazzaville perceived them as white men with black skin.[16] Their patterns of consumption and dress inspired the term "*popo* fashion."[17]

In contrast to the *coastmen*, those participating in the new dress culture movement in colonial Brazzaville began to extend beyond the mere act of wearing clothing. This fact was well established by Ch. Didier Gondola when he stated, "Following in the wake of these houseboys, clerks, and then musicians, ardently competed to recreate identities for themselves through clothing."[18] People beyond the original scope of the movement began to forge complex identities that centered on the juxtaposition of traditional culture,

---

11. Martin discusses the food riots and shortages in great depth in *Leisure and Society in Colonial Brazzaville* from pages 39–50.

12. Martin, "Contesting Clothes in Colonial Brazzaville," 404.

13. Ibid., 416.

14. Gabrielle and Joseph Vassal, *Français, Belges et Portugais en Afrique*, (Paris: Pierre Roger, 1931), 153.

15. Gondola, "Dream and Drama: The Search for Elegance among Congolese Youth," 27.

16. Both Gondola and Martin discuss the *coastmen* in their work. *Leisure and Society in Colonial Brazzaville*, 158–161. "Dream and Drama: The Search for Elegance among Congolese Youth," 27.

17. *Popo* (*coastman*) fashion represented the lifestyle of the *coastmen* and became quite popular during the 1920s and 1930s in colonial Brazzaville.

18. Gondola, "Dream and Drama: The Search for Elegance among Congolese Youth," 27.

modern politics, and progress. They did not simply attempt to erase their Africanity like the *coastmen*; instead, they were creating a cultural hybrid that was informed by their cultural past and understanding of the world during a time of change and development.

Unlike the *coastmen*, the movement that expanded in the 1930s was characterized by the unique outfits the followers assembled. While they pieced together European components, the outcomes were vastly different from the outfits of the colonizers and the *popo*. As Martin states, "All the men wore trousers and shirts, but there the similarity ended."[19] Those that followed the movement during the 1930s thoroughly expressed their creativity through popular dress by wearing a wide variety of clothing including sports apparel, beautiful poplin suits, smoking jackets, helmets, silk shirts, and waistcoats.[20] This is significant because their patterns of dress represented a cultural history that was not erased by the presence of the colonizer. They had embedded ideas about dress culture that they maintained and instituted despite the incorporation of Western clothing into their wardrobes.

Subscribing to this new fashion movement created a sense of community within the oppressed sections of colonial Brazzaville.[21] People visited dancehalls in Brazzaville and Kinshasa wearing their Western clothing and listened to *popo* music, and the segregated ethnic neighborhoods of Bacongo and Poto-Poto attempted to out-dress each other in nightclubs. Despite the fact that those within Brazzaville were using a European dress as a medium to express themselves, this movement was crucial because it united the people during a difficult time in Congolese history. The sort of fashion exhibitionism that arose in Brazzaville was distinctly different from any sort of European expression to date.

The decision to participate in this new movement was not as simple as purchasing a few items of high-end clothing. While the second-hand clothing industry entered Congo-Brazzaville during the 1920s, these clothes only accounted for some of the clothing worn by fashionable Congolese men during this period. Those deeply involved in the movement preferred expensive fashions and aspired to purchase clothing from European stores in the colony.[22] An example of this was Mario de Figueiredo's store on the *Avenue de Commerce* in Brazzaville named 'Kitoko,' which means elegant in Lingala and Kikongo.[23] Kitoko provided a wide variety of desirable products for the African population that could afford to patronize the store.[24] At the same time, many fashion-conscious men of Brazzaville travelled to Kinshasa to find better deals on cloth that they could use to construct high-end garments.[25] Men went to great lengths to participate in the exhibition of high-end fashion in Brazzaville. Despite their meager incomes, they sacrificed their wages to impress others with their highly coveted wardrobes.[26]

By examining the historical roots of the *sapeur* movement, one can see the intricacies that allowed African men to have a monopoly on the access to European goods, including

---

19. Martin, *Leisure and Society in Colonial Brazzaville*, 164.

20. Ibid., 164–65.

21. Ibid., 165–66.

22. Martin, 154–55.

23. Ibid., 164.

24. Ibid.

25. Ibid.

26. The Report of the Government Hospital in Brazzaville in 1930 stated that clerks, interpreters, and typists employed by the government made approximately twelve francs a day; whereas, according to Martin and Gondola, some of the individual pieces acquired by men during the 1920s and 1930s ranged from 50 to 300 francs. *Leisure and Society in Colonial Brazzaville*, 166. "Dream and Drama: The Search for Elegance among Congolese Youth," 27.

clothing. This can be attributed to the initial role of houseboys and their access to European castoffs and the spread of the movement to jobs typically held by men in the colony, in addition to the fact that Brazzaville had a disproportionately large population of males from was 1911 to 1945 due to labor migration from other parts of AEF. As a result of these factors, working men in Brazzaville began to set the groundwork of the *sapeur* movement. The origins of the *sapeur* movement originally centered on the intersection of Western fashion and African tradition in colonial Brazzaville. While this is not something that necessarily disappeared from the *sapeur* movement in the decades to follow, another major factor entered the discourse on dress culture during the mid-twentieth century: World War II.

World War II exposed Africans to new ideas regarding politics and philosophies, allowed African soldiers to rethink the patterns of discrimination thrust upon them by the hypocritical doctrine of the colonizer and express themselves to their peers through written and oral language, and helped Africans acquire new technical skills that they brought back to their homes following the war. The shared experiences of African soldiers empowered them to think beyond daily oppression within the colony. One example of the re-conceptualization of daily life and society as a result of war-time experiences was the emergence of the *sapeur* movement.

World War II fundamentally altered conceptions of dress among soldiers and citizens of Brazzaville. According to Gondola, "The *sape* was made visible during the war years with the emergence of social clubs whose inception is linked to the dawn of bar-dance halls in Brazzaville and Kinshasa, and which would serve as the stage for the acting out of the *sape*."[27] Congolese veterans revitalized and reshaped conceptions of dress culture and politics following their return to Brazzaville. The *sapeur* movement during this time truly began to have philosophical roots and organizations based on the common theme of fashion emerged in Brazzaville. According to Martin, "The proto-*sapeurs* clubs of the 1950s expressed the burgeoning interests of the urban youth. Through their 'cult of elegance' young men sought to define their social distinctiveness, while at the same time deriving a great deal of personal pleasure from wearing stylish clothes, admiring each others' dress and, hopefully, attracting girls."[28] As superficial as these organizations may seem, they also served as mutual-aid associations, addressed the interests of the participants, and some were inspired by European concepts and thinkers.[29] An example of this was the group entitled "Existos," which was founded by students inspired by Sartre, a French thinker whose work they undoubtedly came into contact with in France. According to Martin, there were several groups like Existos in existence in Colonial Brazzaville, including *Cabaret* and *Simple et bien*.[30] Through these groups, they engaged in discussions regarding fashion and modernity that were initiated by veterans following their return from the war.[31]

Due to the fact that the men that returned from the war had a unique set of experiences that united them, it is evident that this furthered the gender imbalance in the *sapeur* movement. This was especially crucial, because the movement was becoming increasingly popular and the factor that united its participants was something that was inherently exclusive to men. This is not to say that men had exclusive access to European goods. However, the major difference between the *sapeur* movement and the act of wearing

27. Gondola, "Dream and Drama: The Search for Elegance among Congolese Youths," 26.
28. Martin, *Leisure and Society in Colonial Brazzaville*, 171.
29. Ibid.
30. Ibid.
31. Martin, "Contesting Clothes in Colonial Brazzaville," 423.

Western dress is the fact that those in the *sapeur* movement were wearing clothing in a distinctly different manner that represented a set of unique experiences that shaped the *sapeur's* understandings of fashion, culture, and politics.

With these broader historical implications, the *sapeur* movement expanded from Brazzaville into Kinshasa with relative ease due to their shared cultural background and similar colonial histories that reflected a long history of violence and discrimination. While the movement changed over time and began to represent a subculture relating to poverty and the dream of advancement in the oppressive Zairian state, the general demographic of its followers primarily continued to be male. The expansion of the *sapeur* movement in Mobutu's Zaire coincided with the Authenticity program, but it would be foolish to assume that Authenticity alone prevented women from participating in the *sapeur* movement. Rather, it is important to examine the undercurrents in Congolese society that facilitated a male-dominated *sapeur* movement. As it has become evident, the act of dressing elegantly thrived among Brazzaville Africans initially because of modes of access that centered upon male-dominated professions. The involvement of men increased as Congolese veterans returned from World War II with new perspectives on colonialism, modernity, and fashion. As time progressed, the political landscape of Mobutu's Zaire and the level of oppression that stifled the masses led to the movement shifting into Kinshasa, where it thrived among the socioeconomically disadvantaged males that suffered the most from Mobutu's nepotistic system.

Despite the long lineage of a male-dominated *sapeur* movement in Congo-Brazzaville and Mobutu's Zaire, it is evident that the political sentiment behind dressing elegantly was not something that solely existed among the male working class of Brazzaville, Congolese World War II veterans, or young poor urban males in Kinshasa. Rather, the movement and its followers were strongly influenced by oppression, and as a result, exerted their identity, political stances, and agency through the act of dressing elegantly. However, discrimination and oppression were not exclusive to males in colonial and postcolonial Congo-Brazzaville and Congo-Zaire. Women felt the pangs of abuse, racism, and discrimination from the colonial government, and in the case of Congo-Zaire, Mobutu's regime. However, their relative absence from the formation of a political discourse based on dress in the two Congos does not negate their politicization. Rather, it reflects a longer history based on the racism and sexism of the colonizer and misogyny in the postcolonial state.

By simply looking at the modern *sapeur* movement without considering the intricacies that led to its emergence and expansion, the aspect of gender and the relative lack of women in the movement cannot explain the absence of women in the movement even though women were involved in politics and the colonial and postcolonial state. By examining the longer history of the *sapeur*, one can contextualize and forge an understanding of why this movement was predominately male and the implications of gender discrimination and imbalance related to its emergence and expansion in the colonial state.

Authenticity and Self-Awareness: Gendered Inequality and Dress Culture in Mobutu's Zaire

Authenticity is the Zairian people's awareness of return to its own sources, of the need to seek out ancestral values in order to select those which can contribute to its own natural and harmonious development. It is its rejection of the blind adoption of imported ideologies. It is the self-affirmation of Zairian man, or rather of man pure and simple, with his specific location, character, and mental and social structures.[32]

The Congo Crisis influenced Mobutu Sese Seko in a number of ways; most importantly, he saw how quickly a civil war could tear the country apart. Due to this understanding, he recognized the importance of creating a sense of unity that the Congolese population could accept. This would not only help him attain sovereignty, but also serve as something that would prove to the international community that the country was progressive, stable, and prosperous. According to a *New York Times* article from August 1, 1967,

> The 36-year-old general's desire to bring order to the habitual chaos of the Congo came out in an interview the other day. He listed as his greatest achievements since 1960 his action to reform the army and give the Congolese a feeling of 'national pride.' 'Congolization is no longer a bad word,' he said proudly. An intimate later explained that 'it tears him apart' to see foreign newspaper reports of Nigeria or any other African country in crisis as 'another Congo.'[33]

In order to achieve this revolutionary sense of nationalism, Mobutu began a number of programs ranging from the renaming of cities to mandatory dress codes.

Mobutu's first step in his revolutionary movement was the re-naming campaign, which began in May 1966. The titles of cities began to shift towards uniquely African names rather than maintaining titles filled with the ghosts of colonialism. An example of this was the shift from Leopoldville to Kinshasa. Kevin C. Dunn described this process as a "re-baptism," which ideally helped citizens of the Congo wash away the legacy of colonialism in the new republic.[34] The Authenticity campaign became one of the major focal points of Mobutu's policies in the 1970s, beginning in 1972 with the forced abandonment of European names for authentically African ones. In January 1972, for example, Joseph-Désiré Mobutu changed his name to Mobutu Sese Seko Nkuku Ngbendu wa Za Banga. The policy of Authenticity was originally described by Kangafu-Kutumbagana, a party theorist for the MPR, "Authenticité sought to move away from borrowed or imposed ideas towards an increased awareness and privileging of indigenous cultural beliefs and values."[35]

Despite the altruistic emphasis the state placed on the necessity of nation-building, it is evident that there were more powerful forces that influenced Mobutu's decision to implement Authenticity in Zaire, including his severe and legitimate fear of receding into the chaos that defined the First Republic until 1965. Nevertheless, the goal of this paper is to create an understanding of the role of women in Zairian society during this period rather than simply focusing on the corrupt nature of Mobutu's policies. Much of the literature that emerged following the emergence of Authenticity centered upon the role of men and how men needed to know themselves in order to solve the problem of culture. This was especially evident in the UNESCO study on cultural policy in Zaire in the 1970s.

---

32. Dr. Bokonga Etanga Botombele, *Cultural Policy in the Republic of Zaire* (Paris: The UNESCO Press, 1976), 55.
33. "Mobutu Seeking Stronger Federal Control in Congo," *New York Times*, 1 August 1967, 6. (ProQuest).
34. Kevin C. Dunn, *Imagining the Congo: The International Relations of Identity* (New York: Palgrave Macmillan, 2003), 110.
35. Ibid., 111.

Throughout the document, there are countless quotations that focus on man's ability to know himself, "In this context, the problem of culture is seen to arise from the desire of every man to know himself, to be known by others, to locate himself in time and space."[36] Similarly, "It is consequently difficult, if not impossible, to understand the black man without recalling those accidents of history which have so marked his personality and which to this day continue to exert an influence on him."[37] Finally, "Its central point is man himself, the fullest development of whose personality it ensures. It is a 'humanism of struggle', a humanism of community, an act of self-transcendence, even sacrifice, for the sake of the nation."[38] The use of the words "man" or "him" in political discourses throughout history is not unique to Mobutu's Zaire. Some of the most influential political speeches or texts of all time have used these words; yet, the gendered inequality in Mobutu's Zaire did not end with the said diction.

In an attempt to safeguard the cultural heritage of the Zairian state, Authenticity banned all Western clothing. Men were forced to wear the *abacost* and women had to wear traditional clothing in public. The *abacost*, essentially a Mao-inspired tunic, was supposed to replace Western suits in the workplace and empower Zairian men with a common cultural heritage. Beyond the hypocrisy of utilizing an imported style of dress to denote a cultural heritage unique from the West, the enforced regulation of dress in the Authenticity movement was problematic because it favored men, and overlooked women and their significant roles in Zairian society. This was especially problematic because the acceptance of the *abacost* was clearly a way to attempt to forge a sense of national unity; yet, women were simply told to dress in traditional clothing.

Zaire was an immensely diverse country with hundreds of languages and ethnic groups. Thus, the words "traditional clothing" could be interpreted in a number of ways depending on one's ethnic background. It is clear that Mobutu was aware of the immense cultural diversity within Zaire, as evidenced by a statement made by Botombele, the State Commissioner for Culture and the Arts, in a report on the cultural policies of Zaire in 1976. He stated, "It was for the State in particular to promote the sentiment of cultural unity. The particular cultures of the different tribes, in which the collective aspects of tribal consciousness were expressed, had to be brought closer together by providing every possible occasion for a feeling of cultural nationhood to assert itself."[39] If the Zairian state's focus was truly on providing occasions for the feeling of cultural nationhood, then having women wear 'traditional clothing' would have been counter-productive to the cause of creating national unity because it would only reinforce prominent ideas of ethnic and regional identities. Thus, when one considers the half-hearted approach to national unity and how women were included in the program, it is evident that Mobutu and the government gave little attention to women and their role within the home, workplace, and society during the Authenticity movement.

During my interviews with Congolese men and women in the neighborhood of Matonge in Brussels during the summer of 2009, the issue of dress culture was central to the discussion of the implementation of Mobutu's Authenticity campaign. Many of the men and women interviewed saw the *abacost* as synonymous with the Authenticity program. Furthermore, those from the region of Katanga, which was central to the Congo Crisis and seceded from the Congo in the 1960s, felt as though they were a colony of Mobutu's Zaire during this period. They attempted to resist the forced adoption of the *abacost*, but

---

36. Botombele, *Cultural Policy in the Republic of Zaire*, 55.
37. Ibid., 56.
38. Ibid., 64.
39. Ibid., 46.

were often thrown in jail. Eventually the men of Katanga began to wear the *abacost*, and women continued to wear traditional clothing.

With the example of Katanga, it becomes clear that Mobutu's cultural policies were in place to instill a sense of national unity to safeguard his position as the head of the state. When one considers the relative lack of attention given to women and dress culture during the launch of the Authenticity campaign, it becomes clear that Mobutu's government did not give much attention to women because they felt that creating a nation among men would decrease the chances of a revolt or another secessionist attempt. The sexist mentality of the Zairian state was especially problematic due to the immense role of women within traditional African societies, including those within the borders of Mobutu's Zaire. Furthermore, the relative neglect of women contrasted the emphasis the government placed on family and the nation.

In a speech given by Botombele on November 24, 1974 regarding the National Festival of Culture and Animation, he stated, "The Festival symbolizes a Zairian reality in which all Zairian citizens, notwithstanding the diversity of their tribes, languages, and customs, consider themselves members of a united family within the People's Revolutionary Movement."[40] Botombele's understanding of the nation as a united family was something that ran throughout Mobutu's policies in Zaire. That being said, the half-hearted approach to women, dress, and politics is interesting because it essentially neglected one of the most prominent members of the family from the metaphorical equation.

Despite the lack of attention given to women by the government in the launch of Authenticity, it is clear that many women were active revolutionaries in Mobutu's Zaire. Michael Schatzberg's, *Political Legitimacy in Middle Africa*, discusses two instances of women directly resisting the Mobutu regime. The first instance, which occurred in 1975 during a national conference on women, involved a woman from Mobutu's ethnic group that stood and openly called for the removal of Mobutu as head of state. The second instance, recalled by Mobutu in 1988, included a number of women that gathered to protest the terrible conditions of the country. In a speech following the incident, Mobutu stated:

> When ... I was still at Gbadolite I heard that a dozen women ... had demonstrated ... You see a demonstration. What do you do, you, JMPR [party youth]? ... You are not going to wait for the gendarmes, you are not going to wait for the soldiers or the JMPR. You know the meaning of our dearly acquired peace. You have shoes, kick them. I'm not saying disorder, but kick them. I'll say it again, kick them. You have hands, hit them.... You remove them from the road in the name of peace.[41]

Clearly, women revolted and resisted against Mobutu's government, which is interesting because it was clearly a sector of the population that Mobutu did little to address. He implemented programs for youth service, development, and indoctrination and paid attention to the creation of a nation among men; yet women were clearly removed from the discussion of nation-building.[42]

This is not to say that had Mobutu addressed women in his Authenticity campaign, it would have removed the ability for women to revolt or resist. However, the neglect given to women during this period symbolizes a greater issue in Mobutu's Zaire and an overall

---

40. Ibid., 46.
41. Michael Schatzberg, *Political Legitimacy in Middle Africa* (Bloomington: Indiana University Press, 2001), 28.
42. Examples of these programs can be found in Botombele's *Cultural Policy in the Republic of Zaire.*

theme of disregarding women in the political sphere. Furthermore, the lack of attention given to women as active participants in the state represents a larger issue dealing with the framework of Authenticity. Mobutu's Authenticity program was poorly conceptualized and implemented because it was primarily a way to counter growing ethnic regionalisms and secessionist attempts while maintaining a positive image among western powers. Mobutu's intentions were not completely altruistic, as his main goal was to stay in power. This is especially clear when one considers the half-hearted nature of the Authenticity movement in general.

One of the major problems that faced Authenticity was reaching the entire population. While Mobutu attempted to control potentially inflammatory information in newspapers and radio broadcasting for the sake of national unity, he neglected other projects that may have actually fostered nation-building. Ultimately, had Mobutu placed more of an emphasis on strengthening radio and television broadcasting in the vast country, it would have furthered his goal of creating a sense of national unity. It is evident that as a personal-coercive leader, Mobutu focused too much on squashing the opposition due to his immense fear of losing control in Zaire.[43]

Another factor that contributed to the failure of Authenticity was the emphasis that Mobutu placed on the international community. The introduction of Authenticity in Zairian society could have been perceived as positive change; however, shortly after its implementation Mobutu showed increased interest in the opinions of foreign powers and decided to focus on making an impression in the international community rather than expanding or improving his cultural and social program in Zaire. Kevin C. Dunn states, "Tellingly, the policy of authenticity was not announced at home. Rather, Mobutu unveiled his foundational philosophy in 1971 in Dakar, Senegal at the National Congress for Senghor's Union Progressiste Sénégalaise."[44] This is especially problematic because Mobutu embraced the platform of "One Zaire for a Great Zaire;"[45] yet, he sought to broadcast this expression and ideology to the international community.

What is interesting about Mobutu's interest in appealing to the international community is the fact that the entire premise behind Authenticity was that it demanded the citizens of Zaire to turn their backs on the West and embrace their collective Zairian identity. It is evident that Mobutu contradicted this sort of thinking by ensuring that the world, including the West, acknowledged the progress, strength, and potential of Zaire. This is evidenced by Mobutu's trip to the Sorbonne in Paris during April 1974, where he spoke about his campaign during a conference on Zairian authenticity.[46] Another instance of this was in April 1974 when Mobutu publicly decided to suspend relations with Belgium. Newspapers around the world covered this event, and would later cover the French taking the place that the Belgians once held in Zaire. It is evident that Mobutu wanted to show the world an independent Zaire that did not need Belgian intervention to persevere.

---

43. Naomi Chazan describes personal-coercive regimes in *Politics and Society in Contemporary Africa*. She states, "Personal-coercive rule, unlike any other forms of authoritarian government, may be understood as a sign of the absence of any clear concept of institutionalization or of recognized norms of political behavior" (153). Furthermore, "political concepts were most evidently promulgated as rhetorical props for precarious heads of personal-coercive regimes who almost uniformly chose to forward crude military-nationalist precepts as a substitute for coherent political ideologies. They justified their actions as genuinely African and independent — as the first steps in the formation of a truly autonomous national existence" (153).

44. Dunn, 117.

45. "Une Foire au Service du Développement," *Jeune Afrique*, 20 July 1974, 60.

46. "Confidentiel: Authenticité à Paris," *Jeune Afrique*, 11 May 1974, 29.

The main problem with Mobutu's orientation towards the West is the fact that Authenticity was not successful in creating a Zairian nation, yet the international community perceived it as one. Dunn states,

> By and large, the nationalist rhetoric produced by the Mobutu regime was aimed at other African and Third World countries in order to alter their views of both the regime and the country as a whole ... The Congo may have been perceived as a symbol of neocolonial intervention, but Zaire now projected itself as a leader of Third World Nationalism.[47]

Similarly, Mobutu's shallow efforts behind his Authenticity program can be seen in his decision to host the "Rumble in the Jungle." It did not take long for Mobutu to realize that an event of this nature would become a landmark event in boxing history and would bring hundreds of thousands of spectators to Kinshasa. Not only was it the first time that an African country had the opportunity to welcome a competition that sparked such high levels of international interest, it was also a chance for Mobutu to dazzle the international community with a façade of progress towards development and nationalism via authenticity in Zaire and ultimately command the respect of the world. The spending that occurred as a direct result of the "Rumble in the Jungle" occurred in a manner very similar to other state-funded projects in Zaire during the period. "[Investment projects] were launched without sensible and comprehensive economic planning and institutional support."[48] The state allocated money towards the "Rumble in the Jungle" without examining what other areas of the budget would suffer as a result. This is significant because by failing to properly finance an event of this size, it would become seemingly impossible to adequately maintain a number of other ventures taken on by the state in the future, including the institution-alization of nationalism through Authenticity.

Frederick Cooper states, "Mobutu's downfall might not have happened if Mobutu had not lost his ability to insert himself into the social relations by which people survived."[49] Cooper's argument is valid, because Authenticity, as Mobutu originally envisioned it, could have attained political stability and legitimacy within Zaire, but the popular disregard for the movement reflected its motives and poor implementation. Cooper's premise is abundantly clear, especially when one considers the relative neglect of women in Mobutu's authenticity campaign. Failing to adequately address women in the Authenticity movement hindered the ability to actually build a nation that could unite the vast reaches of the country. Nevertheless, popular disapproval and the failure of Authenticity did not immediately force Mobutu from his seat of power; yet, instead of trying to salvage political legitimacy, his focus shifted from the façade of nation building to outright acts of corruption.

Conclusion

The *sapeur* movement and Mobutu's Authenticity program were interesting movements, especially because they emerged around the same time in Congolese history. Furthermore, they represented a struggle between international politics, traditional culture, and modernity. By relatively excluding women from these discussions, one cannot fully grasp

---

47. Dunn, *Imagining the Congo: The International Relations of Identity*, 116.
48. Sandra W. Meditz, *Zaire: A Country Study* (Washington D.C.: U.S. Government Printing Office, 1994), 154.
49. Frederick Cooper, *Africa Since 1940: The Past of the Present* (Cambridge: Cambridge University Press, 2002), 167.

the cultural and social histories of the region and the implications these movements had on daily life. While Authenticity struggled to negate the Western influence, in regards to the *sapeur* movement, it attempted to strip its people of a new uniquely African movement that was expressed using a Western medium. One of the major parts of Mobutu's Authenticity program was the emphasis on traditional dress culture. Yet, he invented a suit, the *abacost*, for men to wear in an attempt to create a nation. On the other hand, he simply told women to dress in traditional clothing.

This was problematic because of the immense diversity in the country and growing ethnic regionalisms following independence and the Congo Crisis. It is clear that Mobutu's intent was to instill a sense of national unity to safeguard his position as the head of the state; yet, the absence of a deep discourse regarding dress culture and women clearly dismissed women as political activists or participants within the state. At the same time, the *sapeur* movement was a cultural and political movement that emerged out of a context of colonial and postcolonial abuses. Nevertheless, the movement was primarily composed of men. As we have seen, it is clear that this was not because women were not politicized or actively involved in political discourses. Rather, the origins of the *sapeur* were built upon a gender imbalance in the capital of the AEF, jobs in Brazzaville that were primarily dominated by men, and the shared experiences of Congolese veterans returning from World War II.

It was not African men that necessarily discriminated against women in the *sapeur* movement; instead, it was a sexist colonial history that led to the forging of a movement that was dominated by males. These drastically different movements represent a history and process of gender discrimination that involves colonialism, urban migration, development, neocolonialism, and dictatorship. The ongoing history of politics and dress culture is significant because clothing is much more than pieces of cloth, especially in the case of Central Africa. According to Phyllis Martin, "Many Brazzaville workers came from Central African societies where ... clothing and personal ornamentation conveyed identity, status, values and the significance of the occasion ... personal display through dress was essential in the wielding of power, in statements of identity and in displays of well-being."[50] Understanding this cultural and political history is important because it reminds us of strong identities forged around the mere act of wearing clothes.

References

American University (Washington D.C.). Foreign Area Studies, Irving Kaplan, H. Mark Roth, and Gordon C. McDonald. *Zaïre, a Country Study*. 3rd ed, Area Handbook Series. Washington: FAS : for sale by the Supt. of Docs., 1979.

Anderson, Benedict R. O'G. *Imagined Communities: Reflections on the Origin and Spread of Nationalism*. Rev. ed. London; New York: Verso, 2006.

Balandier, Georges. *Daily Life in the Kingdom of the Kongo from the Sixteenth to the Eighteenth Century*. 1st American ed. New York: Pantheon Books, 1968.

Bokonga Ekanga, Botombele. *Cultural Policy in the Republic of Zaire: A Study*. Studies and Documents on Cultural Policies. Paris: UNESCO Press, 1976.

Chazan, Naomi. *Politics and Society in Contemporary Africa*. 3rd ed. Boulder, CO.: Lynne Rienner Publishers, 1999.

50. Martin, *Leisure and Society in Colonial Brazzaville*, 155.

"Confidentiel: Authenticité à Paris." *Jeune Afrique* Vol.11 (1974): 29.

Cooper, Frederick. *Africa since 1940: The Past of the Present.* Cambridge, UK; New York: Cambridge University Press, 2002.

Dunn, Kevin C. "Imagining the Congo: the International Relations of Identity." New York: Palgrave Macmillan, 2003.

Fanon, Frantz. *The Wretched of the Earth.* New York: Grove Press, 2004.

Fisher, Angela. *Africa Adorned.* London: Collins, 1984.

Gondola, Ch Didier. *The History of Congo.* The Greenwood Histories of the Modern Nations. Westport, CN.: Greenwood Press, 2002.

Gondola, Didier. "Dream and Drama: The Search for Elegance among Congolese Youth." *African Studies Review* Vol 42. 1 (1999).

Hendrickson, Hildi. *Clothing and Difference: Embodied Identities in Colonial and Post-Colonial Africa.* Durham: Duke University Press, 1996.

Martin, Phyllis. *Leisure and Society in Colonial Brazzaville.* New York: Cambridge University Press, 1995.

Martin, Phyllis. "Contesting Clothes in Colonial Brazzaville." *The Journal of African History* Vol. 35.3 (1994).

Mazrui, Ali Al, Amin, and Ricardo René Laremont. *Africanity Redefined.* Classic Authors and Texts on Africa. Trenton, NJ: Africa World Press, 2002.

"Mobutu Seeking Stronger Federal Control in Congo." *New York Times.* Vol. 1 (1967): 6.

Roberts, Allen. "'Authenticity' and Ritual Gone Awry in Mobutu's Zaire." *Journal of Religion in Africa.* Vol. 24 (1994): 134–59.

Schatzberg, Michael G. "Political Legitimacy in Middle Africa: Father, Family, Food." Bloomington: Indiana University Press, 2001.

Stewart, Gary. *Rumba on the River: A History of the Popular Music of the Two Congos.* London; New York: Verso, 2000.

Tordoff, William. *Government and Politics in Africa.* 4th ed. Bloomington, Ind.: Indiana University Press, 2002.

"Une Foire au Service du Développement." *Jeune Afrique* Vol. 20 (1974): 60.

Vassal, Gabrielle and Joseph. *Français, Belges et Portugais en Afrique.* Paris: Pierre Roger, 1931.

Chapter 13

Le Femmes Libre and *Mama wa Taifa*: Constructions of Gender in Mobutu's Zaire and Nyerere's Tanzania: 1965–1979

Jonathan Shaw

Neighboring nations Tanzania and the Democratic Republic of the Congo emerged from the colonial period with two markedly different national contexts.[1] Tanzania's bloodless independence struggle produced one clear choice for head of state, Julius Nyerere, who moved into independence as the head of his highly mobilized, multi-ethnic Tanzania Africa National Union party. Educated in Scotland and Uganda,[2] brilliant, philosophical, and calm, Nyerere's rise to national leadership was predetermined with colonial officials and peaceful, but would not have been possible without sustained political pressure and grassroots organization.[3]

By contrast, the abrupt Belgian withdrawal from the Congo was marked by violence and chaos, and a severe lack of premeditation. Only 26 Congolese in a population of over thirty million had completed higher education by independence in 1960.[4] Numerous powers vied for control of the nation during the Congo Crisis of 1960–61, and the elected president, Patrice Lumumba, was assassinated within his first year in office. Foreign powers, in the fervor of the Cold War, attempted to control Congolese proxies who in turn attempted to manipulate their supposed puppeteers. Out of this maelstrom emerged an unlikely leader: a man who had not completed secondary school for disciplinary reasons, achieved power through establishing client networks within the military, and had no major ethnic base to consolidate his political influence. In light of these challenges, Joseph Desiree

Mobutu, despite intense support from the United States, seemed destined to be another victim of Congo's exceptionally bloody political history within a short time. This, of course, would not be so.

Twenty-five years later, both men were still major forces in their respective nation's politics, albeit in the twilight of their influence.[5] Their legacies today, however, are as

---

1. Zaire in 1960 and Tanzania in 1963.
2. At Makerere University in Kampala and the University of Edinburgh.
3. For example, see Isaria N. Kimambo and A. J. Temu, *A History of Tanzania* (Nairobi: East African Publishing House, 1969), 209. *Nyerere's push to the UN for independence formally began in 1955 through a direct appeal to end trusteeship and place power in the hands of indigenous political groups.*
4. Barbara A. Yates, 'Structural Problems in Education in the Congo (Leopoldville),' *Comparative Education Review* 7, no. 2 (October 1963): 159.
5. Nyerere steps down from the presidency in 1985, but remained chairman of the party in power, *Chama Cha Mapinduzi*, until 1990. Mobutu loses U.S. carte blanche as the Cold War ends in 1990 and is so weakened he falls to rebels backed by Rwanda in the First Congo War in 1997.

divergent as were the conditions of their emergence into national leadership. Julius Nyerere's beatification to sainthood in the Catholic Church is ongoing in Tanzania and Mobutu's vilification continues unabated as the world's deadliest conflict since World War II continues in the Congo, ignited in the wake of his violent fall from power.[6] The role of women in society was a key element of cultural legislation by the central government in both Tanzania and Zaire during the first fifteen years of power, but with substantively different intentions and outcomes in each nation.[7]

This chapter will examine three areas of connection and comparison in constructions of gender in Tanzania and Zaire from 1965 to 1979: the presentations of gender in the Arusha Declaration and the N'Sele Manifesto; the use of dance and dance groups as a culturally legislated medium of gender control and expression; and the concept of childhood and fatherhood in each state.[8] The chapter seeks to approach the issue of gender construction from the perspective of both the women in the country who were being "acted upon" and the two men who dominated the political scene of each nation for decades, and the way they perceived and influenced gender in their respective nations.

Women in the Lives of the Big Men

Mobutu's highly tuned pragmatic political sense, anchored in egocentrism, led to constructions of gender that served Mobutu's own conservative views of women, while paying lip service to progressive notions of gender equity.[9] This division between personal and political created an institutionally complex dichotomy between supposedly "traditional" and "modern" ideas of women. By merging his personality with the state, Mobutu's own instincts about gender, and his attempts to present gender in a "modern" way, were frequently at odds. Mobutu's *authenticite* campaign included the requirement that all Zairians shed their Christian names. His wife, Marie-Antoinette Mobutu, however, refused to "Africanize" her name.[10] Even as he could control the nation through cultural legislation, he could not coerce his own wife to participate. Later, the pseudo-deification of his mother and the concept of *femme libre*[11] as an appropriate goal for gender equity, were challenged by satirical political songs that presented Mobutu's own mother, Mama Yemo, as a *femme libre*, much to the deep frustration of Mobutu.[12]

---

6. Richard Brennan, *Mortality in the Democratic Republic of Congo*, Report (New York: International Rescue Committee, 2008).

7. Indeed, gender finds its way into the key 'foundational' documents of each nation: the N'Sele Manifesto and the Arusha Declaration.

8. The study begins in 1965 because this is when the Arusha Declaration and N'Sele Manifesto are released, after which both nations enjoy a period of growth until the mid-70s, when both experience disastrous economic meltdowns. Thus, the time period gives a view of the formation of policy in a time of optimism and the effects of gender constructions as the fortunes of each country wane dramatically.

9. Mobutu disenfranchised women from political power, and personally pushed back against instances of the *femme libre* in popular culture.

10. Crawford Young and Thomas Turner, *Rise and Decline of the Zairian State* (Madison, Wis: University of Wisconsin Press, 1985), 360.

11. This was the term used to describe the liberated female ideal in Zaire, but became double edged with its increased association with sexually 'loose' women.

12. Mobutu's birth mother, whose single parenthood of Mobutu left her open to suggestions that she was a prostitute or 'loose' woman for many years, particularly by Mobutu's political opponents.

The frustration was borne from personal offense and because Mama Yemo was "given extraordinary prominence in regime hagiography," held up as a model of womanhood, in the vein of the Virgin Mary.[13] Beyond Mobutu's personal inconsistencies there were also disputes in the collective Zairian imagination of "authentic" perceptions of gender. This must be seen as a product of perceptions that modern women lacked "traditional" morality, and that in fashion, music, sexuality, and opinions about their role in the family, modern women could not be trusted to preserve important cultural elements of the kind that Mobutu constantly suggested were integral to the "primordial" Zairian identity. Mobutu's cabinet members and staff frequently reported Mobutu's proclivity for pursuing and seducing their wives, aware that his subordinates had full knowledge of it. They had no possibility of denial or reprisal, and the wives, of course, had no say in the matter—their husband's careers, and lives, were at stake. On reflection, one felt that Mobutu's adulterous interests was not sexual *per se*, rather he pursued these women "to weaken their husbands and strengthen himself."[14]

By contrast Nyerere understood the essential political role women could play in his vision of Tanzania, no doubt related to women's prevalence in agrarian societies within Tanzania.[15] Beyond labor, however, Nyerere sought to reform the role women played in individual families, and with *Ujamaa* (or "familyhood") the nation's guiding political philosophy, what role women were to play in the "family" of Tanzania. *Ujamaa*, in order to be more than mere political jargon, had to reflect and reference deeply ingrained perceptions of the family in broad swaths of Tanzanian society. The concept of *mama*, therefore, became essential component in the definitions of political, social, and religious terms related to the *Ujamaa* state. Nyerere's sincere distaste for the kind of personality cult Mobutu actively fostered decentralized his own parentage in the story of Nyerere, making him far less susceptible to problems associated with re-creating his own nuclear family structure as the supposed model for all societies within the state.

Much of Nyerere's personal history with women must be extrapolated from his political philosophy and comments he made on the subject later in life. One key is Nyerere's contention that only two elements of 'traditional' society needing major revision before implementation in progressive Tanzanian politics: poverty and the equality of women. Although Nyerere's Zanaki natal culture was, by many accounts, highly egalitarian regarding economics, political leadership, and communal property, it was male-dominated and controlled. Late in life Nyerere reflected, "When I first started to write about liberation, I wrote about the liberation of women."[16] The claim that Nyerere's motivation in pushing for self-rule had much to do with empowering women has some evidentiary basis. The independence movement in Tanzania was pervaded with powerful women, many of whom became the backbone of the organization of the movement, as documented in Susan Geiger's *TANU Women*.[17] Nyerere owes much, in particular, to Geiger's primary subject,

---

13. Young and Turner, *Rise and Decline*, 154.

14. *Mobutu, roi du Zaire*. DVD. Directed by Thierry Michel. Featuring Mobutu Sese Seko. France: Canal, 1999.

15. See the section below on the Arusha Declaration for Nyerere's perception of women's role in agrarian (especially rural) life.

16. Quoted in Viktoria Stöger-Eising's " 'Ujamaa' Revisited: Indigenous and European Influences in Nyerere's Social and Political Thought," *Africa: Journal of the International African Institute* Vol. 70, no. 1 (2000): 134.

17. Geiger is preeminent on the subject of women and TANU political organization from her monograph, *TANU Women*, and three excellent articles on the subject, "Tanganyikan Nationalism as Women's Work," "Women in Nationalist Struggle," and "Umoja wa Wanakawe wa Tanzania and the Needs of the Rural Poor." Geiger's work on the subject is comprehensive and captivating. This paper

Bibi Titi. The presence of women in the movement's leadership, despite strident objections from some men, supports Nyerere's claim. This is not to say there is agreement about the prevalence of women in Tanzania's independence movement. While scholars like Gieger have centralized female involvement in Tanzanian nationalist politics, others, like James Brennan, have countered that the nationalist movement was "overwhelmingly male."[18] When women's and youth auxiliaries were added to TANU (then TAA), the clear implication was that men had been the guiding force and originators of the movement, and women could be added into the mix, along with youth, as the project matured.[19] Whatever structural labels given to female actors in the independence struggle, the involvement of women was ultimately belittled when Nyerere remarked in his inaugural address that during the independence movement some men were even able to persuade their wives to join TANU, clearly placing prime agency on men in the movement, and suggesting that women had to be cajoled into nationalist participation.[20]

The preponderance of martial action in the violence prior to Congolese independence and the subsequent Congo Crisis meant that men would dominate the process, as women were barred from military service. The legacy of this exclusion would continue through the entire lifespan of Mobutu's Zaire, despite late attempts to legitimize claims of gender equity with "the inclusion of a greater number of women [as a] symbol of progressive 'regime orientation,'" which ultimately proved hollow as only one women ever had significant power in Mobutu's Zaire.[21] Even as women from Tanzania were still under colonial control, they viewed women in Congo as being oppressed, placing in the same status as other states still under colonial control in 1962, even though Congo had been independent for two years.[22] This presupposed that despite still being members a colonized state, Tanzanian women perceived themselves as both more free from colonial rule and intra-state oppression than their Congolese counterparts. At least some of this must be attributed to the integration of women into Tanzania's independence movements and the wholesale exclusion of women in Congo's post-colonial organization.

Loving Such Fathers, Birthing Such Sons

Both Mobutu and Nyerere self-consciously presented their nationalizing legislations in the context of 'traditional' African approaches to community. Much confusion exists about who Mobutu's father was, although it is clear he was treated as a son by a respectable local butcher in his home town of Lisala. Mobutu's primary familial relationship was with

---

begins in 1965, the year Geiger concludes her study of women in the TANU nationalist movement in her seminal book on the matter.

18. James Brennen, "Youth, the TANU Youth League and Managed Vigilantism in Dar es Salaam, Tanzania, 1925–73," *Journal of the International African Institute*, Vol. 76, No. 2 (2006): 221–46.

19. Initially proposed in 1954, and later implemented in Mobutu's MPR in the 1960s. See Young and Turner, *Rise and Decline*, 228.

20. Susan Geiger, "Tanganyikan Nationalism as 'Women's Work': Life Histories, Collective Biography and Changing Historiography," *The Journal of African History* Vol. 37, no. 3 (1996): 472.

21. Young and Turner, *Rise and Decline*, 193. The woman was Lusibu Zala N'kanza, who gained some power in the 1990s, as Mobutu's power waned dramatically.

22. Susan Geiger, *TANU Women: Gender and Culture in the Making of Tanganyikan Nationalism 1955–1965* (Portsmouth, NH: Heinemann, 1997), 164. Other countries under discussion were Northern Rhodesia and Nyasaland.

his mother, who came to be known as Mama Yemo. When, as dictator, Mobutu increasingly sought to replace Christian representations of spirituality with his own cult of personality, Mama Yemo was given a role very similar to the Virgin Mary in national mythology— Mobutu and Jesus Christ even shared the legacy of "complex" paternal origins. As Interior Minister Engulu Mpongo said, "In all religions, and at all times, there are prophets. Why not today? God has sent a great prophet, our prestigious Guide Mobutu ... our Messiah ... Our gospel is Mobutuism. This is why the crucifixes must be replaced by the image of our Messiah. And party militants will want to place at its side his glorious mother, Mama Yemo, who gave birth to such a son."[23] Mobutu himself spoke with tremendous admiration for his mother, and once said he was inspired to be "a son worthy of his mother."[24] This was high praise indeed from a claimant to deity. All this reverence made it intolerable to him when Mama Yemo, parodied in a satiric take on the national anthem, *La Zariose*, was accused of at one time being a prostitute, a claim that may well have been accurate.[25]

Nyerere's mother, the fifth wife in her household and thus not a prominent member of it, has been accounted for variously in histories of his life, and some modern revisionist histories claim her to be an important practitioner of "witchcraft" in her community.[26] In fact, she was an important rain summoner, and was well respected in her larger community for this skill. Nyerere clearly admired her greatly, but attempted none of the elevation techniques employed by Mobutu to venerate her legacy. Nyerere's own devotion to Catholicism made Mobutu's deistic constructions of his parentage deeply heretical, but nonetheless, spiritual mothers became part of his origin mythology as well. Most important of these mothers were those women who participated in TANU's early push towards independence. These women came articulated themselves as *Wamama Nyerere*, "Nyerere's Mothers," and Tanzanian female political activists called Nyerere *mwanangu*, "my son," placing them in a guardianship role over their leader.[27] Even his standard honorific, *Mwalimu* (Teacher), is not particularly masculine, especially when compared to Mobutu's insistence on being called *Baba*, or father. The agrarian life elevated by Nyerere was one that concerned both male and female members of society equally, whereas the hunt (embodied by Mobutu's leopard skins) was the provenance only of the men. Working for the common good, rather than for the leader, became a national project both genders could partake in equally in Tanzania.

Mobutu's paternalistic cult of personality was ultimately both ineffective and unconvincing despite its enforced dominance. His family model of governance did not resonate with an increasingly impoverished and alienated populace. Mama Mobutu, Mobutu's second wife, became mother of the state. Mobutu was the state embodied, and claimed spiritual paternity for all of Zaire's people. Thus Zaire's women merely worked their father's land, cultivated his crops, and paid his bills. The inherent distance generated by these roles presented Mobutu as an overseer of the women of his nation. But if he could not care for 'his women,' then how could they respect him as a father?

---

23. Young and Turner, *Rise and Decline*, 169; quoting Interior Minister Engulu, 74–75, *Zaire-Afrique* Vol. 91 (January 1975): 25.

24. *Mobutu, roi du Zaire*. DVD. Directed by Thierry Michel. Featuring Mobutu Sese Seko. France: Canal, 1999.

25. Young and Turner, *Rise and Decline*, 174. The parody went, "Tricolored flag in the wind, which revives party dances, which links us to the prostitute Yemo."

26. Robert Mugagga, "Yes, Nyerere Could Make a Great Saint!" *The Observer* (Kampala), October 29, 2009.

27. Gregory H. Maddox and James L. Giblin, (Eds.) *In Search of a Nation: Histories of Authority & Dissidence in Tanzania*. (Athens, Ohio: Ohio University Press, 2006): 284.

Finding Women in the Manifesto at N'Sele and the Arusha Declaration

Language, particularly as used in the production of policy, was an important element of both men's nationalist visions. The predominance of Swahili under Nyerere and the continued utilization of French despite strong indigenous *linguae francae*, Lingala and Swahili had profound effects on each project. Recognizing Mobutu's own passion for semantics requires no deeper analysis than noting the process of wholesale re-naming that occurred as a part of his *authenticite* campaign, inaugurated in 1965 and in full force by the mid-1970s, with other key "revolutionary" reforms. Serious consideration must be given to the specifics of language used to construct ideas of gender in the context of the state in each nation. In contrast to French, Swahili is a non-gendered language. The universal singular pronoun *yeye* is neutral, and gender can only be determined through context. This gender neutral principle extends to all pronoun usage in Swahili. The French language, of course, genders every noun.

Before exploring the way gender and the role of women were presented in the two most important ideological documents in each independent nation's early history, it is necessary to establish the role of these documents in the national mythology of their respective nations. Just as the Declaration of Independence outlined key principles that would come to be interpreted as the character of the United States, at least as it aspired to be, the Arusha Declaration and N'Sele Manifesto were meant to outline the burgeoning characters of independent Tanzania and Congo, respectively. The chronology of the production of these documents is instructive. Nyerere delivered the Arusha Declaration in February of 1967, and in May of that year Mobutu released the N'Sele Manifesto. Clearly, Mobutu recognized the impact the international response to the Arusha Declaration had on Tanzanian consciousness, and wanted to emulate its embrace of African "tradition" in the "modern" context.

One of the key twelve objectives of TANU, as outlined in the Arusha Declaration, is "equal opportunity to all men and women."[28] Later Nyerere made the point that women in the villages worked very hard, much harder than the men. In fact he said that "women who live in the villages work harder than anybody else in Tanzania."[29] He encouraged all Tanzanians to emulate the work ethic of village women. These mentions are the only places in the Arusha Declaration that Nyerere specifically highlights women's role in the structure of the new nation. Other than the loose allusion to it at the introduction to the text, and the later reference to work ethics in one paragraph towards the end, women do not figure into the Arusha Declaration. By contrast, an entire section of the N'Sele Manifesto was devoted to the role of women in Zaire. Even as the document begins, one of the four overall goals of the "revolution" in Zaire was the "effective liberation of Zairian women and youth."[30] The section on women begins with the statement that women were "the number one victim of colonialism."[31] Women were called the "hope of the nation" in their role as educators and that "with respect to traditional family links" the revolution would emancipate "millions of Zairian women to fulfill their potential."[32] The specific methods that would be utilized to generate this liberation were never articulated. The

---

28. Julius K. Nyerere, *Ujamaa: Essays on Socialism* (Oxford: Oxford University Press, 1974), 15.

29. Ibid.

30. Makanda Kabobi, *Manifesto at N'Sele*, by Mobutu Sese Seko (N'Sele, 1967), 6. This is the author's translation in conjunction with Emily Brandon at Georgetown College.

31. Ibid., 23.

32. Ibid.

section on women closes with a reminder that "through the action of MPR's founder [Mobutu], spectacular results have been achieved in the liberation of women."[33] What these spectacular results might have been was left to the reader to imagine.

The Gender Politics of Dance: *Animation* and *Ngoma*

In promoting 'traditional' dance in Tanzania, *ngoma*, and repudiating Western imports, Nyerere said in his inaugural address that it was "hard for any man to get much real excitement from dances and music which are not in his blood."[34] Perhaps Nyerere did not intend sexual metaphor when talking about the "real excitement" of traditional dance, but pre-colonial dance cultures in both nations was often inextricable from sexual display.[35] In the elevation of *ngoma* to a celebration of traditional culture, the government unwittingly centralized expressions of female sexuality as crucial to the national character. Elements within the nascent government noted this unintentional celebration of female sexuality early on, and reacted to it by having TANU Youth League members engage in the moral policing of female behavior. Leaders "instructed male youths to patrol urban areas and 'arrest all women wearing [indecent] clothing and artificial hair.'"[36] The attempt to contain and control female sexual expression, despite the pretense of increased freedom and equality belied much of the spirit of Tanzania's new state. Nothing, by contrast, was done to prevent the expression of male sexuality often present in *ngoma* performance, and, in fact, the emphasis on male sexual power was perhaps heightened.[37]

It is worth noting that Tanzania's most famous female nationalist, Bibi Titi, emerged from a Dar es Salaam based dance group, "Bomba," to help lead the emergent TANU party in 1955.[38] Bibi Titi's association with *ngoma* as an entree to politics was not unique.[39] Despite whatever de-sexualizing efforts were made to reform *ngoma* dancing and dance groups, the power of dance in placing women in positions of influence in Tanzania cannot be denied. This likely has to do with the fact that *ngoma* groups were one of the few colonial-era mechanisms for Tanzanian women to organize, interact formally, and collaborate on political, social, and personal projects. Laura Edmonson suggests, interestingly, that "the rural and the female body, both located on the margins of the Tanzanian state, serve as objects of obsession and uncertainty" and were thus subject to legislation and regulation.[40] Edmonson also argues that some dance themes, such as "the twirling hoes," came from agrarian reforms instituted by Nyerere in the 60s, under the guise of a revival of "work songs" from the pre-colonial era.[41]

33. Ibid.

34. Julius Kambarage Nyerere, *Freedom and Unity: Uhuru Na Umoja A Selection from Writings and Speeches 1952–65* (New York: Oxford University Press, 1966), 186.

35. Laura Edmonson, "National Erotica: The Politics of 'Traditional' Dance in Tanzania," *TDR (1988–)* Vol. 45, No. 1 (Spring, 2001):153–70.

36. Brennen, "TANU Youth League," 238.

37. Edmonson, "National Erotica," 158.

38. Geiger, *Women's Work*, 467.

39. Ibid., 470.

40. Edmonson, "National Erotica."

41. Gunderson, "From 'Dancing with Porcupines' to 'Twirling a Hoe': Musical Labor Transformed in Sukumaland, Tanzania," *Africa Today* Vol. 48, No. 4, Musical Performance in Africa (Winter, 2001): 3–25.

It is important to note that within the context of the nationalist *ngoma* dance the state, as an ideological constructs was passive—the key agents in the political dances were women. Through this dance process, then, women engaged in a sexual monologue about the state where women were the penetrative agents in the sexual conversation, exerting their sexual energies upon the passive state. While men may or may not have been a part of the *ngoma* display, women organized, choreographed, and presented the *ngoma* dances— thus it was their dance, and their expressiveness, and their relationship to the state being negotiated through dance groups and exhibitions. Moreover, this was a productive sexual encounter. The women who ran and participated in these *ngoma* groups became vital grassroots organizers in the TANU movement and in galvanizing early support for Julius Nyerere. Through this process a deep bond was formed, as was shown in the usage of the familiar term *mwanangu*. By using the possessive form of the word child, *mwana*, these women claimed themselves as Nyerere's mothers, and he became the product of the con- summation of relationship between women and the nascent state of Tanganzania negotiated through *ngoma* dancing.

One of the many mandated public proclamations of affection for Baba Mobutu in Zaire was the saying, "We will sing and dance to honor our guide [Mobutu] and express our love for him."[42] This dancing was not meant to hearken back to a bygone era of Zairian culture: rather it was a premeditated "national consecration of our vital force and the arrival of the national spirit."[43] Pre-colonial songs, which celebrated "the founding ancestors or the goodness of life," were co-opted into odes to the state and to Mobutu.[44] *Animation* was the name given to this process, the word intended to infer a kind of spontaneous energy that begged immediate release, borne of the supposed fervor of passion and joy that came with being a part of the Zairian populace.

Unlike *ngoma* groups, *animation* groups had tightly controlled messages, which were often explicitly political. The leaders of these groups were part of the state/party apparatus, never able to operate with some independence like the *ngoma* leaders. Nonetheless, like in Tanzania, traditional dance was often connected to fertility, family, and sexuality, and these embedded values could not be erased with a whitewash of politics. What makes these embedded qualities troubling in the Zairian context was that, just as was true in Tanzanian *ngoma*, these dances served as an articulation of social relationships—ideas about gender and sex were communicated clearly through the movements of dance. Like in Tanzania as well, this *animation* conversation ended up being a monologue, this time with Mobutu dictating the terms and discussion and even the movements displayed in this embodied relationship. Thus the content, whatever its supposedly innocuous political message, was much more transgressive. The women who participated in *animation* were exerting sexual energy through the medium of dance, similar to *ngoma*, but rather than directing it at the state, they could only direct their efforts at Mobutu, who positioned himself as the human proxy for the nation. Rather than being the active agents, Mobutu's power became the dominant discourse in animation. Thus we see the subtext being the daughters of the nation engaging in sexual dialog with their national father. This kind of twisting and transgressing of traditionality in the guise of progressivism is a hallmark of political discourse in Mobutu's Zaire.

---

42. *Mobutu, roi du Zaire*. DVD. Directed by Thierry Michel. Featuring Mobutu Sese Seko. France: Canal, 1999.

43. Editorial, *Salongo*, March 22, 1974, 2.

44. Kenneth Adelman, "The Recourse to Authenticity and Negritude in Zaire," *The Journal of Modern African Studies* Vol. 13, no. 1 (March 1975): 135.

Conclusion

This chapter provides an introduction to the complex relationship between emerging independent African states and the women who were finding their place in these fledgling societies. When discussing gender in Zaire it would be irresponsible not to reflect for a moment on the potential origins of the current crisis in eastern Congo: the site of the highest rates of sexual violence ever recorded. The situation is highly complex, and multiple national actors and their proxies are engaged in this conflict, which has much to do with resource exploitation and complex ethno-political claims. When the nation lived for over three decades with a political philosophy based solely on the study, reverence, and emulation of Mobutu it is not irresponsible to connect some of the social and political exploitation of women in the Mobutu regime to the use of rape as a tool of societal disassembly in the modern conflict in the Congo. Ultimately, this chapter is intended to be the beginning of a discussion about the ways in which gender constructions in Tanzania and Zaire in the Mobutu and Nyerere era influenced and interacted with one another. Much more needs to be done to flesh out the implications of gender utilization and construction in the post-colonial era, and how these constructions are currently impacting Tanzanian and Congolese society today.

References

Adelman, Kenneth. "The Recourse to Authenticity and Negritude in Zaire." *The Journal of Modern African Studies* Vol. 13, no. 1 (March 1975): 135.

Brennen, James. "Youth, the TANU Youth League and Managed Vigilantism in Dar es Salaam, Tanzania, 1925–73." *Africa: Journal of the International African Institute*, Vol. 76, no. 2 (2006): 221–46.

Brennan, Richard. *Mortality in the Democratic Republic of Congo.* Report. New York: International Rescue Committee, 2008.

Bogues, Anthony. "Julius Nyerere: Radical African Humanism, Equality, and Decolonization." *Black Heretics, Black Prophets: Radical Political Intellectuals.* New York: Routledge, 2003.

Edmonson, Laura. "National Erotica: The Politics of 'Traditional' Dance in Tanzania." *TDR* Vol. 45. (1988).

Geiger, Susan. "Tanganyikan Nationalism as 'Women's Work': Life Histories, Collective Biography and Changing Historiography." *The Journal of African History* Vol. 37, no. 3 (1996): 465–78.

_____. *TANU Women: Gender and Culture in the Making of Tanganyikan Nationalism 1955–1965.* Portsmouth, NH: Heinemann, 1997.

Gunderson, Frank. "From 'Dancing with Porcupines' to 'Twirling a Hoe': Musical Labor Transformed in Sukumaland, Tanzania." *Africa Today.* Vol. 48, No. 4, (2001): 3–25.

Maddox, Gregory H. and James L. Giblin, (Eds.) *In Search of a Nation: Histories of Authority & Dissidence in Tanzania.* Athens, Ohio: Ohio University Press, 2006.

Mobutu, roi du Zaire. DVD. Directed by Thierry Michel. Featuring Mobutu Sese Seko. France: Canal, 1999.

Mugagga, Robert "Yes, Nyerere Could Make a Great Saint!" *The Observer* (Kampala), October 29, 2009.

Nyerere, Julius K. *Ujamaa: Essays on Socialism*. Oxford: Oxford University Press, 1974.

Stöger-Eising, Viktoria. "'Ujamaa' Revisited: Indigenous and European Influences in Nyerere's Social and Political Thought." *Africa: Journal of the International African Institute*, Vol. 70, no. 1 (2000): 118–43.

Yates, Barbara. "The Origins of Language Policy in Zaire." *The Journal of Modern African Studies*. Vol. 18, no. 2 (June 1980): 257–79.

Young, Crawford and Thomas Turner. *Rise and Decline of the Zairian State*. Madison, WI: University of Wisconsin Press, 1998.

Chapter 14

On the Promotion of "Certain" Ugandan Women: Was Idi Amin Feminist or Foe?

Alicia Decker

It has been more than thirty years since Idi Amin and his ragtag band of soldiers poured across the Ugandan border into the Sudan. Hundreds of heavily armed men and women crammed into dozens of dilapidated vehicles piled high with looted goods, all in an effort to find safety in exile, to escape the carnage they had left behind. And carnage they did leave. Between 1971 and 1979, Amin and his military henchmen were responsible for the murder of up to 300,000 Ugandans—or one in every thirty-six.[1] Indeed, the thousands of bodies thrown into the River Nile or buried in shallow graves in Namanve Forest serve as evidence of an extremely violent era. And yet, despite the prevalence of violence, Amin was also one of the first post-colonial African leaders to elevate women to high positions of political power. He appointed them as cabinet ministers, permanent secretaries, sub-county chiefs, and even bodyguards. Did his actions indicate a progressive social agenda—an ironic feminist sensibility of sorts? Or were they a reflection of a different type of political strategy, something far more sinister and complex?

Although Amin's actions might suggest a certain level of respect for women, he was definitely *not* a feminist. Instead of promoting any type of genuine empowerment, he strategically manipulated ideologies about femininity and masculinity in order to consolidate and maintain his tenuous grasp on power. While there were numerous arenas in which this played out, this essay focuses specifically on gendered patterns of promotion (and demotion). I argue that Amin elevated a limited number of women to high political positions for four key reasons: 1) to normalize and legitimate military rule by incorporating intelligent, civilian women into the government; 2) to bolster his reputation as a "manly" leader who could surround himself with

beautiful women; 3) to humiliate and emasculate his male colleagues, thus reinforcing his own masculinity; and 4) to demonstrate his "commitment" to women's rights. Although these promotions were important symbolic victories for women, they did not significantly alter the masculine power structure, and therefore, were politically "safe." Over time, however, as the security situation waned, Amin experienced a leadership crisis which threatened his legitimacy as a ruler *and* as a man. He responded by lashing out at his closest friends and allies.

One such target was Princess Elizabeth Bagaya, a remarkable woman whose rise to power and fall from grace provides a striking illustration of this gendered pattern of pro-

---

1. Amnesty International, *Human Rights in Uganda* (London: Amnesty International, June 1978), 13.

motion. Appointed first as roving ambassador and then later as the nation's first female cabinet minister, Bagaya seemed to represent the limitless possibilities that were available to hard-working Ugandan women. Within a few short years, however, she became a symbol of something very different—the "dangers" of female sexuality writ large. Although press coverage of Bagaya's plunge into the so-called "abyss of immorality" was intended to humiliate her and serve as a warning to other "wayward" women, it inadvertently underscored the state's anxieties about single, powerful women.[2] The media's relentless attention to Bagaya's alleged gender transgressions simply reinforced the point that in Amin's military state, gender mattered.

This chapter considers *why* gender mattered. I begin with a discussion of Amin's gender positioning, focusing on the ways in which the military as an institution profoundly influenced his personal and professional life. I argue that his understandings of masculinity and femininity were inherently militarized, or shaped by military values. The next section provides readers with an abbreviated biographical sketch of Bagaya's life through the mid-1970s. I consider the high and low points in her early career, focusing particularly on her work within Amin's military state. In the penultimate section, I analyze why Amin promoted and later demoted women like Bagaya. As I have suggested above, these types of decisions were strategic and reflected a particular type of militarized gender logic. The conclusion then returns to the question posed in the title of this essay: was Amin feminist or foe? I suggest that although Amin was not a feminist, he was not necessarily a foe either. Instead, his actions had contradictory effects on women, empowering some, while disempowering others. By highlighting these complexities, I hope to make the case for a more nuanced understanding of Amin's military rule.

Militarized Masculinity: The Making of a Man

Amin's military regime was different from a lot of other military states because of its messiness. Although the structure of power was ultimately hierarchical, the lesser chains of command were never consistent. Amin regularly shuffled cabinet ministers and high-ranking military officers from one position to the next. People got into the habit of listening to the radio every morning to find out whether they needed to report to work or go into hiding. Many of the Ugandans that I interviewed in 2005 and 2008 agreed that it was chaotic at best.[3] And yet, if we were to revisit Amin's Uganda—this time wearing a pair of Cynthia Enloe's famed "gender goggles"—things would look quite different.[4] We would undoubtedly see a distinct type of logic at play—that of gender. Indeed, it is fair to say that gender was one of the crucial organizing factors in Amin's military regime, influencing who he was as a man *and* how he governed as a ruler. By thinking about Amin's rule from a gender perspective, we get a much better sense of the complexities that have thus far been hidden—beyond the violence—beyond the barrel of a gun.

---

2. "Radio Comment on Miss Bagaya," *Voice of Uganda*, 24 January 1975. See also Elizabeth Nyabongo, *Elizabeth of Toro: The Odyssey of an African Princess* (New York: Simon and Schuster, 1989).

3. Many scholars also agree that Amin's regime was chaotic in various ways. For a recent interpretation of Amin's rule, see Mark Leopold, "Sex, Violence and History in the Lives of Idi Amin: Postcolonial Masculinity as Masquerade," *Journal of Postcolonial Writing* 45, no. 3 (2009): 321.

4. Cynthia Enloe, *The Curious Feminist: Searching for Women in a New Age of Empire* (Berkeley: University of California Press, 2004), 105.

It is important to mention at the outset that gender is not a static category of analysis, nor can it be reduced to simplistic definitions of male and female. Instead, it is a far more complicated mix of culture, place, and time. To understand gender, we have to understand how a specific society has constructed and interpreted the multiple meanings of masculinity and femininity over time. To understand how gender operated during Amin's rule, we need to look at how the militarization of society affected local constructions of manhood and womanhood. Which types of masculinities and femininities were hegemonic during this historical moment? Which were repressed? Given Amin's martial background, it is not surprising that militarized gender identities would be privileged.

Amin came from a militarized society. His home region of northwestern Uganda had long been used by the British colonial government as a labor reserve.[5] They recruited men from the north in order to counterbalance the administrative strength of the Baganda in the south. Since military service was one of the primary ways that men could provide for their families, manhood became intimately tied to militarism. Like many of his neighbors, Amin grew up poor with very limited exposure to formal education.[6] He joined the King's African Rifles in 1946 at the age of twenty-one and quickly earned the respect of his superiors.[7] The British appreciated Amin because of his strength, loyalty, and ferocity and steadily promoted him through the ranks. By independence in 1962, he had become the army's second-in-command. By 1966, he was commander-in-chief. And less than five years later, he seized power in a military coup and became head of state.

Ali Mazrui argues that Amin represented a resurrection of the so-called "warrior tradition," which measured adulthood and masculinity through violent rites of passage.[8] As a warrior-cum-military leader, Amin embodied "political masculinity":

> As a personal quality political masculinity is a powerful image of manliness in a political leader, which tends to affect his style of leadership and his impact on his followers … The political masculinity of the General [Amin] does not lie merely in his size, though he is impressively tall and broad. Nor does it lie merely in his insistence that he fears no-one but God. Yet these factors are part of the story, combined with the additional factor that an affirmation of fearlessness and an athletic build have indeed been part of the total picture of martial values within African political cultures.[9]

Mazrui's attempt to connect Amin's political masculinity to an ancient warrior tradition is interesting, but a partial explanation at best. Amin spent all of his life in and around army barracks, so whatever warrior tradition he might have possessed was overlaid by

---

5. Mark Leopold, *Inside West Nile: Violence, History and Representation on an African Frontier* (Oxford: James Currey, 2005).

6. Despite Amin's lack of formal education, he was incredibly clever and had an innate talent for languages. He was fluent in Lugbara, Kakwa, Lugbara, Lusoga, Langi, Acholi, Swahili, and English. Timothy Parsons argues that the King's African Rifles had been an important source of education for East African soldiers. It was here that many soldiers learned to read their vernacular languages. It is unclear whether Amin received formal educational training through the army. See Parsons, "Dangerous Education? The Army as School in Colonial East Africa," *The Journal of Imperial and Commonwealth History* 28, no. 1 (2000): 112–134.

7. Judith Listowel, *Amin* (Dublin: IUP Books, 1973); James Mittelman, *Ideology and Politics in Uganda: From Obote to Amin* (Ithaca: Cornell University Press, 1975).

8. Ali Mazrui, "The Resurrection of the Warrior Tradition in African Political Culture," *The Journal of Modern African Studies* 13, no. 1 (1975), 67. See also Aidan Southall, "The Bankruptcy of the Warrior Tradition," in *The Warrior Tradition in Modern Africa*, ed. Ali Mazrui (Leiden: E.J. Brill, 1977).

9. Ali Mazrui, *Soldiers and Kinsmen in Uganda: The Making of a Military Ethnocracy* (Beverly Hills: Sage, 1975), 169.

years of advanced military training. Instead of attributing Amin's gendered behavior to a so-called primordial warrior tradition, it may be more useful to look to the military as an institution of socialization.[10]

The military taught Amin to equate manhood not only with courage and strength, but also with sexual virility. Indeed, hyper-sexuality is one of the key characteristics associated with militarized masculinity (and the warrior culture described by Mazrui). Soldiers often learn to demonstrate their power through their sexual prowess. As such, a man's status among his peers increases with each sexual conquest. Although this type of posturing is not unique to military men, it is highly celebrated in military environments. Amin surrounded himself with beautiful women in order to bolster his masculinity. Former cabinet minister Henry Kyemba explains:

> Besides his five wives, Amin has had countless other women, many of whom have borne him children. His sex life is truly extraordinary. He regards his sexual energy as a sign of his power and authority. He never tries to hide his lust. His eyes lock onto any beautiful woman. His reputation for sexual performance is so startling that women often deliberately make themselves available, and his love affairs have included women of all colors and many nations, from schoolgirls to mature women, from street girls to university lecturers.[11]

Kyemba argues that "his treatment of women has its counterpart in his treatment of the country. His urge to dominate by force, his vindictiveness, his peacock flamboyance— all suggest that he has seized and ravaged the country as he has possessed his scores of women."[12] This suggests that Amin did not respect women, but instead, used them to satisfy his personal and political lusts. Although he incorporated women into the state at very high levels, he did so in ways that would not threaten his tenuous grasp on power. The rise and fall of Elizabeth Bagaya clearly demonstrates that the promotion of women in Amin's military state was strategic, but not necessarily empowering for the individuals involved. It is to her story that we now turn.

Militarized Femininity: The Unmaking of a Woman

Elizabeth Bagaya enjoyed a privileged upbringing. As the eldest daughter of the King of Toro and the niece of the King of Buganda, she received a first-class education, both in Uganda and abroad. She was one of the first three African women to be admitted to Cambridge University, where she graduated with a degree in law in 1962. Three years

---

10. Other scholars have found Mazrui's analysis problematic for different reasons. Aidan Southall, for example, argues that the celebration of an essential warrior tradition is dangerous because it reinforces racist stereotypes about the "savagery" of Africans. Timothy Parsons, on the other hand, rejects the idea of an African martial tradition altogether. He argues that officers of the King's African Rifles invented martial traditions among particular ethnic groups to bolster recruitment. Parsons suggests that ethnic groups in this part of Africa did not possess innate warrior qualities, but instead, enlisted more soldiers because of economic need. This economic need was a product of inequitable development. See Aidan Southall, "Social Disorganization in Uganda: Before, During, and After Amin," *The Journal of Modern African Studies* 18, no. 4 (1980): 627–656; Timothy Parsons, *The African Rank-and-File: Social Implications of Colonial Military Service in the King's African Rifles, 1902–1964* (Portsmouth, NH: Heinemann, 1999).

11. Henry Kyemba, *A State of Blood: The Inside Story of Idi Amin* (London: Corgi Books, 1977), 163–164.

12. Kyemba, *A State of Blood*, 165.

later, in November 1965, she was admitted to the bar, thus becoming the first female barrister in all of East and Central Africa. Before she had an opportunity to celebrate her tremendous achievement, however, Bagaya received word that her father had passed away unexpectedly. She was asked to return home immediately to help her brother, the future king, with the transfer of power.[13]

Bagaya's homecoming was challenging, not only because of her new responsibilities as chief royal advisor, but also because of mounting political tensions within the country—a period of time known as "the 1966 crisis." During this crisis, Prime Minister Milton Obote suspended the constitution and assumed all executive powers. He also arrested five of his cabinet members and replaced the army's commander-in-chief with a more "loyal" soldier—Idi Amin. Given that the King of Buganda was the country's ceremonial president and the central government was located on their traditional land, the Baganda were outraged. They ordered the government to leave, but the state refused to give up "their" land. Things came to a head when Obote ordered Amin to attack the royal palace. Although the king was able to escape into exile, the kingdom fell into shambles. The following year, in September 1967, Obote abolished the institution of kingship completely, promulgating a new constitution based on a "republican" system of government. The political environment had become highly precarious for royalty and many, like Bagaya, decided to flee.

Bagaya's period in exile began in London, where at the invitation of Princess Margaret and Lord Snowden, she took part in a Commonwealth fashion show. Being one of the few black models on the runway, her appearance created quite a buzz and soon she was inundated with modeling offers. Within a short period of time, she began gracing the pages of the world's top fashion magazines, including British and American *Vogue*. With the assistance of Jacqueline Kennedy, she met the editor-in-chief of American *Vogue*, who invited her to come to New York City. Once there, she signed on as a model at the Ford Agency, appearing in *Look*, *Life*, and *Ebony* magazines. She also began taking acting lessons, ultimately winning the lead role in the film version of Chinua Achebe's classic, *Things Fall Apart*.

By the time that Amin seized power in early 1971, Bagaya had become an international superstar. Given her tremendous success and popularity—both in Uganda and abroad—it was no surprise that she would be courted for a position in the new government. The new Minister of Planning and Economic Development, Apollo Kironde, suggested to Amin that Bagaya would make an excellent roving ambassador. Although the two had never met, Amin invited her to return to Uganda, along with a number of other royal exiles. Without hesitation, she jumped onto a plane and returned home. In the months that followed, Bagaya met with Amin on numerous occasions, discussing the various ways she might involve herself in the nascent government. The two came to an agreement and on July 21, 1971, Amin formally appointed her as the country's first roving ambassador.[14] He knew that she would lend respectability to his regime abroad and "soften" his image on the home front, thus making the military dictatorship more palatable to Ugandans. His decision was immediately popular among the nation's women. The Uganda Council of Women (UCW) hailed Bagaya's appointment as "one of the biggest steps women in Uganda have attained," a political move that would "show the world that women of Uganda are at the same rank with the men."[15]

---

13. Most of the biographical information for this section comes from Bagaya's autobiography. See Nyabongo, *Elizabeth of Toro*.

14. "Liz Bagaya Gets Top Job," *Uganda Argus*, 22 July 1971.

15. "Women's Biggest Step," *Uganda Argus*, 28 July 28 1971.

Although Bagaya's position required her to promote the regime on the diplomatic front, much of her time was spent at home, mobilizing Ugandan women for national development. She regularly traveled the country, giving speeches to various women's groups about their responsibilities as "mothers of the nation." In an address to the UCW, the national women's organization at the time, she stated that "the role that mothers of the nation can play in terms of culture is more important than that of the leaders of this nation."[16] As such, they needed to make an effort to pass on their indigenous languages, poetry, proverbs and songs. Otherwise, she argued, the nation would disappear. Bagaya also encouraged women to embrace modernity. During a speech at a women's leadership seminar held at Makerere University in early 1972, she told women not to be afraid of losing their femininity if they competed with men. Instead, they should utilize it to pursue their goals. In other words, it was possible for women to be educated and modern, as well as moral and cultural guardians.[17]

Over the course of Bagaya's first year in office, Amin became increasingly interested in her personal and professional affairs. Although it was standard protocol for the roving ambassador to brief the president after every diplomatic mission, Amin found ways of keeping a close watch on her movements. He selected a number of security personnel to accompany her on each of her trips, presumably so that they could report back to him on her behavior. He also issued warnings to various government officials to keep their distance from her. When Bagaya took a short leave of absence in early 1973, Amin had her followed. Once she returned, he confronted her about a series of rumors that had been circulating about the two of them at the highest levels of government. He was not angry, but merely surprised that onlookers should think it was even a big deal. According to Bagaya's retelling of the story, Amin asked the rumor mongers the following: "Am I not a man, and is Bagaya not a woman, what is wrong with that?"[18] Before she had time to respond to his recap, he invited her to join him on a trip to the Middle East. When she told him that she did not want to accompany him, he announced that he no longer needed a roving ambassador. Instead, he wanted her to focus her attention on domestic women's issues. In her memoir, *Elizabeth of Toro: The Odyssey of an African Princess*, Bagaya interpreted her new responsibilities as evidence that Amin was taking Ugandan women seriously. I tend to think that his actions were less an expression of his commitment to women's issues than they were a reflection of his desire to keep closer tabs on her movements.

Over the following year, Bagaya maintained a busy schedule, not only working on various women's issues, but also, maintaining her duties as roving ambassador. Although Amin had reassigned her to other tasks—at least in theory—he continued sending her on various goodwill missions throughout the world. And as always, her delegations included top-ranking military and security personnel. Despite his insecurities, Amin needed her diplomatic skills. After briefly flirting with the idea of making Bagaya his ambassador to Egypt in late January 1974, Amin quickly changed his mind. On February 19, 1974, Amin shocked the nation with a bold announcement: Bagaya was to become the new Minister of Foreign Affairs, the first female cabinet member in the nation's history.[19]

Although there are a number of theories as to why Amin made such an unprecedented move, the most likely explanation is that he promoted her in order to publicly humiliate

---

16. "Mothers Big Role," *Uganda Argus*, 27 November 1971.
17. "'Let Us Put More Emphasis on Women's Education' Plea," *Uganda Argus*, 29 March 1972. See also "Role of Modern Women in Our Society," *Uganda Argus*, 27 April 1972.
18. Nyabongo, *Elizabeth of Toro*, 135.
19. "Ambassador Bagaya Replaces Lt. Col. Ondoga," *Voice of Uganda*, 20 February 1974.

Michael Ondoga, the then-current Minister of Foreign Affairs. This occurred at a time when the army, and indeed the entire nation, had been riddled by ethnic tensions. One former minister, Paul Etiang, told me about a cabinet meeting in which Amin chastised the ministers for neglecting their portfolios and for engaging in "tribal activities," petty behaviors that Amin claimed were typical of women.[20] French filmmaker Barbet Shroeder captured this tirade while he was shooting footage for his documentary *General Idi Amin Dada: A Self-Portrait* (1974). Amin told the ministers:

> All of you, you are in very high ranking governmental posts. Your duty is not to be very weak. You must not be like a woman who is just weak and he [sic] can't speak, even talk … You should not be like [the] Minister of Foreign Affairs … This is the weakness of the Ministry of Foreign Affairs. If I see the minister is [a] coward, automatically I kick you out of my office because I know that you have got something wrong with you. I will put another person straight … whether you hide, you will be known.[21]

Unfortunately for Ondoga, this warning was no joke. After the meeting ended, Amin ordered the ministers to go to Makerere University for an important announcement. Once there, he asked Bagaya to join him at the podium as his new Minister of Foreign Affairs. According to Etiang, the students did not know how to react. One asked what would happen to Ondoga. Amin assured the student that he would be reassigned. Within twenty-four hours, however, he was dead. It seems likely that Amin promoted Bagaya solely for the purpose of insulting and humiliating an ethnic rival. His actions demonstrated that even a "weak" woman could do a better job.

While this changing of the guards was intended to emasculate Ondoga, it also served to enhance Bagaya's reputation as a strong woman. Amin declared that he wanted the new minister to be powerful—not "like a woman who is just weak." He confirmed this sentiment when he swore her into office. He challenged her to be as tough as the women prime ministers in Israel, India, and Sri Lanka, warning that if she failed she would have "let down the country and down-graded [her] womenfolk."[22] In the months that followed, Bagaya demonstrated her fierce loyalty to the regime, garnering significant support for the government, particularly within the Arab world. One of her crowning achievements as minister came in September 1974, when she delivered a biting indictment of "western imperialism" before the United Nations' General Assembly. Amin was delighted by her speech and awarded her with a prestigious medal, the Order of the Source of the Nile (Second Class).[23] Before she could accept the award, however, she needed to complete the remainder of her diplomatic mission, which involved travel to Canada, West Germany, France, and the United Kingdom. Amin wanted her to return to Uganda as soon as possible and asked her to cut short her tour, worried perhaps, that she would defect like so many other members of his regime. He had also heard rumors about "misdeeds" committed while she was abroad, and wanted to confirm that her behavior had been appropriate.[24]

---

20. Etiang served as Minister of Foreign Affairs (1973–1974), Minister of State in Charge of African Affairs (1974–1976), and Minister of Transport, Communication and Works (1976–1978). Paul Etiang, interview by author, Kampala, 26 July 2005.

21. Barbet Shroeder, *General Idi Amin Dada: A Self Portrait*, DVD (Criterion Collection, 1974).

22. "Challenge to Bagaya," *Voice of Uganda*, 21 February 1974.

23. "Thousands Mark Uganda's Uhuru Day," *Voice of Uganda*, 10 October 10 1974. The First Class award was reserved for heads of state.

24. Nyabongo, *Elizabeth of Toro*, 169–172.

Contrary to many people's expectations, Bagaya did not defect. When she returned home, she found that Amin had sent all of his ministers on leave. He did this on occasion in an attempt to weaken their control over their ministries, demonstrating that he alone was the one in charge. After debriefing the president, she too was sent on a one-month furlough. Shortly after settling into her new routine, Bagaya received a phone call from one of Amin's close friends — Roy Innis, the American-born leader of the Congress of Racial Equality (CORE). Innis asked if he could stop by to chat. Bagaya was surprised, but obliged his request. When he arrived at her door, he got straight to the point: "If Amin asks you, will you marry him?" Bagaya said that it was out of the question, since he was a married man. Innis responded by saying, "If he asks you, I shouldn't refuse if I were you. It will be very dangerous." And with that, he left.[25]

At the end of Bagaya's leave, she returned to her office to resume work. Almost immediately, Amin summoned her to his chambers and relieved her of her duties. A group of police officers escorted her to her official residence and then proceeded to search her house. They returned that evening to arrest her. After spending one night in jail, she was released on house arrest. According to a declassified report issued by the U.S. Department of State, Bagaya had been tortured while in police custody. A Ugandan informant told the U.S. Ambassador to Kenya that she showed signs of "being badly beaten and having her head shaved with broken glass."[26] Bagaya's memoir mentions nothing of violence so it is difficult to corroborate this part of the report.

Meanwhile, Amin announced to the state-run newspaper that he had fired her for "the good of the country and the interests of the security of Uganda and Africa as a whole."[27] He alleged that she had inappropriately utilized government funds while attending the United Nations' General Assembly Meeting in New York. In addition to spending exorbitant sums on lavish dinners and expensive clothing, Amin claimed that she met with CIA operatives who had succeeded in brainwashing her. He said that on her way back to Uganda, she passed through Orly Airport in Paris and "made love to an unknown European in a toilet." Amin stated that her behavior "ashames [sic] and degrades the standard of women in Uganda." Her actions, he said, were immoral and therefore dangerous to the nation's security interests.

While Bagaya was on house arrest, she was asked to account for all the money that she spent during her trip. Because she and her accountant kept detailed receipts, she was able to account for all expenses. At the same time, French authorities issued a formal statement that the "toilet incident" never took place, as she was under diplomatic escort the entire time. The Ugandan state was never able to charge her with a crime, so she was released from house arrest. Although she did not plan to go into exile, everything changed on January 24, 1975, when her "nude" photograph was plastered across the front page of the daily newspaper.[28] The photo had been published as "proof" that Bagaya had had sex with an unknown man in a Paris bathroom. Several months later, they reprinted the picture to remind readers of her "guilt."[29] The regime strategically utilized the doctored image of her naked body to symbolize the dangers of women's sexuality writ large and to promote a more acceptable version of femininity (i.e. docile, asexual, and "weak"). Bagaya had no choice but to flee. She went into hiding and eventually made her way across the Kenyan

---

25. Nyabongo, *Elizabeth of Toro*, 175–176.

26. Declassified/Released US Department of State EO Systematic Review 30 JUN 2005, R 021341Z DEC 74.

27. "Miss Bagaya Loses Her Ministerial Post," *Voice of Uganda*, 29 November 1974.

28. "Radio Comment on Miss Bagaya," *Voice of Uganda*, 24 January 1975.

29. Photograph. *Voice of Uganda*, 7 April 1975.

border on February 8, 1975. She did not return to Uganda until the overthrow of Amin in April 1979.

Reflections on the Gender of Military Power

What does Bagaya's story tell us about the gender of military power? And likewise, what does militarism teach us about gender? Although I am continuing to explore both of these questions in greater detail, I am prepared to make a number of preliminary assertions about gender and military rule. Let me start by saying that it is reasonable to assume that Amin was not necessarily cognizant of the extent to which gender influenced his rule. After all, most of us "do" gender without thinking about it. As an analytic tool, however, it is important because it helps us to better understand *how* Amin organized the state and maintained power. His ideas about what a man or a woman should or should not do were reflected in his policies, as well as his political appointments. His decision to promote women like Bagaya to high-level positions was strategic and reflected a particular type of militarized gender logic. It was hardly a reflection of Amin's feminist sensibilities, but instead, a defense mechanism—a means of protecting his image as a fearless ruler *and* as a powerful man.

What was the gender logic behind Amin's decision to incorporate intelligent, civilian women into the government? First, it was a way for the state to normalize and legitimate military rule. Because Amin seized power in a coup, he needed to establish his reputation as a better leader than his predecessor. Amina Mama suggests that military leaders often incorporate elite women into the state in order to accomplish these goals.[30] In her research in Nigeria, she demonstrates how various military leaders appointed their wives to high political positions in order to "soften" the image of the state, thus making it seem more like a family affair. Maryam Babangida, wife of the former Nigerian military leader Ibrahim Babangida (r. 1985–1993), suggests that "gradually his *militariness* rubs off on her and stands her in good stead as an ambassador both of the man and his profession."[31] Although Amin never appointed his wives to high administrative posts, they served an important function as role models for the nation's women. Bagaya also did a great deal of work on behalf of the women of Uganda. In addition to her diplomatic duties, she traveled across the country giving speeches and chairing meetings of various women's clubs. She was popular in domestic and international arenas, and therefore, represented a softer side of militarism.

Amin also promoted women into high political positions in order to bolster his reputation as a "manly" leader who could surround himself with beautiful women. He routinely bragged about his sexual exploits, claiming that no woman could resist "Big Daddy." By working closely with Bagaya—an international fashion model and movie star—he stoked the rumor mills. Even though Bagaya refutes all claims that she ever had a sexual relationship with Amin, many people thought otherwise.[32] Whether the two were

---

30. Amina Mama, "Khaki in the Family: Gender Discourses and Militarism in Nigeria," *African Studies Review* 41, no. 2 (1998): 1–17.

31. Maryam Babangida, *The Home Front: Nigerian Army Officers and Their Wives* (Ibadan: Fountain Publishers, 1988), 35.

32. One sixty-year old woman, for instance, told me that Bagaya was his girlfriend and that "he loved her." Another fifty-year old woman explained that she was his mistress and that "Amin wanted to kill her ... because she got another boyfriend." See Mother 28, interview by author, Kampala, 24 June 2005 and Mother 42, interview by author, Kampala, 31 July 2005. The late Abu Mayanja, Amin's former Minister of Education from 1971–1972, also believed that the two had been intimately involved. Abu Mayanja, interview by author, Kampala, 13 June 2005. Other former ministers denied that this

intimately involved is almost irrelevant. What matters is that many Ugandans believed this to be true. This pattern of self-aggrandizement through the "possession" of women is certainly not unique to Uganda. In Rafael Trujillo's military dictatorship in the Dominican Republic (r. 1930–1961), for instance, women were an important form of symbolic capital. As Lauren Derby poignantly argues, Trujillo's power was directly proportional to the number of women to which he could lay claim. The higher the status of the woman, the more the dictator's macho stature grew.[33] There are undoubtedly countless parallels that can be found in other military dictatorships throughout the world.

Militarized societies are often marked by rigid gender roles and relations, meaning that there is generally little overlap between the two social worlds. If a man engages in "women's work" or begins "acting like a woman," he threatens the existing gender order. The Minister of Foreign Affairs was fired for transgressing these boundaries. According to Amin, he was acting like a "woman who is just weak."[34] He was replaced *not* by another man, but instead, by a woman. Gender logic suggests that Amin did this in order to put Ondoga in his place—to show him that he was less qualified than a "mere" woman. He used similar rhetoric when announcing the appointment of other women to high-level positions. For instance, when he appointed Helen Oyeru to become the permanent secretary in the Ministry of Provincial Administration, he publicly acknowledged that "some women were proving to be better officers than a number of men officers because a number of men in high ranking government and military positions indulge too much in heavy drinking."[35] Later, when he announced the promotion of Ellen Pharas Awori to the rank of Provincial Commissioner for Culture and Community Development in Karamoja District, he said it was because women had become more hard-working than men.[36] The promotion of women emasculated men.

Given the importance of Bagaya and other high-ranking women to the maintenance of state power, why would Amin get rid of them? The most logical explanation is that he was experiencing a crisis of masculinity—an inability to maintain control over the women who were closest to him, as well as the country more generally. Amin was furious at the thought that Bagaya may have had sex with another man, especially a white, "imperialist" man. He had to find a way to humiliate her, just as he thought she had done to him. He therefore orchestrated the publication of the "nude" photographs in order to show the world the depths of her depravity. As if that were not enough, he later made a series of scathing comments about her at the OAU Summit, which was held in Kampala several months later. To the Palestinian Liberation Organization's delegate, he insisted that she was "African in colour, but imperialist at heart."[37] To the foreign press, he said that "she thinks she is still queen or something," insinuating that the disgraced princess was uppity and deserved what she got.[38] Amin's actions and comments seem to suggest that he was a wounded man who was lashing out due to frustration and fear.

---

was true. See, for example, Henry Kyemba, interview by author, Kampala, 2 February 2005; James Zikusoka, interview by author, Kampala, 26 May 2005; William Banage, interview by author, Kampala, 8 July 2005; and Paul Etiang, interview by author, Kampala, 26 July 2005.

33. Lauren Derby, "The Dictator's Seduction: Gender and State Spectacle during the Trujillo Regime," *Callaloo* 23, no. 3 (2000): 1113.

34. Shroeder, *General Idi Amin Dada.*

35. "Oyeru Becomes Second Woman Permanent Secretary," *Voice of Uganda*, 15 May 1975.

36. "Dynamic Lady Promoted," *Voice of Uganda*, 6 September 1976.

37. Benoni Turyahikayo-Rugyema, *Idi Amin Speaks: An Annotated Selection of His Speeches* (Madison: African Studies Program at the University of Wisconsin, 1998), 47–48.

38. Anthony Hughes, "Field Marshal Idi Amin Dada, President of Uganda," *Africa Report* 20, no. 5 (September–October 1975), 7.

It may come as a surprise to learn that after Bagaya's dismissal, Amin continued promoting women to important political positions. Far from altruistic or even feminist, this was really just an attempt to tap into the momentum of the global women's movement. By hiring a limited number of women to key administrative posts, Amin was able to demonstrate an on-going "commitment" to women's rights that predated the U.N. Decade for Women. Because Uganda's international reputation had fallen to an all-time low, Amin needed all the political capital he could muster. He therefore used women to reinforce the "legitimacy" of his regime. And, once again, we see that women and *ideas about women* were central to the maintenance of state power.

Conclusion

Throughout this essay, I have argued that gender was a crucial organizing factor within Amin's military state. It influenced who he was as a man and how he governed as a ruler. I have also argued that Amin's ideas about gender were profoundly shaped by military values. His decision to promote certain women to high-level positions was strategic and reflected a particular type of gender logic — one that used women to advance the needs of the military state. Women such as Bagaya were militarized, but not empowered.[39] Because empowerment was never the goal, it is fair to assume that Amin was *not* a feminist. But does this mean that he was necessarily a foe? I would suggest not. Many of his policies were actually liberating for some Ugandan women. When Amin expelled the Asian population in late 1972, for instance, many women began working in the informal sector. Some women received shops that had been "abandoned" by the departing Asians, while others were forced to work out of necessity. In either case, many women gained valuable skills as a result of Amin's policies, something I have described in other work as an "accidental liberation."[40] I am not suggesting that this liberation was complete or enjoyed by all, but it did alert me to the fact that women did not necessarily perceive Amin as a foe. Many older women that I interviewed remembered Amin fondly, either for "teaching us how to work," or for banning miniskirts and restoring "morality" to a rapidly changing society. Many younger women, of course, found the bans offensive and relayed numerous stories about the violence that accompanied the anti-mini operations. These stories suggest that Amin's regime had contradictory effects on women. In a sense, then, he was neither feminist nor foe.

References

Amnesty International. *Human Rights in Uganda*. London: Amnesty International, June 1978.

Babangida, Maryam. *The Home Front: Nigerian Army Officers and Their Wives*. Ibadan: Fountain Publishers, 1988.

---

39. Uta Klein discusses this process in relation to women's involvement in the Israeli Defense Forces. See Klein, "War and Gender: What Do We Learn from Israel?" in *The Women and War Reader*, ed. Lois Ann Lorentzen and Jennifer Turpin (New York: New York University Press, 1998), 153.

40. Alicia C. Decker, "An Accidental Liberation? Idi Amin, the Asian Expulsion, and the 'Empowerment' of Ugandan Women in the 1970s" (forthcoming).

Decker, Alicia C. "An Accidental Liberation? Idi Amin, the Asian Expulsion, and the 'Empowerment' of Ugandan Women in the 1970s." Forthcoming.

Derby, Lauren. "The Dictator's Seduction: Gender and State Spectacle during the Trujillo Regime." *Callaloo* 23, no. 3 (2000): 1112–1146.

Enloe, Cynthia. *The Curious Feminist: Searching for Women in a New Age of Empire.* Berkeley: University of California Press, 2004.

Hughes, Anthony. "Field Marshal Idi Amin Dada, President of Uganda." *Africa Report* 20, no. 5 (September–October 1975): 2–7.

Klein, Uta. "War and Gender: What Do We Learn from Israel?" In *The Women and War Reader,* ed. Lois Ann Lorentzen and Jennifer Turpin, 148–154. New York: New York University Press, 1998.

Kyemba, Henry. *A State of Blood: The Inside Story of Idi Amin.* London: Corgi Books, 1977.

Leopold, Mark. *Inside West Nile: Violence, History and Representation on an African Frontier.* Oxford: James Currey, 2005.

_____. "Sex, Violence and History in the Lives of Idi Amin: Postcolonial Masculinity as Masquerade." *Journal of Postcolonial Writing* 45, no. 3 (2009): 321–330.

Listowel, Judith. *Amin.* Dublin: IUP Books, 1973.

Mama, Amina. "Khaki in the Family: Gender Discourses and Militarism in Nigeria." *African Studies Review* 41, no. 2 (1998): 1–17.

Mazrui, Ali. "The Resurrection of the Warrior Tradition in African Political Culture." *The Journal of Modern African Studies* 13, no. 1 (1975): 67–84.

_____. *Soldiers and Kinsmen in Uganda: The Making of a Military Ethnocracy.* Beverly Hills: Sage, 1975.

Mittelman, James. *Ideology and Politics in Uganda: From Obote to Amin.* Ithaca: Cornell University Press, 1975.

Nyabongo, Elizabeth. *Elizabeth of Toro: The Odyssey of an African Princess.* New York: Simon and Schuster, 1989.

Parsons, Timothy. *The African Rank-and-File: Social Implications of Colonial Military Service in the King's African Rifles, 1902–1964.* Portsmouth, NH: Heinemann, 1999.

_____. "Dangerous Education? The Army as School in Colonial East Africa." *The Journal of Imperial and Commonwealth History* 28, no. 1 (2000): 112–134.

Shroeder, Barbet. *General Idi Amin Dada: A Self Portrait.* DVD. Criterion Collection, 1974.

Southall, Aidan. "The Bankruptcy of the Warrior Tradition." In *The Warrior Tradition in Modern Africa,* ed. Ali Mazrui, 166–176. Leiden: E.J. Brill, 1977.

_____. "Social Disorganization in Uganda: Before, During, and After Amin." *The Journal of Modern African Studies* 18, no. 4 (1980): 627–656.

Turyahikayo-Rugyema, Benoni. *Idi Amin Speaks: An Annotated Selection of His Speeches.* Madison: African Studies Program at the University of Wisconsin, 1998.

Chapter 15

"The Beauty and Rightness of Our National Costume": Dress, Modernity, and Women's Activism in Northern Sudan

Marie Grace Brown

In 1952, the Sudanese Women's Union—the Sudan's first political party for women—declared that the adoption of the tobe as the national costume for women was an integral part of women's progress in attaining increased economic and social rights. Meaning "bolt of cloth," the tobe is a garment four meters long and two meters wide, which Sudanese women wrap around their bodies when outside their homes or in the presence of non-related males. Formerly predominately worn by married women in northern Sudan, by the middle of the twentieth century, the tobe had become the preferred uniform of midwives, nurses, and students. For women activists of the 1950s, swept up in Sudan's bid for independence from British colonial rule, the tobe became an appropriate representation of the nation.[1]

My work seeks to elevate Sudanese women from their assumed role as passive cultural vessels in political movements and argues that through the creation and manipulation of new national symbols like the tobe, Sudanese women became active participants in constructing national identity. Current scholarship on the development of Sudanese nationalism is limited to the activities of intellectual male elites and largely overlooks the role women played in nationalist movements. When women activists (both feminist and nationalist) are mentioned, they are often cast as passive symbolic representations of the newly formed nation. Yet, this gendered symbolism performed active political work. Women activists manipulated the tobe as an important symbol of national distinction and cultural authenticity. Unlike other forms of native dress, which, in the eyes of nationalists and imperialists alike, symbolized backwardness, the tobe satisfied western standards of modernity (such as modesty and discipline) while remaining authentically "Sudanese." The term "manipulate" is used advisedly; in the same way that women arranged the tobe around their bodies each day, so too did women activists construct and negotiate new national meanings for the garment. This chapter has two aims. First, it argues that Sudanese women were equally inventors of national tradition and crafters of standards of modernity. Second, it suggests that non-textual sites of analysis, such as clothing and dress, amplify unheard or under-heard voices in nationalist struggles.

---

1. The Sudan is a country of numerous ethnicities and over one hundred languages. No monograph can do justice to the complexities of these multiple identities.

Why Study Cloth and Clothing?

Historians have yet to capitalize on clothing and fashion as analytic tools. We treat clothing as a cultural symbol—a marker, or outward sign, of identity. In contrast, this chapter sees sartorial behavior as an active choice, which reaffirms family connections, solidifies communal networks, and broadcasts political support or protest. Thus, clothing is not a passive representation of social status—but a creative force. Dress is not only a marker of social connection, but also the very bond itself. This active understanding of clothing delimitates dress as a functional body covering, from fashion, a selective collection of garments whose popularity rises and falls with the rhythms of production and consumptive trends. Unlike studies of dress, which focus on the garment itself, analysis of fashion examines a person's socio-political aspirations as expressed in his/her clothing preferences. In foregrounding the possibility of choice in cut, texture, color, and place of production, analysis of fashion grants agency to what is otherwise assumed as an apolitical, unimaginative daily act.

Historically, studies of dress in Africa have suffered from the restrictive opposition of traditional verses modern. In works that span the shift from colonial to post-colonial, heavily laden words such as indigenous, tradition, authentic, modern, and progressive are inevitably used. These words can lure a scholar into creating analytical binaries (tradition/modernity; East/West). However, the transnational character of African dress and fashion render the simple division between authenticity and modernity obsolete. Put another way, "traditional" dress cannot be simply classified as antagonistic to western colonialism and influence. Secondly, fashion studies are largely ignored in favor of ethnographic analysis of so-called traditional clothing. Dress only seems to become politically meaningful during struggles for independence in which nationalists wear traditional costumes in opposition to the western-styled dress of imperial sympathizers. Taken together, these assumptions isolate African dress as a simple, static cultural symbol.

Recent scholarship presents a new complexity of African fashion, which challenges categories of global/local and public/private. In her analysis of "traditional" hand-dyed Senegalese cloth, anthropologist Leslie Rabine writes, "Far from embodying the timeless, closed society evoked by colonialist notions of tradition, however, these fashions result from a centuries-old history of weaving together influences from many African, European and Arabic cultures." Moreover, the production and consumption of traditional garments become the "focal points for the anxieties, attachments, and criticisms that attend the ever-changing status of tradition in a society in crisis."[2] It is in these crisis moments that fashion choice becomes political choice. Thus, clothing compels scholars to reconsider the notion that 'the public' and 'the political' are primarily male spaces. As Jean Allman notes in her introduction to *Fashioning Africa: The Power and Politics of Dress*, fashion and dress place women in the center stage and bodily praxis makes women's political praxis visible.[3] This chapter highlights the dynamism of African fashion and argues that in choosing the tobe, Sudanese women activists incorporated modern behaviors with cultural authenticity.

The re-conceptualization of the seemingly standard categories of public/private is critical for scholars of post-colonial nationalisms. The current state of scholarship on nationalism within Africa and the Middle East is largely conservative; historical narratives

---

2. Leslie W. Rabine, *The Global Circulation of African Fashion* (Oxford: Berg, 2002), 28.

3. Jean Allman, "Introduction," Jean Allman, (Ed.), *Fashioning Africa: Power and the Politics of Dress* (Bloomington: Indiana University Press, 2004), 5.

trace a rise of nationalism, which does little more than mirror than transplant European-styled nations and nationalisms onto the African continent. However, in analyses of the transitional periods from colonial to post-colonial, the scholar must be careful not to assume the inevitability of the establishment of the nation-state. A methodological question arises: how to convey the uncertainty of a historical moment when the outcome is widely known. The answer lies in focusing on alternate experiences or ideologies.

A renewed focus on women as active creators of national identity is one such alternate experience. This study treats the nation as an entirely modern concept of group identity, one that relies fully on the canonization of local practice into "tradition." Benedict Anderson's seminal work on the nation as an "imagined community" provides a valuable starting point for this research.[4] However, the limited focus of Anderson and others on the primacy of print culture in creating national consciousness has yielded nationalist narratives, which overly emphasizes the role of intellectual (predominately male) elites. The privileging of print culture precludes the role of women in the formation of national identity. In moving from texts to textiles, I am de-centering the voices of male intellectual elites and foregrounding the experiences of Sudanese women as they engaged with non-textual sites of nationalism. This shift away from texts liberates the concept of "the nation" from western measures and standards. Using dress as an analytical lens challenges scholars to reconsider "the public" and "politics" as male spaces. Though formally excluded from participating in government, northern women activists engaged in politics through the creation and negotiation of bodily practices. As these women adorned themselves, so too did they fashion their ideas for a new nation.

Women's Activism in Northern Sudan

Though the tobe in the Sudan dates back to the beginning of the eighteenth century at least, the tobe's character as a 'traditional' costume is much more recent. The tobe was not a locally produced garment. Sudanese merchants traveled to Cairo and traded luxury items such as slaves and ivory for large quantities of unbleached cloth. The cloth was then taken south to Asyut to be dyed before finally being sold in the Sudan. Pacification and consolidation of the Sudan during the Turkiyya period encouraged and facilitated trade and the importation of new clothing varieties. Throughout the nineteenth century, lower class women and young girls wore little more than a cotton cloth wrapped around their waist. As connections to global trade networks grew, upper class women and older women were distinguished by a loose cotton wrapper, a tobe, which they wore in public. The tobes themselves varied in material from fine calico to thin cotton. During this time of relative stability and regional cohesion, a newly rising middle class of land-owners sought to mimic the nobility and increasingly turned to imported cloth and clothing as status symbols.[5] At the end of the nineteenth century, the religious and nationalist reforms of the Mahdi called for a rejection of foreign imports. However, it would appear that after two centuries of growing popularity, the tobe, though an imported good, had come to be considered a Sudanese cultural object. Additionally, as religious fervor increased under the Mahdi, the tobe aptly satisfied a preference for chaste clothing. The tobe proved remarkably adaptive

4. Benedict Anderson, *Imagined Communities: Reflections on the Origin of Nationalism* (London: Verso, 1991).

5. George Michael La Rue, "Imported Blue Cotton Cloth: Status Clothing for Rural Women in Pre-Colonial Darfur," African Studies Association Annual Meeting (Boston, 1993).

in the face of drastic socio-political shifts during the eighteenth and nineteenth centuries. In fact, its very authenticity is derived not from its status as a locally produced garment, but from the tobe's ability to mirror the currents of Sudanese history. As will be demonstrated below, in the twentieth century, the tobe continued to provide viable and visible solutions to important socio-political questions of nationalism and authenticity.

In 1952, the call for the adoption of the tobe as the national dress occurred during a period of strong political and social activism. Influenced by the Egyptian nationalist movement, educated, urban elites began a campaign for Sudanese self-rule in 1920s. However, Sudanese inhabitants were far from united as to what form that rule should take. British colonial rule had followed a conscious program to isolate culturally southern Sudan from the North. Christianity and the English language were promoted in the South, while Islam and Arabic held primacy in the North. In addition, British irrigation schemes and strict control of local economies significantly stunted the development of the South. These divergent colonial policies yielded deep suspicions between northern and southern Sudanese. Despite these factions, on December 31, 1955, the Sudanese Parliament passed a transitional constitution and declared independence from both British and Egyptian rule on January 1, 1956.

Before the transition to independence, the late colonial period had introduced new notions of domesticity, companionate marriage, and civic duty, which significantly altered the way Sudanese women viewed themselves and their roles in the family. Beginning with the founding of the League of Cultured Girls in 1947, Sudanese women began to work collectively to establish new social positions for themselves. Over the next few years, a handful of other women's organizations were founded. In spite of common goals such as increased education for women and girls, equality in the work force, and increased domestic rights, the early women's organizations succumbed to competition and partisan disputes. In 1952, a small group of women agreed to establish the Sudanese Woman's Union, a network that would become one of the most enduring and recognizable Sudanese women's organizations. Local newspapers reported on the formation of the Union and publicized the first meeting at which the organization's mission and constitution would be laid out. Like the organizations that had come before, the Sudanese Women's Union (WU) participated in charity work and aimed to improve Sudanese women's lives socially, economically, and politically.[6] As a sister organization to the Sudanese Communist Party, the WU was intimately bound to party politics. Unlike other national political parties at the time, the Sudanese Communist Party allowed women to become full party members. Previously, Sudanese women participated in politics only as extensions of their male relatives; even the more active women and women's groups were limited to a "Greek chorus" role to give support to the male dominated party line.[7] Though the leadership of the WU and the Communist Party did not always agree, the WU's proposed social reforms were unique as part of a larger political project.

One of the foremost concerns of the Women's Union was to elevate the social and economic status of Sudanese women by prescribing appropriate behaviors for a new type of woman—one who was defined by her distance from perceived harmful local practices. The union utilized the press, specifically their own journal, *The Woman's Voice*, to identify causes of women's "backwardness" and suggest solutions.[8] At a time when many still

---

6. Haga Kashif Badri, *Women's Movement in the Sudan* (New Delhi: Asia News Agency, 1986), 89.

7. Sondra Hale, *Gender Politics in Sudan: Islamism, Socialism, and the State* (Boulder, CO: Westview Press, Inc., 1996), 84.

8. Marjorie Hall and Bakhita Amin Ismail, *Sisters Under the Sun: The Story of Sudanese Women* (London: Longman, 1981), 106.

considered the voice of the woman to be sacred, *The Woman's Voice* was particularly subversive with the suggestion of the forbidden blazoned across its masthead. Yet, the popularity and strength of *The Woman's Voice* was sizable; circulation numbers varied but ranged from 12,000 to 17,000 readers at the height of the journal's popularity.[9] Equally suggestive was the journal's content, which was noted for "forceful" stance of articles that "attempted to educate its female readership away from certain traditions ... like the practice of facial scarification and female circumcision."[10] This rejection of perceived harmful traditions was not unique to the WU. Another women's leader, Zeinab el Fateh el Badawi, writes,

> When the women's movement started in 1947 we felt at the time that the Sudan was the most disagreeable of all countries in which to be a woman. Women in mass were isolated in the hareem [sic] ... with no education and with superstition as a dominating power in their lives ... Girls, backward and uneducated, had to endure the inhumane operation of pharaonic circumcision, their right nostrils were pierced to hold heavy wedding rings, their lips were tattooed, and they had to go through the agony of the eventful forty days of the marriage.[11]

Superstition and backwardness are mentioned repeatedly as dangerous forces, which threaten the health of Sudanese women and the success of the women's movement. As envisioned by many women activists, the new Sudanese woman would not be defined by harmful practices; she would be educated and freed from the isolation of the harem. The problem facing women activists was how to abandon customs now deemed harmful, while retaining a uniquely Sudanese identity during the years of nation building.

The rejection of local traditions such as pharaonic circumcision, facial scarification, and tattooing has vast implications for scholars' understandings of the development of Sudanese national culture. In her recent work, "Activating the Gender Local: Transnational Ideologies and 'Women's Culture' in Northern Sudan," Sondra Hale has begun to trace current intellectual developments of the Ideal Muslim Woman as envisioned by the Sudanese Communist Party and the National Islamic Front in the 1980s. Similar inquiries could be made of the process for fashioning new images of the ideal Sudanese woman at the height of the Sudan's nationalist and independence movement. Hale theorizes that transnational ideologies such as communism and Islamism are built up and popularized at the expense of existing local practices, especially "women's culture." She attributes this to male leaders seeking to position women in ways that will be most beneficial to the broader goals of the movement.[12] Thus, in the name of progress, women lose their connection with particular cultural markers. Conversely, male dominated political institutions can also circumscribe women in roles as carriers of an authentic culture and code of morality. Tied to an invented sense of enduring tradition, women become static and evoke continuity. In contrast, men are viewed as dynamic agents of change.[13] As outlined by Hale, both the erasure of women's culture and the essentialising of traditions treat women as passive recipients of a male defined culture. However, the call of Sudanese

---

9. Carolyn Fluehr-Lobban, "The Women's Movement in the Sudan and Its Impact on Sudanese Law and Politics," *The Ahfad Journal* Vol. 2. 1 (June 1985): 58.

10. Ibid.

11. Zeinab el Fateh el Badawi, *The Development of the Sudanese Women Movement* (Khartoum: Ministry of Information and Social Affairs, 1966), 1–3.

12. Sondra Hale, "Activating the Gender Local: Transnational Ideologies and 'Women's Culture' in Northern

Sudan," *Journal of Middle East Women's Studies* Vol. 1. 1 (Winter 2005): 30.

13. Hale, *Gender Politics in Sudan*, 7, 77.

women leaders for the rejection of certain cultural practices left no doubt that women were also involved in defining images of a new Sudanese woman. Thus, scholars must be careful in assuming that culture is an instrument of control wielded by men or male dominated structures. Women were equally engaged in manipulating cultural norms to assert new roles for themselves or strengthen old ones.

At the same time that women activists were rejecting certain traditions, they upheld and promoted the tobe as a valued symbol of cultural authenticity. In the first year of the organization, the Sudanese Women's Union defined a particular brand of feminism, which combined political rights with local traditions. Fatima Ibrahim's description of that project has been quoted often:

> We do not consider men our enemies. We do not consider Islam our opponent ...
> We demanded political, economic, and social rights for women, equal opportunities for employment, and an equal role for women within the family ...
> We held that feminism is indigenous to our culture, and full equality can be reached on the basis of our own religious and cultural precepts. We knew we must reassure our people that we did not mean to change the basic tenets of our traditions.

Many scholars stop quoting Ibrahim there; however, she ends her recollection with this line, "We stressed the beauty and rightness of our national costume, the toab [sic]."[14] When Ibrahim's lines are read in their entirety, it is evident that donning the tobe was part of a larger project combining feminism and nationalism. Ibrahim's use of the term "stress" suggests that in 1952 women had not fully subscribed to the idea of tobe as national dress. Yet, photographs and travelogues reveal that, by the 1950s, the majority of northern Sudanese women were wearing tobes regularly. Thus, Ibrahim's call for the "rightness" of a national costume suggests that the WU sought a discursive shift and not a material one. The vocabulary of unity and authenticity employed by the Women's Union disguises the disruptive side of national identity formation. In the first half of the twentieth century, the tobe was not popular in the South. While the tobe as national costume indicated a change in the garment's meaning in the North, in the South, the adoption of the tobe as the national costume required a paradigmatic shift in the standards of dress. Thus, the tobe is not a marker of Sudanese cultural authenticity, but, more accurately, Northern Sudanese cultural authenticity.

The beginnings of this move to new meanings can be seen in women's recollections of the political events surrounding the nationalist movement. In 1954, a procession to celebrate the signing of the Sudan's Independence Agreement marched from Khartoum to Omdurman. The march was one of the first instances in which women took part in public demonstrations. Among the marchers were members of the Women's Revival Society in Sudan, one of whom recalls, "Hundreds of women with their national toob [sic] took part shouting loudly 'Long Live the Sudan.' So it was a great task to be done by the Society."[15] Here, the threads of nationalism and feminism are closely interwoven in the tobe. In fact, it is impossible for the historian to separate the national act of celebration from the feminist act of taking part in a demonstration for the first time. The tobe, as the nascent national costume for women created a safe space in which Sudanese women could participate in the project of nation building.

---

14. Fatima Ahmed Ibrahim, "Arrow at Rest," Mahnaz Afkhami (Ed.), *Women in Exile* (Charlottesville: University Press of Virginia, 1994), 197–98.

15. Badri, *Women's Movement in the Sudan*, 92.

New Public Spaces

In order for the tobe to succeed as a 'national costume,' it had to satisfy the standards of modernity for Sudanese nationalists and the departing British imperialists. For former colonies in the twentieth century, the success (or even acknowledgment) of nationhood depended upon fluency in the Westernized language and in the signs of modernity. British colonial policy was framed around rhetoric of "moralpolitik." In response and in order to prove themselves conversant in the modern world, nationalist leaders adopted many of the values of the power they sought to overthrow.[16] In the eyes of British imperialists, appropriate clothing was both a "sign and an instrument" of a corporeal "metamorphosis" from ignorant barbarism to self-conscious civility.[17] For Sudanese nationalists, the adoption of correct clothing signaled to themselves and the world a readiness to rule.

However, the standards of correct dress for Sudanese men and women differed dramatically. Though Sudanese clothing has a long history of importing fabrics and styles, minimal contact between British and Sudanese women limited exchange of fashion trends. Sudanese women often viewed British women as "infidels" whose outfits were considered foreign and indecent.[18] As a result, Sudanese women did not discard the tobe in favor of European dress. The experience for Sudanese men is quite different. Folklorist Ali-Dinar's work in contemporary Darfur details the level of freedom men have in making clothing choices. A man's decision to wear a suit, shirt, and trousers, or a jallabeya, rested upon social context: leisure vs. work and formal vs. informal.[19] Today's familiarity with western dress began during the colonial period as Sudanese men assumed the positions of civil servants. The western styled uniforms, which were distributed to soldiers and guards, continue to have a "lasting effect in the interplay between traditional and western items of dress."[20] These distinctions in sartorial preferences, one "traditional" and one varied with western influences reveal the highly gendered experiences of colonialism. However, it would be a mistake to assume that the traditional character of women's dress rendered the tobe static or limited the opportunities for the women wearing it.

As general education for girls increased in the middle of the twentieth century, the tobe gained new significance for young girls who had not worn tobes previously. A crucial element to the advance of girls' education was the rise of night schools, which allowed women and girls to tend to their responsibilities in the home and receive an education. "The girl students could move about with their toobs [sic] on after 9 o'clock in the evening without fear and without anybody escorting."[21] Taking the place of a chaperone, the tobe provided a safe and modest way for women and girls to walk in the streets. British officials similarly stressed the connection between education and orderly dress. Ina Beasley, Controller of Girls Education, faced incredible obstacles in instituting and expanding education for young Sudanese women and girls in the 1940s. Not the least of these was

---

16. For an example of how the moralpolitik operated in Egypt, see Lisa Pollard, *Nurturing the Nation: The Family Politics of Modernizing, Colonizing, and Liberating Egypt, 1805–1923* (Berkeley: University of California Press, 2005).

17. John L. Comaroff and Jean Comaroff, *Of Revelation and Revolution: The Dialectics of Modernity on a South African Frontier*, Vol. 2 (Chicago: The University of Chicago Press, 1997), 227.

18. Griselda el-Tayib, "Women's Dress in the Northern Sudan," In Susan Kenyon, (Ed.) *The Sudanese Woman* (Khartoum: Graduate College, University of Khartoum, 1987), 40–66.

19. Ali Bahr Aldin Ali-Dinar, *Contextual Analysis of Dress and Adornment in Al-Fashir, Sudan* (Philadelphia: University of Pennsylvania, 1995), 75.

20. Ibid., 28.

21. Badri, 25–26.

reluctance on the part of parents to send their daughters to school. Yet, amongst accounts of her campaign to counter prevailing prejudices, Beasley's diaries are filled with observations about the lack of proper dress for her students. Under their tobes, many girls wore little at all. Though some schools did provide uniforms for their students, the most effective means of combating immodest dress was simply to teach girls to sew. The standard domestic science curriculum included lessons on how to cook with less waste and the basics of sewing. Durable calico material was provided by the colonial government, and then paid for in installments by the parents. It was imagined that at the end of four years a dedicated student would have made herself an entirely new set of clothes.[22] A student's new dress was much more than a practical school project. It was tangible evidence of the success of the civilizing mission.

The tobe's character as an authentic garment permitted women and girls to enter public spaces that were previously closed to them. Here, the tobe and girls' education are critically linked; without such a covering, female students could not have made their way to and from school. The tobe maintained an appropriate level of modesty and granted women and girls increased access to public spaces without a chaperone. In times of political crisis, the image of women in the streets has often been used as a symbol of a world-turned-upside-down.[23] However, the modest and traditional character of the garment may have worked to temper what would otherwise have been disruptive social behavior. Building upon Michel Foucault's theories of discipline and social order, Timothy Mitchell, an historian of Egypt, argues that imperialists aimed to socio-political order out of perceived disorder. However, colonial disciplinary power functioned "not at the level of an entire society, but at the level of detail, and not by restricting individuals and their actions but by producing them."[24] For example, the regular appearance of school uniforms, equally spaced as students sat on benches, created discipline within the classroom.[25] Mitchell's analysis can also be moved outside the classroom. A student in a uniform (or, in this case the tobe) creates a singular space of social order within the chaos of the streets. Viewed in this light, the tobe did not just facilitate entry into the streets, but rather created the very public space that women and girls entered.

Just as the tobe permitted girls to enter the streets to attend school, so too did it allow members of the Women's Union to enter the public debates of independence and nation building. Fatima Ibrahim fully understood the importance of adhering to newly adopted standards of modernity. At the same time, she was keenly aware of Sudanese women's potential social and political leverage as bearers of an authentic culture. After being the first woman elected to Parliament in 1965, Ibrahim strategically drew upon the modest intentions of the tobe to enhance her own position, she writes, "I had chosen to uphold an image of myself as a traditional, respectable, family-oriented woman in my private life. This image gained me the credibility that allowed me to be radical and outspoken in my public life." The tobe provided an acceptable framework for what otherwise might have been unpalatable ideas. To avoid the possibility of rumors, which would have destroyed her image and thus her effectiveness, Ibrahim never travelled alone in a car with another

---

22. Ina Beasley, *Before the Wind Changed: People, Places, and Education in the Sudan* (Oxford: Oxford University Press, 1992), 357.

23. See Palmira Brummett, "Dogs, Cholera, Women, and Other Menaces in the Streets: Cartoon Satire in the Ottoman Revolutionary Press," *International Journal of Middle East Studies* (November 1995): 433–60; and Lynn Hunt, *The Family Romance of the French Revolution* (Berkeley: University of California Press, 1992).

24. Timothy Mitchell, *Colonizing Egypt* (Berkeley: University of California Press, 1991), xi.

25. Ibid., 79.

colleague, nor attended a meeting in which there was no other woman present.[26] Both the tobe and these modest behaviors mutually reinforced Ibrahim's image as an activist who sought progress for women within Sudanese traditions and values.

Women activists sought to situate their demands for women's rights in a manner that would not challenge local traditions. Recall Ibrahim's earlier quote, "We held that feminism is indigenous to our culture, and full equality can be reached on the basis of our own religious and cultural precepts. We ... did not mean to change the basic tenets of our traditions. We stressed the beauty and rightness of our national costume, the tobe."[27] Ibrahim's notion of an indigenous feminism is a provocative rejection of Western imported structures of feminism as well as transnational ideologies of feminism. Thus for Ibrahim and the members of the WU, the tools of the women's movement needed to be located within pre-existing cultural practices. As a marker of Sudanese culture, the tobe allowed women activists to cloak literally themselves as upholders of tradition. The close association with tradition put women in direct opposition to Western—attired male politicians and activists. In a 1969 speech addressing a conference on literacy, President Numairi criticized Sudanese women leaders for importing Western ideals. Taking the podium after Numairi, Ibrahim stated, "It is symbolic that the president who is dressed top to toe in imported Western clothing assigns the label 'foreign' to the indigenous demands of Sudanese women, all of whom happen to be dressed in the toab."[28] Here, the tobe is not only an indication of authenticity, but also a guarantee of Ibrahim's cultural sincerity. Because she has grounded herself in local tradition, Ibrahim's progressive demands are cast with an air of authenticity and rendered less threatening.

Bodily Knowledge and Alternate Ways of Knowing

It is vital to note that the tobe was not seen as a political costume, but understood as the national dress. Therefore, a complete analysis of the tobe and its meanings must move past the overtly strategic use of women activists and examine its everyday use among Sudanese women. Nation building is about much more than evoking local traditions. Its members must also be united in shared daily behaviors. Here, one must return to the premise that has been used throughout this essay: fashion is a creative force that opens up new spaces for socio-political interaction. New behaviors of capitalist consumption allowed non-activist women to engage with shifting meanings of the tobe as well. The tobe does not exist in isolation, but is a crucial component of family networks and responsibilities. Specifically, new tobes mark the most important stages of a Sudanese woman's life: the onset of puberty, marriage, and the birth of children. For most of the twentieth century, tobes for these occasions were purchased by men and to be given as gifts for their wives or daughters.

As a result, Sudanese men had great economic control as well as a "choice of delaying or accelerating women's access to new goods and styles." This dependence on male buying power resulted in slow, gradual shifts in textures and styles.[29] However, colonialism

---

26. Ibrahim, "Arrow at Rest," 199, 203.
27. Ibid., 197.
28. Ibid., 201. This public outburst earned Ibrahim negative attention from the government.
29. el-Tayib, 41.

brought changes in patterns of purchasing and consuming goods. In their noted work on colonialism in South Africa, Comaroff and Comaroff argue that the primary goal of eighteenth and nineteenth century imperialists and mercantilists was "to conquer by implanting new cultures of consumption … [through] trade that might instill needs, which only they could satisfy, desires to which only they could cater, signs and values over whose flow they exercised control."[30] Many of these desires were aimed at a new class of consumers: Sudanese women. Historian of consumption in Africa, Timothy Burke, explains that as men were drawn into the imperial labor force, women gained "new leverage over household and family economies."[31] Thus, Sudanese women sought greater political participation at the same moment that they gained a larger presence in an ever-widening global economy.

New modes of consumption enabled Sudanese women to learn more about themselves and the world around them. Each year, new styles of tobes were given names that reflected current events or important issues of the day. Some of the most popular casual styles, named "Bengali" or "Japonez" not only reveal the origins of the cloth, but also allude to past colonial trade routes.[32] Ali-Dinar has compiled a list of popular tobe names of the 1960s that reveals just how creative tobe names can be. Labels such as "The Sound of Music (released in 1965)," "The London Message," and "The Russian Satellite" reflect global connection and awareness. Moreover, names such as "The Week of Women" and "The Female Unions" carried clear messages of political affiliations and aspirations.[33] Through their tobes women engaged with politics, culture, and world events in ways that were not possible with other forms of clothing. Put another way, tobes facilitated a uniquely gendered way of learning about the world. This knowledge was not limited to the wearer of the tobe, but would have been disseminated throughout the community. One of the most common ways for new styles to be advertised was through songs performed at weddings. In this way, even those who did not possess the tobe itself could learn of its name and the meanings behind it. Thus, in a strange twist, by wearing her national costume, a Sudanese woman gained a better understanding of herself on an international stage. Taken collectively, tobes served as veritable shared archive of history and culture.

Tobes also provided the means for a Sudanese woman to learn about herself intimately. Both British colonial and Sudanese nationalist campaigns rejected critical aspects of women's culture. Traditional customs such as pharaonic circumcision, facial scarring, and spirit possession were condemned as 'primitive.' Yet, these rites provided a woman with valuable information about her body, sexuality, and reproduction. Divorced from these traditions, a woman lost touch with her body. However, new modes of consumption granted new avenues for gaining bodily knowledge. In keeping with the imperial civilizing mission, the most popular goods in colonial markets were those connected to dress and hygiene. Sudanese women, an entirely new group of potential consumers, were the prime audience for soap, lotion, and perfume advertisements. Burke writes, "Women bore the burden of ensuring their own purity and the purity of their households through the use of soap and cleansers. Equally, the 'beauty' of their bodies and the 'modernity' of their manners were a major subject of domestic and hygienic training."[34] Commodities stepped into the void created by the abandonment of traditional customs.

---

30. Comaroff and Comaroff, *Of Revelation and Revolution*, 219.
31. Timothy Burke, *Lifebuoy Men, Lux Women: Commodification, Consumption, and Cleanliness in Modern Zimbabwe* (Durham: Duke University Press, 1996), 70.
32. el-Tayib, 55.
33. Ali-Dinar, *Contextual Analysis of Dress and Adornment*, Appendix A.
34. Burke, *Lifebuoy Men, Lux Women*, 194.

Consumption supplemented or replaced ritual as women began to learn about their bodies through new products and behaviors of consumption. There is no doubt that new markets and products were disruptive, even destructive, of local women's culture. However, I want to suggest that consumption is an arena in which Sudanese women may indulge in their bodily desires. This argument is taken from Dorothy Ko's revisionist work on footbinding in China. Standard arguments assert that footbinding lasted for over half a century due to men's sexual fantasies. In opposition, Ko argues that the painful tradition was kept alive because of the joy that women took in forming and fashioning their bodies: "Women applied their imagination and skills to the pursuit of perfect pairs of footwear ... vying to outdo their sisters and neighbors in the choice of fabric, novelty of style, and workmanship. To them, the appeal of footbinding is located in the fantastic lives of shoes as fashionable and ritualized objects."[35] Similarly, the chance to buy a new tobe presented a joyful opportunity to browse with friends among the latest colors, textures, and styles. This modesty garment was not wrapped around the body casually. Sudanese women experimented with folds and tucks so that the fabric might flutter around her shoulder, or so her hips and buttocks would be accented as she walked. Through adornment, a Sudanese woman was once again familiar with the desires and contours of her body.

Both the global and intimate messages of the tobe presented unique sites of knowledge production for Sudanese women. These alternate ways of knowing were distinct from male-dominated state and social institutions, and reveal a gendered encounter with nationalism and modernity. The parallel projects of modernity and nationalism were not confined to government offices, public halls, or even protests in the streets. Sudanese women, even those who may not be considered politically active, participated in national identity formation each time they went to their closets. Nationalist celebrations of tradition, colonial standards of progress, and new behaviors of consumption all combined in the tobe to create a garment that was equally authentic and modern. Sudanese women became active payers in the nationalist movement through a dynamic and non-textual site of identity formation: the tobe. At its most functional level, the tobe permitted schoolgirls and women activists to enter the public spaces of education and politics. Yet, the tobe itself was also a site of learning. For women in northern Sudan, knowledge about themselves and their world was received and transmitted through the tobe.

The multiplicity of meanings of dress is both daunting and an invitation to scholars. Sudanese women's alternate ways of knowing speak to the importance of seeking alternate lens of academic analysis. Studies of post-colonial nationalisms must not be defined and proscribed by western standards and measures. Only by analyzing new sites of nationalism can we begin to construct narratives with local resonance. In the case of the Sudan, multiple national identities still compete for dominance and recognition. The tobe, though a powerful mobilizing symbol, is tied to a particular brand of nationalism, which still struggles to fully incorporate the ethno-cultural diversity of the Sudan. Therefore, this study does not narrate the end of the Sudanese nationalist movement, but rather, its beginning.

References

Ali-Dinar, Ali Bahr Aldin. *Contextual Analysis of Dress and Adornment in Al-Fashir, Sudan.* Philadelphia: University of Pennsylvania, 1995.

---

35. Dorothy Ko, *Cinderella's Sisters: A Revisionist History of Footbinding* (Berkeley: University of California Press, 2007), 228–29.

Allman, Jean. "Introduction." In *Fashioning Africa: Power and the Politics of Dress*. Bloomington: Indiana University Press, 2004. 1–10.

Badri, Haga Kashif. *Women's Movement in the Sudan*. New Delhi: Asia News Agency, 1986.

Beasley, Ina. *Before the Wind Changed: People, Places, and Education in the Sudan*. Oxford: Oxford University Press, 1992.

Burke, Timothy. *Lifebuoy Men, Lux Women: Commodification, Consumption, and Cleanliness in Modern Zimbabwe*. Durham: Duke University Press, 1996.

Comaroff, John L. and Jean Comaroff. *Of Revelation and Revolution: The Dialectics of Modernity on a South African Frontier*, Vol. 2. Chicago: The University of Chicago Press, 1997.

el Badawi, Zeinab el Fateh. *The Development of the Sudanese Women Movement*. Khartoum: Ministry of Information and Social Affairs, 1966.

el-Tayib, Griselda. "Women's Dress in the Northern Sudan." Susan Kenyon, (Ed.) *The Sudanese Woman*. Khartoum: Graduate College, University of Khartoum, 1987. 40–66.

Fluehr-Lobban, Carolyn. "The Women's Movement in the Sudan and Its Impact on Sudanese Law and Politics." *The Ahfad Journal* Vol. 2, no. 1 (June 1985): 53–62.

Hale, Sondra. "Activating the Gender Local: Transnational Ideologies and 'Women's Culture' in Northern Sudan." *Journal of Middle East Women's Studies* Vol. 1., No. 1 (Winter 2005): 29–52.

Hale, Sondra. *Gender Politics in Sudan: Islamism, Socialism, and the State*. Boulder: Westview Press, Inc., 1996.

Hall, Marjorie and Bakhita Amin Ismail. *Sisters Under the Sun: The Story of Sudanese Women*. London: Longman, 1981.

Hunt, Lynn. *The Family Romance of the French Revolution*. Berkeley: University of California Press, 1992.

Ibrahim, Fatima Ahmed. "Arrow at Rest." Mahnaz Afkhami, (Ed.) *Women in Exile*. Charlottesville: University Press of Virginia, 1994. 191–208.

Ko, Dorothy. *Cinderella's Sisters: A Revisionist History of Footbinding*. Berkeley: University of California Press, 2007.

La Rue, George Michael. "Imported Blue Cotton Cloth: Status Clothing for Rural Women in Pre-Colonial Dar Fur." African Studies Association Annual Meeting. Boston, 1993.

Mitchell, Timothy. *Colonising Egypt*. Berkeley: University of California Press, 1991.

Rabine, Leslie W. *The Global Circulation of African Fashion*. Oxford: Berg, 2002.

Chapter 16

Breaking the Walls of Tradition: Male Braiders in Nigeria

Sati U. Fwatshak

Gender studies have grown through time from the 1960s and early 1970s, when the concept of gender first gained prominence in feminist studies.[1] It has spread in Nigeria since the 1980s. However, a number of weaknesses characterize gender studies in Africa in general, and in Nigeria in particular, which in part explains my interest on work choice, an ignored aspect.

Firstly, gender studies have been dominated by studies on women,[2] identifying and chronicling various forms of discrimination against them, especially in the public domain of political participation.[3] A recent Nigerian publication on gender, for example, portrays women as victims of discrimination, domination, oppression, and exploitation in a world generally characterized and driven by patriarchy, and, in the case of Nigeria, the dominance of both patriarchy and cultures (social, economic, political, and religious), among other factors that offend the status of women.[4]

Secondly, cross-gender role studies have focused mainly on the successful entry of women into traditionally male jobs, showcasing the roles of women as rulers/chiefs and traders (in pre-colonial Africa), nationalists and politicians (in colonial Africa), politicians, engineers, mechanics, computer programmers, and chief executives of major industrial and financial institutions (in the post-colonial period). This leaves a gap in gender studies: the roles of men. In Nigeria, documentation of males engaged in roles regarded as traditionally belonging to the female sex are just emerging, and largely remains on the pages of newspapers and the Internet. The fact that the walls of tradition are crumbling and that what matters is how human beings in their daily activities respond to change, makes a study of males in traditionally female jobs also imperative. In this study, I focus on males in the braiding industry.

The verb "braiding" derives from the Middle English (thirteenth century) word, "Breidan," meaning "to dart, twist, and to pull." Since then it has also been associated with making sudden jerky movements from one side to another, weaving, knitting, brandishing, moving quickly, and turning about, among others. Its contemporary usage in the narrow sense as hair plaiting has been dated to the sixteenth century.[5] This means

---

1. Yakubu Aboki Ochefu, "'Men Work Harder but Women Work Longer': An Analysis of Gender Relations, Labor and Production In Idoma and Tiv Societies," in Okpeh Ochayi Okpeh and Dung Pam Sha (eds.) *Gender, Power and Politics in Nigeria* (Makurdi: Aboki Publishers, 2007), 59.

2. Much of the literature cited by Toyin Falola in chapter 10 of his book, *The Power of African Cultures* (Rochester, NY: University of Rochester Press, 2003), 271-73, treat women as their main subject matter.

3. 1 Adagba Okpaga, "Women Empowerment, Citizenship and Political Participation," in *Gender, Power and Politics in Nigeria*, 248.

4. 1 See generally, Okpeh and Sha (eds.), *Gender, Power and Politics in Nigeria*.

5. 1 "Braids," *http://dictionary.reference.com/browse/braids*. Accessed on January 8, 2010.

that the practice of braiding has been with us for a long time. In its long history, it has been associated mainly with the women, the gender that braids and is braided. However, things have changed. Some men, especially African-Americans and African sportsmen, especially highly rated footballers (soccer stars) playing in clubs in Europe, are braided. That is not news now in Nigeria. What is news, though, is the fact that men also have taken to braiding as an enterprise, a means of livelihood. *The Punch*, a local newspaper, has only tangentially told the Nigerian story.[6] However, essential details and national profiles are still missing. Although men are in the practice of various aspects of women's body decoration such as palming, pedicure, and manicure, fixing weave-on, etc., the choice of braiding is deliberate. It is the only one with roots in old Africa. The others are recent inventions from non-African worlds imported into the continent. In order to set the discussion of men's entry into braiding as breaking the walls of tradition in the gender division of labor in proper perspective, a profile of the gender division of labor in Nigeria in Nigeria's history is imperative.

The Walls of Tradition: A Profile of Gender Roles in Nigerian History

Gender roles are established norms and activities of social groups constructed and assigned along lines of biological sex. Thus, they define how males and females should dress and behave, their roles in decision-making processes, and the kind of work they should engage in.[7] Gender roles have indeed characterized all human societies at different periods in their histories but remain awash in the sea of controversies. For instance, it is argued that "maleness and femaleness are integral parts of our human design" and that males and females differ in several respects: men have a higher level of testosterone (responsible for the male drive for dominance) than women do.[8]

Support for the division of labor based on sex and justification for the exploitation of women among the Tiv and Idoma of central Nigeria is expressed in their local saying that although women put in more hours of work, men do the hardest jobs.[9] Opponents argue that sex-based division of labor is not realistic nowadays, as switches in gender roles are old in history and are elaborating due to social and economic change, occasioned by industrialization that are expanding the roles of women in national economies, though slowly.[10] The two positions have some relevance in Nigerian gender roles over time. Patriarchy, which loomed large in the past, assigned different roles to men and women, but change processes have ensured that such divisions of labor did not remain stagnant.

With respect to the rule of biological sex differences, pre-colonial Nigerian societies, like many other old societies, had traditions in which gender roles were classified by sex in many spheres of life and livelihoods. It has been argued that in Nigeria such a division

6. 1 *Punch*, *http://www.nigeriansinamerica.com*. Accessed on January 9, 2010.
7. 1 Ochefu, "Men Work Harder," 58.
8. 1 Frank York, "Gender Differences Are Real," *http://www.narth.com/docs/york.html*. Accessed on January 7, 2010.
9. Ochefu, "Men Work Harder," 65.
10. 1 Gerald M. Meier and James E. Rauch, *Leading Issues in Economic Development* (New York: Oxford University Press, 2000), 272-74.

of labor assigned men the roles of clearing new lands, cultivating crops, hunting, production of iron and other tools and utensils, trading slaves, leadership of the family, decision-making, and control over women and children.[11] In Africa generally, Toyin Falola has identified some roles like hunting, blacksmithing, and carving, which were reserved for men.[12] In the colonial period, the power base of men was consolidated. At the political level, male colonial officers dealt with African men as political leaders—Native Authorities, tax collectors, police, soldiers, etc.[13] At the economic level, men enjoyed wage-attractive occupations like the civil service, the army, and the police; they also focused on cash crop production, again gaining economic advantage over women in access to income. At the social level, men received more access to western education than women, thereby gaining advantages in civil service and white-collar job employments. Men were also earlier exposed to the emergent colonial cities as workers, only to be joined later by their wives. By these advantages, men became breadwinners of their families,[14] and consequently dominant figures in society.

By the same token, women in the pre-colonial period were assigned the roles of clearing of virgin lands, planting and harvesting of crops, cultivation of vegetables, food processing, and other home-based economic activities; small-scale trade; the gathering of firewood and some fruits, mushrooms, berries, and medicinal herbs; the making of pottery, brewing of beverages, and fetching of water; family and child care; serving as the mistresses of men; and cooking meals.[15] African women generally seemed to have shared the same experiences in gender roles with their Nigerian counterparts with respect to performing domestic chores, assisting men with harvests, and processing food.[16] In the colonial period, women's marginalization was intensified, as the colonial economy, administration, and wage employment favored men, while women were relegated to the roles of housekeepers and petty jobs.[17] John Agaba supports Falola's position on the colonial regime as the root of widened marginalization of African women in general and Nigerian women in particular in the political sphere.[18]

The post-colonial African state inherited the gender inequality of the colonial period, as the second-class citizens status of women, the perception by men of women as weak and incapable of leadership, the belief by men that women should be limited to the home

11. 1 Ochefu, "Men Work Harder," 64; Patricks Ogiji, "Gender Integration and the Socio-Economic Construction of Politics in Nigeria: A Generic Approach," in *Gender, Power and Politics in Nigeria*, 116; Simon Kpelai Tersoo, "Women Entrepreneurship, Power and Politics in Benue State," In *Gender, Power and Politics in Nigeria*, 145; Ezekiel Gaya Best and Uthman A. Abdul-Qadir, "Socio-Cultural Obstacles to Engendering Democracy in Nigeria," in *Gender, Power and Politics in Nigeria*, 236.

12. Falola, *The Power of African Culture*, 262-63.

13. Ibid., 264.

14. 1 Ibid., 265.

15. 1 Ochefu, "Men Work Harder," 64-65; John Ebute Agaba, "Nigerian Women and Politics: The Colonial Experience," in *Gender, Power and Politics in Nigeria*, 73; Patricks Ogiji, "Gender Integration and the Socio-Economic Construction of Politics in Nigeria: A Generic Approach," in *Gender, Power and Politics in Nigeria*, 118; Simon Kpelai Tersoo, "Women Entrepreneurship, Power and Politics in Benue State," in *Gender, Power and Politics in Nigeria*, 145; Okpeh, Ochayi Okpeh, "Patriarchy, Women's Quest for Political Leadership, and the Democratization Process in Nigeria," in *Gender, Power and Politics in Nigeria*, 185; Anthony Zaayem Apenda, "Culture as a Barrier to Women Leadership," in *Gender, Power and Politics in Nigeria*, 220; Ezekiel Gaya Best and Uthman A. Abdul-Qadir, "Socio-Cultural Obstacles to Engendering Democracy in Nigeria," in *Gender, Power and Politics in Nigeria*, 236.

16. Falola, *The Power of African Cultures*, 262-63.

17. 1 Ibid., 265.

18. 1 Agaba, 79-87.

front, etc. were entrenched and continued the marginalization of women.[19] Besides, west-ernization, capitalism, Islam, and Christianity as change agents have also worsened women's situations. Capitalism continued to exploit women, as did patriarchy, through low pay for women because without education, women lack the skills to be in highly paid employment and are limited to mainly farming jobs. Islam secludes women and reduces their chances of economic independence; Christianity ascribes to the male the leadership of the family.[20] Thus, according to Falola, the current marginalization of women in Africa is the product of a historical process in which colonialism deepened pre-colonial patriarchy and its successor; the post-colonial state, inherited such a legacy. The import of these research findings is that gender roles have not remained static. A survey of cross-gender roles in Nigerian history is proof of this.

A Survey of Cross-Gender Roles in History

Cross-gender roles are manners and actions of individuals that do not conform to ascribed gender roles. Although, even in plays, cross-gender roles pose difficulties. For example, several female gamers on the Strange Aeons mailing list asked, "How does one role-play having a penis?" Indeed, one could just as easily ask, "how does one role-play anything other than yourself, in the real world?"[21] The dynamism of societies has caused older forms of gender divisions of labor to crumble, as cross-gender roles have been evolving in different societies, though at different paces. Thus, while in pre-industrial and nineteenth century Europe, women were engaged mainly in the domestic sector, from the twentieth century and especially since the end of World War II, they constitute a large part of the modern sector employment and occupation.[22] In the United States of America, males have also in the last twenty years increasingly entered into traditionally female jobs as nurses, midwives, telephone operators, and pre-school and kindergarten teachers.[23] This suggests a significant shift in gender roles.

In the specific case of African women, Falola has convincingly argued, "It is misleading to talk about issues of exploitation and empowerment of women as if their role has been static. Evidence is clear that women's roles have changed over time and that we now have women who are as well educated as men."[24]

According to Falola, Africa's pre-colonial "economy and politics gave women visible roles and privileges." Women played crucial roles, as did men, in the agrarian system and enjoyed some level of independence where they had direct access to land or had established occupations. Women played some of the roles played by men such as warriors (Dahomey), house builders (Kenya Massai), long distance traders (Yoruba), chiefs/rulers (exemplified by Queen Amina of Zaria, Sabro women chiefs of Sierra Leone, and women chiefs of Da-homey Kingdom), and religious priests (Yoruba women priests of Sango, Osun, and

---

19. 1 Falola, *The Power of African Cultures*, 266.

20. 1 Ibid., 267.

21. 1 Sandy Antunes, "Leaping into Cross-Gender Role-Play," *http://www.mud.co.uk/richard/ifan195.htm*. Accessed on January 07, 2010.

22. 1 J. Robert Wegs, *Europe Since 1945: A Concise History*, 3rd ed. (New York: St Martins Press, 1991), 172.

23. 1 ABC News, "Labor Market," *http://abcnews.go.com*,.Accessed on January 15, 2010.

24. 1 Falola, *The Power of African Cultures*, 262.

Obatala).[25] In the remote past, examples of women leaders/rulers included Meroe Queens, who ruled at Musarawat, for example, Amanirenas, Amanishakhete, Naldamak, and Amanitere.[26] In the colonial period, in spite of their marginalization, African women contributed to the nationalist struggles in Africa as politicians. And despite all odds, in the post-colonial period, many women are moving to occupations initially regarded as men's occupations such as engineering and computer programming.[27] Examples of females in "male jobs" in contemporary Nigeria are not in short supply. Nigerian women have improved on their cross-gender role statuses, as members of the armed forces, security guards, vice chancellors of Nigerian universities, one governor (in Anambra state), deputy governors, auto-mechanics, cab drivers, barbers, and photographers.[28] Since the colonial period, men have also made successful entries into traditionally female jobs as house helps, cooks, bar and restaurants attendants, etc.

Although the evidence above shows that women have pioneered and have been more successful or innovative in cross-gender role occupations, the sad story is that, on a general note, change has been slow in guaranteeing gender equity, as women in less developed countries are still below men in wages and in job positions, and are in large part agricultural, domestic, and low-skilled workers.[29] While a few educated women have been moving into skilled jobs, rural uneducated women are still in the old order. From the pre-colonial period through to the present, Nigeria has remained largely rural-based and agricultural, while literacy rates show there is still room for improvement. According to a 1999 estimate, agriculture accounted for 70% of the country's workforce, while industry and services accounted for 10 and 20% respectively. A 2003 estimate on the nation's literacy figures for those aged 15 and over who can read and write in one form or the other are 68% males and 75.7% females.[30]

Breaking the Walls of Tradition: Male Braiders in Nigeria

It has been quite some time since men started doing business in women's hair in the form of Jherri curls and palming. However, these activities have no roots in "traditional" Africa. Doing business in braiding is relatively new, but has roots in "traditional" Africa in the sense that African women have been braiding hair for a very long time. When did men start braiding as an occupation? Why did men take to braiding as an occupation? In which Nigerian city or town did it start? In what other Nigerian cities is it practiced and

---

25. 1 Ibid., 262, 264.
26. 1 Basil Davidson, *The Lost Cities of Africa* (Boston/Toronto: Atlantic Little Brown, 1959), 39-40.
27. 1 Falola, *The Power of African Cultures*, 266, 268.
28. 1 For evidence of female barbers see Craig Wilson, "Women make the cut," *USA TODAY* http://www.usatoday.com/life/lifestyle/2004-06-27-female-barbers_x.htm. Accessed on February 9, 2010; and "Quote from Kelvin," *http://www.nairaland.com/nigeria/topic-4475.0.html*. Accessed on February 9, 2010. The material from Kelvin provides only an inference for the existence of a female barber in Abuja. For females in auto-mechanics see, "Female Auto Mechanic with Class and Style," http://awuraba.com/profiles/101/295-female-auto-mechanic-with-class-and-style.html. Accessed on February 09, 2010.
29. 1 Meier and Rauch, *Leading Issues in Economic Development*, 271-74.
30. 1 See Nigeria's economy/Nigerian economy for the occupational distribution at: *http://www.travelblog.org/Africa/Nigeria/fact-econ-nigeria.html*. Accessed on February 9, 2010.

how did it spread to these other cities in the country? Are there any challenges and opportunities? I will try to answer some of these questions in the sections that follow.

Origins and Development of the Male Braiding Occupation

It is not clear when males started braiding as an occupation in Nigeria. However, the evidence points out to the late twentieth century as the commencement of this cross-gender role activity. According to the newspaper *Punch*:

> The business of making a variant of hairdos called braiding was until recently the exclusive preserve of women. But not only are men involved in the business these days, they have literally hijacked it from the womenfolk. This is particularly so with Ivorian braids, which remains the toast of many fashion freaks. Introduced to the Nigerian market a few years back, Ivorian braids are made by extending the hair with the aid of attachments that are woven into long tiny stretches. Hence in Nigeria, the hairdo is popularly called One Million Braids.[31]

Punch was indeed hyperbolic in stating that men "have literally hijacked it from the womenfolk." This statement is both sensational and misleading. This is because even though statistics are lacking, my data on the braiding profession in many Nigerian cities, including Lagos and Makurdi, where I work, shows that there is a large number of women braiding, and male practitioners stand in an inferior relationship to the women in terms of numbers. At the Wadata market in Makurdi, for instance, I witnessed about twenty women on one spot practicing the craft daily, apart from those operating in their own shops.[32]

As to where the business started in Nigeria, informants point to Lagos. And as to how it spread to other Nigerian cities, informants say that it was the desire and decision of former apprentices of practitioners to set up their own businesses in locations they chose outside Lagos. Thus, outside Lagos, the business thrives in major cities like the Federal Capital Territory (FCT), Abuja, Jos, Makurdi, and Port-Harcourt, among others.[33] The credit for the foundation of the business in Lagos has been claimed by the Benin Republic, from where non-Nigerian but ECOWAS citizens came to Lagos and launched it. Thus, according to the *Punch*, "This hairstyle (one million braids) that has been so warmly embraced in Nigeria originated from Cotonou, the capital of neighboring Republic of Benin." This was based on the claim by Seun and Togbe, male practitioners from Benin Republic, who asserted that they imported the business to Nigeria from Cotonou, where they learnt the trade from women, serving as their apprentices or assistants.[34] Lagos might

31. 1 *Punch*, "How Cotonou Boys Dethroned Nigerian Women in Braiding Business" *http://www.nigeriansinamerica.com/vbulletin/showthread.php?t=14543*. Accessed on January 9, 2010.

32. 1 All my informants confirmed that there were more females than males in braiding in their respective cities. However, none was certain about the numbers of females or males in the profession.

33. 1 *Punch*, "How Cotonou Boys Dethroned Nigerian women." I know one male who does the business in Jos. He is by name Yaptu, a Mupun person like me. However, all attempts to meet and interview him failed. The first time I went to the shop on January 4, 2009, he was sick and was not fully recovered until the Jos religious crisis of January 17-20, as I continued to contact him on phone for an appointment. I went to the shop again on February 11, 2009 but missed him and returned to Makurdi.

34. 1 *Punch* , "How Cotonou Boys Dethroned Nigerian women " *at:http://www.nigeriansinamerica.com/vbulletin/showthread.php?t=14543*. Accessed February 9, 2010.

have been the Nigerian springboard, but not every male practicing in other cities learnt the trade there. Agama Iji Moses, interviewed in Makurdi, confirmed this by stating that he learnt different aspects of women's hair-do and nail fixing in different Nigerian cities like Lagos, Jos, Abuja, and Makurdi. Terna Tyam and Caleb Sesugh Abui, who both practice the trade in Makurdi, learnt it in Gboko, Headquarters of Gboko Local Government Area of Benue State. Ikwu George Ejugwu and Mike Bufer, who both practice in Abuja, learnt the trade in Makurdi and Gboko respectively.[35]

A Narrative of Male Braiders in Three Nigerian Cities

Lagos

Lagos, once Nigeria's administrative capital, now stands as the nation's commercial capital. Located on the shores of the Atlantic, it is home to a population of 9,013,534, according to the 2006 national head count.[36] Among its nine million people are the rich and the poor, industrialists and petty traders, workers, the self-employed, the underemployed, and the unemployed. The Lagos story of the braiding business as presented by the Saturday *Punch* is as follows. That braiding the hairstyle called one "million braids" originated from Cotonou, capital of Benin Republic, one of Nigeria's French speaking neighbors from which Nigerians import much of their second hand cars. Togbe, one of the Beninoise in the business in Nigeria, claimed that their decision to come to Nigeria was due to high demand for male braiders from women who used to travel across the border to make braids in Cotonou. Subsequently, the braiders decided to move to Badagry and then also to Lagos, Abuja, and Port Harcourt in search of bigger market opportunities. The "Cotonou boys," as the pioneers from Benin Republic are called, made a headway into the business due to their skill and fine finishing, which earned them fast patronage and incomes, as well as a competitive edge over women braiders.

Some of the leading names in the Lagos business among the Cotonou male hair-braiding entrepreneurs are Seun, Togbe, and Mautin. Seun claimed that in the Benin Republic itself, men do not practice the occupation and that he and many other men learnt the business as apprentices to women. Seun further claims that he holds a National Diploma certificate (called OND in Nigeria). His business name in Lagos is Ronstar Braiders, located at Ogba market. He ventured into the business due to lack of funds to continue his education. He is satisfied with the job, which helps him earn a living and to provide for his siblings, but he aspires to export his skill to Europe or the United States of America. He attributes his success to his ability and those of his colleagues to work continuously for long hours, which enables them to finish fast, as the women patrons often feel too tired if it takes longer. Their speed helps them to do at least two hair-styles (a million braids) a day, each taking about six hours with three braiders working on each woman's hair.

---

35. 1 Agama Iji Moses, interviewed in his shop: Gracious Hair Clinic, No. 15 Konshisha street, 3rd Avenue, off Katsina Alla street, Makurdi, January 15, 2010, Terna Tyam, interviewed in his shop: Flex Salon, No. 7, 1st Avenue, off Katsina Ala street, Makurd, January 16, 2010, Caleb Sesuh Abui, interviewed in his shop: *Sandiz*, at No. 39, 2nd Avenue, Iyorkaa Ako street, Makurdi January 16, 2010. Ikwu George Ejugwu, interviewed January 26, 2010 at his work place, Dansville Plaza, Apo legislative Quarters, opposite AP filing station, FCT, Abuja, January 26, 2010. Mike Bufer, interviewed at his work place, Essence Plaza, Wuse Zone 6, Abuja on January 26, 2010.

36. 1 "2006 Population Census," *http://www.nigerianmuse.com*. Accessed on February 13, 2010.

However, Togbe, the other Beninoise in the business, learnt the job in Lagos under his aunt. Togbe is the owner of Philip Final Touch Braiders, located off Wemco Road, Ikeja, Lagos. He started at Badagry but left for Lagos out of frustration over some customers' inability to fully pay for his services. He said the decision to leave Badagry was enhanced by some of his customers who used to come from Lagos and persuaded him to try other Nigerian cities including Lagos and Abuja. The business is run as a family business with three of his brothers working with him. He charges N30000 to train apprentices and his aspiration is, like Seun's, to export his skill to Europe to meet the demands of Nigerian women in the Diaspora, as some patronize him each time they come home on vacation or other visits. Togbe and his brothers specialize only in twisting.[37] This contrasts with the practice of the craft by Nigerian men who do other aspects of women's hair, as we shall see later.

Why do Nigerian women like the twisting hairstyle or the one million braids? Again, our lead source, the Saturday *Punch*, has the women's side of the story and all came to one thing: their husbands love it. According to Mrs. Oluwadipe Alao, "I do this style, at least, five times in a year. I opt for it each time my husband gives the signal that I should, because he likes it. It is painful, but I endure it because of him. He picks the bill. But I keep it for just one month because I love to pour water on my head." Mrs. Lovena Agu, a Nigerian resident abroad, said that besides making her look younger, braids gives her the needed break from frequent visits to the salon: "My husband also says it makes me look younger and fashionable." Corroborating Agu, a newlywed woman who identified herself simply as Kemi, told Saturday *Punch* that she was at the braiding center at the behest of her husband: "He told me that he wanted me to do the tiny, long, twisting style that he sees some ladies do." [38] As to service charges, the practitioners said that when they started some years back in Badagry, they charged N1200 per person, but that the cost had risen to N3500 due to the increases in the cost of the imported Ivorian attachment, which they preferred to use. According to one of them, it relaxes better in hot water, and was lighter on women's head and could last for as long as six months, depending on how the bearer managed it.[39]

Abuja

Abuja has been Nigeria's political capital since the early 1990s, when Ibrahim Babangida, then head of the military government, relocated the nation's capital from Lagos, a move started by his predecessors in the 1970s. Unlike Lagos, which is commercial in orientation, Abuja is largely administrative, with businesses mainly located in neighboring Karu Local Government of Nasarawa State, indicated by a pillar separating the local government from the FCT. According to the 2006 census, the population of the FCT is 1,405,201.[40] Beninoise has partly told the story of the beginning of males' entry into the braiding business in Abuja as a part of the establishment of the business in Lagos. According to their story, the movement to Abuja and Port-Harcourt was occasioned by their desire to find new opportunities in the large Nigerian market.[41]

---

37. 1 *Punch*, "How Cotonou Boys Dethroned Nigerian women."
38. 1 Ibid.
39. 1 Ibid.
40. 1 "2006 Population Census."
41. 1 *Punch*, "How Cotonou Boys Dethroned Nigerian women."

Nevertheless, as earlier stated, some practitioners in Abuja learnt the profession in Benue State. Ikwu George Ejugwu, who holds the northern Nigerian A Level certificate called Interim Joint Matriculation Board (IJMB) from the School of Remedial Studies, Makurdi, is from a family whose parents are farmers and traders. After completing his A Levels, he took up appointment as a seller of textile wrappers in Oju LGA of Benue State, and later changed to sales representative in a beer distribution shop, also in Oju. He later on moved to Jos, the Plateau State capital, and worked with a cold stores company selling frozen fish. He returned to Makurdi and became an apprentice to Agama proprietor of Gracious Hair Clinic for six months, learning braiding and other aspects of hair styling for free. From Makurdi he moved to Abuja, where he first worked for a wage at REPHICAL HAIR SALON, at Wuse Zone 6, and later moved to his new place of employment called GSPOT HAIR SALON, also in Abuja, where he is also working for wages. He has spent three–and-a-half years as an employee (as of January 2010) because he has been unable to set up his own due to shortage of start-up capital, but he hopes to establish his own shop.[42]

Another practitioner in Abuja is Mike Bufer. He holds the Nigerian Senior School Certificate (SSCE), which he obtained at Government Secondary School, Gboko, also in Benue State. His parents are like those of Ikwu, farmers and businesspeople. He trained for five months as an apprentice on the job in Gboko, and paid 3000 naira (N3000) and bought two crates of soft drinks as the fees. He is four years as an employee (as of January 2010) due to shortage of start-up capital and is desirous to set up his own.[43] The two males interviewed in Abuja were unable to tell which male started the business in the city and in which year the pioneer started it. This lack of knowledge should be understood within the context of the fact that they are employees who both came to Abuja from Benue State.

Makurdi

Makurdi is the capital of Benue State, in Nigeria's Middle-Belt or Central Region as it is so-called in official circles. Benue State, which was carved out of Benue-Plateau State in 1976, prides itself as the "food basket of the nation." This is symbolized by an art work displaying a basket containing various food items in the state capital located at a major junction linking Makurdi to Lafia (capital of Nasarawa State to the north), Enugu, (capital of Enugu State to the southeast), and Calabar, (capital of Cross-Rivers State to the south). The population of Makurdi is 292,645,[44] while Benue State's population total is 4,219,244. Agama Iji Moses holds a degree in Sociology and Anthropology from Benue State University, Makurdi (2007), and Diploma in Law (Benue State Polytechnic, 2003). He had his secondary school education at Government Secondary School, Ikachi, Oju, Benue State, and his primary education at Pilot Primary School, also in Oju. His father is a farmer and his mother is a civil servant. He started his career as a Sales Representative for Guinness, Nigeria, Lagos, from 1997-1999.

Moses picked up the interest in styling hair while schooling and learnt different aspects of hairdo in different cities: retouching, washing and setting, and fixing weave-on in Lagos for three weeks in 1999; pedicure, manicure, and braiding in Jos in 2001; twisting

---

42. 1 Ikwu George Ejugwu (27) interviewed January 26, 2010 at Dansville Plaza, Apo legislative Quarters, opposite AP filing station, FCT, Abuja.
43. 1 Mike Bufer (32) interviewed at Essence Plaza, Wuse Zone 6, Abuja on January 26, 2010.
44. 1 "2006 Population Census."

in Abuja in 2002; fixing short weave-on in Makurdi, also in 2002. Thus, unlike the "Cotonou boys" in Lagos who specialize only in braiding, Agama is a hairstylist as well. In two of the cities where he trained, he paid fees in kind and in cash as follows: N22000, one crate of soft drinks, one carton of wine, and one packet of cabin biscuits (in Lagos), and N2500 and a crate of soft drinks in Makurdi. In Abuja and Jos, he practiced as a freelancer with friends. He set up his own business called Gracious Hair Clinic in 2005 with about N500000, after working for a woman he convinced to start the business with him as an employee/part owner on Calabar Street, High Level, Makurdi. He raised money from the joint venture with the woman and also personal home services he rendered to customers in and outside Makurdi, including Abuja.[45]

Terna Tyam holds B.Sc. in Crop Science, Lagos State University (LASU). His father is a schoolteacher while his mother is a farmer and businessperson. He started his career as a sales representative in a company in Lagos called Harvest Field, where he worked for three years but was not satisfied with the job. He left for Gboko, where he trained in hair-do as an apprentice under his elder brother for three years and paid no fees for the training. He has been in the business for 15 years, including periods of working as employee for other people and being on his own. His business name is FLEX SALON, and is located at No. 7, 1st Avenue, off Katsina-Ala Street, Makurdi, set up at the cost of N150000.[46]

Caleb Sesugh Abui is a secondary school graduate with an O certificate. His father is a civil servant, his mother is deceased. He has been in the business since 1998. He started the business as an apprentice in Gboko, under his friend who did not charge him for the training, which took him three months. After his training, he worked for other people as an employee until 2009, when he set up his own. The business is called SANDIZ and is located at No. 39, 2nd Avenue, Iyorkaa Ako Street, Makurdi. He declined to disclose the sum he used to set up the business.[47]

Which male started the business in Makurdi and when? The answers to these questions are hard indeed. My informants in Makurdi do not know the first male to start the business there. However, most of them point to Terna Tyam as the oldest male in the business in Makurdi. According to Agama Iji Moses, the entry of males into the business was enhanced by the Poverty Alleviation Program, which started in the first tenure of Olusegun Obasanjo as the civilian president of Nigeria. Associating the origin of male entry into the business with Terna Tyam seems correct as he has spent more years (15) in the business than any other male I interviewed. However, this evidence is subject to further confirmation, as the interviewees do not even know how many males are in the business in Makurdi, which means it is possible that some persons exist in the business but that I was unable to locate them. Until a proper register of male entrants is produced showing entry years, the issues will remain a matter of conjecture with Terna Tyam on the top. It is difficult to trace the male who started the business in Makurdi and the date of the commencement of male participation in braiding.

---

45. 1 Interview: Agama Iji Moses (30), single, interviewed at his shop: Gracious Hair Clinic, No. 15 Konshisha street, 3rd Avenue, off Katsina Alla street, Makurdi, January 15, 2010.

46. 1 Terna Tyam (35), married with children, interviewed at his shop, No. 7, 1st Avenue, off Katsina-Ala street, Makurdi, on January 15, 2010.

47. 1 Caleb Sesugh Abui, interviewed, January 16, 2010, at his shop, No. 39, 2nd Avenue, Iyorkaa Ako Street, Makurdi.

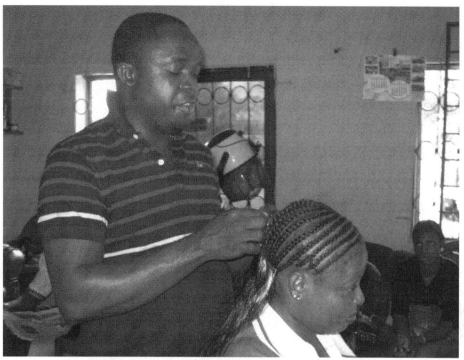

Figure 1: Hair Braiding. Courtesy of the author.

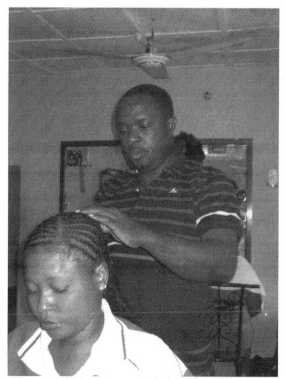

Figure 2: Two Male Braiders at Work. Courtesy of the author.

Port-Harcourt

Port-Harcourt is the capital of Rivers State in the oil-rich Niger-Delta region. Two male braiders were interviewed in this city: one a Ghanaian and the other a Nigerian. The Ghanaian, Thomas Hettey, is Christian and married. He declined to disclose his age and educational attainments. He claimed that he formerly worked in Ghana as an accountant (most likely as a clerk) before branching into braiding after learning the new occupation from another Ghanaian in Port-Harcourt, Nigeria, for a period of two years. In 2000, he started his own salon in a shop jointly rented with another practitioner. He raised his start up capital from practicing the trade by braiding. His patrons are mainly females who heard about him from fellow women. The fee he charges depends on the style he makes for each customer and he attributes his success (the business sustains him) to the grace of God.[48]

Prosper Chigozie Wodo is a Nigerian braider who granted me an interview in Port-Harcourt. Born in June 1985, his highest educational qualification is Nigeria's Senior School Certificate (SSCE), obtained at Kenneth Commercial Secondary School. His father is a civil servant, while his mother is a trader. His initial economic activity was making costumes for the movie industry on a part-time basis. He later took to braiding, which, according to him, is a natural endowment. In his own words, "I did not choose it [braiding]; it is just a gift that I have. I believe I started making hair from my mother's womb." Like some other Nigerian participants in the job, his parents, who are from different cultural backgrounds, initially did not support him but when he started making it and they became beneficiaries, their initial reaction turned to approval. He started the braiding and other hair dressing trades in 2005 at Mgbundukwu in Mile 2, Dibou, Port-Harcourt. He also attributes his success to the grace of God. His fees depend on the hairstyle and the occasion for it is meant. He charges between N2000 and N3000 for routine hairdressings but charges between N30000 to N40000 for wedding hairdos.[49] Thus, like other male braiders, he also does other types of women's hairstyle.

Explaining the Entry of Males into Braiding

Scholars examining gender roles have tried to explain cross-gender or sex-atypical roles, expressed in the choice of work as behavioral problems and associated stress. In these contexts, according to Christine S. Koberg and Leonard H. Chusmir, pioneer studies focused on the issue of whether a relationship exists between a person's choice of an occupation that is contrary to what society regards as appropriate to that person's biological sex and the person's sex role conflict, or a personality conflict caused by that person's biological sex, whereby an individual's internal values do not cohere with those imposed by the society. Koberg and Chusmir have summarized the arguments of pioneers in this endeavor as follows. The first is that which looks at sex-atypical roles as dysfunctional and personal and organizational results of factors like job dissatisfaction and role conflict. Second is that sex-atypical roles have the propensity to increase levels of stress in the individuals involved. Third, people who choose sex-atypical roles will encounter and fight

---

48. 1 Thomas Hettey, interviewed at his shop, No. 21, Egede Street, Mile 2, Dibou, Port-Harcourt, February 2, 2010.

49. 1 Prosper Chigozie Wodo, interviewed at his shop, Mgbundukwu in Mile 2, Dibou, Port-Harcourt, February 21, 2010.

strong internal battles leading to sex role conflicts, whether or not there are external societal pressures. Using the results of empirical studies, Koberg and Chusmir concluded that sex-atypical roles have no clear links with sex role conflicts.[50]

In the Nigerian case, no single model explains the entry of males into braiding. As noted earlier in our story about the business in Lagos, Seun, one of the practitioners said he was in it because he could not raise funds to further his education.[51] For Agama Iji Moses, the issue is just that he was driven by interest in the profession. This interest has propelled him to forge ahead in spite of his parents' initial reservation and rejection. Both of his parents wanted him to study first and pick up an occupation later. For his mother, who had a strong Christian conviction, braiding is for the female gender, and that it was a big source of temptation to men entering it.[52] Thomas Hettey and Prosper Chigozie Wodo were also moved by a similar consideration. Caleb Sesugh Abui was stimulated by a combination of factors including interest in the job and because, according to him, "it is lucrative." Like Agama, his entry, which was driven by these two factors, helped him stand out against his parents who regarded braiding as a feminine job.[53]

For Terna Tyam, the issue was not interest but lack of gainful employment. According to him, "when I left school, I had no better job to do." Unlike Agama, Terna did not face opposition from his parents because, already, his elder brother was in the profession.[54] Ikwu George and Mike Bufer are in the job because of several reasons, principal of which is gainful employment for income generation. While the additional reason for Mike Bufer was personal interest in the profession, Ikwu's additional reasons were his love for imagination and creativity, which the job offers, and he wanted to know the secret of women and to make them happy.[55] Like the others except Terna Tyam, the interest they had and the desire to be gainfully employed helped them to withstand the pressures from their parents who all felt braiding was not for men.

Two major factors stand out clear from the various practitioners as their reasons for entry into braiding: the issue of interest and of gainful employment. The issue of interest in a particular profession has been instrumental to many people choosing one career or the other. Some of the females in "male jobs" also showed this to be the case in their respective professions. Two examples, one in the USA and one in Nigeria, prove this point. For example, Winfield, a female barber in the USA who owns her own shop, Vera's Full Service Barber Saloon, is in the profession because, "I went into it because I enjoy providing a service. I enjoy the art of cutting hair."[56] Sandra, who claims to be the first female mechanic in Nigeria, got into the job for two reasons: divine inspiration and her love for the job. According to her, she started the job at age 14 years when God told her in a dream to be a female mechanic. "The idea came to me through dreams, and fortunately I was able to pursue it. I dreamt that God said, 'Sandra, I want you to be a female mechanic.'

50.   1 Christine S. Koberg and Leonard H. Chusmir, "Sex Role Conflict In Sex-Atypical Jobs: A Study Of Female-Male Differences," *Journal of Organizational Behavior*, Vol. 12 (1991): 461-65.

51.   1 *Punch*, "How Cotonou Boys Dethroned Nigerian women."

52.   1 Agama Iji Moses, interviewed at his shop: Gracious Hair Clinic, No. 15 Konshisha street, 3rd Avenue, off Katsina Alla street, Makurdi, January 15, 2010.

53.   1 Caleb Sesugh Abui, interviewed at his shop, No. 39, 2nd Avenue, Iyorkaa Ako Street, Makurdi, on January 16, 2010.

54.   1 Terna Tyam, interviewed at his shop, No. 7, 1st Avenue, off Katsina-Ala street, Makurdi, on January 15, 2010.

55.   1 Ikwu George Ejugwu (27) interviewed at Dansville Plaza, Apo legislative Quarters, opposite AP filing station, FCT, Abuja, on January 26, 2010; Mike Bufer (32) (interviewed at Essence Plaza, Wuse Zone 6, Abuja, on January 26, 2010.

56.   1 Wilson, "Women made the cut."

I told Him I could not do it—but He said, 'You can.'" She adds that when one day she visited a mechanic garage with her dad and was later asked to come home with him, her reaction was, "I said no. I love this job." As she observed, "In that workshop, I saw a big engine on a top of a table, dismantled, with black engine oil running down the table. I fell in love with that black engine oil."[57]

The employment explanation is verifiable and has basis in the unemployment realities in Nigeria. Indeed, unemployment has been a major feature of the Nigerian state, as shown in the tables below.[58]

General Unemployment Rates

Year	Unemployment Rate (%)
1985	4.3
1986	5.3
1987	7.0
1988	5.1

Urban Unemployment

Year	Unemployment Rate (%)
1985	8.7
1986	9.1
1987	9.8
1988	7.3

The falls in general and urban unemployment rates in 1988 are credited to measures taken under the Structural Adjustment Program (SAP), the implementation of which began in 1986. In the 1980s, generally rural unemployment was highest among secondary school leavers who constituted about two-thirds of rural farm labor, also called "disguised unemployed." At the macro level, unemployment among secondary school leavers ranged between 35% and 50%. The unemployment rate among urban youth aged 24 years was about 40%, while the rate was 31% for youth aged 15 and 18 years old.[59] For the 1990s, the youth unemployment rate, according to Alana, is 11.5%.[60] The unemployment rates for the years 2003 to 2009 are provided in the table below.[61]

At a meeting of senior and junior researchers on the Volkswagen Sharia Debates project in Bayreuth in the summer of 2007, the comment by one of the senior researchers on a

57. 1 BBC, "Female auto-mechanic in Nigeria; Sandra Aguebor Edokpayi, the Chief Executive of Sandex Car Care and the founder of Lady Mechanic Initiative has proven a point," (2005), *http://awuraba.com/profiles/101/295-female-auto-mechanic-with-class-and-style.html*. Accessed on February 9, 2010.

58. 1 O.O. Alanana, "Youth Unemployment: Some Implications for the Third Millennium," *http://ajol.info/index.php/gjss/article/view/22763*. Accessed on February 6, 2010.

59. 1 "Nigerian unemployment," *http://www.country-data.com/cgi-bin/query/r-9405.html*. Accessed on February 06, 2010.

60. 1 Alanana, "Youth Unemployment."

61. 1 CIA World Factbook, *http://www.indexmundi.com/nigeria/unemployment_rate.html*. Accessed on January 05, 2010.

Federal Unemployment from 2003 to 2009

Year	Unemployment Rate	Rank	Percent Change	Date of Information
2003	28.0%	30		1992 est
2006	2.9%	27	-89.64%	2005 est
2007	5.8%	65	100.0%	2006 est
2008	4.9%	65	-15.52%	2007 est
2009	4.9%	60	0.0%	2007 est

junior scholar's presentation on primary school enrollment in Northern Nigeria was that figures from public authorities in Nigeria are not to be trusted on their face value but subjected to empirical verification. The statement seems justified in the case of the unemployment figures for the twenty-first century. For instance, the federal government accepted the 28.57% unemployment figure provided by the World Bank, as 40 million Nigerians out of its 140 million people were unemployed.[62]

Scope, Challenges, Opportunities, and Contributions of Males in Braiding

Males in the hairdo business cover a wide range of female and male hairstyles. Their male customers do dreadlocks, generally called "Bob Marley." Their female customers do a lot more styles. Female customers do the popular "one million braids," "slant," "short Egyptian cut," "Rihanna," "Bob Marley," "Anita Becca," "Shaku," "Sade Adu," "all back," "dog cut," "side fringe," "full fringe," etc., which mainly derive from the names of popular artists and their hairstyles.[63] While the Beninoise specialize in only the one million braids, their Nigerian counterparts are responsible for the other patterns. Some of these patterns, like Rihanna, are not braided, but fixed or woven as attachments to women's hairs after "traditional" Nigerian braiding has been done. While some, like Caleb Sesugh, do only women's hair, others, like Agama Iji Moses and Prosper Chigozie Wodo, do both women and men's hair and in addition do manicures and pedicures and hair dying.

Males in braiding, like other cross-gender occupations, confront challenges. One of these is stigmatization and rejection/lack of encouragement from parents and sometimes society. In the United States, males who choose traditionally female occupations like

---

62. 1 Daily Trust Editorial, "Nigeria: The Unemployment Crisis," *http://allafrica.com/stories/200903160028.html.* Accessed on February 6, 2010.

63. 1 The different male and female interviewees gave me these style names. Agama actually also showed me a Rihanna disc plate on which case were her different hairstyles.

nursing and midwifery confront the challenge of stereotyping, these jobs being initially termed as "sissy" professions. At worse, they might be thought to be predators. In the Nigerian case, except for Terna Tyam and Thomas Hettey, all male braiders interviewed faced initial challenges in the form of lack of encouragement and outright rejection from their parents, who did not agree to their sons entering into it because they regarded the occupation as belonging to women and therefore not for men.

Capital is another challenge. Generally, the business is costly to establish, being capital-intensive. Agama Iji Moses set up his with the sum of about half a million naira; and Terna Tyam spent about N150,000 to set up his. Consequently, prices for braiding and other hair-do services differ according to the style or pattern a customer wants. Agama Iji Moses charges N2000 for one million braids; N7000, including the cost of materials, for Rihanna,; and N13000 for Brazilian hair, excluding materials (i.e., Brazilian synthetic hair, which costs N65000 for one and a woman needs two). Ikwu George charges N1700 for full fringe and adds that in Abuja, Rihanna costs N5000, while artificial dread locks cost N7000. The least charge by Caleb Sesugh is N1000.[64] The three women interviewed in Makurdi and Abuja said that they were paying N2500 for braiding (excluding the weave-on or synthetic hairs). This means they were doing the average category and avoiding the costly categories from N5000 to N13000 (both also excluding synthetic hairs). The women, however, claimed that the N2500 represented an increase over time. All the three also claimed that they started making their hairs for N1500 some years back, with Mary-Ann Agada adding that a friend of hers made her hair for N30 for her wedding.[65] Just as prices differ by style and materials, so do the time taken to start and finish the different styles. The one million braids seems to take more time than others; it takes at least six hours. Some styles, like Rihanna, take between four and five hours, some others like Anita Beca take between one and two hours.[66] The women confirmed some of these claims, saying that they spend between two hours and five hours depending on the type of hair they want to make.[67] Considering the fact that the one million braids takes longer time to complete, the fee of N2000 charged by Agama Iji Moses seems low. However, considering also the fact that Makurdi, his business location, is not an expensive town, the amount is not too low. Competition is another challenge that males have had to overcome. The occupation is competitive to the extent that it is an open, free market, with women already well-established in it in every city. To attract women and other customers, different strategies were adopted by different male practitioners interviewed. The proprietor of Gspot Hair Salon, where Ikwu George works, initially printed and circulated handbills. Subsequently, pioneer customers told others about the shop. The other male practitioners did not use the medium of advertising through handbills. Agama Iji Moses could only attribute his being known to "the work of God, because Calabar street (where he started) was obscure."[68] But since he established his own, he has continued to attract customers, especially women, through his jokes, doing their hair well, and giving out gifts like make-up, hair clips, etc. during festive periods like Christmas. In the case of Mike Bufer, surviving the competition has been through doing the women's hair well and this advertises

64. 1 Interviews with Caleb Sesugh, Agama Iji Moses, and Ikwu George.

65. 1 Mary-Ann Agada, interviewed in Makurdi on January 15, 2010; Faeren Jato, interviewed in Makurdi on January 16, 2010; Juliet Aghariagbon, interviewed in Abuja on January 26, 2010.

66. 1 Interviews: Ikwu George, Agama Iji Moses.

67. 1 Interviews: Agada, Jato, Aghariagbon.

68. 1 Invoking the name of God is typical of small-scale businesspeople in Nigeria. On several occasions in Jos, Makurdi, and Kaduna, I have passed through groups of Christian shop owners organizing prayer sessions during the day. Their Muslim counterparts say, *Allah ya bamu sa'a*: "May God grant us good luck," when boarding commercial vehicles on business trips to local markets.

his skills to new customers, as old ones are retained. Terna Tyam shares the same experience with Mike Bufer. Additional reasons for males' competitiveness, according to them, include their creativity/innovation, patience, politeness, being caring and cordial, and making customers happy.[69] Togbe attributed his and his brothers' competitiveness and success to being thorough as experts. In addition, he told the *Punch*, "Customers say they prefer the seriousness, speed and focus with which we work on their hair. Some say they detest the habit of ladies talking while making their hair."[70]

Some females' preference for men was confirmed by two Nigerian customers of the "Cotonou Boys." Accordingly, Oluwadipe Alao "preferred Cotonou Boys to Nigerian women because they were focused and they kept to the time they set to finish the braids. They don't gossip or talk while braiding. They hardly get tired and you don't find them going about when they should be working. So, if they tell you they'll be through in six hours, you are sure it will be so."[71] Lovena Agu added strength to the female preference for male braiders by stating, "I have been making my hair with them for more than eight years. Generally, I preferred men doing my hair because they concentrate more and are more serious-minded. Their work is neat and perfect. I like their touch."[72] Juliet Aghariagbon, a businesswoman who patronizes male braiders between two and three times a month, said she was introduced to the male braider in Abuja (Mike Bufer) by her friend who also patronizes him. Her reasons for preferring males is that "they do it better. They do it the way I want it." And in the specific case of Mike, she says, "He knows the job and he is very patient."[73]

In the same vein, Mary-Ann Agada, a public servant in Makurdi, patronizes Terna Tyam because, according to her, "I am more comfortable with the way this man makes my hair. He is patient, and clam. Lady plaiters cannot take the nastiness we women sometimes exhibit." Like Aghariagbon, Agada was introduced to Terna Tyam by a female customer of his who was her elder sister.[74] Faeren Jato, a student of Benue State University, does her hair with Caleb Sesugh Abui. Her reason for patronizing him is that "he is an expert in this business." She was introduced to Caleb by her neighbor, who told her that Caleb is "excellent in hair business" and that "men are more tolerant of us."[75] Deborah Ogbonna, a third year student of the University of Port-Harcourt, preferred her male braider to females because, according to her, the male braider takes his job seriously and he is very good at the job.[76] Chinyere Constance said that she left her former female braider for a male because he gives her hair a tender and gentle touch and that he is patient and hardworking.[77] A female braider familiar with the popularity of male braiders said that males are succeeding because they are consistent and work hard.[78] The testimonies of the

---

69. 1 Interviews with Ikwu George, Agama Iji Moses, Terna Tyam, and Mike Bufer.

70. 1 *Punch*, "How Cotonou Boys dethroned Nigerian women."

71. 1 Ibid.

72. 1 Ibid.

73. 1 Juliet Aghariagbon, interviewed at Essence Plaza, Wuse Zone 6, near Dayspring Hotel, Abuja, on v.

74. 1 Mary-Ann Agada, interviewed at FLEX SALON, No. 7 1st Avenue, off Katsina Ala street, Makurdi, on January 15, 2010.

75. 1 Faeren Jato, interviewed at SANDIZ, No. 39 2nd Avenue, Iyorkaa Ako street, Makurdi, on January 16, 2010.

76. 1 Deborah Ogbonna, interviewed on the University of Port-Harcourt campus, on February 28, 2010.

77. 1 Chinyere Constance, interviewed on the University of Port-Harcourt campus, on February 26, 2010.

78. 1 Esther David Akpan, interviewed at her shop, No. 7, Abakaliki, Mile 1, Dibou, Port-Harcourt, on February 26, 2010.

women confirm the claims of male practitioners that they know the job well and are patient with the women. Thus, men are competitive in the business.

Another challenge is inefficiency of public essentials like electricity and water. Erratic power supply is a major feature of Nigeria. This causes delays for those doing Jherri curls or palming and those braiding when darkness comes. This problem often irritates some customers and those hair braiders and stylists without alternative power sources could lose customers. Maintaining generator sets to keep electricity going is very costly in terms of fueling, as gas supply is also erratic and costly. The inadequate supply of potable water is another problem. In most cities, there is no regular water supply from public utilities authorities. City dwellers rely on water sold by water vendors (called *mai ruwa* in Hausa as most of the vendors are Hausa people) who fetch and sell this essential need in jerry cans. Unpredictable access to electricity and water raise the cost of doing the business. The circulation of fake materials, especially synthetic hair, is yet another problem. The fake materials make the braiding or weave-on job very difficult as they break easily.[79]

In spite of all these challenges, the business, which recently (2009 in Makurdi and Abuja) set up a central union,[80] with male and female members numbering more than one hundred, established leadership structures consisting of both male and female. Terna Tyam is the president and their regular monthly meeting, sustained through members' fixed monthly dues,[81] is lucrative and has great potential. According to their stories, male braiders are succeeding. Agama Iji Moses has a large rented shop, a car, and trains 12 male and female braiders in Makurdi, some of whom have gone to other cities to practice. He also has some apprentices and two workers under him, whom he pays monthly allowances of N5000 each plus additional daily transport and subsistence allowances of N200.

All other men claim as their successes their ability to raise money for their upkeep and those of their families (for married ones), such as food, electricity bills, house and shop rents, and children's school fees. Of all the people interviewed, only Agama Iji Moses keeps books of accounts in which daily incomes are recorded. He showed me the current book of accounts, which was not professionally done as accountants would do it, showing income and expenditure columns separately but rather is an entry of what each customer has paid for the services rendered on each particular day. Based on its potential for income generation, male practitioners and their female customers suggested that young males who are jobless should seek alternative means of livelihood through practicing the trade.

Beyond individual gains, male participation in the business has other positive linkage effects in the following areas:

- Entrepreneurship training. With various numbers of apprentices training under them, they provide a source of skills acquisition to the growing Nigerian population in search of gainful employment.

- Job creation. Those who are established on their own employ some workers, the least being two employees who are on regular salaries. To this extent, they are small-scale enterprises helping to reduce Nigeria's unemployment figures.

---

79. 1 Interviews with Mike Bufer, Ikwu George, Agama Iji Moses, Terna Tyam, Caleb Sesugh.

80. 1 According to Terna Tyam, before 2009, unions in the trade in Makurdi were organized by different branches like Wurkum and North Bank, but that in 2009 the branches came together and formed the Benue State Hair Saloon Association.

81. 1 Agama Iji Moses said the monthly dues are N200 in Makurdi; Ikwu George and Mike Bufer say the dues are N500 for Abuja. The differences in dues in the different towns are a reflection of differences in the cost of living in the two areas. It is cheaper to live and work in Makurdi than in Abuja, the Federal Capital.

- Revenue sources. The taxes they pay to governments at the LGA and state levels and the rents they pay to landlords for their accommodation and shops provide revenues to their respective recipients.

Conclusion

The entry of Nigerian males into braiding, formerly regarded as women's role in the gender division of labor, is part of the general process of change associated with the dynamism of society stimulated principally by personal interest and the search for gainful employment. Although an emerging trend in the Nigerian economy and society, it is gaining popularity as the male practitioners devise ways of capturing the patronage of some women, through devotion, skillfulness, and patience. The mainly city-based male practitioners face challenges including initial competition from females who dominate the business, shortage of capital, and inefficiency of public utilities like water and power distribution. However, they have weathered the storms and are succeeding; they are generating their own incomes, training and employing others; and they are generating revenues to state and local governments. As society grows in sophistication and struggles for sustenance intensify, male braiders demonstrate that gender roles may fizzle out while skill/competence in jobs of whatever description and categorization rule.

Bibliography

Books and Articles

Ajayi, Ademola S. (ed.) *African Culture and Civilization*. Ibadan: Mantis Books, 2005.

Davidson, Basil. *The Lost Cities of Africa*. Boston/Toronto: Atlantic Little Brown, 1959.

Engels, Frederick. *The Origin of the Family, Private Property, and the State*. Moscow: Progress Publishers, 1983.

Falola, Toyin. *The Power of African Cultures*. Rochester, NY: University of Rochester Press, 2003

Koberg, Christine S. and Leonard H. Chusmir. "Sex Role Conflict in Sex-Atypical Jobs: A Study of Female-Male Differences." *Journal of Organizational Behavior*, Vol. 12, (1991): 461-65.

Meier, Gerald M., and James E. Rauch. *Leading Issues in Economic Development*. New York: Oxford University Press, 2000.

Okpeh Ochayi Okpeh and Dung Pam Sha, (eds.) *Gender, Power and Politics in Nigeria*. Makurdi: Aboki Publishers, 2007.

Wegs, Robert J. *Europe Since 1945, A Concise History*. 3rd Edition. New York: St Martins Press, 1991.

Internet Sources

ABC News. *http://abcnews.go.com/WNT/story?id=129474&page=2*. Accessed on September 15, 2010.

"2006 Population Census." *http://www.nigerianmuse.com*. Accessed on February 13, 2010.

Alanana, O. O. "Youth Unemployment: Some Implications for the third Millennium." *http://ajol.info/index.php/gjss/article/view/22763*. Accessed on February 6, 2010.

Antunes, Sandy, "Leaping Into Cross-Gender Role-Play," *http://www.mud.co.uk/ richard/ifan195.htm*. Accessed on January 7, 2010.

BBC. "Female auto-mechanic in Nigeria; Sandra Aguebor Edokpayi, the Chief Executive of Sandex Car Care and the founder of Lady Mechanic Initiative has proven a point." *http://awuraba.com/profiles/101/295-female-auto-mechanic-with-class-and-style.html*. Accessed on February 9, 2010.

Bello, Muhammad. "Nigeria: Rivers Police Warns Against Harassing Female Drivers." *Daily Trust*, September 4, 2009. *http://allafrica.com/stories/200909040320.html*. Accessed on February 9, 2010.

"Braids." *http://dictionary.reference.com/browse/braids*. Accessed on January 8, 2010.

"CIA World Factbook." *http://www.indexmundi.com/nigeria/unemployment*. Accessed on January 5, 2010.

Daily Trust Editorial. "Nigeria: The Unemployment Crisis." *http://allafrica.com/stories/ 200903160028.html*. Accessed on February 6, 2010.

"Female Auto Mechanic with Class and Style."

http://awuraba.com/profiles/101/295-female-auto-mechanic-with-class-and-style.html. Accessed on February 9, 2010.

Nigeria's economy/Nigerian economy at: *http://www.travelblog.org/Africa/Nigeria/fact-econ-nigeria.html* and http://www.travelblog.org/Africa/Nigeria/fact-ppl-nigeria.html. Accessed on January 9, 2010.

"Quote from Kelvin." *http://www.nairaland.com/nigeria/topic-4475.0.html*. Accessed on February 9, 2010.

Punch. "How Cotonou Boys Dethroned Nigerian Women in Braiding Business." *http://www.nigeriansinamerica.com*. Accessed on January 9, 2010.

Wilson, Craig. "Women Make the Cut." *USA TODAY*

http://www.usatoday.com/life/lifestyle/2004-06-27-female-barbers_x.htm. Accessed on February 9, 2010.

Part IV

Womanhood, Motherhood, Femininity, and HIV/AIDS

Chapter 17

Motherhood, Women's Bodies and "Eating Well": Pregnancy, a Metaphor of Life in the Cameroon Grassfields

Bridget A. Teboh

Introduction

Post-colonial Africa has witnessed through ever growing literature fundamental differences in people's socio-political and economic relations, cultural experiences, and public sentiment. In the Cameroon Grassfields during the late nineteenth and early twentieth centuries, a woman's body had symbolic meaning, her lifecycle clearly defined, and her journey had an ultimate destination—motherhood. Any discussion of women's bodies in that region necessarily included a related discourse on the reproduction of society and an interest in the symbolism of procreation. Today much of the literature, often by women and about women, has been pivotal in questioning Western representations of gender subordination, traditional female roles and their importance, and advocating for the empowerment of women in the political, social, and economic fields.

African proverbs, laments, and songs are used as part of an interdisciplinary methodology that combines both written and oral sources to shed some light on how Moghamo people and 'others' have constructed real womanhood and motherhood and their perceptions of women's body and pregnancy. These roles/institutions and their meanings are discussed anew regarding the significance of the female principle of life. Women's health and re-production emerge from the discussion as tools for negotiating gender power as well as social relations in Moghamoland and for strengthening kinship ties in the Cameroon Grassfields. Within this socio-cultural context, pregnancy becomes a metaphor of life, and in/fertility a tool used to reveal the dynamics of gender inequality and notions of success or failure for both women and men in Africa.

This chapter is thus about three things: motherhood, women's bodies, and pregnancy. These three things are tied together by a common factor, women's clout or power, *ikah-meyi*, among the Moghamo, and not all broad issues of power. While these three themes remain the focus of this chapter, it also addresses reproductive health and wellbeing; links maturity, women's body and power; and examines the symbolic repertoire of procreation and fears regarding infertility and its impact on women; pregnancy as a powerful stage in a woman's lifecycle; and links to the female principle of life. I argue that Grassfields women have always asserted clout or *ikah* as females, as fertile beings and potential mothers. Glimpses of that clout are also brought to bear in this chapter. These issues transcend the field of history, cutting across the disciplinary boundaries of African Studies, women's history, gender studies, and ethnographic history.

Structurally, after this brief introduction followed by an overview of Moghamoland, other sections of this chapter include: a review of some literature on motherhood, history, and fertility studies; the female power; maturity, women's bodies, and power; averting misfortune, *ndo'on,* and culinary symbolism procreation imagery in Moghamoland; engendering power in twentieth century Moghamoland; and finally, 'eating well,' pregnancy as a metaphor of Life. What really does 'eating well' signify for the Moghamo? This chapter unveils benefits to fertile women and the challenges they face as infertile beings, as well as exploring how fertility and reproductive health as tools for negotiating social relations have shaped women's well-being. It uncovers controversial issues and debates relevant to women's bodies, women's lives, gender relations, and sexuality in Africa and how women handle them.

Moghamo Grassfields of Cameroon: An Overview

The Grassfields of Cameroon comprise primarily the North-West Province (known as Bamenda grassfields in Anglophone Cameroon) and parts of the Western Province (in Francophone Cameroon), which are two of the ten provinces that make up the Republic of Cameroon today. This paper centers mostly on the Bamenda Grassfields and the Moghamo. Since the nineteenth century, this region has also been known as the former British colonial Bamenda Division; the Western Grassfields; the Bamenda Grasslands; the Bamenda Division; and the Bamenda Province.[1] It covers a relatively large surface area that is approximately 17,409 square kilometers, 3.7 percent of the total surface area of present-day Cameroon.[2] Moghamoland is made up of twenty-two original villages, and some recent additions.[3] It has a surface area of about 485 square kilometers and today it is constituted as part of the North-West Province of Cameroon. The Bamenda Grassfields comprises five ethnic groups: the Tikars, the Widikums, the Tivs, the Mambilas, and the latest arrivals to the area, the Chambas, according to British colonial administrative officers in the field.[4] The Moghamos are part of the Widikum ethnic group that occupies most of the south-central portions of the Bamenda plateau, and also includes the Menemos, Ngembas, Ngies, Ngwos, and some communities in the Menchum valley like the Beba-Befang.[5] All Widikum people share the same forefather, Mbeka, who settled at Tadkon,

---

1. The term grassfields was first coined by German colonial authorities in reference to the vegetation type in that part of Cameroon, characterized by highlands with extensive grasslands.

2. Provincial Services of Statistics and National Accounts (henceforth PSSNA), *Statistics Year Book for the North West Province: 1987/88–1993/94* (PSSNA — Bamenda, December 1995), 5.

3. Original Moghamo villages include Batibo (Aighwi), Bessi, Guzang, Ashong, Anong, Mbunjie, Nyenjie, Ambo, Bessom, Enyoh, Ewai, Kurlabei, Kuruku, Mbengok, Ngen-Muwah, Numben, Enwen, Oshum, Tiben, Efah, and Kugwe. Additions include Angwe, Diche I, Diche II, Elum, and Tikom near Nigeria.

4. E. M. Chilver and P. M. Kaberry, *Traditional Bamenda: The Precolonial History and Ethnography of the Bamenda Grassfields,* Vol. 1, Ministry of Education and Social Welfare and West Cameroon Antiquities Commission (Buea: Government Press, 1967), 6.

5. Colonial Office London (henceforth CO), *Cameroons Under United Kingdom Administration: Report for the Year 1955* (Colonial Office, London: her Majesty's Stationery Office, 1956), 3. Also, CO 846/5/6, St. Joan's Social and Political Alliance, "Questionnaire on the Stus of Women;" and CO 694/1-31, "Cameroons: Correspondences 1915–1926."

their original settlement on the southern stretches of the Grassfields from whence his sons by marrying wives who bore children for them spread out to found the original twenty-two Moghamo villages and other Widikum peoples. From the late nineteenth century, it has been through the mechanism of the female body imagery that society was able to express the multiple and sometimes conflicting characteristics of women, mothers, and the family in that particular social setting:[6]

> We women have been — and are repositories
> of the essential virtues of this Moghamoland.
> We are the backbone of its survival.[7]

As in other Grassfields communities, the contributions of Moghamo men and women to the well-being of their respective families had been carried out in separate but complementary spheres. Such division of labor by gender was neither superior nor inferior until European colonization and subsequent interpretations. In general, a man's responsibilities were to provide for the material needs of his family and protect the family patrimony, especially its women, from predatory outsiders.[8] Correspondingly, a woman's duties involved performing household (domestic) functions and farming duties, and exhibiting chaste and modest behavior at all times.[9] The latter was especially important since, according to Moghamo norms, the honor and social worth of a family and its members was largely determined by the (sexual) comportment of its women. Such norms allowed people to construct real womanhood, motherhood, and wellbeing in Cameroon. For example, when I asked, all elderly Moghamo women said they were virgins when they got married and that was a good thing for them then.[10]

The social and cultural institutions found in Moghamoland during the late nineteenth and early twentieth century is characteristic of much of the Cameroons Grassfields according to earlier anthropological and ethnographic studies. These studies document the ecological conditions, economic exploitation, and political separation that have structured social relations within and between family units.[11] Furthermore, they attest to the cultural significance associated with the family and the sexual behavior of its women.

---

6. See, Bridget Teboh, "Women and Change in the Cameroons Grassfields: A Social and Economic History of Moghamoland c. 1889–1960" (Ph.D. Diss. University of California Los Angeles, 2002). See chapter two for details on Moghamo social setting.

7. Ma Wumunjong, interview by author, tape recording, Batibo, North West Province, Cameroon, December 22, 1998. See also, Miriam Goheen, *Men Own the Fields, Women Own the Crops: Gender and Power in the Cameroon Grassfields* (Madison, Wisconsin: The University of Wisconsin Press, 1996), 71–72.

8. Mama Chusana, interview by author, tape recording, Batibo, North West Province, Cameroon, August 26, 1996; Rebecca Njah, interview by author, tape recording, Batibo, North West Province, Cameroon, December 27, 1998. For more details on a similar process, see Peggy Reeves Sanday, *Female power and Male Dominance: On the origins of sexual inequality* (Cambridge: Cambridge University Press, 1981).

9. Ndi Jonas, interview by author, tape recording, Batibo, North West Province, Cameroon, December 22, 1998; Woed Mbebaghi, interview by author, tape recording, Batibo, North West Province, Cameroon, December 22, 1998.

10. All these women were 60 years old or above. Cecilia Dassi (henceforth Ma Wumunjong), interview by author, tape recording, Batibo, North West Province, Cameroon, December 22, 1998; Mama Chusana, interview by author, tape recording, Batibo, North West Province, Cameroon, August 26, 1996; Rebecca Njah, interview by author, tape recording, Batibo, North West Province, Cameroon, December 27, 1998.

11. Edwin Ardener, "Belief and the Problem of Women," in Ardener Shirley (ed.), *Perceiving Women* (London: Mallaby, 1975); Goodridge Richard, "Women and Plantations in West Cameroon since 1900," in Shepherd, V. and Brereton, B. and Bailey, B. (eds.), *Engendering History: Current Directions in the Study of Women and Gender in Caribbean History* (New York: St. Martin's Press,

While these authors acknowledge the roles that women played in the family as cooks and cultivators, etc., rarely do they attempt to explain the complex nature of symbolism and representation, nor do they explain process within Moghamoland. A notable exception is Shirley Ardener's edited volume, with chapters that provide an analysis of the dynamic association between material factors, social institutions, and cultural constructs in West Cameroon, Mongolia, and South Africa. Briefly, she argues that in these societies, pre-occupation with female chastity serves to define family units and organize family members around a common objective, guarding the virginity of their women. She goes on to suggest that this "shared concern may have the adaptive advantage of reinforcing intra-familial co-operation in the face of potentially disruptive external forces."[12] While Ardener's study is illuminating, it does not cover Moghamo women, and topics such as *ikah-meyi* (women's clout/power) are unexplored. For women to be perceived historically in Moghamoland as symbols, they have to be logically capable over time of serving as a vehicle for meaning.[13] What was the relational position of women as a symbol within the wider cultural nexus?

I address these issues by applying models of symbolic and structural analysis[14] to the ethnographic and historical data collected in Moghamoland. Girls and women are at the same time pure and capable of pollution.[15] They embody purity and danger, and here I concern myself mostly to explicate the symbolic configuration formed by women as vehicles of family meaning rather than to account for the actual position held by women in Moghamoland. Drawing upon the work of Victor Turner, I propose to treat women as a dominant symbol within Moghamo culture.[16] According to Turner, "a dominant symbol is one which occupies a central position within the wider cultural system: it serves to condense meaning, unify disparate significata under a single form."[17] Furthermore, dominant symbols are multi-vocal and thus able to represent a wide range of significata, some of which may even contradict one another.

For a better understanding of such symbolism, a discussion of fertility, procreation and their meanings and impact is necessary. Using Moghamo women's laments regarding dangers to procreation as window to wellbeing, let me examine the significance of both gender and procreative imagery beyond the confines of house or compound, kitchen, and birthing. The metaphors of cooking ingredients and stories of plugged fallopian tubes

---

1995), 384–402; Elisabeth Chilver, Paul Nkwi, J.-P. Warnier, Mitzi Goheen, "Gender and Accumulation in Nso," *Paideuma*, no. 41 (1995): 73–82.

12. Shirley Ardener (ed.), *Persons and Powers of Women in Diverse Cultures: Chapters in Commemoration of Audrey I. Richards, Phyllis Kaberry and Barbara E. Ward* (New York/Oxford: Berg Publishers Limited, 1992), 5.

13. For a definition of a "vehicle" and meaning cross-culturally, see Susanne Langer, *Philosophy in a New Key* (Cambridge, Massachusetts: Harvard University Press, 1971).

14. This strategy was first proposed and later refined and used by anthropologists. See, for example, Mary Douglas, *Purity and Danger* (London: Routledge & Kegan Paul, 1966); Mary Douglas, *Natural Symbols* (New York: Random House, 1970); Eva Hunt, *The Transformation of the Hummingbird* (Ithaca: Cornell University Press, 1977); Claude Levi-Strauss, *The Savage Mind* (Chicago University Press, 1966); Nancy Munn, "Symbolism in a Ritual Context: Aspects of Symbolic Action," in *Handbook of Social and Cultural Anthropology*, J. Honigmann (ed.), (Chicago: Rand McNally, 1973); Victor Turner, *The Forest of Symbols* (Ithaca: Cornell University Press, 1967); Victor Turner, *Forms of Symbolic Action* (Seattle: University of Washington Press, 1969); and Victor Turner, *Dramas, Fields, and Metaphors: Symbolic Action in Human Society* (Ithaca: Cornell University Press, 1974).

15. For a discussion on the anthropology of menstruation, see Mary Douglas, *Purity and Danger*; and Thomas Buckley and Alma Gottlieb (eds.), *Blood Magic: The Anthropology of Menstruation* (Berkeley: University of California Press, 1988).

16. Victor Turner, *The Forest of Symbols*; Victor Turner, *Forms of Symbolic Action*.

17. Turner, *Forest of Symbols*, 27–31.

and stolen fetuses "evoke cultural typifications, simultaneously providing a framework for action and controlling it i.e. infertility and procreation."[18] Through the lens of ways of speaking about fertility, childbearing, and pregnancy, I examine in detail how rural Moghamo women, as one (often itself differentiated) voice among many, comment on political and economic changes and the impact these have had on their lives, their health, and their fears.

Motherhood, History, and Fertility Studies

The focus on complex connections in work on motherhood in anthropological demography, and on infertility in medical anthropology, has gained greater attention among scholars. While early twentieth century socio-cultural and economic history of Africa has engaged a number of scholars,[19] fewer historians have taken up ordinary women's and cultural history as key factors in African history.[20] Building upon insights from social theory regarding agency and structure,[21] and from feminist anthropology regarding the politics of reproduction, Susan Greenhalgh has called for a multidisciplinary "political economy of fertility."[22] Her approach draws heavily on anthropological concepts and methodology to examine the relation between fertility, gender, and "the political-economic dimensions of social and cultural organization,"[23] of which gender itself is a "pervasive force."[24] Africanist demographers are ever more mindful of social, cultural, and economic change, largely in an attempt to explain the relative (and anomalous) stability of high fertility in Sub-Saharan Africa. The Caldwells, for example, suggest that in many Sub-Saharan African societies, belief in the efficacy of ancestors to dispense fortune and misfortune and the importance of extended kin relations support high fertility. Frank and McNicoll describe high fertility as a strategy women use to ensure access to land and labor within the context of marriage, bride-wealth, inheritance, and land tenure institutions. However, economic insecurity may erode these social institutions and erode women's motivations to maintain a strategy of high fertility.

Studies of infertility in medical anthropology emphasize the effects that infertility has on the lives of infertile men and women. For women, reproductive mishaps (e.g.,

---

18. Rasmussen, *Spirit Possession and Personhood among the Kel Ewey Tuareg* (Cambridge: Cambridge University Press, 1995). He makes a similar point for the symbolism involved in Tuareg spirit possession. These idioms are not just 'mere' idioms. The way people think and talk about procreation can be highly significant in shaping decisions and actions regarding marriage, sexuality, and childbearing. Moreover, these decisions are often statements (or are perceived as statements) regarding the politics of cultural identity.

19. See, for example, Jeanne Marie Penvenne, *African Workers and Colonial Racism: Mozambican Strategies and Struggles in Lourenco Marques, 1877–1962* (Portsmouth: Heinemann, 1995).

20. See *Interpreting Women's Lives: Feminist Theory and Personal Narratives*, edited by the Personal Narratives Group (Bloomington: Indiana University Press, 1989); Berger and White, *Women in African History*; Toyin Falola, *The Power of African Cultures* (Rochester, NY: University of Rochester Press, 2003), 250; and Catherine Coquery-Vidrovitch, *African Women: A Modern History* (Boulder, Colorado: Westview Press, 1997), 34.

21. See, A. Giddens, *New Roles of Sociological Method : A Positive Critique of Interpretive Sociologies* (New York: Basic Books, 1976).

22. Susan Greenhalgh, "Toward a political economy of fertility: Anthropological Contributions," *Population and Development Review* 16 (1) (1990): 85–106.

23. Greenhalgh, "Toward a political economy," 95.

24. See, M. Inhorn, *Infertility and Patriarchy: The Cultural Politics of Gender and Family Life in Egypt* (Philadelphia: University of Pennsylvania Press, 1996).

miscarriages, stillbirths) are a problem. They use infertility as a tool to reveal the dynamics of gender inequality and family life, notions of success and failure, and cultural conceptions of kinship. Infertility allows anthropologists to examine how people make sense out of unexpected and unfortunate events, manage experience associated with prenatal loss and prenatal diagnosis of disability, and respond culturally to the 'never enough' quality of conception-assisting new reproductive technologies.[25] Thus, I ask, if medical anthropologists can "use infertility as a tool to reveal the dynamics of gender inequality and family life,"[26] why can't historians use fertility to question wifehood and motherhood construction in twentieth century Cameroon, while also revealing the dynamics of gender relations, inequality and notions of success or failure, and conception of things in place?

These scholars have used motherhood, women's bodies, and women's agency in Africa to further western feminist theories and views. By treating motherhood simply as "the traditional role of women" in Africa, through uncritical emphasis on "the inferior place of the woman in society and her role" as being in the kitchen and in the home, out of the public arena (i.e. politics) and as mothers only (i.e., bearers of children), these scholars have portrayed women as always subordinate to men and second class citizens in these existential roles. In contrast, I discuss these roles and institutions and their meanings anew in terms of the significance of the female principle of life. This approach locates women, motherhood, and pregnancy as central in the Moghamo belief system and to the survival of Moghamo lineage and society.

Female Power: Problematic and Persistent Perceptions

African women have historically and generally in African studies been labeled as "submissive, the weaker sex, marginalized and powerless." There is no denying that some truth lies in these labels. However, in the polarizing literature African women are weak and submissive or too headstrong, powerful, or dangerous. The inadequacy of these commonly applied terms, "submissive, weaker sex, powerless," as if women were one homogenous group, and the "hegemony and counter-hegemony" in feminist and national studies, begs for further investigations. These terms are too general and too limited to elucidate completely the actual distribution of power and authority between African men and women, especially as exemplified by the Grassfields of Cameroon.

A number of perspectives have been advanced regarding the concept of women's power and status in African societies. Some of these perspectives share a common problem: the fact that motherhood, wifehood, and womanhood have been used interchangeably by western feminists.[27] Oyewumi writes in her book *The Invention of Women*, that the idea that "the woman in feminist writings is a wife" is not a new one.[28] She continues that a "number of researchers on gender in African societies have shown that feminist anthropologists of Africa tend to focus on social categories that they perceive to be defined

25. For a cross-cultural comparison, see L.L. Layne, "Motherhood Lost: Cultural dimensions of miscarriage and stillbirth in America," *Women and Health* 16 (3/4) (1990): 69–98.

26. Feldman-Savelsburg, *Plundered Kitchens*, 41.

27. Margaret J. Hay and Stichter, Sharon (eds.), *African Women South of the Sahara* (London: Longman, 1984).

28. Oyewumi Oyeronke, *The Invention of Women: Making an African Sense of Western Gender Discourses*, (Minneapolis: University of Minnesota Press, 1997).

by men, equivalent to the category of wife in the West. What is new is the identification of its point of origin within the West."[29] I could not have said it better. However, while the discourse on motherhood continues, it needs to be placed within the context of socioeconomic and cultural change in twentieth century Africa. Oyewumi has argued that in most feminist anthropological research, "*woman* is used as synonym for *wife* both conceptually and linguistically, and *husband* as a synonym for *man*," as demonstrated in the following comment by Rosaldo on Yoruba women:

> In certain African societies like the Yoruba, women may control a good part of the food supply, accumulate cash and trade in distant and important markets; yet when approaching their husbands, wives must feign ignorance and obedience kneeling to serve the men as they sit.[30]

The problem is that the *oko*, the Yoruba category rendered as *husband* in English, is not gender specific; it encompasses both males and females. Females, too, assume the role of husband; thus some of the 'husbands' alluded to in the above quote are women. There is thus little understanding that African social arrangements, familial and otherwise, derive from a different conceptual base. Husbands indeed could be both males and females.

In Moghamoland as in much of Africa, *wife* is a stage in a woman's life cycle. Even though it is a stage of relative power for one in the 'prospect of full bloom,' it is quintessentially a subordinate category. Consequently, many women traditionally have not privileged it in identifying themselves. Wifehood tends to function more as a role than as a deeply felt identity, and it is usually deployed strategically. Across Africa, the category generally translated as *wife* is not gender specific but symbolizes relations of subordination between any two people. As a result, in the African conceptual scheme it is difficult to conflate woman and wife and articulate it as one category. Mother is the preferred and cherished self-identity of many African women.[31] That is where the subtle power of women is lived and experienced on a day-to-day basis. In all African family arrangements, including matrifocal ones like the Akan of Ghana,[32] "the most important ties within the family flow from the mother, whatever the norms of marriage residence. These ties link the mother to the child and connect all children of the same mother in bonds that are conceived as natural and unbreakable."[33] It is not surprising then, that, the most important and enduring identity name that African women claim for themselves is 'mother.'

In Moghamoland, for example, when a woman gets married, she is assigned a title-name beginning with *ibort*, mother, which she took only after she gave birth to her first child. If she did not have children, she remained an *iweik*, a wife. Let us examine the case of Lydia Njeukeu who got married to Shadrack Mbah. When she had her first child she became *Ibort* Njeik. In the event that another mother was given the same name *Ibort* Njeik, as indeed was the case, Lydia, in order to distinguish between the two mothers, became *Ibort* Njeik Guka (her place of residence) or *Ibort* Njeik Shadrack (her husband).

---

29. Oyeronke, "Family Bonds/Conceptual Binds: African Notes on Feminist Epistemologies," *SIGNS*, Journal of Women in Society and Culture, Volume 25, Number 4 (Summer 2000): 1093–98.
30. Oyewumi, "Family Bonds," 1096.
31. Ma Wumunjong, interview, December 22, 1998; Ibort Ndam, interview, December 26,1998.
32. Takyiwaa Manuh, "Wives, Children, and Intestate Succession in Ghana," in Gwendolyn Mikell (ed.), *African Feminism: The Politics of Survival in Sub-Saharan Africa* (Philadelphia: University of Pennsylvania Press, 1997); Gwendolyn Mikell, "The State, the Courts, and Value Caught Between Matrilineages in Ghana," in *Money Matters, Instability, Values, and Social Payments in the Modern History of West African Communities*, Jane Guyer (ed.) (Portsmouth, NH: Heinemann, 1994).
33. Oyewumi Oyeronke, "Family Bonds," 1094.

In this case, it is obvious that the identity and honorary title of mother came before the wifehood connection, which was implied by the name of the husband at the end. Even then, we found that the Moghamo preferred to use the location or place of birth before marriage of the woman instead, as in *Ibort* Njeik Guka. However, motherhood was not constructed in tandem with fatherhood. The notion that mothers are powerful is thus a very defining characteristic of the institution of motherhood and its place in society.

African constructions of motherhood are therefore different in significant ways from the "nuclear motherhood" that has been articulated by feminist theorists such as Chodorow.[34] In a critique of Chodorow's assumptions, Oyewumi writes:

> In her account, there is no independent meaning of motherhood outside the mother's primary and sexualized identity as the patriarch's wife. The mother's sexual ties to her husband are privileged over her relationship to her child; she is not so much a woman as she is a wife.

Maturity, Women's Bodies, and Power in Moghamoland

Like their ancestors, Moghamo people recognized the mother and her role in the process of production and reproduction of society. Moghamo attitudes towards the female body and motherhood shed light on women's power, *ikah*. Bamenda Grassfields women attained maturity as their bodies developed and they were ready to be plucked, like juicy, ripe fruit. This allowed them to accrue respect in society and derive certain privileges from their status as mothers. Such privileges in practical terms constitute *ikah*, women's power recognized by all Moghamo. For this to happen, fertility came to the forefront of every discourse. A mother was honored at public occasions and rituals and other ceremonies performed for her, thus creating and strengthening strong family ties and relationships, through network groups. This was possible because in Moghamo worldview men and women complemented to each other; therefore, no conflict existed between home and the world outside before European interventions of 1900s. What existed was a gendered division of labor with women and men participating in ancestral prayers as well as rituals for the survival, reproduction and sustenance of the Moghamo.[35]

Time and food were set aside to honor mothers through rituals in order to avoid *ndo'on* and to please the gods of the land. This was also an acknowledgement of biological difference between men and women and the fact that there were certain tasks that only women could do: "very important things, like carrying a child to term in one's stomach and giving birth to this child."[36] Motherhood in this context therefore emerged as a system of knowledge, one that women were sole custodians of, and childrearing became a closely related corollary. There is no denying that motherhood and childbearing/rearing vary widely, both historically

---

34. For details see, Nancy Chodorow, *The Reproduction of Mothering: Psychoanalysis and the Sociology of Gender* (Berkeley: University of California Press, 1978). See also, CO 847/9/5 and CO 847/11/12, "Correspondence Relating to the Welfare of Women in Tropical Africa," 1935–37.

35. Ma Wumunjong, interview, Batibo, January 15, 1999; Bah Quadi, interview, tape recording, Batibo, North West Province, Cameroon, January 15, 1999; Woed Mbebaghi, interview by author, tape recording, Batibo, North West Province, Cameroon, January 15, 1999; Mama Chusana, interview, Batibo, February 14, 1999.

36. Mama Chusana, interview by author, tape recording, Batibo, Northwest Province, Cameroon, January 15, 1999.

and cross-culturally. However, for the Moghamo motherhood was not only the culmination of a series of ritual events that were all linked together, but it also conferred an identity, and represented a very important stage in the lifecycle of a woman.

Engop ngup bi nyii bom

May the little chick grow to become a hen.

The above is a Moghamo proverb regarding motherhood and fertility. It is indicative of what matters in the Moghamo belief system vis-à-vis women's bodies and procreation as well as survival of the lineage. A real woman ought to be able to bear children and procreate, that is what makes her a woman. That is what makes her sexy, desirable in the eyes of all men. When I visited Cameroon and Moghamoland during 1998–1999, the most cited of fears among women was infertility. Individuals were worried about the conception, birthing-troubles, and survival of their own children and were anxious about the decreasing population. In addition, women used these complaints in their everyday negotiations with kin and with neighbors to talk about what it meant to be a woman, what it meant to be Moghamo, and how the Moghamo could survive and get ahead in the economic and political upheavals that have rocked Cameroon over the past twenty years.

The fear of infertility is common in the Grassfields of Cameroon as it has serious consequences for the survival of the family and marriages. Working among the Bangante of the northwest Grassfields, Feldman-Savelsburg's findings uncover a similar fear of infertility and the impact of the latter on women's lives. She writes,

> The fear that worried women included biological infertility as well as social and supernatural impediments to good marriage, bringing a pregnancy to term, and socializing offspring to further reproduce a Bangante life-style.[37]

However, because she paid most of her attention to the study of infertility and the search for a remedy, she failed to discuss the clout or *ikah* that women have as fertile beings and mothers. Birth and fertility were not only natural or biological events, they were also social processes with culturally and historically specific meanings. The Moghamo woman at the center of my research revealed a core of shared images of procreation and social reproduction centered on 'cooking.' They also demonstrated that not all Moghamo worried about infertility and reproduction in the same way or to the same extent. Their concerns were shaped by the multiple and changing realities within the society, and complex meanings of fertility for the lives of women, their vulnerability and economic decline exacerbated by the legacy of colonialism.

Realizing these interconnections for the case of the Moghamo has convinced me that women's and gender studies need to be firmly grounded in a holistic, multi-dimensional, and socio-cultural history. Representations of motherhood thus emerged as a theme of central interest to present-day Moghamo women as well as to diverse actors with divergent interests over time. My work reflects this intense involvement in both present and past. As I investigated women's expressions about fertility, threats to procreation as well as infertility, I discovered dimensions of *ikah*, and indigenous conceptions of fertility-power and vitality linked to a strong belief system. This belief system contradicts the labeling of African women as "the weaker sex," through conceptions of illness and misfortune, *njo'om* and *ndo'on*,[38] and of the close relation between cooking, feeding/eating, and procreation, a metaphor of life itself in the Moghamo worldview.

---

37. Pamela Feldman-Savelsburg, *Plundered Kitchens, Empty Wombs: Threatened Reproduction and Identity in the Cameroon Grassfields* (University of Michigan Press, 1999), 25.

38. *Njo'om* in Moghamo is an oath, the power of the spoken word. It was also the term for the mechanism used to activate mystical powers, which could lead to *ndo'on*. *Ndo'on* is bad luck, misfortune,

Averting Misfortune, *Ndo'on* and Culinary Procreation Imagery/Symbolism

Moghamo political and cultural ideology in the nineteenth century was (and still is) a complex and diffuse theory of mystical power and danger, *njo'om* and *ndo'on,* which provided a system of sanctions that not only reinforced most political roles and prerogatives, but also reinforced the importance of rituals in Moghamoland.[39] In its negative aspect, *Ndo'on* was manifested in illness, death, poverty of those targeted, and the infertility of women and men, etc. Rituals surrounding marriage practices and the practice of motherhood thus abound in Moghamoland (for example, *ibu'uh, inami, idziin no'oh, ayimbangha,* etc.) and highlight Moghamo conceptions of mystical power and danger, as well as serving as a window to an understanding of *ikah-meyi,* women's power derived from motherhood. Rituals emerge as tools of empowerment of women, as well as the only means to avoid *ndo'on* in individual families and in Moghamoland as a whole.

The rhetoric of misfortune and a culturally specific symbolism of procreation were tied to socially structured experience. Such rhetoric focused on how women used fertility symbolically to comment on their lives as successful mothers, and, if barren, how they struggled with such misfortune. Through proverbs and idioms of fertility they found a language that gave meaning and made comprehensible the ways their lives were affected by social change. These women emphasized concepts of personhood, social status, and cultural identity through tales of reproductive threats and through their quest for fertility. In so doing, they drew upon a symbolic repertoire of procreation imagery focused on metaphors of the kitchen, the pot, and cooking. These metaphors, elements of which were common to several central and east African societies, included visions of sex as heat; the womb as hearth or a cooking pot; ova/egg, sperm, and blood as ingredients; gestation as cooking and stirring the pot; and birthing as serving a delicious meal. The imagery of marriage referred to the kitchen simultaneously as a physical and metaphoric locale that drew the wife inside the husband's village, kin group, and compound. In Moghamoland for example, marriage, *enami,* means "cooking inside," as the wife's marital duties were to produce crops and cook food for her family while metaphorically making babies, i.e. "something is cooking" within the bounds of the nuptial kitchen.

Understanding this culinary symbolism of procreation in Moghamoland was essential to solving the puzzle of fear of infertility in an area of high fertility, and to specifying the connection between social structural factors and demographic outcomes. What people do is the link between social structure and demographic outcomes such as fertility rates. Human agency is the product of "knowledgeable actors" and their "knowledge" is culture. Recent theory in anthropological demography seeks to take culture seriously, but could be advanced by more attention to the content of that culture. Twentieth-century anthropological explorations of the imagery of procreation have been embedded in studies on kinship, rites of passage, and more recently rites of affliction or spirit possession.[40] Concern

---

or a kind of curse or suffering with which the traditional God of the Moghamo, *Nwighe* afflicted people who had violated the rights of others in certain ways.

39. Bah Quadi, interview, Batibo, January 16, 1999; *Fon* G. T. Mbah II, interview, Batibo, January 16, 1999; *Fon* of Bessi, interview, Bessi, January 17, 1999; *Atah*-Nyen, interview, Nyen, North West Province, Cameroon, December 22, 1998; *Dong* Ngubighe, interview, Batibo, September 14, 1996.

40. R. Devisch, *Weaving the Threads of Life: The Khita Gyn-eco-logical Healing Cult among the Yaka* (Chicago: Chicago University Press, 1993); J. Boddy, *Wombs and Aliens Spirits: Women, Men and The Zar Cult in Northern Sudan* (Madison: University of Wisconsin Press).

with the broad cultural significance of gender "has motivated a reemerging interest in the symbolism of procreation,"[41] and the romance of the sperm and the egg, to deconstruct biomedical metaphors and discourses surrounding reproductive biology. Delaney on the other hand relates the imagery of coming-into-being (procreation) to gender definitions, cosmology, and everyday life in a Turkish village.[42] In what is the most comprehensive book to date on the symbolism of procreation, Delaney asks why human reproduction, and women's role in it, is so devalued in the Judeo-Christian-Islamic world. Delaney seeks her answer in the symbolic link between men and God as "monogenetic" life-givers, and thus critiques the conflation of patriarchy and male dominance in much feminist anthropology as intellectually sloppy,[43] a profound if sometimes disputed challenge.[44]

After several conversations with research informants it became clear to me that the symbolism of procreation and women's experience of their bodies were intimately tied up in social relations.[45] Fear of infertility emerged as a recurrent theme in Moghamo discourse, a barometer of anxiety about personal fate, the future of the chiefdom and one's cultural heritage, and of ambivalent response to modernity and cultural imports. Infertility stigmatized women and could contribute to their impoverishment. Even if most Moghamo women were not infertile (on the average they had four children each), they feared reproductive threats more than men, or well-to-do women, because the consequences of infertility were so grave and could deprive them of land.

Infertility disrupted a Moghamo woman's expected life course and denied her the pride and full adult status that came with childbirth. In addition, infertility put women at greater risk of impoverishment in Moghamoland, through the changes it initiated in relations between husbands and wives, among *ifu'uh*, co-wives, or *mbanyas*, and between divorced women and their natal kin, and through the loss of potential assistance that children provide. The stigma and impoverishment associated with infertility has a specific historical context in Moghamoland: the economic crisis and sharpened identity politics of the 1980s and 1990s. Tales of the theft of food from women's kitchens and farms, and children from their wombs, permeated Moghamo women's accounts of dangers to procreation in the 1980s; in the 1990s these accusations of theft implicated the state and commercial elite in stealing the means to health and success via harmful economic policies and new forms of witchcraft.[46] This violent imagery suggested that the serious consequences of infertility found symbolic expression in a particular form of discourse. With the language of infertility and the imagery of thieves and witches interfering in the process of "making babies," women discussed social processes they perceived to be just as threatening as infertility itself. Women were more vulnerable than were men to changes in their situation.[47] For Moghamo women and the Moghamo in general, fertility was an indicator of "things

---

41. Feldman-Savelsbury, *Plundered Kitchens, Empty Wombs*, 4. See, Martin's *The Woman in the Body*, 19.

42. Delaney, *The Seed and the Soil: Gender and Cosmology in Turkish Village Society* (Berkeley: University of California Press, 1991).

43. Delaney, *The Seed and the Soil*, 35.

44. See M. Inhorn, *Infertility and Patriarchy*, 25.

45. Ma Wumunjong, interview, Batibo, January 15, 1999; Rebecca Tikwe, interview, Bessi, February 10, 1999. For parallels from Bangante, see Feldman-Savelsburg, *Plundered Kitchens*, 5.

46. Feldman-Savelsberg, *Plundered Kitchens*, 20–28.

47. See, S. Leith-Ross, *African Women: A study of the Igbo of Nigeria* (London: Routledge and Kegan Paul, 1965). For further reading on the subject of vulnerability, see also, Ada Mere, "Status of Igbo Women," in *A Year to Remember: Symposium Proceedings*, International Women's Year (University of Nigeria, Nsukka, 1975), 38–45.

in place" whereas infertility was an indicator of "things out of place" or "things falling apart."[48]

En-Gendering Power in Twentieth Century Moghamo Grassfields

Ikah a gheu? Imbangha keu kai ayi gwi?

What power? Didn't a man come from a woman's belly?

It was an eye-opener for me to hear men minimize their 'powerful' status as men. This Moghamo proverb indicates the gender sensibilities of Moghamo people their specific socio-cultural setting (Moghamoland). The notion of women's power, *ikah-meyi,* and influence is borne out in the generalized examples of ritual praise and ceremonies in honor of the female (woman). The following concepts stand out in relation to Moghamo women's power and the ability to bear children, the lifeline to continuity in their belief system: child/daughter*hood,* woman*hood,* wife*hood,* mother*hood,* and grand-mother*hood.*[49] This categorization is necessary in Moghamoland as it demonstrates the stages in a woman's life cycle.[50] Every stage in her lifecycle had corresponding duties, obligations, responsibilities, benefits, and privileges. I argue that women have *ikah* by virtue of the fact that they are female. How they negotiated this *ikah,* whether as individuals in society or collectively as women, determined the cultural, political, social, and economic tempo of Moghamoland and shed light on the formulation and reformulation of gender roles.

Womanhood, for example, is a concept closely associated with *ikah,* which attains its apogee when a female becomes a mother, *ibort* or *abu'u,* through marriage and childbirth. *Ikah-meyi* is not static. *Au contraire,* it increases during a woman's lifetime. It hardly ever diminishes (except in cases of divorce, adultery, or abominations).[51] In this sense, and only through an understanding of the various stages of a woman's lifecycle, can the full meaning and impact of *ikah-meyi* and pregnancy be understood.[52] Similarly, the complex correlation between womanhood, motherhood, proper marriage, and power only becomes truly evident when viewed through this prism.[53]

I am a daughter, I am a wife, and I am a mother ...
My duties and responsibilities are MANY and diverse

48. The idea of things falling apart as a result of a clash of two cultures during colonization is borrowed from, Chinua Achebe, *Things Fall Apart* (Everyman's Edition, 1992).

49. Evidence from Moghamo interviewees has shown that these *-hoods,* or states of being/life stages, a name that I adopted for practical reasons, held the key to women's power, *ikah,* during the 19th century, *ishu'uwe,* and persisted throughout the colonial and post-colonial period.

50. For further explanations see also, Oppong, *Marriage, Fertility and Parenthood,* 30–34. Also see Green, *Igbo Village Affairs,* 150.

51. Stages in life also refer to 'office' or 'status' thus used here for lack of a better English word. However, they describe social hierarchy or ranking of women in Moghamo Grassfields.

52. See, Teboh, "Women and Change in the Cameroons Grassfields."

53. For a detailed discussion of the use of life histories see Susan Geiger, *TANU Women: Gender and Culture in the Making of Tanganyikan Nationalism, 1955–1965* (Portsmouth, NH: Heineman, 1998), 11; See also, David William Cohen, *The Combing of History* (Chicago: the University of Chicago Press, 1994).

I am powerful in more ways than meets the eye ...
What will our land be without me? (Song by Moghamo Women)[54]

In Moghamoland as the above song indicates, women's duties are multi-faeted. However, their power or *ikah* is equally acknowledged in areas that count the most—childbearing.[55] Women's lives are full of contradictions. Confused, I asked my collaborators: "How could you be burdened with so much work, and still feel and think that you have power?" I got my answer in the form of a Moghamo proverb as follows:

Mba nwan ya ibort meud kerri.

Only the mother knows the father of her child.

That is a powerful statement. The fact that such a saying or proverb exists, goes to show that women did have power linked to pregnancy, childbearing and motherhood. As Woed Mbebaghi a king-maker calmly, yet bluntly put it:

What else do we men or fathers have as proof? Nothing really ...
We are helpless and depend on the word of our wives.
For that reason, we must therefore claim ownership of our
children by insisting that they look like us or resemble us.[56]

Pregnancy was and still is a time of great power for women, a time they used wisely and negotiated for more benefits within the household and family. This statement testifies to the ultimate power and control that women have over their children and their husbands. Given that the male ego could easily bruise in such situations, men felt much better by claiming ownership of children, saying: "oh ... my baby looks like me! He or she has my eyes and my father's mouth," and thus showing off their 'power' and virility in public.

In Moghamoland, the transition from adolescent to motherhood was a journey towards an ultimate goal, a mark of achievement and social accomplishment for Moghamo women enabled by rituals and initiation.[57] This was the position and status that all women in aspired or wished to attain, and this was where barrenness and infertility became a stigma, and fertility and marital bliss a sign of success since women's age grade structures were based on the childbearing cycles.[58] An interesting component regarding views about women and women's bodies in Africa is the idea that women are "the weaker sex." I asked

---

54. Mama Maria, interview by author, tape recording, Batibo, North West Province, Cameroon, February 10, 1999. Mama Maria knew many old songs in praise of women that she willingly shared with me.

55. Female collaborators told me in 1999 that it was very important for a child to resemble its parents, including its mother. The said child indeed becomes the 'love child' of the husband, who sees in the child (if it is a girl) his beloved wife of yester years, and if a boy a mirror of himself, a testament of truth; the maternal grand-parents see in her their little girl and if a boy, an heir who belongs to them. Ma Wumunjong, interview, Batibo, December 22, 1998; Ibort Acha, interview, Batibo, December 22, 1998; Ibort Ndam, interview, December 1998; Ibort Nyah, interview, January 15, 1999; Ibort Ndam, interview, January 17, 1999.

56. Woed Mbebaghi, interview, Batibo, January 15, 1999. DNA testing is still very rare in rural areas.

57. In this sense, initiation such as *ibuu, idzin minoh, inami*, etc. meant the presentation of a child to the ancestors for blessings as they entered the difficult space of adult life. In Moghamoland, this initiation or presentation was done at three specific moments in a person's life: at birth, after puberty, and at death. Bah Quadi, interview, Batibo, December 22, 1998; Ma Kurondong, interview, Ashong, December 27, 1998.

58. See, Nkwain, "A Kom man Weds," in Chilver, *Fieldnotes* (1957); Paul Nkwi, *Traditional Bamenda*, 25; Chilver, *Pre-colonial Bamenda*, 38–45. Ma Wumunjong, interview, Batibo, December 22, 1998.

men in Moghamoland this question: Are women the "weaker sex" in the Cameroon Grass-fields? Here is what some men and women said to that effect:

> Women have the reputation of being physically weaker than men ... but that is not the point. They can control men. Women do not dispute this fact that they are weak. Instead it is something, a strategy they use to avoid the more difficult tasks around the home and ... to attract attention of the husband.[59]

It was therefore not uncommon to hear the wife 'lamenting,' in a voice totally broken with fatigue, while she did some work in her back yard or in her kitchen. The least discomfort as she tried to split firewood for cooking, or to lift a big bunch of plantain, knowing that the husband was home or around, was pretext for this famous Moghamo women's lament:

> *Yoo-uuhh-oui, meu borrt ...! A fah-i bi zweti ...!*

Oh dear, I am tired, I am very tired! This task will kill me ...![60]

At the sound of such lament, a good husband often seized the moment and went to the rescue of his wife. He knew better than to sit back and do nothing. Whether the concern he showed her then was faked or genuine is open for debate. What is obvious is the fact that he quickly found very comforting words for his 'tired and over-worked' wife, and quite often brought gifts of palm wine to boost her moral and to remain in her favor. This is *ikah-meyi* at work, subtle yet firm, as this husband might not be given food otherwise. Moghamo cosmological conceptions of procreation or 'making babies,' pregnancy, and child-birthing, leave no doubt in any man's mind about the 'godlike' capabilities of the woman and mother.

> God left with each female [human, animal and plant], the possibility of continuing God's work of creation and procreation task.[61]

Everyone knew that both the male and female had to transmit in variable quantity and quality hereditary characteristics to the unborn child.

> Cheuyi Mbangha kwehe chen ichugi.

> Men do not sit down or squat to urinate.

The above proverb provides a reason why the Moghamo believed that women were godlike, *Ichigeu Nwighe*. Such a belief also explained the meticulous stages within a marriage ceremony, and justified the elaborate rituals and praise in honor of the mother and child, such as *ibu'uh, inami, idziin no'oh, ayi-mbangha*. As one elderly man at Guzang put it in a nutshell through yet another proverb, *mbangha keu kwehe chen ichugi*, "do men sit down to urinate?"[62] The process of urinating was a metaphor for childbirth, and Moghamo men did not pretend to have those powers. While this was a factual statement because men did literally stand up to urinate, symbolically it meant something else: something profoundly linked to Moghamo belief system and procreation concept, a metaphor for childbirth. During the child-birthing process, it was believed that squatting or "sitting down" was the best method. For a man to say that he too urinated while sitting

---

My findings show that the husbands in these cases really have little control over the situation, and so absolutely depend on the wives.

59. Pa Munji, interview by author, Guzang, North West Province, Cameroon, December 27, 1998 ; Ma Wumunjong, interview, 1998; Bah Quadi, interview, 1998; Ibort Acha, interview, 1998.

60. Interview, Ibort Acha, interview, Batibo, December 22, 1998.

61. Ma Wumunjong, interview, December 22, 1998; Bah Quadi, interview, December 22, 1998; Woed Mbebaghi, interview, Batibo, December 22, 1999.

62. Jonas Tita, interview by author, Guzang, North West Province, Cameroon, December 22, 1998.

down meant that he was claiming that he could physically give birth, an impossible thing for a man in Moghamo belief system. While acknowledging the importance of his 'seed' in the whole process, man accepted his limitations and honored through rituals the miracle of childbirth and the mother of his child.

Pregnancy and birthing were things that were beyond man's comprehension, and he did not insist on finding answers, for he knew them. As the Moghamo would say, *Ayi ya Ichigeu Nwighe*, "Woman is mystical, woman is like god, and woman is God's gift to us, humankind."[63] This belief was used to also justify why men went to great lengths to ask women's hand in marriage. Men needed women to bear children for them, while they hoped and prayed that the children were really theirs. It re-emphasized what I call the Female Principle of Life. Every proper union between a man and woman, therefore, was reminiscent of the union between God and the Earth, and should bear fruit. However, in this case the woman was predestined by God to continue God's creation, and the man thus only played the role of a human conduit or egg donor. Life-giving capacity, or the female principle of life, was perceived as a gift deposited in the womb of every woman.[64] Conversely, a husband's sexual neglect of his wife was frowned upon. It was interpreted as refusal to enable procreation, an interruption of the pre-destined course of nature in a marriage.

"Eating Well": Pregnancy, as a Powerful Stage

Pregnancy for Moghamo women is a powerful condition and stage. Once a young woman became pregnant, through "eating well" and "feeding sufficiently," the grain or egg lodged inside her womb, attained maturity, and she births a healthy child. This maturity was determined by the lateness of the "one who knows everything," menses, *isheik*.[65] During this time the woman had dual functions. Not only must she augment what the Moghamo conceive of as "her personal seminal juices," *igheu nyeud ayi*, (amniotic fluid), she must also do everything in her power to increase her husband's sexual appetite and desire.[66] It was believed that the husband must communicate via the amniotic fluid almost all the characteristics of the unborn child. The said communication started with the sex of the child: was the quantity of sperm sufficient? The lineage and clan knowledge system for which the husband was the support and vehicle, depended on the quality of his juices and hers. Herein lies the legitimate quest for physical pleasure in Moghamoland

---

63. Bah Quadi, interview, December 22, 1998. Other Moghamo informants agreed with Bah Quadi with respect to the mystery of women's powers in the birthing process. See, Interview, Number One, Batibo, December 1998; Interview, Woed Mbebaghi, Batibo, January 17, 1999.

64. Patrilineal households depended on the ability to have heirs to continue the family name, men had to marry wives and have children. Most Moghamo women confirmed that sterile women were treated differently and blamed for their infertility. More than 60 percent of forty-five childless wives that I encountered during my fieldwork were divorced, while only 20 percent were still married, and that they said was because they had independent wealth (land, real estate property, businesses), and/or were sheltered by the husband's family.

65. *Isheik* in Moghamo means menses or the period, the blood that is shed during menstruation. Every woman before menopause had a period every month, and if she missed it or was late, that was proof of pregnancy. It was called the "one who knows everything" because it served as a symbol, a marker or proof that a woman was not only fertile, but had also been sexually active.

66. For a similar interpretation of local practices, see also Chantal Guilmain Gaulthier's discussion of the Fali of Northern Cameroon "Le jeu de la femme," in *Fonction de la Femme dans L'Ordre Social* (Paris Khartala, 1987), 41–43.

and the Bamenda Grassfields. The sex of the child was determined during intercourse by the quantity and quality of emitted genital fluids. Woed Mbebaghi explained the idea to me as follows:

> If these fluids are more abundant from the maternal source, then the child will be a girl, if abundant from the paternal side the child will be a boy ... a man who produces only daughters is considered weak and said to be lacking in virility.[67]

At a micro-analytic level this was interpreted to mean that seduction and enticement were tools used on a regular basis by both partners for personal gains. However, during pregnancy a woman had a lot of power, since her husband and everyone around gave her whatever she wanted. The female principle of life was nowhere as evident as during the time that a woman got pregnant. Pregnancy was a most anticipated moment and stage in a married woman's lifecycle, and from the above discussions, it was obvious that during pregnancy a woman had a lot of power to negotiate her status and economic standing within the family. She thus became an *ayi-bumeu*, a pregnant woman, loved by all. In Moghamoland, the pregnant woman paid special attention to her food and also the food that her husband ate. She made sure that he ate foods reputed to be rich in sperm count such as he-goat meat, cow leg, bone marrow, *foufou*, bananas, as well as encouraging him to drink palm wine and the "drecks," *aton mino'h*. During the third and last trimester, that is, from the seventh to the ninth month, snakes, especially the, viper, *atangha*, as well as tadpoles, okra, and other slimy and soft vegetables were delicacies consumed to enable the baby 'slide out' with relative ease during the birthing process.

It was a husband's responsibility to get his pregnant wife needed meats and rare fruits, sometimes from far away. Usually, these were accompanied by kola nut, which they mutually shared as a sign of love and unity, as well as the bitter kola, known as "kick starter" or in French, "*le demarreur*," reputed aphrodisiac noted for giving strength and stamina to the man.[68] Some men alleged that pregnant women used pregnancy as a ruse to "do nothing," besides cook food for themselves and their husband. Others became so capricious and lazy that they left all other tasks to their co-wives if they had any, or to young female relatives.[69] In any case, the good husband never let his pregnant wife do strenuous work during her pregnancy. This song by an old woman in one of the villages, Mbuhnjei, recounts and captures this whole idea behind pregnancy and power:

> I am not sick. I am in [with child]. I am not sick, I just ate too much.
> But if you say I am sick, maybe I am. I will just lie here and rest.
> Please, bring me some cold water. I am feeling very hot![70]

Incidentally, the Moghamo expression for pregnancy is *iwi ngah,* meaning "she is in" or "the seed is implanted inside." This expression is also a metaphor for feeling secure in one's marriage. Figuratively, it means that finally she has arrived and she is really in the house, and so can bargain and negotiate better deals for herself. Using a culinary metaphor as did old women, this was interpreted to mean that the pregnant woman had something

---

67. Woed Mbebaghi, interview, Batibo, December 22, 1998. Other elderly Moghamo shared this same notion and corroborated the idea. Ma Wumunjong, interview, Batibo, December 22, 1998; Bah Quadi, interview, Batibo, December 22, 1998.

68. The bitter kola is a species of kolanut, very bitter in taste and liked by men all over Africa. The bitter-kola is called "the kick-starter" among English-speaking Africans, and "le demarreur" among the French-speaking Africans because, for centuries, it has earned a reputation for giving strength to weak men, in the same way that the magic pill, viagra, has done today around the world.

69. Pa Number One, interview, Batibo, December 29, 1998.

70. Mami Suzanna, interview by author, Mbunjei, North West Province, Cameroon, December 20, 1998.

'meaty' and good cooking in her pot. The next nine months were critical as the woman tried to cook and serve a delicious meal, thereby making babies (inside her marital home) and attaining the envied status of mother, *ibort*. Given that failure to conceive or bear children were grounds for bringing in another wife or for divorce, getting pregnant was cause for celebration. The pregnant woman was pampered by her family and especially husband, and given her heart's desires because the pregnancy validated the husband as a virile, fertile, and real man.

Conclusion

From the above discussion, it is evident that Moghamo women and men were in a relationship of permanent complementarity, negotiation, and exchange. However, women had power in an area that mattered most to them (procreation), and as such held the key to *ikah* and decision-making. This chapter has rendered explicit the role of mothers, while simultaneously contributing to the theoretical understanding of categories such as *ibort* (mother) and *iweik* (wife), two of the crucial stages in the lifecycle of a woman. Far from being the definitive statement on the origins, nature and exercise of power in Moghamoland, this chapter has sought to extend the boundaries of discussion regarding gender and power relations in Africa. In the process it addressed the construction of real womanhood, motherhood, and wellbeing through such phenomena as *ndo'on*. Moghamo belief system recognized a shared and complementary power base, with such power originating in the spiritual realm. I have argued that health and reproduction are tools for negotiating gender and social relations and for strengthening family and kinship ties.

Drawing upon a symbolic repertoire of Moghamo procreation imagery focused on metaphors of the kitchen and cooking in a marriage, this chapter examined women's infertility challenges. It has thus contributed to the understanding of pregnancy, its links to a proper marriage and women's power in the African context by critically examining how recent and existing works have shaped perspectives on African subjects, pregnancy, and motherhood. This chapter is also a welcome contribution to the dialogue on African fertility/infertility, pregnancy, the importance of women in human reproduction, and gender equality and relations. Through African ways of speaking, the complex nature and exercise of power in Moghamoland have been demonstrated. Pregnancy represents a powerful stage in a woman's lifecyle, and therefore can be used to deduce and infer the importance of mothers in society, and the dependence on the female for its survival and reproduction.

Women filled a space that no one else could fill and for that reason, they were invaluable and had *ikah*. These associations not only shaped the way people conceptualized mothers but also shaped their expectations from mothers and women's bodies. To fully assess the concept of *ikah-meyi* it was necessary to re-visit the role that women played in society in terms of the female principle of life and to analyze the hidden meanings inferred by the recognition of their social and cultural functions in Moghamoland. Pregnancy thus emerged as a privileged space, which when manipulated properly signified a lot of power for women. The female principle of life has remained a constant in Moghamoland in spite of some changes (delays in age of marriage, education, etc.). Having children and carrying on the family and lineage name enhanced women's status in the home and in the society, and are part of a system of knowledge that mothers' control.

It is clear from the above analysis that the roles women assumed during their life cycle were multi-faceted and often were perceived by western scholars as contradictory. I challenge historians, therefore, to deal carefully with these contradictions, and to avoid jumping to hasty conclusions because, in Moghamoland as elsewhere, there is room for such contradictions. Female scholars and Africanists have the responsibility to provide the kind of information that will enable non-Africans to understand the nature of the universe in which African women live. This discussion of Grassfields Moghamo women's *ikah*, and related topics, has done just that by contributing to the discourse on motherhood, women's body and pregnancy/fertility, and power in society. This chapter offers a poignant corrective to the tendency, even in recent works on Africa, to define women as weak and powerless, terms that are too inadequate to elucidate the reality of African women's lives.

References

Primary Sources

Basel Mission Archive (BM). Basel.

Colonial Office (CO). Public Records Office, Kew Gardens, London, UK.

Hook, S.R. Divisional Office, Bamenda, Comments on the Moghamo Intelligence Report, p. 6, (no date) *BA* ab 21a. *The National Archives (BA)*, Buea.

Isherwood, Francis. "The Story of the Diocese of Bamenda," mimeo. Nov. 1979. *The Cameroonian National Archives (YA)*, Yaoundé.

Provincial Services of Statistics and National Accounts (PSSNA), *Statistics Year Book for the North West Province: 1987/88–1993/94.* (PSSNA: Bamenda, December 1995), 5. The Provincial Archives (BSR), Bamenda Station.

Secondary Sources

Ardener, Edwin. *The Coastal Bantu of the Cameroons. Ethnographic Survey of Africa, Western Africa.* Part X1. London: International African Institute, 1956.

Ardener, Shirley. *Eyewitnesses to the Annexation of Cameroon: 1883–1887.* Buea: Government Press, 1968.

Austen Ralph A. and Jonathan Derrick. *Middlemen of the Cameroons Rivers: The Duala and their Hinterlands, c. 1600–c.1960.* Cambridge: Cambridge University Press, 1999.

Chilver, Elizabeth M. and Phyllis Kaberry M. *Traditional Bamenda: The Precolonial History and Ethnography of the Bamenda Grassfields.* Vol. 1. Ministry of Education and Social Welfare and West Cameroon Antiquities Commission. Buea: Government Press, 1967.

_____. "From Tribute to Tax in a Tikar Chiefdom." *Africa: Journal of International African Institute.* Vol. 30 (1960): 1–19.

Chilver. "Native Administration in the West Central Cameroons, 1902–1954." In K. Robinson and F. Madden (eds.) *Chapters in Imperial Government.* Oxford: Blackwell, 1963.

Cowan, Gray L. (ed.) *Education and Nation-Building in Africa.* New York: Praeger, 1965.

Gann, H. L. and Duignan, P. *Colonialism in Africa, 1870–1960.* London: 1970.

Hansen, T. K. (ed.) *African Encounters with Domesticity.* New Brunswick, New Jersey: Rutgers University Press, 1992.

Hunt, R.N., Liu, T. P. and Quataert, J. (eds.) *Gendered Colonialisms in African History.* Oxford: Blackwell Publishers, 1997.

Jayawardena, K. *The White Woman's 'Other' Burden: Western Women in South Asia during British Rule.* New York: Routledge, 1995.

Kaberry, Phyllis M. *Women of the Grassfields: A Study of the Economic Position of Women in Bamenda, British Cameroons.* Colonial Research Publication, No. 14. London: HMSO, 1952.

Mama, Amina. "Women's Studies and the Studies of Women in Africa during the 1990s." Working Paper Series 5/96, Dakar, Senegal: CODESRIA, 1996, 28.

Nkwi, Paul. *Elements for a History of the Western Grassfields.* Yaoundé: University of Yaoundé Press, 1982.

Rudin, Harry. *Germans in the Cameroons, 1884–1914: A Case Study in Modern Imperialism.* New Haven: Yale University Press, 1938.

Sharwood-Smith, Sir Bryon. *Recollections of British Administration in the Cameroons and Northern Nigeria, 1921–1957: But Always as Friends.* Durham: Duke University Press, 1969.

Strobel, Margaret. *European Women and the Second British Empire.* Bloomington: Indiana University Press, 1991.

Teboh, Bridget. "Women and Change in the Cameroons Grassfields: A Social and Economic History of Moghamoland, c. 1889–1960." Ph.D. Dissertation, University of California Los Angeles, 2002.

Thomas, Lynn. "'Ngaitana (I Will Circumcise Myself)': Lessons from Colonial Campaigns to Ban Excision in Meru, Kenya." In B. S. Duncan and Y. Hernlund (eds.). *Female Circumcision in Africa Culture: Controversy, and Change.* Boulder: Colorado, Lynne Rienner Publishers, 2001: 129–50.

Werner, Keller. *The History of the Presbyterian Church in West Cameroon.* Victoria: Press book, 1969.

Zintgraff, Eugen. *Nord Kamerun.* Berlin: Paetel, 1895.

Articles

Ardener, Shirley and A. Warmington. "The Political History of Cameroon." *The World Today* (1982): 43–53.

Dillon, Richard. "Ideology, Process, and Change in Pre-Colonial Meta Political Organization." Ph.D. Dissertation, University of Pennsylvania, 1973.

Hunt, Nancy R. "Domesticity and Colonialism in Belgian Africa: Usumbura's Foyer Sociale, 1946–1960." *Signs: Journal of Women in Culture and Society.* Vol. 15. 3 (1990): 469.

Gaitskell, D. "Housewives, Maids, or Mothers: Some Contradictions of Domesticity for Christian Women in Johannesburg, 1903–1939." *Journal of African History.* Vol. 24. 2 (1983): 241–56.

Kaberry, Phyllis. "Retainers and Royal Households in the Grassfields of Cameroon." *Cahiers d'etudes africaines* 3, no. 10 (1962): 282–98.

O'Neil, Robert J. "A History of Moghamo, 1865–1940: Authority and Change in a Cameroon Grassfields Culture." Ph.D. Dissertation, Columbia University, 1987.

Pedersen, S. "National Bodies, Unspeakable Acts: The Sexual Politics of Colonial Policy-making." *Journal of Modern History*, Vol. 63 (1991): 647–80.

Sheldon, K. "I Studied with the Nuns Learning to Make Blouses: Gender Ideology and Colonial Education in Mozambique." *The International Journal of African Historical Studies*. Vol. 31. 3 (1998): 595.

Special Issue on "Gendered Colonialism and African History," *Gender and History*, Vol. 8. 3 (1996).

Special Issue on "Revising the Experiences of Colonized Women: Beyond Binaries." *Journal of Women's History*. Vol. 14. 4 (2003).

Tripp, A. "A New Look at Colonial Women British Teachers and Activists in Uganda, 1898–1962." *Canadian Journal of African Studies*. Vol. 38. 1 (2004).

Warnier, Jean-Paul. "Histoire du Peuplement et Genese des Paysages dans L'Ouest Camerounais." *JAH*. Vol. 25. 4 (1984): 395–410.

Interviews and Personal Communications

*All interviews were conducted by author in the UK, U.S., and Cameroon between 1998 and 2004.

Acha, Emmanuel, interview by author, Guzang, North West Province, Cameroon. December 27, 1998.

Acha, John. Teacher. Interview by author. Tape recording. Batibo, Momo Division, North West Province, Cameroon. December 22, 1998; December 23, 1998; January 17, 1999; February 10, 1999.

Bah Ikan. Quarter/lineage head, Farmer. Interview by author. Tape recording. Batibo, North West Province, Cameroon. December 28, 1998; December 30, 1998; January 15, 1999; February 10, 1999; 14 February 1999.

Bah Quadi [Ndi, Jonas.] Quarter head, Farmer, Court clerk. Interview by author. Tape recording. Batibo, Momo Division, North West Province, Cameroon. December 22, 1998; December 27, 1998; December 28, 1998; December 29, 1998; January 17, 1999; 26 January 1999; February 11, 1999.

Chilver, Elisabeth. Professor Emeritus of History, Oxford University, England. Telephone conversation with author. 22 January1998; February 9, 1999; March 14, 2000; February 8, 2001; April 19, 2001.

Chilver, Elisabeth. Professor Emeritus of History. Interview by author. Tape recording. Oxford University, Oxford, England. August 12, 1998; August 14, 1998.

Fokabo, Esther, interview by author, Batibo. January 18, 1999.

Fon Agwenjang Timah of Anong, Graduate student, Peace corps worker, interview by author, Houston, Texas, June 16, 1999; April 23, 2001; 29 July 2000; 30 July 2000.

Fon Enoh of Ashong. Civil Servant, Farmer. Interview by author. Tape recording.

Ashong, Momo Division, North West Province, Cameroon. December 26, 1998, January 15, 1999.

Fon Forkum of Bessi. Farmer. Interview by author. Tape recording. Bessi Palace, Momo Division, North West Province, Cameroon. December 23, 1998; December 28, 1998.

Fon G. T. Mba II of Batibo, Interview, Batibo, Momo Division. December 20, 1998; December 22, 1998; December 23, 1998; January 15, 1999; January 17, 1999, December 27, 1998; December 29, 1998, 13 January 1999; January 16, 1999.

Fon of Ambo. Interview by author. Tape recording. Ambo, Momo Division, North West Province, Cameroon. December 27, 1998; March 20, 1999.

Fon of Enyoh. Interview by author. Tape recording. Enyoh Palace, Enyoh, Momo Division, North West Province, Cameroon, December 17 and 26, 1998.

Fon of Ewai. Interview by author. Tape recording. Bamenda, Mezam Division, North West Province, Cameroon, December 22, 1998; December 23, 1998; January 15, 1999; January 18, 1999.

Ibort Chu'u. Queen, first wife of the *Fon* of Batibo, mother, grandmother, Mother, Farmer. Interview by author. Tape recording. Batibo Palace, Momo Division, North West Province, Cameroon. December 22, 1998; December 27, 1998; January 15, 1999; January 17, 1999; February 12, 1999.

Ibort Ndam-Shadrack. First Wife, Mother of four, Grandmother, Farmer, Interview by author. Tape recording. Batibo, Momo Division, North West Province, Cameroon. December 22, 1998; January 10, 1999; January 15, 1999; January 17, 1999.

Ma Kurubab, First Wife, Mother, Grandmother, Farmer. Interview by author. Tape recording. Bali, Mezam Division, North West Province, Cameroon. January 16, 1999; January 17, 1999.

Mama Chusana, Mother, Farmer. Interview by author. Tape recording. Kurgwe, Momo Division, North West Province, Cameroon. December 29, 1998; January 15, 1999.

Ma Wumunjong [Dassi, Cecilia]. Princess of Aighwi/Batibo, Daughter of the late *Fon* Acha-Mbah II, First Wife, Mother, Grandmother. Interview by author. Tape recording. Batibo, Momo Division, North West Province, Cameroon. December 22, 1998; January 17, 1999. February 11, 1999.

Mokom, Grace, Interview by author, tape recording, Guzang, North West Province, Cameroon. January 17, 1999.

Njeik, Stanley, Interview by author. Batibo, North West Province, Cameroon. December 22, 1998.

O'Neil, Robert. Historian, Reverend Father. Saint Mary's Parish, New York. Telephone conversation with author. February 12, 1999; 11 March 1999; 15 September 2000.

Pa Anokamba. Bag Weaver, Trader, Farmer. Interview by author. Tape recording. Bessi, Momo Division, North West Province, Cameroon. December 27, 1998; January15, 1999.

Tebit, E. K. Teacher, Farmer. Interview by author. Tape recording. Quojuh, Batibo, Momo Division, North West Province, Cameroon. December 23, 1998, February16, 1999.

Teboh, Esther. Retired Midwife/RNP, Deputy-Mayor Batibo. Former WCNU President, Interview by author. Tape recording. Batibo, Momo Division, North West Province, Cameroon. December 23, 1998; December 27, 1998; 05 January 1999; January 15, 1999; February 15,1999.

_____. Telephone conversation with author, July 8, 1999; September 18, 2000; November 10, 2000; January 17, 2001; March 18, 2001; April 7, 2001; May 28, 2001; August 5, 2001.

Woed Mbebaghi. Kingmaker, Quarter/lineage head, Farmer. Interview by author. Tape recording. Batibo, Momo Division, North West Province, Cameroon. December 22, 1998; December 26, 1998; January 12, 1999; January 15, 1999; January 17, 1999; February 26, 1999.

Chapter 18

Mothers and Grandmothers: Strategies of the Construction of Motherhood in Cape Verde

Andréa de Souza Lobo

Introduction

Among the elderly women I met in Boa Vista,[1] Mrs. Lúcia[2] was special. We bonded in a way that enabled me to visit her home, participate in family events, have an occasional chat, or simply sit on her porch together and watch people coming and going. Mrs. Lúcia is a mother of three. Her husband is a former emigrant who returned from abroad for health reasons and currently lives off memories and limited financial resources saved up during his time abroad. Mrs. Lúcia makes a living doing laundry, which pays household and child-raising expenses. The two youngest children are still in school and the oldest, Zefa, works in the local government. Zefa has a daughter of five and both mother and daughter live at Mrs. Lúcia's house. The young woman maintains a conjugal relationship with the child's father. Every night she leaves home to sleep with him and every day she sends him food by means of a child. Mrs. Lúcia always has her granddaughter at her side, who calls her *mamã* (mommy), while calling her mother by her name.

Mrs. Lúcia often talked to me about caring for a child. In her opinion, young women do not pay proper attention to the little ones; to illustrate, she gave the example of her own daughter:

> Zefa has no time for the girl, too much going on in her head, she has so little time, she gives the girl a cold bath in the middle of the yard, she has no patience to put food in her daughter's mouth, and the child is left hungry. Mrs. Lúcia says the young ladies in Boa Vista have too much on their minds, and that, were it not for grandmothers, who knows how the little ones would get by … The girl sleeps with me, since her mother lies (sleeps) in the father-of-child's bed. I do not trust Zefa to take care of my little granddaughter alone, she has no patience and ends up hitting the girl. She has her own problems, which she needs to work out.

African kinship studies that focus on generation issues are not new in Anthropology. Among the classics, Alfred Radcliffe-Brown suggested equivalence of alternated generations and opposition among close generations. According to the author, friendly equality

---

1. Boa Vista is one of the ten islands that form the Cape Verdean Arquipelago in Africa.
2. All names in this study are fictitious.

between grandmothers and grandchildren has the function of reducing stress resulting from the relationship between parents and children, which in turn are marked by parental authority and severe obligations.[3] Meyer Fortes, in his description of the Tallensi, points to conflicts between parents and children, while Tallensi grandparents 'spoil' their grand-children, are caring and congenial, leaving the responsibilities of discipline and resource allocation to the parents.[4] They see their role in the child's education, personality formation, and reproduction of sociability as important.

Recent studies in the African context, in turn, seek to reflect upon the generational issue through dialogue with our ancestors. The Africa volume under the title "Grandparents and Grandchildren," organized by Susan Whyte, Erdmute Alber, and Wenzel Geissler in 2004, is a reflection of the importance this topic has in contemporary production. In the volume's introduction, the organizers draw attention to the fact that while many authors continue to reproduce the classical image of the relationship between grandmothers and grandchildren as sympathy and friendship, ethnographic situations paint more complex pictures.[5] This is due to the fact that new ethnographies pay attention to everyday practices and the concreteness of substances shared among relatives. These studies focus less on the institutional structure of kinship systems and more on relations constructed in everyday practice. Thus, in addition to perceiving construction of everyday life, they draw attention to the importance of seeing grandmothers and grandchildren in a temporal context, regarding changing patterns in the societies under analysis.

In my case study, involving the Creole society of Cape Verde, in order to understand the central role of women and the relations among women for reproduction of family relationships, the role of grandmothers cannot be overlooked. With arguments in this direction, this article seeks to demonstrate how maternity is not restricted to the mother figure, but involves other women in the sharing of substances which are essential for everyday life—food, bed, house, goods, and values. In this context, an important strategy arises that makes maternity in Cape Verde a particular case: the fact that one generation is not enough to fulfill motherhood, since it requires the joint effort of two generations of women within the family structure. Mother and grandmother are complementary in the task of rearing children and this union defines the local meaning of what a child needs in order to feel happy and supported. Likewise, the exercise of maternity in both stages of life means fulfillment of motherhood for a woman. The article thus presents the argument that being a mother in Cape Verde is a cycle, which begins with the birth of a child and only ends in a definitive manner when the woman becomes a grandmother.

Context

Before proceeding with the analysis of what I call process-oriented maternity and at-tempting to cover relationships among mothers, daughters, and grandchildren, it is necessary to briefly describe the social context in which women become mothers and grandmothers. Throughout 2004 and 2005, for 15 uninterrupted months, I carried out fieldwork on one of the ten islands that make up the Cape Verdean archipelago—the

---

3. Alfred Radcliffe-Brown, "Introduction," Radcliffe-Brown and Darryl Forde (eds.), *African Systems of Kinship and Marriage* (London: Oxford University Press, 1952).

4. Meyer Fortes, *Web of kinship among the Tallensi: The second part of an analysis of the social structure of a trans-volta tribe* (London: Oxford University Press, 1969).

5. Susan Whyte, Erdmute Alber and Wenzel Geissler, *Africa*, 74 Vol. 1 (2004).

Island of Boa Vista. Research was carried out in the population of Vila de Sal-Rei on the topic of female migratory flows and their influence on transformations, which have taken place in local family organization.[6] Sal-Rei is the main village on the island and has approximately 2,500 inhabitants, among the 4,209 residents scattered among the seven small villages in the arid landscape typical of the archipelago.[7] The main economic activity is subsistence farming, although it is not the activity with the most intense financial resource transfers, a place reserved for money sent by emigrant women who live, for the most part, in Italy, working as housemaids.

Cape Verde is an archipelago located on the Atlantic and inhabited since its discovery by the Portuguese in 1460. Its effective occupation took place later in the context of slave trafficking from the African continent to Europe and the Americas. Its process of social formation is, therefore, a result of the meeting between Portuguese and Africans, which started a Creole society, marked by heterogeneity. The country is characterized as a diaspora society, considering its historical specialization of exporting people to all four corners of the world. It is within this context that a type of family organization with apparent ambiguities gains structure—one that is essentially patriarchal, albeit with heavy traits of matricentrality.

In summary, local family organization has the following general characteristics: the significant unit is the extended family. Priority is given to blood relations over conjugal relations; mobility of men, women, and, especially, children among several households is part of family dynamics. The concept of motherhood is more social than biological, considering that a combination of two generations of women is necessary to fulfill social maternity. The household is the central unit, strongly associated with women and children and men have a relationship marked by absence and distance from the children's daily lives, as well as those of the mothers of these children, contributing financially and socially in a sporadic manner. Adult women emigrate, leaving behind family members, children, and the fathers of their children on the island.

Domestic units are heavily centered on the mother or grandmother figure. Women play an important economic role, and, furthermore, predominant conjugal arrangements encourage instability and circulation of men among several domestic units throughout their adult lives. All of this gives women greater weight in family structures. Female centrality is reinforced by family networks, which due to the relative absence of men, are formed by exchanges and sharing of objects, values, and persons. Within this context, sharing is a fundamental category to understand family relations, and this is not limited to genealogical bonds. Analysis of sharing practices, mutual assistance, and solidarity among persons and domestic groups bring forward the fundamental concept of "making families," i.e. strengthening bonds among relatives and creating kinship where there once was none. Given the characteristics of the reality found in Boa Vista, focus should be placed on the family system as a process, which is constructed on a daily basis.

As part of a Creole society, and therefore, the result of a social dynamic in which forces, processes, values, and symbols originating from two civilizations, African and European,

---

6. Andréa Lobo, *Tão Longe e Tão Perto. Organização família e emigração feminina na Ilha de Boa Vista—Cabo Verde* (Doctoral Dissertation presented to the PPGS of the Department of Anthropology of the University of Brasilia, Brasília, 2006).

7. Lobo, *Seca, Chuva e Luta. Reconstruindo a Paisagem em Cabo Verde* (Master's degree dissertation paper presented to the PPGS of Department of Anthropology of the University of Brasilia, 2001), regarding the meaning of arid landscapes in formation of Cape Verdean identity.

are mixed, clashing and interpenetrating, giving birth to a third entity,[8] family organization in Boa Vista reveals competing practices and models that shift between one civilization's orientation and the other. Thus, along with practices that reproduce a family system such as the one described above, there are also values based on a nuclear family model, consisting of a couple residing with their children, as in Europe, and regarded as ideal, especially by women. We have, on the one hand, practices reproducing traditional forms (coherent with what is understood as African custom) of family organization, and, on the other, existence of an ideal model coveted but never attained.

The Value of Grandmothers

In order to understand the central role of women and of the relationship among women for reproduction of family relations in Cape Verde, grandmothers cannot be overlooked. Differently from what takes place in Western culture,[9] in which elderly women are often regarded as inactive and even marginal, grandmothers in Boa Vista play an important role in decision-making processes and exert strong influence on the household. When considering having children, it is a given that the mother will not raise the child by herself, but he or she will be *agüentado* (taken care of) by family members, ideally the maternal grandmother.

Responsibility over children of their daughters is an important aspect in the life of Boa Vista women. This responsibility begins with the daughter's first pregnancy, which nearly always happens when she is still living in the family household, and comprehends the child's entire lifecycle. Prior to giving birth, which is a period during which doubts may arise regarding paternity, it is the mother of the pregnant woman who provides the most emotional and financial assistance. She is also the one who takes charge of negotiations involving recognition of paternity by the likely father and his family. After birth, particularly in the first years, the maternal grandmother is a central figure in the child's daily life.

Differences in the relations between grandmothers and grandchildren depend on temporal factors—and the position of each person in the family context—children of children in marriage or not, children of emigrated daughters, children of sons, or children of daughters, etc. Nevertheless, even when full sharing between grandmothers and grandchildren is not possible, the strong relationship between them will take place due to the centrality of the woman-grandmother in the family context in question. When all three generations—grandmother, daughter-mother, and child-grandchild—live in the same household, both adult women share responsibilities in caring for the child. It generally falls upon the mother to breast feed and search for means for supporting the child. The main assistance of the grandmother is concentrated on the practical day-to-day aspects;

---

8. Wilson Trajano Filho, "Some problems with the Creole Project for the Nation: the case of Guinea-Bissau," Paper presented at the Seminar Powerful Presence of the Past, at the Max Planck Institute, Halle, Germany in 2006.

9. Recent studies have approached changes in the Western family context, in which the role of grandparents in grandchild rearing has undergone significant changes. For more information regarding this topic see Myriam Lins de Barros, *Autoridade e afeto: avós, filhos e netos na sociedade brasileira* (Rio de Jan eiro: Jorge Zahar, 1987); Catherine Goodman and Merril Silverstein, "Grandmothers raising grandchildren: family structure and well-being in culturally diverse families," *The Gerontologist,* Vol. 42. 5 (2002): 676–89; Ewellyne Suely de Lima Lopes, Anita Neri Liberalesso, and Margareth Brandini, "Ser avós ou ser pais: os papeis dos avós na sociedade contemporânea," *Textos Enbelhecimento,* Vol. 8. 2 (2005): 1–10.

it is she who spends the most time with the child, cares for hygiene and, after the breastfeeding period, feeds, puts to sleep, and reprehends. Caring for children, as well as doing *mandados* (household chores) and preparation of food in a Boa Vista home, are not responsibilities of a single woman, but are shared between them. In turn, like women, children are at the center of attention in the domestic universe, receiving care from different people.

I fail to see, in Boa Vista, a fixed differentiation, which classifies relationship as grandmother/grandchild equals proximity and affection and mother/son and equals distance and authority. Affection and authority characterize both relations. Children are given care and attention, but authority is also imposed. In this regard, mothers and grandmothers are not different. What changes is the form in which they experience this, the manner in which they give care and how this feeling is seen by children or grandchildren. The feelings involved in *agüentar* (caring for) a child vary over time, experienced in a different manner by mothers and grandmothers. In daily life, it is not alarming or controversial if the maternal grandmother *agüentar* (takes care of) one or more grandchildren. Differently from the western ideal that "whoever gives birth to the child should care for it," being a grandmother in Boa Vista presupposes effective participation in the process of raising the child, and, in most cases, a feeling of responsibility toward the grandchildren. In times of crisis, this is seen with more clarity, for example, when the mother and father fight over guardianship of a child in justice, and it is given to the maternal grandmother. On the other hand, when a grandmother refuses to *ajudar* (help) the daughter with her child and is reprimanded by community members by means of gossip.

Daughters, in turn, expect *ajuda* (help) from their mothers raising their children. It should be made clear that this is not a source of anxiety or debate, but simply how things happen and should happen. In everyday situations, taking care of a grandchild or allowing a mother to take care of one's child is not the topic of negotiations between the two women, it is a given. If there are deviations from this expected behavior, negotiations are started and there may be rumors and conflicts, which mobilize the family and even the entire community. The case presented at the start of this article highlights an important factor in the relationships among mothers, daughters, and grandchildren: grandmothers are calm. I heard this a few times when these women attempted to explain the reason behind their dedication to grandchildren, often-leaving little space for mothers to perform daily tasks such as feeding, bathing, and reprimanding their children. As they explained, young women are not calm enough to take care of a child, since they are too concerned and anxious about other things (work, fun, and men). They thus lose their temper, hit children needlessly, and do not take proper care of them. The expression used by them is that the women *do not have time* for these things.

In the account by Mrs. Lúcia, this expression is employed a few times to define the type of relationship between the young mother and her daughter. Not having time marks the ambiguity of being a mother in a conjugal context characterized by male instability and mobility, in which the woman is, at the same time, the center of reproduction of family relations, responsible for economic aspects, and the source of emotional intimacy. The complex universe of a young mother, therefore, justifies her lack of time and the need for a network structure, which complements their functions in rearing children. Grandchildren can tell the difference. Grandmothers are stable, usually not going beyond the space of their houses and neighborhoods, therefore being associated with the domestic universe. Furthermore, they are no longer occupied with unfaithful companions or rival women. They *have time*, since they are no longer involved in constant demands coming from outside the household. At an age in which children are a part of, and dependent upon, the household and the female universe, identification with the grandmother is total.

It is important to clarify that mothers are not regarded as negligent toward their children—one must bear in mind that the mother is identified as a central figure in the child's process of formation, and she is the main person responsible for supporting and transmitting values and emotional comfort to this child. The position of the mother is justified by her situation, i.e. part of the experience of being a woman is a period in which she should be more dedicated to other tasks than daily care for children. In order for this to happen, the structural system of Boa Vista families enables them to step out strategically without this causing traumas or feelings of abandonment in children.

The reasons for living with the grandmother are many, from situations in which everyone lives together in a house, going either through financial difficulties or due to the mother's emigration, or even the simple wishes of grandmothers or children. Living with one's grandmother is a valid option, not restricted to special occasions. Mobility seems to be the key here; the child may be with the mother or the maternal grandmother, as well as spending periods with the paternal grandmother or in the house of another family member. One way or the other, 'living with' does not necessarily imply a fixed or permanent arrangement in one's life, and this is valid for a child's life. What makes the maternal grandmother special is the fact that she is identified as the central member in concepts of house and family.

The Value of Grandchildren

Nha Celeste had ten children. Three of them have lived in Italy for many years. One made a living for herself there, married a white man, had a son who is also married, and who has given her a great-granddaughter. They have never come to Boa Vista and Nha Celeste does not know her granddaughter. Nevertheless, the daughter is considered a good daughter, since she sends support to the mother whenever possible. In our conversations, the topic of choice for Nha Celeste was her grandchildren; she told of the love they all have for her and how proud she was to be called *mamã*. All 17 grandchildren call her this way and she beams with pride whenever she mentions it. She also told me that all of them, even after becoming adults, come visit her every day, because they like to see *mamã* and enjoy her cooking. Some grandchildren still live with her, while others only spend the day in her house when their mothers are out working. When I asked if she did not get tired of having to *agüentar* (caring for) grandchildren, she found my question strange, limiting her response to: "they are my company, my children are out making a living! Were it not for them, I don't know what my life would be like, or this man's here (pointing to the sick husband on a chair)." Having grandchildren who partake in food, room, and board make a grandmother out of a woman. If she cooks for her grandchildren and provides comfort, in turn, it is up to the grandchildren to assist the grandmother in all household chores, giving in return respect, emotional comfort, and ensuring reproduction of the home.

Having a daughter's child nearby is a central characteristic in the organization of a home and is a common means of strengthening social relations and bonds and exercising motherhood in this society. Grandchildren are generally integrated in daily chores; boys and girls help in women's tasks such as cooking, cleaning, and transporting water, firewood, or food. In summary, they are important for completing many *mandados* (household chores) that grandmothers are no longer fit to accomplish. The presence of grandchildren also helps guarantee transfers of resources from the older generation, such as food and financial assistance, particularly if the parents of the children are abroad.

Lastly, it is also up to the grandchildren to take care of and keep the grandmothers company, i.e. they mediate duties between one generation and the next, between daughters and their mothers.

It is important for children to live close to their grandmothers and find in them a safe haven of emotional support. Likewise, children are fundamental links between generations. In this system, children of unmarried daughters are of special importance to grandmothers. As the young woman matures and builds a stable conjugal relationship, the possibility of grandchildren who are no longer living with their grandmothers increases, coming by to visit only. Physical proximity and sharing turn a woman into a grandmother in the meaning giving to it in Boa Vista. Grandmothers enjoy the presence of grandchildren and take pleasure from the company of children during a stage of life in which their own children are dedicated to construction of their adult lives in a society, which sees in emigration the best alternative for their reproduction. However, in addition to emotional comfort, being together with grandchildren guarantees maintenance of rights. Not having grandchildren at home means abandonment and loss in various ways. Grandchildren ensure that children maintain substantial financial contributions for economic security at an advanced age. Among families with which I maintained regular contact, 84 per cent of the grandmothers supported one or more grandchildren, 37 per cent of which received financial support from mothers or fathers of the children.

A good life for these women is one surrounded by children and grandchildren. Children are a type of link between relations, making them add up. Development of the domestic cycle, as understood by Fortes,[10] ends with the dispersion stage, in which grown children tend to form new units and elderly parents tend to be left alone. The ideal structure in Boa Vista involves children staying for a long time and grandchildren becoming incorporated into the unit. In a sense, grandchildren represent continuation of the relationship with daughters, taking on daily functions that were once the daughters', and ensure their fidelity at a stage of the domestic cycle characterized by dispersion and 'empty nests.'

Children of Emigrated Daughters

We have seen that the central role of grandmothers is not limited to special or crisis situations. We have also seen that relations between grandmothers and grandchildren, although always central, vary according to situations and choices in life. Thus, the question of how the relations among grandmothers-mothers-children take place should be explored in the case of emigrant mothers. I understand that the focus on grandchildren should be regarded in two senses: firstly, being a grandmother is part of a woman's inter-subjective experience, a time of intimacy with grandchildren and maintenance of bonds with daughters; secondly, the relationship with children of daughters has a mediated character. This second aspect is fundamental for understanding the role grandmothers play in cases of emigration.

The grandmother is the ideal candidate to take care of children of a mother who wishes to emigrate. Ideally, she is best suited to take the place of the mother in case of her absence. An important factor for a child's stability is the fact that he or she is already accustomed to the grandmother, since even in the presence of the mother; he or she spends most of his or her time with the grandmother, making them used to her and not wishing to leave

---

10. Fortes, *O Ciclo de Desenvolvimento do Grupo Doméstico* (Brasília: UnB, 1974).

her. Therefore, this is the ideal situation for the child's well-being. On the other hand, it is also the ideal situation for mothers and grandmothers. Children regret living apart from their mothers and being more intimate with their grandmothers, aunts, or older sisters. However, if there is a feeling of loss on the part of children, there is also in their accounts a profound feeling when it comes to mothers. They acknowledge and appreciate not only the effort made by these women to give them a better life, but, especially, the concern they have, even from a distance, to be a part of their lives and someone who can be relied upon. This proximity between mothers and their children is constructed and encouraged by the maternal family in the child's daily life, particularly by grandmothers. Grandmothers play a fundamental role in this context of mediator between mother and child.

Grandchildren call their grandmother *mamã* and, on many occasions, claim that the grandmother is their "true mother." Some of these children do not recall living with the biological mother, since she emigrated early in their lives. Such facts could lead us to believe that in emigration situations there would be generational confusions between mother and grandmother. However, field data demonstrate that this is not what happens. It is clear from the accounts of these women that being a mother is different from being a grandmother and that the fact that *agüentar* (caring for) children is part of the context of assistance, a central category in the female family universe and in the perception of motherhood as social.

It is clear that the division of tasks takes on new arrangements when the mother is not present, including the relationship of the child with extra-domestic contexts. In addition to becoming the main (and sometimes only) source of emotional support for a child, the grandmother ends up accumulating positions administrating contexts of their grandchildren's lives that would normally be the responsibility of the mother. All of these factors may lead to generational confusion between mother and grandmother, and, in fact, this may happen at some stage in the child's life. However, the role expected of grandmothers is of mediating mother and child relationships in order to guarantee that the role of the former is well defined and appreciated by the latter. Let us proceed to an ethnographical case.

Mrs. Joaninha's daughter left for Italy before Joyce was one year old. The grandmother took in the child and, due to difficulties in regularizing her situation as an immigrant, the woman had been gone for four years when I met Mrs. Joaninha and her little granddaughter. Seven other people lived in the house, including children and other grandchildren, since Mrs. Joaninha was a widow. The other grandchildren were jealous of the relationship between Joyce and her grandmother, since according to them the girl was her "royal granddaughter." When Mrs. Joaninha heard such complaints, she justified herself by saying:

> I like all my grandchildren and children the same, they are all mine! But Joyce's mother is away, and the burden is mine! Although my daughter is always present in her life, sending little things whenever she can and helping me bear the burden! That is why I always tell her: girl, it was your mother who sent you this outfit, resulting from a lot of hard work in Italy, working in other people's houses just to help us out! I do this because it is the mother who bore the child, right? Every mother needs her value acknowledged and I know my daughter suffers a lot abroad! The poor girl, were it not for the pictures I show her everyday, wouldn't recognize her mother on the street if she saw her.

I met many grandmothers with behavior similar to that of Mrs. Joaninha. Despite taking pride in their grandchildren's acknowledgement, the clearest expression of which is calling them *mamã*, they take on the responsibility of keeping the biological mother constantly alive in the lives of the children. In order to accomplish that, they constantly talk about the mothers, reporting on their sacrifice, showing pictures. They stress additionally that this or that piece of clothing or toy was sent by the mother abroad. In spite of that, it is common for a child to become confused up to a certain age. Chico, raised by his grandmother and apart from his mother since the age of one, told me that when he was little he could not really tell who was who in his life. He knew he had a mother in Italy and that she sent him things and paid for his education, but he "had this mother thing a little mixed up, since I lived with my grandmother and rarely saw my mother. As I grew up with my grandmother explaining everything, I understood the role of each woman in my life and the place they hold."

It is therefore necessary to take into consideration the mediated quality and complement this relation. Understanding this aspect is fundamental to understanding the place of the grandmother. Being a grandmother is not the same as being a mother, but a grandmother is also a mother. On the other hand, a grandchild is not a child, but a daughter's child. Differently from other African societies that consider there to be a confusion of roles between mothers and grandmothers, accounts by Boa Vista women insist that there is a clear distinction between grandmothers' relationships with grandchildren and mothers' relationships with children. My data show that, and as stated by Catrien Notermans, when speaking of generational confusion in African societies, for these women, being a mother and being a grandmother are distinct experiences.[11] Although mothers and grandmothers are fluid categories, they are experienced in distinct manners in a woman's life cycle. As for children, they speak to their grandmothers as if they were their 'mothers' and can often not identify a mother other than the grandmother. It is up to the latter to be careful enough to make the child aware of his or her biological mother and to nurture feelings of love. As experienced in the case of Mrs. Joaninha, I frequently heard grandmothers reminding grandchildren of their mothers, putting the children on the phone with them and insisting that there is no ambition to take the place of the mother, since "the mother is she who bore the child." Reinforcing this picture, I recall that every time children talk about their *mamã* to someone else, they use the term *nha avó* (my grandmother).

How, then, should this apparent confusion of roles between women and children be understood? Rather than simply discussing generational confusion or equivalence of roles, I see tension in this context. There is tension between a system that emerges from a local practice based on a structure of relations between matrifocal families, which employ the concept of social maternity and a Christian and biologized model of family in which the "mother is she who bore the child." In Boa Vista, two generations are required to fulfill the role of *agüentar* (caring for) children. Maternity cannot possibly be exercised in a single generation because it is centered on complementarity between women. Since children are an important value in a context in which conjugal relations are not stable and there are no corporate groups — i.e. a bilateral yet matricentered system — tension is observed between grandmother and mother rather than equivalence between grandmothers and grandchildren. The place of mediation between mother and children occupied by grandmothers is fundamental for those involved, but emerges against a background of tension between the two models. Mother and *mamã* are two faces of maternity. Being a *mamã* comes later, when one becomes a grandmother. When younger, this woman

---

11. Catrien Notermans, "Sharing home, food and bed: paths of grandmotherhood in East Cameroon," *África*, Vol. 74. 1 (2004): 28–46.

was a mother, but could not have been a *mamã*. The maternity cycle is a process only concluded, thus, when one becomes a grandmother. The grandmother-daughter-grandchild relationship therefore has a special character, not excluding or diminishing the importance of the mother. On the contrary, it joins the women, in the end strengthening the network of relations, which might be broken in the absence of one of its members. Is this complementarity, however, free of tensions?

Competition or Complementarity?

During my fieldwork, at times I was able to observe that the bonds between children and grandmothers living in the same household are stronger in terms of affection than those with mothers. This observation resulted from practical factors, which I monitored, such as everyday rites of sharing and naming. Grandmothers and grandchildren share the daily life of the household (domestic production, consumption, and daily care) and grandchildren refer to the grandmother by using the term *mamã*. Both are central in the daily life of an individual and constitute what I call relatedness. In this context, if kinship in Boa Vista has a strong character of a relationship constructed over the daily life of living together, could we affirm that the grandmother holds a more central place than the mother in the life of a child?

It does not strike me as correct to claim that there is some kind of competition between mothers and grandmothers, in which the latter holds an advantage over the former. Although tensions inherent to the system cannot be denied, what indeed exists is complementarity of functions and forms of treatment, which result from situations in the lives of these women. Maternity, as it is regarded in Boa Vista, is not limited to the figure of the mother, but has a meaning that encompasses other women sharing substances that are essential for daily life—food, room and board, goods, and values. Additionally, the particular nature of this case is that one generation is not enough and that maternity requires the coordinated efforts of two generations of women within these matrifocal families.

In the absence of men as stable figures (i.e. someone who can be relied upon), the union of two women in different stages of life is necessary in order to raise a child. Mother and *mamã* come together in the task of caring for and feeding. This union gives meaning to the local sense of what a child needs in order to be happy and supported, with differentiated attention from mother and *mamã*. Likewise, exercising maternity at both stages of life means complete exercise of maternity for a woman. Being a mother is a cycle, which starts with the birth of a child and the possibility of being a mother is only fulfilled when a woman has the opportunity to become a *mamã*.

Being a mother and being a grandmother are distinct yet complementary. They are distinct stages of the experience, which complement each other in everyday rites of taking care of the house, family, and children. If development of the domestic cycle is taken into account, it becomes possible to better understand this argument. When young women begin to bear children, the mother is on her way to a stage of greater tranquility and relative stability. With or without a partner, this woman is already responsible for her domestic unit and for maintenance of those living in it. As in the case of our informant (Mrs. Lúcia), the grandmother-woman takes on the responsibility of daily care for the grandchildren living in her unit since she believes she is in better conditions to *agüentar* (caring for) the children. In the cases of grandchildren not living in the same house, relatedness is also nurtured, both being charged with obligations of visiting and reciprocal exchanges.[12]

It is important to make clear that this relationship is not simply defined by the generational position, rather being molded socially depending on the domestic context, and, especially, on gender relations. The life of an adult woman is divided into two stages. The stage when the woman is a young mother, she is under the authority of another (or others), but in spite of that she is the center of production and reproduction of the household; and when she is a grandmother, she gradually steps away from the productive and sexual-reproductive context and into that of domestic authority. This context of sexuality is fundamental for the type of relationship between woman and child at both stages of a woman's life, as well as for the relationship of complementariness between the two women involved. A woman generally becomes a mother while still very young and at a stage in which conjugal relations are marked by instability. Additionally, this stage is also marked by economic instability of the woman. She, therefore, must divide her time between her job, which generates income, and the household, children, and the man with whom she maintains a relationship as well as do her tasks in the household of origin. Therefore, during a day, she circulates between house and work, or in situations in which income is generated from domestic production, she occupies herself with the various daily chores. At night, as seen in the account at the start of this article, the mother dedicates herself to her man. Since it is common for them to live in different houses, women leave home to sleep in their partners' beds, leaving children behind with their grandmothers. Sleeping together plays an important role in maintenance of a conjugal relationship. It nurtures the feeling of proximity in the couple, giving the woman a sense of stability, in addition to allowing her to keep her partner in her attention—after all, if he is sleeping with her, he is not out with other women.

Therefore, a mother has to divide herself to be with family, men, and children, both in daily chores and in bed. According to grandmothers, this division leaves them anxious and tense; a state, that is not aligned with the care a small child needs. For young women, concerned with conjugal life, they require time and mobility, and a child could be a hindrance. It is common, in pregnancies, for friends and family members to judge the young woman as stupid, since a child makes a woman *get stuck* after pregnancy, which facilitates mobility of men in their relationships with other women. On the other hand, having a child is an important value for men and women, and is often seen by them as a potential link of stability in a conjugal relationship.[13] In this regard, organization of the domestic routine itself, with great emphasis placed on relations between women, removes exclusivity of the biological mother with children and presupposes circulation of responsibilities with them among women in the family, especially the grandmother. The child, who under these circumstances could be seen as a burden, is regarded as a gift or an asset

---

12. The relationship with the paternal grandmother is a good example. Once conflicts regarding paternity have been worked out, the relationship with the paternal grandmother is also of great importance. As in most cases the child lives with the mother in the house of the maternal family, the paternal grandmother being expected to visit the grandchild and the grandchild to visit her, being regarded as good if grandchildren spend a few nights with her, and, depending on circumstances, live with her. Children and grandmothers establish a fundamental connection between families, a connection that overcomes matters related to conjugality, but that is connected to it by the male figure.

13. In a mother-father relationship, although a child is no guarantee of stability, he or she is a link, which may ensure that the man always returns to this woman. Furthermore, through the relationship with the paternal grandmother, the child is an important link between both families.

for mothers and grandmothers who balance system tensions by means of complementarity of functions.

If the notion of matricentrality with which we have been working is taken into consideration, and the accounts of these grandmothers are analyzed, we see that a grandmother is also a mother. This, of course, is experienced in a distinct manner by grandmothers, daughters, and grandchildren. The perspectives regarding the value of children change depending on the position individuals hold within the social structure. It is worthy of note that within traditional standards, grandmothers and mothers complement each other in the domestic context, in a notion of maternity as a process not limited to a single woman, but extended to other women in the family, causing no emotional losses to the children, who always have someone to fill the role of *mamã*. This structure becomes a problem when analyzed from the standpoint of tension between it and an idealization of the Western Christian model of a nuclear family, which is increasingly present in Boa Vista as a sign of 'modern times.'

Modern Times

Substantial changes have taken place in the local context since discovery of the island's natural beauty by Europeans and the resulting inflow of tourists, with reflections affecting not only relationships between grandmothers and grandchildren, but also family relations in general. These changes are seen in a differentiated manner depending on the position of individuals in the domestic group and their position in the social structure: grandmothers are the ones who see the process as the most negative, as a loss of something. For younger people, changes are positive, since they bring about new possibilities of interaction with the outside world. Mothers have an ambivalent view. Although they wish to meet their children's needs, they are not considered fit to take on the responsibility of a child without making use of assistance networks.

One factor that has influenced traditional standards of grandchildren living with grandmothers is the Western image of family transmitted by the Catholic Church and media. Younger women begin to show signs of wanting what they call a *normal* family; one in which the conjugal couple lives in the same house and parents help raise children together. One of the greatest inconveniences, in the parents' opinion, of leaving children in the care of an older person is the low value given to modern aspects of life, which have started to become incorporated into the daily life of the island: school, entertainment, and hygiene. Grandmothers do not monitor grandchildren's performance in school, and due to household chores, they take children's attention away from what should be primarily from education. On the other hand, due to the generational distance, they do not feel fit to control and keep up with the novelties in terms of juvenile entertainment (pubs and nightclubs). Grandchildren use this in their favor and claim they prefer to be with their grandmothers not only because they are more patient and attentive, but also because with them they have greater freedom to go out. However, there is a downside: they must lead their life in a traditional fashion, do *mandados* (household chores), and share their food, living spaces, and resources with a greater number of people. In a traditional context, when speaking of their own lives, conversations with elderly ladies can go in one of two opposite directions: (1) concern about aging, waning health, intense poverty, solitude, loss of caring and respect; and (2) benefits of aging. Being 'grown up' is something positive, a synonym of stability and authority. The elderly woman is able to center her performance on the family and is, thus, identified as its center.

However, when their lives are put into a context of changes brought about by modern times, the balance is broken. Faced with new options, houses with more resources lure children and teenagers, removing them at increasingly younger ages from the universe the grandmother provides. Their interpretation is that traditional rules of respect no longer have the strength they once did. A concern thus arises: who can help grandmothers with daily chores in these new times? Nha Tereza raised nearly ten grandchildren in her house and currently complains about how they are all grown and no longer need her, she has no one helps her with chores anymore:

> If I want to buy two pounds of rice, young lady, I have to sit in this yard and hope that one of God's children will come knocking at my door so I can ask this someone to run an errand for me! Granddaughters (there are four still living with her) wake up early, have breakfast and go out into the world, telling me they are going to school, but I think they are wandering around all day long! What I do know for sure is that they no longer need their grandmother for anything and that's why they don't even ask if I need an onion to prepare lunch! No one but these two cats here keeps me company nowadays, young lady! This is how the world is now, when we are no longer useful, we get tossed out.

In the daily life at Nha Tereza's home, she observes that granddaughters respect her and do not talk back to her, although they no longer enjoy her company as children used to. What I saw in this relationship was a type of formal respect that younger ones should show toward elders, but there is little sharing in daily life. This takes us to a reflection about reciprocity between grandmothers and grandchildren at different stages of life.

The theoretical transmission line I use to discuss family organization in Cape Verde is the concept of proximity (and consequently, distance). To that end, I have reflected on notions of kinship in modern anthropology by means of the concept of relatedness by Janet Carsten.[14] Having something in common is the basis of relatedness—sharing, exchanges of goods, services, emotions, reproduction, and meaning make up the essence for construction of relations among blood relatives. The matricentered family is thus the ideal space for reciprocity. However, if reciprocity is broken, kinship relations fade to the point of becoming mere memories. Regarding relationships between grandmothers and grandchildren, the quality of the affection and the importance of grandmothers in vertical offspring relations are fundamental factors for their reproduction and reproduction of the system as a whole.

Nevertheless, family relations are generally contextual and contingent, relative to strategic positions, which are constantly being reconstructed. Different perspectives regarding grandmothers and grandchildren demonstrate that roles are not fixed, but fluid and flexible, with room for negotiations, which alter relations. Personal and social identities are influenced by the forms with which others see them and behave in relation to them. It is not given, but constructed and reconstructed on a daily basis. Social and historic processes affect relations between grandmothers and grandchildren. As we have seen, the meaning of being a grandmother is not the same in situations of daily life as in cases of emigration or family crises. As with all other social relations, the quality of the relation between grandmother and grandchild is not static, but must rather be understood over time and regarding changing patterns.

---

14. Janet Carsten, *After Kinship* (Cambridge: Cambridge University Press, 2004).

The *Other* Family

The quality of the relations between grandmothers and grandchildren is closely related to the ease with which children find mobility in Cape Verdean society—a topic widely discussed in several African contexts. Esther Goody,[15] in her study of the Western African Gonjas, shows that children circulate with the objective of intertwining geographically dispersed branches of the family group. When speaking of circulation of children, the author differentiates crisis circulation and volunteer circulation. In the latter case, the objective is to solidify kinship bonds, the child being one of the family's assets. Fostering, thus, could not be understood in terms of children's micro-movements, but as a means of reproduction and replication of society. This hypothesis leads us to a reflection about some aspects of the Boa Vista case. The ease children have of circulating among homes makes up for several tendencies, which might otherwise weaken the solidarity of the family group as a whole. When caring for a grandchild, for example, a grandmother justifies her requests that their own children provide support, be it material or affection. Grandmothers receive special benefits when caring for a grandchild: chances of receiving support from their children increase and the right to demand support from the network of relatives is consolidated.

In emigration situations, depending on the relationship established between mothers and children at a distance, mothers do not feel that they have abandoned their children, who, in turn, do not feel abandoned. Leaving children with their grandmothers, even the maternal (preferred) grandmother, implies sacrifice by the mother in exchange for the benefit to the children and family group. Whoever keeps the children sees this act as solidarity and a possible way to maintain and intensify relations. Furthermore, the company of children gives a special meaning to the daily routines of grandmothers, adding pleasure and fun. Children are not a burden, but a gift. *Agüentar* (caring for) a child fills one's day, ensuring social interaction with neighbors, enabling sharing of household errands, providing a source of affection, and creating a link between mothers and daughters.

Among other strategies, sharing children reduces the threat of loosening solidarity among relatives originated from appreciation of social mobility. Understanding movement of children through time and space, between generations and homes, is not a problem, but a process, which is part of the social dynamics. This allows us to see Boa Vista family organization not as an alternative model (which exists only if there is an ideal model), or much less as an anomaly, rather, simply as a different form of social organization. Like ours, it is a system among many others. In a context in which relations among relatives are more constructed than biologically established, the concept of motherhood is also more social than biological.

The relationship between mother and child, albeit central, is only one element within the family context. Each individual is involved in a network of shared blood, which requires constant demonstration of solidarity (blood ties take precedence over contractual relations), and children are important parts in these relations. The woman who gives birth has a network of solidarity to raise the child, since one rarely takes care of a child alone. Judith Modell states that circulation of children is a means of reproduction and, as such, an appreciated resource subject to various competing interests.[16] Therefore, more

---

15. Ester Goody, *Parenthood and social reproduction: fostering and occupational roles in West Africa* (Cambridge: Cambridge University Press, 1982).

16. Judith Modell, "Rights to the children: fosters care and social reproduction in Hawaii," Sarah Franklin and Helena Ragoré, (Eds.), *Reproducing Reproduction. Kinship, towers and technological innovation* (Philadelphia: University of Pennsylvania Press, 1998).

than production of children, their distribution must be taken into account. In Boa Vista, both are facilitated by the organization of domestic routines, which favors circulation within the maternal family, since it does not idealize conjugality as a pre-requisite for procreation, which means children are born, generally, when the mother is still living with her parents.

The figure of the maternal grandmother is the main point of support for a young mother, and, ideally, this grandmother is entitled and charged with sharing maternity with her daughter. This results in the fact that it is not necessarily the mother who will raise the child and that both biological mother and maternal grandmother (or, occasionally, the other), can share the social identity of mother. Depending on the context, this can be a source of tension between those involved. Particularly in cases of emigration by the mother, a situation in which (in spite of efforts and strategies to maintain proximity at a distance) she is at risk of seeing her influence diminished in the daily lives of children, although this relationship is better defined by complementarity.

Studies about African societies demonstrate that people are greatly appreciated, and more importantly, are seen as a sort of social and political 'capital,' each individual adding many advantages to the group. With the person as a fundamental value, rights in persons are brought, in this context, into the spotlight, with the possibility of the status of each individual being thought of as the set of rights he or she has over other persons or objects, as well as additional corresponding duties. It is important to bear in mind that rights in persons may be transferred, resulting in compensation or indemnization. In the scope of kinship, there is a possibility of manipulation of these rights to increase the number of people under control of one individual and the forms with which transfers of rights take place are of fundamental importance in the African context.[17]

This discussion, regarding Boa Vista families, allows us to see children as a fundamental value, by observing the value of people in a society characterized by scarce resources, exporting of its members and the importance of family life. Women who have children know the immediate and long-term value of that child. That is, a baby is at the center of reproduction of relations among relatives and neighbors, encourages visits, creates reasons for festivities, and brings together women from the mother's and father's families; the child, from the age of six or seven, performs household services, keeps company and circulates among homes; and the adult sons or daughters help support the elderly. Faced with the impossibility of taking care of a child alone, created by the family system itself, the ideal person with whom a mother may share the value of children is her own mother, the child's maternal grandmother. As demonstrated here, for the maternal grandmother, a grandchild is an asset, which ensures her centrality in the domestic context. For the child's mother, leaving her child with the maternal grandmother may be a guarantee of always being remembered as a good mother, even in cases of long-lasting physical distance. The value of children also extends geographically, since they are a fundamental link between the families of mother and father, other relatives and neighbors. The woman should, therefore, share her children the same way she shares food, material goods, and information. In a matrifocal system, all female production involves creation and maintenance of relations and mobility of children is a component of this: it reproduces female centrality and increases the number of women to whom an individual owes loyalty.

---

17. For more in this regard, see Igor Kopytoff and Suzanne Miers, "African Slavery as an Institution of Marginality," Kopytoff and Miers, (Eds.), *Slavery in Africa: Historical and Anthropological Perspectives* (Madison: University of Wisconsin Press,1979); David Parkin and David Niamwaya, *Transformations of African Marriage* (Manchester: Manchester University Press, 1987); Radcliffe-Brown, 1952.

In turn, children and teenagers have, by means of their relations with women (from the paternal and maternal families), a safe source of emotional comfort and transmission of material goods and values.

Fortes and Radcliffe-Brown explained belonging as a fundamental part of the life of individuals in African societies. For instance, among the Tallensi, the principle of lineage enables one to seek support from his or her kin on any subject, i.e. individuals sharing a lineage grow up together, visit one another, identify themselves with others, and behave in the same manner in corporate dealings. Furthermore, they know each other's stories in detail, which is a real strength in the corporate life of lineage and community. In a society such as Boa Vista, marked by the absence of groups with these characteristics, other mechanisms for producing and reproducing solidarity are necessary. Family groups thus assume a special character, a fruitful space for construction of relations of belonging and transmission of goods and values. If this privileged space is marked by the distant character of man as father and companion, female centrality seems to be, by excellence, the space of belonging.

Naming is important in this context. As stated by Christian Geffray, all members in a society are categorized by means of a series of distinctive linguistic operations that identify them. Words allow the speaker to name people who emerge at each of the structural moments of material and social reproduction of his or her community.[18] When calling grandmothers *mamã*, grandchildren are simply making a generational confusion, but they understand the category of mother as transcending the figure of the biological mother and incorporating women from a different generation. In other words, two generations are necessary in order for maternity to be fulfilled in Boa Vista.

However, it should be made clear that categories are fluid and there is always a possibility that individuals will use the options their system provides depending on their interest or the position they hold in the social structure. By observing the cycle of domestic development, it is possible to see that individuals change positions and perspectives depending on the stage they are in their life. Likewise, in today's Boa Vista, in order to talk about families, it is necessary to take into consideration not only their internal cycle, but also several aspects of the social structure in times of rapid changes. The main tension points, which emerge from this social framework, have to do with the shock between a traditional model as the one characterized and analyzed here and the growing reference to an ideal Western nuclear family, present in the accounts of individuals, under the category 'new times.' As a result, of this tension, new forms of establishing a position in everyday practice arise. Grandmothers, when asked about their relationship with grandchildren, emphasize that the "mother is she who bore the child," opposing, at the level of discourse, the characteristic of shared motherhood that I observed in the daily lives of the families. Grandchildren, especially when younger, begin to appreciate what they call a "normal family" and to lose interest in what grandmothers have to offer. Mothers, at increasingly early stages, seek options to construct their domestic space according to European standards of residence and family organization.

Upon approaching the relations between grandmothers and grandchildren in the Cape Verdean context, their characteristics, and modifications that have taken place in the quality of these relations, we have reached an important point: the nuclear family model is an analytical concept manifested not only empirically in some cases, but also as an idea defined in social imagination.[19] The process-oriented maternity or circulation of children

---

18. Christian Geffray, *Ni pere ni mere: Critique de la parente: le cas makhuwa* (Paris: Du Seuil, 1990).

19. Claudia Fonseca, "Mãe é uma só? Reflexões em torno de alguns casos brasileiros," *Psicologia USP*, Vol. 13. 2 (2002): 1–12.

analyzed in Boa Vista are, therefore, categories for analysis ethnographically apprehended from a social practice that reproduces itself in opposition to this model, allowing us to ponder—always considering classical ethnology—the complexity of kinship dynamics. The case presented here is only one more example.

References

Barros, Myriam Lins de. *Autoridade e afeto: avós, filhos e netos na sociedade brasileira*. Rio de Jan eiro: Jorge Zahar, 1987.

Carsten, Janet. *After Kinship*. Cambridge: Cambridge University Press, 2004.

Fonseca, Claudia. "Mãe é uma só? Reflexões em torno de alguns casos brasileiros." *Psicologia USP*. Vol. 13. 2 (2002): 1–12.

Fortes, Meyer. *Web of kinship among the Tallensi: The second part of an analysis of the social structure of a trans-volta tribe*. London: Oxford University Press, 1969.

_____. *O Ciclo de Desenvolvimento do Grupo Doméstico*. Brasília: UnB, 1974.

Geffray, Christian. *Ni pere ni mere: Critique de la parente: le cas makhuwa*. Paris: Du Seuil, 1990.

Goodman, Catherine and Silverstein Merril. "Grandmothers raising grandchildren: family structure and well-being in culturally diverse families." *The Gerontologist*. Vol. 42. 5 (2002): 676–689.

Goody, Esther. *Parenthood and social reproduction: fostering and occupational roles in West Africa*. Cambridge: Cambridge University Press, 1982.

Kopytoff, Igor and Miers Suzanne. "African Slavery as an Institution of Marginality." Kopytoff and Miers, (Eds.) *Slavery in Africa: Historical and Anthropological Perspectives*. Madison: The University of Winsconsin Press, 1979.

Lobo, Andrea. 2001. *Seca, Chuva e Luta. Reconstruindo a Paisagem em Cabo Verde*. Master's Thesis, PPGS of Department of Anthropology of the University of Brasilia, Brasília. 2001.

_____. *Tão Longe e Tão Perto. Organização família e emigração feminina na Ilha de Boa Vista-Cabo Verde*. Doctoral Dissertation, PPGS of the Department of Anthropology of the University of Brasilia, Brasília. 2006.

Lopes, Ewellyne Suely de Lima, Neri Anita Liberalesso, and Park Margareth Brandini. "Ser avós ou ser pais: os papéis dos avós na sociedade contemporânea." *Textos Envelhecimento*. Vol. 8. 2 (2005): 1–10.

Modell, Judith. "Rights to the children: fosters care and social reproduction in Hawaii." Sarah Franklin and Helena Ragoré, (Eds.) *Reproducing Reproduction. Kinship, Towers and Technological innovation*. Philadelphia: University of Pennsylvania Press, 1998.

Notermans, Catrien. "Sharing home, food and bed: paths of grandmotherhood in East Cameroon." *África*, Vol. 74. 1 (2004): 28–46.

Olwig, Karen Fog. "Narratives of the children left behind: home and identity in globalised Caribbean families." *Journal of Ethnic and Migration Studies*. Vol. 25. 2 (1999).

Parkin, David and Nyamwaya, David, (Eds.) *Transformations of African Marriage*. Manchester: Manchester University Press, 1987.

Trajano Filho, W. "Some problems with the Creole Project for the Nation: the case of Guinea-Bissau." Paper presented at the Seminar, Powerful Presence of the Past, at the Max Planck Institute, Halle, Germany in 2006.

Radcliffe-Brown, Alfred. "Introduction." Radcliffe-Brown and Darryl Forde (Eds.), *African Systems of Kinship and Marriage*. London: Oxford University Press, 1952.

White, Susan R. Erdmute Alber and P. Wenzel Geissler. "Lifetimes Intertwined: African Grandparents and Grandchildren." *Africa*. Vol. 74.1 (2004): 76–95.

Chapter 19

The Good Mother and the Contaminating Mother: Experiences and Expectations of Motherhood Following an HIV-Positive Diagnosis

Gretchen du Plessis & Heidi Celliers

Sarah Wilson's study of motherhood and illness has the provocative title: "When you have children, you're obliged to live."[1] Many notions of womanhood and motherhood are hidden in these words. In general, women have unwritten obligations to protect their health for the sake of their societies but have limited control over the conditions of their lives. They tend to be economically and socially dependent, struggle to protect themselves (and often their children too) from violence, and have little say about the circumstances under which they first become sexually active or become mothers. Despite their subordination and exploitation, in recent years, many of the public campaigns to address the HIV/AIDS pandemic recognize women as key players in sexual negotiation, reproduction, family health care, cultural transition of normative behaviors, social support, and care-giving. In other words, women as mothers are seen as crucial to slowing the spread and managing the consequences of the pandemic.

In this chapter, we report on a qualitative study of a group of women following an HIV-positive diagnosis. Our goal is to highlight the tension between reproductive autonomy and the disease-containment directive for HIV-positive mothers on the one hand, and the tension between reproductive self-determination and the socio-cultural framing of motherhood in a patriarchal society on the other. Almost from the onset, it was apparent that gendered notions of reproduction offer conceptual tools for understanding the evolving HIV/AIDS pandemic. Such notions also add weight to an understanding of HIV-infection as more than merely an individual experience of disease. Moreover, gendered notions of reproduction underpin most of the epidemiological models used in describing HIV/AIDS. Nowhere is this more apparent than that of, in the absence of general population testing in South Africa, pregnant women who are still the major sentinel groups for testing the incidence and prevalence of HIV in the total population. Underlying this is the more general notion that the social construction of gender provides limited ways in which women can recognize and legitimate their bodily experiences and practices. Ultimately women can resist these constructions, but in order to do so, they must be adequately empowered and have effective strategies to acquire and secure their empowerment.

In this regard, what would the barriers to empowerment for an HIV-positive woman be in South Africa? An HIV-positive woman is expected to come to terms with her status,

---

1. Sarah Wilson, " 'When You Have Children, You're Obliged to Live': Motherhood, Chronic Illness and Biographical Disruption," *Sociology of Health and Illness*, Vol. 29 (2007): 610–26.

disclose her status to her sexual partner(s), convince her partner(s) to go for testing and use condoms, access health information, and involve her doctor(s) in any future planned pregnancies. It thus seems that all prescriptions for slowing down the pandemic conspire to make women bear the burden of the epidemic. A biomedical study of HIV-positive women in Burkina Faso illustrates this point:

> Counseling recommends the adoption of a responsible sexuality and the choice for a combined approach (condom and hormonal contraception) to avert the transmission of the infection to others, most particularly to the husband and, above all, to limit the possibility of a new pregnancy that would expose the new child to the risk of HIV infection and to the risk of becoming an orphan.[2]

However, individual female responsibility for reproductive health can only make sense in a context of reproductive autonomy and self-determination, which cannot be assumed in patriarchal societies.[3] Ward makes the important observation that many women's reproductive illnesses are in fact vertically transmitted if viewed in terms of power in sexual relationships.[4] The emphasis on vertical transmission should therefore be seen against the wider backdrop of the social construction of HIV/AIDS and the feminization of sexually transmitted infections (STIs).

HIV-positive mothers are thus defined as individuals who should be monitored, objectified in surveillance studies, and educated. Since femininity is construed as nurturing and protective, a mother who fails to protect her babies against a killer disease is seen as pathological.[5] Even so, these same women are rendered dependent on the medical profession to define their health status and to provide expertise in reproduction, health care, and childbirth.[6] Concerns about mother-to-child-transmission of HIV invoke old assumptions about male invulnerability and female responsibility in respect of fetal health or risk. Consequently, maternally mediated risk is emphasized whereas father-fetal associations are underplayed. Clearly, given the prevalence of heterosexual transmission of HIV, for every HIV-positive mother that is at risk of infecting her current and possible future fetuses with HIV there is (potentially) a male partner who contributed to the infection. In the parlance of HIV/AIDS, official reports still shift between using the term mother-to-child-transmission (MTCT) and parent-to-child-transmission (PTCT) to address this issue. These concerns about women and reproductive health are explored in this paper. First, we describe the methods. Then we report on how the interviewees experienced their diagnosis, what they perceived living with HIV as a woman of reproductive age is like, their notions of motherhood, and of having children and breastfeeding.

---

2. Yacouba Nebie, Nicolas Meda, Valerie Leroy, et al., "Sexual and Reproductive Life of Women Informed Of Their HIV Seropositivity: A Prospective Cohort Study in Burkina Faso," *Journal of Acquired Immune Deficiency Syndromes*, Vol. 28 (2001): 367–72.

3. Tamsin Wilton, *Sexualities in Health and Social Care: A Textbook* (Buckingham: Open University Press, 2000).

4. Martha C Ward, "A Different Disease: HIV/AIDS and Health Care for Women in Poverty," *Culture, Medicine and Psychiatry*, Vol. 17 (1993): 413–30.

5. Michele Travers and Lydia Bennett, "AIDS, Women and Power," in Lorraine Sherr, Catherine Hankins and Lydia Bennett (eds.) *AIDS as A Gender Issue: Psychosocial Perspectives* (London: Taylor & Francis Ltd, 1996), 64–78.

6. Susan E Bell, "Sexual Synthetics: Women, Science and Microbicides," in Monica J. Casper (ed.) *Synthetic Planet: Chemical Politics and the Hazards of Modern Life* (New York: Routledge/Taylor & Francis, 2003), 197–212; Nancy Krieger, "Gender, Sexes, and Health: What are the Connections— and Why Does it Matter?" *International Journal of Epidemiology*, Vol. 32 (2003): 652–57.

Details of the Study

The study encompassed a qualitative approach informed by critical social theory. In particular, critical ethnography as described by Carspecken[7] was used in order to look further than people's meanings, experiences, and subjective understandings to include elements of structure that, according to Layder "represent the standing conditions confronting people in their everyday lives — and representing what Marx and Engels describe as circumstances transmitted and inherited from the past."[8] A critical ethnographic approach was chosen to uncover hegemonic legitimacy-claims of "knowing" and "framing" reproductive behavior. This demanded a focus on situational and structural issues as meaningful, constraining, and/or enabling in terms of the reproductive behavior.

Applying this meant investigating how HIV/AIDS and women's reproductive choices and options are inherent from past systemic arrangements (stemming from patriarchy, institutionalized racism, and technocratic control of disease) that comprised a disempowering landscape for women. The methodology choices enabled the discovery of structures of power and privilege that extended beyond the immediate social and institutional arrangements of health information and service delivery and access for women living with HIV. The production of meaning (that is meanings of a reproductively healthy life in the presence of HIV/AIDS) could thus be seen in its temporal and historical "situatedness." Furthermore, it enabled the location of the choices made by the research participants as far as their reproductive lives were concerned in a series of social, political, cultural, and economic relations. It made possible the exposure of decision-making about reproductive health as fractured processes characterized by disjuncture, rupture, and contestation.

The study entailed in-depth interviews with a group of volunteer research participants over a period of two years, commencing in 2006 and ending in 2008. By working through a community-based organization in Gauteng, South Africa, research participants were recruited through referrals in a snowball sampling technique. Volunteer participants were women between the ages of 18 and 49 years and of a known HIV-positive status. They all relied on public health care, were willing to participate in the study, and consented to be interviewed more than once. Eventually ten research participants were available for follow-up interviews. These women gave rich descriptions of their experiences of living with HIV. Multiple, in-depth interviews were conducted — either at the public health clinic or at a venue suggested by the interviewees. All interviews were tape-recorded and notes were taken as back-up. The tape recorded interviews were transcribed verbatim and word-processed as computer files. Interviews typically lasted between 40 minutes to an hour.

The research proposal and ethical considerations of the study were submitted to the Ethics Review Committee of the Department of Sociology at the University of South Africa (UNISA). In addition, written permission to undertake the research was obtained from the Gauteng Department of Health. Informed consent was sought from each research participant and re-negotiated at each encounter. Participation was voluntary and the research did not interfere with the participants' ability to receive medical care at the public health care facilities. In addition, observation methods were used during visits to voluntary

---

7. Phil F. Carspecken, *Critical Ethnography in Educational Research: A Theoretical and Practical Guide* (New York: Routledge, 1996).

8. Derek Layder, "The Reality of Social Domains: Implications for Theory and Method," in Tim May and Malcolm Williams (eds.) *Knowing The Social World* (Buckingham: Open University Press, 1998), 95.

counseling and testing (VCT), service sites, and at support group meetings. The critical social framing of the study prescribed constant reflection on the difference between exploration and exploitation. Some of the tensions between the insider and outsider roles were resolved through keeping a field diary, engaging in reflexive debriefing sessions with some of the participants, and being actively involved in assisting the support group for women living with HIV that formed as an outcome of the study.

Motherhood Following an HIV-Positive Diagnosis

For the women participating in our study, receiving an HIV-positive diagnosis initiated a profound status passage—from being mothers, wives, and women to being "women-wives-mothers-living-with-HIV." The diagnosis presented a biographical disruption dislocating relationships, marriages, practical concerns, and taken-for-granted assumptions about gendered embodiment and everyday life. The diagnosis forcefully drew the women into encounters with public health care giving and set the moral context within which they had to negotiate their new identities as women living with HIV. The diagnosis not only marked a status passage for the research participants, but the shock of it also rendered them involuntarily receptive to a socialization process intended to inculcate in them the core values of the biomedical technocratic control over the disease. During counseling sessions, they were encouraged to disclose their status (to at least) a confidant that could act as a 'treatment buddy' when embarking on an antiretroviral (ARV) treatment regime. For the research participants, being poor and dependent on a public health care system spilled over into not possessing the power to control their disclosure.

For some of the women in the study, HIV-testing was seen as a 'normal' part of antenatal testing. This problematizes the notion of informed consent for voluntary testing for HIV. A few others spoke about the psychological pain of a HIV-seropositive diagnosis heaped upon the shock of an unplanned (and in some cases for the father also an unwanted) pregnancy. Six of the research participants tested due to health complaints and not as part of antenatal screening. They were not regarded by health care practitioners as fitting the profiles of 'at risk' groups, since they already had children and were in stable relationships at the time of their consultations. Because they were not pregnant at the time, they were also not part of the sentinel group (that is the antenatal testing group). This perceptual block that defines the best candidates for testing for HIV-infection is a legacy of biomedical hegemony that obscures the possibility of an HIV-infection to the point where a woman's health has deteriorated to such an extent that testing for HIV-infection becomes the only feasible option left to explain her ill health. It also demonstrates a bias towards antenatal testing for the epidemiological tracking of new infections. Given the reactions of shock to their diagnosis it is also likely that many of the research participants shared these perceptual blocks and did not see themselves as being at risk of HIV-infection.

The women who had used Nevirapine antenatal as part of the MTCT program regarded the experience as positive and saw it as part of responsible motherhood, for example one of the respondents indicated:

I used Nevirapine with my daughter [now aged 5]. She is HIV-negative and I had no problems. I will use Nevirapine again, because really I tell you no mother would like to give her baby this illness. (Participant 1)

Accessing an ARV-treatment regime due to serious opportunistic infections and/or a low CD4-blood count, however, was seen as a low point in the illness trajectory. Although all the research participants attested to the potential value of the life-prolonging effect of the treatments, they also regarded it as indicative of serious illness.

Assessing a Life as an HIV-Positive Woman of Reproductive Age

Economic considerations influenced the research participants' perceptions on ideal family sizes. For example, participants gave the following perspectives:

It is so expensive out there. You know I would even have liked to have only two children, because life is so very expensive and I worry about the children who are still at school. (Participant 2, a mother of four children and wanting no more children)

I see so many people struggling today without money and jobs. I think we are suffering more from poverty now than from AIDS. People must think about money for their children when they plan their family, because school is expensive and the young people take a long time to find jobs. (Participant 3, a mother of one and wanting no more children)

No, I don't want another baby soon. Right now, life is a struggle for us financially and another baby will make things even harder for us. I haven't thought much about another baby. I would like to get a better place to stay. Living in a shack is no life for a baby and life is so expensive. I would like to get a job and earn money. I first have to look after my child and when he goes to school I might be able to find a job, I don't know. I would like to have a job where they also offer training, since I left school before I finished Grade 9. I am worried every day about rent and food. Bringing up a child is too expensive and that is the main problem. (Participant 4, a 23 year-old mother of one child)

In the last-quoted case the young woman was abandoned by her baby's father. He did not pay child maintenance and her current male partner was unable to find full time employment. In addition to being the main caregiver to her baby, this young woman became the sole income-bearer in the household, which consisted of several young people who did not participate in waged labor. She accessed a social disability grant. Representing a discourse of self-sufficiency—by thinking about finding suitable employment that would also offer training—in her narrative, she displayed the kind of positioning of a morally responsible mother-living-with-HIV that is embedded in the prescriptive discourse on living positively with HIV. This discourse is incompatible with the way that she actually negotiated the demands of her domestic life. She narrated her ambitions in reference to a future in which her child will be able to attend school. Without actual help with childcare, housing, training, and access to waged labor, this young woman's hopes will remain unrealized.

The study revealed that HIV-positive women are inundated with a deluge of messages about condom use. For the most part, however, the narratives conformed to the heterosexual dominant discourse in which women were required to curtail and be the passive recipients of aggressive male sexual attention. The majority believed that they were infected with HIV by their husbands. Here are some examples:

My husband no longer sleeps with me. He does not want to get tested [for HIV]; although I know that he has given this to me. When he gets sick, I can see in his eyes how afraid he is that he has AIDS. But he is in denial and does not want to be tested. I see him watching me when I take my [ARV] medicine and he insists that I keep on taking it, but he does not want to test himself. (Participant 2)

My husband left two years ago. I think he must have given me this virus. I only slept with him and was never sick before I met and married him. But I don't see him anymore. I think men think that this is a woman's disease and that they can't get it. I wish I could know his status too. I should have asked him to get the blood test a long time ago, before he left. My youngest she is 5 years old and she has never been sick—never. So I don't think that I had HIV with my pregnancy. So now I think I got this virus later—after she was born. I think that is when I got it from my husband because he had many, many girlfriends. I even know about some of them.... I think husbands must be tested, you know. Just look around you here. There are only women at the clinic—only a few men here and there—but there are mostly women, young women and old women and women with babies. (Participant 5)

In these narrations, the women placed themselves closer to the position of a victim of HIV-infection than to the position of a vector for HIV-infection. Counseling at public health care clinics privileges the self-sufficient woman living with HIV who has dealt with her anger. Some of the participants, however, voiced their anger at contracting the infection in what they regarded as not particularly risky sexual relationships. For them, risk-taking implied autonomy in action, but none of the women willingly exposed themselves to infection. No one wanted to pass the infection onto their children. Although the interviewees' experiences of heterosexual sexual relationships as revealed in their narrations were varied and complex, they were not indicative of promiscuous, high-risk sexual relationships. Although it was not possible to ascertain whether the blame put on husbands for being the infective partner or for their infidelity had any basis in reality, for many of the interviewees their heterosexual relationships precluded dialogue or negotiation about their own health concerns. The participants' feelings of anger and disappointment also stemmed from expectations that being a wife or a partner to a man implied a contractual relationship in which the woman would bring her sexuality and reproductive power into a hierarchical heterosexual relationship and the male would reciprocate with economic support. Infection, abandonment, material neglect, and rejection were brutal affronts to these expectations.

Most of the participants experienced relationship breakdowns of varying degrees following their HIV-positive diagnosis. Most broke up with a partner, whereas some stayed with their original husband or partner, but reported that the relationship had changed. In cases where the relationship broke down, the women consistently reported that the men did the leaving. That is, the men physically moved away, a state of affairs that was normalized in the narrations. Some formed new relationships with partners they regarded as supportive, suggesting that the disease itself changed expectations and perceptions of intimate interpersonal relationships and its affective dimensions. One woman, for example, believed that she would remain celibate following her diagnosis, since:

I am living alone. I don't have a boyfriend and I also don't want a boyfriend. The men leave when there is trouble or when they think that you or the baby is sick. (Participant 6)

Another made a conscious choice to restrict her friendships and close relationships to other people living with HIV, as she explained:

I have told you that my daughter's father and I have split up before she was born. Actually, I knew for a long time that the relationship was not working and after the diagnosis, he left. I have met someone a while ago who is also HIV-positive and he is very supportive. After I was identified [diagnosed as HIV-positive], I decided only to meet other people who are HIV-positive. I will not take a boyfriend who is not HIV-positive … (Participant 7)

Interviewer: Please explain to me why you feel this way. Why would you not date a man who is HIV-negative?

Participant 7: Because you can only understand what it is like to be HIV-positive if you yourself are positive, you see.

Interviewer: Is that the most important reason for you?

Participant 7: Yes, my boyfriend understands what it means to live with this disease and he is so supportive—he always tells me not to feel sorry for myself.… [Laughs].… He is the only one that can tell me that—I won't take that from anybody.… [Laughs].… We live with this virus together. We met at a support group meeting, and when I saw him I knew that I wanted to be with him. I was the one that asked him to go out with me and I persisted.

This last narrative shows the type of in-group alignment that Goffman associates with the consequences of experiencing stigma.[9] This over-identification with "the aggregate of persons who are likely to have to suffer the same deprivations," is intrinsically contradictory as it serves to deepen the social chasm between the stigmatized group and the 'normal others' and consequently to deepen stigma. Of particular interest is the moral authority that she ascribed to her HIV-positive boyfriend to be the individual sanctioned to tell her to refrain from self-pity. Read in conjunction with her later comments (not in this quotation) about her fears that this man would leave her should she refuse to have sex with him the hierarchical nature of this relationship becomes clear. At the same time, however, her story positioned her as the one who actively pursued the man for a relationship—yet this very attempt at rewriting the taken-for-granted codes of a heterosexual relationship left her feeling psychologically vulnerable. For her, a safer relationship as a woman living with HIV implied a relationship with someone who biomedical shared her fate.

Those research participants who were in heterosexual relationships at the time of the fieldwork regarded the men in their lives as protectors, providers, comfort-givers, pleasure-givers, and key players in their social support systems. Being in a relationship served affective needs, offered opportunities for shared problem solving and sharing of resources, and provided a semblance of normalcy. For example, some participants stated:

I have never had a husband, but I have a boyfriend now. He supports me. He sometimes gives me money for food. He understands how I feel. You know it is not good to be alone. Now I can still go out with my boyfriend to the beer hall. We laugh and sit there like everybody else—like normal people. (Participant 8)

The person I can talk to about my illness is my boyfriend, because he understands how I feel. He is better for me, since my parents, they have so many problems … really they have too many problems. (Participant 4)

My first one [referring to her eldest son, aged 23 years] does not understand this thing about relationship, you know? He says, 'Why don't you just sit Mommy,

---

9. Erving Goffman, *Stigma: Notes on the Management of Spoiled Identity* (Englewood Cliffs, NJ: Prentice-Hall, 1963), 112.

without anyone? We will look after you.' But I tell him: 'No but I need somebody. I need a friend that I can share some of these things with.' You can't have that same relationship with a child. (Participant 1)

Some interviewees, however, confirmed that their post-HIV-diagnosis heterosexual relationships were as disabling as the relationships they had had prior to the diagnosis. Heterosexual relationships were constructed in the narrations as dangerous, non-monogamous, transitory, precarious, and inequitable, but paradoxically also as sought after. Insights about gender roles in intimate relationships from the narratives show the four types of contradictory positioning and simultaneously conflicting subjectivities. Firstly, that of hope and fear: for example, hope for a better, more stable relationship versus the fear of abandonment, loneliness, and rejection. Secondly, that of risk and responsibility: for example, the risk of being abused, rejected, or abandoned versus being responsible for protecting their children against stigma, transmission, and abandonment. Thirdly, that of power and weakness: for example, the power to pursue a relationship or to rewrite the codes of hierarchical heterosexual relationships versus weakness by failing to negotiate a more egalitarian relationship. Finally, that of innocence and guilt: for example, blamelessness due to being the victim of a trusted partner's unfaithfulness versus guilt and remorse for not avoiding risky relationships. The latter is revealed in the words of an interviewee: "We women we want to have husbands and boyfriends."

The question that arises is whether the interviewees' talk about their sexual relationships following their HIV-positive diagnoses revealed conscious shifts towards safer sex? There seems to be evidence in support of this, although it is not the kind of agency-led, active adoption of infection containment as favored in counseling in all cases. Many of the participants were using condoms, although the use of the male-controlled barrier method was not without problems. Some chose sexual abstinence, not as a safer sexual practice in terms of containing infection, but because they dreaded a further abandonment. Some reported that they abstained, but mostly because their husbands or partners allegedly no longer had sexual relations with them. Some of the women voluntarily chose new relationships with male partners who were also HIV-positive. These women were aware of the possibility of re-infection, but such zero-concordant relationships were preferred for complex reasons of in-group alignment, affective needs, and needs for acceptance.

In their talk about gender roles, the research participants did not regard themselves as disembodied subjects. Instead, their narrations revealed bodies that were shaped and limited by socio-cultural constructions of gender. Such constructions, which had started long before HIV entered their lives, prescribed the ways in which a woman should dress or act. HIV-infection challenged and reshaped some of these constructions and the interviewees reflected on the loss of a former image of themselves as women. They also told of attempts to reclaim that image, for example:

What is really troubling me is the swelling in my legs. I now have to walk with a stick, you see. It is really difficult, because we don't have a car in the family and I go to the clinic on the taxi and I find it difficult to walk. I used to be such a strong woman—I could do everything—the cooking for the family. Everyone loved my cooking and I liked doing that. Now I am so weak and tired and I must ask the children to help. I don't like to ask them, although they are supportive. I wanted to be the one that did things for them.... My daughter is my biggest support. She is my eldest and she takes care of me and helps me with house work and so on. She brings me clothes and says that we must dress smart, because that helps us feel stronger. (Participant 2)

My stomach is so big, but my arms, legs and face are so thin now. I don't look like me anymore—I used to be a big woman.... I am a weak woman now. I am not like I used to be. (Participant 3)

I show people that I can live a full life with this disease. I look well now and I always walk fast and upright. This is the way people have always known me to be—a woman who runs instead of walking. So this is still the way I am even with the HIV. I take the stairs instead of the lift. People see that I am always smiling and that I have energy. They see me and not the virus. (Participant 9)

I am not well now. I have sores in my mouth and throat that will not go away. I feel weak and I have become very thin.... I really feel sad all the time now. You see I dress nicely and I even put the make-up, and people see me and they see a proud woman. But inside I am sad that I have this problem now. I ask myself all the time why this happened to me. I'm a very nice person and help others all the time. So how and why has this illness be placed upon me? (Participant 5)

I do not have many friends, not like before. Only a few people come to my house nowadays. Then I make sure that it looks really nice at my place and so on. They see I am good with the house and with my baby. But those who do visit don't talk about the disease with me. As long as they see that I am happy, smiling and strong, they don't think about the disease. (Participant 4)

Clothing, doing housework, having a given body shape, and being a strong woman were culturally legitimized instructions on corporeality. In contrast, counseling strives to inculcate acceptance of the appearance of markers of disease on the body (such as weight loss, skin blemishes, or weakness). Living-with-HIV and traversing the abyss between the ideal woman living with HIV and 'passing for normal' thus required a studied posturing for a particular configuration of femininity. This posturing is a blend of cultural prescriptions and of unconscious self-surveillance to render a particular subjectivity.

Notions of Mothering

Before HIV entered their lives, many of the research participants regarded mothering as a natural extension of female personhood. After their HIV-diagnoses, motherhood (including conception, antenatal care, childbirth, birth care, postnatal care, and breast-feeding), along with so many aspects of their lives, became constituted primarily as medical events in their lives. As opposed to 'natural' mothers, these women became 'contaminating' mothers. Some of the narrations reflected this, for example:

This thing of HIV will make it hard for women to be women. When I was a young girl, this is what you know how your life will be—to get married and have babies. Yes, you know there was illness around then too. Young children got sick and so on. But this HIV and AIDS is a different thing to worry about. (Participant 3)

I will have another child soon, but I will talk with the doctor about it first. It is not the right thing to do—to just fall pregnant just like that. So it's better if you know your status and the status of your partner, so if you make a baby you both of you must sit down with the doctor and inform that doctor that you want to have a baby. Then that doctor will give you options, you know? And the doctor will check all those things—viral load and CD4-counts. It is different now with my condition, I cannot just fall pregnant. (Participant 1)

For some of the interviewees, having a healthy child as a HIV-positive woman became a marker for being a responsible woman. The caring, concerned mother preventing the vertical transmission of the infection to her child became emblematic of the ideal embodiment of the conscientious woman living with HIV. Two of the research participants who discovered their HIV-positive statuses during antenatal testing, gave the following accounts:

> This is a good thing that the government is doing with the ARVs for pregnant women. I want to say really that it is okay to have a baby and use medicine to prevent that baby from getting the virus. I did it and it was not bad to take that medicine. This is what we women can do for our children — to take that medicine so that they don't get the same virus. It is not the children's fault that there is this thing of HIV. So they should not be the ones to be suffering. But you know, the trouble we are really having as women is that bringing up a child is too expensive. That is the main problem. These are women's troubles, this thing of taking care of the children and the men run away from the problems. (Participant 4)

> I have no problems with the [ARV and VCT] services, they are really okay. I like talking to the doctors and nurses about my child and they can see that he is doing well. When they say that he is well, I feel proud and I think that I am a good mother. I was scared, because at the hospital where he was born some of the people were talking that the medicine [Nevirapine] is like a poison for your baby. But I took that medicine and I did everything that the nurses told me to do with my baby. (Participant 6)

The construction of child-care as exclusively 'women's troubles' is indicative of patriarchal ideology and a normalization of this burden placed on women. The woman in the last quotation had used Nevirapine during her pregnancy, but feared the possibility that her child's HIV-seronegative diagnosis had somehow been a false result and that the virus would return. This dreaded 'return of the virus' was interpreted by her not as a possible failure in testing and/or treatment but rather as a signal that she as a mother was not responsible enough to keep her child alive:

> I am so worried about my child all the time. I worry that the virus will come back and kill him and that people would say that I could not take care of him. Sometimes I worry so much I cannot sleep. I sit and look at him all the time. When we were children we got sick and then we got better — without medicine even. But with this it is different — when he gets sick now I must take him to the doctors and it costs money and every time I think the doctors they are thinking by themselves that it is the virus returning in him but they are not telling me. (Participant 6)

Breastfeeding was regarded by the research respondents as an important form of female labor. Before HIV/AIDS entered the picture, breastfeeding conferred immunizing advantage. Yet HIV and the infection-control focus of public health interventions restricted decision-making autonomy in this sphere of mothering and the participants saw this as another loss suffered by HIV-positive women. They followed advice that contextualized breastfeeding as feasible, desirable, and advantageous only if done according to medical instruction. For the interviewees this threw doubt on taken-for-granted norms and rituals in infant feeding practices. Bottle-feeding was regarded as a sign of possible HIV-infection and was hidden. Some women followed medical advice, but felt confused about traditional infant feeding practices and feared the stigma associated with bottle-feeding. Others, by contrast, regarded their own contamination by the HIV-infection and their extreme poverty as precluding them from safely breastfeeding their babies. In all the narrations it was clear that infant feeding is a socio-cultural practice:

> When I was diagnosed [as HIV-positive] they [public health care personnel] told me that you can breastfeed or get formula milk from the clinic. You must choose only one of these and stick to it: you choose breast or formula. Before, when my sister had her baby, I went with her to the clinic and the nurses there they were so happy that we women breastfeed our babies. They used to say that this is good, it is healthy. This is what a woman gives to her baby—her breast and her milk. Even the mother, it helps her to be healthy after the birth. They talk at home amongst themselves now, you see. People see there is a woman with bottles and they say to themselves that woman she is HIV-positive. You see it's not our culture. So I myself I breastfed my baby also and you see there is no problem now. (Participant 7)

> I did not breastfeed my baby. My health was too bad after the birth. I think I did not have enough milk for him. My body was fighting this infection. So I got the milk formula from the clinic. It was a worry about the water and so on. Also, I came to the clinic many times so that I did not run out [of formula]. But it is okay now, because my child is eating now. That time [referring to when the baby was small and bottle-fed], I kept to myself, so people did not know. When anybody asked why you don't breastfeed, I just say that there was a problem with my breast. I think it was better with the food and things they give at the clinic, because we are very poor and the things they gave us at the dietician helped us a lot. (Participant 4)

Notions of maternal practice were found to continue and change in the narrations. Moreover, HIV and AIDS shape such notions as many elderly women and grandmothers are forced to become primary care-givers to children orphaned by AIDS. Mothering, therefore, extended to thoughts on how to care for children once the HIV-positive mother passes away. One woman decided to set goals for herself to help her retain a positive outlook and these goals were linked to events in the lives of her children. Her notions of mothering reached past her children's ages of dependence:

> Then [referring to a period approximately six months after her HIV-positive diagnosis] I started to know the reasons why I want to live, you know. I started to say: I won't die until my first child is 21. I set goals for myself and for my children and it's happening every day. And then my other important goal is that I want to pick my youngest child [referring to her 5-year old] up from school when she starts school. (Participant 1)

One of the women decided not to have another child of her own and was concerned about children left orphaned due to HIV/AIDS. Her narrative introduced another dimension of the embodied maternal that is neglected in the HIV-therapy discourse, namely that of adoptive mothers:

> I don't know how it would have been without the virus and I don't think on that at all. I just think how to live now and how to take care of my family. I want to be a good mother to my child and to my sister's child. I know that I am ill and I think the best I can do for now is to take care of these children while I still can. You know I think that every person must decide for herself what to do, but I myself would not have another baby of my own. I would suggest that people adopt the children out there who need a family. You know there are many children who need taking care of. (Participant 9)

She also felt empathy for those women with HIV who were not mothers but desired a child. From her narration, and from the other quotations, it can be seen that the transformation of a woman into a mother is a process of exceptional normative and cultural richness and significance.

> You know what; I think that a person's heart always hurts for that thing that you think you cannot get. So if you have never been pregnant, or never had a child of your own, then as a woman this will be the thing that you want most of all. You will want to be a mother. So I am not going to judge someone and say you must not have a child because you have HIV. People must decide for themselves. Nobody has the right to tell a woman that she cannot be a mother. (Participant 9)

Motherhood as a specific kind of female embodiment was revealed in the narrations as firstly subjected to biomedical control, structural constraints, cultural rules, tenets of social acceptability, and stigma. Secondly, mothering was revealed as a medium through which social relations are reproduced and caring of the vulnerable is enacted. Finally, motherhood was positioned as a signifier inscribed with cultural meanings, through which identity is produced and according to which benchmarks for "good" or "bad" mothering can be set.

The embodied maternal thus includes women who are trying to conceive, pregnant women, birthing women, adoptive mothers, lactating mothers, bottle-feeding mothers, women who donate gametes or breast-milk to other women, women who care for infants, children, and adult children, and elderly maternal bodies who are key figures in women's support systems. The bias of disease containment privileges some of these embodiments, and silences others. Moreover, the continued importance of mothering over the life-course is an important discovery from the narratives.

Having Children

Reproductive interventions, processes, and decisions happen in and through the bodies of women.[10] In the narrations, a pregnancy for a woman with a known HIV-positive status was often depicted as a dangerous undertaking. Even those research participants who desired future childbearing were not completely confident about the efficacy of risk reduction strategies. Both the actual and the desired number of children show low fertility aspirations for the research participants. Decisions about future pregnancies divided the research participants in two groups, namely those who wanted to keep their childbearing options open, and those who definitely wanted no more children.

Few women wanted another child: One wanted to adopt a child, another did not want her daughter to be an only child, and some wanted to please their partners' desire for a child.

> Maybe I will have another child one of these days, but it depends on my partner's health status as well. I don't want my daughter to grow up alone, so yes I think it will be good to have another child in the house. But I am worried—you see I don't know how safe it would be to have another child with my status. When

---

10. Jyotsna Agnihotri Gupta and Annemiek Richters,"Embodied Subjects and Fragmented Objects: Women's Bodies, Assisted Reproduction Technologies and the Right to Self-Determination," *Bioethical Inquiry*, Vol. 5: (2008) 239–49.

I know that my daughter is healthy, then it would also influence my decision to have another child, since they can look after one another. A child alone in this world is not safe ... My boyfriend is very supportive. We will make the decision together. He will be angry if I got pregnant without talking to him about it first.... I haven't discussed this with the doctor or the nurse, because I want them to first see that I am doing well and that the HIV is under control. They stress all the time that we should use condoms and I don't want to talk about it now. When we decide to try to get pregnant, I will bring my boyfriend along so that we can talk with the doctor together. Here in this hospital the staff is much better about this. When I used to go to [name of a clinic] the nurses were so strict about telling women that they should not fall pregnant when they are HIV-positive. But you see now I am still young and I will think about having another baby at some time. Anyway, people will ask why I am still young with only one child. (Participant 7)

This narrative reveals woman's perceptions about public health care practitioners' dismay at the prospect of a woman wanting to have another pregnancy or more children whilst dealing with a compromised immune system, poor nutritional status, homelessness, unemployment, and other dependent children to take care of. At the same time, her decisions were shaped by her health concerns and concerns about her partner's health. In addition, her decision to keep her childbearing options open was also influenced by her concern for her child to have a sibling to offer support. Finally, anticipated stigma against a young woman with only one child also featured in her considerations for another pregnancy. Decision-making about future childbearing for a woman living with HIV is therefore not influenced by one factor only, but by many complex considerations.

Some women's thoughts about a future pregnancy were greatly influenced by their need to entertain their current partners' wishes. Their partners' expectations outweighed their confidence in their own opinions and their own health fears. It demonstrates a difficulty to break with normative gendered assumptions and expectations about women as reproducers. The resulted stress was narrated by one woman as feelings of guilt for going against these expectations.

Actually I am not sure. My new partner wants me to have a baby with him. He said I used ARVs with my last baby and there were no complications. My daughter tested positive at birth, but after some time she tested negative. My partner says this means we can also have a healthy baby—he wants a child of his own with me. But I don't know ... I don't know what another pregnancy will mean for me. But I have been in this relationship for two years now and it is a very good relationship. That is why I am thinking it is the right thing to do now—to have another child within the next two years with this man. I will feel guilty if I don't have a baby with him. Due to this condition that I have, I do not want to postpone a pregnancy any longer. The age is also running—I don't want a baby when I'm 45. My boyfriend really wants to have another child. (Participant 1)

Concerns about the deleterious effects of pregnancy on the health of a HIV-positive mother were expressed in some of the narratives. This reveals the tension between gendered norms that stress nurturing and putting the needs of others (like male partners' needs for children) first on the one hand and individualist concerns to prioritize one's own health on the other hand. Many of the research participants did not want any more children. The reasons mentioned were fertility as God's will, the burdens of childcare, not wanting to have another heterosexual relationship, and economic considerations. Thus a positive HIV-status was not the sole determinant of reproductive decisions.

Although not all the respondents were in stable heterosexual relationships at the time of the interviews, there was only one woman who expressed the wish to obtain a sterilization to rule out future pregnancies. The other research participants had to be either supremely confident in their own abilities to plan (or avoid) a next pregnancy according to their or their partners' health and economic statuses or they might have misperceived their own risks of falling pregnant again. The women who wanted to keep future childbearing options open placed currency in their ability to reproduce. In this way, some women living with HIV may actively collude with patriarchal expectations of women as reproducers in the face of tenuous economic situations.

Conclusion

Much of the obsession with reproductive health in HIV/AIDS has been inherited from the twentieth century's efforts to improve reproductive health, limit population growth, lower maternal and child mortality, and lower the burden of STIs. As this paper has shown, at the level of individual experience and decision-making for women as mothers or potential mothers, a picture emerges of women facing the paradox of fulfilling their reproductive responsibilities but in a biomedically prescribed and regulated way. They exhibited low fertility preferences and their HIV-statuses were not the only or main considerations in their future reproductive decision-making. Access to goods and resources, power to control disclosure of a stigmatized status, and abilities to perform as "normal" or negotiate safer sex differed between the research participants.

Disease containment rhetoric undermined the empowerment of women by perpetuating women's subordination through an overemphasis on women's responsibilities in curtailing new infections and caring for the sick and vulnerable. The research participants were not empowered with knowledge about how to deal with side effects, condom failures, and the reluctance of husbands and male partners to be tested for HIV. Whereas disease curtailment and care are certainly points to consider, the empowerment of women does not imply that women living with HIV should be considered as therapy-activated soldiers in the fight against the epidemic. Instead, empowering women living with HIV requires making visible their multiple invisible burdens and labor in a society plagued with single mothers.

Some of the interviewees found the absolution of men problematic and as discursively legitimizing men's less important responsibility for safer sex. As one of them remarked during a support group meeting:

> Taking Nevirapine is for women only. Only the women take it to prevent her baby from getting HIV, but what about the father of that baby? Who will know if he is HIV-positive or not? He has to do nothing to protect that baby. So the men think it is only the women's responsibility. (Participant 5)

Our study demonstrated that issues such as informed consent for antenatal testing, adherence to ARV-treatment regimes, infant feeding practices, and reproductive decision-making for women living with HIV are shaped by individual needs, social circumstances, cultural contexts, and material resources. In all four of these issues (testing, treatment, infant feeding, and reproductive choice), the interviewees experienced tensions between biomedical and socio-cultural prescriptions. The future success of VCT and ARV treatment therefore depends on paying attention to these tensions and finding creative solutions to them without ignoring the rights and empowerment of women.

Self-efficacy for the woman living with HIV implies a belief that her considered actions will have the desired, intended effects. This can be achieved through concerted efforts to expand the contraceptive choices available to women living with HIV (irrespective of their ages and parity) and by paying attention to emergency treatments for condom failure. Greater attention should be given to the development of microbicides that can prevent HIV- and STI-transmission and to the availability of male and female condoms. In addition, the use of ARV-therapies should be seen as a life-long practice. Furthermore, public programs directed at eradicating HIV/AIDS stigma should address the themes of victimization and transmission stigma. Women should not be regarded as disease vectors or as passive victims because pity and guilt are not liberating notions.

HIV/AIDS claims lives and destroys individual, families, and communities. At the same time, however, as Baylies and Bujra point out, this epidemic harbors liberatory potential to provide a platform for the transformation of gender relations and the encouragement of greater democratic participation.[11] To be most effective, prevention and treatment strategies should address injustice and inequality and restore human dignity. In the early years of the global HIV/AIDS epidemic, Allan Brandt (1988, 168) indicated, "AIDS will be a standard by which we may measure not only our medical and scientific skill, but also our capacity for justice and compassion."[12] The empowerment of women, as mothers, nurturers, and career women, requires vision and political will, but is crucial in order to address the problems of HIV/AIDS with justice and compassion.

References

Baylies, Carolyn and Janet Bujra. *AIDS, Sexuality and Gender in Africa: Collective Strategies and Struggles in Tanzania and Zambia*. London and New York: Routledge, 2000.

Bell, Susan E. "Sexual Synthetics: Women, Science and Microbicides." In Monica J. Casper (ed.) *Synthetic Planet: Chemical Politics and the Hazards of Modern Life*. New York: Routledge/Taylor & Francis, 2003, 197–212.

Brandt, Allen M. "AIDS: from Social History to Social Policy." In Elizabeth Fee and Daniel M Fox (eds.) *AIDS: the Burdens of History*. Berkeley: University of California Press, 1988, 147–71.

Carspecken, Phil F. *Critical Ethnography in Educational Research: A Theoretical and Practical Guide*. New York: Routledge, 1996.

Goffman, Erving. *Stigma: Notes on the Management of Spoiled Identity*. Englewood Cliffs, NJ: Prentice-Hall, 1963.

Gupta, Jyotsna A. and Annemiek Richters. "Embodied Subjects and Fragmented Objects: Women's Bodies, Assisted Reproduction Technologies and the Right to Self-Determination." *Bioethical Inquiry*, Vol. 5 (2008): 239–49.

Krieger, Nancy. "Genders, Sexes, and Health: What are the Connections—and Why Does It Matter?" International Journal of Epidemiology, Vol. 32 (2003): 652–57.

---

11. Carolyn Baylies and Janet Bujra, *AIDS, Sexuality and Gender in Africa: Collective Strategies and Struggles in Tanzania and Zambia* (London and New York: Routledge, 2000).

12. Allen M Brandt, "AIDS: from Social History to Social Policy," in Elizabeth Fee and Daniel M. Fox (eds.) *AIDS: the Burdens of History* (Berkeley: University of California Press, 1988), 168.

Layder, Derek. "The Reality of Social Domains: Implications for Theory and Method." In Tim May and Malcolm Williams (eds.) *Knowing the Social World*. Buckingham: Open University Press, 1998, 86–102.

Nebie, Yacouba, Nicolas Meda, Valeriane Leroy, Laurent Mandelbrot; Seydou Yaro; Issiaka Sombie; Michel Cartoux; Sylvestre Tiendrebeogo; Blami Dao; Amadou Ouangre; Boubacar Nacro; Paulin Fao; Odette Ky-Zerbo; Philippe Van de Perre; and Francois Dabis. "Sexual and Reproductive Life of Women Informed Of Their HIV Seropositivity: A Prospective Cohort Study in Burkina Faso." *Journal of Acquired Immune Deficiency Syndromes*, Vol. 28 (2001): 367–72.

Travers, Michele and Lydia Bennett. "AIDS, Women and Power." In Lorraine Sherr, Catherine Hankins, and Lydia Bennett (eds.) *AIDS as A Gender Issue: Psychosocial Perspectives*. London: Taylor & Francis Ltd, 1996, 64–78.

Ward, Martha C. "A Different Disease: HIV/AIDS and Health Care for Women in Poverty." *Culture, Medicine and Psychiatry*, Vol. 17 (1993): 413–30.

Wilson, Sarah. " 'When You Have Children, You're Obliged to Live': Motherhood, Chronic Illness and Biographical Disruption." *Sociology of Health and Illness*, Vol. 29 (2007): 610–26.

Wilton, Tamsin. *Sexualities in Health and Social Care: A Textbook*. Buckingham: Open University Press, 2000.

Chapter 20

The 'Weaponization' of Rape and HIV/AIDS in African Conflicts

Obijiofor Aginam

> In the one hundred days of genocide that ravaged the small Central African nation of Rwanda ... an estimated 250,000 to 500,000 women and girls were raped ... [R]ape was the rule, its absence the exception. Sexual violence occurred everywhere, and no one was spared.—Anne-Marie de Brouwer & Sandra Ka Hon Chu[1]

> For 60 days, my body was used as a thoroughfare for all the hoodlums, militia men and soldiers in the district.... Those men completely destroyed me; they caused me so much pain. They raped me in front of my six children.... Three years ago, I discovered I had HIV/AIDS. There is no doubt in my mind that I was infected during these rapes ...—Testimony of a Rape Victim during the genocide in Rwanda.[2]

While the history of wars and conflicts is replete with systematic incidents of sexual violence against vulnerable women, modern-day wars have witnessed large-scale indiscriminate deployment of rape as a "weapon" of war by combatants. Focusing on the linkages between wars, conflicts, and HIV/AIDS, this chapter argues for effective and adequate reparation for victims of rape in the reconstruction of post-conflict societies in the process of Disarmament, Demobilization, and Re-integration (DDR). That the AIDS crisis is exacerbated in complex ways by violent conflicts and civil wars is a truism that is manifested in the indiscriminate deployment of rape by combatants, the breakdown of public health infrastructure in war/conflict zones, and in sexual relations between peace-keepers/combatants and either commercial sex workers or vulnerable women/girls who are desperate to survive.

One conspicuous phenomenon of recent armed conflicts in Africa and elsewhere is the widespread deployment of rape as a systematic tool of warfare in conflicts. Evidence abounds from the former Yugoslavia, Liberia, the Democratic Republic of the Congo, Sudan, the Central African Republic, Sierra Leone, and Rwanda. One striking difference between the use of rape as a weapon of war in pre-1990 conflicts and latter-day wars is the emergence, and "willful" transmission, of HIV to the victims—an incurable virus that decimates the immune system of the human body. Although serious questions have been raised in social science literature about the actual time of transmission or infection, and whether the "intent" of the perpetrators could conclusively be to infect the victim with HIV, there is evidence from the victims' accounts that confirm the deliberate nature

---

1. Anne-Marie de Brouwer and Sandra Ka Hon Chu, *The Men Who Killed Me: Rwandan Survivors of Sexual Violence* (Vancouver: Douglas & McIntyre, 2009), 11.
2. Reported in F. Nduwimana, *The Right to Survive: Sexual Violence, Women and HIV/AIDS* (Montreal: Rights & Democracy, 2004), 75–76.

327

of these acts. In the context of Rwanda, the two quotes above offer some persuasive proof that rape was widespread during the conflict, and that there was clear intent by the perpetrators to infect the victims with HIV.

This chapter argues that women who were victims of rape during conflicts have an inalienable right to reparation, psychological and physical rehabilitation, and access to social measures and health security. Since cash payments are often made to ex-combatants to induce them to de-mobilize and lay down their arms, there is no reason why cash payments should also not be made to HIV-infected victims of rape to enable them survive on anti-retroviral therapies. In efforts to reconstruct post-conflict societies, DDR processes should include sustainable policies and programs aimed at holistic reparation for victims of rape during wars and conflicts.

Conflict, War, and Disease in Historical Perspective

Throughout recorded history, diseases have posed enormous challenges during wars and conflicts. Historians have recorded how the decimation of human lives by disease during conflicts led to the collapse of states, cities, and empires. In one of the earliest historical accounts of wars, Thucydides demonstrated how plague devastated the city of Athens during the Peloponnesian War in 430 BC.[3] Historians postulated that plague of Justinian led to the collapse of the Roman Empire.[4] Smallpox and other 'exotic' diseases devastated the native populations of North America and led to the collapse of the Aztec and Incan Empires during their conquest by European forces.[5] During the American War of Independence in 1776, smallpox prevented the American forces from capturing Canada.[6] As Brundtland stated:

> Cholera and other diseases killed at least three times more soldiers in the Crimean war than did the actual conflict. Malaria, measles, mumps, smallpox, and typhoid felled more combatants than did bullets in the American Civil War.[7]

According to Hans Zinsser,[8] throughout history, soldiers have rarely won wars; rather, microbes have. The epidemics get the blame for defeat, the military generals the credit for victory.[9] While the linkages between wars and disease is almost as old as human history,

---

3. Thucydides, *History of the Peloponnesian War*, transl. by R. Warner (Harmondsworth: Penguin Books, 1954).

4. W.H. McNeill, *Plagues and Peoples* (New York: Doubleday, 1976).

5. A.W. Crosby, *The Columbian Exchange: Biological and Cultural Consequences of 1492* (Westport, CT: Greenwood Press, 1972)

6. Andrew Price-Smith, *The Health of Nations* (Massachusetts: The MIT Press, 2002).

7. Gro Harlem Brundtland, "Global Health and International Security," *Global Governance* Vol. 9 (2003): 417.

8. Han Zinsser, *Rats, Lice and History* (London: George Routledge, 1937).

9. C. Coker, *War and Disease*, (Unpublished) Senior Fellow's Report, "Disease and Security" Conference, 21st Century Trust, Varenna, Lake Como, Italy, April 23–May 1, 2004. See also Stefan Elbe, *Strategic Implications of HIV/AIDS*, Adelphi Paper 357 (New York: Oxford University Press, 2003),13 (stating that "American microbiologist Hans Zinsser advanced the provocative thesis that soldiers have only rarely won wars; rather they mop up after a barrage of epidemics. And typhus, with its brothers and sisters,—plague, cholera, typhoid, dysentery—has decided more campaigns than Caesar, Hannibal, Napoleon, and all the inspector generals of history. The epidemics get the blame for defeat, the generals the credit for victory").

modern-day wars and conflicts, as the quotes above illustrate, have witnessed an increased and indiscriminate use of rape, and the willful transmission of HIV/AIDS as weapons of war by combatants. The emergence of HIV/AIDS in the past two decades, and the complex interaction between the virus and conflicts, has reinforced both the human and state security dimensions of disease. While the state security dimension focuses on the collapse of the apparatus of governance, the human security dimension focuses on threats to the vulnerable groups, especially women and girls, during conflicts. As Brundtland observed:

> [W]e should broaden debate to accept that health is an underlying determinant of development, security, and global stability. We must consider the impact of armed conflict and, perhaps more importantly, the silent march of diseases that devastate populations over time... The explosion of conflict immediately brings to light the links between health and security.[10]

Although the history of wars and conflicts is replete with massive and systematic sexual violence against vulnerable women, modern-day wars in Africa and elsewhere are increasingly characterized by the use of rape as a weapon of war, the intentional or willful transmission of the HIV to innocent victims, and the neglect of these victims in post-conflict reconstruction programs.

HIV/AIDS and Rape in Recent African Conflicts

The "securitization" of HIV/AIDS has led to intense academic and policy debates since the popularization of the notion of human security by the United Nations Development Programme (UNDP) in 1994.[11] In the post-1994 human security discourse,[12] the link between disease, especially HIV/AIDS, and conflicts has elicited voluminous literature.[13] Human Security recognizes the emergence of new threats to the security of peoples: safety from chronic threats such as hunger, environmental degradation and natural disasters, disease, and repression.[14] The International Crisis Group, in its 2001 report entitled

---

10. Brundtland, "Global Health and International Security," 417.

11. United Nations Development Programme (UNDP), *Human Development Report 1994: New Dimensions of Human Security* (New York: Oxford University Press, 1994).

12. For a discussion of human security, see Commission on Human Security, *Human Security Now: Protecting and Empowering People* (New York: Commission on Human Security, 2003); Fen Osler Hampson, *Madness in the Multitude: Human Security and World Disorder* (Oxford University Press, 2001); R. McRae & D. Hubert (eds.), *Human Security and The New Diplomacy: Protecting People, Promoting Peace* (Montreal: McGill-Queen's University Press, 2001); B. Ramcharan, *Human Rights and Human Security* (The Hague: Martinus Nijhoff, 2002); Lloyd Axworthy, "Human Security and Global Governance: Putting People First" *Global Governance* Vol. 7 (2001): 19–23. For critique of human security, see R. Paris, "Human Security: Paradigm Shift or Hot Air," *International Security* 26 (2001): 67.

13. Price-Smith, *The Health of Nations; Jennifer Brower & Peter Chalk, The Global Threat of New and Reemerging Infectious Diseases: Reconciling U.S. National Security and Public Health Policy* (Santa Monica: RAND, 2003); Stefan Elbe, "HIV/AIDS and the Changing Landscape of War in Africa," *International Security* 27, 2 (2002): 159; Stefan Elbe, "HIV/AIDS: A Human Security Challenge for the 21st Century," *Whitehead Journal of Diplomacy and International Relations* 7 (2006): 101–13; Stefan Elbe, "Should HIV/AIDS be Securitized? The Ethical Dilemmas of Linking HIV/AIDS and Security," *International Studies Quarterly*, 50, 1 (2006): 119–44; Laurie Garrett, *HIV and National Security: Where are the Links?* (New York: Council on Foreign Relations, 2005); Obijiofor Aginam, "Bioterrorism, Human security and Public Health: Can International Law Bring them Together in an Age of Globalization," *Medicine and Law*, 24, 3 (2005): 455–62.

14. UNDP, *Human Development Report* (1994), 24–25.

"HIV/AIDS As a Security Issue," categorized HIV/AIDS as a personal security issue, an economic security issue, a communal security issue, a national security issue, and an international security issue.[15] Influenced by the UNDP report, the Commission on Global Governance argued that "the security of people recognizes that global security extends beyond the protection of borders, ruling elites, and exclusive state interests to include the protection of the people."[16]

The Commission on Human Security noted that human security embraces far more than the absence of violent conflict. It encompasses human rights, good governance, access to education and health care, and ensuring that each individual has opportunities and choices to fulfill his potential.[17] One of the core policy conclusions advanced by the Commission on Human Security focuses on the health challenges for human security in three key areas: global infectious disease, poverty-related threats, and violence and crisis.[18] HIV/AIDS neatly fits into these three categories because it is a global pandemic; it is poverty-related at least in most poor countries, and the pandemic is exacerbated in complex ways by violent conflicts and civil wars that are marked by rape of women by combatants, breakdown of health infrastructure, and sexual relations between peacekeepers/combatants and commercial sex workers.

Although one school of thought led by some prominent African and Africanist scholars, especially Whiteside, de Wall, and Gebre-Tensae, has strongly contested the common assertion that wartime rape is a significant factor in the spread of HIV either by design or as a by-product of systematic sexual violence, they nonetheless concede that there is strong evidence to support and prove this assertion at least in the case of the Rwandan genocide.[19] The case of Rwanda, Whiteside, de Wall, and Gebre-Tensae argue, was a concerted and systematic attempt to completely eradicate a population and is an exceptional case by any standards.[20] The structural problem with this scholarship and school of thought is the fact that, as de Brouwer and Chu stated, "the magnitude of sexual violence in conflict situations will never be fully known, since the stigma associated with being a victim discourages women and girls from reporting the crime."[21] This is particularly true of most African conflict situations where cultural and traditional practices, beliefs, and norms shape societal values and ethics. While rape is systematically deployed in past, recent, and ongoing conflicts in Sudan, the Democratic Republic of Congo, the Central African Republic, Sierra Leone, Liberia, and others, we may not be able to determine empirically the linkages between these acts and transmission of HIV. As persuasively argued by Elbe:

> One of the most striking aspects of recent armed conflicts in Africa is the deliberate targeting of civilians and the widespread use of rape, which has been deployed as a systematic tool of warfare in conflicts in Liberia, Mozambique, Rwanda, and Sierra Leone.[22]

---

15. ICG, *HIV/AIDS As a Security Issues* (ICG: Washington/Brussels, 2001).

16. Commission on Global Governance, *Our Global Neighborhood: The Report of the Commission on Global Governance (Oxford University Press, 1995)*, 78, 81.

17. *Human Security Now: Protecting and Empowering People (New York: Commission on Human Security, 2003)*, 4.

18. Ibid.

19. Alan Whiteside, Alex de Wall, and Tsadkan Gebre-Tensae, "AIDS, Security and The Military in Africa: A Sober Appraisal," *African Affairs* 105 (2006): 201–18.

20. Ibid., 214.

21. de Brouwer and Chu (eds.), *The Men Who Killed Me: Rwandan Survivors of Sexual Violence*, 23.

22. Stefan Elbe, "HIV/AIDS and the Changing Landscape of War in Africa," *International Security*, Vol. 27, No.2 (Fall 2002): 167.

Relying on unofficial statistics and data, Elbe observed that human rights workers in Sierra Leone reported that "during the country's eight-year civil war, armed rebels and insurgent forces raped thousands of women."[23] It is estimated that between 200,000 and 500,000 women were raped during the genocide in Rwanda that lasted 100 days.[24]

In the eastern region of the Democratic Republic of Congo, various civil society groups and the United Nations agencies have reported widespread systematic rape involving thousands of women and young girls. These rapes and other acts of sexual violence are being carried out with impunity, brutality, and in flagrant violation of age-old laws, customs, and norms of war by virtually all sides to the conflict — civilians, militiamen, armed groups, and members of the Congolese Armed Forces. During the Liberian civil war, between 1999 and 2003, about 49 percent of women between ages fifteen and seventy experienced at least one act of sexual violence from a soldier or armed militia member.[25] In Sierra Leone, about 64,000 internally displaced women experienced war-related sexual violence between 1991 and 2001.[26] When compared with the atrocities and gross violations of the dignity and basic rights of vulnerable women in the conflicts in the Balkans and elsewhere, which often involved mass rape and cleansing of ethnic minorities, it is fair to state that this is therefore not an African phenomenon. Going as far back as World War I (1914–1918), Brouwer and Chu stated that rape, forced prostitution, and other forms of sexual violence were prevalent in Europe (largely by the German army and the armies of other Axis powers); in Asia during World War II (involving the Japanese Imperial Army); in Europe during World War II (involving the German army); and in Bosnia-Herzegovina and Kosovo during the Balkan conflicts in the 1990s.[27]

It is, however, unique that armed militias and combatants may have started using HIV as a weapon of war, as seen in evidence from the Rwandan genocide and the ongoing conflict in the Democratic Republic of Congo. Notwithstanding the seriousness of the questions that have been raised concerning whether the actual intent of the perpetrators of rape could have been to infect the victim with the virus, Elbe cites the account of one rape victim in Rwanda that the rapists taunted, "We are not killing you. We are giving you something worse. You will die a slow death."[28] There is also another account that captured women, in Rwanda, were taken to HIV-positive soldiers specifically to be raped.[29]

These types of incidents, driven by the 'weaponization' of HIV, raise serious human security issues in post-conflict societies. The complementary nature of human and state security therefore makes HIV less recondite in security discourses because the virus strikes

---

23. Stefan Elbe, "HIV/AIDS and the Changing Landscape of War in Africa." citing Douglas Farah, "A War Against Women," *Washington Post* (April 11, 2001), 1.

24. Lisa Sharlach, "Rape as Genocide: Bangladesh, the Former Yugoslavia and Rwanda," *New Political Science*, Vol. 22, 1 (March 2000): 28; de Brouwer and Chu (eds.), *The Men Who Killed Me: Rwandan Survivors of Sexual Violence*; Nduwimana, *The Right to Survive: Sexual Violence, Women and HIV/AIDS*.

25. Shana Swiss, et al., "Violence Against Women During the Liberian Civil Conflict," in Anne-Marie de Brouwer & Sandra Ka Hon Chu (eds.), *The Men Who Killed Me*, 25.

26. Marie Vlachova and Lea Biason (eds.), *Women in an Insecure World* (Geneva: Geneva Centre for the Democratic Control of Armed Forces, 2005).

27. Ibid., 23–26.

28. Elbe, "HIV/AIDS and the Changing Landscape of War in Africa," 168, citing Margaret Owen, "Widows Expose HIV War Threat," *Worldwoman News* (June 12, 2001), 1.

29. Elbe, "HIV/AIDS and the Changing Landscape of War in Africa," 169. For an insightful discussion of the willful transmission of HIV to rape victims during the Rwandan genocide, see V. Randell, "Sexual Violence and Genocide Against Tutsi Women, Propaganda and Sexual Violence in Rwandan Genocide, An argument for Inter-sectionality in International Law," *Columbia Human Rights Law Review* Vol. 33, 3 (2002): 733–76.

soldiers and civilians because of the breakdown of infrastructure and the indiscriminate deployment of rape as a weapon of war by combatants.[30] In International Humanitarian Law—the set norms that generally criminalize genocide, war crimes, and crimes against humanity—precedents now abound on the criminal conviction of individuals who systematically deployed rape as a weapon of war in Rwanda and former Yugoslavia.[31] In the trial of Jean-Paul Akayesu for genocide before the International Criminal Tribunal for Rwanda, the Tribunal found the accused guilty of aiding and abetting acts of sexual violence involving the systematic rape of Tutsi women. These acts of systematic rapes of Tutsi women, carried out in areas under the authority of Akayesu, were accompanied with the intent to kill the women who were on Tutsi ethnicity. Despite the legal precedents of cases like Akayesu, do international legal mechanisms offer a holistic paradigm for the reconstruction of post-war societies? Has the link between HIV, victims of rape, and psychological and other reparation been taken into account in post-conflict reconstruction and peace-building processes?

Postscript: DDR and Victims of Rape in Post-Conflict Societies

The United Nations and other important actors have now recognized DDR programs as an integral component of post-conflict peace building and reconstruction processes. Nonetheless, DDR programs remain complex simply because of their multidimensional nature that involves military, humanitarian, and other socio-economic components. The DDR process raises many challenges for its non-military components. In the context of victims of rape during conflicts, Francoise Nduwimana, in her study of the victims of rape during the Rwandan genocide,[32] interviewed 30 women who were among the thousands of victims of rape infected with HIV. Writing in 2004, more than a decade after the Rwandan genocide, Nduwimana queried whether we can accurately refer to these women as survivors of the genocide when, every day, "these women, linked by the miserable three-pronged destiny of genocide, rape and HIV/AIDS, witness their friends, acquaintances, neighbors, and family members dying in anonymity, with the world utterly indifferent to their fate."[33] Are these women survivors of genocide, when in the absence of treatment for HIV/AIDS, those who are alive see only death in the horizon? What is the point of surviving only to die slowly a few years later completely dehumanized?[34] In the absence of health and social measures, Nduwimana argues.

> [W]omen who have been raped and who are living with HIV/AIDS are condemned to death ... As it is blatantly clear that between 66.7% and 80% among surviving women, is closely linked to rape and other physical violence suffered by these

---

30. Virginia van der Vilet, *The Politics of AIDS* (London: Bowerdean, 1996). Van der Vilet states that "wars and anarchy create ideal conditions for the transmission of HIV. Soldiers and civilians, many moving without partners or families for extended periods, live outside of conventional morality, many resort to satisfy their needs. War brutalizes human relationships ... and brings sexual violence in its wake."

31. See the judgment of the International Criminal Tribunal for Rwanda (ICTR-11996-4), October 1998, where the Tribunal convicted Jean-Paul Akayesu, former Prefect of Taba, Rwanda for the crime of genocide involving acts of rape and sexual violence.

32. Nduwimana, *The Right to Survive*.

33. Ibid., 9.

34. Ibid.

women during, the justice system must include HIV/AIDS as one of the consequences of these crimes and adopt the appropriate legal and reparation measures.[35]

Rwanda is not an isolated event. Similar calls and proposals have been canvassed for victims of rape during the civil wars in Liberia and Sierra Leone. DDR (disarmament, demobilization, and reintegration) processes, in the case of Rwanda and other post-conflict societies mostly in Africa, have overly emphasized the disarmament and demobilization to the detriment of the reintegration. Even where reintegration receives attention and resources, it often neglects the victims of rape by focusing more on re-integration of child soldiers and ex-combatants into their communities. Victims of rape as a weapon of war, I argue, have an inalienable right to reparation, psychological and physical rehabilitation, and access to social measures and health security. If, as in most DDR programs, cash payments are made to ex-combatants to induce them to de-mobilize, there is no reason why similar payments should also not be made to HIV-infected victims of rape to enable them survive on anti-retroviral therapies. The "right to survive," as Nduwimana calls it, should take the center stage in contemporary AIDS diplomacy. The DDR process in most post-conflict African societies must strive to integrate this very important social problem—the psycho-medical rehabilitation of HIV-infected victims of rape during conflicts.

References

Aginam, Obijiofor. "Bio-terrorism, Human Security and Public Health: Can International Law Bring them Together in an Age of Globalization." *Medicine and Law* Vol. 24, 3 (2005): 455–62.

Axworthy, Lloyd. "Human Security and Global Governance: Putting People First." *Global Governance* Vol 7 (2001): 19–23.

Brower, Jennifer and Peter Chalk. *The Global Threat of New and Reemerging Infectious Diseases: Reconciling U.S. National Security and Public Health Policy.* Santa Monica: RAND, 2003.

Brundtland, Gro Harlem. "Global Health and International Security." *Global Governance* Vol. 9 (2003): 417.

Coker, Christopher. "War and Disease." *Our Global Neighborhood: The Report of the Commission on Global Governance.* Disease and Security Conference.

Commission on Global Governance.Oxford: Oxford University Press, 1995.

Commission on Human Security. *Human Security Now: Protecting and Empowering People.* New York: Commission on Human Security, 2003.

Crosby, A.W. *The Columbian Exchange: Biological and Cultural Consequences of 1492.* Westport, CT: Greenwood Press, 1972.

de Brouwer, Anne-Marie and Sandra Ka Hon Chu. *The Men Who Killed Me: Rwandan Survivors of Sexual Violence.* Vancouver: Douglas & McIntyre, 2009.

Elbe, Stefan. "HIV/AIDS and the Changing Landscape of War in Africa." *International Security* Vol. 27, 2 (2002): 159–77.

---

35. Ibid.

_____. "HIV/AIDS: A Human Security Challenge for the 21st Century." *Whitehead Journal of Diplomacy and International Relations* Vol. 7 (2006): 101–13.

_____. "Should HIV/AIDS be Securitized? The Ethical Dilemmas of Linking HIV/AIDS and Security," *International Studies Quarterly* Vol. 50, 1 (2006): 119–44.

Garrett, Laurie. *HIV and National Security: Where are the Links?* New York: Council on Foreign Relations, 2005.

Hampson, Fen Osler. *Madness in the Multitude: Human Security and World Disorder.Oxford:* Oxford University Press, 2001.

International Criminal Tribunal. *Judgment of the International Criminal Tribunal for Rwanda.* ICTR-11996-4. 1998.

International Crisis Group (ICG). *HIV/AIDS as a Security Issue.* ICG: Washington/Brussels, 2001.

McNeill, W.H. *Plagues and Peoples.* New York: Doubleday, 1976.

McRae, Rob and Don Hubert (eds.). *Human Security and The New Diplomacy: Protecting People, Promoting Peace. Montreal: McGill-Queen's University Press,* 2001.

Nduwimana, F. *The Right to Survive: Sexual Violence, Women and HIV/AIDS.* Montreal: Rights & Democracy, 2004.

Paris, Roland. "Human Security: Paradigm Shift or Hot Air." *International Security* Vol. 26 (2001): 67.

Price-Smith, Andrew. *The Health of Nations.* Massachusetts: MIT Press, 2002.

Sharlach, Lisa. "Rape as Genocide: Bangladesh, the Former Yugoslavia and Rwanda." *New Political Science* Vol. 22, 1 (2000): 28.

Thucydides. *History of the Peloponnesian War.* Transl. by R. Warner. Harmondsworth. Penguin Books, 1954.

United Nations Development Programme (UNDP). *Human Development Report 1994: New Dimensions of Human Security. New York: Oxford University Press,* 1994.

Van der Vilet, Virginia. *The Politics of AIDS.* London: Bowerdean, 1996.

Vlachova, Marie and Lea Biason (eds.). *Women in an Insecure World.* Geneva: Geneva Centre for the Democratic Control of Armed Forces, 2005.

Whiteside, Alan, Alex de Wall, and Tsadkan Gebre-Tensae. "AIDS, Security and the Military in Africa: A Sober Appraisal." *African Affairs* Vol. 105 (2006): 201–18.

Zinsser, Han. *Rats, Lice and History.* London: George Routledge, 1937.

Chapter 21

Femininity and the Practice of Medicine: The Asante Experience

Yaw Sarkodie Agyemang

This chapter examines how the social construct of femininity is used in the practice of medicine among an African people, the Asante of Ghana. The objective of relating femininity to medicine is to bring to the fore the ambiguities and the contradictions in the concept of femininity and to point out that the ambiguities and contradictions are purposefully constructed. One of these purposes is to aid in the practice of medicine. Therefore, this chapter argues that one way of understanding the notion of femininity is to examine the concept and practice of medicine because it opens a window to understanding femininity. While it is admitted that the practice of medicine also throws light on masculinity, the chapter will focus on femininity. In pursuing its objective, the chapter first examines the concept and practice of medicine among the Asante. Afterwards, it situates the place of femininity in the practice of medicine. Finally, it examines the Asante conceptualization of femininity from earlier discussions by drawing out some qualities of being female as captured from the relationship between the practice of medicine and femininity.

The Asante of Ghana

The Asante is a sub-ethnic group of the Akan, the largest ethnic group in Ghana. The Akan ethnic group is situated in the central and southern part of modern day Ghana. The Asante is the largest sub-ethnic entity of this group and speak a dialect of the Akan language called Twi. Most of the Asante are found in the administrative region called Ashanti Region with some of them called the Ahafo, a part of the Brong-Ahafo Region. The Asante view the world as being one with two components, the spiritual and the material or the sacred and the profane. The sacred part of the world is arranged hierarchically, with *Onyame* (the Creator or God) at the top, followed by the spirits of the dead, *Nananom Nsamanfo* or simply the ancestors, and then the lesser divinities called the *Abosom*. In addition, they believe that the world is populated by numerous spirits with some inhabiting every created thing, including humans. There is mutual influence of these two aspects of the universe; however, the sacred has a tremendous influence on the profane world and, therefore, much attention is given to this aspect of the universe in the religious life of the people.[1]

In Asante religious thought, relationships are very important. True existence is achieved only when there are good interpersonal relationships: a good vertical relationship with

---

1. Yaw Sarkodie Agyemang, "The Influence of Aspects of Akan Religious Thought on the Lives of the Akan: A Case Study of the Sekyere," Master's Thesis, University of Ghana, 1994, 202–205.

the sacred world; a good relationship between humans and the environment; and a harmony between the material and spiritual components of the human person. When these interconnected relationships are working, then the Asante are able to realize the goal of their indigenous religion: total well-being at the individual and cooperate levels. This total well-being, according to Gaba,[2] in the context of the Anlo Ewe of Ghana, which also applies to the Asante, is tangibly manifested in the absence of life's negating factors such as diseases, hunger, death of infants and the youth, lack of social harmony, defeat in war, and outbreak of epidemics. In their place there should be factors that make life meaningful and worth living. These factors include the abundance of food, success in all life endeavors at the level of the individual, good physical and psychological health, long life and, most importantly, at the communal level, communal peace and harmony. Certain actions of humans can either induce God to grant or refuse this goal of religion. Among these actions is the practice of medicine, which we shall focus on next.

Defining *Aduro*

The Asante name for medicine is *aduro* (or *aduru*), which translates into English as "medicine." *Aduro* is a generic term denoting various kinds of practices ranging from the use of herbs and barks of trees to the use of mystical forces for benevolent or malevolent purposes. Categories of deities could also be referred to as *aduro*. According to Asare Opoku, these deities are "medicine" in the sense that they were previously magical objects, which, over time, have been deified.[3] In Asante thought *aduro* has various and sometimes opposing meanings. To unearth these various meanings, it is imperative for a detailed understanding of what the practice of medicine entails.

The Asante use parts of plants and animals to cure or prevent physical or mental diseases. This is termed as *aduro*. At other times, however, objects such as rings, anklets, and waist and wristbands are used for the same purpose of either curing or preventing physical or mental illness. This practice is also described as medicine and falls within the WHO definition of medicine as

> ... the sum total of all the knowledge and practices, whether explicable or not, used in diagnosis, prevention and elimination of physical, mental and social imbalance and relying exclusively on practical experience and observation handed down from generation to generation, whether verbally or in writing.[4]

Aduro simply means the herbs, roots, bark of trees, animal droppings, parts of animals, and other substances that are used for prophylactic or curative purposes.

In another sense, *aduro* also means the use of mystical forces for the protection of life and properties or anything beneficial to an individual or society. In this instance, Rattray describes important Asante chiefs and queens who symbolically sacrificed their individuality to establish a stronger Asante nation in a ritual where each person cut a piece of his/her hair and nails that was mixed with "medicine."[5] Such use of mystical forces is deemed to

2. Christian R. Gaba, "Prayer Among the Anlo Ewe," *Orita: Ibadan Journal of Religious Studies,* Vol. 2, 2 (December 1968): 75. See also Laurenti Magesa, *African Religion: The Moral Traditions of Abundant Life* (Maryknoll, N. Y.: Orbis Books, 1997).

3. Kofi Asare Opoku, *West African Traditional Religion* (Accra: FEP International, 1978), 56.

4. As quoted by E. Evans-Anfom, *Traditional Medicine in Ghana: Practice and Prospects* (Accra: Academy of Arts and Sciences, 1986), 15.

5. R. S. Rattray, *Ashanti* (London: Oxford University Press, 1923), 289.

be beneficial to society and hence is described as *adu(ro)pa* (good medicine). The other side of the coin is the use of these mystical forces to cause harm to life and property. Since this practice is harmful to society, it is termed as *adu(ro)bone* (bad medicine or sorcery).[6] Such a medicine is sometimes related to adjudication of cases, including one called *nkamre* (easy saying). The medicine prevents an opposing party in a court case from an accurate statement of his/her case. Another one is called *siri*, which is used to win a court case even if the party using the medicine is guilty.[7] To win a case in Asante court does not depend only on having a strong case but also having spiritual assistance that would compel the panel of judges to give judgment in the favor of a party. *Aduro* can be used by a guilty party to mystically influence judgment. Chiefs must resist this tendency of mystical control over their judgments; hence a chief and his elders must be mystically above their subjects by having a stronger *aduro*. There is an Asante saying that *aduro bi twa aduro bi*, "one medicine cuts (is stronger than) another medicine." This explains a hierarchy in *aduro* with the one more powerful holding sway over the one less powerful. *Aduro* is also used to win war. The greatest priest of Asante, Okomfo Anokye is said to have sacrificed some important Asante chiefs to prepare *aduro* for the Asante to win their freedom from their then overlords, the Denkyira. *Aduro* is sometimes used as the building foundation of important markets, towns, and to ensure the success of any project. This type of medicine can be referred to as "foundational medicine."

Priests and priestesses, chiefs, and other people use *aduro* to protect themselves against diseases, to safeguard the life and property of the citizens and the community against 'spiritual' attack, which includes witchcraft and bad 'medicine.' An object used for protection, this type of *aduro* is sometimes called *suman* (fetish). It comes in the form of man made objects such as charms, amulets, and talismans, intended for various purposes. They may be worn on the body, put under seats, rubbed on the body, or buried on the compound or farm. Those with these objects are described as being mystically powerful are feared in the community. Asare Opoku regards these objects as magic, "because they signify the means through which occult forces are generated into action."[8] The appropriateness or otherwise of this description will be examined later in the chapter.

The concept of *aduro* in some respects is morally neutral in terms of what it does because it can be used for either a good course (*adupa*: good medicine) or a bad one (*adubone*: bad medicine). One use of bad medicine is *aduto* (literally "to throw" medicine or hexing), which is a negative use of this mystical force to cause harm. This has been described as sorcery or bad magic.[9] Therefore, some observers of African Traditional Religion, as earlier on noted with reference to Opoku, describe this practice as being magical.[10]

The question to ask is how appropriate is it to describe this aspect of Asante medicine as being magical? There is no doubt that magic, understood as the act of applying the knowledge of the mystical forces in nature and utilizing these forces to serve both benevolent

6. Samuel Awuah-Nyamekye, "Magic: Its Nature and Meaning in Traditional Akan Society of Ghana," *Orita: Ibadan Journal of Religious Studies*, Vol. 40, 1 (June 2008): 30.

7. D. M Warren and K. O. Brempong, *Ghanaian oral Histories: The Religious Shrines of Techiman Traditional State* (Papers in Anthropology, Department of Sociology and Anthropology, Iowa State University, 1988), 29 and 31.

8. Opoku, *West African Traditional Religion*, 147–48.

9. Awuah-Nyamekye, "Magic: Its Nature and Meaning," 38.

10. Geoffrey E. Parrinder, *West African Religion: A Study of the Beliefs and Practices of Akan, Ewe, Yourba, Ibo and the Kindred Peoples* (London: Epworth, 1969), 27.

and malevolent human ends,[11] as part of the indigenous belief system of the Asante falls under the genre of *aduro*. However, like Ellis and ter Haar, I take the position that Tylor's definition of religion "as a belief in the existence of an invisible world, often thought to be inhabited by spirits that are believed to affect people's lives in the material world"[12] seems to be the definition that helps us to understand many practices, including the practice of indigenous medicine in African societies. Consequently, the use of charms, amulets, and talismans needs not be magic or superstition. The use of these objects expresses a religious thought. They express the idea that the supernatural powers like *Onyame*, the Creator, the *abosom*, lesser divinities, and *Nananom nsamanfo*, the ancestors, among others, use these objects as media to effect a cure or prevent life from being threatened.

Obviously, some aspects of the practice of medicine could be described as being magical, but not all medicinal practices can be described as such. For example, though morality is secondary in medicine, it must, however, be noted that the efficacy of the good medicine depends on good moral conduct. Among the taboos of *ayera aduro* (vanishing medicine), according to the priest of the *Kopo* deity of Sekyere Kwaman are murder, sleeping with another person's wife, and evil thoughts. These offenses are all moral in nature. It was also observed that the taboos associated with the good medicine are moral in nature. The deities, who are the source of medicinal knowledge, warn priests who practice it not to use it to do evil and to maintain their efficacy by refraining from evil activities. Users are also required to exhibit a high moral conduct. An example of this is a ring given by the river deity *Atonsu* of Gyeduako. According to the priest of the shrine, those who come for the ring are told to mention the name of the deity whenever they are in mortal danger and the deity would intervene to save them. This is clear evidence that the ring in itself cannot protect the wearer. It symbolizes the belief in the deity to save those under its tutelage. The ring is a reminder of the ever-saving presence of the deity and a medium for sacred manifestation in human affairs. Such a practice is obviously not magical.

Lastly, scholars often see one main distinction between magic and religion is the notion that magic is mechanical and has an emphasis is on human effort, while religion is supplicatory and the stress is on the sacred.[13] The above discussions on morality and the role of the sacred in medicine are ample testimonies that aspects of medicine described as magical are indeed religious expressions. In conclusion on this issue, there is the need to consider the caution by Hammond that a clear cut conceptual distinction between religion and magic is not helpful in the discourse on magic and religion, because "[M]agic is not an entity distinct from religion but a form of ritual behavior and thus an element of religion."[14] The discussion so far reveals that *aduro* is any substance that is used to cure or prevent physical ailment and a media for the supernatural intervention in human affairs, be it for good or evil.[15] One fact and a major pre-occupation of this paper is that the various understandings of 'medicine,' be it magical or non-magical, are deeply intertwined with ideas of femininity. The Asante understanding of what constitutes femaleness is explored below.

---

11. Parrinder, *West African Religion*, 157.
12. Stephen Ellis and Gerrie ter Haar, *Worlds of Power: Religious Thought and Political Practice in Africa* (London: Hurst & Company, 2004), 3.
13. Dorothy Hammond, "Magic: A Problem in Semantics," *American Anthropologists* New Series 72, 6 (June 1970): 1349–56; and E. Bolaji Idowu, *African Traditional Religion: A Definition* (London: SCM, 1973), 189–202.
14. Hammond, "Magic: A Problem in Semantics," 13, 55.
15. See Ellis and ter Haar, *Worlds of Power*, 95.

Aduro and Femininity

Femininity must be differentiated from feminism. Femininity certainly concerns femaleness and femininity has something to do with women. However, feminism as a social philosophy is normative, because it assumes the posture of a certain level of unfairness against women in the male and female relationship and prescribes a certain kind of action geared towards the liberation of women, children, and the entire society.[16] Femininity, on the other hand, is not normative. The concept of femininity falls within the concept of gender. Though it is centered on humans, it goes beyond anthropomorphism. Gender is socially constructed roles and attributes given to men and women depending on a given society's understanding of what constitutes being a male or female.[17] Femininity therefore, is equated with womanliness, where womanliness does not only refer to being female because a man can be described as being a woman and vice versa.[18]

One aspect of femininity and medicine that has been amply captured by the literature is the role of women as witches. Women are often regarded as the major players in the practice of witchcraft.[19] The practice of witchcraft is of importance to the chapter as its perceived activities are chiefly to cause harm to life and properties and medicine is needed to counteract witchcraft and the perceived harm it causes. The role of women as priestesses, diviners, and other ritual functionaries, which makes them to be healers and practitioners of traditional medicine, is well noted in the literature.[20] Though women share this role with men, there are certain rituals that are the preserve of women.[21] The sacred world of the African is also gendered as some deities are regarded to be females and others as males. Even the Supreme Being, regarded to be the creator, is given either male or female attributes or sometimes both.[22] The special place of human life in African religious belief especially the sacredness of the female life is also noted.[23] Gaba reports of a gendered symbolic religious language among the Anlo Ewe of Ghana. A good example is the symbolism of

---

16. Molara Ogundipe, "Indigenous and Contemporary Gender Concepts and Issues in Africa: Implications for Nigeria's Development," CBAAC Occasional Monograph No. 2 (Lagos: Malthouse Press, 2007), 8.

17. Maggie Humm (ed.), *The Dictionary of Feminist Theory* (Columbus: Ohio State, University Press, 1990 repr. 1997).

18. Among the Asante an aggressive or an assertive female is described as *Obaa-barima* (woman-man) or *Obaa kokonini* (a female cock) because the quality of being aggressive or assertive is a masculine one. Conversely, a male who is gentle, caring, and loving, qualities associated with women, is also called *Obaa* (woman). For further discussion on this issue see Ogundipe, "Gender Concepts," 12–14 and, especially, Virginia Bruce, "The Expression of Femininity in the Male" *The Journal of Sex Research,* Vol. 3, 2 (May, 1967): 129–39.

19. E. Bolaji Idowu, "The Challenge of Witchcraft," *Orita: Ibadan Journal of Religious Studies,* Vol. 4, 1 (1970): 10; Dominique Zahan, *The Religion, Spirituality, and Thought of Traditional Africa* (Chicago: University of Chicago Press, 1979), 93; Evan M. Zuesse, *Ritual Cosmos: The Sanctification of Life in African Religion* (Athens, Ohio: Ohio University Press, 1979), 69.

20. The following are examples of such works: Zahan, *Traditional Africa*; S. N. Ezeanya, "Women in African Traditional Religion," *Orita: Ibadan Journal of Religious Studies,* Vol. 10, (1976): 105–21; and Parrinder, *West African Religion.*

21. Gaba, "Women and Religious Experience," in Ursula King (ed.), *Women in the World's Religion: Past and Present* (N.Y.: Paragon House, 1987), 187.

22. John Mbiti, *Concepts of God in Africa* (London: SPCK, 1970), 115; Ezeanya, "Women in Traditional Africa," 114–15; and Gaba, "Women and Religious Experience," 187.

23. Ogundipe, "Gender Concepts," 30.

"wife," which denotes either a male or female priest or sometimes the entire worshipping community.[24] These ideas are explored in relation to the subject under discussion— femininity and medicine among the Asante.

Femininity and Medicine among the Asante

Femininity is explored in the healing of some physical ailments, especially as it occurs in the childbirth. The pawpaw (papaya) is regarded to be either male or female. In a situation where a woman experiences a difficult childbirth, the roots of a female pawpaw are cut by a woman and used to prepare a medicine that aids in the delivery. The male pawpaw is never used in this medicine.[25] It has also been observed that women dominate in the area of birth attendants—male medicinemen only come in when labor is extremely difficult. While there is an obvious reason for women to dominate this trade of traditional birth attendants, some women play major role. They are women who have given birth to many children without suffering any infant mortality and those who have experienced infant mortality hardly become midwives. These women midwives are those who have exhibited the true quality of being female, because those who have not given birth are regarded as being masculine. The qualities of femininity include giving birth to many children and nurturing all of them to health and life.

Gendering the spiritual world enables the co-operation of the profane and the sacred to address the fertility needs of women. Children who die before the customary naming ceremony, which often occurs on the eighth day, were in the past buried in the female latrine but not the male one. After the burial of such a child, the maternal grandmother of the bereaved mother performs a rite to the female spiritual mother in the ancestral world to grant another child to the woman.[26] Women who suffer frequent infant mortality are believed to be troubled by the spiritual mother of the children who takes them back to the spiritual world out of jealousy.[27] Medicine is given to such children to prevent their spiritual mother from snatching them. This practice is consistent with the worldview of some West African cultures such as the Ibibio of South Eastern Nigeria. Justin Ukpong reports that the Ibibio believe that every child has a spiritual mother called *Eka-Abasi*, who has a strong link with a newly born child till the age of seven.[28] The Ibibio therefore sacrifice to this 'mother', who is believed to be jealous and could cause the death of children. Ambivalently, she protects the child till it gets to the age of seven.

This is not the only way the feminine spirits are related to infants among the Asante. Rattray reports that upon passing urine, an infant's urine is mixed with soil and used to make the sign of the cross at the back of the child as a form of symbolic prayer to the feminine deity, the Earth Goddess, to protect the child from waist pains.[29] The sign of

---

24. Gaba, "Women and Religious Experience," 180–84.

25. The male pawpaw does not bear fruit and, therefore, is regarded to be sterile and un-productive.

26. R. S. Rattray, *Religion & Art in Ashanti* (London: Oxford University, 1927), 60.

27. Friday Mbon, "Women in African Traditional Religions," in Ursula King (ed.), *Women in the World's Religion: Past and Present* (N.Y. Paragon House, 1987), 17.

28. Justn S. Ukpong, "Sacrificial Worship in Ibibio Traditional Religion," *Journal of Religion in Africa*, Vol. 13, 3 (1982): 178.

29. Rattary, *Religion & Art*, 67.

the cross is used to drive away evil and is called *musuyidie* (something to remove evil).[30] Therefore, the prayer to the Earth Goddess was not for the prevention of waist pains alone but also any misfortune that could afflict the child. The discussion above shows that taking care of infants is largely a feminine role. Protecting and nurturing infants are feminine roles and gendering the spirit world enables the Asante to exploit the resources of feminine spirits in the practice of medicine.

The practice of witchcraft adds another dimension to femininity and medicine. The Asante consider witchcraft to be mainly a female domain, though there are male wizards. Considering the perceived activities of witches of causing harm to life and properties, witchcraft becomes the target of medicine. In addition to cursing witches in prayer, as enemies of society, another way of dealing with their activities is the use of medicine. In particular, the executioner gods (*suman brafo*)[31] specialize in catching witches.[32] Medicine is procured in the form of charms and amulets to protect communities, homes, businesses, and individuals against the activities of witches. Sometimes, it is believed witches themselves can be a source of medicinal knowledge, because they know the antidote to any disease or harm they have caused. Medicine is also needed to purge witches of the craft.[33] Related to this negative use of mystical power is *sika aduro* (money medicine). *Sika aduro* is a type of medicine that ensures physical prosperity. In Asante thought, those who possess this medicine get rich quickly and seemingly without any effort. It is regarded as 'bad medicine' as it is an anti-social behavior, in which only the lazy and the wicked would engage. Those (mostly men) who go for this medicine would trade parts of their bodies, in particular, their phallus, for money. It is like entering into a pact with the mystical world where the human agent who needs help offers something very valuable to him to the mystical world in exchange for material wealth. The valuable *thing*, in addition to sacrificing the manhood, is often a loved one, such as a loved wife or daughter. When queried why females suffer such a fate, it was explained that females often receive the affection of men, and since the object of sacrifice for wealth must be valuable to the person, women are those who are offered as sacrifice.

A further explanation is needed here because often in this kind of medicine parts of the female associated with reproduction and nurturing, such as the womb, vagina, and the breast, are removed for the ritual preparation of *sika duro*. Moreover, among the Asante and some African cultures, women expose their nakedness, especially the vagina, as a form of protest. This form of protest, more often than not, compels men who are at positions of influence to give in to the demands of women.[34] There seems to be something special about the body of women. Ogundipe is, therefore, right in her analysis that the practice of exposing the nakedness of women reflects the idea that the body of women, most especially, the life giving parts is sacred. She remarks:

---

30. Ibid., 266. One may suspect Christian influence on the use of the sign of the cross. However, it is likely to have originated from the place where aspects of rituals to ward off evil or to remove the effect of sin (*musuyie*) are performed. These rituals are often performed at cross roads, *nkwanta nan* (four cross-roads). Thus, it is not likely to be a syncretic practice.

31. Opoku, *West African Traditional Religion*, 56.

32. See T. C. McCaskie, "Anti-Witchcraft Cult in Asante: An Essay in the Social History of an African People," *History of Africa*, Vol. 8, 137 (1981): 125–54. M. J. Field also makes a similar observation. See her work "Some New Shrines of the Gold Coast and Their Significance," *Africa: Journal of the International African Institute*, Vol. 13, 2 (Apr. 1940): 138–49.

33. William C Olsen, "Children for Death: Money, Wealth, and Witchcraft Suspicion in Colonial Asante," *Cahiers d'Études Africaines*, Vol. 42, 167 (2002): 530–38.

34. Ogundipe, "Gender Concepts," 29–31.

It is this sacred concept of the body of the woman that is found potent in political struggle all over Africa ... regrettably, this concept can and has led to the unfortunate murders of women and their mutilation in the pursuit of using their bodies for powerful potions and magic in contemporary times.[35]

Thus, in addition to the value attached to the woman as a wife or as a daughter or a niece, it is also the mystery or sacredness associated with the body of the woman that is exploited in this kind of medicine.

Menstrual blood is also utilized in medicine. Menstrual blood is believed to have the capacity of making any medicine impotent. Deities and all sacred objects are rendered desacralized by this substance.[36] This explains why menstruating women are forbidden to go to certain places or get into contact with certain objects and personages. This property associated with menstruation has implications for the practice of medicine. Some medicines are supposed to harm others (*aduro bone*). A standard way of neutralizing the efficacy of bad medicine is bringing it into contact with menstrual blood or the loincloth that has been used by a menstruating woman. Men who eat food prepared by a menstruating woman are believed to become imbeciles (*gyimigyimi*) and their good medicine is neutralized. Rattray observes, "An unclean woman is capable of breaking down all barriers that stand between defenseless man and those evil unseen powers, which beset him on every side."[37] However, at the same time, the men fortify themselves against any medicine that could harm them. Zuesse notes this in respect to hunting among the Epulu Pygmies of D. R. Congo and describes this feminine power as *sacral power,* which manifests itself negatively when a woman breaks a taboo.[38] This quality of neutralizing medicine is also associated with the Earth Goddess. A taboo of most Asante protective medicines is the medicinal objects coming into contact with the earth. *Asase Yaa* is a female spirit that shares this attribute with her human counterparts. The earth has sacral power.

The Asante further explore femininity in another type of medicine: medicine to ensure that trading activities are successful in markets. In the past, this medicine required either a pregnant woman, or a cow as a substitute, to be buried alive in the market before business commenced. Sometimes instead of a pregnant woman or animal, a human virgin was used. In each case, the sacrificial object was buried alive. Virginity was also utilized in the area of war medicine. The Asante engaged themselves in various wars for various purposes. In some of these wars, the sacrifice of human beings was involved to prepare *eko aduro* (war medicine). This type of medicine is supposed to ensure success in war, with the sacrifice of three prominent Asante chiefs to win the Asante war of liberation being the most famous example. Among those sacrificed were often virgin girls (*obaa onnhu barima da*) or pregnant women or animal (often a cow). A virgin animal substitute can be used, but the difficulty is determining the virginity of the animal. This practice does not pertain to only the Asante. Among the Anlo Ewe, vestal virgins are offered as sacrifice to wipe away sins that demand the sacrifice of a human being.[39]

In the Asante worldview, water bodies are also gendered. Some rivers are male while others are female. As part of the ritual to graduate a trainee priest or priestess, the water in a pot, which contains various objects for divination, is regarded as feminine.[40] The

---

35. Ibid., 30.
36. Rattray, *Religion & Art,* 75.
37. Ibid., 75.
38. Zuesse, *Ritual Cosmos,* 68.
39. Gaba, "Religious Experience," 184.
40. Rattray, *Religion & Art,* 46.

gendering of water bodies plays a functional role in medicine. Bodies of water regarded as female are often perceived to have the power of curing females with problems of infertility. *Kwaabena*, a stream in Sekyere Kwaman, is a notable example. The water snakes in the stream are called "children of *Kwaabena*" (*Kwaabena mma*). Infertile women who drink from this stream are believed to be blessed with some of the children of the stream. Rivers regarded as female are good sources for succor for couples looking for children.

Days are gendered. Mondays (*dwoda*—cool day) have feminine quality of "coolness," while Fridays (*Efida*—dirt day) are given a masculine quality. Thus, in the past marriage was preferred to be performed on an auspicious day like Monday and Saturday (a male day but dedicated to the Supreme Being, *Nyame*) but not on Thursday (*Yawda*—painful day) or Friday, both of which are given masculine qualities. The earth and water bodies that are regarded to be feminine play an important role in rituals that symbolize death and resurrection and, therefore, regeneration. It should be noted that the Akan, of which the Asante form part, regard the sea as a female born on a Tuesday. Thus, Tuesdays are the resting days for fishermen among the costal Akan. Rituals that are meant to wash away "filth" (*fi*) caused by, for example, sin, the death of a spouse, or some sicknesses, are performed around such water bodies. In these rituals, old clothes or some items associated with the old life are either buried in the earth or thrown into the sea or feminine rivers. These rituals bring out one feminine quality of being merciful or forgiven. This is captured by an Akan proverb that *Akoko baatan nan nkum ne ba* (the leg of the fowl does not kill its chick). Consequently, the Supreme Being, *Nyame*, who is a male, is giving feminine attributes of being *Obaatan*—a nursing mother. Like a nursing mother, *Onyame* is merciful, forgiving, and sustaining. The earth and feminine water bodies accept the "filth" of society so that individuals and the entire society could be re-born and purified. The above discussion on femininity and healing opens a gate to understanding the quality of femaleness as understood by one African people.

The Meaning of Femininity among Asante

Femininity, in Asante thought, connotes life, fertility, production, growth, and regeneration. These ideas are taken from the African woman's role as life bearer and nurturer. Thus, in the ritual that gives life, the physical parts of females that are associated with birth and nurturing—the genital organ and the breast—are the most preferred parts. Since society is multiplied from females, it is the quality of being female that could also help in the multiplication of wealth either legitimately (as in medicine to ensure trading activities in a market) or illegitimately as in "money medicine."

It is within this understanding of the qualities of being feminine that the female pawpaw is used to ease childbirth instead of the sterile male pawpaw. In the same vein, while male deities are often consulted in times of war where aggression is needed, the female goddesses are utilized when children are needed to populate the community. The use of virgin girls and pregnant women for the *aduro* of the building foundation sacrifice of towns and villages also highlights the same qualities of femaleness. In addition to the virgin girl having the quality of purity, she embodies the totality of life, as all life-giving potentials are still intact in her. Pregnancy is a drama of creation and regeneration as the pregnant woman holds life in her. Thus, in creative "medicine" (such as to save the life of a threatened community), since the pregnant woman already participates in creation, using her in a ritual would ensure the re-creation of a threatened life or ensure the perpetuity of life. This practice reinforces the belief that femininity connotes life.

One other understanding of femininity is "destruction" in both negative and positive senses. Negatively, the sacral power associated with femaleness, as seen in the menstrual blood or the earth, is a taboo to almost all good mystical medicine. The sacral power neutralizes their potency and renders them ineffective. It destroys good medicine, including objects and personages that participate in the sacred. Ambivalently, the sacral power destroys bad medicine that is intended to harm life and property. The ambivalence in the construction of femininity makes the quality of femaleness to be loathed, as attested to by the numerous femininity-related taboos to which users of medicine are expected to adhere. Nevertheless, it is cherished because of its life-protective power of destroying life-threatening medicine. Gaba makes a similar observation among the Anlo Ewe of Ghana.[41]

This conceptual ambivalence of femininity is shared with the concept and practice of medicine. Medicine as a concept is ambiguous in the sense that, on the one hand, it refers to the act of healing or safeguarding of life in general. On the other hand, it also refers to the act of threatening or destroying life and property. Both the ambiguous conceptions of femininity and medicine make the two concepts to be so elastic as to include many things that are either humanly explicable or inexplicable. One can humanly explain the use of herbs, roots, and tree bark to induce a cure, but one cannot humanly explain the use of charms, amulets, and talismans to prevent either the destruction or restoration of life and properties. The practice of medicine is mysterious; hence, it is *aduro,* a mystery. In the same way, femininity cannot be totally explained because of beliefs associated with pregnancy, child bearing, and, especially, menstruation. Hence, Ogundipe remarks that the nine-month pregnancy of a woman makes her "awe-inspiring."[42] Femininity, like the practice of medicine, has its profane aspects but in a sense remains a mystery.

The quality of being mysterious makes both femininity and medicine share the sacred the quality of being inscrutability or unknowable. Both participate in the sacred, and femininity, for example, is regarded to be sacred by some African peoples such as the Yoruba.[43] There is a power associated with the sacred that can be found in the practice of medicine and the concept of being female. The power gives femininity its mysterious nature. However, the mystery surrounding females has one major implication for femininity. Femininity has come to be associated with darkness, the uncanny, evil, and these partly account for the accusation of witches as being most women. Notwithstanding the fact that femininity in Asante thought is anthropocentrically conceptualized, the concept goes beyond the human realm to include all of creation since existence is gendered in the life and thought of the Asante. Gendering existence causes femininity to represent two opposing ideas—life and death. Femininity is creative and regenerative on the one hand, but on the other hand, it is life threatening and destructive. This ambivalent conceptualization of femininity enables it to be permeable so that it could be exploited by society for many purposes, including the practice of medicine.

References

Agyemang, Yaw S. "The Influence of Aspects of Akan Religious Thought on the Lives of the Akan: A case study of the Sekyere," Master's thesis, University of Ghana, 1994.

---

41. Gaba, "Religious Experience," 185.
42. Ibid.
43. Ogundipe, "Gender Concepts," 26–31.

Amadiume, Ifi. *Male Daughters, Female Husbands*. London: Zed Publishing, 1997.

Amoakohene, Margaret Ivy. "Violence against Women in Ghana: A Look at Women's Perceptions and Review of Policy and Social Responses." *Social Science & Medicine*. Vol. 59, no. 11 (December 2004): 2373–2385.

Awolalu, Omosade J. "Women from the Perspective of Religion." *Orita: Ibadan Journal of Religious Studies*. Vol. 10, no. 2 (Dec, 1976): 95.

Awuah-Nyamekye, Samuel. "Magic: Its Nature and Meaning in Traditional Akan Society of Ghana," *Orita: Ibadan Journal of Religious Studies*, XL, no. 1 (June 2008): 25–46.

Bruce, Virginia. "The Expression of Femininity in the Male." *The Journal of Sex Research*. Vol. 3, no. 2 (May, 1967):129–139.

Ellis, Stephen and Gerrie ter Haar. *Worlds of Power: Religious Thought and Political Practice in Africa*. London: Hurst & Company, 2004.

Evans-Anfom, E. *Traditional Medicine in Ghana: Practice, Problems and Prospects*. Accra: The Academy of Arts and Sciences, 1986.

Ezeanya, S. N. "Women in African Traditional Religion." *Orita: Ibadan Journal of Religious Studies*. Vol. 10, no. 2 (1976): 105–121.

Field, M. J. "Some New Shrines of the Gold Coast and Their Significance." *Africa: Journal of the International African Institute*. Vol. 13, no. 2 (April, 1940): 138–149.

Gaba, Christian. "The Religious Life of the People." In Francis Agbodeka, ed. *A Handbook of Eweland Volume1: The Ewes of Southeastern Ghana*. Accra: Woeli Publishing Services, 1997. 85–104.

_____. "Women and religious experience among the Anlo of West Africa." In Ursula King, ed. *Women in the World's Religion: Past and Present*. New York: Paragon House, 1987. 117–95.

Hammond, Dorothy. "Magic: A Problem in Semantics," In *American Anthropologists*. New Series. Vol. 72, no. 6 (June 1970): 1349–56.

Humm, Maggie, ed. *The Dictionary of Feminist Theory*. Columbus: Ohio State, UP, 1990 repr. 1997.

Idowu, E. Bolaji. *African Traditional Religion: A Definition*. London: SCM, 1973.

Magesa, Laurenti. *African Religion: The Moral Traditions of Abundant Life*. Maryknoll, N. Y.: Orbis Books, 1997.

Mbon, Friday. "Women in African Traditional Religions." In Ursula King, ed. *Women in the World's Religion: Past and Present*. N.Y. Paragon House, 1987, 7–23.

McCaskie, T. C. "Anti-Witchcraft Cult in Asante: An Essay in the Social History of an African People." *History of Africa. Vol. 8*, no. 137 (1981): 125–54.

Ogundipe, Molara *Indigenous and Contemporary Gender Concepts and Issues in Africa: Implications for Nigeria's Development*. CBAAC Occasional Monograph., Lagos, 2007.

Olsen, William C. "Children for Death": Money, Wealth, and Witchcraft Suspicion in Colonial Asante," *Cahiers d'Études Africaines*. Vol. 42, no. 167 (2002): 521–50.

Opoku, Kofi Asare. *West African Traditional Religion*. Accra: FEP International, 1978.

Parrinder, Geoffrey E. *West African Religion: A Study of the Beliefs and Practices of Akan, Ewe, Yourba, Ibo and the Kindred Peoples*. London: Epworth, 1969.

Rattray, R. S. *Religion & Art in Ashanti*. London: Oxford University, 1927.

_____. *Ashanti,* London: Oxford University, 1923.

Ray, Benjamin C. *African Religions: Symbol, Ritual, and Community.* Englewood Cliffs, N. J.: Prentice-Hall, 1976.

Ukpong, Justin S. "Sacrificial Worship in Ibibio Traditional Religion." *Journal of Religion in Africa.* Vol. 13, no. 3 (1982): 161–81.

Warren, D. M. and K. O. Brempong. *Ghanaian Oral Histories, The Religious Shrines of Techiman Traditional State.* Papers in Anthropology, Department of Sociology and Anthropology, Iowa State University, 1988.

Zahan, Dominique. *The Religion, Spirituality, and Thought of Traditional Africa.* Chicago: University of Chicago Press, 1979.

Zuesse, Evan M. *Ritual Cosmos: The Sanctification of Life in African Religion.* Athens, Ohio: Ohio University Press. 1979.

Index

A

Abimbola, Wande, 155
Abiodun, Rowland, 74; Alaafin, 76, 78; Orompoto, 93
abolition, 27
abortion, 111, 113, 136
Abuja, 254-258, 264-265
Accra, 14, 163, 166-170, 172-175
Achebe, Nwando, 4; Chinua, 84, 229
Adepegba, Cornelius O., 73
Adesanya, Aderonke Adesola, 13, 79, 90, 95, 69
Ado, Adele, 22
adultery, 107, 116, 262
Agaba, John, 251
Agikuyu, 141
Aginam, Obijiofor, 17
agrarian, 71, 217, 219-220, 253
Agyeman, Yaw Sarkodie, 18, 335
AIDS, 109, 111, 120, 123, 141
Akamba, 105
Akan, 166, 173, 277, 335, 343
Akayesu, Jean-Paul, 332
Akinola, 161
Alber, Erdmute, 294
alcoholism, 40
Algeria, 157
Al-hijab, 114, 118
Ali-Dinar, Ali Bahr Aldin, 243, 246
Allah, 112, 118
Allman, Jean, 238
Altman, Dennis, 181
Amanirenas, 253
Amanishakhete, 253
Amanitere, 253

Amin, Idi, 15, 225, 229, 231
Amina of Zaria, 252
Amoah, Elizabeth, 104
Amutabi, Maurice, 137
Amuyunzu-Nyamongo, Mary, 140
ancestors, 77, 106-107, 159, 222, 275, 278, 294, 335, 338
Anderson, Benedict, 239
anglophone, 170, 272
Anlo, 336, 339, 342, 344
An-Na'im, Abdullah Ahmed, 114
anthropology, 24, 59, 156, 258, 275, 281, 293, 305
anti-colonial, 43, 48
Aole, 76
Aquinas, Thomas, 115
Arab, 59, 63, 65, 112-113, 118-119, 134, 156
archaeology, 71
archipelago, 294-295
Ardener, Shirley, 274
aristocracy, 61,
Aristotle, 114
Arnfred, Signe, 9, 36
Arowa, Omoboyode, 80, 94-95
Arthur, John W., 127
Arugba, 88, 91; Sango, 84; Osun Osogbo, 85, 89
Arusha Declaration, 220, 216
Asante, 18, 169, 170, 173, 335-344
asexual, 117, 233
Ashanti, 335
Asian-Americans, 165
Asyut, 239
Athens, 328